D1539113

THE ESSENTIAL HISTORY OF
IPSWICH TOWN

FOREWORD BY KEVIN BEATTIE

MEL HENDERSON AND PAUL VOLLER

First published in 2001
by HEADLINE BOOK PUBLISHING
for WHSmith, Greenbridge Road, Swindon SN3 3LD

1 3 5 7 9 10 8 6 4 2

ISBN 0 7553 1021 7

Design by designsection, Frome, Somerset
Picture credits: pages 158 (top), 166, 167, 168 (top) Action Images; pages 4, 125, 147, 168 (bottom), 191, 216 *East Anglian Daily Times/Ipswich Evening Star*; pages 5, 8, 11, 19, 35, 40, 53, 55, 65, 72 courtesy David Kindred Collection; pages 14, 20, 21, 22, 23, 27, 28, 43, 44, 49, 51, 56, 58, 86-7, 96, 108, 123, 124 taken from Ken Rice's book *Ipswich: An Illustrated History of Ipswich Town FC*, Wensum Books, 1973
While every effort has been made to trace and acknowledge all copyright holders, we would like to apologise should there have been any errors or omissions
Memorabilia provided by Paul Voller
The authors would like to thank everyone who helped in putting this book together, including Julian Flanders, Chris Hawkes, David Kindred, Sandra Morgan, Samantha Savage and Kathie Wilson

Printed and bound in Great Britain by Clays Ltd, St Ives PLC, Bungay, Suffolk

HEADLINE BOOK PUBLISHING
A division of Hodder Headline
338 Euston Road
London NW1 3BH

www.headline.co.uk
www.hodderheadline.com

Contents

Foreword
By Kevin Beattie

My love affair with Ipswich Town started in 1969 and will last until my dying day. I was proud to represent them and honoured to be named their best-ever player. It hardly seems possible that 32 years have elapsed since I first pulled on the blue shirt, and I can honestly say there was never a dull moment during my time with the club.

I was also fortunate enough to play for England and on occasion entertained my international colleagues with tales of life at Portman Road. They were envious of the close association between the Ipswich players and the chairman, Mr John Cobbold, who was a renowned prankster, best illustrated by an outrageous incident at a party at his house. 'Mr John', Allan Hunter, myself and three donkeys were involved in a race and, while Bobby Robson tried not to be impressed, even he was rendered speechless by the sight of the chairman and his partners in crime.

Not that a party atmosphere prevailed at Portman Road all the time. It was never a hindrance to the club's on-the-field ambitions, and such was the warm atmosphere generated, players felt like family members and were inspired to achieve. I was part of an exciting era at Ipswich, during which we challenged for the League Championship, won the FA Cup and the UEFA Cup, and travelled throughout Europe.

Now, after the sort of lull that most clubs experience, Ipswich are back. Under the dynamic leadership of chairman David Sheepshanks and manager George Burley, I envisage many successful and eventful years ahead. This updated history is a useful reminder of how Ipswich Town Football Club rose from the amateur ranks and rapidly blossomed to become one of the foremost clubs, not only in England but also Europe.

Chapter One: 1878-1907
In the Beginning

When a group of former Ipswich School pupils convened a meeting at the Town Hall on Wednesday, 16 October 1878, it was for the purpose of forming a club to enable them to continue the game they had played and enjoyed as schoolboys. The new club, now known the world over as Ipswich Town, started life as the Ipswich Association Football Club, thus avoiding confusion with the Ipswich Football Club which was, in fact, a rugby club that had been formed eight years earlier.

The following day's *East Anglian Daily Times* reported that Mr J.H.H. Knights had been elected honorary secretary and that Messrs F.G. Bond, J.M. Franks, G.S. Sherrington and C. Fisher had formed the first committee. It also stated that the club's first game had been fixed for Saturday week and further commented: 'This will be rather a novelty to the Ipswich public, who have been used to the very different play of the Ipswich club under the Rugby rules. Without giving an opinion on the relative merits of the two systems, we may express our pleasure that the young men of the town have resolved to afford themselves, and the public, a taste of the old, original style of football. There is plenty of room in the town for both clubs and we hope that the young one will not fail through want of support – much less from jealousy – from the direction of Portman's Road.'

Ten days after its formation the new club staged a practice game between 'The Secretary's team' and 'The Club' which resulted in a 2-2 draw, a remarkable scoreline since reports suggested that the former side comprised of merely seven players while the latter, bizarrely, had 12. Mr T.C. Cobbold, who had accepted

Mr T.C. Cobbold was invited to become the club's first president.

an invitation to be the first president, not only handed over a brand new ball beforehand, but was also one of The Club's dozen players.

He could have had no idea what he was starting. The great, great uncle of future chairmen John and Patrick Cobbold, he was educated at Ipswich School and Charterhouse. He was Conservative MP for Ipswich from 1 January 1876 until his death on 21 November 1883 at the age of 50, and the Cobbold family has retained an active involvement in the club ever since.

The club's first home was Brook's Hall, Broom Hill, off the Norwich Road, but there were no dressing rooms, the players instead crossing the road to The Inkerman public house and changing there. Their opening fixture was at Harwich on 9 November 1878, when a brief report in the *East Anglian Daily Times* revealed that it had lasted only an hour due to the late arrival of the Ipswich team. B. Burton – Bunnell Henry Burton, who later became chairman of Burton, Son and Saunders, one of Ipswich's most prominent firms – achieved the distinction of becoming the club's first goalscorer and R. Peecock added a second past the hosts' goalkeeper, Major Brine, in a 2-0 victory. The club completed 12 fixtures in the 1878-79 season, winning eight, drawing one and losing the other three, at Woodbridge, Framlingham College and Ipswich School.

Intriguingly, an Ipswich Football Club (the rugby club) press advertisement on 14 December 1878 informed readers that 'a match will be played by aid of the electric light' on the following Tuesday, at the Orwell Works Ground, Brook's Hall, Norwich Road, kick-off 7.30pm. The advertisement further informed that the game would be played between Ipswich and United Suffolk, and that the electric machines were to be supplied by Mr Paterson, of London, and driven by two of Messrs Ransomes, Sims and Head's patent portable engines (kindly lent for the occasion). When one considers that floodlights were not installed at Portman Road until February 1960, it is not difficult to imagine the level of interest that such an occasion would have aroused.

Admission was fairly expensive, from 1s 6d for a reserved space bought on the day down to sixpence for an unreserved ticket purchased in advance, and organisers arranged for Teale's conveyances to run to the ground from the Cornhill every five minutes. Remember, this was an ambitious project undertaken by the Ipswich Football Club, as opposed to the Ipswich Association Football Club that was the forerunner of the club in residence at Portman Road today. Several association members took part, but reports do not clarify under which rules the game was played, although from the fact that goals were scored and each side comprised 13 players, it is reasonable to assume that it was a combination of both. Indeed, for some years, several athletic young men were members of both clubs and enjoyed playing both games.

The 'electric light' game was played on a slippery, snow-covered pitch and a newspaper report confirmed that 'both teams expressed themselves as thoroughly satisfied with the result'. It added: 'For the United Suffolk team, A. Sidgwick (captain), played remarkably well, and his men won the game by five goals to three. The goals were kicked by G. Sherrington, L. Turner, J.H. Knights and F.W. Wrinch for United Suffolk. Knights had the honour of making two of the five. For the Ipswich team the goals were made by A. Turner (captain), E. Turner and H.B. Peecock.' While the report suggested that the occasion was a great success, it later transpired that several prominent businessmen lost money on the venture – it would be called sponsorship today – because too few spectators had attended for the books to be balanced.

Ipswich School provided the bulk of the club's first players, notably S.A. Notcutt, F.C. Peecock, P.P. Cornell, C.L. Alexander and the Sherrington brothers, G.S. and W.S., and it was also one of many schools to provide opposition. George Sherrington was an outstanding forward who scored four goals on his debut for the club in 1878 and captained it the following season while still at school. Later he played for Cambridge University, Crusaders, and the famous Corinthians, while as a lawyer he was to prove a valuable member of the Football Association, on which he served as the Suffolk and Norfolk representative from 1887 to 1907 and as a vice-president from 1897 to 1907.

A League is Formed

By 1885 there were sufficient clubs operating within the county to enable the formation of the Suffolk County Football Association, its first members including Beccles Caxton, Bury St Edmunds, Cowell's, Orwell Works, Ipswich Rangers, Ipswich School, Long Melford, Newmarket, Stowmarket, Sudbury, Woodbridge Town and, of course, Ipswich Association Football Club. The introduction that season of the Suffolk Senior Cup provided the first competitive football within the county and was clearly to the liking of Ipswich Association who, although beaten 3-1 by Woodbridge Town after two replays in the first round, were successful in the 1886-87 final when they beat Ipswich School 2-1.

The Suffolk Senior Cup began to attract more and more spectators and when Ipswich again reached the final in 1888-89 a record crowd of

An early shot of the Portman Road ground, which Town shared with the rugby club on alternate Saturdays until 1891, but was still the venue thereafter for other events.

3,000, many of whom had gate-crashed the event, ringed the Portman Road pitch to see a 4-0 victory over a Newmarket side reported to average 12 stone a man.

It was at their annual general meeting on 18 September 1888 that the Ipswich Association Football Club began moves to amalgamate with the rugby club, based at Portman Road, which then, as now, belonged to the Corporation (Borough Council) of Ipswich, and where the playing surface was considered to be far superior. George Sherrington, along with team-mate and fellow solicitor Stephen Notcutt, were instrumental in the amalgamation with the rugby club.

It was confirmed on 1 October 1888 that an agreement had been reached, with the new club being called Ipswich Town Football Club. Initially, the two clubs agreed to share Portman Road on alternate Saturdays and this was the case until 1891, when the rugby club departed and Ipswich Town moved into Portman Road on a permanent basis. After the amalgamation, Oxford blue and white stripes were adopted as the club's colours. Blue and white were the colours from the start, but in the beginning the 'uniform' comprised dark blue shirts with a white shield.

It was announced in September 1890 that Ipswich Town would not be competing in the Suffolk Senior Cup competition, but would instead enter the FA Challenge Cup for the first time. They won their opening tie, in the first qualifying round, defeating Reading by two goals to nil, and made further progress in the second by seeing off Norwich Thorpe to the tune of 4-0. A 5-2 victory over Huntingdon County put them within one game of the first round proper.

The Huntingdon game kicked off late, because Francis Peecock's train from Stowmarket was delayed, but Town were still forced to start with ten men. Despite falling behind, they recovered well to record a convincing win, but hopes of advancing to the first round proper were firmly dashed when the 93rd Highlanders won 4-1 at Portman Road. Unfortunately, this was to remain the club's best performance in the competition for 46 years.

Town's record in the Suffolk Senior Cup, prior to the First World War, was far more impressive.

They appeared in 15 Suffolk Senior Cup finals, winning 13, and they established a record, so far unmatched, of victories in five successive seasons from 1904 to 1908. Two players, W.E. Double and A.E. Bailey, played in all five finals and, together with the rest of the side who defeated Haverhill Rovers 6-1 in 1906, each received a gold medal from the Suffolk County FA to commemorate their cup hat-tricks.

Three Town players – Ernest Kent, Stephen Notcutt and Arnold Haward – were in the Suffolk County team to take on Preston North End, the first Football League champions and the first professional side to play at Portman Road, on 24 March 1892, which the visitors won 3-0. Town met Woolwich Arsenal on 23 November that year and the game, which resulted in a 5-0 defeat for the home side, was marred by the sending-off of visiting forward A. Elliott for 'deliberately holding after twice being cautioned'.

A Debate over League Status

There was a significant development in April 1895 when a special meeting of the club was called to consider an invitation, extended from some time earlier, to join the Southern League, which was envisaged as an alternative to the Football League, by then almost seven years old and comprised entirely of northern clubs. The influential George Sherrington, unable to take part in the meeting as a county official, nevertheless led opposition to the move, writing a letter to the *East Anglian Daily Times* in which he explained that overnight travel and professional opposition would be involved, and added that the landlords at Portman Road 'may not wish professionals to appear there'.

He was supported by Francis Peecock who, in opening the following evening's meeting and proposing that Ipswich Town should not join the Southern League, voiced the opinion that 'football was played for fun and was not to become a business'. Laughter reverberated round the room when he added: 'Soon we shall be having Ipswich Town Limited.'

All, however, were not opposed to joining the new league, although businessman R.D. Hendry's was a lone voice when he proposed an amendment that Town should accept the invitation and there was silence when the chairman called for a seconder. Rather than take the route into professionalism, therefore, the club decided, by an overwhelming majority, to reject the invitation and continue as before.

George Sherrington was one of five members on the committee of the new FA Amateur Cup competition that was introduced in the 1893-94 season and the first trophy was purchased at a cost of £30. Ipswich were one of the original 81 entries, alongside Tottenham Hotspur, but their progress was brief. They gained a bye in the first qualifying round and lost 1-0 to Ilford in the second at Portman Road, but they had better luck the following season, reaching the second round proper before going out to Old Etonians, 7-3, in a replay at Wimbledon.

In 1895-96, Town beat Old Harrovians 6-2 at home to earn a second-round trip to face the eventual winners, Bishop Auckland. The official party set off for the North East, travelling on the Great Eastern Railway to York, whereupon they changed to the Great Northern Railway for the final leg to Darlington. No executive travel in those days: the Ipswich team emerged from a third-class carriage and startled GNR officials exclaimed that such conditions were only fit for the transport of cattle to market.

The players only reached their overnight hotel at midnight, which may or may not have contributed to their 3-1 defeat in front of 2,000 fans. Either way, it was an historic occasion as it represented Town's longest journey to complete a fixture and the first time an overnight stay had been deemed necessary.

By far the biggest game to have been staged at Portman Road was the visit of Aston Villa, reigning Football League champions and FA Cup holders, on 26 February 1898. They fielded a full-strength side against a Suffolk County side that included four representatives from Ipswich Town – P.P. Cornell, C.F. Woods, E.A. Kent and C.L. Alexander.

More than 5,000 spectators paid almost £235, of which the visitors were paid £150, and it was Villa, hardly surprisingly, who won 4-1. The occasion was regarded as being sufficiently important for the Great Eastern Railway to organise special trains to ferry supporters from outlying areas. A special stand was even erected and wagons were placed around the ground, a measure that became normal practice at the ground for many years thereafter.

A Time for Change

The move for change was gathering pace and at the club's annual general meeting, held at the Town Hall on 30 August 1898, secretary Philip Cornell was criticised and was labelled 'a fossilised amateur' by Mr H.H. Gibbons, secretary of the Ipswich and District League, who was angered to learn that the Town reserve side would not be participating in his competition.

It was in May the following year that the club eventually decided, with some degree of reluctance, to move into league football, and they finished a creditable fourth in their first season as members of the eight-club Norfolk and Suffolk League. Town regularly fielded two clergymen in those days – Rev M.W. Murray and Rev H.A.P. Gardiner – and there was at least one occasion, a Suffolk Senior Cup-tie at Sudbury which they won 3-1, when they were forced to play the entire 90 minutes with just ten men, Rev Murray, the curate of Bramford, deciding that rushing to the bedside of a dying parishioner was more important than playing football.

Ipswich Town Football Club 1906-07 with the Suffolk Senior Cup that they had just retained for the fourth successive season. Back row (left to right): G. Lewis, W.S. Cotton, V.J. Lewis, A. Baxter, A.E. Bailey, P.S. Green, I.S. Double. Front row (left to right): E.L. Brown, C.M. Phillips, J.W. Malden, W.E. Double (captain), H. Potter, G.D. McGhee.

Town's membership of the Norfolk and Suffolk League was to last for eight seasons. In 1901-02 they lost 9-0 on the final day of the season, to champions Lowestoft Town, and finished third. That game was significant in as much as it was the last played for the club by Ernest 'Toby' Kent, who had scored more than 200 goals in roughly the same number of games, including friendlies.

He became the first Ipswich player to receive a testimonial when, in January 1903, secretary George Wilding circulated a letter that contained the paragraph: 'Mr Kent is intending shortly to be married, and it is felt to be a fitting occasion upon which to make the presentation to him.' Born on 1 September 1868, he died at his daughter's home in Finningham on 14 June 1960. By special arrangement with the club his ashes were scattered at Portman Road and in the following two seasons Ipswich won the Second Division and First Division titles.

In the 1902-03 campaign they lost 5-1, in what turned out to be the championship decider, to Lowestoft in their penultimate game and had to settle for the runners-up spot. A newly-formed club, Norwich City, were third, but had the distinction of completing a league double over Ipswich as East Anglian derby rivalry got under way in earnest.

At this stage in the club's history, it was the committee, rather than the players, who were making the most telling contributions to the club's future. For example, before the 1904-05 season got under way, major improvements were made to the Portman Road ground when two-and-a-quarter acres of adjacent wasteland owned by the Corporation was levelled and turfed to provide a pitch exclusive to football, leaving the remaining area free for cricket, hockey, tennis and athletics.

The Ipswich Cricket, Football and Athletic Ground Company Limited was formed in November 1905, with capital of £2,000, and it was responsible for the construction of the first Portman Road grandstand, a project completed by Mr W.G. Fisk at a cost of £230 during the 1906-07 season.

The new company's first chairman was William Parker Burton, of Burton, Son and Saunders, and the vice-chairman was Philip Wyndham Cobbold, great uncle of future chairmen John and Patrick Cobbold and himself destined to take control, briefly, at Portman Road. Born in Ipswich on 5 January 1875, he attended Eton College, played first-class cricket for Cambridge University, and from 1902 he represented Suffolk, captaining the side on many occasions. A new, 21-year ground lease, dated 24 June 1905, was obtained from the Corporation.

Chapter Two: 1907-36
The Long Road to Professionalism

In the summer of 1907, Ipswich were caught in the middle of a power struggle between the FA and the newly-formed Amateur FA, which owed its existence to a small, but influential, group of amateur clubs in Middlesex and Surrey. The FA were felt by some to be favouring the northern professionals and clubs, county associations and competitions throughout the country had to decide whether to affiliate to one or the other.

The Norfolk and Suffolk League remained loyal to the FA, as did both the Norfolk and Essex County FAs, but the Suffolk County FA found itself divided. For the seven years 'the split', as the breakaway was known, lasted, there were in effect two county associations.

Town defected to join the Amateur Football Association, the decision being taken at a special meeting held at Ipswich Town Hall on 16 August 1907, over which Sir Frederick Wilson, a pioneer of both the Ipswich and Felixstowe Golf Clubs, presided. There was a turnout of 140 members, including George Sherrington and Stephen Notcutt, both of whom had severed their links with the FA over the dispute.

Following that meeting, representatives of the club were invited to attend the inaugural meeting of the new Southern Amateur League at the Clarence Hotel, Whitehall, on 23 August 1907, at which the club was elected to Section A of the new competition for the start of the 1907-08 season.

A sum of £280 was invested on the building of a new pavilion, which was still being used as the dressing rooms 58 years later, by which time the team had been crowned champions of the Football League. With the exception of Eastbourne, all Ipswich's other opponents were from London and some took the unusual step of electing to pay two visits to Suffolk, where attendances were generally higher, thereby ensuring financial gain, and because they were guaranteed a good day out. The club's long-standing reputation as generous hosts was starting to take root.

A New Era
Eastbourne were the opponents when Ipswich made their Southern Amateur League debut at Portman Road on 14 September 1907,

The Ipswich Town side that lined up in the Southern Amateur League in 1907-08. Back row (left to right): W. Cotton, C.M. Philips, I. Double, W.E. Double, J. Fraser, Mr S.A. Taylor (secretary). Front row (left to right): A.E. Bailey, H. Butcher, J.W. Malden, W.K. Sampson, C.A. Fenn, F. Turner.

an occasion made all the more memorable by a 4-1 home win and remarkable in that not a single foul was committed by either side.

Billy 'Swanky' Malden gave Ipswich the lead within 30 seconds and the visiting captain complimented the home crowd at the end when he said: 'They cheered our goal as much as their own.' Malden, blessed with a powerful shot, netted 12 times in as many games that season and in a total of 168 appearances, between 1901 and 1911, he netted 133 times. He joined Town from Ipswich Rangers and had been a member of the England amateur team that toured Bohemia in 1905.

A schoolmaster by profession, towards the end of his career Malden made the journey from London at weekends, but following a club decision to cut back on travelling expenses, he left to join Civil Service, who were based in the capital.

The gap Malden left in the Town side was plugged, eventually, by Ernie Bugg, a plumber by trade, who was signed from Westbourne Mills and went on to score 79 goals in the three seasons prior to the outbreak of the First World War. Tragically, his career was brought to a premature end when he lost a leg during the fighting in France.

The Ipswich team that defeated Eastbourne in the club's first Southern Amateur League fixture was: I.S. Double, W.E. Double, A.E. Bailey, W.S. Cotton, C.M. Phillips, V.J. Lewis, C.D. Fenn, W.H. Dunnett, J.W. Malden, H. Butcher and F. Turner. Several of the players were new to the club, Butcher having joined from Orwell Works and Fenn from St Mary's Stoke, while Turner was a local youngster who made light of the fact that he was deaf and dumb.

Others, meanwhile, were more familiar, with Bill Double remaining as captain and the experienced pair of Albert Bailey and Walter Cotton maintaining their places throughout the season. Charlie Fenn, whose brother Cyril also signed, was absent only once. A talented winger, Charlie represented the Southern Amateur League select side several times alongside club colleague Malden, and he was a very versatile sportsman who also excelled at cricket, rowing, athletics and lawn tennis. He sailed for India in 1912. Charlie, who received an inscribed gold watch and chain upon his departure, later returned to live in Ipswich, where he died on 2 November 1974 at the age of 85.

Within three days of defeating Eastbourne at the start of a new era for the club, secretary George Wilding, who had been in the job since the start of the 1900-01 season, resigned. Town finished the season third from bottom in the nine-team league, which was won by New Crusaders, but far more worrying was the club's financial position. They incurred huge losses, primarily because their rent had risen to £240 per annum and they began the following season with just £3 in their kitty.

After some members questioned the wisdom of maintaining Southern Amateur League status, subscriptions were increased by 50 per cent, although the five-shilling fee had remained in place since the very first meeting in 1878. A reduction in rent, to £150, was also welcomed, but easing the financial burden did little to improve on-the-field matters. Not even home advantage – Town played 12 of their 16 games at Portman Road – could bring about a change of fortune, although they did improve their league position by one place to finish fourth from bottom.

Only by winning their last three games of the 1909-10 season did Ipswich avoid relegation, eventually finishing third from bottom having won just six, and lost nine, of their 16 games. There was a significant change behind the scenes, with Ivan Double, the goalkeeper who had succeeded George Wilding as secretary, indicating that he had too many commitments to continue. He was replaced by Frank Mills, who worked for the local clothing firm, Phillips and Piper, and who was to remain in office until 1936.

Among the new players were H.G. Rowsell, from Cambridge; Alf Liffen, a former soldier who was employed by Ransomes, Sims and Jefferies; Norwich-based Claude Sennitt; and Allan Bowman, who hailed from Ipswich but who was working in London.

One incident worthy of mention occurred in a 4-0 home defeat by Casuals, on 23 October 1909, when Ipswich were awarded a penalty for an alleged handling offence. Bill Double, the Town captain, took the spot-kick and made no attempt to score, his way of indicating that he thought the penalty should not have been awarded.

In another game, the referee came in for some loud criticism for his interpretation of the offside rule. This prompted former referee, Mr W. Kemp, to rise to his feet and deliver a rebuke to the offenders, and the *East Anglian Daily Times* correspondent added to the debate when he penned these words: 'It is really surprising what an exhibition some spectators do make of themselves at matches – "see all and say nuffin" is surely the safest motto at football matches.'

The 1909-10 season also saw Ipswich suffer the heaviest defeat in their history, going down 15-1 to Corinthians in a friendly fixture played at Portman Road on New Year's Day. Ipswich player Vernon Lewis, meanwhile, made news for an event in no way associated with football. It was when Bostock and Wombwell's Menagerie came to town in December 1909, at the Palace Rink in the Old Cattle Market, that Lewis volunteered to enter the lion's den – not once, but nightly at 8.30 prompt. He kept his word and was rewarded with a gold medal, handed over by the famous lion tamer, Captain Wombwell.

Ipswich finished fourth from bottom in the 1910-11 season, but this time without the threat of relegation. They started the campaign, during which 13 of their 16 games were played at home, with a new captain, Billy Garnham succeeding Bill Double, who managed only one game, in which he collapsed and had to be carried from the pitch. His brother, goalkeeper Ivan, also had to quit playing because of injury.

New players were again recruited to bolster the team's strengths, among them F.E. Dann, a full-back from Beccles; C. Tilbrook, another full-back from Bury St Edmunds; goalkeeper Billy Masterson, from Westbourne Mills; and Cecil Potter, an inside-forward from Melton, who left at the end of the season to sign as a professional for Norwich City. He stayed with the Canaries until the outbreak of the First World War, after which he managed Hartlepool, Derby County, Huddersfield Town and Norwich, where he remained until resigning on 19 January 1929.

Meanwhile, Vernon Lewis played his last game for the club on Saturday, 11 March 1911, and shortly afterwards was on a boat bound for Montreal in Canada. His parting gift was a gold sovereign case, but there was bad news when it was revealed that his seven Suffolk Senior Cup medals had been stolen from a London hotel.

Ipswich embarked on their first tour abroad, departing on 3 May 1911 and travelling via Harwich, Antwerp and Dresden to Prague, where they arrived two days later. They played two games against Slavia Prague, losing one 4-0 and drawing the other 1-1.

Without the services of consistent marksman Malden, the club started the 1911-12 season with Ernest Bugg, who had been included in the touring party to Bohemia some months earlier, in the No. 9 shirt and he went on to score 17 goals, 12 of them helping Ipswich to finish a league-best fifth and the other five in cup competitions. There was a quick reminder of what Town were missing, however, when Malden scored a hat-trick in Civil Service's 4-2 win at Portman Road on 14 October 1911, the season having started just a week previously.

On 6 November that year, at the height of a severe south-westerly gale, the corrugated iron roof of the Portman Road grandstand was blown away, with damage extending to the trees lining the adjacent road and overhead tramway lines which were brought down. The glass sides of the stand fell inward, but the lower structure remained intact and it was not long before the grandstand was restored at a cost of £60.

It was a wet summer in 1912, with rain almost every day, and one of the few people who did not complain was the club's groundsman, Walter Woollard, who had decided it was necessary to returf the pitch.

An upbeat annual general meeting on Friday, 19 July heard that the club had an improved cash balance of £28 4s 11d and that both attendances and membership contributions had also increased. It was decided to hold the membership fee at 7s 6d and season tickets went on sale, at five shillings each.

On the playing side, long-serving full-back, Albert Bailey, decided to hang up his boots and was elected a life member. With Billy Masterson having moved back to Great Yarmouth, the club had to find a new goalkeeper and local lad, A. Durrell, was an adequate replacement, going on to play in every competitive game during the 1912-13 season.

Billy Garnham remained as captain, while other regulars included Ernie Harbord, a teacher of whom it was claimed that his speed off the mark was so great that his fellow forwards could not keep up with him. Apparently, he often crossed the ball without a colleague in sight and his pace often caused him to run right off the end of the pitch.

Town finished in their highest Southern Amateur League position to date, fourth, winning half of their 18 games, but it was a false position, since records were incomplete and some of their rivals were lagging behind in terms of games played, including the Malden-inspired Civil Service who finished top, despite having completed four games less.

During a game against Casuals at Portman Road on Saturday, 19 October 1912, Billy Garnham kicked the ball into the road and it struck a small girl. A policeman was called and five minutes elapsed before he returned the ball and allowed the game to continue.

Ipswich reached the AFA Cup semi-finals for the first time in their history, with New Crusaders the visitors on 8 March 1913 to a packed grandstand and a further 2,000 spectators behind the ropes all the way round the pitch. Ernie Bugg had a goal disallowed before the visitors netted twice in the second half and all Town could offer in reply was a consolation goal from Ernie Harbord.

The club said goodbye to another stalwart, Cyril Fenn, brother of Charlie, who headed for British Columbia on 18 April 1913, after being presented with a gold watch, to try his luck at fruit farming. A crowd, including Ipswich captain Billy Garnham, gathered at the railway station to see him off. Sadly, Cyril was a casualty of the First World War.

Ipswich again finished fourth in the 1913-14 season, winning half of their 16 games. Billy Masterson returned in goal, deciding to travel down each week from Great Yarmouth, and R.J. Hemmell made the journey from Norwich, while S.J. West's weekly trip was from Felixstowe.

The split between the FA and the AFA, dating back to the summer of 1907, was eventually over by the time the season finished, at which point another tour of Bohemia was undertaken. All three matches were lost and those in the party that crossed the English Channel would be doing so again in the First World War. The conflict signalled the end of football at Portman Road and Ipswich were denied a return to action until early 1920, by which time the ground was in a serious state of disrepair.

It seemed it might be necessary for the club to play their fixtures at another venue – both Sidegate Lane and Gippeswyk Park were mentioned – but neither ground was suitable, since it was not possible to control admission. As a result, Ipswich Town did not function at all during the 1919-20 season.

After a six-year gap due to the First World War, the Town side that took to the field in 1920 contained a number of new faces.

Having finally agreed a compensation figure with the War Office, and with Stephen Notcutt and his team of volunteers having made the pitch playable again, Town were forced, because of casualties, to issue an appeal for new players to come forward for the 1920-21 campaign and it transpired that not one player who had taken part in the final Southern Amateur League game of the 1913-14 season was present when the club kicked off a new season seven years later.

A cash crisis – the balance stood at a mere £31 7s 7d – forced the club to increase the annual membership fee to one guinea (£1 1s) in the summer of 1920, although members would all be able to watch games from the grandstand. A further concession for members was that they were allowed to be accompanied by a female.

Bert Haste, a long-time servant for Town, who was renowned for his explosive shot.

Starting Afresh

It was a new-look Ipswich team that took to the field on 4 September 1920, for the first game to be played at Portman Road in more than six years, a friendly against Old Bancroftians that ended 1-1. The side included several new faces, among them W.H. Gillespie and Tom Stepney, who was known affectionately as the 'Old Warhorse', both having been signed from Orwell Works.

Other new players were D. Hutcheson, who had moved to Ipswich from London; H. Taggart, who had experience in Ireland with Belfast Celtic; Charlie Spindler, from Stoke Athletic; and Herbert 'Bert' Haste, who worked as a clerk at Churchman's, and who was signed by secretary Frank Mills from the Life Brigade Old Boys in 1919 and was widely acknowledged as one of the finest players in the area at the time.

Bert Haste played for Ipswich for six years, during which time he rejected offers to turn professional with both Hull City and Chelsea. He later recalled that the offer from the London club had been particularly attractive – £5 5s a week – but he had a good job and his main ambition was to become a clergyman. Haste was renowned for his explosive shooting and even managed to burst the net from a powerfully struck penalty against Eastbourne. His brother, Beauford 'Beau' Haste, also appeared for Town in the early post-war years, and both later entered the ministry, Bert spending 20 years as a missionary in India before retiring to Weymouth, while Beau resided in Felixstowe.

Other new faces included the former Clacton Town and Essex centre-half, Adrian Gilling, and centre-forward Len Mizen, a soldier from the local barracks who did not enjoy the best of health and died in 1929 at the age of 33. In 53 games for the club he scored 46 goals, the most memorable of which was from a free-kick and which earned an unexpected 1-0 win over Chelsea, then in the First Division, at Portman Road on 10 May 1921.

Mizen netted a hat-trick in the third replay of an AFA Cup first round tie against Old Lyonians on 15 January 1921, after the teams had drawn 3-3, 1-1 and 0-0. The decisive game ended 5-2 to Town after extra time and the second round was another marathon, with three games being required to see off Aquarius and earn a third round meeting with Ealing, who came to Portman Road in front of a record 5,000 crowd and won comfortably, 4-0.

The Southern Amateur League committee agreed to extend the 1920-21 season after Ipswich were late in applying to join. Early-season form was poor, but it improved during the second half of the campaign and Town eventually secured third place. Mizen was top goalscorer with 15 goals and he was a huge favourite with the crowd.

Team captain H.A. Dix, an Army officer at Landguard Fort, left for a tour of duty in Ireland soon after the season started and was replaced by recent recruit Hutcheson, only for

Len Mizen averaged almost a goal a game during his time at the club.

him to suffer a leg injury that saw Billy Garrard, previously with Eastbourne and who had moved to the town to help his father run the Ipswich Gas Company, take over. Garrard was also a county tennis player.

Town only lost one of their last ten games and other players of the time included Fred 'Windmill' Smith; printer Percy Rozier; Adrian Gilling, who later opened a tailor's shop in the town; and Len Robinson, a goalkeeper who was the only player to turn out for the club in competitive matches both before and after the First World War.

Earl Cadogan, president of Chelsea and whose country seat was Culford Hall, near Bury St Edmunds, arranged the visit of the London club. The game was staged in aid of the Ex-Officers' Association and the Ipswich and East Suffolk Hospital, and the opportunity to see such top-class opposition pulled in a record attendance of over 8,000. Chelsea were captained for the day by Vivian Woodward, a former England international who had previously played for Clacton Town and was still living there. Earl Cadogan, incidentally, soon became a vice-president of Ipswich, in addition to his role with Chelsea.

A First Title Beckons

There was no lack of confidence as Town approached the 1921-22 season, although three players, including Mizen, were declared unavailable because all were soldiers and would be required to play in the RFA (Royal Field Artillery) team. The club secured excellent replacements in local lad Sammy Fenn; Jimmy Gardner, signed from Walton United; and Frank Johnson, who was recruited from Halstead.

Fenn and Gardner played in every Southern Amateur League game en route to the title, without doubt the club's greatest achievement at the time.

Johnson, meanwhile, marked his first season with the club by finishing as leading scorer, netting a total of 27 times, including five in the 7-0 win over Lowestoft Town in the fourth qualifying round of the Amateur Cup, which constituted a new club scoring record.

Eric Wilsher, a teacher who had just completed his training at St Mark's College in London, was another new signing, and Ipswich remained unbeaten in the league until 22 April 1922, when Cambridge Town won 1-0 at Portman Road. Despite such a strong run, however, they still found themselves in the position of having to win their final two games in order to secure their first-ever Southern Amateur League title.

New recruit Sammy Fenn played in every game in 1921–22 as Town secured the title.

After beating bottom club Old Parkonians 2-0 in a game when they missed an early penalty, Town headed for the south coast to meet second-placed Eastbourne whose ground, the Saffrons, was bathed in sunshine and ringed by a 4,000 crowd. Arthur Fenn opened the scoring after 24 minutes, but the hosts equalised and had it remained 1-1 they would have taken the league crown. Fenn, who was later to captain the club, added a second (controversially, as many thought that there was an element of handball) and Ipswich held out, thanks in no small way to some excellent saves by goalkeeper Oscar Reeve, who had made his way into the team via the reserves.

Thousands of jubilant supporters could not wait to celebrate the club's biggest achievement to date. A large crowd gathered at Ipswich Railway Station, cheering the players as they disembarked from the 10 p.m. train from London and made their way on to a lorry that was bedecked in blue and white for a tour of the town. An estimated 4,000 people followed and the Ex-Servicemen's Band completed the victory procession on a second lorry. The parade made its way to the Cornhill, where the players entered the Golden Lion Hotel, made their way upstairs and waved to the happy throng gathered outside.

Fenn, whose two goals had ensured victory over Eastbourne, was a particular favourite. He was a clerk with the local firm of Burton, Son and Saunders and in 157 appearances for the club, between 1920 and 1927, he scored a total of 108 goals, an impressive strike rate by any standards. He formed part of a feared trio alongside Mizen and Haste, all of them formidable marksmen.

Having clinched their first major title, the Ipswich amateurs were quickly put in their place when Chelsea returned to town on 9 May 1922 and triumphed 7-1, in front of a crowd of approximately 7,000, to avenge their surprise defeat a year earlier.

The club's annual general meeting on 21 July 1922 heard that the bank balance stood at a very healthy £451 14s 6d, the highest-ever, and it was also reported that the average attendance at Portman Road during the championship-winning 1921-22 season had been 3,080. The mood of the meeting was understandably upbeat, and there was little cause for concern that the ground rent was now £425, as gate income more than covered outgoings.

On the playing side, Billy Garrard sportingly suggested that Adrian Gilling should succeed him as captain, while Frank Johnson returned to Halstead and Jimmy Gardner accepted an offer to turn professional with Yeovil and Petters. Several professional clubs also approached Bert Haste, and it was his father who was instrumental in him staying put and combining his football with his job at Churchman's.

With Mizen replacing Johnson at centre-forward and V.L. Garnett coming in at outside right, Town set about their defence of the league crown in determined fashion

Billy Garrard led the side to their first title success in 1922, but an injury the following season ended his career.

and only narrowly failed to retain it, eventually finishing second to Eastbourne as the previous season's top two swapped places. The pair also met in the first round of the AFA Cup, with Eastbourne winning 4-1 at Portman Road in a game that was marred by an injury to Billy Garrard, as a result of which he never played again. Tommy Whitehead, a local lad, replaced the stricken Garrard for the remainder of the season and eventually he, too, became the club's captain. Mizen was another casualty, which meant that the main goalscoring responsibility had passed to Bert Haste. He responded magnificently to net 30 times.

The rivalry between Ipswich and Eastbourne was intense. Town won the first game of the season, 3-1, at home, but, remarkably, the return was never played. It was originally scheduled for mid-February, but the south coast outfit had to cancel because they were involved in an AFA Cup-tie. As the season drew to a close, and all other fixtures had been completed, Eastbourne were declared champions and there was no protest from Ipswich, despite the fact that they were just one point in arrears, meaning that victory in the final game would have earned them the title for a second successive year.

To this day, it remains a mystery why the fixture programme was never concluded, although it has been suggested there was an arrangement between the two clubs' respective committees. It will never be known for certain, but some people close to the situation were of the opinion that because Fenn's second goal, in the decisive game the previous season, was clouded in controversy – it was felt he had handled the ball – officials had come to a convenient arrangement for the following campaign, although such a theory, no matter the eventual outcome, seems incredibly far-fetched.

New Blood

The Town committee found it necessary in the summer of 1923 to appeal for youngsters to come forward and play football, because they were concerned with the long-term effect of the decision by both Ipswich School and Framlingham College that rugby should be their official sport. Their lead was followed by several local authority-run schools, the reason for the switch being that football, unlike rugby, had continued during the war years and was thus seen as unpatriotic.

Arthur Fenn was elected captain for an indifferent 1923-24 season that saw several new players introduced. They included George Harris, who took over in goal from Oscar Reeve and who was to make quite an impact.

He rejected offers to turn professional from several Football League clubs, including Hull City, and opinion to this day is divided as to whether he, or successor George Nicholls, was the best amateur goalkeeper ever to appear for the club.

On the subject of goalkeepers, Town used four against Aquarius on 17 November 1923. Harris was carried off injured to be replaced by Eric Wilsher and when he, too, was hurt, it was Bert Haste's turn to deputise, but only until the interval when groundsman Walter Woollard took over. Amazingly, despite Town only having eight men on the field at times, they only lost 3-1 after their opponents managed to find the net twice in the closing stages.

Other new faces in the 1923-24 season belonged to Lionel Turner, a centre-half who worked for the Great Eastern Railway; Vic Harman, who had turned out for the Tottenham reserves and travelled up from London each week; and local lad Keith Harman, from Leiston. A series of injuries contributed to Town finishing a disappointing fourth from bottom, having won just seven of their 20 league fixtures.

They fared much better the following season, claiming fifth place and with a points tally just four adrift of that of the champions, Midland Bank. A supporters' club was formed, with the intention of arranging events at which both supporters and players could socialise together, although there was some reluctance to the proposal that Ipswich should follow the example of other clubs and organise trips to away games.

Again there was an influx of new blood to Portman Road. W.W. Dempsey arrived from RAF Felixstowe, scored 13 goals in 14 league games, and later in the season accepted an offer from Norwich City to turn professional, making several appearances in the Canaries' first team.

Goalkeeper Harris was selected to play for an England Amateur XI, while other new recruits included Billy Hawkes and S. Sharman from Orwell Works and J. Reilly from Brantham, while Fred Hunt, George Doulton, Bill Jarrett, Vic Page and Frank Cotterell were promoted from the reserves. It was only over the final two games of the season that Town's title prospects faded.

Despite coming close to the title the previous season, there were problems to be resolved at the beginning of the 1925-26 campaign. Captain Tommy Whitehead's appearances were limited through injury, and George Harris took over the team leadership, while ex-player Tom Stepney struggled in the role of trainer and the first four league games all resulted in defeats, including a 9-3 away hammering by old rivals Eastbourne.

Harris, who was again selected to play for an England Amateur XI, featured in two extraordinary incidents. On 21 November 1925, he became the first Town goalkeeper to score, from a penalty, and he did it again the following week, also from the spot, a feat never since emulated. The circumstances of the first penalty were bizarre. Town were awarded a penalty in a home friendly against London Caledonians and, since they did not believe the decision to be correct, Harris ran from the other end of the pitch and simply rolled the ball to the opposing keeper. The intention was for the Caledonians custodian to collect the ball, but he stepped out of the way to allow it to cross the line, thereby indicating that he, at least, felt the award to be justified.

Ipswich struggled to climb away from the bottom end of the Southern Amateur League in the 1925-26 season, and only the fact that both Aquarius and Merton fared even worse spared Town the indignity of relegation. Several youngsters were introduced, among them Alf Baker, Clem Burch, Percy Bugg, Ray Colby, Jackie Green and Bernard 'Tricky' Taylor, who went on to manage the Ipswich Greyhound Stadium before his death in 1977.

If 1925-26 was depressing for Ipswich, the following season was a roller-coaster affair, as can be seen from some extraordinary league results. For example, although Toc H visited Portman Road and were beaten 8-1, they returned six months later to triumph 8-2, and while Ealing beat Town 10-5 at their ground, the corresponding fixture at Portman Road resulted in a 9-0 home win.

Part of the explanation for such an up-and-down state of affairs was that RAF and Navy players regularly appeared, but when they were not available their places went to untried reserves and, as a result, team strength suffered. Flight-Lieutenant S.N. Webster, stationed at RAF Martlesham, was one of the servicemen who appeared in the side, and he gained international fame in 1927 when he won the Schneider Trophy, in Venice, averaging a speed of 281.656 miles per hour in his Napier-Lyon seaplane. He became an instant hero, both locally and nationally, and received the AFC 'Bar' from Prime Minister Stanley Baldwin at 10 Downing Street.

The committee turned to Sammy Fenn, who had first played for the club in the 1921-22 season and had been playing for Ipswich Works for two years, to be captain and he accepted, going on to enjoy a good season, although Town finished second from bottom after winning just eight and drawing three of their 22 league fixtures.

There were rumblings of discontent on two fronts. Firstly, there were suggestions that the club would be on the move to a new home at Belvedere

Road as a result of not seeing eye to eye with their landlords at Portman Road, although peace was quickly restored. Secondly, the topic of professionalism was raised yet again and it was even claimed that Ipswich was the biggest town in the country that was not home to a professional club.

Norwich City, of all people, even offered help, but the offer was declined and the Town committee stuck to their guns, pointing out that it was preferable to have a first-rate amateur side to a third-rate professional one. It was claimed in a letter to the *Green 'Un* that wages would account for half the estimated £100-a-week running costs and other doubters expressed concern at crowd potential.

S.N. Webster who appeared in the side between 1925 and 1930, gained international fame when he broke the world air speed record in Italy in 1927.

When Ipswich played Chelmsford in the first round of the East Anglian Cup on 16 October 1926, the kick-off was delayed because the referee's motorcycle had broken down. Only after he hitched a lift to Portman Road did the game get under way, although Town were trailing 5-0 at half-time and eventually lost 8-0. Come the end of an indifferent season, it was time for drastic action.

Time for Change

In the summer of 1927, Frank Mills placed an advertisement for a professional trainer and the successful applicant was Edwin Dutton, the 37-year-old former trainer of South Shields who had been on the books of Newcastle United alongside Scott Duncan, a future Ipswich manager.

Dutton had been spotted by Newcastle in Germany and he returned there in 1913, the fact that he had represented Germany against Hungary four years earlier seemingly counting for nothing as his more recent connections with England led to him being interned in a prisoner-of-war camp for the duration of the First World War.

Edwin Dutton became Town's first professional trainer in 1927.

Town's rent increased to £500 for the 1927-28 season and, because the pitch was in such a poor state, Freddie Blake was appointed groundsman, taking up his new role on 1 September 1927. He immediately set about creating the best playing surface in the country and even after retiring as groundsman he continued to work on a part-time basis – his enthusiasm for virtually any task belying his seniority. He went on to receive an official Football League award at their annual dinner in London and there can have been no more loyal, nor more dedicated, employee in the history of the club.

As their landlords refused to meet the cost of much-needed improvements to the pavilion, it meant that the club had no alternative but to pick up the £700 bill for a major refit that included the installation of a sunken bath. It was a major expense at the time.

On the field, there was an improvement under Dutton's direction, and Town averaged a point per game as they finished sixth in a 13-club Southern Amateur League. They also won the Suffolk Senior Cup, defeating HMS *Ganges* 2-0 in front of 11,669 spectators – a record for the competition – on Easter Monday. Clem Burch, who later in life was to join the Metropolitan Police, scored both of the goals. The game also signalled the end of HMS *Ganges*' 20-game unbeaten run. It was not all joy in the cup competitions, however, and Town were beaten 10-1 by Harwich & Parkeston at the second round stage of the East Anglian Cup.

That defeat was soon forgotten, though, as Ipswich began their AFA Cup campaign against Northampton Nomads and advanced to the final, where their opponents were the Bank of England. Having defeated them 4-1 in a league game three weeks earlier, Town were favourites to win the final at Dulwich Hamlet on 31 March 1928. However, in ankle-deep mud they were beaten 4-2 and with 2,300 people having travelled from Ipswich, it was hardly surprising that there were renewed calls for the formation of an official supporters' club.

Dutton's influence on a team captained by Alf Baker, and in which Clem Burch, Ray Colby, Jackie Green, Reg Colby, Len Gibbs, 'Tricky' Taylor, Percy Bugg and George Nicholls all had key roles to play, was clearly being felt, and a significant improvement in fortune was anticipated at the start of the 1928-29 season.

Flight-Lieutenant Webster was selected by Dutton to be Town captain and he proved to be an inspired choice. The team won 13 of their opening 14 league games, and by the end of the campaign had suffered just three defeats. Despite such an impressive record, however, it was only good enough to earn the runners-up spot behind champions Cambridge Town, who remained undefeated throughout their 22-game campaign. The rivalry between the two sides was best demonstrated on Good Friday when Ipswich lost 2-1 in front of a Milton Road crowd of 11,961, around 4,000 of whom had travelled by rail and road from Ipswich. The ground was literally bulging at the seams and it was a relief that no one was seriously injured when a corrugated iron roof collapsed, causing 50 spectators to crash to the ground.

Back at Portman Road, the construction of a new stand on the West side of the ground – modest by today's standards, but nevertheless welcome at the time – saw numbered seats introduced for the first time. Dutton also introduced a new, matching kit for the team, discarding the amber socks that had looked strangely out of place alongside blue-and-white striped shirts.

First Time at Wembley

History was also made when Town made their first appearance at Wembley Stadium. Those who assumed the FA Cup final of 1978 to be the club's first visit to the hallowed stadium were quickly reminded by older supporters of the events of 13 October 1928. Opponents Ealing, their own ground consistently waterlogged, were pleasantly surprised when a request to play at nearby Wembley was granted and a report of the game in the *East Anglian Daily Times* suggested there were 'some empty seats' as a crowd of only 1,200 witnessed a 4-0 win for Ipswich, Harold Rogers (2), Len Gibbs and Percy Bugg all achieving the same feat as Roger Osborne almost 50 years later, in scoring at the national stadium.

Town also regained the Suffolk Senior Cup, beating Woodbridge Town 5-0 in the final at Portman Road, and there was no lack of optimism in the summer of 1929 when Dutton was appointed for a further two years. In his acceptance speech he promised that he would do 'everything possible' to land the Southern Amateur League title, which he duly did.

There were the usual crop of new faces at the start of a memorable season, with A.A. – Alfred Arthur – Green making the most impact, and it would be no exaggeration to state that he ranks as one of the most popular players in the history of the club. Known throughout his time at Portman Road by the nickname 'Dammo', he was the younger brother of another player, Billy Green, and the son of Harold Green, who had played for the club in the early 1920s.

Dammo was a stonemason by trade. His premises were in Cemetery Road and the columns fronting Lloyds Bank on the Cornhill, in Ipswich town centre, are a lasting memorial to his craft. From a football point of view, his career statistics – 163 goals in 159 games between 1929 and 1936 – say it all and confirm he was one of the most consistent marksmen ever to don the club's colours.

In his first season, Dammo scored 13 times in the league, but was actually upstaged by his attacking partner, Fred Birtchnell, who had been signed from Clacton Town and weighed in with a league tally of 17, with another 15 spread between three cup competitions. He was one of the first players to develop a special goal celebration and performed many a cartwheel on the way to creating a new scoring record of 44, including goals in friendlies. Goals were certainly not in short supply that season, with Eric Talman also netting 22 times in competitive games.

Ipswich lost the first game of the 1929-30 campaign, 2-0 at home to Midland Bank, but then triumphed in 15 games in succession and eventually lost just four times in 22 fixtures to clinch the title with a six-point cushion separating them from runners-up Eastbourne. Sidney Webster missed the climax, having been posted abroad and played his last game on 26 March 1930 when Barclays Bank were beaten 3-0 at Portman Road.

Billy Green also went abroad, to Singapore to supervise a contract on behalf of his employers, Ransomes, Sims and Jefferies, before the end of a season that saw Town regain the Suffolk Senior Cup. They defeated Sudbury Town at Portman Road in front of an 8,858 crowd on Easter Monday, when Talman claimed a hat-trick in a comfortable 6-0 stroll, and the club completed a hat-trick of honours when a Birtchnell goal was enough to defeat King's Lynn in the final of the Hospital Cup.

The captain at the start of the 1931-32 season was 'Tricky' Taylor, who had taken over when Sidney Webster had departed, and the club decided to enter the FA Cup, rather than the Suffolk Senior Cup, after several clubs, including Sudbury, spoke with one voice, to suggest Ipswich were too strong and should withdraw to give the others a chance.

Town also suffered what would today be termed a goalkeeping crisis. George Nicholls had moved away from the area and George Harris had retirement on his mind, so Len Harvey came in to plug the gap. Two early meetings with Cambridge Town, both resulting in defeats for Ipswich, went a long way towards deciding the Southern Amateur League title and when the same two sides occupied the top places at the end of the season there was a 12-point gap, although finishing runners-up was regarded as quite an achievement for an Ipswich side who had lost four of their opening five games, including two to the eventual champions.

Ipswich had a settled defence, with full-backs Billy Milne and Fred Chambers ahead of goalkeeper Harvey, and a regular half-back line of 'Tricky' Taylor, Norman Rowland and Neville Groom. There were problems in attack, however, with Fred Birtchnell deciding to move on half-way through the season. Despite this setback, Dammo Green responded magnificently to net 21 times in 17 league games with a further nine in the FA Cup, where Town's interest was ended at the second qualifying stage by Crittalls Athletic.

A Supporters' Club is Formed

One significant development that season concerned, at long last, the establishment of an official supporters' club. It was formed at a meeting in the town's Crown and Anchor Hotel on 24 November 1930, which was attended by 80 people, and Major Harold R. Hooper, who was to play a prominent part in helping to form the professional club a few years later, became the first president. Mr Murray Walker was appointed chairman, and Mr Jack Eggett, at whose instigation the meeting was called, accepted the post of secretary.

Billy Milne inherited the captaincy for the 1931-32 season and Town started their Southern Amateur League campaign with an 8-2 win at Carshalton, with right winger A. Rodwell scoring four times. That seemed a modest feat, however, when compared to the eight-goal haul of Dammo Green in an emphatic 10-0 defeat of Eastbourne in the penultimate game of the season, the 9-0 half-time scoreline suggesting that Ipswich eased up considerably after the break. Green's own personal tally was a Southern Amateur League record.

Cambridge Town retained the championship, with Ipswich slipping to third place and they also had the briefest of FA Cup runs, losing 3-2 in a preliminary round tie against Leiston Works, a game in which 'Tricky' Taylor missed a penalty. Ted Jones from Stowmarket, Bob Stopher and George Burch, Clem's brother, were new signings, but Ipswich also failed to hold on to the Hospital Cup, going down 4-3 in the final to the 4th Div Signals, for whom Jock Sowerby made such an impression that Town could not wait to sign him.

Title Success

They had to wait until December 1932 to do so, however, by which time he had left the Army and was living in Ipswich. Another new recruit was Jack Cowley, who had been playing for Newark Town. The Ipswich captaincy that season passed to Neville Rowland, as Billy Milne had sustained an injury from which he failed to make a proper recovery, and Rowland marked his first campaign as skipper by leading Town to the Southern Amateur League title.

Only three league games were lost, and they finished with a four-game flourish in which they recorded a 100 per cent record, scoring ten goals for the loss of none. All four were played at Portman Road and for the penultimate game, opponents Midland Bank broke new ground when they travelled by air.

It was ironic that the championship success was achieved without the services of Edwin Dutton after he had retired to his native Newcastle in the summer of 1932 following five years at the club. He could claim, however, that in his time as trainer, Ipswich had progressed considerably. Dutton was presented with a rosewood clock in front of the pavilion, at which point his successor, Herbert Dainty, was also introduced.

Dainty had been a member of Dundee's Scottish Cup-winning side in 1910, which remains to this day their only success in the competition, and went on to represent the Scottish League before coming south of the border to play for Nottingham Forest, Leicester City and Southampton. Prior to his arrival at Portman Road he had been coaching in South America.

The league title apart, Ipswich also won the Hospital Cup. They defeated Harwich & Parkeston 1-0 in the final at Portman Road – with Dammo Green scoring in extra time – and a large crowd of 8,763 also enjoyed the antics of the clown, Funny Harry. Generally, however, attendances continued to drop and the cry for a change to professionalism was becoming ever louder.

The decline in interest was reflected in a poor turnout at the club's annual general meeting on 30 June 1933, although this hardly made sense since the members of the previous season's Southern Amateur League-winning side were present to collect their medals. The club president, Mr H. Jervis White

Jervis, provided the souvenirs because the league did not even have a trophy to present. Norman Rowland remained as captain and Herbert Dainty as trainer, and even the rent stayed the same – £500.

Ipswich again decided not to enter the Suffolk Senior Cup, because the final was scheduled for Easter Monday and would clash with the game against Cambridge Town, a source of vital revenue. They were early victims of an FA Cup knockout, by Gorleston Town in the extra preliminary round, but managed to advance to the semi-final stage of the AFA Cup where they were beaten 2-1 by St Albans City. In the Hospital Cup, Harwich & Parkeston beat them in the final, 2-0.

By winning the Southern Amateur League title for the second successive season, Ipswich completed a remarkable six-year run in which they never finished lower than third. It was Town's fourth such championship and also their last, clinched by a one-point margin from Hastings St Leonards, one of only four teams to beat them that season.

When goalkeeper Len Harvey was injured in January 1934 he was replaced by youngster Harry Duke, from Orwell Works, and he went on to make a name for himself when, in August that year, he signed professional forms for Norwich City, newly-crowned champions of the Third Division (South) and promoted to the Second Division of the Football League for the first time.

The annual general meeting of 1934 was dominated by two events. Tom Mullins paid tribute to the work of long-serving committee member, Murray Walker, who had died the previous March, while there was a lengthy discussion on the subject of Ipswich perhaps relocating to a different league. Several unsuccessful attempts had been made to gain admission to stronger competitions, including the Isthmian and Athenian Leagues, and some supporters even organised a petition to indicate their support for a withdrawal from the Southern Amateur League, stating that a town the size of Ipswich deserved a better standard of football.

The summer of 1934 also saw another change of trainer at Portman Road, with Herbert Dainty departing to be replaced by Bob McPherson, son of one-time Newcastle United trainer, James McPherson, and a brother-in-law of Town's first professional trainer, Edwin Dutton. The new man had been with Dutch club HBS, from the Hague, for ten years, and it was there, in 1931, that Ipswich had first come across him, as HBS were their first opponents on a short tour of Holland.

In October 1934, Charlie Wells, a centre-forward who had played for Ipswich in the previous two seasons, died of pneumonia. Injured in a trial match at the start of the season, it was following surgery that the pneumonia developed. Collections were taken at matches to help his mother with the cost of travelling from the family home in Newark to Ipswich. The death also occurred of Mr Herbert Jervis White Jervis, the club president since the start of the 1913-14 season.

On the field, Town failed to make it a hat-trick of league titles when they could manage no better than fourth position in the Southern Amateur League, although it seemed fitting that they should finish with a game against Eastbourne, their very first opponents back in 1907 and against whom they had played some memorable matches during what had been a long and mainly happy association with the SAL.

Another New League

It was on 16 February 1935 that representatives of several East Anglian clubs gathered in Ipswich to discuss the formation of the new Eastern Counties League and one week later, at another meeting, the move was completed as Ipswich, along with King's Lynn, Lowestoft Town, Harwich & Parkeston, Crittalls Athletic, Chelmsford, Colchester, Bury Town, Gorleston and Yarmouth Town all voted to proceed. Cambridge Town and Thetford Town were also invited, bringing the number of clubs to 12. When Cambridge decided against the move, Clacton Town were enlisted in their place.

The following month saw the celebration of another important landmark, this time the Jubilee of the Suffolk County Football Association. It was marked by a visit to Portman Road on Wednesday, 20 March 1935 of Arsenal, for whom the brothers Dennis and Leslie Compton featured and the former scored twice. Fred Chambers, Cecil Dorling, A.E. Brunt, Dammo Green and Herbert Clements were the Town representatives in a match won 6-1 by the Gunners in front of an appreciative 8,000 crowd who paid £293 1s 3d for the rare privilege of seeing top professionals in action.

On 21 June 1935, Ipswich Town appointed Captain John Murray Cobbold as their new president, to succeed the late Mr Jervis White Jervis. Known as Captain Ivan, he was the father of two sons, John and Patrick, both of whom were to become future chairmen of the club. Captain Cobbold, born at Holywells, Ipswich, on 28 January 1897, attended Eton and joined the Scots Guards in 1915. Two years later, he was promoted to the rank of captain and he left the Army in 1919 to become chairman of the family brewing firm. He had been president of the Suffolk County FA for two years before accepting a similar post at Portman Road.

It was a time of change for the club: a new man at the top and a new league in which to take part. Fred Chambers was appointed captain and while the first team would be competing in the inaugural Eastern Counties League, the reserve side was also destined for pastures new, the Essex and Suffolk Border League. Ipswich were busy recruiting new players in the summer months, among them Harry Burns, a centre-half from Easington Colliery, Bob Hetherington from Bishop Auckland, Jack Edwards from Norwich CEYMS, Jock Henderson from Leyton and the RAF, Jackie Little from Needham Market and George Knights from Hadleigh who, many years later, was chairman of the official supporters' club until his retirement in 1985.

Captain John Murray Cobbold became the club's president in 1935.

Ipswich started life in the Eastern Counties League by losing 4-0 away to eventual champions Lowestoft Town on 7 September 1935, but they recorded three straight victories to get into their stride and were sitting second at one stage before finally finishing sixth in the new 12-club league. Their biggest win was a 10-2, Portman Road drubbing of Thetford who, not surprisingly, occupied bottom position at the end of the season. Jock Sowerby scored four that day, yet his end-of-season league tally was only seven, although he did add 13 more in the various cup competitions.

Town's 2-0 defeat at Yarmouth on 2 November 1935 was significant for the dismissal of goalkeeper Henderson, who retaliated after being fouled by a home forward. Interestingly, that remained the only time an Ipswich goalkeeper had received his marching orders in almost 57 years, until Canadian international, Craig Forrest, was sent off in the goalless draw with Sheffield United at Portman Road on 26 September 1992.

A Move Towards Professionalism

As far as Ipswich were concerned, the first Eastern Counties League campaign was played to a backdrop of debate about the prospect of professional football in the town. A letter was written to the local newspaper on 28 February 1936 outlining, for the first time, how much a switch would be expected to cost. Its writer was Leonard P. Thompson and he estimated that it would cost £5,000 if Portman Road could be the professional club's home and twice as much if new headquarters would have to be sought.

Thompson had done his homework and suggested in his letter that 'all of us who have written letters and any others who may be interested, convene a preliminary informal meeting at which we could discuss frankly and fully the several possibilities which I know to exist of further action'. Just 21 years old at the time, Thompson was secretary of the building firm, Parkington & Sons Limited, and he received a sufficiently encouraging response for an entirely new club, Ipswich United, to be formed by the end of the following month.

The new club's registered colours were Sunderland-style, red-and-white stripes, they would seek membership of the Southern League and, if Portman Road was not going to be available, its home would be the Suffolk Greyhound Stadium. A further meeting was arranged for 9 April, when in the region of 1,500 people squeezed into the Public Hall in Westgate Street, with many others locked out and forced to follow events via loudspeakers.

Thompson was joined on the platform by various local dignitaries, including Alderman R.F. Jackson, greyhound stadium proprietor Mr Nat Shaw, Mr Robert N. Cobbold and Lt Col Harold R. Hooper, all of whom were to become directors of the first professional club. The meeting heard Thompson appeal to Ipswich Town to join the drive towards professionalism and it was claimed that the new club already had cash pledges totalling £5,000, which must have impressed the three-man Town deputation of Charlie Bunn, Bob McPherson and G.T. Flatman, who sat silently during the proceedings.

Thompson further claimed that 2,000 football fans travelled across the county border to watch Norwich City's home games and he felt sure they, and many others, could be enticed to the greyhound stadium to watch the new club in action. Plans had even reached the drawing board stage to increase the greyhound stadium's capacity to accommodate 30,000 spectators, while a pricing structure for admission – 9d for the ground,

1s for the covered stand and 2s for seats – was also in place. The new club clearly meant business and, without the support of Ipswich Town, was committed to going it alone.

Lt Col Hooper, an architect by profession, played a leading part in smoothing the way towards professionalism and he used his skills as an orator to good effect when he addressed the meeting with an appropriate message: 'This meeting will, I am sure, lead to an amicable arrangement between lovers of football in Ipswich which sooner or later will see a successful professional team running in the town, with amongst its keenest supporters those men who have, for so many years, kept the spirit of amateur football alive in Ipswich.'

But his words appeared to have fallen upon deaf ears at Portman Road, because when Town held a meeting on Friday, 17 April 1936, at the Town Hall, it was decided that they would remain a separate organisation and retain their amateur status. It was further agreed that a six-man deputation would approach the proposed professional club with a view to thrashing out an agreement for them to use Portman Road on alternate Saturdays.

The situation remained unresolved until the saga took a dramatic new twist, one week on, with the publication of a letter in the *Evening Star* from an entirely unexpected source. Captain Cobbold, the Ipswich Town president, had been in Canada while the initial series of meetings had unfolded and upon his return officials of the new Ipswich United club had approached him to seek his opinion. It was to prove a significant turning point in the route towards professionalism and he confirmed his views in print as follows:

'Sir, On my return from Canada today, I am delighted to hear that the question of a professional football side for Ipswich has come to a head. For many years I have been convinced that a town the size and importance of Ipswich must have professional football and it is distressing for supporters of the game to have to go to London or Norwich to see a match. Being interested in the game in general, and particularly in this endeavour to introduce better football at Ipswich, I shall certainly be pleased to give the scheme my utmost support.'

So, within days of Ipswich Town apparently dismissing the prospect of them playing any part in the switch to professionalism, the club's president – absent, remember, from any of the meetings that had been convened – was broadcasting an entirely opposite view to what had been heard before. He was in favour and giving his blessing to the venture, and that very same night Lt Col Hooper presided over yet another get-together, this time between representatives of the two sides, which was to go a long way towards bringing the matter to a conclusion.

It led to one more meeting, at the Town Hall on 1 May, at which Ipswich Town's previous resolution, to remain as an amateur club, was rescinded and replaced by the following: 'That the Ipswich Town Football Club amalgamate with the proposed Ipswich United Football Club Ltd, and Ipswich Town Football Club Ltd be formed to run a professional team in the Southern League and an amateur team in the Eastern Counties League at Portman Road, Ipswich, and a combined committee be formed without delay with a view to working out the necessary details; and that the consent of the Ipswich Corporation and the Ground Syndicate be obtained as soon as possible.'

Two weeks later, the board of directors was announced: Captain J.M. Cobbold (Chairman), The Rt Hon Lord Cranworth, The Hon Douglas A. Tollemache, Sir Charles H.N. Bunbury, Lt Col Harold R. Hooper, Sir John Ganzoni MP, Robert N. Cobbold, Alderman Robert F. Jackson and Nathan (Nat) Shaw. The new club's vice-presidents included Sir Samuel Hill-Wood, chairman of Arsenal and whose own role in the introduction of professional football to Ipswich should not be under-estimated.

It was Sir Samuel who persuaded Captain Cobbold to abandon visits to his London club, and to see his horse run, and instead attend Highbury as his guest, at which point Captain Cobbold, extremely impressed with what he witnessed there, privately promised himself that if a campaign was mounted to bring professional football to Ipswich he would do everything within his power to ensure its success. Sir Samuel offered no lack of support or advice and even provided his London home for the purpose of interviewing prospective managers.

Clearly, the advent of professionalism signalled the start of a new era and the end of an old one. Almost 58 years had passed since the club had been formed and it was a time in which many outstanding individuals ensured its success both on and off the field. While playing achievements are recorded elsewhere, the contribution of loyal club servants must also be noted. Frank Mills was secretary for 26 years from 1910, Mr H. Jervis White Jervis president from 1914 to 1935, and Mr W. Stanley Brand was treasurer from 1901 to 1921 before being succeeded by Mr C.A. Bunn from 1924 to 1936. In addition, Tom Mullins was an excellent chairman for 12 years to 1936 and it seemed appropriate that he was to continue to serve the new professional club in the role of vice-president.

Chapter Three: 1936-43
March to the Football League

Town moved quickly to embrace their new status and accepted Sir Samuel Hill-Wood's invitation to use his London home to interview managerial candidates. It was on 29 May 1936 that the directors announced the appointment of Michael Terrence O'Brien, the assistant boss of Brentford and coach to the Middlesex County FA. O'Brien, an Irishman, was born in County Down in 1893 and apart from playing ten times for Northern Ireland he also represented the Republic on four occasions. An imposing defender, he had played for a number of clubs, including Brentford, Celtic, Norwich City (twice), QPR, Leicester City, Hull City, Derby County, Walsall and Watford, and had spent two years as manager of QPR before a disagreement with the board led to him joining Brentford.

When the Ipswich directors asked O'Brien whether he would be able to assemble a team, he replied confidently: 'Yes, most definitely, and I can promise you to a team to be proud of.' His appointment confirmed, Town's new board held their first formal meeting on 2 June, the venue being 30 Lower Brook Street, Ipswich, in a building later demolished to make way for the present offices of Eastern Counties Newspapers. One week later, the club was represented by Mr Robert Cobbold, Mr E.J.H. Steele, chairman of the management committee, Mr H.W.P. Cutting and new boss O'Brien as they were unanimously elected into the Southern League, newly constituted and in one division of 16 clubs.

O'Brien's immediate task was to sign a squad of players and, since the club had not even staged a game, funds were limited. O'Brien's recruitment drive got under way on 15 June when Ipswich signed their first professional player, Ossie Parry, from Crystal Palace. He was approaching his 28th birthday at the time, but the club informed the local press that he was several years younger and the truth did not emerge until he retired, with his 42nd birthday on the horizon, in 1950, by which time he had played well over 200 times for the club, a number that may well have doubled but for the intervention of the Second World War.

Parry was interviewed at the age of 79 and admitted that Ipswich had made him a cash offer he was in no position to refuse. The club further

The Cobbold Brewery, not only the family business of the Cobbolds, but also a place of work that was to prove a useful aid in attracting big names to the club.

looked after him by awarding him a testimonial, in the shape of an organised collection when supporters filled buckets and blankets with £300 of cash. He went to work at the Cobbold Brewery and collected another bonus when he was declared redundant just months before his retirement, thereby entitling him to a golden handshake.

One week after Parry became an Ipswich player, goalkeeper Fred Houldsworth arrived from Stoke City and George Perrett, just 20 at the time, was signed from Fulham. On 1 July Charlie Cowie, who was later to become reserve team trainer, was signed from Barrow and fellow countryman Bobby Bruce, a 29-year-old Scotland international, was persuaded to leave Sheffield Wednesday. Jack Blackwell, from Boston, also joined the brand new adventure.

But one signing, above all others, signalled Ipswich's intention to make an immediate impact. The national press of 10 July could not ignore the fact that Scottish international Jimmy McLuckie was prepared to leave Aston Villa for Portman Road, a real coup for the new boys. To swell the professional ranks O'Brien then brought in George Dobson (Rotherham), Jackie Williams (Aston Villa), Jock Carter (Reading) and yet another former Scotland international Bob Thomson, who arrived from Racing Club de Paris but who had also played for Falkirk, Sunderland and Newcastle United.

None of the players had cost a penny in transfer fees, but they had been guaranteed attractive wages in order to come to Suffolk and the club's next move was to set about raising the necessary funds to pay them.

An announcement was made on 21 July that the club was issuing £10,000 worth of 5 shilling shares. Directors were required to invest £25 each, for 100 shares, and the applications to invest in the club through share purchase came from as far afield as Egypt. The club also negotiated a new 21-year lease on their Portman Road ground, costing £120 for each of the first seven years, £150 for each of the next seven, and £200 for each of the final seven. Season tickets then, as now, were a vital source of revenue – supporters could have their own numbered seat in the grandstand for £2 2s and ground passes costing half that sum were also eagerly snapped up. The new club banked a further £314 14s, the closing balance of the amateur club.

The players reported for pre-season training on 4 August 1936 and while O'Brien worked hard to prepare a squad that also included Jock Sowerby, Jackie Little and Darkie Clements, survivors of the amateur regime, Portman Road was a hive of activity as the club worked overtime to ensure that everything was right for the opening game. Freddie Blake took enormous pride in preparing a playing surface that could not have been bettered, while the pitch was enclosed by new 4ft 6ins-high iron railings, made and installed by the local firm, Cocksedge & Co. Further improvements included new goalposts, while new stoves were installed in the dressing rooms and the entire area was given a fresh, new look thanks to gallons of blue and white paint.

One of the biggest tasks was to bank the terracing and erect a roof at the Portman's Walk end of the ground, which later became known as the North Stand. Supervising the work was Leonard Thompson, prime instigator of the switch to professionalism, who had been appointed secretary of the new club and also took on the additional responsibility as chairman of the newly-formed supporters' club, which had well over 1,000 members paying 1s per year for membership.

Dawn of the Southern League

And so to 29 August 1936, the historic day when professional football finally came to Ipswich after years of stubborn refusal by the amateur regime to bow to the inevitable arrival of professionalism. Incredibly, the club had rejected offers for new signing McLuckie before he had even played for Ipswich, but while Town refused to even consider selling him at what would have been a substantial profit, the player was also adamant that he would be sticking to his agreement with manager O'Brien and was installed as the club's first-ever professional captain.

It was bright and sunny on the big day, and a celebratory lunch was held at the Great White Horse Hotel, which was also intended as a thank-you to guests who had played a part in steering the club towards professionalism, and would prove to be a tasty appetiser for what was to follow. Apart from the loyal toast, another, entitled simply 'football', was proposed by Mr Stanley Rous, the Suffolk-born secretary of the Football Association who would later be knighted for his services to the game. Captain Cobbold responded.

With the music of Captain Cobbold's former regiment, the Scots Guards, adding to the carnival atmosphere of Portman Road, Jimmy McLuckie led out his team, resplendent in a new kit of royal blue shirts with white sleeves, white shorts and royal blue socks with white hoops. Ipswich could not have asked for a better start, with George Dobson ensuring his place in the record books with the first goal against Tunbridge Wells Rangers. Jackie Williams, Bobby Bruce and Jack Blackwell added further goals and Town were convincing 4-1 winners in front of 14,211 spectators, a crowd only bettered once that season, when Norwich City Reserves visited Portman Road on Boxing Day.

Town lost that game 3-1, suffering their first league defeat of the season in the process, but on Christmas Day they had crossed the border into Norfolk and beaten the same opposition 2-0, thanks to goals by McLuckie and Carter. An 11-game unbeaten run came to an end when they lost 1-0 at home to Folkestone on 20 March, but they were clear at the top of the table and although they lost 3-0 at Barry Town, their only away defeat, and on the last day of the season, it did not matter as they finished five points clear of Norwich City Reserves to capture the Southern League title at their first attempt and crown a momentous first season in professional football.

An important factor in the club's success was the fervent backing of a support that was the envy of several Second Division clubs at the time. The biggest attendance was for the 2-1 win over Watford in the first round of the FA Cup, a fixture that attracted a then record crowd of 18,229. It was hoped that the result, together with such a large turnout, would reinforce the case for admitting Ipswich into the Football League. It was further felt that a 3-2 Hospital Cup win over Norwich City, who paraded their regular Second Division line-up, may help to tip the scales their way. However, their application to join the Football League was unsuccessful and at a meeting on 7 June 1937 it was revealed that Exeter City and Aldershot, the two clubs seeking re-election, had achieved their goal, polling 40 and 34 votes respectively to Town's 24.

Great Managers – 1936-37

MICHAEL O'BRIEN

Michael O'Brien was appointed manager upon the club's switch to professionalism and his immediate task was to recruit a team, which he did with such effect that he led the club to the Southern League championship at the end of what proved to be his only season at the helm.

A charismatic character, O'Brien was a centre-half, standing over six feet tall, in his playing days. Born in Kilcock, County Down, on 10 August 1893, he was a much-travelled player, even having a spell in the USA with Brooklyn Wanderers in 1926, when he left Britain during the general strike.

Capped ten times by Northern Ireland and four by the Republic of Ireland, he was regarded as outstanding management material and he returned to former club QPR in May 1933. He had two years in charge before joining another of his previous employers, Brentford, as assistant manager and in 1936 came the chance to join Ipswich.

O'Brien's range of contacts within the game was a powerful weapon when it came to recruiting players and he proved to be an astute judge as he quickly moulded the players into a title-winning unit that helped to propel Ipswich towards Football League status. Not only that, but he also took over the duties of secretary when Leonard Thompson was struck down by ill health on the eve of that momentous 1936-37 campaign.

Within days of the start of the 1937-38 season, and after the official club photograph had been taken, came the bombshell news that O'Brien had parted company with the club. To this day, the exact circumstances leading to O'Brien's departure have never been clarified, although popular rumour has it that he was disciplined for an off-the-field misdemeanour when he struck up a friendship with the wife of a local publican, a liaison frowned upon by Captain Cobbold who, as brewery boss, moved quickly to nip any potential scandal in the bud.

O'Brien's wife had died shortly after he took up his post at the club and his own death occurred in September, 1940, at Uxbridge, Middlesex, when he was only 47.

Captain Cobbold's determination to see Ipswich elected to the Football League was underlined when he announced that manager O'Brien had been instructed to make new signings who would, hopefully, ensure that a similar application in a year's time would not meet with similar disappointment. Ground improvements were also sanctioned – 650 tip-up seats were bought from Arsenal and were installed in the main stand, while around half the Churchmans Stand was covered over by local firm Cocksedge & Co. at a cost of £1,450. O'Brien, meanwhile, got to work in preparation for the new season by signing Len Astill from Blackburn Rovers, Gilbert Alsop from West Bromwich Albion and Bob Rodger from Rhyl – three star signings that boosted to 16 a strong staff that had been depleted by the decision of England amateur international Jock Sowerby to reject the professional terms offered by Town in favour of a move north of the border to join Rangers.

Managerial Moves

It was a bombshell when Captain Cobbold revealed on 11 August 1937 that manager O'Brien was no longer with the club and after a failed attempt to lure the leading manager of the time, Major Frank Buckley of Wolverhampton Wanderers, it was almost three months later, on 10 November, that the announcement came of Scott Duncan's appointment. His transfer fee was a case of vintage port, dispatched to Manchester United by Captain Cobbold after he had sent a car to collect Duncan, virtually kidnapping him, and then informing the Old Trafford directors that he had no intention of returning him.

Not that Duncan was in any hurry to return, either, since he sat down to negotiate a bumper contract, guaranteeing him an annual salary of £2,000, with a further bonus of £1,000 if he could mastermind the club's entry to the Football League. In addition, he was promised £2,000 extra if they were

A case of vintage port was enough to prise Scott Duncan away from Manchester United to lead Town.

promoted to the Second Division and £3,000 if they should ever climb as high as the First. Not only were such sums way in excess of the average worker's pay at the time, they also dwarfed the earnings of the Town players who earned £8 a week, with bonuses of £1 for a draw and £2 for a win.

Don Read was running the club at the time, having joined as assistant secretary on 1 October 1936, and after being thrust into the spotlight when O'Brien, then secretary-manager after Leonard Thompson's ill-health forced him to step down, departed. He was interviewed in May 1988, at the age of 78, and remembered: 'It was really the Captain Cobbold-Scott Duncan partnership that did the trick. While one provided the necessary financial backing, the other had the contacts throughout the world of football. They couldn't have done it without each other. Captain Cobbold was an inspirational figure who headed a good board of directors. He was a terrific ambassador and the club owes him and his family a tremendous debt of gratitude.'

Read felt the same about Duncan, adding: 'Scott might have been paid a lot more than the average working man, but he was worth every penny because of his tremendous pull in the game. He was a very careful man where money was concerned. He could never be accused of throwing his cash around. He was a damned good housekeeper. Scott looked more like a bank manager than a football manager. He was an immaculate dresser. He always wore a dark suit, a homburg, white collar and dark tie. And you should have seen the shine on his shoes. When I look back 50 years some things are a bit of a blur. But the day Scott arrived and the time we worked together is something I'll never forget.'

While Duncan's appointment was something of a coup, from a football point of view Town were unable to match the achievements of the previous season and had to settle for third place – Guildford City were the champions – in an expanded Southern League that now comprised 18 clubs. Colchester United were one of the newcomers and they proved quite an attraction at Portman Road on 5 February 1938 when a remarkable crowd of 23,890 – beyond the numbers Town could attract upon their return to the Premier League in 2000 – was somehow shoe-horned into the ground to see the first-ever professional meeting of two clubs whose rivalry has remained intense, even if they no longer meet on a regular basis.

The Drive to Join the Football League

Not for the first time, it was off-the-field matters that dominated the thinking of everyone connected with the club and the Football League meeting could not come soon enough. On 30 May 1938 a six-man deputation from Portman Road – Captain Cobbold, Robert Cobbold, Herbert Foster, Nat Shaw, Scott Duncan and Donald Read – travelled to London, where they were pitted against the bottom two clubs, Walsall and Gillingham, in the battle to win a place in the Third Division (South). It was crunch time. Would Town's ambitious election campaign succeed or fail?

The application to join the Football League was submitted on 9 April, the same day it was announced that former full-back, Bob Thomson, had been appointed as assistant to trainer Bob McPherson, after former Leicester,

Bolton and Norwich player Stephen Wright, who had been Lincoln's trainer for four years, had a brief spell in the job. While glamour friendlies against top-class opposition like Wolverhampton Wanderers and Sunderland had demonstrated the crowd potential at Portman Road, the club's average attendance in the Southern League during the 1937-38 season had been a healthy 9,000-plus and, the club felt, confirmed the Suffolk public's appetite for big-time football.

All this, and more, was pointed out in a glossy brochure produced by the Ipswich directors and forwarded to every other club who would have a say in which clubs were elected. No expense was spared. The publication included a specially-commissioned aerial picture of a packed Portman Road; a brief survey of industrial Ipswich; and a statistical section showing how the club's crowds compared favourably with those who currently enjoyed League status. Furthermore, it was pointed out that the town's convenient geographical position would enable the majority of visiting clubs to make the return trip in one day.

It was an ambitious campaign that cost thousands of pounds, such was the directors' determination to succeed, but it would never have borne fruit without the input of manager Duncan who, accompanied by Captain Cobbold and Herbert Foster, clocked up thousands of miles in his new club car – a Wolseley 16, registration number PV 4939 – in visiting clubs to establish personal contact with officials.

In most cases, they were people Duncan already knew, but others were quickly won over – and precious votes were secured – as he put forward the club's case in a forthright, but friendly, manner. Considering how reluctant Ipswich had been to embrace professionalism, the whirlwind campaign to bring League football to the town could not have offered a starker contrast.

Such was Duncan's confidence that Ipswich would succeed that, on 24 May, he was able to persuade Mick Burns to join the staff. A goalkeeper who had been in the Preston North End side beaten 3-1 by Sunderland in the FA Cup final of 1937, his signing represented yet another coup for the club.

Duncan's persuasive tongue continued to work to the very last minute as the Town deputation waited for more than an hour for item six on the agenda – the election of clubs. As a former Newcastle United player, not only was he able to convince the Geordies to change their mind at the 11th hour and vote for Ipswich, but their decision also prompted five others to throw their support behind the new boys.

Despite Duncan's insistence that all would be well, however, Captain Cobbold and the others did not share his confidence. As the other clubs deliberated, a wager was struck. Duncan predicted that Town would not only succeed, but would top the poll, and Captain Cobbold agreed to hand over a sovereign in the event of him being proved correct. The bet was quickly settled in Duncan's favour as the voting was announced. Ipswich were top with 36, two more than Walsall, and Gillingham were the unlucky losers with 28 votes who dropped out of the League. Four of the Ipswich deputation returned by rail to amazing scenes in the town, while Duncan and assistant secretary Read remained in the capital for another meeting at which the following season's fixtures were unveiled.

Plans to mark the historic occasion in style were quickly set in motion and there was a happy throng at Ipswich Railway Station to greet Captain Cobbold and his colleagues on their return from London. The streets were lined with cheering crowds as a procession, led by an open-top bus carrying some of the Town players, brought traffic to a standstill en route to the Cornhill and even more ecstatic scenes. From the Town Hall balcony, Captain Cobbold told the huge crowd: 'I hope what we have accomplished will be of benefit to this town, not only this year or next, but for generations to come. We don't want to stay in the Third Division longer than we can help.'

Preparing for a New Challenge

Having secured Football League status, Ipswich then embarked on a campaign not only to strengthen their squad, but also to update the ground. Fifty years on, Read recalled: 'We installed some extra turnstiles, but the main change was that we had to open the gates early once the season got under way, in order to cater for the extra demand. It might seem strange these days, but we never had any crowd problems. Our supporters came along to watch the football and to enjoy themselves. In all honesty we seemed to take promotion to the League in our stride. We had no great problems.'

Read also remembered how he was accompanied by just one policeman and two gatemen as he toured the turnstiles after half-time to collect the day's takings. Other ground improvements saw the Churchmans Stand extended to the full width of the pitch, an additional section to the main stand and the enclosure in front of it properly terraced.

Duncan, meanwhile, was stepping up his recruitment drive by signing centre-half Tom Fillingham from Birmingham, former Wolves centre-forward Fred Chadwick from Newport County and Billy Dale, considered to be one of the country's best uncapped full-backs, from Manchester City.

Dale, who had started his career with neighbours United, helped City to win the FA Cup in 1934 and had been absent just once in the Maine Road club's 1936-37 League Championship triumph. Left-winger Ellis Rimmer also arrived from Sheffield Wednesday, with whom he had won an FA Cup medal three years earlier, and his pedigree was further strengthened by four England caps during his time at Hillsborough.

Other new faces belonged to teenager Trevor Morris from Caerphilly Town, but he made little impact and was much better known in his later role as secretary of the Welsh FA. The signing of former Chelsea half-back Jock Hutcheson was not without its problems, as the Football League refused to accept his registration because two years previously he had been seriously injured and, with his career apparently over, he had been compensated under the League's insurance scheme, which meant he was barred from League action. However, there was nothing to stop him from appearing in the FA Cup and, in keeping with the romance of the oldest knockout competition, he was to make quite an impact on his Town debut, while occupying the rest of his time by helping with training and skippering the second string side.

Town could accommodate 600 season ticket holders and decided that ground admission would be one shilling (sixpence for youngsters) with the enclosure costing 1s 6d and a seat in the stand two shillings. They made their Football League baptism at home on 27 August 1938 against a Southend United team who chose to travel to Ipswich by boat. Fred Jones, who had cost £150 from Chelmsford City the previous season, had the distinction of scoring the club's first League goal. He went on to add another, with further goals by Gilbert Alsop and Bryn Davies, who had been signed from Cardiff three months earlier, ensuring a 4-2 win in front of 19,242 spectators. It was a perfect start and Town followed it up with a 1-0 victory over Walsall just two days later, when Ambrose Mulraney's ninth-minute goal was enough to secure both points.

The early joy was short-lived, however, as Ipswich went on a run of five successive defeats. A goalless home draw with Bristol Rovers, on a day when the Football League instructed that the National Anthem should be played to celebrate the Munich Pact, temporarily halted the slide, but three more defeats meant that Town had collected a mere one point from a possible 18 and had slumped to within one place of the bottom of the table. Duncan made three new signings; right-winger Pat Curran cost £800 from Sunderland and failed to live up to expectations, but he had better luck with wing-half Dave Bell, at £1,075 from Derby County, and Charlie Fletcher, a left-winger from Plymouth who had helped Brentford to win the Second Division title in the 1934-35 season.

To help control a spiralling wage bill, Town offloaded Jackie Williams to Wrexham and Gilbert Alsop to his former club, Walsall, while Bell and Fletcher, who scored nine times in his 29 League appearances, sparked an almost immediate improvement that saw Ipswich eventually finish a very creditable seventh, the highest position achieved by any side in their first season as Football League members, after taking ten points from their last six games. Fred Chadwick finished as top scorer with 17 goals in 34 league

A crowd of 28,194 crammed into Portman Road and witnessed the home side fall 2-1 to First Division giants Aston Villa in the 1939 FA Cup third-round replay.

appearances and also netted five times in the FA Cup, four of them coming in the 7-0 first-round dismissal of Street and the other in the 4-1 defeat of Torquay United at the next stage, which earned a glamour third-round clash with Aston Villa at Villa Park.

It was Ipswich's biggest game so far and defeat seemed a foregone conclusion, since they were third bottom of the Third Division (South) when they travelled to take on the First Division giants. No player anticipated the game more eagerly than Town captain Jimmy McLuckie, returning to his former club, but the talk was more of Town making a graceful exit from Villa Park rather than causing an upset on a pitch sprinkled by snow. Some supporters were put off travelling by the excessive rail charges – 12 shillings for a return ticket – but Captain Cobbold had a brainwave and announced a free trip for 1,000 supporters who would otherwise have been forced to stay at home and they took their places among a 34,910 crowd, at the time the biggest ever for a Town game, on 7 January 1939.

Hutcheson came in from the cold to make his senior debut at right-half, a late replacement for Bell who had, in turn, moved into the middle of the defence to deputise for broken rib victim Fillingham. Ipswich had terrible luck when Mulraney suffered an early injury, but they were encouraged to go in at half-time without conceding a goal. Early in the second half the match exploded in controversy when Town were awarded a penalty. Fletcher ran up to take the spot-kick, but was distracted when Villa full-back Ernest Callaghan threw a lump of mud at the ball and his effort came back off a post. The referee, Mr S. Hadley of Leicester, refused the Town players' appeals for the kick to be retaken and there was further misery, seven minutes from the end, when Villa took the lead through captain James Allen's header from a corner. But, in the 88th minute, never-day-die Town were level, the debut-making Hutcheson heading in a Fletcher free-kick to earn a replay at Portman Road four days later.

It remains a mystery how a crowd of 28,194, which was to remain a record until the League Championship-winning season of 1961-62, managed to squeeze into the ground for the second game, but some were perched precariously on the roof of the Alderman Road stand in anticipation of a giant-killing act. But again Ipswich were cursing their luck. They went down to ten men after Bell sustained a broken leg soon after the interval and then fell behind to Fred Haycock's opener for the visitors. Fred Jones, only in the starting line-up because of Mulraney's injury at Villa Park, levelled after 74 minutes with a superb goal, but Haycock struck again with seconds remaining to clinch a 2-1 replay success for the First Division side. The controversy was maintained right to the bitter end, however, with Town goalkeeper Burns so convinced that there had been a handling offence that he raced to confront the referee on the half-way line. His protest fell on deaf ears, however, and it was Villa who progressed to meet holders Preston North End in the next round.

Later that year, on 8 May, Villa were back in town for the Ipswich Hospital Cup game and it proved to be a popular attraction with 19,209 spectators, paying £1,185 16s 6d, flocking into the ground.

Scottish international Frank O'Donnell, who had been a team-mate of Town goalkeeper Mick Burns in Preston's side for the FA Cup final of 1937, took the scoring honours when he bagged a hat-trick in just four second-half minutes. Ipswich had led at half-time through what proved to be Bryn Davies' last goal for the club and Jackie Little was the other marksman on a night when a Trooping of the Colour ceremony, as performed at His Majesty's birthday parade, was a popular pre-match attraction.

Despite a satisfying start to life in the Football League, such was Town's ambition to do even better that manager Duncan was busy adding to his staff throughout the summer of 1939. By far the most significant signing was that of former Irish international Matt O'Mahony from Bristol Rovers who had been rated as the best centre-half in the Third Division (South) the previous season. Jack Hick (Bristol City), Fred Mitcheson (Plymouth), David Edwards (Gloucester City), John Friar (Norwich) and John Wardlaw (Morton) further strengthened the squad, while Pat Curran and Frank Shufflebottom both departed, to join Watford and Nottingham Forest respectively. But Town had played just three league games at the start of the 1939-40 season when war was declared on Germany and the Football League competition was officially suspended.

Suspension of League Football

Ten days after war was declared on 3 September 1939, the Ipswich Town board of directors issued a statement informing supporters that they had unanimously decided to suspend football indefinitely. The decision disappointed fans and the supporters' association, the largest such organisation in the country with around 10,000 members, wrote to the club begging them to reconsider. When the Home Office and the football authorities relaxed the rules a little, permitting friendly games, there was optimism of a change of heart among the Town directors. However, after a special board meeting was convened, a second statement on 29 September declared that operations would be closed down at Portman Road as from

Jackie Little was one of many players whose careers were affected by the outbreak of the Second World War.

the following day. Town became the first League club to shut their gates, kit was removed to the Cobbold Brewery and players were only allowed to take their boots home.

Jackie Little remembered it well. A member of the Town side on the momentous day when they defeated Southend United in their first Football League fixture, he was 80 when he recalled the events of September 1939. 'There were 35 players, plus the office boy, sitting in the dressing room, listening to the radio. When the announcement came over, our insurance cards were stamped and we were sacked on the spot. Captain Cobbold was adamant there would be no more football at Portman Road until Hitler had been defeated.'

During the war years Jackie played a handful of games for Chelsea and also turned out for Norwich along with Ipswich colleagues Billy Dale, Ossie Parry, Ambrose Mulraney, Mick Burns, Jimmy McLuckie and Fred Chadwick. He was 34 when football reconvened in 1946, but still managed to clock up over 100 games in the following four years before retiring.

If the news was a blow to supporters, it was even more devastating for the players who had no alternative but to put their careers on hold. Several stayed in the area and found employment at the Cobbold Brewery or at Churchmans, where Scott Duncan also took up a post but who was also in receipt of a weekly retainer from Captain Cobbold's own pocket. The brewery boss had risen to the rank of Lieutenant-Colonel when he chaired the annual meeting held on 22 January 1943 and reported a financial crisis. The club's debt had soared to £14,195 and he was reluctant to put the company into liquidation. He proposed, instead, that the debt should be repaid and after donations of either £250 or £500 from his boardroom colleagues he was left with a staggering £11,195 bill which he promptly settled in an amazing act of generosity that was, tragically, to be the last of his many good deeds on behalf of the club.

Lieutenant-Colonel Cobbold did not survive to see his dreams on behalf of Ipswich Town fulfilled. He served in the Welsh Guards and on 17 June 1944 he was attending a service at the Guards Chapel in London when it was struck by a German bomb and he was one of many casualties. His enthusiasm, drive, foresight and generosity represented a massive contribution to the Ipswich Town success story and can never be under-estimated. He was succeeded as chairman by his uncle, Philip Cobbold, whose own son, Robert, a Major in the Welsh Guards, had been killed on active service just ten days earlier in Italy.

Chapter Four: 1945-49
A Time to Rebuild

Professional football resumed at Portman Road in the 1945-46 season, but Ipswich were still in the dark about their fixture list just four weeks prior to the start. The decision was made to regionalise the Third Division (South) to ease travelling problems and Town took part in the northern section with ten other clubs, as well as a cup competition during the second half of the season. Rules were flexible, with professionals still in the services able to turn out for the club nearest to their station, so long as permission was granted by their own club. This enabled Ipswich to make great use of sailors based at HMS *Ganges*, Shotley, and soldiers from Colchester.

Among Town's guest players during the transitional 1945-46 season were Harry Baird and Albert Day, who had played for Huddersfield and Brighton respectively prior to the Second World War, and both of whom later signed on as full-time professionals. Irish international Baird, who went on to make over 200 appearances for the club, was stationed in the Army at Saxmundham and it was no surprise that he turned out for Scott Duncan, the manager who originally brought him to England to play for Manchester United. Day, a Physical Training Instructor at Colchester, scored regularly to become the club's leading marksman, and West Bromwich

Christmas 1945 brought the sad news of Philip Cobbold's death.

Albion full-back, Jimmy Southam, was another well-known guest player. In a 4-3 defeat at Watford on 3 November 1945 a young player making his debut scored twice and no one could have imagined the future impact that Tommy Parker would make at Portman Road, both on and off the field. As one illustrious career was starting, another ended as Jimmy McLuckie bowed out at the age of 38 in the 2-2 home draw with Watford on 13 April 1946.

The club, and the Cobbold family, suffered another terrible blow with the death of Philip Cobbold at Christmas, 1945. He had been in poor health when he had been appointed chairman, after having suffered from a heart attack, and it was to his enormous credit that he agreed to take charge at a time when he was also running the family brewing business. His sterling efforts ensured that Town were quickly back into their stride after the war ended. He was succeeded by Peter Chevallier, a current board director and managing director of Fisons, who had been awarded the DSO and MC during the First World War, and who had played tennis for Suffolk. Philip's son, Alistair, was co-opted to fill the vacancy on the board.

Ipswich had been members of the Football League for eight years, but the 1946-47 season was only their second proper campaign and it turned out to be the longest on record, lasting from 31 August all the way to 14 June, the extension being necessary because of a severe winter and the banning of midweek fixtures by a government anxious not to disrupt production in the factories. Sensibly, the League made use of the fixture programme that had been drawn up for the ill-fated 1939-40 season and one of the undoubted highlights came in the third game when Norwich City, relegated from the Second Division in 1939, were trounced 5-0 at Portman Road. An injury to their goalkeeper, Hall, handicapped the Canaries, who were forced to seek re-election at the end of a season in which Town did well to finish sixth. The injury to Hall was caused by a collision with Jack Connor whose grandson, Phil Whelan, was to star for Ipswich in the 1990s and win England Under-21 recognition before moving to Middlesbrough, and then on to Oxford and Southend.

The fans' thirst for football was demonstrated by a turnout in excess of 8,000 for a reserve game on the first day of the new season and that was exceeded the following month when a crowd of 10,501 saw Arsenal's second string win 4-2. Another attendance record was set when the Boxing Day 1-1 draw with QPR attracted 20,267 spectators, just 24 hours after Town had won 3-1 in the corresponding game in London and the Rangers programme carried the following message: 'Welcome Ipswich! Infants by

50 Greatest Players

JIMMY McLUCKIE   Inside-forward

Joined Ipswich Town: 9 July 1936   **From:** Aston Villa

Debut: v Tunbridge Wells Rangers, 29 August 1936, League

Appearances: 57   **Goals:** 3

Left Ipswich Town: 3 July 1947   **For:** Clacton Town

Jimmy will always have a special place in the club's history, as the first professional captain and by far the most respected player to have joined the club at the time. His transfer captured the imagination of not only Ipswich supporters, but fans around the country, because he was still regarded as one of the top players in the game. He was only 28 when he agreed to step down from the First Division to the Southern League and he had won a Scottish international cap just two years earlier when he was with Manchester City, to whom Villa paid £5,000 for his signature. Soon after his move to Ipswich had been completed, and before he had made his debut for the club, Bolton tried to tempt Town with a cash offer that was promptly rejected. Jimmy stayed loyal to Ipswich, helping them to win the Southern League in his first season, and within two years they were in the Football League. The Second World War interrupted his career and soon after his 38th birthday he played his last game for the club. Jimmy combined his time during his final season between scouting and office duties, then joined Clacton Town as manager. He returned to his native Scotland and lived in Edinburgh until his death in November 1986.

reason of time alone, your hospitality and grand sportsmanship have, since your baptism into League football, earned the highest praise and enhanced the prestige of England's national game. Truly the right spirit for Xmas. None others would we choose with whom to do friendly battle on this day of Peace.'

The £300 it took to secure Albert Day's signature proved to be money well spent when he was the club's top scorer in the 1946-47 season, netting 14 times in 25 league games. He was followed by Tommy Parker on 11 and Stan Parker, no relation, on ten, the latter having been signed from the local Life Brigade Old Boys. Jimmy McLuckie turned scout for a while and was instrumental in signing full-back George Rumbold from Leyton Orient and the new recruit never missed a game in his first two seasons, becoming the first Ipswich player to make 100 consecutive appearances – 119 in total – before injury halted his proud, ever-present record. Age was no barrier in those days, either, with Tommy Lang, a Scot who had played for Newcastle and Manchester United before the war, arriving from Queen of the South in October 1946 and making his debut at the age of 40!

In November that year Town were lying 14th in the table after a 4-1 defeat at Aldershot, a game in which Ossie Parry, the club's first professional player ten years earlier, was injured and managed only a handful more games that season. The final fixture, a 2-2 draw at Northampton, was played in 90-degree heat and the biggest home crowd was the 22,012 who attended the Ipswich Hospital Cup clash with Charlton Athletic, fresh from their victory in the FA Cup, fielding ten of their Wembley winners and parading the famous trophy. It was an all-time record crowd for the competition and the game ended in a 2-2 draw.

Ipswich's own FA Cup campaign was ended at home by Walsall, in a second-round replay that only went ahead after a steamroller was used to level a frosty playing surface protected at both ends by straw and tarpaulins. It was a disappointing outcome after Town had done well to draw 0-0 at Fellows Park and were hopeful of landing a mouth-watering home clash with a Liverpool side sitting second in the First Division and who would eventually be crowned champions.

Off the field, an historic ceremony had taken place the previous month in the boardroom at Portman Road when Lieutenant John C. Cobbold, son of the late Captain Ivan and home on leave from service with the Welsh Guards in Palestine, accepted a cheque for £298 15s 9d. The cash had been put in trust by the old amateur club 'just in case professionalism did not catch on' and was handed over by Frank Challis King OBE, a former player, linesman and committee member in the club's amateur days who was clearly of the opinion that the professional set-up was here to stay.

It was announced that Jimmy McLuckie would depart from Portman Road in July 1947, having been made redundant from his job as scout, and a further backroom change saw Wally Gray appointed as assistant secretary. A former Town goalkeeper in the club's amateur days, he went on to become secretary in June

Tommy Parker was ever present during season 1948-49.

1963 and served under six managers, as he remained in the post until his retirement in 1975, when present secretary David Rose, who has been with the club since leaving school, succeeded him.

There was much to cheer during the 1947-48 season, when Town finished fourth, and both Harry Baird and Tommy Parker recorded perfect attendance records. Bill Jennings, signed in the summer from Northampton Town, was the leading scorer with 14 goals in 36 league games and it was felt that just a little more consistency might have resulted in promotion. A new attendance record was set when 24,361 spectators watched a 1-0 home win – Jennings was the scorer – over leaders and eventual champions QPR on 25 October. The previous month, Ipswich achieved a record away win when they defeated Norwich City 5-1, although the return fixture on 31 January saw the Canaries gain revenge courtesy of a 2-1 scoreline that earned them their only away success of the season. As if to underline the fact that it had been an erratic second half of the season, Town finished with three successive defeats.

The threat of a players' strike had been removed when arbitration resulted in an increase in the maximum wage, to £12 a week during the season and £10 in the summer, when it was by no means rare for players to supplement their wages with other employment. Lack of suitable housing in Ipswich was costing the club, as manager Scott Duncan observed: 'We could sign a good strong player straight away if we could find an unfurnished flat.'

The newly-wed Matt O'Mahony asked for a transfer because he could not find a house and the supporters' association tried to ease the problem by purchasing a property in Christchurch Street to rent to players from outside the area. They called it Glemham as a tribute to Captain Cobbold, whose family home was Glemham Hall.

Ipswich were not short of experience as they entered the 1948-49 campaign with a team comprised mainly of thirty somethings – skipper Dave Bell was almost 39 and his full-back partner, George Rumbold, 37 – with Tommy Parker the baby of the side at 24. Town started the campaign in style with a 6-1 win at Bristol Rovers, a new record for an away game. When they followed that triumph with 5-1 successes at home against Torquay and Newport County the talk, not surprisingly, was of promotion. The man orchestrating the play was right-winger Jackie Brown. Belfast-born and capped pre-war by both Northern Ireland and the Republic, he was 33 when Scott Duncan signed him from Barry Town in May that year, after he had played for Belfast Celtic, Wolverhampton Wanderers, Coventry and Birmingham.

After a 1-1 draw at Torquay and a 2-0 defeat at Swansea came a third successive away fixture, with Ipswich crashing 9-2 at Notts County, for whom England centre-forward Tommy Lawton scored four times. Two games later and County were beaten 3-2 at Portman Road, in front of a crowd of 21,262 – the highest to watch an evening home game. Another attendance record was set at the East Anglian derby on 16 October 1948 when 24,569 spectators witnessed a 2-1 win for the Canaries. They completed the double – the only team to do so against Town that season – with a 2-0 win in front of a bumper 35,126 crowd at Carrow Road. Yet more records were established when top scorer Bill Jennings netted 23 times in the league and Tommy Parker made 123 consecutive appearances before he was forced to miss the last game of the season at Brighton through injury.

Town finished seventh, but many supporters voiced concern that the team's average age was so high. The club seemed to agree and adopted Barry Island Youth Fellowship in South Wales as a nursery club and it was from Wales that they made two inspired signings. Doug 'Dai' Rees was a Welsh amateur international centre-half from Troedyrhiw, who managed six appearances in the 1948-49 season, while John Elsworthy was a 17 year-old from Newport Colts who would have to wait before going on to make a huge impact at Portman Road. Another new face belonged to John

Cobbold, at 21 the youngest director in the country, and he was joined in the boardroom by Ernest Steel, while ex-QPR captain George Smith was appointed assistant manager.

Alarm Bells Start to Ring

The danger of having to seek re-election accompanied Ipswich throughout a depressing 1949-50 season in which only one player, goalkeeper Tom Brown, managed to turn out in every league game. New assistant boss Smith, a wartime international and brought to the club for his coaching skills, actually turned

Alistair Cobbold replaced Peter Chevallier as club chairman in October 1949.

out and took over the captaincy from Dave Bell in a move designed to halt an alarming form slump that had left Town as the only team without a point just three games into the campaign. It did not succeed and Smith, who appeared to be on a different wavelength to manager Duncan, resigned in November, although he continued to honour his contract as a player. But in the new year there was an official statement from chairman Alistair Cobbold – who had replaced Peter Chevallier, who had resigned the previous October because other commitments prevented him from attending Saturday games – stating that Smith had been given 14 days' notice to terminate his agreement with the club 'on the grounds of his misconduct and breach of disciplinary rules at the club'.

The club also expressed its total confidence in manager Duncan, while Smith's dismissal caused uproar among supporters. But, just as Smith twice failed with appeals, the fans' attempts to have him reinstated were also doomed as the Football League backed the club. Smith's 'crime' was that he had gone into print in December 1949 with a scathing article in the *Green 'Un* which, since it was heavily critical of the secretary-manager and the board, was considered a serious breach of contract.

Smith departed for the Channel Islands, later managing Portsmouth between 1961 and 1970, and there were plenty who were sorry to see him go, mainly the youngsters who were benefiting from the training sessions he introduced at Portman Road, and young professionals he was keen to promote into the first team.

Len Fletcher, new to Portman Road at the time, later recalled: 'George Smith was too go-ahead for Ipswich in those days. All his attention was geared towards the fitness of the players, and as most of the team were in their thirties the training programme was too stiff for them. They were not able to perform on Saturdays. Players like Jackie Brown and Harry Baird were run into the ground during the week. George wanted 11 players like Tommy Parker who, like the other youngsters, lapped it up. When I came out of the RAF I weighed 15-and-a-half stone. George told me to lose weight and I would be included in the team. I came back for training in the afternoons and was soon down to ten-and-a-half stone. It was a bit of a blow to the younger players when George resigned. George was persuaded to play again and that was his downfall. The team just could not respond.'

It was a time of grave concern, by far the worst season in Ipswich's brief professional history. By the end of 1949 they had managed just three wins from 23 games, and were marooned at the bottom of the table after a miserable run of 11 games without a win. The cry went up for the club to enter the transfer market, but Duncan, never one for extravagance, had expressed the view: 'In these days of fantastic transfer fees, fancy figures are not necessarily the hallmark of a good player.' He was forced to relent, however, as the relegation alarm bells started to ring and in came inside-forward Allenby Driver from Norwich and two Irishmen, full-back Jim Feeney and inside-forward Sam McCrory, from Swansea for a combined fee of £10,500. All made their mark, while John Elsworthy, Vic Snell and Neil Myles made their debuts, and Jackie Little, the last survivor from the old amateur set-up, bowed out to join Stowmarket as player-manager.

Despite the overall gloom during the first half of the season, the visit of Norwich was a highlight. Not only was it watched by a new record crowd of 26,161, but Jackie Brown scored a hat-trick to earn Town a 3-0 success. Fortunately, there was a significant upturn in the team's fortunes after the turn of the year and Ipswich collected 22 points from their last 19 games to scrape clear of trouble, with three wins from their last four games lifting them to 17th place, but they were still just one point better off than second-bottom Newport. New signing McCrory achieved the dubious distinction of becoming the first Town player ever to be dismissed since the club's entry into the Football League, when he was sent off in the penultimate fixture, a 5-0 defeat at Aldershot. The FA Cup brought welcome relief as they reached the third round for only the second time in their history, only to be dumped out of the competition after a 5-1 defeat at West Ham.

Chapter Five: 1950-62
Cinderella Comes of Age

In an effort to avoid a repeat of the problems of the previous season, when the team flirted with relegation until the very last lap, manager Duncan invested in several new faces. The most significant change saw the appointment of Jimmy Forsyth, who hailed originally from Bathgate in Scotland but who had worked south of the border for many years, as trainer-coach. He had played for Portsmouth, Gillingham and Millwall, for whom he appeared in an FA Cup semi-final in 1937 when they became the first team from the Third Division to progress so far in the competition. He remained at the Den as assistant trainer, taking his length of service to 24 years – and as a fully qualified masseur and physiotherapist he was seen as a valuable acquisition. Forsyth, nicknamed 'Chisel' because of his distinctive jaw-line, became one of the most popular characters at Portman Road and went on to serve five different Town managers until his retirement in 1971, and even then he continued to assist the ground staff on a part-time basis.

On the playing side, Duncan also went to Millwall to strengthen his squad. The signing of full-back Len Tyler had a stabilising effect on the defence. Scottish import Ron Murchison, from Perthshire junior club Auchterarder, was also recruited, but had to wait until December for his debut.

The price of admission was increased to 1s 6d, with season tickets costing £5 10s, and there was also a new face on the board, that of Cecil Robinson, a former referee and Suffolk County FA official who was also prominent in local bowls circles after being a founder member, then treasurer, of the Suffolk EBA. Cecil made a habit of travelling with the reserve team and was a director for 25 years, which earned him both an FA Medal of Merit and life membership of the club. He retired in 1975 and died, at the age of 90, just a few months before the club's FA Cup success of 1978.

Town hardly made an impressive start to the 1950-51 season, winning just two of their opening nine league games, but they recovered to take 13 points out of a possible 14 during a seven-game run and duly climbed the table. They achieved a best-ever run of seven away games without defeat, but the attacking problems that had blighted their progress in the previous campaign were never fully overcome.

There was an improvement, however, in their goals tally – 69 in the league compared to 57 a year earlier – but they still lagged some way behind champions Nottingham Forest, who hit 110, and even Southend United, who scored 92 times to pip Ipswich for seventh spot on goal average. Town's top scorer was Sam McCrory with 21 goals from 45 league games, while Ray Warne had an impressive strike rate of 11 goals in 22 league games after being signed from Leiston in October 1950. Ipswich-born, he was surprisingly released within two years to join Sudbury Town.

Allenby Driver was the only other Town player to manage double figures and rugged Welsh centre-half Dai Rees was alone as an ever-present. The biggest win was 5-1 at home to Gillingham, the club Ipswich had replaced in the Third Division (South) in 1936, but who had been re-elected along with Colchester United in the summer of 1950. McCrory missed a penalty and Warne, having scored twice, was forced to withdraw through injury, leaving Town to complete the final 35 minutes with ten men. A 3-1 win at Carrow Road in the penultimate league game not only ended the Canaries' unbeaten home record, but cost them promotion as they finished runners-up to Forest, who dropped their first home point in a goalless draw with Ipswich.

The popularity of Town pair Feeney and McCrory with supporters of their former club, Swansea, was underlined as a coach load of them travelled to Newport for Ipswich's 2-1 win and, wearing Town colours, cheered them on to a 2-1 success. Afterwards, manager Duncan allowed the pair to travel back to Swansea on the coach and he returned there himself during the summer, to sign goalkeeper Jack Parry for £750, although Mick Burns, at the age of 43 and starting his 25th year as a professional, retained his place for the first 12 games of what was to prove to be a disappointing 1951-52 season.

Parry's start was anything but encouraging, as he suffered defeat in each of his first five games for the club, and the supporters' handbook summed up the campaign, when Town finished 17th, as 'a season of promise unfulfilled'.

Although McCrory again finished as leading league scorer with 16 goals, the overall top marksman was Tom Garneys, a £2,700 summer signing from Brentford who bagged 20 in total. Manager Duncan also introduced younger players, including Basil Acres, David Deacon and John Elsworthy, but he clearly had a problem at outside-right, where no fewer than nine different players were fielded. With Tommy Parker now established as captain and as the veterans of the war period were being replaced, 5 January 1952 proved to be a record-breaking day for Ipswich, as they fielded a side comprising 11 players under the age of 30 for the first time in their history, in a 3-2 win over Northampton.

It was a see-saw season, Town beating Southend 4-1 at home on the opening day and then losing 5-0 in the return the following April, while Brighton were crushed 5-0 at home and then a week later gained revenge at the Goldstone Ground when they triumphed 5-1. A run of ten defeats in 13 games saw Town slump as low as 20th in the table, but they arrested the slide and nine games without defeat towards the end of the season took the heat out of a potentially difficult situation.

Town's interest in the FA Cup ended in the third round as they went out to Gateshead in a second replay staged at Sheffield United's Bramall Lane ground, the first match Ipswich had played at a neutral venue. Other new faces at the club included Jimmy Gaynor and Billy Havenga, signed from Shamrock Rovers and Luton Town respectively.

More history was created on 30 April 1952, when the first testimonial match for the benefit of professional players was staged. Tommy Parker, so influential that he was dubbed 'the Billy Wright of East Anglia', and Harry Baird shared the proceeds of a game against a select side.

The Ipswich Hospital Cup was revived and a visit from Tottenham Hotspur – fielding nine of the side, including Alf Ramsey, who had finished runners-up in the First Division – brought down the curtain on another season. The game ended 2-2, as McCrory netted twice after Spurs had raced into a 2-0 lead, and receipts were divided between the Ipswich branch of the Royal College of Nursing and the Ipswich Nurses' Amenity Fund. Despite failing to challenge for promotion, Town were continuing to win friends throughout the footballing world. As an article in Plymouth's programme stated: 'With their beautifully-kept ground, sporting crowd, and distinguished manager in Mr Scott Duncan, Ipswich have these past few seasons become among the most popular clubs in the country.'

Supporters Voice Their Concern

Disgruntled supporters, who had been warned at the annual general meeting that the club would be bankrupt without generous donations from the supporters' association, were in for further disappointment before the 1952-53 season even started. They were amazed to hear, firstly, that Sam McCrory was being transferred to Plymouth for what they believed to be a 'chicken feed' fee of £5,000, and then that Allenby Driver and Jimmy Roberts were also departing, which meant that three of the previous season's four top scorers were no longer at Portman Road. There was further misery to follow, when Tom Garneys missed the last part of the season with a slipped disc. Ipswich, who had suffered financial losses for three years in a row, covered the £3,000 cost of concreting the new West Stand terracing with yet another supporters' association handout.

On the field, injuries took their toll as Jack Parry, Jimmy Gaynor, Dai Rees and David Deacon all joined Garneys on the casualty list. Parry was unlucky, suffering a fractured left wrist at Norwich in September, then a fractured and dislocated right thumb on his return to the first team two months later at Walsall. Part-timer Eric Newman took over in goal and helped Town to a run of five successive wins that took them to seventh in the table, but they eventually finished 16th as the form slump at home, which in turn affected attendances, put the club under further financial pressure.

Town did manage to equal their biggest home win, however, when they defeated Walsall 5-0, but fewer than 7,000 people – the estimated break-even gate at the time was 12,000 – witnessed the goal spree, many having been turned off by the sight of Bristol Rovers and Millwall winning 5-1 and 6-1 respectively at Portman Road.

The FA Cup provided the season's high spot. Two first round draws with Bournemouth took the teams to neutral Highbury, where a crowd of less than 5,000 was scattered around the famous stadium to see Town triumph 3-2. Ipswich were drawn away to Bradford City in the second round and fell behind to a goal by Brian Close, the Bantams' centre-forward, but far better known for his cricketing exploits for Yorkshire, Somerset and England. John Elsworthy equalised to book a replay, which Town won 5-1 to earn a third round trip to face Everton at Goodison Park.

Ipswich had never played in front of a larger crowd – only 430 members of the 42,252 crowd had travelled from Suffolk – but they certainly rose to the occasion. They fell behind, recovered to take a 2-1 lead and then, after Tom Brown had a goal controversially disallowed, Everton hit back through two goals from Dave Hickson to win 3-2. It was a game in which Elsworthy turned in an outstanding individual display that was noted by many scouts, in particular the Liverpool representative, and it was rumoured that the Anfield board were on the brink of making a £10,000 bid until the player's form dipped later in the season.

Suffice to say that the 1952-53 season was not one of the club's most memorable; indeed the flood of the weekend 31 January and 1 February was by far the most dramatic event. The Town party arrived back from their 4-1 defeat at Torquay on the Sunday and found themselves marooned at the railway station for more than four hours after the River Gipping burst its banks. Within minutes Portman Road was under three feet of water, but things were back to normal the following week and the home match against Watford went ahead. A collection raised £153 7s 3d for flood victims and three weeks later the club staged a game that raised a further £158 2s 6d for the East Coast Flood Relief Fund.

Upturn in Fortunes

The disappointments and false dawns of previous years were quickly forgotten in the victorious 1953-54 season, when Town won the Third Division (South) to claim their first professional title and also advanced beyond the third round of the FA Cup for the first time. Everyone was optimistic from the start as Ipswich claimed four successive wins, dropped just one point in their first seven league fixtures and suffered a mere two defeats in 32 league and cup games to go seven points clear of their closest rivals at the turn of the year.

Manager Duncan made three new signings, bringing in George McLuckie, Billy Reed and Alex Crowe from Blackburn, Brighton and St Mirren respectively, and he was clearly confident that the new forwards could help bring about a transformation, as he commented before the big kick-off: 'In this Coronation year, I feel sure our players will play their part in bringing success to the club.'

The championship-winning side of 1953-54. Back row (left to right): W. Reed, J. Feeney, T. Garneys, J. Parry, G. McLuckie, J. Elsworthy, D. Rees. Front row (left to right): A. Scott Duncan, B. Acres, A. Crowe, T. Parker, N. Myles, T. Brown, J. Forsyth.

Little could he have realised, however, how the team's form would improve as they swept all before them during the opening four months and played a brand of football totally unrecognisable from anything that had gone before. However, just when it seemed as though Town would carry on relentlessly to capture the title, they wobbled as a result of the demands of their FA Cup heroics.

Following a less than convincing start, when they conceded a penalty – saved by Parry – after just 45 seconds in the first round tie at home to Reading, they needed a penalty of their own to ignite a comeback in the second round tie against amateur outfit Walthamstow Avenue.

Trailing 2-0 to the London club, Neil Myles reduced the leeway from the spot and Town went on to force a replay in the capital, which was decided by Crowe's 86th-minute goal. Former England star George Hardwick, player-manager of Oldham, missed a penalty as Ipswich booked a fourth round place for the first time in their history when they won a Boundary Park replay. Birmingham were beaten 1-0 before the plucky underdogs more than met their match in the fifth round, when star-studded Preston, twice FA Cup winners and five times runners-up in the competition, cruised to a 6-1 success at Deepdale, although a catalogue of injuries within Town's ranks did not help their cause.

On the same day that Town were going out of the FA Cup, Brighton took over the leadership of the league and it was obvious Ipswich were going to have to fight to the end. They suffered three defeats in a row to make their task even greater, but stormed back to remain unbeaten in their last ten games and eventually landed the crown with three points to spare. While the new-look attack gelled from day one, the contribution of the defence, which remained unchanged for the first 31 games of the season, cannot be overlooked.

By the end of the season, Messrs Parry, Acres, Myles and Parker were all ever-present in 53 league and cup games. Parker was an inspirational captain who made an immense contribution that season, filling in for Rees when the centre-half was injured and also scoring eight goals from his wing-half role. Right-winger Reed also made a massive impact, and was quickly hailed as 'the Stanley Matthews of the Third Division'.

The final match of the season resulted in a 2-1 win over Northampton, with Ted Phillips netting the first and then seeing his deflected shot beat the keeper for the second. Phillips had been signed from Leiston before Christmas, upon completion of his National Service, much of which was spent in Malaya and Trieste. He made his senior debut in March and ended

Town's players celebrate with the 1953-54 Third Division (South) Championship shield.

the season with four appearances, and two goals, to his credit – a mere appetiser to what was to follow in later years.

After the final whistle, Football League committee member Joe Mears, who was also chairman of Chelsea, handed over the Championship shield. On the Monday there was a civic reception for the team and, 24 hours later, they made a triumphant tour of the town, cheered by thousands of supporters.

It was an action replay of what had happened after the trip to Newport the previous week, when promotion had been clinched and the players were feted at a party hosted by the supporters' association. Within two days, Brighton's draw with Crystal Palace finally confirmed that the crown was coming to Portman Road and among many congratulatory letters received by Scott Duncan was one from England manager Walter Winterbottom, originally signed for Manchester United in the mid-1930s by Duncan.

Rarely, if ever, can there have been two successive seasons of such contrasting fortunes. From being a mediocre side who finished 16th in the table in 1953, Ipswich were unrecognisable as they took the division by storm and won back the fans who had been staying away in their droves. Town won 12 away games, more than any other club in the Football League and the Portman Road average rocketed from 9,355 to 15,535, ensuring that the club's bank manager was wearing one of the biggest smiles in Suffolk. The official presentation of championship medals was delayed until 5 August 1954 at a celebration banquet staged at the Great White Horse

Hotel, and the upbeat mood – more than 10,000 members were enrolled in the supporters' association – remained in place as the 1954-55 season, Town's very first in the Second Division, got under way.

Ipswich, with £3,000 of ground improvements at the Portman's Walk end funded by a supporters' association donation, seemed committed to sticking by their promotion-winning heroes and in the early stages they appeared to be taking the step-up in their stride. A 3-2 defeat on the opening day at Rotherham was followed by three wins in succession, over Middlesbrough (twice) and Luton, that left Town in fourth position and led to talk of promotion all over again. This was soon forgotten, however, as they plunged to ten straight defeats that sent them to the bottom of the table and it was clear, even then, that they were destined for a relegation battle.

The depressing run of defeats would have numbered 11 but for a last-gasp equaliser by Wilf Grant to earn a 3-3 draw at Port Vale. It was Grant's first goal for the club following a £7,500 move from Cardiff City that made him Scott Duncan's most expensive signing, but the main scoring burden was again shouldered by Tom Garneys, who netted 21 times in his 25 appearances. He rewrote the record books when he scored four against Doncaster, the first time an Ipswich player had netted more than three times in one game, but he was absent when Town needed him most, for the last ten games of the season, because of a recurrence of his back problem. Ken Malcolm, signed for £2,000 from Arbroath in May 1954, quickly made his mark at the club, making only 21 appearances but spreading them between eight different positions and only failing to line up in goal, at centre-half and outside-right.

With 12 games to go that season, Town seemed to be in a hopeless situation as they languished at the bottom of the table, five points behind their nearest rivals and eight points worse off than the team in 20th place. But a run of just one defeat in six games boosted their slim survival hopes and, remarkably, they went into their final fixture at Notts County still in with a chance of survival. Pushing for the win they needed, however, they were caught on the break in the dying seconds, and the fact that Plymouth's win rendered the Meadow Lane clash meaningless was scant consolation as Town were relegated. On the plus side, Billy Reed won his only two Welsh caps that season and Tommy Parker's achievement in playing 400 games was marked by the presentation of a canteen of cutlery by chairman Alistair Cobbold, who remarked: 'No club in football has had a better servant.'

An embarrassing FA Cup third round defeat in the snow at Bishop Auckland, who were coached by ex-Town player Jock Sowerby, went hand

Great Managers – 1937-55

SCOTT DUNCAN

Ipswich Town were signing more than a manager when they appointed Scott Duncan in November 1937, for here was a highly-respected figure, a charming, persuasive character, who unlocked the door to the Football League through a network of friends in the game whose support was ultimately decisive.

It seems remarkable now to record that Duncan was managing Manchester United when Ipswich – still a non-league club – made their move and his appointment was confirmed on 12 November 1937, when he was 49 years old.

Duncan still had three-and-a-half years of his Old Trafford contract to run, but that was of little concern to the Ipswich board, whose generosity in terms of what they were offering as a salary prompted him to ask if they could really afford to pay a rumoured £2,000 per year – a figure that would have made him one of the three best-paid managers in the country. Undoubtedly influenced by the financial incentives, he quickly warmed to his dual task of continuing the on-the-field progress made under his predecessor and smoothing the way for the club's entry to the Football League.

Duncan had considered a legal career, but he excelled in football while attending Dumbarton Academy and although he did go to work in a local solicitor's office, he duly signed for Dumbarton in 1907. In March 1908, he was transferred to Newcastle United for £150 and had instant success at St. James' Park, helping them to the Football League title in 1909 and the FA Cup in 1910, although he was absent from the final itself.

A fast and skilful right winger, he made 81 appearances and scored 12 goals for the Geordies, and when he returned north in May 1913, Rangers had to pay £600 for his signature. His career was interrupted by the First World War, during which he served as a signalling instructor in the Royal Field Artillery, although he earned a special place in Scottish football history by guesting for Celtic and therefore becoming one of a select group of players to represent both Old Firm clubs.

He had another spell as a player with Dumbarton, then Cowdenbeath, before commencing his managerial apprenticeship with Hamilton Academical and Cowdenbeath. He joined Manchester United in 1932, at a time when they were marooned in the Second Division. Duncan did, however, assemble a team good enough to win the Second Division in 1936. He stayed at Portman Road for 21 years and in that time not only kept his promise to secure League status, but masterminded their meteoric rise from non-league to Second Division in just nine seasons. He resigned as manager in 1955, but remained as secretary for a further three years alongside his successor, Alf Ramsey. A crowd of more than 10,000 attended his testimonial match against Norwich City on 28 April 1958, after which he returned to his native Scotland to spend his retirement in Helensburgh, where he died in October 1976.

in hand with a depressing league campaign and Town's relegation back to the Third Division (South) after just one season signalled the end of Scott Duncan's 18-year reign as manager, although he stayed on for a further three years as secretary.

New Man at the Helm

It was announced on 26 May 1955 that the club had received permission from Spurs to offer the job to their famous international full-back, Alf Ramsey, but it took until 9 August for the appointment to be confirmed because the player capped 32 times by England had been coaching in Rhodesia.

One of Duncan's last acts as manager was to complete the signing from Brighton of former Chelsea player Jimmy Leadbetter, a Scot who could never have imagined the success he was about to enjoy as a key member of Ramsey's revolutionary side.

Other new players were recruited, among them Doug Millward from Southampton, ex-Welsh international Billy Baker from Cardiff, Ron Blackman from Nottingham Forest and Charlie Ashcroft, an England B international goalkeeper from Liverpool, but Ramsey insisted it was his intention to allow the previous season's players – forced, incidentally, to take

Scott Duncan was a tough act to follow for new man Alf Ramsey. But players like (left to right) Roy Stevenson, Ray Crawford, Doug Moran and Jimmy Leadbetter strengthened the team.

a cut in wages – an opportunity to impress. One notable absentee was keeper Jack Parry, who had cracked a rib in a game at Fulham and never played for Town again. He refused the terms on offer and joined Chelmsford instead.

Ramsey was allocated space in the supporters' association handbook. He wrote: 'May I begin by saying "Pleased to meet you" and I sincerely hope that our association will be a happy and successful one. In the past you have supported the club 100 per cent and I would like to feel that in this, my first year as manager, you will do the same. May our slogan, as Mr Scott Duncan has said in previous years, still be "Up the Town".'

The hoped-for winning start did not materialise, however, as Torquay won 2-0 at Portman Road, but a 4-2 home win over Ramsey's former club, Southampton, was to prove more indicative of the direction in which the club was headed under its new leader.

Town made a bold bid to regain Second Division status, but eventually finished third, two points adrift of champions Leyton Orient and only one point behind runners-up Brighton. The influence of their new manager was there for all to see and neutral observers acknowledged Ipswich as the classiest side in the division. Their scoring statistics were particularly impressive, hitting four goals or more on nine occasions – the 5-0 scorelines at Northampton and Millwall equalled the club's previous best away wins – en route to an end-of-season total of 106, compared to the previous best tally of 82 which was overtaken with almost a quarter of the season still to be played. Six hat-tricks were scored, three by Wilf Grant, including two against Millwall, and one each by Tommy Parker, Billy Reed and Tom Garneys.

The season's main success story centred on a positional switch that saw John Elsworthy turn in one polished display after another at left-half, which enabled skipper Parker to revert to his original position of inside-left, and he responded by smashing the club's scoring record. He netted 30 in the league and one in the FA Cup (when a Town team kitted out in black and white hooped change shirts went down 3-1 to Peterborough United, then of the Midland League, at London Road), and exceeded by six Bill Jennings' 25-goal tally of 1948-49.

Having lost the services of new goalkeeper Ashcroft with a broken arm sustained in a reserve game at Coventry in March 1956, Ramsey moved to beat the transfer deadline by signing Roy Bailey from Crystal Palace. Bailey had been living in a caravan at Lewisham and was to have a long, successful stay with Ipswich, as was another new recruit, Larry Carberry, a Liverpudlian full-back doing his National Service with the Army in Bury St Edmunds and signed, initially, as an amateur.

A Roller-coaster Ride

Given a taste of life under new manager Ramsey, no one connected with Ipswich could have anticipated what lay in store during the 1956-57 season, when Town pulled off one of the most amazing recovery acts in the history of the English game. Fears of re-election gave way to a spectacular climb up the table that culminated in them reaching the top, with immaculate timing, on the very last day of a roller-coaster campaign. Of course, it was a team effort, but the huge contribution of new scoring sensation Ted Phillips could not be overlooked as he netted 41 times in as many league games, and contributed 46 goals in 44 games, to shatter the club's goals record set the previous season by Tommy Parker. He was also the leading marksman in the entire Football League and equalled the post-war record for goals scored in a season that had been set by Derek Dooley of Sheffield Wednesday.

Phillips' story was the stuff of comic book heroes. He had been farmed out to Stowmarket the previous season and suddenly, from performing in the Eastern Counties League, he was thrust into the first team spotlight. Tall and powerful, he packed a ferocious shot with either foot and many an opposition keeper became a quivering wreck as Phillips prepared to let fly. He scored five hat-tricks that season and became one of the most talked-about players in the English game as he inherited Parker's No.10 shirt. The one-time forestry worker will always be remembered, not only for his prowess in finding the net, but as the dressing room joker who always had a prank or two up his sleeve. If Phillips' emergence was a major plus, however, Parker's decision to retire on medical advice took at least some of the gloss off Town's splendid achievement.

Ipswich Town with the Third Division (South) Championship Shield in May 1957.

50 Greatest Players

TOMMY PARKER **Wing-half/Inside-forward**

Joined Ipswich Town: November 1945 (as an amateur)

Debut: v Wisbech Town, 17 November 1945, League

Appearances: 465 **Goals:** 100

Left Ipswich Town: 30 June 1957 (retired)

A chance telephone call led to Tommy joining Ipswich and he not only went on to captain the club, but set an appearance record that stood for years. A Royal Navy volunteer, he was stationed at a naval training base at Shotley, when Town manager Scott Duncan rang and asked the commanding officer if there were any budding footballers there. Tommy declined the invitation, preferring to play cricket, but three months later he turned out as an amateur and then became a part-timer while working as a clerk at a local railway goods department. He eventually became full-time and in the 1953-54 season was ever-present in leading Ipswich to the Third Division (South) title. A player renowned for his total commitment and sportsmanship, he was never cautioned in a career that came to a premature end because of a back injury at the age of 33. He returned to the club in 1965 to run the development association. He later became Town's first commercial manager before retiring in 1985. He died in April 1996.

By October, with three points from eight matches, Town were at the bottom of the table. There were murmurings of them having to seek re-election, but by Christmas the talk was of promotion; so convincingly had Ramsey's team turned the corner. If one game summed up the metamorphosis, it was the 6-0 home defeat of a Torquay team who were second in the table at the time, the result rocketing Ipswich from 12th place to seventh. Consistency during the next few months saw Town emerge as genuine contenders for the crown.

It was a three-cornered fight for the championship that also involved Torquay and Colchester United, and the Devon club went into the last day of the season with a one-point lead. Despite several injury problems, Ipswich turned in a wonderful display to beat Southampton at the Dell and then had an anxious 45-minute wait at the nearby Polygon Hotel before learning that Torquay had been held to a 1-1 draw by Crystal Palace at Selhurst Park, thereby ensuring Town were champions, their goal average of 1.87 being superior to that of Torquay on 1.38, although had goal difference been the deciding factor Ipswich, who smashed the 100-goal barrier, would have triumphed by the not insignificant margin of 22 goals.

The following day, the team emerged from their train to be greeted by a 3,000-strong army of fans as they boarded a bus for Portman Road.

Despite Phillips' invaluable contribution, it was by no means a one-man show and the new boy was helped by co-striker Tom Garneys, ten years his senior, who, despite missing around a third of the season through injury, still managed to finish second in the scoring stakes. Winger Billy Reed recaptured the form that had attracted the Welsh selectors the previous season, while one of the great unexplained mysteries surrounded John Elsworthy, whose dynamic displays at left-half were amazingly overlooked by those same Welshmen. Goalkeeper Roy Bailey was an ever-present and his penalty save from Colchester player-manager Benny Fenton in a 0-0 draw at Layer Road was one of the season's key moments. The gates were closed half an hour before kick-off that day and had Fenton scored there would have been no end-of-season celebrations for Bailey & Co.

While a second Third Division (South) Championship Shield in the space of four seasons was a tremendous feat, Ipswich's FA Cup run that year ended in controversy, with the club reported to the FA for misconduct.

The flashpoint came right at the end of an absorbing third round tie against Fulham at Portman Road, when Billy Reed swept a Tom Garneys cross into the net and thought he had levelled the scores at 3-3. However, referee Stokes had blown for full-time before the ball entered the net and not only did Alf Ramsey head for the referee's room at the end, to seek an explanation, but a large crowd of home supporters chanting 'We want the ref' also assembled outside the dressing room area. The angry scenes prompted a report to the FA, which resulted in the club having to publish a warning in a future issue of the official programme warning spectators as to their future conduct. What made it all the more irritating was that Fulham, with Johnny Haynes, Roy Bentley and Tosh Chamberlain in their ranks, had been outplayed for most of the game. As Alf Ramsey, who accepted the referee's decision with dignity, put it: 'I don't think I have ever seen a side have so much of the play and yet be beaten.'

At 29, John Cobbold became the youngest chairman in the country when he took over from his cousin Alistair.

Soon after the season ended there was a significant change in the boardroom, as John Cobbold succeeded his cousin, Alistair, as club chairman. At 29, he was the youngest chairman in the country and was to prove an inspiration for many years to come with his unique brand of leadership. He stayed at the helm for 19 years, during which time the club's hospitality and friendliness was without equal, before making way for his younger brother, Patrick. Former manager Scott Duncan finally received the Football League's long service medal and, in preparation for their return to the Second Division, the club embarked on an ambitious ground improvement plan that saw the construction of a new stand on the west side of the stadium.

Life in Division Two

It was boom time at Portman Road as the 1957-58 season loomed, with every one of the 1,406 season tickets being snapped up by an eager public and with manager Ramsey reinforcing his squad with the addition of four new players: Derek Rees and Reg Pickett from Portsmouth; Brian Siddall from Bournemouth; and Bobby Johnstone from West Ham.

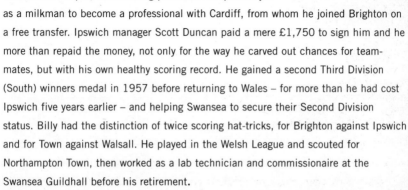

50 Greatest Players

BILLY REED   **Winger**

Joined Ipswich Town: 14 July 1953   **From:** Brighton

Debut: v Walsall, 19 August 1953, League

Appearances: 169   **Goals:** 46

Left Ipswich Town: 26 February 1958   **For:** Swansea Town

Billy was the first Ipswich player to win senior international honours when he represented Wales against Yugoslavia in September 1954 after helping the club to capture their first-ever honour, the Third Division (South) title. He was twice capped as an amateur, and rejected the chance to join Tottenham Hotspur, before being persuaded to quit his job as a milkman to become a professional with Cardiff, from whom he joined Brighton on a free transfer. Ipswich manager Scott Duncan paid a mere £1,750 to sign him and he more than repaid the money, not only for the way he carved out chances for team-mates, but with his own healthy scoring record. He gained a second Third Division (South) winners medal in 1957 before returning to Wales – for more than he had cost Ipswich five years earlier – and helping Swansea to secure their Second Division status. Billy had the distinction of twice scoring hat-tricks, for Brighton against Ipswich and for Town against Walsall. He played in the Welsh League and scouted for Northampton Town, then worked as a lab technician and commissionaire at the Swansea Guildhall before his retirement.

The fans' excitement, however, was tempered with concern that Town, as before, would be hard-pushed to maintain their loftier status, although the pessimists had not bargained for the astute managerial skills of the forward-thinking Ramsey and his penchant for improving the existing players, while at the same time paving the way for the integration of his new signings.

That Ipswich eventually finished eighth was a tremendous achievement, especially as they were forced to soldier on for most of the campaign without the services of their prize asset, Ted Phillips. His season lasted only 11 games, although, typically, he averaged a goal per game in that time, helped by a hat-trick against Bristol City, before he succumbed to a knee injury. The problem originally flared up in pre-season, then he damaged it again in December at Charlton and was told a cartilage operation was necessary. All those years ago it was a career-threatening situation and it was a tribute to the skills of the surgeon, as well as to the player's strength of character, that he recovered to become even more effective in subsequent years.

Phillips' return to action in a reserve game at Portman Road boosted the attendance to 7,369, well above the 4,388 average that season, to underline his immense popularity with the supporters.

A flu epidemic that swept the country took its toll at Portman Road, with ten of the club's 24 professionals laid low at the same time, and it also cost Ted Phillips an appearance for an FA team against the RAF at Notts

50 Greatest Players

TOM GARNEYS　　　　　**Forward**

Joined Ipswich Town: 25 May 1951　　　**From:** Brentford

Debut: v Southend United, 18 August 1951, League

Appearances: 273　　　　　　　**Goals:** 143

Left Ipswich Town: 7 February 1959 (retired)

Tom Garneys was the club's leading marksman in each of his first four seasons at Portman Road, as well as in the 1957-58 campaign – his penultimate season. He won two Third Division (South) medals. Tom had moved to his previous club, Brentford, from Notts County after the arrival of a certain Tommy Lawton at Meadow Lane and he was certainly missed by Ipswich when he was absent from the final quarter of the 1952-53 season with a slipped disc. After his retirement he moved into the licensed trade and was a landlord at Ipswich public house, the Mulberry Tree, before settling down in Billericay.

50 Greatest Players

DOUGLAS (DAI) REES   Defender

Joined Ipswich Town: 9 April 1949   **From:** Treodyrhiw

Debut: v Leyton Orient, 9 April 1949, League

Appearances: 385   **Goals:** 1

Left Ipswich Town: June 1959 (retired)

Dai was a miner until becoming a footballer at the age of 24, having been spotted playing for Wales against England in an amateur international, by then Ipswich manager, Scott Duncan. He signed the necessary paperwork at the local railway station and after winning a regular place at centre-half in 1951, went on to win two Third Division (South) Championship medals. In 1958, he was named in Wales' 40-strong preliminary squad for the World Cup finals, but his name was missing from the travelling party of 22. After leaving Ipswich, he spent seven years in the Eastern Counties League with Sudbury, then two years as with Essex and Suffolk Border League side, Halstead. He also had a spell in the Ipswich and District League with Browns and by the time he finished playing with Sunday League outfit Corinthians, his 50th birthday was on the horizon. He continued to live in the town until his death in March 2000.

County, although team-mate Larry Carberry was able to turn out and appeared again when the Army were the opponents at Old Trafford.

Not for the first time, Town were grateful to veteran striker Tom Garneys as he finished as top scorer with 19 goals in his 33 league outings. New signing Rees grabbed 13 and the club's only ever-present player was Jimmy Leadbetter. The Welsh selectors named both Dai Rees and John Elsworthy in a party of 40 for the World Cup finals in Sweden, but both were missing when the travelling squad of 22 was unveiled.

Billy Reed, meanwhile, returned home to help Swansea stave off relegation in a deal that suited all parties, with Town making a handsome profit collecting £3,000 for a player who had only cost them £1,750. Reg Pickett, who had won a First Division Championship medal in his time at Fratton Park, took over as captain from Rees during the season and Town had good reason to remember bumping into a certain Brian Clough, as he scored four times in Middlesbrough's 5-2 win at Ayresome Park and then netted his side's only goal in a 1-1 draw between the sides at Portman Road.

There was an emotional farewell at the end of the season for Scott Duncan who, at the age of 69, decided it was time to retire. His former club, Manchester United, were Town's opponents in the FA Cup, in what proved to be the Busby Babes' last home appearance before the Munich air tragedy that cost so many their lives.

As Town fought so bravely in a compelling fourth round tie, no one could have had any idea of the horror that was to unfold less than a fortnight later. An heroic defensive display to win 1-0 at Crystal Palace had earned Ipswich their trip to Old Trafford, where the attendance of 53,550 was the biggest to have witnessed a Town game. Not surprisingly, the prospect of the country cousins taking on probably the best side in Europe at the time had Suffolk in a spell, and four special trains ferried almost 2,000 fans north through the ice and snow.

The pitch was in a terrible condition after bulldozers and an army of 100 volunteers had worked by daylight, and again under floodlights, to clear hundreds of tons of snow. Wet in places, frozen in others, and liberally sanded, it was by no means an ideal playing surface, but although it may have been seen as a leveller, no account of the game failed to mention how magnificent Ipswich, minus Ted Phillips, were in failing only narrowly to pull off what would have been the No.1 shock of the competition. Bobby Charlton fired United in front after 39 minutes and Jimmy Leadbetter, making his 100th appearance for the club, came close to an equaliser when his 58th-minute shot came back off a post. Five minutes from the end of an epic tussle, Charlton's shot was deflected past Roy Bailey off the unfortunate John Elsworthy, who was in fine form that day, to make it 2-0.

Time for Consolidation

Having enjoyed a season of consolidation in the Second Division, Town set about further improving their stadium and the West Stand was extended to provide accommodation for 4,000 spectators. Surprisingly, though, that was the number by which the club's average attendance fell in the 1958-59 season, supporters proving hard to please at a time when crowds, generally, were on the increase, thanks in part to television coverage of the World Cup that summer. Ipswich dropped to 16th in the table, but there were several plus points, not the least of which was their survival in the Second Division, while they also progressed to the fifth round of the FA Cup for only the second time in their history and welcomed a new goalscoring hero to Portman Road.

Alf Ramsey had made four new signings – Peter Berry, brother of Manchester United forward John Berry, and Jimmy Belcher from Crystal Palace, together with young full-back Len Garrett from Arsenal and Dermot Curtis from Bristol City. But it was the capture on 6 September 1958 of centre-forward Ray Crawford from Portsmouth that was to have by far the greatest impact. The son of a professional boxer, he cost £5,000 and went on to average nearly a goal per game by the end of his first season.

Curtis took over after four games from Tom Garneys, whose goal on the opening day of the season was to prove his last for the club, and after scoring four times in six appearances, he became the second Ipswich player to win international honours when he was picked for the Republic of Ireland's game against Poland. Ironically, that was to cost him his Town place as Crawford made his debut in replacing him at Swansea and marked the occasion with both goals in his side's 4-2 defeat.

Former office boy and building worker Crawford stayed in the team thereafter, and his goals endeared him to supporters who in turn tagged him 'Jungle Boy' after learning that their new hero had spent part of his National Service in the Malayan jungle, although he played it down, saying: 'I only did two patrols and nothing happened!'

The goals flowed – 25 in 30 league games – and it was unfortunate that Ted Phillips' injury problems prevented the pair from forming what was to prove to be a deadly partnership until late in the campaign. Phillips, struggling to hit form after his cartilage operation the previous season, also suffered a ligament strain and played only 22 games. That was still twice as many as John Elsworthy, who was plagued by knee trouble, a broken cheekbone and a calf problem. It was also a season when Town said farewell to Tom Garneys, who took over as landlord of the Mulberry Tree public house, and Dai Rees, who continued playing with Sudbury Town.

Ipswich made it into the fifth round of the FA Cup for only the second time in the club's history, first of all accounting for a Huddersfield team managed by the great Bill Shankly but hampered by the absence of two key players through injury – right-half and future Town boss Bill McGarry, and young forward Denis Law, who had missed the sides' league meeting earlier in the season because he was creating a new record by winning his first Scottish cap at the age of 18 years and 236 days. The Portman Road pitch was rock-hard after a severe frost and the game was decided when referee Denis Howell, a future Labour MP and Minister of Sport, awarded a penalty after 41 minutes, which Crawford converted.

Chairman John Cobbold was holidaying in Switzerland when Town travelled to Stoke in the fourth round, but he sent a telegram which read 'I insist on a win' and Derek Rees' 23rd-minute goal was enough to do the trick. Rees took just 23 seconds to give Ipswich the lead at the next stage, but visitors and eventual runners-up Luton hit back four times within the next 17 minutes and the Hatters went on to triumph 5-2.

Ipswich rejected a Liverpool bid for Ted Phillips during the summer of 1959, the Merseysiders being given the same answer Fulham had received when they had tried their luck the previous season. Rather than allow key players to move on, Alf Ramsey was more interested in entering the transfer market to plug the gap caused by Dai Rees' departure and he did so when he bought Andy Nelson from West Ham for a then record fee of £8,500. Vic Snell had also filled in at the heart of the defence the previous season, but he lacked height, and relished his new job running the A team. Another newcomer was defender John Laurel from Tottenham Hotspur, but he was to make virtually no impact, appearing just six times in total compared to Nelson, who celebrated his first season at Portman Road as an ever-present and was to go on to make an even greater impact.

Soon after the start of the season Town had started work on an ambitious project to install floodlights at Portman Road. With the work initially expected to be completed by Christmas, the switching-on ceremony eventually took place on 16 February 1960 and was performed by Lady Blanche Cobbold. To mark the occasion, Town arranged a friendly game against Arsenal, which was attended by close on 16,000 spectators and

The Ipswich team for the club's first visit to Villa Park on 12 September 1959. Back row (left to right) Neil Myles, Basil Acres, Roy Bailey, Andy Nelson, Jimmy Belcher. Front row Brian Siddall, Dermot Curtis, Ken Malcolm, Ray Crawford, Ted Phillips, Jimmy Leadbetter.

Dermot Curtis (left) and Ted Phillips became the first Town players to score hat-tricks in the same game (against Sunderland in 1959-60).

resulted in a 4-0 home win thanks to goals by Ted Phillips, Ray Crawford (2) and Doug Millward. The new floodlights – on four pylons 110 feet high – cost £15,000, which was covered by the supporters' association. The tendency at the time was for clubs to automatically increase admission prices each season, but Town chose to buck the trend and, by freezing costs, were offering the cheapest football in the Second Division.

Ipswich made an unhappy start to the league campaign, suffering five defeats in their first seven games to occupy a place just outside the relegation zone, but they picked up as a run of ten games without defeat reaped 18 points and took them into a group of clubs bunched behind the runaway top two of Aston Villa and Cardiff, who were coached by ex-Ipswich forward Wilf Grant.

With seven games to go, Town were actually fourth, but having taken a miserable three points from a possible 14 they had to settle for a final place of 11th. Among the highlights were a 2-1 home defeat of champions Villa and a 6-1 success over Sunderland, also at Portman Road, which equalled the club's best Second Division win and, since the visitors only scored in the closing stages, was almost on a par with their best since joining the Football League. The Sunderland victory also marked the first occasion that two Ipswich players – Ted Phillips and Dermot Curtis – had scored hat-tricks in the same game. Irish international Curtis, whose wife presented him with a son on St Patrick's Day, went one better when he netted all four against Stoke.

The 2-0 home win over Sheffield United was the first league game to be staged under the new lights after Town decided on a Saturday night slot to avoid clashing with that afternoon's Grand National. Goalkeeper Roy Bailey, another with a 100 per cent appearance record that season, saved penalties in four games, and Ipswich were one of only two Football League clubs to complete the campaign without having collected even a single caution.

Town's unluckiest player was Peter Berry who, having scored two goals against Lincoln, was carried off on a stretcher before the end of the game and never figured at first team level again. There was a place in the side during the second half of the season for Aled Owen, a native of Bangor in North Wales who never actually learned to speak English until he was 14. On a sad note, in May 1960 the death occurred of Tom Fillingham, who had captained Ipswich in their first-ever Football League match. He was 58.

Completing the Jigsaw

There was plenty of transfer activity at Portman Road in summer 1960, prior to the club's silver jubilee season that was to prove more successful than anyone could have dared to imagine. Out went Neil Myles, to Clacton, while new faces belonged to Wilf Hall, a £2,000 goalkeeper from Stoke; Bill Baxter, who had just completed an engineering apprenticeship in his native Scotland and was preparing for his National Service when Ipswich handed over £400 to junior club Broxburn; experienced winger Roy Stephenson, who cost £3,000 from Leicester; and John Compton, who had been with Chelsea since leaving school and for whom Town paid £1,000. There was also a new captain, with Reg Pickett voluntarily stepping down to be replaced by Andy Nelson, and as the season began to unfold, it seemed as though Town had acquired exactly the right blend for success. Indeed, when he met Stephenson at Liverpool Street station, Alf Ramsey told him, 'You are the final piece of the jigsaw.' It was to prove an accurate assessment, as all concerned pooled their resources to trigger one of the English game's most remarkable and unexpected success stories.

The opening-day success at Leyton Orient was significant, since it was the first time since 1953 that Town had started the season with a win, and five games into the campaign they were fourth, which was as low a position as they occupied for the rest of a season that got progressively better. Between 27 August and 15 October they put together a ten-game unbeaten run that included wonderful performances to beat Leeds United 5-2 – the first time since the war that a visiting team had scored so many goals at Elland Road – and Charlton Athletic 2-0.

Ray Crawford (left) and Ted Phillips scored 70 of Town's 100 goals in the 1960-61 campaign.

Then from 10 December to 18 March they remained undefeated in 13 games and dropped a mere three points, a scintillating spell that included a double over Norwich, chasing promotion themselves that season, and a 3-1 away win over league leaders Sheffield United, who had won 1-0 at Portman Road and seemed uncatchable as they opened up a six-point lead before Christmas. The Bramall Lane triumph, in front of more than 35,000 spectators at what was then a three-sided ground shared with Yorkshire County Cricket Club, took them to the summit and they never looked back.

Paramount to Town's success were twin marksmen, Ray Crawford and Ted Phillips, who between them contributed 70 of the team's 100 league goals. There were only eight occasions all season when neither player scored and they were both on target in 16 games. They thrived on service from the flanks, but not in the way that one might imagine. Wingers Roy Stephenson and Jimmy Leadbetter were not hell-bent on reaching the by-line to deliver crosses; instead they supplied a series of diagonal passes from just over the half-way line that were invariably turned into goals by the lethal front pair. Crawford played in every one of the 42 league games, scoring 40 times, while Phillips, also ever-present, added 30.

Promotion was assured with a 4-0 home win over Sunderland on 22 April 1961, which left Town requiring just one point from their final two games to clinch the title. The players didn't waste any time, winning 4-1 in a rearranged game at Derby that had first been postponed, at a time when Ray Crawford was injured and feared he would lose his 100 per cent appearance record, and then abandoned with Town trailing 2-1.

Ipswich ended with a defeat at Swansea, where the home players formed a guard of honour to applaud their visitors on to the pitch, but nothing could detract from their historic triumph. It was a season in which Bill Baxter, stationed at Aldershot with the Royal Engineers, emerged to claim a regular place at the expense of the injured Reg Pickett, and the £100 bonus promised to his first club 'if he makes the grade' was duly dispatched. His Army duties meant that he missed full-time training and the benefit of Alf Ramsey's renowned coaching, while his fitness was put to the test with almost endless travelling between the barracks, Portman Road and the family home in Edinburgh, where his wife Dot and baby son William were based. Winning the Second Division Championship also erased painful memories of a 7-1 FA Cup trouncing at Southampton and another embarrassing display in going down 2-0 at home to Barnsley in the inaugural League Cup.

Chairman John Cobbold, who had predicted promotion after the first game of the season, had a perfect response to those writers and commentators who appeared to take great delight with their constant references to Ipswich as a Cinderella club. 'Cinderella is getting quite a big girl now, isn't she?' he quipped.

In readiness for their debut season in the top flight, Ipswich made just one major signing, paying £12,000 for inside-right Doug Moran after he had scored 33 goals to help Falkirk secure promotion north of the border, but his arrival did nothing to prevent most people outside Suffolk predicting the briefest of stays in the big-time. But anyone thinking it would be impossible for Ipswich to survive was in for a huge shock as the fairytale continued. First Division consolidation – or just one place above the relegation zone – may well have been most people's goal, but Alf Ramsey's miracle men swept all before them to become the champions of England at their very first attempt – a feat that is never likely to be matched.

Mind you, those predicting a quick return to Division Two were probably smiling contentedly when, after three games in the first week of the season, Town had accumulated just one point and were sitting 20th in the table. But a 6-2 win over Burnley in which all five forwards found the net – the last time it had happened was in April 1939 – proved the launching pad towards glory and it was a case of steady progress thereafter.

Early in 1962 it seemed the title race was to be contested by five clubs, but Town's consistency removed the challengers one by one, until only Burnley blocked their path. Top at the end of March, Town led the Lancashire side by two points, but had only six games to play, compared to Burnley's ten. When Ipswich slumped to their biggest defeat of the season, 5-0 at Manchester United, it enabled Burnley to regain pole position, but the leadership changed hands yet again a week later as United won 3-1 at Turf Moor.

The race went right to the wire, Ipswich going into their final game at home to Aston Villa knowing that nothing less than a win would do, while also praying that Burnley would slip up at home to already-relegated Chelsea. The miracle happened, as Ray Crawford's two late goals secured victory for Town and Burnley's 0-0 draw left them three points worse off with just one game left to play.

There was no doubt – Ipswich were Football League Champions and thousands of jubilant fans flooded on to the Portman Road pitch to hoist their heroes shoulder-high back to the dressing room. For players and supporters alike, it was the biggest day of their lives. Back in the dressing room, trainer Jimmy Forsyth was thrown, fully clothed, into the bath and champagne, much of it supplied by BBC commentator Kenneth Wolstenholme as he settled a bet that Ipswich would not finish ahead of Tottenham, flowed like water.

It was a clear case of rewriting the record books. Ipswich were the first club to win the First Division title at their first attempt since Preston in 1888-89, the year the Football League was formed. They also equalled the record of Everton and Tottenham of winning the Second and First Division crowns in successive seasons, and they shared with Wolves the distinction of being the only two clubs to win the Third, Second and First Division titles, although Town's feat in doing so in a six-year period hardly compared to that of the Molineux club as their treble haul had spanned 30 years.

Roy Bailey, Larry Carberry, John Elsworthy, Ted Phillips and Jimmy Leadbetter became the first players to win Third, Second and First Division medals, and in Elsworthy's case he could boast two Third Division successes. Furthermore, only 16 players – the lowest number ever – had been used in the entire campaign, only six points were dropped at home and they managed to find the net in every single league outing at Portman Road, something never before achieved. Phillips scored all nine penalties awarded to Town that season, taking his spot-kick record to 23 successes from 24 attempts.

Home and away defeats of champions Tottenham were among many highlights – how Alf Ramsey enjoyed those twin successes over his former club – and it was the first time in three seasons that Spurs had been doubled in this way. Oddly enough, however, it was the 4-3 defeat at Burnley on 22 August 1961 that most observers voted the season's outstanding game. Alf Ramsey claimed it was the best performance by any Ipswich team in his time at the club after he saw his side roar back three times, and Ted Phillips crash shots against the woodwork, before Jimmy McIlroy's late clincher. It was in the return fixture a week later that John Compton, a half-back,

Great Matches

FOOTBALL LEAGUE FIRST DIVISION   Portman Road, 28 April 1962

Ipswich Town 2   **Aston Villa 0**   **Attendance: 28,932**

Crawford 2

Ipswich went into their debut season in the First Division with most people convinced it would be an achievement not to finish bottom. Instead they finished top, completing the miracle thanks to a dramatic last-day win – but they made their supporters wait.

Aston Villa boss, Joe Mercer, had promised beforehand that Ipswich would get the fight of their lives and for a long time the visiting defence was more than equal to anything a frantic home forward line could conjure up. Indeed, the nearest thing to a goal had come when Villa half-back Deakin headed towards his own goal before Sims leapt to get his fingertips to it.

There were 72 minutes on the clock when Bill Baxter was fouled out on the right. Roy Stephenson swung over the free-kick and the lanky figure of John Elsworthy soared above everyone else in the penalty box. His header beat Sims, but came back off the crossbar and Ray Crawford reacted instinctively to throw himself forward and head the ball across the line. Just four minutes later the points were wrapped up as Crawford controlled a clearance and finally got the better of John Sleeuwenhoek before firing his own, and Town's, second goal past Sims.

Burnley's draw at Chelsea left them in a hopeless position, three points worse off than Town and with only one game left to play. Ipswich had achieved the impossible and were crowned champions of the Football League.

Ipswich Town: Bailey, Carberry, Compton, Baxter, Nelson, Elsworthy, Stephenson, Moran, Crawford, Phillips, Leadbetter.

Aston Villa: Sims, Lee, Aitken, Crowe, Sleeuwenhoek, Deakin, MacEwan, Baker, Dougan, Thomson, Ewing.

Referee: E. Crawford (Doncaster).

was drafted into the side at left-back to replace the injured Ken Malcolm, and retained the No.3 shirt for the remainder of the season.

The victorious Town players were all heroes, of course, but the real star of the show was Alf Ramsey. Just as he later promised that England would win the World Cup under his leadership in 1966, he had issued a similar rallying call when he addressed members of the Ipswich Town Supporters' Association one month prior to the commencement of the First Division

Town hero Ray Crawford dives forward on his hands to put the rebound past Sims and into the Villa net to score one of the most famous goals in the club's history.

campaign. He told an attentive audience: 'We have certainly got something on our plate and sometimes, when I look at our fixture list and the places we have got to go, I am frightened and ask what I have done to deserve this. Then again, I think that this is something really worthwhile to fight for. We have got to improve, but I am certain that we shall improve. We have a great chance. To those who say we shall go down as quickly as we came up, I say "wait and see". I think we shall show some people we are quite a team.'

Ramsey was idolised by his players, all of whom called him Alf and were quick to heap praise on him for his tactical foresight and his ability to bring out the best in them. His plan to utilise spindly-legged Jimmy Leadbetter as a deep-lying winger, for example, was a masterstroke with which opponents struggled to come to terms. Ramsey pinpointed the wiry Leadbetter as a key man and added: 'I hope he plays as long as Stanley Matthews. He puts in more work, especially in tackles, than any other forward in the side.'

One-time Portsmouth reserve Ray Crawford credited Ramsey with converting him into an international after he became the first Ipswich player to represent England, winning his two caps in the championship season, and on his debut against Northern Ireland supplying the pass from which Bobby Charlton scored in a 1-1 draw. Later that same season Crawford was on target at Wembley, in a 3-1 defeat of Austria, but he was never to play for England again. Many questioned Walter Winterbottom's judgement, not only in restricting Crawford's appearances but in not partnering him with Ted Phillips.

Crawford led the tributes to his former boss when he died in May 1999, stating: 'I was rather naive when I left Portsmouth. I had never had what I would call proper coaching, but Alf helped me tremendously. It was simple stuff, really. Where to run, when to run, positions to take up, that sort of thing. Every Thursday Alf would run through what I had done wrong in the previous game, telling me how I should put it right in the next one. He always had plenty of advice and there's no doubt he made me a better player. I liked Alf a lot, but I knew that if I didn't heed his advice he would go out and get someone else who would. He didn't suffer fools. He would help if he thought you needed it, but if he felt you weren't appreciative he wouldn't do it. I'll never know for sure, but I think he would have replaced me if I hadn't been receptive. I had a very good relationship with Alf. He was a gentleman and he was quietly determined, too. He knew what he wanted. He left me out of the side several times, when I was having a bad run. I would go in to see him and argue my point, but he would stick to his guns and when you came out of the office you had to admit to yourself that he was right.

'I remember I asked for a transfer once. I'd been with the England boys and knew what they were getting. But the board turned me down and again Alf stuck to his guns. I just accepted it. Alf took me from nothing, to be fair. We came to Ipswich, saw a lovely house and the club bought it for us. We rented it and we had a good time there. What Alf did was like a fairytale, turning a club like Ipswich into champions. He kidded everybody on. He had a system he believed in. It took the others about three years to sort it out and before they sussed it we had come from the middle of the

Second Division, won it and then won the First Division title. There's an old John Wayne movie in which he plays an old football coach. He gets players from here and there, bits and pieces, and puts them together to win things. Every time I see it I think of Alf and those days at Ipswich.'

Crawford remembered how he was accompanied by Alf as he returned to Ipswich by train from each of his two England appearances at Wembley. He recalled: 'Alf wasn't the England manager then, but he spoke as if he was. All the way back he was going through the game. He wasn't giving me a rollicking, but he was saying I should have done this and I should have done that. I remember him saying I was doing all Johnny Haynes' running for him. It was always short and sweet with Alf. It never developed into a slanging match. I've been in some dressing rooms and seen players come to blows with a manager, or the tea go flying up the wall, but that wasn't Alf's way. Alf was regarded as being a bit aloof, but he didn't look down on people. He knew the right time to say something. He would give us time to think about it and he always got his point across.'

Ted Phillips was another who had good reason to be grateful to Alf. He admitted: 'I would have been nothing without Alf. He made me when he took over at Ipswich. He was a god to me. I was better just for talking

---

50 Greatest Players

ROY STEPHENSON   Winger

Joined Ipswich Town: 14 July 1960   **From:** Leicester City

Debut: v Brighton, 13 September 1960, League

Appearances: 163   **Goals:** 26

Left Ipswich Town: 30 June 1965   **For:** Lowestoft Town

When Alf Ramsey signed Roy he told him he was to be the final piece in his jigsaw and the facts bear the truth of that comment. In his first season he collected a Second Division medal and in his second he reached the peak by claiming a First Division medal — two honours that some players never get near to in a lifetime in football.

Roy, known as Rocky by the fans, was thinking of returning north when Ramsey's persuasive tongue got to work and he became a vital cog in the team. Quick off the mark and full of tricks, he was a direct winger whose instructions were to deliver the crosses for goal-hungry forwards Ray Crawford and Ted Phillips to feast upon. Roy left his native North East to join Burnley, then had spells with Rotherham and Blackburn, where he also won a Second Division medal and helped them reach the FA Cup semi-final in 1958. His next stop was Leicester, from where he made the best move of his career in teaming up with Ipswich. He died in February 2000.

to Alf, never mind how he put me right in training. He chatted to me and built up my confidence. He taught me when to run and when I went through the middle the others – Jimmy (Leadbetter), big John (Elsworthy) or Roy (Stephenson) – would thread the ball through. I just went "Bang" and hit it as hard as I could. If it didn't make the net and the keeper got his hands to it, Ray (Crawford) would follow up and get the rebound.'

Phillips remembered bumping into Alf on a train out of London – 'we had a good old chat' – and it was only the next morning, when he read a newspaper, that he realised Alf had been returning home to Ipswich after being sacked by the FA. 'He never said a dickie bird about it,' recalled Phillips. 'But I wasn't that surprised, to be honest. Alf was such a private man.'

Doug Moran, the club's record signing when he arrived from Falkirk in 1961, said: 'Alf was good for me, giving me the opportunity to play in a better class of football. If he had a secret I think it was that he never asked anyone to do something that was beyond them. He was very astute and knew all his players' individual strengths. He would pick you up on something you might have done wrong, but it was just a quiet word in your ear. I never, ever heard him swear. I think the worst thing he ever said was "That was bloody awful" if we hadn't played well. That's unusual in a dressing room. Alf never lost his rag. I can understand why people regarded him as aloof, but that wasn't how the players saw him.'

Larry Carberry, plucked from the Army to become a professional footballer, said: 'I signed for Alf, not just Ipswich. He was a wonderful person and I will always be grateful for the guidance he gave me. He was very helpful. He was a true gentleman, very loyal and very fair to his players, and I have nothing but fond memories of my time there. Alf was good at planning things. He made everything simple for us. And we stuck together through thick and thin. He came to watch me play at Bury and I was introduced to him as I came off the park. In those days at Bury, the main stand was on the opposite side of the ground, so Alf would have had to leave his seat before the end and walk all the way round so that he was there as I came off. The reason I mention that is because a national paper at the time claimed it was the first time Alf had ever been known to leave his seat before the end of a game. I felt quite honoured.'

Carberry had the chance to sign for either Liverpool or Ipswich. 'I rang home and spoke to my dad,' he recalled. 'He was a big Liverpool fan and took it for granted I'd be going to Anfield. They were in a higher league and they were closer to home, but I was drawn to Ipswich by Alf. I couldn't turn him down and I never regretted my decision.'

Jimmy Leadbetter was Scott Duncan's last signing and he also had good reason to be grateful to Ramsey. He said: 'Alf was a lovely man. He treated me like a man, not as a wee daft laddie, and he gained my total respect. He got it from all the players. Personally, I cannot talk too highly of him. He would never put people in an awkward position. If he had anything to say he would just have a wee blether in the corner. None of this shouting at the top of his voice like some of the big-mouths who are managers today and seem to enjoy belittling their players. When England sacked Alf they made a big mistake, he could have continued to do a good job for many more years.'

Roy Stephenson, who was persuaded to come to Ipswich by the great man, said: 'His attention to detail was amazing. In his Friday team talks he concentrated on trying to find weaknesses in the opposition. There were no long dossiers. He had all the information in his head. He had an incredible memory. It was the attention to detail that set him apart from other managers. In my book, Alf was the tops. It's not easy putting your finger on it, but I remember Bobby Moore saying he would walk to Wembley to play for him. I think we all felt like that. When I met Alf to talk about possibly signing I was really thinking about heading back north. It wasn't the money Alf was offering, or the facilities, that made my mind up for me. It was Alf, plain and simple. He did a good selling job.'

Before moving on, a sobering thought. Stephenson recalled the championship-winning season and said: 'I don't think the town was really ready for the First Division title. Do you know, the players organised a dance to celebrate and we couldn't sell all the tickets. Can you imagine that happening now?'

The monetary rewards could not compare, either. The Town squad received a £1,500 bonus provided by the Football League, with strict instructions that it should be shared in relation to games played. John Elsworthy only missed one game that season, but he remembered: 'It worked out at £2 12s per game. After tax there was just enough to buy a new Hoover washing machine. But I have no complaints. You can spend money, but no one can ever take the achievements away. I remember when Bobby Robson's team won the FA Cup and I congratulated him. He smiled and said "Thank you, but I'd still like your championship medal". That brought it home to me.'

Meanwhile, the club celebrated in style with a civic reception following an open-top bus ride through the town on 14 May. Three days later it was the supporters' association who held another party and on 19 May the club's reputation as generous hosts soared when they held a banquet at the Savoy in London, to which every other club was invited to send two representatives.

Great Managers – 1955-63

ALF RAMSEY

Alf Ramsey oversaw a football fairytale in his time with Ipswich, leading a club from the backwaters to the very top, and it earned him the chance to rewrite the record books all over again as manager of England, on whose behalf he kept his promise to win the World Cup.

Born in Dagenham on 22 January 1920, he became a professional footballer in 1944. He won the first of his 32 senior caps on 1 December 1948 when he played in the 6-0 win over Switzerland in a friendly international staged at Highbury. In May the following year he was transferred to Tottenham Hotspur where, in his first two seasons, he won Second and First Division Championship medals. He went on to make a total of 250 appearances for Spurs and remained a regular choice for England, playing in the World Cup finals of 1950 and making his final appearance at Wembley on 25 November 1953 when Hungary handed out a footballing lesson in winning 6-3.

With Tottenham having agreed to release him from his playing contract, he was unveiled as Town's new manager on 9 August 1955. His influence was quickly felt as players and fans alike warmed to his management style, and a final league position of third was deemed a satisfactory start. The following season Ramsey's team topped the Third Division (South) on goal average after a last-day success at Southampton.

Town established themselves at the higher level over the next three seasons until, in 1961, they won a first-ever Second Division crown. While some people were still getting used to the fact that Ipswich were actually in the First Division, Ramsey's team swept all before them again to stun the football world and capture the League Championship, one of the most remarkable achievements in the history of the English game.

The 1962-63 season was to be Ramsey's last. News of his appointment as England manager was announced on 25 October 1962, but he agreed to stay at Portman Road to guide the club through a difficult period and only departed in April the following year.

Ramsey was unceremoniously dumped by the FA in 1974 after England had failed to qualify for that year's World Cup finals. He made a brief comeback with Birmingham City, and had a short spell as an adviser to Greek club Panathinaikos, before retiring, seemingly enjoying the fact that he was no longer in the spotlight. He snubbed offers to publish his memoirs, only occasionally breaking his silence to comment on the England team at the time. He died in an Ipswich nursing home, following a long illness, in May 1999 and a memorial service in the town attracted most of his World Cup-winning team, together with a host of other friends and admirers from the world of football.

Chapter Six: 1962-68
Managerial Merry-Go-Round

The summer of 1962 saw Ipswich invest a new record fee of £15,000 on Bobby Blackwood from Hearts and, after initially rejecting the terms on offer, both Ray Crawford and Bill Baxter relented to sign new deals. But the highs of the previous season were quickly forgotten as Town started depressingly and slumped to within one place of the bottom of the table after winning just two of their first 16 league games.

In a curtain-raiser to the new season, they met Tottenham in the Charity Shield at Portman Road and it was immediately apparent that Spurs boss Bill Nicholson had done his homework to combat Town's unorthodox pattern of play. He pulled his full-backs in to operate alongside the central defenders, thereby outnumbering the Ipswich attackers, and left his wing-halves to deal with Stephenson and Leadbetter. His plan worked a treat and Tottenham were convincing 5-1 victors.

In contrast to the previous season, when Ipswich were able to field a settled side, they were badly disrupted by injuries and the recognised championship-winning side did not reassemble until the 40th game of the season in early April. They managed nine games – five wins, two draws and two defeats – which emphasised the damage that had been done by injuries, and this enabled Town to climb clear of trouble and finish 17th.

They could do little right in the First Division at Portman Road, where they managed just five league wins, two of which came in the last three home games. There was a sparse four months up to 27 April 1963, when they failed to win in front of their own supporters and when their misery ended with a 2-1 victory over Burnley, such was the ferocity with which Ted Phillips struck the winning goal that the net literally gave way. Strike partner Ray Crawford, who scored almost half the team's league goals, and Bill Baxter, who completed his National Service in September, were the only ever-presents.

Foray into Europe
It was a season when Ipswich enjoyed their first taste of European football, waltzing through their preliminary round clash. Floriana may have earned

It was success for Town first time out in Europe as they defeated Maltese champions Floriana 4-1 thanks to two goals each for Ted Phillips and Ray Crawford.

the Maltese crown without dropping even one point, but they were no match for Town who were comfortable 4-1 winners away from home. The Portman Road facilities may have been modest in those days, but the tiny Empire Stadium did not even have showers or baths, which meant that the Ipswich contingent had to change at their hotel. It was new territory for the entire party, but especially for Ken Malcolm and trainer Jimmy Forsyth, neither of whom had flown before. Skipper Andy Nelson broke his nose in two places as a result of a fourth-minute collision and although he battled on bravely, he was rested for the return leg. Malcolm captained the team to what remains their record win in any competition, 10-0, with Ray Crawford netting five of them, in turn a record for a British player in any European competition.

The following month, it was announced that Alf Ramsey was to succeed Walter Winterbottom as the new England manager, although he was to remain at Portman Road until April the following year and his own successor, Jackie Milburn, was brought in during the second part of the season to learn the ropes and get used to the place. In the European Cup first round, Town were paired with AC Milan and went down 3-0 in the first leg in Italy. It was a night of non-stop rain and Ipswich were not a major attraction, with a paltry 7,607 fans turning out in the atrocious weather at the huge San Siro Stadium.

Great Matches

EUROPEAN CUP FIRST ROUND SECOND LEG

Ipswich Town 2
Crawford
Blackwood

AC Milan 1
Barison

Portman Road,
28 November 1962
Attendance: 25,079

This was, at the time, the most glamorous game ever staged at Portman Road, and the millionaire men of Milan went on to lift the European Cup after surviving this brief scare against Alf Ramsey's team.

Trailing 3-0 from the first leg, it was always going to be an uphill task for Town, but they set about it with relish and were denied any luck on the night.

The English champions made a fantastic fight of it, although the Milan defence, superbly marshalled by Maldini, who would to go on to manage Italy, stood firm against a tide of pressure.

Even so, the Italians were fortunate when a long-distance effort by Ray Crawford skimmed the bar and after 36 minutes Town's luck was out again when Roy Stephenson collected a pass from Doug Moran and cracked his shot against a post. Three minutes later, Ipswich hit the woodwork again, this time a Crawford header coming back off the bar. Ted Phillips followed up with another header and thought he had scored until Trebbi produced a spectacular goal-line clearance.

A long centre from Bill Baxter deceived goalkeeper Ghezzi, but bounced off the far post as Town started the second half in a determined mood.

But their task became all but impossible when Milan established a four-goal aggregate lead, Altafini attacking on the break to give Barison his chance with a shot that was deflected in.

Crawford's low shot through a crowded goalmouth ten minutes from the end pulled Ipswich level on the night and Bobby Blackwood's 84th-minute goal, after Stephenson's rocket shot had come back off the bar, earned them a well-deserved win.

Despite their team's exit from the competition, Town supporters made their way home content that they had seen one of the most thrilling games ever played at Portman Road.

Ipswich Town: Bailey, Carberry, Compton, Baxter, Nelson, Elsworthy, Stephenson, Moran, Crawford, Phillips, Blackwood.

AC Milan: Ghezzi, David, Trebbi, Trapattoni, Maldini, Radice, Pelagalli, Rivera, Altafini, Dino Sani, Barison.

Referee: A. Blavier (Belgium).

Larry Carberry remembered: 'The Italians were up to all their tricks. They even had about 40 photographers behind the goal we were defending. I'm not convinced they were all taking pictures. A lot of them were just popping their flashes to distract us. Every time the ball was in the air we lost it in the light.' Town had the consolation of winning the home leg 2-1, when they struck the woodwork several times, and they could at least claim to have gone out to the winners when AC Milan went on to beat Benfica 2-1 in the Wembley final.

There was further disappointment to come in the FA Cup, although the third round win at Mansfield was memorable for Jimmy Leadbetter's first and only hat-trick for the club. It was also the first by an Ipswich player in the FA Cup since Tommy Parker's three goals against Wisbech in 1945. There was relief that no one was seriously injured when some concrete barriers collapsed and the FA Cup adventure – it is strange that Town never scaled any great heights in the competition under Ramsey – was over when eventual runners-up Leicester won 3-1 in a fourth round tie at Filbert Street.

Dermot Curtis was by no means a regular choice, but he continued to gain Republic of Ireland honours, while Ray Crawford netted a hat-trick as the Football League beat their Irish counterparts 3-1 at Carrow Road. There was also a rare change in the boardroom, as Ernest Steel retired after 15 years as a director and was replaced by Scots-born local farmer, William Kerr.

Milburn Takes the Reins

With Alf Ramsey gone, but certainly not forgotten, Jackie Milburn was in sole charge at the start of the 1963-64 season, and it turned out to be a disastrous campaign. The club's championship success of two years earlier

seemed a distant memory as they fought in vain to avoid relegation and actually finished rock bottom of the First Division, winning just nine league games and conceding 121 goals into the bargain. They did not manage a single away win and their leaky defence was breached 76 times on their travels.

Ramsey had left behind an ageing squad, a problem Milburn set about remedying, but for which he had no quick-fix cure. Looking to the longer

New man at the helm, Jackie Milburn.

50 Greatest Players

TED PHILLIPS   **Forward**

Joined Ipswich Town: 11 December 1953   **From:** Leiston Town

Debut: v Watford, 3 March 1954, League

Appearances: 293   **Goals:** 179

Left Ipswich Town: 16 March 1964   **For:** Leyton Orient

Second only to his former partner, Ray Crawford, in the all-time Ipswich scoring charts, Ted was discovered virtually on the club's doorstep after being recommended by the Leiston manager, former Town player Ian Gillespie. A forestry worker before joining up at Portman Road, he was in the first team within three months but was farmed out to Stowmarket Town before returning to claim a regular place. He netted 41 times in 41 games to help Ipswich capture the Third Division (South) title in 1957 and he carried on scoring to bring the Second Division and First Division crowns to Portman Road.

Renowned for his cannonball shooting, he actually netted a £1,000 prize put up by a national newspaper to find the player with the fiercest shot in the country. Ted went on to play for Leyton Orient, Luton and Colchester, and also had a spell in Malta as player-boss of Floriana. He travelled the country laying cables for British Telecom before his retirement and remains a regular visitor to Portman Road.

term, he was instrumental in launching a youth policy that, having been taken on several stages over the years, continues to pay handsome dividends. At first team level, however, it was a constant struggle, even with new recruits Joe Davin (Hibernian), John Colrain (Clyde) and Danny Hegan (Sunderland) on board.

When they opened the season with a 3-1 win at home to Burnley there was little hint of the trauma to follow. But the decline quickly set in as they embarked on a miserable run of 23 league and League Cup games without a win, the gloom only being lifted temporarily just before Christmas when they recovered from being 2-0 down to West Ham and, thanks to three goals in 14 minutes, won 3-2. But it was only a temporary relief and having slumped to the bottom of the table on 1 October they were never able to climb away from the basement. They did improve towards the end of the season, particularly at home when they won eight and drew one of their last 11 games, but they had accepted their relegation fate long before the last day.

New manager Milburn, chosen from a list of 60 applicants after Wolves player Bill Slater rejected an offer from the Ipswich board, struggled to assert his authority in what was a transitional period for the club. Ted Phillips' goals had dried up – he managed just four in 20 league games

50 Greatest Players

RAY CRAWFORD   **Forward**

Joined Ipswich Town: 6 September 1958   **From:** Portsmouth

Debut: v Swansea Town, 4 October 1958, League

Appearances: 353   **Goals:** 227

Left Ipswich Town: September 1963   **For:** Wolves (re-signed from West Bromwich Albion in March 1966, left for Charlton in March 1969)

Ray netted twice on his Ipswich debut and carried on scoring throughout a Portman Road career that saw him enjoy two successful spells at the club.

Captured from Pompey for a mere £5,000, he struck up an immediate understanding with Ted Phillips and their goals helped Ipswich to the Second Division title in 1961, then the First Division crown one year later, with Ray the leading marksman in each season – a feat equalled only by the legendary Dixie Dean in 1930-31 and 1931-32 since the First World War. The club's all-time leading marksman, Ray was unfortunate to win only two England caps before he joined Wolves. He returned to Portman Road, via West Bromwich Albion, and his scoring exploits again helped earn the Second Division title in 1968. After a spell at Charlton he joined Colchester and was on target in their stunning FA Cup victory over the mighty Leeds United in 1971, which still remains one of the biggest shocks in the competition's long history. His playing days over, he returned to his native Portsmouth and was Pompey's youth coach for a while. He worked in merchandising before his retirement.

and also missed two penalties, both against Harry Gregg of Manchester United, before he departed for Leyton Orient.

Town had cashed in on their other goal machine, the much younger Ray Crawford, who was on his way to Wolves for £42,000 within a month of the season starting, much to the disgust of many supporters. In their next 14 games Ipswich tried five different centre-forwards and Gerry Baker, bought from Hibernian for a club record £17,500, eventually held down the job. He did well in a struggling side, but not even his 15 goals in 20 games – including a hat-trick in a 6-3 defeat at Tottenham – could rescue Town.

Milburn tended to look north of the border for his new players. Goalkeeper Jim Thorburn arrived from Raith Rovers and did not have the happiest of times. Chairman John Cobbold received a letter from an angry supporter who pointed out Thorburn's poor record in Scottish football and, when he brought this to the attention of Milburn, the manager leapt to the defence of his new recruit. 'He was playing behind a poor defence,' Milburn explained, only to return north within a few weeks and sign Raith's centre-half, Jack Bolton.

Winger Joe Broadfoot was one of the manager's few successes, as the speedy ex-Millwall player proved to be a big hit with fans, but it was felt that the influx of Scots had caused a dressing room rift and affected team discipline, which had been strict under Ramsey. Milburn offered to resign, but chairman Cobbold refused to accept it.

There were several embarrassing scorelines, none more so than on Boxing Day when Town crashed 10-1 at Fulham, still the club's heaviest defeat. Graham Leggat scored a hat-trick in under four minutes, with Bobby Robson netting the seventh, although two days later the Londoners came to Portman Road and were beaten 4-2. Other trouncings were 7-2 at home by Manchester United and a trio of 6-0 away defeats at the hands of Bolton, Arsenal and Liverpool. In their next game after the Anfield thrashing, Town were dumped 9-1 at Stoke, the same day Team Spirit triumphed in the Grand National and it prompted the *East Anglian Daily Times* headline, 'Team Spirit at Aintree but Ipswich show none at Stoke.'

Gerry Baker scored an FA Cup hat-trick in a 6-3 third round defeat of Oldham that set up a visit from Stoke, for whom Stanley Matthews was just a week away from his 49th birthday as he paid his only visit to Portman Road and at the same time completed the rounds of all First Division clubs.

50 Greatest Players

ROY BAILEY   Goalkeeper

Joined Ipswich Town: 15 March 1956   **From:** Crystal Palace

Debut: v Norwich City, 2 April 1956, League

Appearances: 346

Left Ipswich Town: January 1965   **For:** South Africa

Roy is one of a select group of players to win a Third Division medal in 1956-57, followed by a Second Division medal in 1961 and, just a year later, the big one, a First Division medal. He was signed by Alf Ramsey towards the end of his first season in charge and he was a regular choice for over eight years. After emigrating to South Africa, he took charge of the national team, as well as working as a TV commentator, a job that took him all over the world. When Town were looking for a manager, following Bill McGarry's resignation in 1968, he received a phone call suggesting he should apply for the job, an invitation he declined. Roy's son, Gary, who was born in Ipswich, went on to play for Manchester United and England, but was unable to complete a family double as a Championship-winning goalkeeper. Roy died in South Africa in April 1993.

John Compton signed from Chelsea as a wing-half. But with Alf Ramsey as his tutor, Compton became a regular as a full-back in the 1962 Championship-winning side.

The game ended 1-1 – a decent result considering Baker had left the field injured after just nine minutes – but Town lost the replay 1-0, the same scoreline that saw them crash out of the League Cup earlier that season to Third Division strugglers Walsall.

Troubled Times

When Town chairman John Cobbold begged the supporters' association for money he did not mince his words, claiming: 'As things are we would obviously have the greatest difficulty in holding a place in the Second Division, let alone the First.' The fans' official organisation stumped up £35,000 in the summer of 1964, towards the cost of work on the North Stand, and it brought to £80,000 the total sum donated to the club in a five-year period.

That summer also saw the departure of title-winning heroes, Roy Bailey and John Compton, to South Africa and Bournemouth respectively, with ex-England full-back Mick McNeil from Middlesbrough, and Frank Brogan from Celtic, checking in at Portman Road. But Town made a sluggish start, losing three of their first four games – twice to newly-promoted Coventry, managed by Jimmy Hill, and 5-1 at home to Preston.

It was all too much for Milburn, whose health was suffering as he struggled to stem the tide, and on 4 September he tendered his resignation.

The following day Town lost 2-1 at Norwich, rather unluckily since the injured Bill Baxter was absent for the entire second half of a game in which Trevor Smith made his debut and, at 18 years and three weeks old, became the youngest player to represent the club.

At a special board meeting on 8 September chairman John Cobbold, who again tried to persuade Milburn to change his mind, and his fellow directors reluctantly accepted their manager's resignation after he had been in charge for less than 17 months. There was genuine sadness that Milburn had failed, at least as far as results were concerned, and maybe it was a step too far from non-league Yiewsley for the affable ex-Newcastle centre-forward. As John Cobbold put it: 'Perhaps his niceness was his weakness.' A true gentleman, but sorely lacking when it came to cracking the whip, he at least had the consolation of seeing several of his signings prosper at Portman Road after he had departed,

50 Greatest Players

KEN MALCOLM   **Defender**

Joined Ipswich Town: 28 May 1954   **From:** Arbroath

Debut: v Hull City, 4 September 1954, League

Appearances: 291   **Goals:** 2

Left Ipswich Town: 6 June 1964 (retired)

Ken was a hard-tackling defender who played most of his games at left-back, although in his first season at Portman Road, when Town were relegated, he played in eight different positions. He lost his reputation as a utility man when Alf Ramsey arrived as manager to install him in the No. 3 shirt and only missed three games in the 1956-57 season, when he won a Third Division (South) Championship medal. Ken went one better with a Second Division medal in a memorable 1960-61 campaign, but he was unable to play any more than the first three games of the League Championship-winning season because of a slipped disc. At the age of 36 he captained the team in the record 10-0 defeat of Maltese club Floriana, the club's first competitive home game in Europe. Ken joined the backroom staff, helping then manager Jackie Milburn to establish a youth system that continues to serve the club well today, and he later coached at reserve level. He left the club in 1966, entered the licensed trade and then returned to Scotland and ran his own business as a wholesale fish merchant. His next stop was Guernsey, where he and his wife enjoyed living close to their daughter and her family, and in 1985 he returned to live in Ipswich, working as a caretaker, driver and chauffeur before retiring in 1992.

although it must be said that other recruits did not distinguish themselves, either on or off the park, during their time in Suffolk.

Change of Direction

The board appointed Jimmy Forsyth, with back-up from Charlie Cowie and Ken Malcolm, to take temporary charge of team affairs and the all-Scottish trio managed to lift Ipswich off the bottom of the table with a first win of the season, at the ninth attempt, at Middlesbrough. It was their first away success in 31 attempts and Larry Carberry clocked up his 300th appearance in another impressive victory, 3-1 over Newcastle, just two days before Bill McGarry took over on 5 October 1964. His first game in charge was at Crystal Palace, who took a third-minute lead, but Town fought back to force a draw and climb out of the bottom two.

Things were different under McGarry. Training was tougher, but it was clearly paying dividends as Portsmouth, then managed by George Smith, briefly assistant boss at Portman Road 15 years earlier, were dumped 7-0, a new Football League record win for Town in which Frank Brogan scored his first hat-trick for the club.

50 Greatest Players

JOHN ELSWORTHY   Wing-half

Joined Ipswich Town: 9 May 1949 (as an amateur)

Debut: v Notts County, 27 December 1949

Appearances: 433   Goals: 52

Left Ipswich Town: 30 June 1965 (retired)

John holds a unique place in the Town record books as the only player to win Third Division (South) medals in 1954 and 1957 as well as a Second Division medal from 1961 and a First Division medal from 1962. He was originally signed after being spotted playing for the youth team at Newport in 1949, where he was an amateur, and he chose football ahead of rugby. John could also have joined Glamorgan Cricket Club and for two years until 1951 he served in the RAF, during which time he was paid as a part-timer. He was a gentle giant, a player at his elegant best creating opportunities for others from the middle of the park, although his record demonstrates his effectiveness in front of goal. His entire professional career was spent at Portman Road, after which he ran a grocery and post office until his retirement. John succeeded former colleague Tommy Parker as honorary president of the supporters' club and continues to watch Town on a regular basis.

50 Greatest Players

LARRY CARBERRY   Defender

Joined Ipswich Town: 19 May 1956 (as an amateur)

Debut: v QPR, 3 November 1956, League

Appearances: 283   **Goals:** 0

Left Ipswich Town: 30 June 1965   **For:** Barrow

Alf Ramsey spotted Larry playing for Bury Town, while he was stationed there during national service with the Army, and he played in the reserves after signing as an amateur. He rejected an opportunity to join Liverpool when he had completed his national service, a decision that may have disappointed his father, a lifelong Red, but Larry had no regrets when he collected a Third Division (South) medal just 25 games into his professional career. He was an ever-present when Ipswich won the Second Division and also had a 100 per cent record in the memorable 1961-62 campaign when the championship came to Portman Road against all the odds. That same season, two of his classmates – Jimmy Melia (Liverpool) and Bobby Campbell (Portsmouth) – also won winners medals in the Second and Third Divisions. Larry was close to international honours, appearing for an FA X1 and also as a reserve for the England Under-23 side when he sat alongside Bobby Charlton on the bench. After two years with Barrow he worked as a docker for a further 18 years before retirement.

Through to the end of the season, Ipswich only lost four of their 31 games under McGarry as the new, no-nonsense manager steered them into fifth place. They drew 17 times in the Second Division, a tally no other Football League team could match, and there was a huge difference between the team that started the season so feebly and the one that finished with a flourish, losing just once during the second half of the league programme.

Not that hard man McGarry, with a vocabulary liberally sprinkled with swear words, was necessarily popular with all the players. Bill Baxter and Gerry Baker both requested moves, while Joe Broadfoot gave serious consideration to driving a taxi in his native London for a living, but all three were eventually persuaded to stay on and be part of McGarry's new-look side. In Baxter's case, he had originally demanded a transfer at the same time as Milburn departed, which forced chairman John Cobbold to comment: 'We are managerless, almost pointless and just cannot afford to be Baxter-less.'

McGarry, whose decision to introduce an all-blue kit failed to find universal approval, sold Larry Carberry to Barrow and Bobby Blackwood to Colchester, while Andy Nelson joined Ted Phillips at Leyton Orient, Jimmy Leadbetter was not retained and joined Sudbury Town and John Elsworthy opted for retirement.

50 Greatest Players

ANDY NELSON   Defender

Joined Ipswich Town: 27 May 1959   **From:** West Ham United

Debut: v Huddersfield Town, 22 August 1959, League

Appearances: 214   **Goals:** 0

Left Ipswich Town: 10 September 1964   **For:** Leyton Orient

Andy holds a special place in the record books as the first, and so far only, player to captain Ipswich to the League Championship. He was an instant success at Portman Road, one of four ever-presents in his first season, 1959-60, and he was only absent on three occasions in leading Town to the Second Division crown the following year. He again recorded a 100 per cent record in the momentous 1961-62 season when Ipswich shocked the football world by winning the big one. Andy proved to be a superb signing after national service interrupted his Hammers career and restricted his appearances in the Upton Park first team. He later played for both Leyton Orient and Plymouth Argyle before moving into coaching with Millwall and management with Gillingham and Charlton Athletic. He later became commercial manager at Charlton, after which he emigrated to South Africa.

In came goalkeeper Ken Hancock from Port Vale, Cyril Lea from Leyton Orient and Dave Harper from Millwall. He also initiated a positional switch, moving Bill Baxter to the role of centre-half, and although he was no giant, the strong-willed Scot was an outstanding success. There were changes, too, in the boardroom as John Cobbold's younger brother, Patrick, became a director along with Harold Smith, who had been a leading light in the supporters' association, and Murray Sangster, an all-round sportsman who had represented Suffolk at football, cricket and hockey. At a lively annual general meeting another new director, Ken Brightwell, was appointed, while Cyril Catchpole, with over 20 years of boardroom experience, resigned because of ill health. He became the club's first honorary vice president and Lady Blanche Cobbold the first honorary president.

Chairman John Cobbold generously paid for the players and their wives to embark on a Mediterranean cruise after the 1965-66 season and before the new campaign got under way the supporters' association made a further donation of £17,500, together with the promise of £1,000 a month for the duration of the campaign. Substitutes were introduced that season – Dave Harper for Frank Brogan at Charlton on 28 August 1966 was Town's first change – but Trevor Smith's arrival as the first 12th man at Portman Road could not prevent Bury from winning 4-3 to condemn Ipswich to their first home defeat in more than a year.

Lowestoft-born Eddie Spearritt made his debut on the opening day of the season and another three teenagers, home-grown pair Roy Walsh and Colin Harper together with Mick Mills, a victim of Portsmouth's cost-cutting exercise in scrapping their youth system, were all introduced to the senior side later in the campaign.

McGarry made a number of personnel changes in addition. He appointed a new coach, Sammy Chung, whose arrival led to the departure of Charlie Cowie after 29 years, thus severing the club's last link with the Southern League era.

Goalkeeper Jim Thorburn left to join Doug Millward at St Mirren and Joe Broadfoot moved to Northampton, while Ronnie Bolton was signed from Bournemouth and Bobby Kellard from Crystal Palace, although the latter was quickly on his way three months later to Portsmouth. By far the most popular of McGarry's decisions saw the return of Ray Crawford and he scored eight times in the last 12 games as Town finished a

50 Greatest Players

JIMMY LEADBETTER Winger

Joined Ipswich Town: 15 June 1955 **From:** Brighton

Debut: v Bournemouth, 8 October 1955, League

Appearances: 373 **Goals:** 49

Left Ipswich Town: 30 June 1965 **For:** Sudbury Town

Jimmy was almost 34 when he won a League Championship medal with Ipswich in the 1961-62 season and there was no more valuable member of the side. Originally an inside-forward and signed by Scott Duncan, it was Alf Ramsey's brainwave to play Jimmy as a deep-lying left-winger, and he confused opponents in setting up chances galore for Ray Crawford and Ted Phillips.

Spindly-legged and wafer thin, Jimmy showed impudent skill in outfoxing full-backs who had never been confronted by a winger in such a withdrawn role. It was the accuracy of his passing, rather than the speed and trickery normally associated with a winger, that made him so effective. He was actually reluctant to switch at Ramsey's suggestion, but the move prolonged his career and earned him success he could never have anticipated as a Chelsea reserve or at his previous club, Brighton. He is one of a select group to have won Third Division (South), Second Division and First Division title medals. Jimmy was Sudbury's player-manager until the age of 43, after which he decided to return to his native Scotland. He worked as a van driver for a leading newspaper group before his retirement.

disappointing 15th. In the FA Cup they were drawn away to Fourth Division side Southport and, despite leading 2-1 with eight minutes left, they were the victims of a giantkilling act as the home side netted two more goals. McGarry could have been on his way to Wolves, but he accepted the Ipswich directors' decision not to release him from his contract, although the episode may have affected his enthusiasm for the job at Portman Road.

The summer of 1966 saw England's football fans celebrating their country's World Cup final win over West Germany at Wembley and Ipswich supporters enjoyed the moment more than most as the success was masterminded by former Portman Road manager Alf Ramsey, who was subsequently knighted in the New Year's Honours. All clubs benefited from a surge in interest – Town's average attendance rose by more than 3,000 to almost 16,000, despite an increase in admission to five shillings, as the team topped the table several times before Christmas. They dropped down, however, as they suffered a run of 12 games without a win – nine of them were drawn – but 15 points from a possible 20 in their last ten games earned them a final finish of fifth.

South African youngster Colin Viljoen made a huge impact when he scored a hat-trick on his debut, a 4-2 win over Portsmouth after Town trailed 2-0 inside the first 15 minutes. The season's most dramatic game, the 5-4 win over Hull City, saw Ray Crawford claim a hat-trick as Ipswich replaced the Tigers at the Second Division summit, and another hat-trick hero, Frank Brogan, rewrote the record books in the 6-1 home win over Northampton, when he became the first Town player to convert two penalties in a game. Brogan scored from the spot against Huddersfield after the referee's decision had been strongly disputed by the visitors, and as the Ipswich players celebrated a supporter ran on, grabbed the trainer's bucket of water and threw it over the visiting manager and substitute on the bench.

Yet again that season McGarry made new signings, bringing in Billy Houghton from his former club, Watford, and successfully converting the wing-half into a full-back to cover for the injured Mick McNeil. He also purchased Tommy Carroll from Cambridge City and Charlie Woods from Crystal Palace, then brought Joe Broadfoot back to Portman Road for a second spell, paying Millwall just £5,000, which was £17,000 less than Town had pocketed from Northampton only 14 months earlier. Those departing included John Colrain, who became player-manager of Glentoran, and another two Scots, Joe Davin and Jack Bolton, both of whom returned north to join Morton.

Injuries took their toll that season – Chris Barnard, Dave Harper and Mick McNeil were all sidelined as a result of knocks in the game at Northampton – while teenager Derek Jefferson, first spotted in the North East during Jackie Milburn's time as manager, made his debut in an FA Cup third round win over Shrewsbury as a replacement for Bill Baxter, only denied an ever-present record when he was injured in a car crash and required five stitches to a gash on his forehead.

The big news during the summer of 1967 concerned a major, and extremely bitter, split within the supporters' association, which claimed to have raised about £240,000 for Ipswich Town. It resulted in ten members of the committee resigning and a new organisation, supported by the football club, being formed.

Manager Bill McGarry had to use all his powers of persuasion when he flew to South Africa to confront Colin Viljoen, recently introduced to the Town first team and apparently reluctant to return to England. The cost of a return ticket to Johannesburg was a small price to pay in return for Viljoen's services and he was a key player in helping Ipswich to land the Second Division crown, his most memorable performance coming in an East Anglian derby match at Carrow Road when he netted a hat-trick in Town's thrilling 4-3 win after they had been trailing 2-0 within the first 28 minutes.

Colin Viljoen's goalscoring and all-round vision were crucial to Town in 1967-68.

During the first part of the season, after the directors had confirmed their ambition to return to the First Division by rejecting Southampton's realistic £60,000 offer for Bill Baxter, Ipswich offered little hint that they would be promotion contenders. True they were tucked in behind the leaders and rarely lost, but they were once again the division's draw specialists and were experiencing problems in attack. Gerry Baker accepted the chance of an instant return to the First Division in November 1967 when he joined Coventry City and McGarry turned to Millwall's Bobby Hunt to replace him, only for the new arrival to be injured in training soon after his debut and to be ruled out for a month. With 15 games left, McGarry decided it was time to act and he plunged into the transfer market to sign John O'Rourke from Middlesbrough for a then record fee of £30,000. It was second time

A sea of spectators celebrate after Town clinch the Second Division Championship in 1968.

lucky, as the Town boss had failed to land the former Arsenal and Chelsea player when he was in charge at Luton.

Former England Under-23 international O'Rourke became the latest in a long line of Town players to mark their debuts by scoring and he grabbed a double in the 4-2 home win over Cardiff that represented a major turning point in the club's fortunes. There was another new face in Town's next line-up – Mansfield wing-half and captain Peter Morris cost £12,000 – and with injured players fully fit again the team never looked back. They not only caught, but overhauled, all rivals and a 1-1 draw with Blackburn in their final home game was enough to ensure the Second Division title, their fifth crown in 15 seasons.

The contribution of O'Rourke – 12 goals in an unbeaten 15-game run – was immense, as Town finished one point clear of QPR, who were promoted for the second year in a row. Ken Hancock was the only ever-present, while Ray Crawford proved that old habits die hard with 21 league and cup goals to finish as the club's leading marksman, seven years after he had first done so. The presentation of the Second Division trophy was carried out by Mr Len Shipman, president of the Football League's management committee, at a civic reception in Ipswich following the traditional open-topped bus ride, and Town became the first holders of a brand new trophy as the original had been destroyed in a fire at Coventry's Highfield Road stadium some months earlier.

A Time of Turmoil

Little did anyone realise, when a John O'Rourke goal beat Wolves at Portman Road on the opening day and gave Ipswich a winning start to life back in the First Division, that the 1968-69 season would be one of considerable upheaval as the club was forced to look for its fifth manager since turning professional 32 years earlier.

By the end of October, with just five wins from 15 games, Town were on the fringes of the relegation zone and soon afterwards came the bombshell news that Bill McGarry was quitting to join Wolves, the announcement coming just 24 hours after Ronnie Allen's resignation at Molineux. Ipswich chairman John Cobbold's statement read: 'The board decided to release him with disappointment and reluctance, bearing in mind that his contract was only signed a few months ago and the board went out of their way to meet his demands. We felt that to bind Mr McGarry to his contract would create difficulties and embarrassment, and would not be in the interests of the club in the long run.'

McGarry, who had signed England Under-23 reserve goalkeeper David Best from Oldham for £15,000 the previous month, said he had always been ambitious and that he could not reject the chance. 'It has caused me quite a headache,' he admitted. 'I have decided to move. The trend in football these days is to go into Europe and that must be my aim for Wolves.'

Coach Sammy Chung was named as Town's caretaker boss, but he was quickly reunited with McGarry, and instead it was Cyril Lea, who had moved on to the coaching staff, who was put in temporary charge – but only after Ipswich had been snubbed by their first choice for the post, Frank O'Farrell of Torquay United. A London meeting between Ipswich directors and O'Farrell had gone well, with his last words to chairman John Cobbold being: 'What time does the bus leave for Coventry?' Since Town's next game was at Highfield Road, the Ipswich contingent returned to base confident that their search for a new manager was over.

In fact, it was only just beginning. Mr Cobbold interrupted a board meeting at Portman Road the very next morning to take a telephone call from his Torquay counterpart, Tom Boyce, which informed him that O'Farrell was declining the move 'for domestic reasons'.

Mr Cobbold described the news as 'a shattering blow' and two weeks later, with Town still searching for McGarry's successor, O'Farrell was on his way to Leicester City.

The Ipswich directors admitted they had no other candidate in mind and the team's displays under caretaker Cyril Lea saw him emerge as an outside bet. Certainly, the players were solidly behind him and it seemed as though the majority of supporters would have endorsed his appointment, but the board were uncertain and decided they wanted a more experienced man.

Lea rejected a cheeky £45,000 bid for midfielder Danny Hegan from Bill McGarry, who had valued the player at almost twice as much a few weeks earlier, as the search for a new manager continued. The Town directors failed to keep things under wraps and on 7 December they were turned down again, this time by Cardiff manager Jimmy Scoular.

There were some reports that Bob Stokoe was being lined up for the job, but he said he preferred to remain at Carlisle, and next on the list was Billy Bingham, then of Plymouth Argyle, who said he was anxious to accept and would meet the directors in London. Town were also committed to interviewing Bobby Robson, unemployed after being sacked by Fulham, out of courtesy to Dave Sexton. It was Sexton, the Chelsea manager who had Robson scouting for him at the time, who recommended him for the job and because Sexton was a friend of Ipswich, it was decided that the interview would proceed. Meanwhile, the football continued and David Webb scored his first goals for Chelsea, a hat-trick, in their 3-1 win on Boxing Day. To make matters worse, Derek Jefferson, who wore glasses off the field and contact lenses on it, became the first Ipswich player to be sent off at Portman Road.

It was just as well the board opted to interview Robson because Bingham had a change of heart and contacted John Cobbold to inform him that he would not, after all, be taking the job. That left Robson as the only candidate and after his interview at the Great Eastern Hotel in London, his appointment was confirmed in a statement from Mr Cobbold, which read: 'We were vastly impressed with Mr Robson and there was no doubt in our minds that he was the man for the job. He is obviously pretty tough but most pleasant and his whole life is bound up with football. We have not given him a contract, but I realise no manager can be judged in less than two years. I sincerely hope Bobby stays with us considerably longer than that.' Coincidentally, Robson had lost his job at Fulham on the same day Bill McGarry joined Wolves and only decided to apply when he was sent to Portman Road on a scouting trip by Chelsea boss Sexton.

Chapter Seven: 1969-71
The Start of the Robson Years

Bobby Robson started work at Portman Road on 13 January 1969 and was to remain at the helm until the summer of 1982 when he succeeded Ron Greenwood as manager of England. In that time he led Ipswich to the FA Cup in 1978, the UEFA Cup in 1981 and in both 1981 and 1982 they finished runners-up in the League Championship. Town only finished outside the top six once in his last ten seasons, in the FA Cup-winning campaign, and European football at Portman Road on a regular basis was

It was the start of a 13-year tenure as manager for Bobby Robson when he checked into Portman Road in January 1969.

an added bonus to the domestic success the club enjoyed during what was, on reflection, a spectacular era.

But times were often hard in the beginning as Robson, a rookie boss of limited experience and at 35 years old not much older than some of the Town players, tried to stamp his authority at a time when the club had suffered defeats in four of their previous five games, including an FA Cup third round tie at Everton that was covered by the BBC *Match of the Day* cameras, and occupied 18th position in the First Division.

Robson, who brought with him ex-Norwich and Colchester player Roy McCrohan, also axed by Fulham, agreed that Cyril Lea would become his assistant and the new managerial set-up was in place for a league trip to play Everton at Goodison Park which resulted in a 2-2 draw, Ray Crawford netting a double.

Off to a Flying Start

Robson's first home match was against Manchester United, who pulled in a new record crowd of 30,837, mainly due to the fact that it was George Best's first appearance at Portman Road, and Town won 1-0 courtesy of an own goal. Another highlight during Robson's early games in charge was a victory at fourth-placed Arsenal – only the Gunners' second Highbury defeat that season – and at West Ham, who had not lost any of their seven previous games. Come the end of the season, Town were 12th, having moved up the table after just three defeats, and 20 points from a possible 32 in their 16 games under Robson's leadership.

The statistics, however, could not mask a series of off-the-field problems for the new man who, as if he did not have enough with which to contend, was left nursing a broken nose following a training clash with Bobby Bell just three weeks into his new job. The behind-the-scenes upheaval saw

50 Greatest Players

DANNY HEGAN   Midfielder

Joined Ipswich Town: September, 1963   **From:** Sunderland

Debut: v Bolton Wanderers, 18 September 1963, League

Appearances: 230   **Goals:** 38

Left Ipswich Town: 5 May, 1969   **For:** West Bromwich Albion

Danny was a ball-playing midfielder with sublime ability, a superb range of passing techniques and the impish skills that mesmerised opponents and delighted Town supporters, winning them over in near-record time. Having failed to make the grade with previous club Sunderland, he was a cost-effective signing who matured as a player at Portman Road, although his dislike of training could never have led to him being described as a model professional. It did not prevent him from graduating to senior international level with his father's native Northern Ireland, however, and he won the first of his caps with West Brom and another six after former Town boss, Bill McGarry, signed him for his new club, Wolves, for whom he appeared in an all-English UEFA Cup final against Tottenham in 1972. Also that year, he was in the Irish team that defeated England at Wembley and there followed a brief spell back at Sunderland before he retired as a player. After working as a soccer coach at Butlin's in Clacton, he returned to the Midlands and is still based there.

Eddie Spearritt move to Brighton just ten days after Robson took charge, then, in March 1969, Ray Crawford, having decided he could no longer cope with the First Division, joined Charlton and Ken Hancock moved to Tottenham as understudy to Pat Jennings. Danny Hegan was also on the move, to West Bromwich Albion in a deal that saw Ian Collard and £30,000 travel in the opposite direction, while Billy Houghton was transferred to Leicester. Joe Broadfoot retired because of a knee injury and a group comprising Tommy Carroll, Peter Morris and John O'Rourke, who felt that he was England material and would have a better chance elsewhere, were all considering their futures. In addition, both O'Rourke and Bill Baxter were disciplined separately at a time when Robson had plenty of problems with which to occupy himself.

Robson was given a further headache in the summer of 1969 when, prior to a five-game tour of Canada, the players reacted angrily to a new wages policy at Portman Road which guaranteed them a moderate basic salary of £40 per week and 'generous incentive bonuses' equivalent to £60 for a win. A number of players threatened to reject the terms, but on the first day of pre-season training only three – Tommy Carroll, Colin Viljoen and Steve Stacey – were absent and they returned to the fold in a matter of days.

But the unrest remained and just days before the new season kicked off David Best joined Carroll, Baxter, Morris and Viljoen in wanting to leave. Given this backdrop, it was hardly surprising that Town made an unconvincing start, and their worst since turning professional, as they collected just one point from their opening seven games and occupied bottom slot in the table.

There was no lack of transfer activity, with Bobby Hunt moving to Charlton and John O'Rourke to Coventry in an £80,000 deal after an exchange deal with Southampton for Mike Channon fell through. Town were suffering from a lack of goals – Colin Viljoen was leading scorer that season with six, three of which were penalties – and the £33,000 purchase of young striker Mick Hill from Sheffield United did not have the desired effect. Town were prepared to pay their first six-figure fee for Alan Birchenall of Chelsea, but he was not keen on the personal terms offered, and it was a season when the heroes were in defence. Tommy Carroll did not miss a game, Bill Baxter was his usual dependable self, Mick Mills reached a career milestone of 100 appearances before he was 21 and Colin Harper broke into the side before damaging ankle ligaments in a testimonial match.

But going into the last lap of the season, with Town locked in a relegation battle alongside Sheffield Wednesday, Crystal Palace, Southampton and Sunderland, Robson made a £90,000 double swoop to sign Jimmy Robertson and Frank Clarke, from Arsenal and QPR respectively. The combination of a fast, direct winger and an industrious centre-forward helped to transform Ipswich. The pair starred in the last seven games of the season, with the highlight being the home win over Arsenal when Town were forced to come from behind, and nine points from a possible 14 enabled them to climb clear of trouble and finish the season in 18th place.

While the Robson era was just gathering momentum, another was ending in the summer of 1970 with the retirement of groundsman Freddie Blake, who had prepared his first pitch, for a game against Clapton Orient A, on 3 September 1927. It was a fitting farewell that when a national newspaper polled 50 of the game's leading players, the majority verdict was that Portman Road boasted the finest playing surface in the country.

Summer activity included the departure of chief scout Reg Tyrrell to become assistant manager to John Bond at Bournemouth, while Ron Wigg and Charlie Woods both joined Watford as several younger players, including Mick Lambert, Trevor Whymark and Clive Woods, who had all had a taste of senior action the previous season, were all expected to feature more regularly. A proposed exchange deal involving Colin Harper, with Portsmouth's George Ley coming to Portman Road, fell through, and although both Ian Collard and Colin Viljoen were on the transfer list, there wasn't exactly a rush for their services.

Off-the-field Clashes

The main focus of attention in the 1970-71 season, however, had nothing

to do with what was happening on the field. Captain Bill Baxter was in the spotlight when he rushed into print, less than 24 hours after an FA Cup fourth round tie at West Bromwich Albion, in a Sunday newspaper article in which he slammed the club, claiming: 'They are going to the dogs.' An angry Robson sought an explanation and, when none was forthcoming, Baxter was suspended for two weeks, placed on the transfer list and the captaincy handed to

The dependable Mick Mills inherited the captaincy after Bill Baxter's outburst.

Mick Mills. It seemed out of character for Baxter, a loyal,

50 Greatest Players

BILL BAXTER   **Defender**

Joined Ipswich Town: 10 June 1960   **From:** Broxburn Ath.

Debut: v Norwich City, 27 December 1960, League

Appearances: 459   **Goals:** 22

Left Ipswich Town: 1 March 1971   **For:** Hull City

To many Ipswich supporters who relished the club's rise under Alf Ramsey, there has never been a finer player than this Scottish defensive rock. He was the youngster in the title-winning side of 1962, having joined up as he commenced his national service with the Royal Engineers in Aldershot, and most weeks he only arrived in Ipswich on the Friday to prepare for the next day's game. He captained Ipswich to the Second Division crown in 1968 and continued to skipper the side after Bobby Robson replaced Bill McGarry as manager in January 1969. He may not have been the biggest or the heaviest, but Baxter was a courageous defender whose commitment was total and his popularity with supporters was underlined when almost 16,000 attended his testimonial match in May 1970. Less than a year later he had moved on, a much-publicised row with Robson speeding his departure and he has never been back to Portman Road since. He was player-manager at Northampton and finished his playing career at Nuneaton Borough before retiring to his native Scotland, where he worked for British Telecom.

dependable, one-club servant, to vent his frustration in this way, but worse was to follow a month later when he was still languishing in the reserves. Following the first team's home defeat by Leeds, a row erupted that proved a turning point in Robson's managerial career as it presented him with a test he simply had to pass.

Baxter stayed silent about the incident for years, until he was tracked down in Scotland in the mid-1990s and was happy to recall the stormy events of the night of 23 February 1971. He said: 'Tommy Carroll and I, together with our wives, made for the players' lounge and were told we were both banned. We were told to consult the notice board in the dressing room. Robson had decided that players who weren't playing on the day couldn't go in the players' room. Tommy went off his head and headed downstairs. I said "Where are you going?" and he just kept going. "You'll see" he said. He marched along the corridor towards the dressing room and burst in. He headed straight for the notice board and ripped Robson's note off it. The next thing I knew, the pair of them fell to the floor, grappling and struggling with each other, and Tommy was laying into him.

Robson was shouting "Get the police, get the police". Then Cyril Lea got involved. Cyril was trying to pull them apart and break up the fight. I pulled Cyril off and pinned him up against the door. When the dust settled Tommy and I went off to the pub for a drink. We were both suspended for two weeks and I decided to go off to Scotland. Before the suspension was up Robson rang and said the club had accepted an offer from Hull. I agreed to move. I was glad to get away by then.'

He returned to take delivery of a new car, but has never been back in more than 30 years to the town where he was a hero, having played his way into the hearts of an adoring public. Baxter wanted to remain at Ipswich for the rest of his career and he admitted: 'I blame Robson. I would have stayed at Ipswich until I was finished. When I left I still had two or three years left as a First Division player. I don't believe I was pushed out because I was lacking ability. In my opinion, it was a personal thing. He didn't like me and I didn't like him. It happens. I just didn't get on with Robson. I was blamed for the incident in the dressing room, but I knew it wasn't my fault. I never wanted to patch things up with Robson at the time, although he did try. He would approach me, but I didn't want to know. I just ignored him. I know I'm a stubborn character, but I'm a man's man. If you've got something to say to me, say it to my face. If I don't like it, I'll have a go back. Robson and I had nothing in common. There was no way I could work with him, and I wasn't going to be two-faced about it.'

Writing in his autobiography, *Time on the Grass*, which was published in 1982, Robson recalled the dressing room fracas. He wrote: 'He (Carroll) and his friend Bill Baxter didn't like me and it showed. I couldn't back down. The rest of the players were watching and gauging my reaction. Baxter joined in and Cyril Lea came to my aid.'

The confrontation came at a time when Baxter was within 20 appearances of breaking Tommy Parker's long-standing record and he is remembered for his achievements as a player of immense quality who endeared himself to supporters with his wholehearted approach, along with his willingness to stick with the club through some miserable times when he could have undoubtedly bettered himself elsewhere, rather than for his part in an unfortunate incident that did no one any favours. Even before his final bust-up with Robson he performed solidly that season, scoring the opening goal as Town recorded their first win, 3-0 against fellow strugglers Burnley, following a dismal start to the campaign.

Ipswich failed to find the net in their first five games, collecting a mere two points as they slumped to the foot of the table, but in their next home match after defeating Burnley they walloped Manchester United 4-0. Seven days later and Town were again hitting the headlines, but this time for an amazing incident at Stamford Bridge, probably the most controversial anywhere that season. Chelsea player Alan Hudson fired in a shot which flew wide, but struck the stanchion and rebounded back into play. Town goalkeeper David Best retrieved the ball in preparation for a goal-kick, only to discover that referee Roy Capey was signalling a goal and even after the Ipswich players surrounded him to protest, whereupon he consulted a linesman, he insisted it should count. It was Chelsea's second goal in a 2-1 win, which only fuelled Town's anger, and while there was no lack of sympathy for the club's appeal to the Football League there was no surprise, either, when the authorities reiterated that the result would stand.

Geoff Hammond, now the father-in-law of former goalkeeper Richard Wright, was making his first team debut for Ipswich that day and recalled: 'It was the daftest decision you'll ever see. To this day I can't believe it really happened. When the ref signalled a goal we thought he was joking. Players on both sides were laughing, until we realised he was serious.'

Town put the setback behind them to continue their impressive home form and they managed to accumulate seven points from four games. In one, the 2-2 draw with West Bromwich Albion, David Best twisted his back and had to be replaced by Trevor Whymark, but in the long term it allowed Lowestoft-born Laurie Sivell, at 5ft 8ins one of the shortest goalkeepers in the country, his big chance. He responded with some stirring displays, in particular at Leeds where he defied the league leaders to earn a clean sheet, and Town might even have nicked both points against the run of play had Jimmy Robertson's last-minute shot not rebounded back off the underside of the bar.

Best, having recovered, asked for a transfer because he wanted first team football, but he was recalled when Sivell broke a finger in the home match against Everton. Town eventually had to settle for 19th place at the end of a season in which they made more impact than usual in the FA Cup, despite having no luck in the draw as they were paired with First Division sides in Newcastle, West Bromwich Albion and Stoke, all away from home. Having earned draws and won home replays in both the third and fourth rounds, there was no lack of confidence when the fifth round clash at the Victoria Ground ended goalless, but it was Stoke who edged home with the only goal in the Portman Road replay just when Ipswich were beginning to ponder a first-ever place in the quarter-finals.

Chapter Eight: 1971-80
Emerging as a Domestic Force

Originally planned to start a year earlier, but abandoned in order to both modify the plans and to keep a careful eye on the exact cost of what was to be the club's most ambitious building project to date, work eventually got under way during the summer of 1971 to erect a new East Stand. Within hours of the 1970-71 season ending, an army of workmen began to dismantle the old wooden 'chicken run', parts of which dated back to before the First World War, before painstakingly reconstructing it at Foxhall Stadium, the home of the Ipswich Witches speedway team. In its place rose a 3,700-seater grandstand, 55ft high and 255ft wide, complete with bar and restaurant, costing £180,000. Remarkably, the project was completed within just 102 days and the new stand was officially opened by Sir Alf Ramsey on the opening day of the season, 14 August 1971.

The playing area was moved seven feet from east to west, and its width trimmed by six feet, as the directors reluctantly agreed to display ground advertising around the perimeter to help speed up repayments.

Long-serving trainer and physiotherapist Jimmy Forsyth had decided to call it a day at the end of the 1970–71 season and was replaced by 26-year-old Brian Simpson – one of a number of backroom changes that summer. Ron Gray, a former Sheffield United player who had also managed both Millwall and Lincoln City, arrived as chief scout, while ex-Newcastle, Derby and Cardiff full-back Bobby Ferguson, who had been player-manager of Newport, was appointed to the key role of youth coach. First team coach Cyril Lea also looked as if he might be on the move. Having been a contender for the job as Bournemouth boss the previous season, it was good news for Town when he dropped out of the running for the managerial vacancy at his former club, Leyton Orient. On the playing front, Bobby Robson spent £30,000 to sign Northern Ireland international Bryan Hamilton from Linfield after he had impressed in the Home International series, but he lost out on Suffolk-born Arsenal star Jon Sammels. Despite increasing his original £60,000 offer to £100,000, Leicester matched the bid and the player opted to move to Filbert Street. On the move from Portman Road was Frank Brogan, the club's longest-serving player at the time, who joined Halifax Town.

Town suffered a goalscoring crisis at the start of the 1971-72 campaign, with the 3-1 home win over Coventry in their second game the only one of their opening seven in which they managed to find the net. Four goalless draws at least ensured that valuable points had been collected, but a 3-1 home defeat at the hands of a George Best-inspired Manchester United in the club's eighth game – a League Cup tie – brought calls for Robson's head.

So vociferous were the protests that Robson was actually convinced the supporters' wish would be granted and, after being summoned to a board meeting the next morning, he returned home and suggested to his wife, Elsie, that perhaps it would be a good idea to commence packing. As he drove to the ground the next morning, he was still of the opinion that it would be his last day as Ipswich manager. But he was in for a shock. In the boardroom, chairman John Cobbold apologised to Robson for the fans' behaviour and assured him that he had the total support of both himself and of his fellow directors. It was a gesture that Robson was to recall more than once in later years as other clubs vied for his services and he chose to repay that show of loyalty by staying put.

Transfer Coup

Robson completed one of his best transfer deals to date when he persuaded Blackburn's Northern Ireland international centre-half, Allan Hunter, to join Ipswich at the beginning of September, heading off interest from Leeds, Everton and Manchester United to do so. As part of the deal, Bobby Bell moved in the opposite direction, together with a cheque for £60,000, as the newcomer was valued at £90,000.

Town chartered a plane and suggested to their latest signing that he should join their officials

Securing the services of Northern Ireland defender Allan Hunter was a major triumph for Bobby Robson.

on the return trip, but Hunter declined the offer and said he would travel by car the next day, not daring to admit to Ipswich officials that he would first have to check his map, since neither he nor wife Carol had the faintest idea where Ipswich was located. Hunter's debut came in the 2-1 home defeat by Leicester and after retrieving the ball from the net he passed grounded goalkeeper David Best, a former colleague of his at Oldham, and quipped, 'I see you haven't changed.' So began a long and happy stay in Suffolk for one of the greatest characters in the club's history.

Robson decided that Tommy Carroll was surplus to the club's requirements and sold him to Birmingham City. His search for a new striker ended in early November when he agreed to a £50,000 fee with Leeds United for the services of striker Rod Belfitt. His presence boosted the attendance at Portman Road by around 5,000 for his debut against Wolves and he marked the occasion in style by scoring a goal in Town's 2-1 win. As Hunter's reputation flourished – to the extent that he was quickly tagged the best centre-half in the country – and as he brought out the best in Derek Jefferson alongside him, Ipswich kept well clear of the danger zone and eventually finished in 13th place, a situation helped by taking nine points from the last six games.

One of the most remarkable and, from Town's point of view, embarrassing games of the season, was at Chelsea. The home sides goalkeeping crisis forced them to field defender David Webb in goal and he had little difficulty in keeping a clean sheet in his team's 2-0 win. There were red faces, too, as Ipswich were thrashed 7-0 at Sheffield United and although the return game saw a dreary 0-0 draw, it did contain one explosive incident. Referee Gordon Kew punished Hunter for what seemed an innocuous challenge and Laurie Sivell saved Billy Dearden's spot-kick. Town full-back Colin Harper, still incensed by the original award, continued to protest and was sent off, at which point he ripped off his shirt and threw it at the referee, who required a police escort at the end of the game as supporters hurled cushions and coins in his direction.

During the season the deaths had occurred of director and former chairman Alistair Cobbold, as well as Charlie Cowie, ex-player and reserve trainer. Both Ian Collard and Colin Viljoen withdrew their transfer requests, clearly feeling that Town were moving in the right direction after two years of struggling to keep their heads above water in the First Division. There was also an increase in the average home attendance, which showed the supporters shared the faith, and the progress of young players like Trevor Whymark and Mick Lambert was a further bonus.

50 Greatest Players

JIMMY ROBERTSON   Winger

Joined Ipswich Town: 13 March 1970   **From:** Arsenal

Debut: v Sunderland, 21 March 1970, League

Appearances: 98   **Goals:** 12

Left Ipswich Town: July 1972   **For:** Stoke City

Jimmy was a player of some pedigree, having scored in Tottenham's FA Cup final victory over Chelsea in 1967 and represented his country at Under-23 and senior international levels, before Bobby Robson persuaded him – at the second time of asking – to leave Highbury's marble halls for the then far less impressive surroundings of Portman Road. His impact was both immediate and considerable as he helped ignite a surge of form that enabled Town to stave off the threat of relegation in Robson's first full season at the helm. Jimmy played in only the last seven league games of an otherwise depressing season, scoring three goals as Town won four games and drew another to climb clear of what had seemed, a few weeks earlier, a pretty hopeless situation. Quick and skilful, and blessed with an alert football brain, he was a regular choice in each of the next two seasons. While Jimmy's stay was relatively brief, supporters have never forgotten his vital contribution in helping the club to become established in the First Division.

He joined Stoke, then went to the States for a spell with Seattle Sounders and upon his return he played for Walsall and Crewe. He became a director of a firm of insurance brokers in the Potteries.

Furthermore, Mick Mills added to his international honours with an England Under-23 cap against Scotland, but a cartilage operation prevented him from appearing against Switzerland at Portman Road. The summer of 1972 saw the departure of Jimmy Robertson and Mick McNeil, to Stoke City and Cambridge City respectively, and before the new season had got under way, Bobby Robson, who had agreed a new three-year contract, failed to meet Blackpool's asking price for Mick Burns.

Town seemed to be shedding their unfashionable tag and a 2-1 away victory over Manchester United, with 18-year-old Kevin Beattie making his debut for the suspended Colin Harper at left-back, gave them the perfect start to the 1972-73 campaign. They were quickly brought down to earth, however, when newly promoted Norwich came to Portman Road just three days later and won 2-1.

But Ipswich rallied well from that disappointment, helped by Bobby Robson's astuteness in the transfer market. First he accepted an £80,000 offer from Wolves manager Bill McGarry for defender Derek Jefferson, but kept the deal on ice while he searched for a replacement. He failed to land Terry Yorath and Willie Maddren, from Leeds and Middlesbrough respectively, and eventually decided that the huge promise shown by Beattie justified completing the Jefferson deal and promptly switched the youngster to partner Hunter, at the same time recalling Harper at left-back. Supporters were stunned by Robson's next move, however, a deal which saw leading scorer Rod Belfitt head for Everton and the Merseysiders' 21-year-old striker, David Johnson, travel in the opposite direction. It seemed a strange move to swap such an experienced marksman for a young player of whom little was known outside of Liverpool – and to throw in a cash payment – but Robson's judgement was quickly proved to be spot-on as Johnson, whose main assets were his pace and aggression, struck up a formidable partnership with Trevor Whymark, a player compared to World Cup hero Geoff Hurst by no less an authority than Leeds manager Don Revie.

David Johnson was unknown outside Liverpool when he signed for Town in 1972.

Johnson – rated as the season's best signing by a number of learned observers – brought more than just his on-field ability to the club. His infectious Scouse humour helped to lift an already vibrant team spirit and it was no fluke that Town were sitting fourth in the table in December 1972, nor that they remained there until the end of an immensely satisfying season. They were seen as one of the First Division's most attractive sides and it was widely acknowledged that Bobby Robson had assembled the club's best line-up since the title-winning achievement 11 years earlier.

The Portman Road crowd record was broken when Arsenal pulled in a 34,636 attendance for a game they won 2-1 to deal a fatal blow to the title hopes of a Town side who went on to manage just one win from their final nine league games. There was still much to celebrate, however, as they qualified for the UEFA Cup and also triumphed in the Texaco Cup – the fact that they defeated Norwich in front of full-house crowds in a two-leg final making victory all the sweeter.

Manager Bobby Robson shows off the Texaco Cup to the appreciative Ipswich fans from the balcony of Ipswich Town Hall. David Johnson and Kevin Beattie also enjoy the moment.

'The first of many,' predicted Mick Mills as he held the trophy aloft. Further indication that Ipswich had established themselves among the First Division elite was that Mills won the first of his 42 senior caps for England, while Kevin Beattie, Trevor Whymark and David Johnson all gained Under-23 recognition. In addition there were youth international call-ups for youngsters Glenn Keeley and John Peddelty (England), Les Tibbott (Wales) and George Burley (Scotland), all members of the Town side that captured the FA Youth Cup under new coach Charlie Woods, an achievement that showed the future of the club was in safe hands.

The 1972-73 Ipswich Youth side with the FA Youth Cup. From left to right: L. Tibbott, G. Russo, J. Stirk, D. McKellar, P. Adams, G. Burley.

The very fact that Ipswich were able to reject Manchester United's £150,000 offer for Mick Mills said a lot about the club's position of strength and the directors moved swiftly when Everton made no secret of the fact that they wanted Bobby Robson to replace retired manager Harry Catterick, awarding him a ten-year contract designed to issue a firm 'hands-off' message to the rest of football. Moving ever upwards, and only too aware of the requirements for European football, the club invested in a new floodlighting system, as well as an indoor training centre, exercise room and players' lounge. Player sales – Robson was to make a habit of cashing in on experienced players and replacing them with home-grown talent – funded the lion's share of the club's developments, with Frank Clarke becoming the latest big-name departure when he joined Carlisle for £35,000 on the eve of the 1973-74 season. In later months, Town boosted transfer income to beyond £100,000 as Mick Hill and David Best joined Crystal Palace and Portsmouth respectively, as Robson saw no need to bring in any reinforcements for what promised to be a demanding season as youngsters Roger Osborne, George Burley, Brian Talbot, Eric Gates and Bruce Twamley, a Canadian international, all made their debuts to plug gaps as they arose.

Future Town boss Burley was just 17 when he made his debut against Manchester United at Old Trafford and he never looked back, making 25 appearances during the season. After seven games Town were down in 19th place, but a nine-game unbeaten run that reaped 15 points saw them climb the table and they eventually looked set to finish third until they surprisingly lost at home to Sheffield United in the final game of the season, although fourth place was enough to earn them another crack at the UEFA Cup.

Their commitment to attack was obvious as they exceeded champions Leeds' goal tally by one to finish as the First Division's top marksmen, but they also conceded ten more than relegated Manchester United. In successive league games they lost 5-0 at Leicester and then defeated Southampton 7-0 at Portman Road. Mick Mills and Kevin Beattie played in all 57 games, the latter heading two goals in a matter of seconds as Town came from behind to beat Sheffield United 3-2 in an FA Cup third-round tie at Portman Road and then netted the only goal at Manchester United in the fourth round. Liverpool crushed Town's Wembley hopes at the next stage, but it was in their first-ever tilt at the UEFA Cup that underdogs Ipswich made the country sit up and take notice.

UEFA Cup Debut

Having seen off the mighty Real Madrid, their next opponents were Lazio, reputed to possess Italy's most organised defence and still remembered for an ugly brawl in a clash with Arsenal in 1970, which earned them a two-year European ban. Their defensive reputation was left in tatters, though, as Trevor Whymark scored all of Town's goals in their 4-0 first leg win, but

Allan Hunter rises above the Real Madrid defence to head towards goal. Ipswich's supremacy was ultimately rewarded by a goal in the 52nd minute.

Great Matches

UEFA CUP FIRST ROUND FIRST LEG   **Portman Road, 19 September 1973**

Ipswich Town 1 Real Madrid 0   **Attendance: 25,280**

Rubinan (og)

It was a dream draw for Ipswich, who were in Europe for the first time under manager Bobby Robson, to be paired with the most famous club side in the world, Real Madrid, the Spaniards being six-time European Cup winners and favourites to land the UEFA Cup that season. It was a dream too for the Portman Road faithful who turned up in force and created a magical atmosphere inside the ground.

Not even a controversial claim by the referee that he had been hit by a missile, fired by from catapult somewhere in the crowd, could remove the gloss from a richly-deserved win, even if the all-important winner was an own goal by Real defender Rubinan. Warsaw-based match official, Stanislaw Eksztajn, insisted on reporting Ipswich to UEFA. Film of the incident, which occurred late in an exciting game, clearly showed the referee receiving an accidental kick in the calf from visiting defender Jose Luis, but the authorities still hit Town with a fine of £685.

One goal was scant reward on the night for Town's almost relentless pressure against a side clearly intent on securing a goalless draw and who had keeper Garcia Remon to thank for not losing more heavily. Remon first came to the rescue within two minutes of the kick-off, to keep out a diving header from David Johnson, as Town started the match strongly. On the half-hour mark Ipswich seemed to have a strong case for a penalty when Trevor Whymark was flattened in the box. But their appeals came to nothing and the referee waved play on.

At the other end Real managed just two shots and two corners all night, against a tide of pressure, but it must be said they were unfortunate twice over as Town earned a precious 52nd-minute winner. Referee Eksztajn surprisingly awarded a free-kick for pushing when Whymark was challenged by Rubinan just inside the visitors' half. Ian Collard took a short free-kick to Mick Mills and the Town skipper cut inside. He only half hit his shot and the goalkeeper had it covered, only for the ball to strike the unlucky Rubinan on the leg and roll into the corner of the net.

Remon produced further heroics to keep out a Bryan Hamilton header and those who predicted that such a slender lead would not be enough were forced to eat their words a fortnight later when an attack-minded Ipswich earned a 0-0 draw in the Bernabeu Stadium to advance into the second round.

Ipswich Town: Best, Mills, Harper, Collard, Hunter, Beattie, Hamilton, Viljoen, Johnson, Whymark, Lambert (Miller).

Real Madrid: Remon, Jose Luis, Rubinan, Pirri, Benito, Hourino, Amancio (Aguilar), Grosso Planelles (Maranon), Netzer, Mas.

Referee: S. Eksztajn (Poland).

in the second game Lazio again became the thugs, attacking the Ipswich players both on the field and in the tunnel, to such an extent that Bobby Robson kept his team in the dressing room for two hours before it was deemed safe enough to unlock the doors. Town won through 6-4 on aggregate and again triumphed in the third round against attractive Dutch opponents FC Twente. The win saw them take on Locomotive Leipzig in the quarter-finals. Ten-man Ipswich – Mick Mills was sent off for retaliation – only lost out on penalties when Allan Hunter, who had performed magnificently in the game, had the misfortune to have his spot-kick saved.

Kevin Beattie's meteoric rise saw him win the supporters' Player of the Year trophy for the second year in a row, collect the first Professional Footballers' Association Young Player of the Year accolade and earn promotion to England's senior squad for a game in Portugal, as well as adding to his Under-23 caps during a summer tour of Turkey, Yugoslavia and France.

Manager Bobby Robson was again in demand, this time wanted by Derby to replace Brian Clough, who had surprisingly resigned, but he made his intention to remain at Portman Road clear, hopefully to build on what had already been achieved. Based on their displays at home and abroad the previous season, Ipswich were considered a worthwhile bet for honours in 1974-75 and it proved to be a tale of heartbreak on all three domestic fronts as they finished third in the league, beaten semi-finalists in the FA Cup and pipped at the quarter-final stage of the League Cup by neighbours Norwich.

Ipswich had made an impressive start in the title race, winning four games on the trot without conceding a goal. Indeed, when their defence was finally breached it was an own goal by Mick Mills, but a run of eight wins in nine games took them to the top of the table. A hiccup saw them go five games without scoring, a sequence that included four 1-0 away defeats, and it was to be their form away from Portman Road that would eventually prove costly. At home, Town were virtually invincible and remained unbeaten until Boxing Day when lowly Luton, who would be relegated at the end of the season, scored the only goal. Ipswich only dropped six home points and conceded just 14 goals – including four in the 5-4 win over Newcastle – in front of their own fans, in each case the best record in the First Division.

They were not helped by a demanding fixture programme, largely brought about by their extended FA Cup run, but by taking 15 points from their last ten games they finished a very creditable third, although the fact that they were just two points short of champions Derby inevitably led to thoughts about what might have been. If only they had done marginally better away from home – at one stage they failed to collect even one point from seven games that saw them score one goal and concede 11 – or not been stunned at home by the Hatters...

Ipswich only added one player to the squad that season, goalkeeper Paul Cooper from Birmingham City, who had impressed during a loan spell towards the end of the previous season. At £23,000 he turned out to be an amazing bargain and the club recouped more than seven times as much from the sales of Johnny Miller and Peter Morris to Norwich City, Glenn Keeley to Newcastle and Geoff Hammond to Manchester City. The upbeat mood was maintained as further ground improvements were made, in the shape of two 800-seat extensions at either end of the Portman Stand. It meant the stand would now stretch the full length of the ground, and underneath there was a squash court, new club shop and further office accommodation – all of which took the total cost beyond the £500,000 mark.

The previous season's League Championship may have slipped from Town's grasp, but manager Bobby Robson said: 'We were in with a chance right to the end. We got off to a great start with eight points from our first four games, including a victory over Arsenal that I rate as the team's finest performance since I came to Portman Road in 1969. There was a levelling up of standards in the league and the lead changed hands regularly. We had bleak spells in the autumn and around Christmas, but from then our FA Cup form provided the stimulus we needed and I honestly believe that from January we were the best team in the First Division.'

As was common at the time, Robson again had the chance to move on. This time it was Leeds who failed to lure him to Elland Road as a replacement for Don Revie, who had succeeded Sir Alf Ramsey as England manager, and Robson reflected: 'I would have been a fool to leave behind all my hard work and let someone else come along and cash in. Also, the directors were very fair with me and I felt I owed them something. They upped my salary when I made up my mind to stay and now my situation is perfect. I really believe I have the best working conditions in the world.'

Allan Hunter could also have moved on, when Ipswich and Leicester agreed a £200,000 fee, but a last-gasp change of heart saw him do a U-turn and stay put. He said: 'I was happy with the terms offered, but when it came to completing the deal I just couldn't do it. The forms were in front of me and I had the pen in my hand. All I had to do was sign my name and I'd have become a Leicester player. But I couldn't go ahead. City manager Jimmy Bloomfield couldn't believe it. I just said I was sorry, that I'd changed my mind and that the deal was off. It was only when I got close to signing that I realised I didn't really want to leave. I said goodbye to a lot of money by not signing, but I reckon it was well worth it. I would have hated not being a part of Town's great season.'

The League Cup semi-finals in the 1974-75 season failed to feature a single First Division club, Town's Wembley dream shattered by Norwich on a miserable December night. Having seen off Coventry, Hereford and Stoke, and then gone to Carrow Road and secured a 1-1 draw, Ipswich were entitled to feel confident about their chances of winning the replay to book a place in the last four. When David Johnson fired Town ahead everything was going according to plan, but Johnny Miller, just weeks after joining the Canaries from Town, struck twice to earn them a shock win.

The fact that Norwich had not finished paying for the player rubbed salt into the wounds. Bobby Robson said: 'I'm not a gambler, but I would have bet my house that we could beat Norwich in that quarter-final replay. My players ran out that night in good mood, but only Colin Viljoen and David Johnson played to form. I'm not making excuses, however, because Norwich deserved their win. They were tactically sound.'

It was short and sweet in the UEFA Cup as Town bowed out in the first round to FC Twente, the Dutch club they had eliminated the previous season. Ipswich lost on away goals after they could only follow up a 2-2 home draw with a 1-1 stalemate across the North Sea. FC Twente made it all the way to the final, but just three minutes from the end of the first round second leg they were close to going out as Brian Talbot's fierce drive looked netbound until their goalkeeper, Henny Ardesch, pulled off a wonderful save.

A Cup Run and Record Crowds

But the disappointments in both the League and UEFA Cups were nothing to the frustration and heartbreak Ipswich had to endure in the FA Cup, a competition in which the club had consistently failed to scale any great heights until the 1974-75 campaign. They overcame a difficult first round draw to beat Wolves away, only to hear their next opponents were to be Liverpool, and, in a pulsating tie that created a new Portman Road attendance record of 34,709, skipper Mick Mills decided it when he prodded the ball over the line from close range. Town were 2-0 down at home to Aston Villa until two-goal substitute Bryan Hamilton intervened and inspired them to a 3-2 win that booked a quarter-final place for the first time in the club's history.

Great Matches

FA CUP QUARTER-FINAL THIRD REPLAY

Filbert Street, Leicester
27 March 1975
Attendance: 19,570

Ipswich Town 3   **Leeds United 2**

Whymark	Clarke
Viljoen	Giles
Woods	

Clive Woods' wonder goal decided an epic FA Cup-tie that lasted seven gruelling hours and eventually saw never-say-die Ipswich clinch a first-ever place in the semi-finals.

The teams met four times in the space of 19 days, including twice in 48 hours at neutral venue Filbert Street, and the scenes of joy in the Town dressing room summed up the players' relief at coming out on top in one of the competition's all-time great marathon ties between two evenly-matched sides. Town had to dig deep into their modest resources to replace injured defender Kevin Beattie, out with hamstring trouble, so 17-year-old John Wark was pulled out of a youth trip to Germany for a daunting debut.

Wark slotted in alongside Allan Hunter to perform magnificently in an enthralling game in which Town made the best possible start, taking the lead after just five minutes when Trevor Whymark drilled home on the rebound after a Woods effort was blocked by Leeds defender Norman Hunter. Leeds levelled after 32 minutes through Allan Clarke and the stalemate continued until half-time, only for Ipswich to regain the lead in the 50th minute when Colin Viljoen's shot deflected off Bryan Hamilton's heel and completely wrong-footed keeper David Stewart.

It was 2-2 after 72 minutes when Laurie Sivell appeared to be impeded by Clarke as he made a vain attempt to reach Johnny Giles' header, but nine minutes from the end came the moment that finally separated the sides. Woods accepted a pass from George Burley to cut inside Giles on the edge of the penalty area and let fly with a curling, right-foot drive that eluded Stewart and crept high inside the far post. Not only did Woods' first FA Cup strike thrill the Ipswich fans, it was also voted BBC's Goal of the Month and brought to an exciting end one of the most gripping ties in the competition's long and colourful history.

Ipswich Town: Sivell, Burley, Mills, Talbot, Hunter, Wark, Hamilton, Viljoen, Johnson (Osborne), Whymark, Woods.

Leeds United: Stewart, Reaney (McKenzie), F Gray, Bremner, Madeley, Hunter, E Gray, Clarke, Jordan, Giles, Yorath.

Referee: J. Taylor (Wolverhampton).

Then came an amazing four-game marathon against Leeds, with the first game goalless in front of another record turnout, 38,010, as the entire Portman Stand was in use for the first time. In the Elland Road replay, Town led until the third minute of injury time. Filbert Street, Leicester, was chosen for the third meeting, which resulted in another 0-0 stalemate, and the teams were back at the same venue just 48 hours later to see Clive Woods' stunning, swerving shot clinch Town's 3-2 win and, at the end of a gripping seven-hour saga, secure a semi-final spot for the first time.

John Wark, just 17, produced a heroic defensive display when called upon at the last minute in the decisive game against Leeds and was to figure again as the semi-final ended in tears. Town's problems started in the first game against West Ham at Villa Park when they were ravaged by injuries and were relieved to escape with a 0-0 draw, although the fact that the replay at Stamford Bridge was just four days later never gave all their casualties time to recover. Wark filled in at the back again, this time for Allan Hunter, while David Johnson was also absent. Bryan Hamilton appeared to net the first goal, but referee Clive Thomas ruled it was offside. Town still went in at the interval level at 1-1 with high hopes of winning through, but Thomas again rocked them by disallowing another goal, and, after a second goal for the Hammers, they were out.

The funereal atmosphere of the dressing room was immediately transferred to the coach as the Ipswich party, some of them crying unashamedly, made their way home. Bobby Robson described it as his most disappointing moment in 25 years of football and added: 'There was a feeling of disbelief and aggravation and I never want to go through that again.'

The silver lining to a tear-stained campaign was provided by the Town youngsters who won the FA Youth Cup for the second time in three seasons, the decisive second leg against West Ham at Portman Road attracting a partisan crowd of more than 16,000. The Ipswich directors marked the occasion by again inviting the players' parents from all parts of the country to attend the game and a victory banquet at a local hotel, after which chairman John Cobbold made one of his briefest speeches.

Having congratulated those who had played a part in the success, he brought the house down when he said: 'I would now like all you parents to adjourn upstairs and create another Ipswich youth team for about 17 years from now.'

That summer also saw the end of an era as secretary Wally Gray, a reserve goalkeeper in the 1930s and a full-time employee since 1947, retired. There were plenty of international appearances during the summer as well, including Kevin Beattie and David Johnson who were both on target in England's 5-1 defeat of Scotland at Wembley. Colin Viljoen also forced his way into the England side that season.

Great Expectations

It was a measure of how far Ipswich had progressed that the club announced record season ticket sales for the 1975-76 campaign, although it started disappointingly with a 3-0 home defeat by Newcastle, the first time Town had lost their opening day fixture since 1959. They were actually bottom of the table after three games, but gradually began to work their way up, without ever achieving the consistency they craved. By the halfway stage they were averaging a point per game, but they fared much better during the second half of the season to finish sixth, although expectancy had been so high beforehand that it was considered a disappointment. Once again, they were guilty of erratic away form, but gaining eight points fewer at Portman Road than in the previous season was also costly and the slump in goals scored was attributed to injuries to key players like Colin Viljoen, Kevin Beattie, David Johnson and Brian Talbot, who broke his leg for the third time in his career, and the decision to accept a £40,000 offer from Everton for Bryan Hamilton.

Laurie Sivell, in particular, had lousy luck. He was injured in the first game, which gave Paul Cooper his chance and the ex-Birmingham man did so well that Sivell was unable to regain his place. When Cooper's form dipped, Sivell was recalled for the trip to Aston Villa, only to receive terrible facial injuries in preventing what seemed a certain goal by Andy Gray, now better known as Sky Sports' resident pundit, but in those days a bustling striker who seemed to know no fear. The equally gallant Sivell came off second best in an incident that took place in the last minute, losing several teeth and requiring 11 stitches in and around his mouth as a result of the worst injury of his career. Trevor Whymark replaced him between the sticks for the closing stages as Town held out for a goalless draw. Sivell's luck was really out, because he aggravated a finger injury and it was this, rather than his many other war wounds, that prevented him from returning to action that season.

Ipswich's best run in the First Division came between November and January, when they were unbeaten for 12 games, including the visit of Norwich that attracted a gate in excess of 35,000, the biggest attendance ever for a midweek game at Portman Road. Despite their inconsistency, there were still some memorable performances by the Town players such as beating title contenders Leeds and Manchester United, as well as taking three points from champions Liverpool, equalising three times to earn a point in a six-goal thriller at Anfield. They also completed the double over Arsenal. In the first game on Boxing Day, not even the absence for 20

50 Greatest Players

BRYAN HAMILTON   Midfielder

Joined Ipswich Town: 12 August 1971   **From:** Linfield

Debut: v Everton, 14 August 1971, League

Appearances: 199   **Goals:** 56

Left Ipswich Town: 27 November 1975   **For:** Everton

Bryan was still playing part-time football with Linfield when he shot to prominence with Northern Ireland in the Home International Championship of 1971 and Bobby Robson was handsomely rewarded when he invested £30,000 to bring him to Portman Road. He was blessed with the knack of getting into scoring positions, most of his goals coming from close range thanks to his accurate reading of situations, and he was the club's leading marksman in three successive seasons. A bubbly character, he left to join Everton and later played for Millwall, Swindon and Tranmere, where he was player-manager. He then took charge of Wigan Athletic, Leicester City and the Northern Ireland national team before returning for a brief, but successful, spell as Town's first team coach in the 1997-98 season. In the summer of 1998 he joined Norwich City as assistant to new boss Bruce Rioch, then became Director of Football at Carrow Road before replacing Rioch in the Carrow Road hot seat until a bad run of results led to his resignation in December 2000.

minutes of skipper Mick Mills, while he received seven stitches for an eye wound, could knock them off course, and their Highbury success was most notable for the first senior appearance of England youth international striker Keith Bertschin. He came on as a substitute and promptly headed home with his very first touch of the ball to ensure his own unique place in the record books.

Powerless to aid their own cause, Town suffered further frustration when Manchester United were stunned in the FA Cup final by Southampton. That upset scuppered any hopes that Town might have had of making the UEFA Cup for the fourth year in a row, but manager Bobby Robson remained upbeat as he stated: 'Only by the high standards we had set the previous year could the 1975-76 campaign be judged a failure.'

Ipswich's League Cup campaign was over at the first hurdle, when they lost at Leeds, and progress in both the UEFA and FA Cups was only marginally better. Having disposed of favourites Feyenoord in the first round – Clive Woods' performance in the 2-1 away win must rank as one of the club's all-time best European displays – Town were in buoyant mood for the second round clash with Bruges. When they established a 3-0 first leg lead, few people even considered the possibility of not making the third round, but after George Burley conceded an early penalty in Belgium the home side were in a rampant mood. The aggregate score was level at the break, then David Johnson crashed a shot against an upright and when the tie seemed to be destined for extra-time, Bruges took advantage of Ipswich's slack marking from a corner to grab a last-minute clincher. In the FA Cup a comfortable third round win over Halifax, including a Mick Lambert hat-trick, earned Town a clash with struggling Wolves, and after a 0-0 home draw they were without both Allan Hunter and Trevor Whymark for the replay. Despite dominating the play, and with goalkeeper Paul Cooper having little to do, Wolves settled it with a freak goal by Bobby Gould.

Ian Collard, who sustained a hip injury during a loan spell at Portsmouth, was forced to retire from football at the age of 28, but in complete contrast Mick Mills' career was on the up when he was recalled to England's senior squad after a lengthy gap, proving his all-round value by adding to his cap collection with appearances in both midfield and at full-back. Mills invited FC Twente to supply the opposition in his testimonial game and the 1-1 draw was watched by a crowd of only 12,564. The club's league average that season had been over 25,000, with the low turnout only partially explained by the fact that the game was staged just two days after Derby County won 6-2 at Portman Road on the last day of the scheduled season.

Allan Hunter captained Northern Ireland and won the supporters' Player of the Year trophy, Kevin Beattie again played for England, David Johnson won Under-23 honours, John Wark captained the Scottish youth team and David Geddis was capped at the same level by England.

Change at the Top

After 19 years as chairman, John Cobbold decided to step down to

Consistently impressive performances by Mick Mills in 1975-76 helped to put him back in the England frame.

be replaced by his younger brother, Patrick, during the summer of 1976, although it was still very much a case of 'as you were' in the boardroom as the pair merely changed seats. There was also a major change to the squad, with David Johnson returning to his roots and joining Liverpool in a £200,000 close-season deal, after the final negotiations had been conducted in Holland while both clubs were on tour there.

Initially, the No.9 shirt was passed to Keith Bertschin and after three games Town were second in the table. But after another three, in which they boosted their points tally by just one, they were 17th and it led to a major rethink. Ipswich faced competition from both West Ham and West Bromwich Albion for Plymouth Argyle striker Paul Mariner, but Bobby Robson's persuasive tongue did the trick and the new man made an explosive start. Following his debut in a win at Manchester United, he scored his first goal in a 7-0 demolition of West Brom that marked his first appearance at Portman Road and also saw new strike partner Trevor Whymark become the first Ipswich player to score four times in a First Division game. That equalled the club's record win and later in the season it was West Ham's turn to suffer when Mariner, by this time an England international, netted his first Town hat-trick in a 4-1 triumph.

Mariner helped Ipswich to record a 15-game unbeaten league run during which they dropped just three points and also topped the table for a time. At the halfway point of the season they had won 13 and drawn six of their 21 games. While Mick Mills was absent through injury for the first time in five years and missed the 3-1 home defeat of Sunderland, George Burley chose that game to score his first Ipswich goal in more than 130 appearances. Laurie Sivell was again in the wars as West Brom dumped Town 4-0 at The Hawthorns, with the keeper having to go off after receiving an accidental kick to the head by home striker David Cross. Allan Hunter replaced him until he felt able to resume, still groggy, whereupon he was on the receiving end of a Bryan Robson hat-trick for the hosts.

Kevin Beattie missed a number of games when knee and back problems flared up, and Town's title hopes went up in flames, literally, when he was seriously injured in a bonfire accident in the back garden of his home on the eve of a crucial home game against Birmingham. The previous day, Beattie had been a giant in Town's hard-earned derby win at Norwich and no one present at Carrow Road had even considered that they had seen the last of him for the season. Although the Birmingham game was won, Beattie's absence proved costly as Town lost away to title rivals Liverpool and

50 Greatest Players

DAVID JOHNSON   **Forward**

Joined Ipswich Town: 30 October 1972   **From:** Everton

Debut: v Leeds United, 4 November 1972, League

Appearances: 178   **Goals:** 46

Left Ipswich Town: 12 August 1976   **For:** Liverpool

Those Ipswich supporters who questioned Bobby Robson's judgement in swapping an experienced forward, Rod Belfitt, for Johnson, who had just celebrated his 21st birthday, quickly realised the Ipswich manager knew exactly what he was doing. Johnson struck up an instant understanding with Trevor Whymark to form one of the most feared striking double acts in the country, and his pace, allied to his courage, was a vital factor in the club's emergence as a major force in the 1970s. David was welcomed by his new team-mates, his infectious Scouse humour having a positive effect on dressing room harmony, and he earned three of his eight England caps with Ipswich. He rejected a move to Tottenham in the summer of 1976, but when boyhood favourites Liverpool offered a record fee of £200,000 he was naturally keen to return to Merseyside. He won honours galore in his six years at Anfield and then returned to Everton before spells with Manchester City, Tulsa Roughnecks and Preston North End. David became a financial adviser and also worked for a local radio station, as well as joining former Liverpool colleagues to act as a match-day host at Anfield.

Manchester City, eventually having to settle for third place. Ipswich won with ease against Bristol City in the third round of the FA Cup but, in an action replay of the previous season's fourth round, they drew at home with Wolves and went out in a Molineux replay.

Progress in the Cup

Ipswich rebuilt the Churchmans Stand during the summer of 1977 at a cost of £300,000, increasing capacity, replacing old wooden steps with concrete terracing and adding crush barriers and new entrances. Every seat was sold as a season ticket and the upbeat mood, as well as confirmation that Town were now perceived as one of the country's leading clubs, came with the signing of a new kit deal with sports giants adidas. But Bobby Robson's team returned some indifferent pre-season results and a spate of injuries meant that Mick Mills, John Wark, Trevor Whymark, Colin Viljoen, Dale Roberts and John Stirk were all unavailable for the big kick-off, while Colin Harper, Keith Bertschin and Pat Sharkey had all moved on.

On the first day of the season, after the Portman Road pitch had been completely relaid and a new drainage system had been installed during the off season, the heavens opened to such an extent that referee Roger Kirkpatrick felt he had no alternative but to lead the teams off. After a short break they returned and no spectator could have anticipated that the scoreline, Ipswich Town 1 Arsenal 0, would be repeated in the FA Cup final at Wembley nine months later.

While the season had the happiest possible ending, so erratic was Town's league form – and so numerous were their injury woes – that for a time there seemed a very distinct possibility that they might be relegated. There was little concern when they opened their campaign by taking six points from their first four games, without conceding a goal, but five straight defeats after Christmas plunged them down the table and it was only a 1-0 home win over Bristol City that ensured their survival. They still had three games to play at that point and lost the lot, finishing 18th and just three points clear of the drop zone. They managed just one away win, at Newcastle, and a week before the FA Cup final they were thrashed 6-1 at Aston Villa, when 17-year-old goalkeeper Paul Overton appeared at senior level for the first, and last, time. The game at Villa Park saw Colin Viljoen restored to the side, as he sought to prove his fitness for the big game at Wembley, but Bobby Robson was pushed into a corner as most, if not all, the other players rebelled against his plan and made no secret of the fact that they favoured Roger Osborne, the main victim of Robson's reshuffle. The players made no attempt to disguise their feelings and on the 20th anniversary of Town's FA Cup success Brian Talbot revealed for the first time the extent of the behind-the-scenes drama.

Talbot said: 'Several of us were annoyed that he (Robson) had changed it, but I was the one who piped up. I got into trouble because I was honest. Viljoen was the best passer of a ball we had at the club. He was quick, too. But when he lost the ball you wouldn't see him chasing back. I don't want to harp on about this, but I haven't spoken to the bloke since 1978. He blamed me because he didn't play at Wembley. I was also concerned about my own position. If Viljoen had played it would have meant me switching to the right. I didn't want that. I admit it – I was selfish. We had a lot of strong characters in the side at the time and most of us thought about ourselves first and foremost. Not Roger. He was the nicest lad in the team, so easy-going, and we didn't want to see him dropped. I made it clear I didn't want Viljoen in the team. Others felt the same and said nothing. Because I spoke up, Bobby Robson had me in his office on the Monday.

He was dead right to do what he did. He was angry that we had questioned his decision and he told me "If you do that to me again I'll leave you out". But Bobby was a good manager. It was him – not me, not anyone else – who picked the team. In the end he made a tremendous decision and it won us the Cup.'

To fully understand the impact of Ipswich's success at Wembley that year it is necessary to consider the position they were in at the turn of the year, at which stage they had exited both the League and UEFA Cups and had long since given up any hope of contesting the title race. Little wonder, then, that Bobby Robson, sensing the effect that being on the wrong end of a giantkilling act would have, labelled the FA Cup third round tie at Cardiff as 'the most important game of the season'. It hardly helped that his squad was ravaged by injuries, with George Burley, Kevin Beattie, Trevor Whymark, Clive Woods, Mick Lambert and Robin Turner all ruled out. It was a big day for skipper Mick Mills, who was playing his 494th senior game to go top of the all-time appearances chart and overtake Tommy Parker, whose record had stood for 20 years. Mills set up the first of Paul Mariner's two goals as an under-strength Town did a thoroughly professional job to win 2-0 and Tommy Parkin made his long-awaited senior debut, coming on as a late substitute for David Geddis. Intriguingly, Town coach Cyril Lea, back in his native Wales, was featured in a match-day programme article and actually forecast a victory for Ipswich – not just on the day but in the competition overall.

Ipswich could not have hoped for a better fourth round draw. Hartlepool were 91st in the Football League at the time and were without a win in 14 away league games that season, so only the most optimistic of the 3,000 supporters who made the long trek from the North East to Suffolk could have anticipated anything other than a comprehensive defeat.

The minnows turned in a spirited display, but the result was never in doubt from the sixth minute, when Colin Viljoen converted from the spot. Paul Mariner added a second before the visitors pulled one back, then four minutes into the second half Brian Talbot restored his side's two-goal lead and Viljoen's second goal clinched a 4-1 win. No one was more delighted at Ipswich's success than defender Kevin Beattie, restored to the side after an eight-week absence and just one practice match, and the entire Town camp was in a positive mood when the fifth round draw paired them with Bristol Rovers.

Only referee Brian Daniels could explain why he decided, after the briefest of inspections, that the game would go ahead on a snow-covered

Eastville pitch. While he gave it the thumbs up without even donning his boots and taking a ball on to the playing surface, the Town players took half an hour to decide which footwear to use. They were amazed, that morning, when club officials who had attended the official inspection returned to the team's overnight hotel to announce that the game would proceed as scheduled. The players were thinking more along the lines of packing their bags and jumping on the bus for the trip home.

Snow had fallen since the Ipswich party had arrived in Bristol the previous evening and had continued to do so at a steady pace. Come the end of the game, Town were mightily relieved that they had survived the pantomime on ice with a 2-2 draw. They scored first, through Robin Turner's first senior goal for the club after 27 minutes, but two second-half corners within six minutes of each other paved the way for David Williams to score twice and put Rovers ahead. It might have been even worse when Bobby Gould had the ball in the net for the home side. It was disallowed for offside, but the goal should have stood because it was a wayward back pass by Allan Hunter that put Gould in the clear. With just four minutes left, Paul Mariner set up Turner for a shot that came back off the foot of a post, but the ball rebounded back to him and he prodded it home to keep alive Ipswich's hopes of FA Cup glory. Their relief at living to fight another day could not conceal the players' anger at being forced to perform in such farcical conditions and Mick Mills summed up: 'What's all this about the pitch being flat? It was like concrete and I don't see what being flat has to do with it. To play such an important match on a surface like that was diabolical.'

Everything went to plan in the replay, however, with Town gratefully accepting a second chance to progress to the quarter-finals, although Rovers' failure to cash in on early chances, when the home side seemed to be stuck in first gear, proved costly. Mick Mills scored Ipswich's first and further goals by Paul Mariner and Clive Woods put the gloss on a display, which according to Mills afterwards, was 'competent without being over-exciting'. Mills added: 'We excited an awful lot of people without reaching Wembley in 1975. This time, quite frankly, I don't care if we fail to excite people as long as we can get there.' Bobby Robson was delighted, although it wasn't for a further 20 years that he owned up: 'We were in the quarter-finals and that was when it really sunk in that we had a tremendous chance of going to Wembley. We had a good draw, at Millwall, and we had a good team. "Bloody hell," I was thinking, "we've got a chance".'

Ipswich had beaten Millwall 6-1 in a pre-season game at the Den, but no one expected they would win an FA Cup quarter-final by the same margin. It was a stroll for Town on a day when the London club were once again let down by a section of their support. Problems had started before the kick-off when Millwall fans, lying in wait as part of an organised plan, stoned Town followers' buses as they arrived close to the ground. Once the game was under way, the violence turned even nastier as a hail of missiles was launched into the section accommodating Ipswich supporters. Some, including women, were led away with blood pouring from head gashes and a pitch invasion by so-called Lions fans prompted the referee to lead the teams back to their dressing rooms for an 18-minute break while order was restored. Town won at a canter after George Burley had opened the scoring, with Paul Mariner claiming a hat-trick and the other goals coming from John Wark and Brian Talbot. At the end, while skipper Mick Mills described the game as a non-event because it had turned into such a stroll, Mariner added: 'We have the feeling that someone up there is looking down on us, saying "Go on boys, go all the way to Wembley".'

The semi-final draw paired Town with West Bromwich Albion, who were well ahead of them in the First Division that season, but it was the choice of referee that seemed of more concern to supporters. Most of them were horrified to learn that Clive Thomas, held responsible by many for Ipswich's failure to reach Wembley just three years earlier, would take charge of the game at Highbury. The club, wisely, distanced themselves from the controversy and declared themselves happy with the appointment. There was no need for the fans to worry about the outcome, however, as Town deservedly triumphed in a game packed with incident.

Bobby Robson will never forget that day, as he recalled: 'We were going to Wembley and I'm not scared to admit I was overcome with emotion. I looked around me and saw so much joy. There was John and Patrick Cobbold. Think what it meant to them. Their father had started the club and they were so excited. And the players really savoured the moment, especially those who had been denied it three years earlier. Our dressing room was different now. Oh yes...'

Robson threw open the dressing room doors to the media, who swarmed round the players for interviews as they sipped champagne, and he promised all present that the squad would enjoy the build-up to one of the biggest days of their lives. Looking back, he said: 'I don't know how we made it back to Ipswich. The coach was trundling up the A12

Great Matches

FA CUP SEMI-FINAL   **Highbury Stadium, London, 8 April 1978**

Ipswich Town 3 West Bromwich Albion 1   **Attendance: 50,922**

Talbot	Brown (pen)
Mills	
Wark	

The realisation that Ipswich had finally made it to Wembley overshadowed the drama of an incident-packed game and the celebrations that followed would have done justice to the final itself. Anxious to wipe out the memory of a tearful exit at the same stage three years earlier, the Town players approached the game in confident, determined mood.

Just seven minutes were on the clock when they went ahead, the indefatigable Brian Talbot hurling himself at a cross from the left by skipper Mick Mills after he, Paul Mariner and Clive Woods had cleverly carved out the opening.

Talbot's diving header beat the challenge of Albion skipper John Wile by a split second and goalkeeper Tony Godden could do nothing to prevent the ball flying past his outstretched right arm. As Town fans jumped for joy, Talbot and Wile lay prostrate on the ground with blood seeping from nasty head wounds and once the respective sponge men had taken a look, both players were led off for further treatment.

Wile was back in the action after five minutes, wearing a turban-like head bandage, and, after a further five minutes, Talbot re-appeared on the touchline, although a brief run up the line was enough to confirm he could not continue and Mick Lambert was summoned to replace him.

Lambert quickly helped to create a second goal for Ipswich when he drilled in a corner from the right. The ball ricocheted off the shins of Cyrille Regis for Mills to spin and fire home from five yards.

Two goals ahead after 20 minutes, it was almost too good to be true, and it was no surprise when Wile was withdrawn in the second half to be replaced by attacker Laurie Cunningham.

When Allan Hunter inexplicably handled inside the area it presented Albion with an opportunity to reduce the leeway, Tony Brown accepting the gift to blast home. But the Midlanders were rocked by the 84th-minute dismissal of Mick Martin and any anxiety in the Town ranks was erased when John Wark rose to meet Clive Woods' corner and head his side's third goal.

Ipswich Town: Cooper, Burley, Mills, Talbot (Lambert), Hunter, Beattie, Osborne, Wark, Mariner, Turner, Woods.

West Bromwich Albion: Godden, Mulligan, Statham, T Brown, Wile (Cunningham), Robertson, Martin, A Brown, Regis, Trewick, Johnston.

Referee: C. Thomas (Treorchy).

at 70 miles an hour and everybody was jumping up and down. It was one of the greatest days of my life.'

Preparing for Wembley

The FA Cup final experience was bigger, far bigger, than anyone at Portman Road had anticipated and it tested the club's modest staff resources to the limit. Picture the scene as supporters lucky enough to hold the necessary vouchers queued for their tickets. The box office staff was supplemented by part-timers and, on one memorable day, even chairman Patrick Cobbold and his brother, John, not exactly *au fait* with proceedings, volunteered to assist. So streamlined is the operation today that it is difficult to believe how several cardboard boxes had to be appropriated and into which notes of different denominations were thrown. Satisfying demand was not as difficult as at would have been for other clubs and Town were quick to guarantee that all season ticket holders would be allocated a ticket for Wembley.

'Suddenly we had 35,000 supporters,' laughed Bobby Robson, recalling the stampede for tickets and the countless begging letters, recounting hard-luck stories, that flooded into his office. 'I wondered where these people had been. They weren't there when we beat Leicester 1-0 just before Christmas, I know that.' Robson and his players were forced to distance themselves for a while, the business of securing vital safety points being of far more importance, and the fact that their First Division status was ensured for another year was a huge load off their minds.

Three days before the final the Ipswich squad set off from Portman Road, bound for their Cup final base, Sopwell House Hotel in St Albans. Colin Viljoen was not on board and, with other players nursing injuries, the Wembley line-up was far from certain at that stage. The coach made a scheduled stop in Colchester to collect the blazers and trousers to be worn by players and officials on the big day. It was anything but routine, however, as the players were the butt of jokes played by the women who had made the clothing to a list of measurements taken weeks earlier. Having switched the names, the women sniggered at the farcical scenes as some players were literally swamped by their outfits and others fitted a bit like Norman Wisdom's stage gear. The players saw the funny side and it all helped to enhance the remarkably relaxed mood the Town players were in as the big day approached.

'Like a group of lads on holiday, not a team preparing for the game of their lives,' said Clive Woods, who was to go on and win the Man of the

Match award. The apparent lack of nerves continued throughout the squad's time at the Hertfordshire hotel and even on the big day, but at least one player, privately, was feeling the strain.

Allan Hunter was an injury doubt until the morning of the match. Recalling those few days, he remembered: 'The night before, my mind was in turmoil. It could have been Christmas Eve for all I knew. I smoked about 40 Embassy to calm my nerves and I remember thinking "If I do play I won't have any wind left". The FA Cup final was a big, big thing in my life. When I was a kid at primary school I wrote an essay about what I was going to do when I grew up. I said I was going to be a footballer, I said I would play for an Irish club, I said I would move to England, I said I would play for my country and I said I would play in an FA Cup final.'

Hunter had more than a pint of fluid drained from his knee after Town's 6-1 defeat at Villa Park the previous week and took no part in the pre-Wembley training. Come match day, he was to have a fitness test at 11am, with young deputy Russell Osman standing by. Hunter added: 'I woke up at seven and I couldn't wait. I feared the worst and had even rung my wife the previous night to tell her I didn't think I would be playing. I wanted it over and done with. If I wasn't going to play, I at least wanted time to get drunk!'

Most of his team-mates were still asleep and Bobby Robson had to be awoken to supervise Hunter's brief fitness test on the hotel lawn. The Northern Ireland defender recalled: 'I did a few sprints, a few twists and turns with a ball and it wasn't a problem. "I don't feel anything" I told the manager and he just said "Okay, you're playing". The uncertainty that week had taken the edge off the build-up, which is a big part of the occasion. But to know I was definitely playing made up for that.' His defensive sidekick, Kevin Beattie, was also a doubt with a knee problem, and he admitted: 'I was only 80 per cent fit, but the gaffer wanted me to play. I had two cortisone injections before the game and another at half-time to kill the pain. I wouldn't have got through without them.'

The players of both sides had to undergo an FA Cup final ritual when they assembled prior to lunch for live television interviews. The BBC's man at the Ipswich hotel was John Motson, who was educated in Suffolk and had a soft spot for the club, and he was genuinely taken aback at how calmly the Town players took a potentially daunting task in their stride. Bobby Robson recalled: 'We saw the Arsenal lads being interviewed and they looked a bit subdued. That didn't do us any harm. We had lunch and Mick Lambert was gathering money to put on a bet. I gave him £20 to put on. We were 5-2, ridiculous odds, and I thought it would show my confidence in the team. I couldn't see us losing.'

Robson had been shrewd enough to guard against any of his players freezing on the big day. A few weeks earlier, when Town faced away games against West Ham and QPR on successive days, he contacted the national stadium to arrange for his players to have a look round, and they also had a training session on the pitch 48 hours before the big day.

There was a lot of rain during the few days leading up to the final, but by Friday evening everyone was assured that the game would go ahead as planned. But there was an overnight storm and few people, therefore, were aware of the scene that greeted referee Derek Nippard when he arrived at Wembley at 11.30am. He remembered: 'The first thing I saw was members of the ground staff pumping water off the pitch. I must admit it immediately crossed my mind that I might be the first referee to postpone an FA Cup final.' But after the morning downpour had subsided, conditions were humid by kick-off time, although despite the brilliant sunshine there was still surface water in some areas.

Bobby Robson recalled his team talk: 'I told the players "We only have one chance and we don't want to come back in here with any regrets about what we didn't do". I told them to make it a performance to remember. They had nothing to be afraid of. We were better than our league position, we all knew that, and I reminded them they had a better semi-final result than Arsenal. Our tactics worked a treat. David Geddis had never played wide on the right before, but he played the game of his life. We could do that because we had Paul Mariner, who was good enough to play on his own up front. The three midfield players took it in turns to get through. John Wark hit the post twice and Roger Osborne got the goal when we wondered if we were ever going to score.'

Before the game, the Town players were touched by the level of support they had on the day, starting with the reception they received as they first emerged from the tunnel to inspect the pitch and be picked out for live television and radio interviews. Most looked to find loved ones in the crowd, and there was a poignant moment for Clive Woods when he spotted his mother. He explained: 'She suffered from multiple sclerosis and never went very far in those days. But I was determined that she would be at Wembley. We managed to get her a special place, in her wheelchair, behind the goal and when I spotted her I had a huge lump in my throat.'

FA secretary Ted Croker had visited the Ipswich hotel to discuss FA Cup final protocol and, as guest of honour Princess Alexandra was introduced to the players, Kevin Beattie heeded the senior official's advice not to shake her hand too firmly. He laughed as he remembered what happened: 'When we were interviewed by John Motson in the morning he brought it up and I just looked into the camera and blurted out something like "Don't worry, love, I'll be gentle with you". When she reached me she said "Mr Beattie, I saw you on television earlier" and I could feel myself going as red as a beetroot.'

The conditions – a heavy pitch with the sun beating down from above – sapped the players' energy as the game wore on, and Osborne's 77th-minute, left-foot shot that beat Pat Jennings was his last kick of the match. He said: 'When I came off it wasn't down to exhaustion. Why should I have been any more tired than, say, Brian Talbot or John Wark? Everybody ran their socks off that day. It was emotion and excitement mixed in with exhaustion, I suppose. It just made sense for me to come off and let Mick Lambert come on. It has caused a lot of confusion ever since, but I asked for it. I wasn't injured, so people are entitled to wonder what was going on.'

Axed the previous week, Osborne was suddenly the hero and he allowed his mind to wander back to the heavy defeat at Aston Villa. As Bobby Robson conducted an instant post mortem in the Villa Park dressing room, he pointed to Osborne and said: 'The only person to come out of this smiling is him.' The training from Monday onwards was geared to Osborne regaining his place at Wembley, although with typical modesty the match-winner shunned the limelight and summed up: 'I was just in the right place at the right time.'

Osborne did a thorough job of marking Arsenal danger man Liam Brady in the big game, although he has always acknowledged that the Irish star was not fully fit, and some newspapers said it was a 1-0 thrashing for the Gunners. Milking the moment, the Town players enjoyed their lap of honour and dressing room party, then it was off to the West End for the club's official banquet. There were plenty of sore heads the next morning, but the bus made its customary stop at the Army and Navy public house in Chelmsford and regulars could hardly believe their eyes as the previous day's FA Cup winners walked through the door with the trophy. It was a popular watering hole for the Ipswich party as they returned home from London venues in the days prior to the Chelmsford by-pass. All the way back on the A12 that day there were supporters waving to the players, who had only a few minutes to freshen up at Portman Road before transferring to an open-top bus for what turned out to be a victory crawl to the

Great Matches

FA CUP FINAL	Wembley Stadium, London, 6 May 1978
Ipswich Town 1 Arsenal 0	**Attendance: 100,000**

Osborne

The 50th FA Cup final to be played at Wembley belonged to Ipswich, but they made their huge contingent of supporters wait before finally pressing home their advantage. The sun beat down on a rain-soaked pitch – referee Derek Nippard had even contemplated a postponement when he arrived at the stadium – and it sapped the players' strength.

There was no doubt, however, that Town were firmly in control, desperate to seize the prize in front of a worldwide television audience on the biggest day in the club's history. Skipper Mick Mills and his players showed no sign of nerves, instead displaying a steely determination as they appeared to revel in their role as underdogs in what the bookmakers saw as a foregone conclusion.

From the 11th minute, when Paul Mariner rattled the Arsenal crossbar, it was as one-sided as any previous final, but it seemed as though Ipswich were destined to outplay the Gunners without gaining any reward. John Wark twice struck the same post with near-identical efforts and, as Bobby Robson's team turned up the heat, only a

Part and parcel of Town's FA Cup final success was the manner in which Roger Osborne stifled Arsenal's danger man, Liam Brady.

Pat Jennings lies helpless on the ground as Roger Osborne (No.7) squeezes his shot into the net to give Town a richly-deserved victory in the 1978 FA Cup final.

magnificent save by Pat Jennings denied George Burley the breakthrough when he arrived unnoticed to meet a Clive Woods cross with his head.

The thought of Arsenal weathering the storm and going on to nick the trophy against the run of play began to enter the heads of Town's frustrated followers – but not the team who drove themselves forward yet again.

Youngster David Geddis, a surprise choice to roam the right flank, crossed low and hard into the goalmouth. Willie Young's clearance flew straight to Roger Osborne, whose first-time effort flew between the diving Jennings and his left-hand post. It seemed right that Osborne, who had worked so hard in marking Liam Brady, should get the goal.

The final 12 minutes seemed like an eternity before the final whistle signalled the start of unprecedented celebrations that were destined to last for days.

Ipswich Town: Cooper, Burley, Mills, Talbot, Hunter, Beattie, Osborne (Lambert), Wark, Mariner, Geddis, Woods.

Arsenal: Jennings, Rice, Nelson, Price, O'Leary, Young, Brady (Rix), Sunderland, Macdonald, Stapleton, Hudson.

Referee: D. Nippard (Bournemouth).

Town's players celebrate for the cameras after their historic victory over Arsenal in the 1978 FA Cup final – one of the finest moments in the club's history.

Cornhill, where the famous trophy was held aloft by each of the players in turn. Bobby Robson found it impossible to make himself heard and immediately jettisoned plans to deliver a carefully-prepared speech. As the huge crowd, estimated at over 100,000, eventually made their way home, the players moved inside for a civic reception to climax an amazing 24 hours that none of them would ever forget.

Their FA Cup final triumph more than compensated for the disappointments Ipswich had suffered earlier in the 1977-78 season, particularly the circumstances of their UEFA Cup exit. Trevor Whymark, for whom the Wembley occasion came round too quickly as he struggled for fitness after tearing knee ligaments in a Boxing Day defeat at Norwich, scored five of the six goals – four in the 5-0 second leg win – as Swedish side Landskrona were brushed aside in the first round and after a 1-0 home win Town shared six goals with Las Palmas to set up a third round clash with favourites Barcelona. European Footballer of the Year, Johan Cruyff, was the Spaniards' main star, but he was kept quiet in the first game at Portman Road by the close attention of Roger Osborne, the same job he had done so effectively against Arsenal's Liam Brady at Wembley.

Kevin Beattie and Allan Hunter parade the trophy to Town's jubilant fans.

Ipswich, with Kevin Beattie restored to the defence just 25 days after a cartilage operation, secured an emphatic 3-0 lead thanks to goals by Eric Gates, Trevor Whymark and Brian Talbot, and afterwards Bobby Robson said: 'Now we must make sure we don't do another Bruges!' In the return game, however, Cruyff was as brilliant as he was ordinary in the first, as Barcelona won 3-0 and progressed after a penalty decider, leaving Town to reflect on some rank bad luck and a poor refereeing display that not only saw a Paul Mariner 'goal' disallowed, but the home side level on aggregate thanks to a dubious penalty decision just two minutes from the end of normal time.

The least said about Ipswich Town's part in the curtain raiser to the 1978-79 season, the Charity Shield, the better. Five of the FA Cup-winning heroes were absent as Town returned to Wembley to be on the wrong end of a 5-0 drubbing by the champions, Nottingham Forest. Back at Portman Road the club were putting the finishing touches to 24 executive boxes as part of

Great Matches

UEFA CUP THIRD ROUND FIRST LEG **Portman Road, 23 November 1977**
Ipswich Town 3 Barcelona 0 **Attendance: 33,272**

Gates
Whymark
Talbot

This win was hailed at the time as the best single result in the club's history, with the mighty Spaniards tamed by Town's flowing football to send a packed Portman Road wild with delight.

Ipswich could never have hoped for a three-goal advantage from the first leg, but the decision to hand willing midfielder Roger Osborne the task of marking one of the world's greatest stars, Johan Cruyff, proved to be something of a masterstroke.

Manager Bobby Robson's gamble to recall defender Kevin Beattie, unable to complete a reserve game just four days earlier, also paid off handsomely as he and colleague Allan Hunter kept things tight at the back.

Town were ahead after 16 minutes when Clive Woods, whose skills overshadowed anything the visitors could offer, raced down the left and beat full-back Macizo on the outside. He crossed low into the box and Eric Gates controlled the ball before beating goalkeeper Artola with a perfect shot that zipped into the far corner of the net.

Woods also set up Ipswich's second goal after 61 minutes with another cross. Paul Mariner headed down, Artola was unable to gather the ball cleanly, and Trevor Whymark was on the rebound in a flash to run the ball over the line.

The scoring was completed after 78 minutes and once again Woods was the architect, turning Macizo and then crossing for Brian Talbot to hurl himself forward and net with a diving header.

Town boss Robson spoke of his delight at the result but added: 'I was very much afraid of Barcelona before the match. They didn't play as well as I had anticipated. I am surprised we won 3-0.'

Opposite number Rinus Michels at first conceded Ipswich were already into the quarter-finals, but later smiled: 'Football is not always normal.'

The wily Dutchman was laughing again a fortnight later at the Nou Camp Stadium after his side had triumphed by the same scoreline and won through in a penalty shoot-out.

Ipswich Town: Cooper, Stirk, Mills, Talbot, Hunter, Beattie, Osborne, Gates (Viljoen), Mariner, Whymark, Woods.

Barcelona: Artola, Macizo (Clares), Migueli, Olmo, De La Cruz, Neeskens, Sanchez, Heredia (Rexach), Cruyff, Asensi, Zuviria.

Referee: A. Prokop (East Germany).

50 Greatest Players

COLIN VILJOEN   **Midfielder**

Joined Ipswich Town: August 1965   **From:** School

Debut: v Portsmouth, 25 March 1967, League

Appearances: 372   **Goals:** 54

Left Ipswich Town: August 1978   **For:** Manchester City

There were few more visionary footballers than Colin, who had an alert football brain and could size up situations quicker than almost any other midfielder in the country. He was at his peak in the mid-1970s when he gained two England caps and he would have added further international honours but for injury. He netted a hat-trick on his debut for Town and another in an away win over Norwich, but it was in creating openings for others that he excelled. Colin's passing, whether short or long, was consistently spot-on, he was supremely fit, worked hard and was able to dictate the pace of most games in which he played. He won the fans' Player of the Year award in 1975, but his Portman Road career was to come to an unfortunate end after he reacted angrily to being left out of the line-up to face Arsenal in the 1978 FA Cup final. He left shortly afterwards to join Manchester City and from there he moved back south again to join Chelsea, where injury forced him to call it a day. Colin went into the pub and restaurant business for three years before returning to his native South Africa to run the FIFA-approved Coerver skills development programme.

a £600,000 project that also saw the club restaurant extended and the standing area in front of the Portman Stand replaced with 1,800 seats. The club had made a profit of £200,000, mainly due to their FA Cup success, and the sales of John Stirk and Colin Viljoen, to Watford and Manchester City, raised a further sum of £130,000. Bournemouth goalkeeper Kieron Baker arrived in a £20,000 deal as Paul Cooper and Laurie Sivell both had fitness problems, but by far the most intriguing transfer saw Town clinch the services of Dutch midfielder Arnold Muhren from FC Twente for a bargain fee of only £150,000. He made his debut in the first home game of the season, rarely touching the ball as Liverpool won 3-0, but once Bobby Robson changed Town's tactics, switching from a more direct style to filter the play through midfield, he was as influential as any player in the country and was a popular winner of the fans' Player of the Year award at the end of his first season with the club.

Town were relatively busy in the transfer market that season. In January 1980 they accepted an offer of £450,000 from Arsenal for all-action midfielder Brian Talbot, who had been on the Gunners' wanted list since before the previous year's FA Cup final, and the following

50 Greatest Players

BRIAN TALBOT   Midfielder

Joined Ipswich Town: 28 July 1970   **From:** Juniors

Debut: v Burnley, 9 February 1974, League

Appearances: 227   **Goals:** 31

Left Ipswich Town: 11 January 1979   **For:** Arsenal

Brian joined the club straight from school and was almost sold to Bournemouth before he made his senior debut, but never looked back. He survived three leg breaks early in his career and also had two spells in the North American Soccer League to gain valuable experience. Having established himself in the side, he quickly gained Under-21, B and senior international honours. His supreme fitness, enthusiasm and forceful running from midfield often overshadowed his other attributes, but Brian became an accomplished footballer whose all-round appreciation of the game saw him carve out a long and successful career. He moved to Arsenal after winning an FA Cup medal with Ipswich, claiming a place in the record books the following year when he was in the Gunners' side that defeated Manchester United to make him the first player to appear in Cup-winning sides in successive seasons with two different clubs. He also played for Watford and Stoke, before becoming player-manager at West Bromwich Albion, then taking charge of Aldershot. He occupied the prestigious role of chairman of the Professional Footballers' Association and for the last four years has been manager of Rushden & Diamonds, eventually leading them into the Football League as Conference champions in 2001.

month they also said farewell to striker Trevor Whymark, who moved to Vancouver Whitecaps in a £150,000 deal. His last appearance was in his own testimonial match, in which Dutch midfielder Frans Thijssen also took part as a guest. Thijssen had been recommended by Arnold Muhren and Bobby Robson eventually forked out £200,000 to FC Twente, for whom he had played against Ipswich in the UEFA Cup in the 1973-74 and 1974-75 seasons, as he continued to reshape his team. Ipswich brought in a further £100,000 from Sheffield United for Les Tibbott that season, but did at least manage to avoid the departure of manager Robson as he celebrated ten years at Portman Road, after Sunderland, Barcelona and Athletic Bilbao all failed to prise him away from Portman Road. Amusingly, he tried to deny Bilbao's interest until being advised he was sporting their club tie, a gift during their failed attempt to lure him to Spain which hinged on the amount of compensation they would be willing to pay Ipswich.

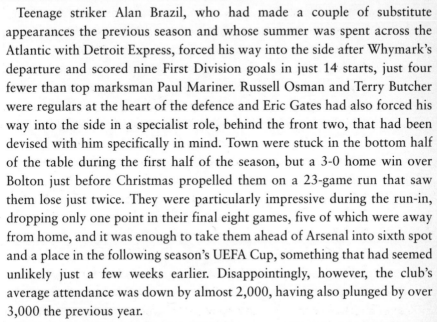

50 Greatest Players

TREVOR WHYMARK   Forward

Joined Ipswich Town: 5 May 1969   **From:** Juniors

Debut: v Manchester City, 28 February 1970, League

Appearances: 335   **Goals:** 104

Left Ipswich Town: February 1979   **For:** Vancouver Whitecaps

From humble beginnings – he was spotted playing for Norfolk against Suffolk in a county youth match – Trevor progressed to the very top. He won seven England Under-23 caps, but his only senior cap came courtesy of a 25-minute appearance as a substitute in Luxembourg. There were other highlights in his nomadic career. At Portman Road he twice netted four goals in a game, against West Bromwich and Lazio in a UEFA Cup-tie, a feat that earned him a special memento from their arch-rivals Roma. Injury denied him a place in the 1978 FA Cup final, but he is remembered for both his aerial prowess and for his deadly partnerships with first David Johnson and then Paul Mariner. He left Ipswich for Vancouver Whitecaps, scoring the goals that earned them the Soccerbowl title and was named Man of the Match. He also played for Sparta Rotterdam, Derby County, Grimsby Town, Southend, Peterborough and Colchester before retiring. He worked as a driver, but retained a football involvement as a coach at Norwich City's youth academy.

Teenage striker Alan Brazil, who had made a couple of substitute appearances the previous season and whose summer was spent across the Atlantic with Detroit Express, forced his way into the side after Whymark's departure and scored nine First Division goals in just 14 starts, just four fewer than top marksman Paul Mariner. Russell Osman and Terry Butcher were regulars at the heart of the defence and Eric Gates had also forced his way into the side in a specialist role, behind the front two, that had been devised with him specifically in mind. Town were stuck in the bottom half of the table during the first half of the season, but a 3-0 home win over Bolton just before Christmas propelled them on a 23-game run that saw them lose just twice. They were particularly impressive during the run-in, dropping only one point in their final eight games, five of which were away from home, and it was enough to take them ahead of Arsenal into sixth spot and a place in the following season's UEFA Cup, something that had seemed unlikely just a few weeks earlier. Disappointingly, however, the club's average attendance was down by almost 2,000, having also plunged by over 3,000 the previous year.

Town's interest in the League Cup came to an abrupt end at Blackpool, after they surprisingly decided to fly north on the day of the game, and their defence of the FA Cup did not last beyond the quarter-final stage. They saw off Carlisle in the third round, but the fourth round home game against Orient only proceeded after a flame-thrower was used to melt patches of ice. Conditions were still difficult as players from both sides struggled to keep their feet, although it was the goalkeeping heroics of John Jackson that earned the visitors a 0-0 draw. Town were far more businesslike to win through in the Brisbane Road replay and for the second year in a row Bristol Rovers were Town's fifth round opponents. They were thrashed 6-1 at Portman Road and the luck of the draw favoured Ipswich again at the next stage, although Liverpool demonstrated why they were leading the league as they soaked up considerable home pressure and eventually won through to the semi-finals thanks to a lone Kenny Dalglish goal.

Ipswich had their only tilt at the European Cup-Winners' Cup in the 1978-79 season and after earning a goalless draw in the first game in Alkmaar they overcame the Dutch side 2-0 at Portman Road. Their next opponents were Innsbruck and all they had to show for their first leg efforts at home was a John Wark goal. On the eve of the return in Austria a group of players who broke a curfew were disciplined by manager Bobby Robson, who dished out a number of £250 fines. It was not the ideal atmosphere in which to prepare for such a key game.

Town showed plenty of professionalism on the pitch, but were caught by an Innsbruck goal 15 minutes from the end that took the tie to extra-time. A 100th-minute goal by George Burley, his first in Europe, took Ipswich through, but only after they had played out the closing stages with ten men after Paul Mariner had been sent off. Having been booked earlier, he was dismissed when he ignored an offside decision and raced through to put the ball in the net, appealing in vain that he had not heard the whistle.

When the Ipswich party arrived back at Heathrow and boarded the bus for the final leg of their homeward journey, even Bobby Robson was forced to smile as Allan Hunter, one of those who had incurred a fine, grabbed the microphone for a one-man cabaret act, at the end of which he announced: 'If you want to join the 250 club see Mr Robson for further details.'

Barcelona, by now without Dutch superstar Johan Cruyff, were back at Portman Road four months later in the next round and two Eric Gates goals gave Town a 2-1 first leg lead as they successfully overcame the absence of the suspended Mariner. But defeat by the narrowest of margins in front of 100,000 fans in the Nou Camp saw Barca edge through on the away goals rule en route to winning the trophy.

George Burley and John Wark became the first Ipswich players to win senior Scotland honours and they both lined up against England at Wembley, with Wark opening the scoring in a game that saw a Kevin Keegan-inspired home side roar back to win 3-1. Allan Hunter won his 50th cap for Northern Ireland, while Russell Osman and Terry Butcher were both selected by England at Under-21 level, but there was more disappointment in store at the start of the 1979-80 campaign, by which time Cyril Lea had departed after 15 years as player, caretaker manager and coach to join Stoke as assistant manager. He was replaced by Bobby Ferguson and Town stuttered during the first half of the season when, following Mick Lambert's £40,000 move to Peterborough and an injury to Clive Woods, there was a gap to be filled on the left wing. Town were actually bottom of the table in October, after five successive defeats, and still in the bottom three after 18 games had been completed, but once the new system featuring Paul Mariner and Alan Brazil as twin strikers, and Eric Gates operating in a more withdrawn role, kicked in, they went 23 games without defeat and eventually finished third.

50 Greatest Players

MICK LAMBERT — Winger

Joined Ipswich Town: 11 December 1967 **From:** Juniors

Debut: v Coventry City, 25 March 1969, League

Appearances: 263 **Goals:** 45

Left Ipswich Town: 12 July 1979 **For:** Peterborough United

Mick was an all-round sportsman who was successful at tennis as a schoolboy and then turned to cricket upon completing his studies, when he joined the ground staff at Lord's. He played football in the winter, first with Cambridge City and then Newmarket Town, where Ipswich first spotted his potential. He was signed as an amateur while still at Lord's and was still there when he made his senior debut. Mick knew it was decision time and the progress he had made in such a short time at Portman Road, together with the financial rewards on offer, tipped the scales football's way. Mick was a direct winger with a good turn of pace who delivered telling crosses and also had a keen eye for goal, although he had a history of hamstring trouble that restricted his progress. It had been his ambition for years to play in the FA Cup final and his dream came true when he replaced goalscorer Roger Osborne for the last few minutes against Arsenal in 1978. He celebrated a successful testimonial before joining Peterborough and also had a spell with Vancouver Whitecaps before retiring. Mick settled in Ipswich and works as a sales representative for a local drinks firm.

50 Greatest Players

CLIVE WOODS   Winger

Joined Ipswich Town: 19 June 1969   **From:** Norwich Gothic

Debut: v Newcastle United, 6 September 1969, League

Appearances: 338   **Goals:** 31

Left Ipswich Town: 13 March 1980   **For:** Norwich City

Clive was an exciting winger for whom the FA Cup final of 1978, when he was named Man of the Match, represented the peak of his Ipswich career, although he insists he played better games on a number of occasions. He was a late starter in the professional game, signing for Town at the age of 21, but only after being plucked out of the Norwich Business Houses League to play a trial that came to nothing. He tried his luck with Wolves and Scunthorpe, where he shared digs with Kevin Keegan, before Ipswich came on the scene again and persuaded him to quit his job in a shoe factory. His dazzling displays for Town – he even filled in at centre-forward when required – earned him an international call-up during Ron Greenwood's time as England manager, but he never won a cap. Clive moved to Norwich before retiring as a professional, although he played to a high local standard well into his 40s. He managed a sports shop in Norwich before becoming distribution manager for a firm of electrical retailers with branches all over the country.

As usual, there were more players departing Portman Road than there were arriving at the club, a successful youth system plugging the gaps as senior players were traded for useful sums. Dale Roberts (£50,000 to Hull), David Geddis (£300,000 to Aston Villa) and Clive Woods (£70,000 to Norwich) were the latest batch of departures and they could have been joined by Allan Hunter, who knocked back proposed £100,000 moves to both Chelsea and Bristol City.

On New Year's Day skipper Mick Mills was piped on to the field for his 600th appearance and later that month the club paid £200,000 for winger Kevin O'Callaghan. In December, Town's long unbeaten run started with a 4-0 home win over a Manchester City side captained by Colin Viljoen. Eric Gates netted a hat-trick that day, and the run ended when the City won 2-1 at Maine Road on the last day of the season. In between, the most memorable league victory saw Manchester United crash 6-0 at Portman Road when Town also missed two spot-kicks. In four games around that time a total of nine penalties were awarded and only two scored. Paul Cooper was partly responsible as he boosted his reputation with two saves against Derby, eventually taking his total to five, which earned him plenty of national publicity.

Great Matches

FOOTBALL LEAGUE FIRST DIVISION   Portman Road, 1 March 1980
Ipswich Town 6 Manchester United 0   Attendance: 30,120

Mariner 3
Brazil 2
Thijssen

Ipswich were third in the table and United second going into a game those Town supporters present at Portman Road that day will continue to talk about for years. It was such an unexpected scoreline that the BBC *Grandstand* teleprinter repeated it in words and, incredibly, it could have been even worse for the visitors had spot-kick expert John Wark been playing. Wark had been given compassionate leave to attend his father's funeral in Glasgow, so there was a recall for Kevin Beattie as part of a minor reshuffle.

But after Frans Thijssen saw a weak, 35th-minute penalty easily saved by Gary Bailey (the Ipswich-born son of ex-Town keeper Roy and making his first appearance at Portman Road), it was Beattie's turn to fail. His twice-taken spot-kick occurred on the stroke of half-time and after his first attempt was kept out by Bailey's foot, he tried to place his next effort and this time was denied again by the young visiting keeper. It might have been a frustrating afternoon for Beattie had things turned out differently.

There was to be no shortage of goals, however, as Paul Mariner helped himself to a hat-trick, while future Old Trafford star, Alan Brazil, added two more as well as missing a sitter. Dutch midfielder Thijssen weighed in with another in what was to be the season's biggest First Division win and enabled Ipswich to equal their club record of 16 games without defeat.

United were trailing 3-0 after 27 minutes and double figures looked on the cards with Eric Gates, in particular, wreaking havoc in his withdrawn role, as the Town players swarmed forward.

While Ipswich boss Bobby Robson emphasised that the visitors had been fortunate to escape so lightly, as his team dominated from start to finish, opposite number Dave Sexton was virtually inconsolable in defeat. Sexton, a good friend of Robson's for years, said: 'I took Martin Buchan out of the back four to mark Gates, but it didn't work the way I expected it to. I cannot fault the players, only myself.'

Just imagine if those penalties had gone in.

Ipswich Town: Cooper, Burley (O'Callaghan), Beattie, Thijssen, Osman, Butcher, Mills, Muhren, Mariner, Brazil, Gates.

Manchester United: Bailey, Nicholl (Jovanovic), Houston, McIlroy, McQueen, Buchan, Coppell, Sloan, Jordan, Macari, Grimes.

Referee: A. Robinson (Waterlooville).

The sight of Paul Mariner and Alan Brazil celebrating a goal was a common one at Portman Road during the late 1970s and early 80s. This is one of the six that Town put past Manchester United in March 1980.

George Burley was one of the first Town players to win international honours with Scotland.

Once again, Town's interest in the League Cup was short-lived as Colchester teenager, Tommy English, scored the only goal in the first leg of a second round tie at Portman Road, with the teams drawing 0-0 at Highfield Road in the return. There were only two trips into Europe that season. The Norwegian side Skeid Oslo were overwhelmed 10-1 on aggregate in the first round before Ipswich were stunned by Grasshoppers Zurich on the away goals rule. The Swiss earned a 1-1 draw at Portman Road after a goalless stalemate in the first game.

The FA Cup was equally frustrating, although Town did make it to the quarter-final stage after wins over Preston, Bristol City and Chester had fans thinking of a return to Wembley. Those dreams were well and truly dashed at Goodison Park, however, just a week after the 6-0 home victory over Manchester United, when Town crashed 2-1 and Kevin Beattie's magnificent header three minutes from the end was scant consolation.

50 Greatest Players

ROGER OSBORNE Midfielder

Joined Ipswich Town: 12 October 1971 **From:** Juniors

Debut: v Wolves, 27 October 1973, League

Appearances: 149 **Goals:** 10

Left Ipswich Town: February 1981 **For:** Colchester Utd

A Hollywood scriptwriter would have been hard-pushed to better the Roger Osborne story. His younger brother, David, had been invited to midweek training sessions and Roger often drove him to Portman Road. Having stood and watched for several weeks, it was suggested that he join in and before long he had impressed sufficiently to sign amateur forms. He then had nine months as a part-time professional before giving up his job as a labourer. Roger slowly forced his way into the first-team scene, an industrious midfielder whose contribution was never greater than in marking an opponent, something he did to great effect when nullifying the threat of Dutch legend Johan Cruyff as Ipswich defeated Barcelona 3-0 in one of the most memorable of several top European nights under the Portman Road floodlights. That was nothing, however, to his part in the FA Cup final of 1978, when he was so overcome with emotion after scoring that he was unable to take any further part in the game. After his playing career ended, Roger worked as a driver before becoming manager of the Rushmere Sports Club in Ipswich.

George Best, on the verge of yet another comeback at the time, guested for Ipswich in Bobby Robson's testimonial match in November 1979 when a crowd of 23,284, the biggest ever for a non-competitive game at Portman Road, turned out to pay tribute to the Ipswich manager.

Following the usual batch of international appearances at the end of the 1979-80 season, a group of Ipswich players spent a fortnight in Budapest filming *Escape to Victory*, which starred Michael Caine and Sylvester Stallone, and Messrs Wark, Osman, O'Callaghan, Beattie, Turner and Sivell all returned sporting short back and sides which set them apart from their team-mates. Paul Cooper had also flown out to Hungary, having been hired as coach to Stallone, but the American star decided that he was sufficiently adept in the art of goalkeeping and told Cooper that his services were not required, although anyone who has seen his performance in the movie will probably disagree with the *Rocky* star's seemingly arrogant stance.

Chapter Nine: 1980–82
The Glory Years

There has never been, and perhaps never will be, a season to compare with the marathon, 66-game 1980-81 campaign when Ipswich were on the trail of an unprecedented treble – League Championship, FA Cup and UEFA Cup – until the closing stages. Many of those privileged to witness the stylish play of Bobby Robson's exciting mix of home-grown talent, shrewd signings and the highly influential Dutch imports only appreciated how special a season it had been when, in years to follow, they had to contend with some very lean times. Gerard Houllier, the Liverpool coach, moaned about his team's workload during the 2000-01 campaign, when they scooped a trio of Cups and also qualified for the Champions League, but it did not compare with the programme Ipswich had to endure 20 years earlier, when they had nowhere near the depth of talent that Monsieur Houllier had at his disposal.

It was their lack of reserve strength, rather than any shortfall in terms of ability, that was to see them fail so narrowly on the domestic front. The extent to which Ipswich dominated, however, is best demonstrated by recalling that John Wark won the PFA Player of the Year poll ahead of Frans Thijssen and Paul Mariner, while the football writers plumped for Thijssen as Footballer of the Year, with Mick Mills as runner-up and Wark third. In both cases, it was the first time that players from the same club had filled all the top three places.

Firing on Three Fronts
Town started the season on a winning note, recording a 1-0 victory at Leicester, and were unbeaten in their first 14 league games. They lost only twice in their first 32 games, but with ten matches to go the pressure finally told as their meagre resources were stretched to breaking point by a spate of injuries from which players had little time to recover as the games came thick and fast.

Two teams, Aston Villa and, almost inevitably, Liverpool, managed to stay in touch, until the Merseysiders fell away and it became a two-horse race to the finish. In the end it was Villa who triumphed in the League

Championship, although they lost both league games to Ipswich and were also dumped out of the FA Cup at the very first hurdle at Portman Road. On reflection, that probably did them a favour as they were not distracted from their main target of landing the title. They stayed clear of injury, manager Ron Saunders rarely having to change his regular line-up, and in using only 14 players all season seven of them were ever-present. Ipswich, in contrast, had to call upon the services of 21 players and were required to play 20 games more than their Midlands rivals.

Town's league form only started to dip at the end of March and they lost three away games on the trot, at Manchester United, Leeds and West Bromwich Albion. But they clawed their way back into contention with a win where it mattered most, at Villa Park, and even after going down at home to Arsenal – Town's first defeat in 47 games at Portman Road – and again at Carrow Road in the East Anglian derby on Easter Monday, they were still in the hunt when they travelled to Middlesbrough on the last Saturday of the season.

Leading 1-0 at the break, they learned that Villa were losing at Arsenal, which meant that if it remained that way at the end, the scene would be set for a title decider at home to Southampton, Ipswich's game in hand. Sadly, the situation had changed drastically after another 45 minutes, with Boro battling back with two goals. It did nothing to soften the blow when news filtered through that Villa had lost at Highbury but, with a four-point lead, they were assured of the league crown and were entitled to their celebrations. Ipswich may have finished as the First Division's leading scorers with 77 goals, but the league table did not lie and they duly lost their final game, finishing runners-up and four points adrift of Villa.

Paul Mariner scored the goal that dumped Villa out of the FA Cup at Portman Road, rounding off a flowing move that was so typical of Town that season, when their refreshing brand of attacking football drew praise from all quarters. In the fourth round Ipswich travelled in style to Shrewsbury, the first journey undertaken in their specially customised £65,000 team bus, one of only 13 in the country and equipped with two televisions, video, card tables, toilet, fridge, hot and cold running water, food preparation area and treatment table. An 18,000 crowd was the biggest ever at Gay Meadow, and while a 0-0 draw meant Ipswich would have home advantage in the replay, there was still a high price to pay.

George Burley landed awkwardly after challenging for a header and was forced to limp through to the end of the game as Town had already used their substitute. It was originally felt that Burley's knee ligament damage would enable him to return in three weeks, but he never played again that season and actually needed the skill of top surgeon David Dandy to save his career.

Ipswich won the replay against Shrewsbury 3-0 and defeated Charlton 2-0 at Portman Road in the fifth round, to earn a quarter-final trip to Nottingham Forest. They led 2-0 there, but eventually needed a Frans Thijssen equaliser to make it 3-3 and it was the other Dutchman, Arnold Muhren, who decided a tense replay when he beat Peter Shilton with a right foot volley. And so to Villa Park for a semi-final date with Manchester City that would turn sour for Town. They failed to find their best form and Kevin Beattie broke his arm after 86 minutes, little realising when he was forced to withdraw that he would never play for the club again. It was the first year that the FA ruled drawn semis should go into extra-time – a replay would have suited Ipswich as they were well below their best – and ten minutes into the additional period Paul Power curled a free-kick past Paul Cooper to make Town's misery complete.

European Dreams

In the end, only the UEFA Cup remained as Town saw their League Championship and FA Cup hopes dashed, but it was in Europe that they turned in some of their best displays of the season. Aris Salonika were their first opponents and John Wark netted four times in Town's 5-0 first leg win, including a hat-trick of penalties. Ipswich were warned that the return game was being staged in Greek bandit country, which explained the presence of an armed policeman alongside the official party at all times. Certainly, the fans were hostile, although they had been fired up by claims that Ipswich had bribed the referee in the first leg, which, some people argued, explained the award of three penalties and the ease of their victory. The 40,000 home crowd bought the propaganda hook, line and sinker, to such an extent that they were baying for English blood by kick-off time, and, as firecrackers added to the atmosphere, there was an emotional appeal over the PA system, begging fans not to set fire to the stadium!

The Greeks were leading 3-0 when Eric Gates eased the pressure with a 73rd-minute reply, but as the Town party left the stadium their bus was stoned, a brick shattered the window right next to George Burley, and everyone was ordered to keep their heads down, or even lie on the floor if they could, all the way back to the hotel.

There was no such trouble in the second round, with Ipswich again taking what seemed to be a comfortable 3-0 first leg lead to Czechoslovakia.

The 1981 FA Cup semi-final against Manchester City, in which he broke his arm, proved to be Kevin Beattie's last appearance for Ipswich Town.

Bohemians felt the full force of substitute Kevin Beattie's left foot as he thundered in the final goal after coming on as a substitute at Portman Road. Laurie Sivell came in from the cold for his first senior game in almost a year and, after light snow greeted the Town party as they flew in to Prague, the game was staged in sub-zero temperatures. This was the famous occasion when most players donned extra layers of clothing, and in some cases tights, in an effort to beat the cold. Kevin Beattie, however, took the field in a short-sleeved shirt!

Ipswich were forced to defend for most of the game, going down 2-0 and scraping through to the third round, where they were back behind the Iron Curtain again, to face Polish side Widzew Lodz, but not before establishing a 5-0 lead at Portman Road. They were taken aback by what they discovered in the Polish mining town – a frozen pitch which was solid and covered in snow – and were even more amazed when they were told the game would go ahead. It was ten degrees below freezing and only the fact that his side were five goals to the good persuaded Bobby Robson not to protest. Conditions were just as difficult, of course, for the Poles who

Great Matches

UEFA CUP QUARTER-FINAL FIRST LEG

Geoffroy Guichard Stadium, St Etienne, 4 March 1981

St Etienne 1   Ipswich Town 4

Attendance: 42,000

Rep

Mariner 2
Muhren
Wark

How good were Ipswich in trouncing St Etienne at their own Geoffroy Guichard Stadium, inflicting only their third defeat in 31 European games?

Listen to the French club's coach, Robert Herbin, who was still in a state of shock when he uttered the words: 'Ipswich were the English steamroller.' Herbin was being quizzed by equally startled journalists in the home dressing room and he admitted: 'We were outclassed by a better team. We have a lot of lessons to learn. Basically, what happened was what I feared would happen.' Herbin had been to England to spy on Town as they defeated Wolves 3-1 at Portman Road, after which he commented: 'We have no chance, but we will do our best.' That was thought to be nothing more than a smokescreen, but his fears were confirmed as Ipswich turned on the style to record a result that manager Bobby Robson predicted would 'cause a stir throughout Europe'.

Yet Town had made the worst possible start in the muddy conditions, falling behind to a 16th-minute goal by Johnny Rep, a World Cup finalist with Holland in both 1974 and 1978. Paul Mariner equalised in the 28th minute with a spectacular header and just two minutes after the break the partisan crowd went silent when Arnold Muhren's shot from 30 yards went in off an upright. After 57 minutes Mariner scored his second of the night, pouncing on the rebound after goalkeeper Jean Castaneda could only parry a shot from Terry Butcher. And John Wark completed the scoring 14 minutes from the end when he

climbed high above the St Etienne captain and French international, Christian Lopez, to head home from 12 yards.

The Town players could not conceal their delight at the end, leaving the field to generous applause from French fans who may have been shell-shocked but still appreciated football of the highest order from the English visitors.

St Etienne: Castaneda, Battiston, Zanon, Gardon, Lopez, Janvion, Paganelli, Larios, Roussey (Zimako), Platini, Rep.

Ipswich Town: Cooper, Mills, Butcher, Thijssen, Osman, Beattie, Wark, Muhren, Mariner, Brazil, Gates.

Referee: M. Rainea (Romania).

Arnold Muhren faces up to Michel Platini as Ipswich claim their greatest UEFA Cup scalp.

skated to a 1-0 win, meaning that Town had comfortably secured their place in the quarter-finals at the expense of a side who had previously eliminated both Manchester United and Juventus.

Town resumed in Europe three months later with probably the most memorable display of that entire season, winning 4-1 in St Etienne, and triumphing 3-1 in the return when young defender Kevin Steggles made his debut. Steggles was in the side again, for the second leg of the semi-final in Cologne, when Ipswich were defending a slender 1-0 lead from the first game at Portman Road, but it was another youth product who stole the glory that night, just when some critics were suggesting Town had gone as far as they could.

John Wark heads the only goal of the first leg of the UEFA Cup semi-final against Cologne at Portman Road in April 1981.

The build-up to the game in Cologne saw Town lose at home to Arsenal and then suffer another defeat on Easter Monday at Carrow Road, after which they headed straight for Norwich Airport and a flight to Germany. In an effort to lighten the mood in the camp, Bobby Robson stunned the players by suggesting a visit to a theme park near Cologne and they let their hair down for a few hours on the day before the game. Then, the next night, they earned another 1-0 win thanks to Terry Butcher's header, to book themselves a place in the final against AZ '67 Alkmaar, the newly-crowned Dutch champions.

Great Matches

UEFA CUP FINAL FIRST LEG   **Portman Road, 6 May 1981**

Ipswich Town 3   AZ '67 Alkmaar 0   **Attendance: 27,532**

Wark
Thijssen
Mariner

Ipswich could not have asked for a better first leg scoreline as they reached out to put one hand on the UEFA Cup. Robson had drummed it into his players that, having seen their hopes of League Championship and FA Cup glory dashed, the UEFA Cup represented their last chance to end a marathon season on a high note.

They responded just as he hoped they would, rising to the occasion to establish a three-goal lead against the newly-crowned Dutch champions (who had beaten Feyenoord 5-1 just three days earlier to earn the title), and raise by far the biggest cheer at Portman Road all season.

Ipswich were in front after 28 minutes, with John Wark converting from the spot after AZ skipper Hugo Hovenkamp had handled on the line to prevent Paul Mariner's shot from entering the net.

Just 46 seconds after the break, Thijssen made it 2-0. Goalkeeper Eddy Treytel blocked his first effort, but the ball spun into the air and the Ipswich midfielder followed up to head home on the rebound. Alan Brazil twisted and turned past defender Richard van der Meer to set up the third goal in the 56th minute, his cross being turned past Treytel by Paul Mariner.

Manager Bobby Robson admitted: 'I would have settled for a 2-0 lead, so 3-0 is a bonus. In a way they're lucky to get away with that because we outwitted them.'

Ipswich Town: Cooper, Mills, McCall, Thijssen, Osman, Butcher, Wark, Muhren, Mariner, Brazil, Gates.

AZ '67 Alkmaar: Treytel, van der Meer, Spelbos, Metgod, Hovenkamp, Peters, Jonker, Arntz, Kist, Nygaard (Welzl), Tol.

Referee: A. Prokop (East Germany).

Despite missing several good chances, like this one from John Wark, Town's first-leg performance against AZ meant that they already had one hand on the UEFA Cup

UEFA CUP FINAL SECOND LEG   Olympic Stadium, Amsterdam, 20 May 1981

AZ '67 Alkmaar 4   **Ipswich Town 2**   Attendance: 28,500
Welzl   Thijssen
Metgod   Wark
Tol
Jonker

Leading 3-0 from the first leg a fortnight earlier, it seemed as though Ipswich were in easy street when Frans Thijssen further extended their advantage just three minutes into the second leg in Amsterdam. But nothing could have been further from the truth as the Dutch side threw caution to the wind, levelled just three minutes later and then played their part in one of the most exciting European finals ever.

More than 7,000 fans had travelled across the North Sea and Ipswich gave them a dream start. Eric Gates took a corner on the left, Peter Arntz headed clear and Thijssen volleyed it home.

Austrian international Kurt Welzl equalised before AZ added a second through Johnny Metgod. John Wark made it 2-2 with his 14th goal in Europe that season, a close-in hook shot.

Pier Tol fired AZ in front five minutes before the break and then goalkeeper Paul Cooper was beaten by a 30-yard free-kick struck by Jos Jonker in the 74th minute. That set up an amazing last few minutes as the Dutch side flung players forward in a desperate attempt to claw their way

Franz Thijssen is mobbed after giving Town a 1-0 lead in the second leg.

level, but nothing was to deny Ipswich as they hung on for their first European success.

AZ '67 Alkmaar: Treytel, Reynders, Spelbos, Metgod, Hovenkamp, Peters, Jonker, Arntz, Welzl (Talan), Nygaard, Tol (Kist).

Ipswich Town: Cooper, Mills, McCall, Thijssen, Osman, Butcher, Wark, Muhren, Mariner, Brazil, Gates.

Referee: M. Weschweiler (Germany).

The final followed the pattern Town had established in earlier rounds, establishing a handsome first leg lead and then being forced to scrap all the way in order to preserve their advantage. Having lost out domestically, however, Ipswich were in no mood to allow another top prize to slip from their grasp and were able to parade the UEFA Cup at a packed Cornhill prior to a civic reception. Ipswich Borough Council insisted it would have gone ahead even if Town had lost in the final, deeming that the team's fabulous football that season was sufficient cause for celebration.

(Right) The morning after the night before ... Bobby Robson was still in the mood to celebrate in Amsterdam the day after Town's historic UEFA Cup victory.

The crowds flock to the streets of Ipswich as the players parade the UEFA Cup.

International Recognition

Transfers that season included Roger Osborne's £25,000 move to Colchester, while both Arnold Muhren and Frans Thijssen were recalled to the Dutch side, Eric Gates joined Mick Mills, Paul Mariner, Russell Osman and Terry Butcher in representing England, both John Wark and Alan Brazil played for Scotland, and Kevin O'Callaghan was called up by the Republic of Ireland.

Before the start of the 1981-82 season, Ipswich announced a major sponsorship deal with Japanese hi-fi giants Pioneer. At the time it was the biggest deal of its kind, the club benefiting to the tune of more than £400,000 over three years in return for wearing the Pioneer name on their shirts, although rules at that time prevented sponsors' names being displayed on television. Town decided to put the cash to good use, unveiling plans for a new stand – to be named the Pioneer Stand – on the West side of the ground. Costing £1.4 million, it would provide seats for 4,800 spectators and dwarf the Portman Stand on the other side of the ground. Work was to start within weeks and it was anticipated that the stand would be ready for use at the start of the 1982-83 season. 'It is a gamble,' admitted Bobby Robson, 'but it is a gamble we consider to be well worth taking.'

Robson also announced that all 30 executive boxes – six more had been added that summer – were booked for the next three years and more season tickets than ever before had been sold. 'It all helps to give the club stability at a time when several others are feeling the pinch,' he added.

Ipswich again set off in pursuit of the League Championship, slipping as low as seventh at one point, but only because they had several games in hand. They also topped the table on a number of occasions as they and Liverpool battled it out for the biggest prize of all. The Anfield men were stubborn opponents who would not be shaken off. Even with 11 wins and two draws in their final 15 games, Town had to be content with finishing runners-up for the second year in a row, once again suffering from injuries to key players as they again fell four points short of the winning total.

Terry Butcher was missed after he suffered an horrific injury in an FA Cup-tie at Luton when he was accidentally kicked in the face by Brian Stein. Typically, although the incident occurred early in the game, Butcher ignored advice and battled on until Town were two goals ahead before leaving the field. He was still in the dressing room, with the Luton club doctor struggling to stem the flow of blood, when the rest of the team trooped in.

Butcher was transferred to hospital but was released later that night and was reported to be in jovial mood as his father drove him home. Within a few hours, however, he was back in a hospital bed, given a blood

50 Greatest Players

KEVIN BEATTIE   **Defender**

Joined Ipswich Town: August 1969 (as an apprentice)

Debut: v Manchester United, 12 August 1972, League

Appearances: 307   **Goals:** 32

Left Ipswich Town: January 1982 (retired)

Three separate supporters' polls have named Kevin as the best
Ipswich player of all time. Further testimony to his tremendous
ability was provided by ex-Ipswich and England manager Bobby
Robson, who had no hesitation in nominating Kevin as one of
England's all-time greats. He served a brief apprenticeship before the first team, and
international recognition, beckoned. Kevin was in the England youth team that captured
the Little World Cup and gained the first of nine Under-23 caps soon after his senior
club debut in the opening game of the 1972-73 season at Manchester United. He went
on to win nine full caps, a total that would have been far greater but for injury, in
particular a series of knee problems. Such was his impact on the English game that he
was the first winner of the PFA's Young Player of the Year award in 1974. A defensive
giant, and an explosive mix of pace and power, he formed a formidable partnership with
Allan Hunter that culminated in the club's historic FA Cup success in 1978, but a series
of injuries restricted his appearances for both club and country. He sustained a broken arm
in the FA Cup semi-final against Manchester City at Villa Park in 1981 and never played
for Ipswich again. A brief comeback, first with Colchester and then at Middlesbrough
under Malcolm Allison, was also doomed to failure. His next stop was Norway, where he
played and coached, and upon returning to Ipswich he entered the licensed trade. He
had a much-publicised health scare in 1991 when he was close to death with
pancreatitis. His fighting qualities helped to see him through and he now writes a local
newspaper column and commentates on Ipswich games for BBC Radio Suffolk.

transfusion and underwent intricate surgery. Then he was rushed to London
for a second operation and lost a total of 15 pints of blood. After visiting
him, Bobby Robson said: 'He's in a bad way, he's fighting for his life.'

It was a full five weeks before he was allowed home, by which time his weight
had plummeted by a stone and a half. He did return to action for the final nine
games of the season and it was a relief that he recovered as well as he did.

There was a further blow, although it was by no means a shock, when it
was announced that Kevin Beattie was quitting. He had undergone five
knee operations in four years, but the medical people could do no more and
he was advised he had no alternative but to call a premature halt to a career
that had promised so much but which, in reality, fell a long way short of

50 Greatest Players

ALLAN HUNTER   Defender

Joined Ipswich Town: 9 September 1971   **From:** Blackburn Rovers

Debut: v Leicester City, 11 September 1971

Appearances: 355   **Goals:** 10

Left Ipswich Town: April 1982   **For:** Colchester United

In more than a decade at the club, Allan was a huge fans' favourite who was a pillar of strength at the back as the club first consolidated in the First Division under Bobby Robson and then emerged to become genuine title challengers in the mid-1970s and early 1980s. He was the fans' Player of the Year in 1976, but faded from the first team scene after the FA Cup final success of 1978, although he remains the most capped Ipswich player of all time, winning all but six of his 53 Northern Ireland caps while at Portman Road. He rejected moves to Leicester and Chelsea, eventually leaving to become player-manager of Colchester United, but he quickly decided management was not for him. He was tempted back, briefly, as assistant to Mike Walker before working as a docker and turning back the clock to pass on his carpentry skills to pupils at an Ipswich special school. He has scouted for Manchester City and Newcastle United in recent years.

expectations. John Wark, who had netted 36 times the previous season, continued to find the net regularly. When Ipswich visited Southampton he scored in just 12 seconds, the fastest goal ever at The Dell, and he also had the distinction of scoring Town's 1,000th goal in the First Division, against Aston Villa at Portman Road. Oddly enough, he fluffed three penalties and the main scoring honours went to fellow countryman Alan Brazil, who bagged all five goals as Town trounced league leaders Southampton 5-2 at home. He claimed a hat-trick in the space of five minutes early in the game to equal Ray Crawford's club record achieved against Floriana in 1962.

Town's home win over Manchester United marked the debut of 39-year-old former Crystal Palace, Orient and Millwall keeper John Jackson, who had been signed as cover for Paul Cooper when Laurie Sivell was recovering from a knee operation. Another new face was that of Tony Kinsella, signed from Tampa Bay Rowdies for £40,000, while David Barnes, who had been raised in Felixstowe, jumped at the chance to move to Portman Road when his Coventry contract was cancelled by mutual consent.

Ipswich's grip on the UEFA Cup was short-lived as Alex Ferguson's Aberdeen drew 1-1 at Portman Road and then completed the knockout blow in front of a partisan Pittodrie crowd. As holders, Town were seeded, but quickly realised that the Scots were by no means inferior opponents.

Great Managers – 1969-82

BOBBY ROBSON

Bobby Robson is Ipswich Town's longest-serving manager, but his appointment was down to sheer luck as at least two other candidates, Frank O'Farrell and Billy Bingham, both rejected earlier offers from the Portman Road board. How Town were to benefit as Robson, ditched by Fulham before he had time to find his feet in management, gradually overcame a series of behind-the-scenes problems to launch the club into a glorious new era. One need only examine his record – Town won the FA Cup in 1978, the UEFA Cup three years later, twice finished runners-up in the League Championship race and consistently qualified for Europe – for confirmation of his impact upon the club.

Robson was one of the best coaches around, a student of the game from an early age when he played for Fulham, West Bromwich Albion and England, who was also an excellent judge of a player. His transfer market dealings on behalf of Ipswich were nothing short of remarkable. 'I spent the club's money as if it was my own,' he used to joke, when quizzed as to why he bought so few players in his 13-and-a-half year reign.

Robson actually showed a transfer surplus of more than £600,000, a remarkable feat, as he shrewdly invested in youth and only bought 14 players, an average of almost one per season, during his time in charge.

'I run this club from A to Z,' was another of Robson's favourite sayings, a reference to the way the board of directors were happy to leave all the decision-making in his capable hands, a unique situation in football either then or now.

Despite being sought-after by top clubs in England and on the continent, he repaid the loyalty of an appreciative board by staying at Portman Road and only ended his love affair with Ipswich to answer the call of his country.

He succeeded Ron Greenwood in 1982 and had to show plenty of resolve to ignore demands for his resignation, enjoying the last laugh when he steered England to the semi-finals of the World Cup in 1990, only to lose out to West Germany in a penalty shoot-out.

Robson spent nine years on the continent, winning plenty of silverware as his travels took him to Holland and PSV Eindhoven, Portugal and Sporting Lisbon then Porto, and finally to Spain and, arguably, the biggest job of all as coach of Barcelona.

After another year at PSV he returned to England and did not have to wait long for his next challenge, managing Newcastle – the club he idolised as a youngster growing up in the North East. Still going strong at 68, he explained his decision not to retire when he said: 'I need football – it's my drug.'

There was another shock in store in the FA Cup, when wins at Birmingham and Luton – the game at Kenilworth Road was skipper Mick Mills' 700th for the club and established a new club record of nine successive victories – earned them a fifth round trip to Shrewsbury, where they were beaten 2-1. Ipswich managed to reach the semi-final of the League Cup for the first time, but lost to eventual winners Liverpool.

Allan Hunter and Kevin Beattie both celebrated testimonials – against Celtic and Moscow Dynamo respectively – and Hunter later departed to become player-manager of Colchester United. In the World Cup finals during the summer of 1982 there was plenty of interest for Ipswich fans – George Burley, John Wark and Alan Brazil were in the Scotland

Mick Mills had the honour of leading his country in the 1982 World Cup finals.

squad, with Terry Butcher, Paul Mariner and Mick Mills, who was given the captain's armband by Ron Greenwood, part of the England 22. Butcher had a hand in the fastest goal in World Cup finals history, when Bryan Robson scored after 27 seconds against France, and Mills, who had earlier turned down a £150,000 move to Sunderland, captained his side in three unbeaten games, yet they still failed to make the second phase.

When Greenwood announced his retirement, the FA turned, as had always been feared at Portman Road, to Bobby Robson to succeed him. While Ipswich had persistently refused some leading club sides permission to speak to their manager, they had always agreed that they would be honoured to supply a second England manager, and less than 20 years after Alf Ramsey vacated the same role they gave Robson their blessing to follow a similar route.

Robson could not refuse the call of his country – it was a job he had coveted for some time and he had been groomed for it by taking charge of the B-international side. He signed a five-year contract, but not before he recommended that his successor at Portman Road should be first team coach Bobby Ferguson, who had moved through the ranks after first joining the club as youth coach and then graduating to reserve and senior levels. Robson's spell in charge had spanned 13-and-a-half years, a glorious era by any standards, as Ipswich emerged as one of the country's leading clubs, and his only frustration was his failure to land the League Championship.

Chapter Ten: 1982-86
Fall from Grace

Bobby Robson may have been a tough act to follow, but he left behind a team packed with international talent who had finished runners-up in the First Division in successive seasons. The new manager, 44-year-old Bobby Ferguson, was steeped in the Ipswich way, having joined the club 11 years earlier, and the policy of promotion from within was compared at the time to Liverpool's famous bootroom dynasty.

A respected coach, Ferguson himself acknowledged: 'I suppose it's a bit like Bob Paisley taking over from Bill Shankly. I'm not a stranger to anyone at the club. I know the players and they know me. Some of them have grown up with me. Continuity is important and I can't see there being many changes.'

But while Ferguson's coaching credentials were never in doubt – he had played his part in what had been achieved at Portman Road over several successful years – he was found wanting in other crucial areas that had seemed like second nature to his predecessor. It was Robson's proud boast that he 'ran the club from A to Z' and he possessed a shrewd business brain that meant he was often likened to the managing director of a major business. He was as at home behind his desk as he was in a tracksuit, and he went to great lengths to deal with a mountain of correspondence, rarely declining invitations to attend events and functions. He had a gift, too, for public relations, and was comfortable in front of a camera, as well as in the company of national newspaper men, many of whom were his close friends.

Passing the Mantle
Ferguson, in many ways a logical choice to take charge, decided on a different approach. He was keen to distance himself, for example, from administrative tasks and Pat Godbold, secretary to every Town manager since Scott Duncan, immediately noticed a diminishing workload. Ferguson treated the media with suspicion, more often than not snubbing requests for interviews and even ordering the club receptionist to inform journalists from national newspapers that he was not available for comment. What had been one of the most media-friendly clubs, featuring regularly on the back pages,

was suddenly shunned as Ferguson tried to tackle the job his way – by concentrating all his his efforts on working with the players on the training ground, in particular devoting a great deal of time and energy to improving those younger members of the staff who were knocking on the first team door. He chose to promote Charlie Woods, another who had previously worked at youth and reserve levels, to assist him, with Brian Owen stepping up to look after the second string and Peter Trevivian, who had been employed by Ipswich Borough Council to run sports schemes for local youngsters, was recruited to fill the vacancy at youth level. An FA coaching badge holder, Trevivian was a former player with Southampton and Hereford who had been forced into premature retirement through injury.

There was a strong case, given Robson's ability to spearhead all areas of the club's activities, for the appointment of a chief executive, who could

50 Greatest Players

ARNOLD MUHREN   Midfielder

Joined Ipswich Town: August 1978   **From:** FC Twente

Debut: v Liverpool, 15 August 1978, League

Appearances: 214   **Goals:** 29

Left Ipswich Town: 26 July 1982   **For:** Manchester United

Arnoldus Johannus Hyacinthus Muhren was one of the most creative and cultured players in the club's history who represented a fantastic bargain at just £150,000. He quickly became a firm crowd favourite, too, with his wonderfully elegant style and won the supporters' Player of the Year accolade at the end of his first season at Portman Road. He had already been capped by Holland before his arrival and he reclaimed his place in the Dutch side on the back of some impressive club displays. His left foot was used to great effect, spraying passes all over the pitch, unlocking opposing defences and unleashing long-distance strikes. He and fellow countryman Frans Thijssen revolutionised the Ipswich style of play and helped to land the UEFA Cup in 1981. He left the following year to join Manchester United, winning an FA Cup medal in his first season as he converted a penalty at Wembley in the 4-0 replay triumph over Brighton, and he was 37 when he  helped to inspire Holland to the European Championship in 1988. He is now coaching youngsters at his first club, Ajax, where he played alongside the great Johan Cruyff and his elder brother, Gerrie, was another key member of their European Cup-winning side.

have enabled Ferguson to concentrate on what he did best. Instead, the club seemed oblivious to the new manager's shortcomings and, far from being a smooth transition, the immediate effect should have set the alarm bells ringing in the boardroom.

In his first programme notes, Ferguson emphasised: 'Quality of performance is our prime target, just as it has always been during my time at the club. We encourage the players to express themselves, but I accept there will be bad times as well as good.'

Prophetic words, as it turned out, because Town were unable to win any of their opening six league games, which left them at the bottom of the table, although when they ended the barren spell they did so in style, with a 6-0 hammering of Notts County at Meadow Lane, the hosts' heaviest home defeat since 1888 and Town's most emphatic away success ever. Town followed that game with the second leg of a UEFA Cup first round tie at home against Roma and, having lost 3-0 at the Olympic Stadium on a night when defensive errors were costly, a battling 3-1 triumph at Portman Road saw them edged out on aggregate. Little did the team of the supporters know that they were destined not to return to the European stage again for a further 19 years.

50 Greatest Players

MICK MILLS MBE   **Defender**

Joined Ipswich Town: February 1966   **From:** Portsmouth

Debut: v Wolves, 7 May 1966, League

Appearances: 741   **Goals:** 30

Left Ipswich Town: 9 November 1982   **For:** Southampton

Mick clocked up more appearances for the club than any other player and was an inspirational captain for most of his time at Portman Road. He was recruited as an apprentice after Portsmouth scrapped their youth set-up and he must constitute one of the greatest bargains of all time. Comfortable in either full-back position, or even in midfield, he represented England in all three positions en route to winning 42 senior caps. He also gained Youth and Under-23 representative honours. He captained Ipswich to FA Cup glory in 1978 and again when the UEFA Cup was won three years later. Mick also skippered England in the World Cup finals of 1982, after which he was surprisingly sold to Southampton. He remained in the game when his playing career ended, managing Colchester and Stoke, then assisting former Town team-mate Terry Butcher at Coventry, and ex-international colleague Trevor Francis at both Sheffield Wednesday and Birmingham City.

Parting of the Ways

The squad Ferguson inherited was only weakened by the summer departure of Arnold Muhren to Manchester United, something the club were powerless to prevent. Having reached the end of his initial two-year contract in 1980, the only way he could be persuaded to remain at Portman Road on another two-year deal was by being guaranteed a free transfer when it expired. The new Pioneer Stand was nearing completion – 1,600 seats were occupied at the first home game and others were added before the official opening on 5 February 1983 – but the project was not without its critics.

The club took the decision to construct it when every seat at the ground was sold as a season ticket and potential customers were being turned away, and they were satisfied that they had in place a financial plan that would enable them to meet the cost. Eventually, though, as big-name stars followed Muhren out of Portman Road, it suited some people to state that the stand was a millstone round the neck of new boss Ferguson and blamed the exodus of stars on the need to raise funds in order to pay for the new structure. Others, however, had a more realistic grasp of things, understanding that Ferguson's often-abrasive nature was not always conducive to building team morale and that there was little point in retaining the services of players keen to depart, for whatever reason.

In the case of skipper Mick Mills, he was sold to Southampton for a giveaway £40,000 and any doubts as to whether he still had plenty to offer were not only dispelled that season, but also the following term when he helped his new club to finish runners-up to Liverpool. He had once again been linked with Sunderland, as well as Chelsea, before deciding in favour of a switch to the south coast. Youth product Irvin Gernon stepped up to inherit the No. 3 shirt, and Paul Mariner became the new club captain, but it seemed a strange decision to part company with someone as loyal and influential as Mills, the most outstanding professional in the club's history, and in particular when it seemed that the new manager appeared to need all the help he could get.

In some quarters the view was expressed that Mills had been sacrificed since he constituted a threat, but whatever the reason it was a move that was to backfire on Ipswich. By early December that season Town had climbed as high as seventh, only to suffer three defeats in a row, but when they recovered to occupy sixth spot at the end of March, it seemed as though they might yet again qualify for Europe. But a run of two points from four games put paid to that dream, although to eventually finish ninth was considered respectable in the circumstances.

50 Greatest Players

FRANS THIJSSEN   Midfielder

Joined Ipswich Town: February 1979   **From:** FC Twente

Debut: v Derby County, 28 February 1979, League

Appearances: 170   **Goals:** 16

Left Ipswich Town: 8 April 1983   **For:** Vancouver Whitecaps

Frans and Arnold Muhren were colleagues at FC Twente, Arnold recommended him to Ipswich and the pair rekindled their midfield partnership at Portman Road. He succeeded his fellow Dutchman as the supporters' Player of the Year in 1980 and also went on to regain a place in the Holland team. Blessed with tremendous balance and dribbling skills, his twisting and turning had opponents in a daze. He became only the second foreign recipient of the Footballer of the Year award when he topped the soccer writers' poll in 1981, the same year he scored in both legs of the UEFA Cup final. After a spell in Canada he returned to England when he was signed by Nottingham Forest manager Brian Clough, an accolade in itself. After his playing career ended he had spells in charge of Malmo (Sweden) and De Graafschap, and was appointed coach of Fortuna Sittard during the 2000-01 season, a position he quit at the end of the campaign.

Among the league highlights was the 6-1 home defeat of West Bromwich Albion, when John Wark scored four times, and the win over eventual champions Liverpool, also at home, by an injury-hit side. Interestingly, only the all-conquering Reds could match Town's impressive statistic of losing just seven away league games, but it was also noticeable that Town lost the same number at home, the highest tally in the First Division, and Portman Road was losing its 'fortress' tag.

The departures of Muhren and Mills were followed by the sale of Alan Brazil to Tottenham for £500,000 in March 1983, after it had seemed that Manchester United would be his most likely destination. The following month, Frans Thijssen took advantage of a similar arrangement to that of fellow countryman Muhren, joining Vancouver Whitecaps on a free transfer.

Brazil decided to ask for a move and Bobby Ferguson said: 'It was with a certain amount of reluctance that the club agreed to his request for a transfer, but I wondered at the time whether there was any point in trying to keep a player who clearly saw his future elsewhere. I cannot conceal the fact, either, that the present financial position had a lot to do with the club accepting Tottenham's offer and the cash we receive for Alan will go a long

way towards easing the burden. It is only natural, after building a new £1.4 million grandstand, that we should be feeling the pinch, but I want to assure all supporters that we have every reason to face the future with confidence.'

Brazil and Ferguson had not always seen eye to eye and on one occasion, when the latter was first team coach, the Scot did not follow his instructions at Stoke. He was amazed, come the end of the game when he

Alan Brazil scores one of the 80 goals he registered in 210 games for Town.

50 Greatest Players

ALAN BRAZIL   **Forward**

Joined Ipswich Town: July 1975   **From:** School

Debut: v Manchester United, 14 January 1978, League

Appearances: 210   **Goals:** 80

Left Ipswich Town: 15 March 1983   **For:** Tottenham Hotspur

There may be a few players who scored more goals than Alan, but there was no more deadly finisher in a one-on-one situation with the goalkeeper and he claimed a place in the record books when he became the first Ipswich player to score five goals in a league match, against Southampton at Portman Road in February 1982. He was on target regularly at youth and reserve levels, and he was at his most prolific in the first team when he developed a near-telepathic understanding with Dutch midfielder Arnold Muhren that helped to bring the UEFA Cup to Ipswich in 1981. He won the club's Player of the Year award in 1982, the same year he represented Scotland in the World Cup finals, and he won a total of 13 senior caps, two of them after he left for Tottenham. He later moved on to Manchester United, Coventry and QPR before retiring at the age of 28 with back trouble. He returned to action with brief spells in both Australia and Switzerland, then tried his luck in estate agency and the licensed trade before joining Sky Sports as their Nationwide League expert. In 2000 he switched to a full-time radio role, anchoring the prestigious breakfast show on talkSPORT, and he still lives in Suffolk.

was having a shower, that Ferguson marched in, fully clothed, to confront him as the water cascaded down on both of them. The loss of Thijssen meant Ipswich were minus four of the team that had finished runners-up the previous season, while a fifth, Eric Gates, was ruled out from January onwards with a broken toe he had sustained in an indoor six-a-side competition. Gates also asked for a transfer before being sidelined, although he later withdrew his request.

All Quiet on the Domestic Front

Town made little impact in the domestic cup competitions during Ferguson's first season at the helm. They could hardly have been given a tougher task in the Milk Cup, being paired with holders Liverpool, and they lost both legs without scoring. In the FA Cup they started with a third round trip to The Valley and a clash with Charlton, then of the Second Division but parading £300,000 signing Allan Simonsen, the Danish international and twice winner of the European Footballer of the Year award. Town were trailing 2-0 after 15 minutes, but fought back to level at the break and John Wark's late winner earned them a fourth round home tie with Grimsby.

The game marked the return to Portman Road of Trevor Whymark, then the Mariners' player-coach, but he lasted only a couple of minutes before having to retire with damaged knee ligaments. Ipswich won 2-0 and were drawn away to Norwich in the fifth round, when ex-Town striker Keith Bertschin scored after just five minutes to book the Canaries a quarter-final berth for the first time in 20 years. A dejected Bobby Ferguson took the defeat badly, moaning: 'There was only one team on the pitch and that team did not win.'

The summer of 1983 saw the first change at boardroom level for eight years, with Willie Kerr resigning to be replaced by his son, John, and just a few weeks into the season the club suffered a devastating blow when former chairman John Cobbold died at the age of 56. He had joined the board in 1948 at the age of 21 and had friends throughout football, which was reflected by the turnout at his memorial service. Fans and famous faces from within the game united with family members and friends to pay tribute to the one person, above all others, who had earned Ipswich its unique place in the game.

'We thank him for his integrity,' said the Rt. Rev. John Waine, Bishop of St Edmundsbury and Ipswich. 'There was no hypocrisy with him, no side to him, only humility and warm friendship. He was a man of great humour and a man who, at the end, showed great courage right up to the time of his death. The fact that so many from the world of football are here today is tribute to someone who made such a contribution to the building up of a club which has not only achieved great things on the field, but has a reputation for friendliness and sportsmanship off it.'

Bobby Robson said: 'If every club had a director like Mr John, football generally would be in a better state. He was my motivator and I just felt I had to succeed for him.' Arsenal chairman Peter Hill-Wood added: 'We will miss, but never forget, his infectious sense of fun. Football has lost its finest ambassador.'

Town were second in the table after four wins and a draw from their first five league games and it may not have been a coincidence that they suffered their first defeat, 1-0 at Birmingham, on the Saturday following John Cobbold's death, as everyone at the club felt a deep sense of loss. Paul Cooper made his 400th Ipswich appearance against his former club and the following week he was beaten four times at home as West Bromwich Albion triumphed 4-3 thanks to two goals, the last a penalty, in the final three minutes. A 2-1 win at Coventry reversed the downward trend, but by the time Town recorded their next victory, at home to Wolves on Boxing Day, they had managed just one win from their previous ten league outings.

It was a traumatic time at Portman Road, because just eight weeks into the season Paul Mariner and John Wark had rocked the club when they both demanded moves after requests for substantial wage rises had been rejected by the board. The players had committed themselves to inflation-proof contracts, but argued that they were underpaid in relation to their counterparts at other leading First Division clubs. While the board had little alternative but to place both players on the transfer list, insisting it would take 'realistic offers' to capture them, Bobby Ferguson's response was to relieve Mariner of the captaincy and when his replacement, Russell Osman, was injured it was Terry Butcher's turn to lead the team.

Balancing the Books

Ferguson praised the commitment of the transfer-listed pair, but Mariner was on his way in February 1984, his last appearance coinciding with the senior debut of Jason Dozzell, at the time when he was still a pupil at the town's Chantry High School. The youngster's chance came sooner than intended, when he replaced the injured Eric Gates in the 29th minute of the home game against Coventry. In true fairytale fashion he netted an

50 Greatest Players

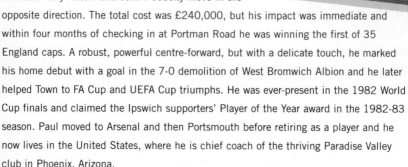

PAUL MARINER   **Forward**

Joined Ipswich Town: October 1976   **From:** Plymouth

Debut: v Manchester United, 30 October 1976, League

Appearances: 339   **Goals:** 135

Left Ipswich Town: 9 February 1984   **For:** Arsenal

Paul was playing non-league football with Chorley, and working in a tin can factory, when he was spotted by Plymouth and was top scorer in two of his three seasons there before Ipswich signed him in a player-exchange deal that saw Terry Austin and John Peddelty move in the opposite direction. The total cost was £240,000, but his impact was immediate and within four months of checking in at Portman Road he was winning the first of 35 England caps. A robust, powerful centre-forward, but with a delicate touch, he marked his home debut with a goal in the 7-0 demolition of West Bromwich Albion and he later helped Town to FA Cup and UEFA Cup triumphs. He was ever-present in the 1982 World Cup finals and claimed the Ipswich supporters' Player of the Year award in the 1982-83 season. Paul moved to Arsenal and then Portsmouth before retiring as a player and he now lives in the United States, where he is chief coach of the thriving Paradise Valley club in Phoenix, Arizona.

89th-minute goal to earn a 3-1 win and capture Town's first points of 1984, with Mariner and midfield youngster Mark Brennan, who netted his first goal for the club, also on target.

There was general disappointment at the news that Mariner was bound for Arsenal in a £150,000 move, although at the time of his and Wark's stance – they were rumoured to be seeking £1,000-a-week pay deals – there was a lot of anger directed at them by Town supporters.

Manager Ferguson described it as a major loss and added: 'Only our present financial plight is responsible for Paul's transfer and the £150,000 we have received makes it impossible for me to replace him with a player of equal class. These are hard times for football in general and we make no effort to deny that here at Portman Road we are certainly feeling the pinch. But I am confident that we have a bright future ahead of us.'

Ipswich plugged the gap in attack caused by the sale of Mariner by bringing a player in the opposite direction, but loan signing Alan Sunderland and his new mates drew a blank in four successive league defeats before extending the miserable sequence to seven straight losses, during which Town had scored just twice for the loss of 16 goals. There was further upheaval with the news that John Wark, who had clocked up a club record 162 consecutive appearances, was joining Liverpool for £450,000.

Although Romeo Zondervan arrived from West Bromwich Albion for £70,000, manager Ferguson admitted: 'Nothing could really compensate for the loss of John Wark and I can only repeat what I have said on a number of occasions in the past – that we were forced to sell for financial reasons. John's departure has saved the club financially and while the money will ease our debt it must be made clear that we are not yet out of trouble completely.'

Ferguson and chairman Patrick Cobbold agreed to take part in a Radio Orwell phone-in, which he described as a useful exercise, but he went on: 'Issues such as the construction of the Pioneer Stand and Mick Mills' departure were allowed to dominate what should have been a more general discussion. As was stated at the time, even without the new stand we would have our cash problems for the simple reason that attendances have dropped dramatically over the past few months.'

The day after Zondervan's arrival, Ferguson spent £60,000 to bring in goalkeeper Mark Grew from Leicester as cover for Paul Cooper, since Laurie Sivell was struggling with knee problems that led to him retiring at the end of the season. There was real concern at this stage for Town's First Division status, but they rallied tremendously in the final few weeks to lose just one of their last ten games. At one stage, when they were 20th and four points adrift of the team above them, with just six games to play, their situation looked next to hopeless. The odds looked to be stacked against Town, who were without George Burley and Terry Butcher through injury, but they took 16 points from a possible 18, including four from their last two away games, when they drew at Liverpool and came from behind at Old Trafford to secure the win that ensured their survival.

Beating the drop was the silver lining to a cloud of depression that hung over Portman Road for much of the 1983-84 season, with the domestic cup competitions offering little respite from a largely uphill struggle. After Blackburn Rovers and QPR had been overcome in the Milk Cup, thanks mainly to the contribution of John Wark in scoring six of Ipswich's nine goals, Norwich came to town and triumphed by the only goal of a fourth round tie when veteran star Mick Channon was on target. Manager Ferguson could not disguise his disappointment when he said: 'I can understand how our supporters felt after that game because I was just as disgusted with the general performance in which one or two individuals, in particular, let us down very badly.'

Town's FA Cup interest was short-lived, too, as they won 3-0 at Cardiff in a third round tie, but crashed out at the next stage to Shrewsbury, the second time in three seasons that the Shropshire club had delivered a knockout blow, and the fact that the game was featured on *Match of the Day* only added to Ipswich's embarrassment. Manager Ferguson, though, played down the result when he said: 'I refuse to scream and shout after going down to a side from a lower division, not like other managers who seem to treat this type of result as the end of the world. Anger sometimes seems to block common sense at times like these.'

Alan Sunderland, whose initial one-month loan deal had been extended to the end of the season, was signed on a permanent basis prior to the 1984-85 campaign. He failed to score in his first nine games, but it was felt that his experience was vital to the many younger players who had forced their way into the side and the fact that his late winner against Manchester United had ended Town's relegation fears was not forgotten, either. Ipswich were also boosted by the news that sponsors Pioneer were prepared to extend their support for a further 12 months, worth a minimum of £100,000, and their name appeared on a new strip that bore more than a passing resemblance to that sported by France in winning the European Championship that year.

Bobby Ferguson, who still had a year of his original contract to run, was given another two-year deal and the only transfer activity on the playing front saw Tony Kinsella return to Millwall, where he had won an FA Youth Cup medal before crossing the Atlantic to join Tampa Bay Rowdies in Florida. John Kerridge, chairman and chief executive of Fisons, joined the board.

Feeling the Pinch

By drawing their opening four league games, Town created a new club record, but whatever happened on the field of play became a mere backdrop to the real drama at Portman Road – an ever-worsening financial situation. It was so serious that when chairman Patrick Cobbold convened a boardroom meeting, to which he invited the various departmental heads, he reported that he was under pressure from the bank to slash costs and reduce the overdraft. Several money-saving ideas were discussed, including an across-the-board ten per cent pay cut that was dismissed as unworkable, and the chairman said he was prepared to hand over to the club the proceeds from the sale of a farm in Scotland which he owned and which he estimated as being worth between £70,000 and £80,000.

Expenses were cut in a number of ways. Tablecloths in the club's Centre Spot restaurant paid one less visit per week to the laundry, while the players' meals were prepared on the bus, rather than incurring the extra cost of stopping at a hotel or restaurant as they returned from away games. Staff numbers were also trimmed, mainly by redundancy. Funds were also raised by the sale of David Barnes to Wolves and Kevin O'Callaghan to Portsmouth, although the £150,000 spent to recruit Kevin Wilson from Derby balanced the books. Wilson was no overnight success, but he more than repaid the fee when he netted five times in less than a week, to help earn the victories over Stoke and Sunderland that virtually guaranteed Town's survival in the top flight, with a goalless draw in the penultimate game at Coventry making absolutely sure.

Town may have only just kept their heads above water in the league, but they progressed well in the cup competitions, to the extent that they were the last team to retain an interest in both. In the FA Cup, a last-minute Mark Brennan goal earned them victory at Bristol Rovers, meaning that Ipswich had survived at this stage of the tournament for 15 years in a row, equalling Liverpool's record that had stood for more than 50 years. A fourth round home tie against Gillingham saw debut-making striker Kevin Wilson celebrate with a goal in a 3-0 win, then the weather intervened and Town found themselves playing Sheffield Wednesday in a fifth round tie just five days before the quarter-final games were scheduled. They trailed to the Owls at half-time but stormed back to claim an exciting 3-2 win and book a trip to face the champions elect, Everton, at Goodison Park.

Town led 2-1 when Steve McCall was unluckily sent off for what was his first foul of the game and, to make matters worse, Everton equalised five minutes from the end. It was another debatable decision, with the referee awarding a penalty when the ball was rammed against Russell Osman's arm from close range, but it gave the Merseysiders a chance to win through in a tense replay.

For real drama, though, the Milk Cup took the biscuit. Town's first opponents were Derby and by scoring in each of the two legs against Ipswich, who won through 5-3 on aggregate, Kevin Wilson probably earned himself the move to Portman Road. Ipswich progressed the hard way in round four, drawing at home with Newcastle and then winning the St James' Park replay, which was their first away success that season.

An Oxford side who had already accounted for Arsenal, and who were pushing for promotion from the Second Division thanks to the financial backing of a certain Robert Maxwell, were overcome before a goalless home draw against QPR – the Portman Road pitch was in far-from-ideal condition after several postponements – had Town heading for London and a replay on the equally tricky Loftus Road synthetic surface. Russell Osman was sent off for retaliation after being punched by Simon Stainrod, who was also dismissed, and Terry Butcher marshalled the troops as they triumphed 2-1. Mich D'Avray's goal in the first leg of the semi-final at home to Norwich was scant reward for Town's superiority and they were made to pay in the return at Carrow Road.

An early injury to D'Avray was a massive blow – not only did he suffer concussion and a broken nose in a clash with Dave Watson, he was also knocked unconscious and almost swallowed his tongue, with only the prompt action of referee Keith Hackett preventing a far more serious problem. It was a very physical contest and Ipswich were beaten by a shot that deflected off Ian Cranson and a late Steve Bruce header. Terry Butcher was so angry – he felt his side had been on the wrong end of some outrageous tackles that escaped punishment – that he kicked a hole in the

50 Greatest Players

STEVE McCALL   Defender/Midfielder

Joined Ipswich Town: 2 October 1978   **From:** Juniors

Debut: v Skeid Oslo, 19 September 1979, League

Appearances: 331   **Goals:** 12

Left Ipswich Town: 3 June 1987

For: Sheffield Wednesday

Steve was a product of the club's youth policy who went on to win a UEFA Cup medal and earn England representative honours at youth level, when Brian Clough was the man in charge, and for the Under-21s. A midfielder with an excellent left foot, he successfully switched to the left-back role before returning to the middle of the park following Arnold Muhren's departure from Portman Road. He made a huge impact in the marathon 1980-81 season, playing in 48 of Town's 66 games, and he never looked back, enjoying a long, uninterrupted run and going on to represent England at B-international level. Steve's career was interrupted by injuries at Sheffield Wednesday and he moved on to Plymouth Argyle before joining Torquay United as assistant manager, a post he later occupied upon returning to Argyle and playing until he was almost 40. He remained in the West Country until accepting an invitation to return to Portman Road as a scouting co-ordinator.

dressing room door. Butcher was also critical of the manager's team selection, claiming: 'I think Bobby Ferguson made one important mistake. He left out Russell Osman when we needed his experience, aggression as well as his determination. It was frustrating for me to know that Russell, with all his fighting qualities, was watching from the stand when he should have been on the pitch.'

Norwich went on to beat Sunderland in the Wembley final, but the celebrations were subdued as both clubs were eventually relegated, the Canaries with just one point fewer than Town.

Terry Butcher was left frustrated by Ferguson's team selection at Norwich.

Butcher, an England regular, was the fans' choice to follow Trevor Putney as

50 Greatest Players

ERIC GATES   Forward

Joined Ipswich Town: July 1971 (as an apprentice)

Debut: v Wolves, 27 October 1973, League

Appearance: 384   **Goals:** 96

Left Ipswich Town: 9 August 1985   **For:** Sunderland

It is remarkably straightforward, for those privileged to have witnessed him at his peak, to conjure up images of Eric doing what he did best, creating goals out of nothing. Bobby Robson used to encourage the other players to feed the ball into Eric, no matter how tightly he appeared to be marked, and he would inevitably come out on top. His trademark turn would be followed by a ferocious shot and most of his goals were scored from just outside the penalty area. He revelled in the role behind the front two, wreaking havoc across Europe to help bring the UEFA Cup to Portman Road in 1981 and it was during that season, when he played the best football of his career, that he deservedly won two England caps. After his playing career ended at Carlisle, he had a spell coaching at Hartlepool, but can now be found sharing his forthright views with local radio listeners in the North East, where he covers Sunderland both home and away.

50 Greatest Players

RUSSELL OSMAN   **Defender**

Joined Ipswich Town: July 1975   **From:** School

Debut: v Chelsea, 3 September 1977, League

Appearances: 385   **Goals:** 21

Left Ipswich Town: 1 August 1985   **For:** Leicester City

Russell was always destined to have a long and successful career after winning an FA Youth Cup medal with Ipswich while still attending his local high school in his native Derbyshire. He was also captain of the England schoolboys rugby union side and he went on to represent his country at football as a youth, Under-21 and senior international, winning a total of 11 full caps. A strong, two-footed defender, as equally adept in the air as he was on the deck, Russell had an uncomplicated style that marked him out as one of the most solid and dependable players of his era. He was the only Town player to appear in every one of the club's 66 games during the memorable 1980-81 season when he won a UEFA Cup medal and that was his second successive 100 per cent season. Russell went on to play for Leicester City and Southampton before joining Bristol City, where he went on to become manager.

Since leaving management he has worked for national radio and Sky Sports as a football pundit and still lives in the West Country.

Player of the Year and apart from Kevin O'Callaghan adding to his collection of Eire Caps, further international honours were won by Steve McCall (England B) and Ian Cranson, who made his England Under-21 debut, while both Jason Dozzell and Andy Crane won England youth caps.

Commercial manager Tommy Parker retired after 30 years' service as player and club official, as did physiotherapist Tommy Eggleston. The decision by Pioneer not to renew their lucrative sponsorship deal was a massive blow, especially as Town failed to attract another big-money backer. Rather than not sport a sponsors' name, the club entered into an agreement with Radio Orwell that guaranteed them air time rather than cash, which was still in very short supply at Portman Road.

Transfers and Relegation

Before the new season started, two more members of the UEFA Cup-winning side, Russell Osman and Eric Gates, were sold. Osman, a reliable

50 Greatest Players

GEORGE BURLEY   **Defender**

Joined Ipswich Town: August 1972 (as an apprentice)

Debut: v Manchester United, 29 December 1973, League

Appearances: 500   **Goals:** 11

Left Ipswich Town: September 1985   **For:** Sunderland

George is the first player to go on and manage the club, and he is set on emulating the achievements of his mentor, Bobby Robson, in restoring Ipswich to the forefront of football, not only in England but abroad. He was lured south after being spotted in a specially arranged trial and was still only 17 when he made his senior debut at Old Trafford with orders to mark the legendary George Best. An attacking full-back, he was the launch pad for many an Ipswich attack and was a regular member of the side for many years, winning the Player of the Year prize in 1977. He won an FA Cup medal the following year but was cruelly denied a place in the UEFA Cup-winning side of 1981 because of a career-threatening knee injury from which he eventually made a successful recovery. Capped 11 times by Scotland, he went on to play for Sunderland, Gillingham and Motherwell before entering management with Ayr United. He returned south to take charge of Colchester United but just six months later, in December 1994, he grabbed the opportunity to become manager of Ipswich.

defender who had never let the club down, joined Leicester for £200,000 and Gates, a dangerous player who had netted several key goals for the club, returned to his native North East to join Sunderland for £150,000, having previously looked set to join their neighbours, Newcastle. He was later joined at Roker Park by George Burley, who cost just £50,000 and who had requested a transfer prior to the big kick-off.

As if the loss of such an experienced trio was not enough, Town also had to contend with an injury to the inspirational Terry Butcher, forced to sit out all but one of the opening 19 games after twice undergoing surgery on his knee. Steve McCall, whose run of 175 consecutive appearances was ended the previous season, was another casualty, breaking his toe in the second game against Manchester United and forced to spend ten games on the sidelines thereafter. Even their deputies, Kevin Steggles and Irvin Gernon, suffered from the injury jinx and Ipswich were grateful for the defensive displays of Ian Cranson, their only ever-present that season, although nothing could stop the slide into the Second Division after 17 years in the top flight.

Bobby Ferguson was a long-term admirer of Ian Atkins, first spotting the player at Shrewsbury, and he kept track of him as he moved on to Sunderland and then Everton. After a successful loan spell, he forked out £100,000 to bring the industrious Atkins to Portman Road, but the new man also had spells on the sidelines because of a stress fracture of the foot.

Alan Sunderland, who had started the season as captain in Butcher's absence, hurt his back in a road accident and never reappeared following the turn of the year, by which time Town were embroiled in a survival scrap. Town landed a real bargain with the £5,000 capture of fireman Nigel Gleghorn from Seaham Red Star, but it did not help that he was introduced into a struggling side.

A depressing run of just two wins from 17 league games since the start of the season looked set to end at relegation rivals Oxford, Ipswich raced into a 3-0 lead after 53 minutes. Experienced keeper Paul Cooper was injured and manager Ferguson surprisingly overlooked Mark Grew in favour of youngster Jon Hallworth, which prompted an angry outburst from Grew, who claimed: 'Even the washerwomen have a better chance than me of being picked.'

Hallworth's debut turned into a disaster as Oxford replied four times, including a John Aldridge hat-trick in the space of nine minutes, and a stunned Bobby Ferguson, unable to watch after the home side scored their fourth goal, walked into the changing room five minutes before the end. That result left Ipswich second from bottom with just eight points from 18 games.

With little choice but to gamble on home-grown talent, Ferguson gave a debut to Mick Stockwell for the Boxing Day trip to Coventry, where Town earned their third win in five games to continue what most people assumed would be a climb clear of danger. They only lost one of their next six games, but two successive defeats by Nottingham Forest and Newcastle United, where Trevor Putney was sent off with 18 minutes left and the scores level at 1-1, proved to be a setback. Once again, however, the team rallied and a four-game unbeaten run that reaped eight points saw them enter April with a decent chance of scraping clear. But the next four games could not have been more different, with Town not even managing a goal as they collected just one point, although a subsequent 3-2 home win over Oxford seemed to convince supporters that they were clear of danger.

But the fans, particularly the hundreds who flooded on to the pitch, had not done their sums. Mathematically, Ipswich were not safe and four days later their prospects of beating the drop were dealt a crushing blow. It was 1-1 at Upton Park when Nigel Gleghorn's 86th-minute challenge on Mark

Sheffield Wednesday's Martin Hodge beats Town's Jason Dozzell to the ball. The Owls goalkeeper put up the shutters all afternoon to deny Town, and the 1-0 defeat all but condemned them to relegation and life in Division Two.

Ward resulted in a penalty which Ray Stewart converted to earn the Hammers a 2-1 win. An incensed Terry Butcher – he felt that Ward was guilty of taking a dive – remonstrated so forcibly with referee Gerald Ashby at the end that he had to be restrained by two policemen, as well as West Ham keeper Phil Parkes and Town boss Bobby Ferguson. The incident resulted in Butcher being charged with bringing the game into disrepute and there was even talk of the FA banning him from the World Cup, but he eventually escaped with a £1,000 fine and a warning as to his future conduct. To make matters worse for Ipswich that night, they learned that Oxford had beaten Everton thanks to an 89th-minute goal and that the relegation issue was anything but resolved.

On the final Saturday of the season Ipswich were at Sheffield Wednesday and a strong travelling support, many of them in fancy dress, returned home devastated by a 1-0 defeat on a day when home keeper Martin Hodge put up the shutters. No one felt the disappointment more than Terry Butcher, who was in tears at the end as he feared the worst. Rivals Leicester and Coventry had both won and Town's fate was in the hands of Oxford, losers at home to Nottingham Forest but with one game, at home to Arsenal, still to play. It was as if Town were on death row. The Gunners' season was dead and the Manor Ground erupted as Oxford raced into a third-minute lead, eventually winning 3-0 to condemn Ipswich to the drop.

50 Greatest Players

TERRY BUTCHER   Defender

Joined Ipswich Town: August 1976   **From:** School

Debut: v Everton, 4 April 1978, League

Appearances: 351   **Goals:** 21

Left Ipswich Town: July 1986   **For:** Rangers

Mention of Terry's name immediately conjures up the image of him playing for England, his head swathed in blood-soaked bandages as he refused to bow to injury. They didn't come much tougher and he formed a solid defensive double act with Russell Osman as Ipswich won the UEFA Cup in 1981, by which time he had already won the first of 77 senior caps. Originally recommended to Ipswich by a supporters' club official, Terry went on to become captain of the club he followed as a boy. He was a key member of the England squad at the World Cup finals of 1982 and 1986, after which he moved to Rangers in a £750,000 deal, and was back in the World Cup finals again in Italy in 1990 when he was skipper of Bobby Robson's side that reached the semi-finals. He led Rangers to numerous Scottish League and Cup successes before returning to England as player-manager of Coventry, then he managed Sunderland before heading north of the border again to run an hotel in Bridge of Allan and coach at Raith Rovers and Dundee United. More recently, he has covered England games for Radio 5 Live.

Butcher reflected later: 'In the end we only had ourselves to blame. We didn't score enough goals – 32 in 42 games – and had lost too many players over the years.'

Butcher also clarified the bigger picture when he added: 'So what went wrong with Ipswich? Why did a club that had been so successful a few years earlier find itself struggling and eventually relegated? Bobby Robson's departure was obviously a major blow. His influence was everywhere and he had been responsible for much more than just team selection. On the pitch, losing Arnold Muhren was the start of our slide. Like Robson he had become vital to the club's success and he was impossible to replace.'

Butcher also tackled the controversial subject of the Pioneer Stand, which was blamed in many quarters for causing the club's demise. He added: 'I believe the decision to build the new stand was taken in the best interests of the club. The idea was to provide better facilities for the fans so they could watch a team that was expected to compete with the best in Europe. Nobody could have envisaged the exodus of top players over the next three or four seasons. It's wrong to say that the players were sold purely to pay for the stand. Each one was ambitious and for their own reasons wanted to get away. I was as sad as the supporters were to see them go as they were all good friends as well as good players.'

Butcher was to join the exodus himself that summer, although it hurt him to move on. Ipswich had knocked back a bid from Manchester United early in 1985 and in the summer Butcher had agreed a new three-year deal, which included a clause that the club would permit him a transfer if they were relegated. After representing England in the World Cup finals in Mexico, he completed a £750,000 move to Rangers and the general consensus among Ipswich supporters was that he had been under-valued, a view that grew stronger when Norwich centre-half Dave Watson moved to Everton for a widely quoted fee of £1 million.

Chapter Eleven: 1986-92
Back to Basics

The 1985-86 season had seen Ipswich create a record by advancing beyond the third round of the FA Cup for the 16th consecutive season, but that mattered little. They were now facing up to life in the Second Division, minus Butcher and with little financial backing, although a brand new sponsorship deal with Fisons – new director John Kerridge was still at the helm there – did help. But the supporters, fed a diet of top-flight fare during 18 consecutive seasons of First Division football, deserted the club and a crowd of only 12,455 attended the opening game of the 1986-87 season at home to Grimsby, which resulted in a 1-1 draw and before which there was a minute's silence in memory of Sir Stanley Rous, the Suffolk-born former FA secretary and FIFA president.

The Grimsby game marked the debut of close season signing John Deehan, a player of some experience who had arrived from Norwich in a swap deal that took the younger Trevor Putney to Carrow Road. The crowd figures were to get worse, with the 9,399 turnout for Shrewsbury's visit to Portman Road on 9 September 1986 the lowest for 20 years. Another two records were created that season, when Town conceded 14 penalties, but not a single goal at the North Stand end of the ground, and in February 1987 the club welcomed 34-year-old David Sheepshanks on to the board – an appointment the significance of which was perhaps lost on most supporters at the time, and who could hardly have envisaged the impact he was to have on the club in the years to follow.

Town's long sequence of FA Cup third round successes was ended when Birmingham City, managed at the time by ex-Norwich boss John Bond, won 1-0 at Portman Road. In the Littlewoods Cup it was Cambridge United who knocked them out, and after seeing off Plymouth Argyle, Reading, Aston Villa and Manchester City in the new Full Members Cup, they were beaten in the semi-final at Blackburn. The main focus was on whether Ipswich could regain First Division status at the first time of asking and despite finishing fifth, which would normally have ruled out such a scenario, they still had a chance via the play-offs, introduced for the first time that season.

In those days the format was to involve the team finishing third from bottom of the First Division, alongside those finishing third, fourth and fifth in the Second Division, and so Town took on Charlton over two legs. The first, at Portman Road, ended goalless thanks to Paul Cooper's penalty save from Colin Walsh. For the return game, the double loss of Ian Cranson and John Deehan, both of whom provided aerial power, was a blow Ipswich could not overcome. Charlton took full advantage, winning 2-1 in what just happened to be Town's first-ever Sunday game, to avoid the drop.

Bobby Ferguson seemed to sense his time was up and did not even travel back to Ipswich on the team bus. Confirmation of his departure came within three days, after the Ipswich directors had tried to protect the club's record of having never sacked a manager since joining the Football League in 1938, when they announced that his contract was not being renewed. The long and short of it, however, was that Ferguson's services were no longer required and in football terms he had been fired.

There are those who believe Ferguson should have been retained, but in terms of results he had under-achieved and paid the price. Ferguson also showed himself to be insensitive in dispensing with the club's Scottish scout,

50 Greatest Players

PAUL COOPER   **Goalkeeper**

Joined Ipswich Town: 18 June 1974   **From:** Birmingham City

Debut: v Leeds United, 20 April 1974, League

Appearances: 575

Left Ipswich Town: July 1987   **For:** Leicester City

It cost Ipswich a mere £23,000 to sign Paul and he repaid them with 13 years' sterling service. A first team goalkeeper at the age of 17 with previous club Birmingham City, for whom he gave up a full-time job as a despatch clerk to become an apprentice, he originally joined Ipswich on loan and did so well that Town were anxious to make the move permanent. After establishing himself as the No. 1 choice, he went on to win both FA Cup and UEFA Cup honours, and many judges considered him unfortunate in having to compete with the likes of Peter Shilton and Ray Clemence or he might have won England honours. Paul established a reputation as a penalty expert, once saving two in a game against Derby in the 1979-80 season, when he stopped five of the seven he faced. It was a major honour that the Ipswich fans voted him their Player of the Year in the 1980-81 campaign when Town won the UEFA Cup and were, until late on, chasing success on three fronts.

George Findlay, who had discovered a trio of international stars in George Burley, John Wark and Alan Brazil. Did Findlay, who had followed Bobby Robson from Fulham, not deserve better than to learn of his axing via a telephone call from an Ipswich-based journalist who rang to offer his sympathies after being given the news by Ferguson?

New Man at the Helm

Ferguson was not alone in departing Portman Road during the summer of 1987. Paul Cooper left for Leicester on a free transfer and Kevin Wilson, who had scored 20 league goals the previous season and won Northern Ireland honours, was signed by Chelsea for £335,000, a fee fixed by a transfer tribunal. Town seemed to be in no rush to appoint Ferguson's successor and were refused permission by Stoke City to speak to their manager, Mick Mills, who was still a hero in the eyes of the Ipswich supporters and their No. 1 choice for the job. Gillingham manager Keith Peacock was in the frame, as was Ian Bowyer as he ended a long and distinguished playing career, while long-serving Town coach Charlie Woods put himself forward and was interviewed for the post.

But almost a month after Ferguson's dismissal, it was Chesterfield manager John Duncan who was appointed. An articulate Scot who had played for Dundee, Tottenham and Derby, he decided to retain Woods as his assistant but carried out the board's orders to pension off 66-year-old chief scout Ron Gray after 17 years' service. Another backroom change saw the departure of physio John Chandler, who joined Colchester after 19 years at Portman Road, 13 years as a part-timer. He was replaced by 21-year-old David Bingham, known to Duncan as he was the son of the Chesterfield chaplain.

Town started the season with three new signings – Neil Woods (Rangers), David Lowe (Wigan) and Graham Harbey (Derby County) – and it was quickly apparent that the new manager's ideas of how the game should be played were at odds with the style of play to which the supporters had become accustomed. He preferred a more direct approach, which was not to the liking of all the players he inherited. In the case of Ian Atkins, who was skipper when Duncan arrived, he missed the start of the season through injury and when he was fit again did not, as he had anticipated, reclaim the captaincy from Ian Cranson. Later in the season Atkins moved to Birmingham on loan, and then permanently in a £30,000 deal. Cranson was also on the move, to Sheffield Wednesday for £450,000 in an eve-of-deadline deal. Another transfer saw young striker Michael Cole join Fulham for £45,000. One move that did meet with the approval of supporters saw John Wark return from Liverpool at a cost of £100,000, with the player taking a significant pay cut to escape the Anfield reserves and putting Town ahead of FA Cup holders Coventry, who had agreed a similar fee.

The 1987-88 season also saw Town blood one of ex-boss Ferguson's signings, Simon Milton, a former paint sprayer who cost just £5,000 from Bury Town, but by far the greatest impact was made by young striker Dalian Atkinson, who had been spotted in Shropshire by former chief scout Gray, ironically after he had been checking on another potential target. Atkinson's mixture of pace and power saw him score twice against both Barnsley and Huddersfield, then he stole the show in a home clash with Middlesbrough that was attended by England manager Bobby Robson, anxious to take a close-up look at Boro's emerging defender, Gary Pallister, who was partnered by Tony Mowbray.

Neither could cope with Atkinson, who scored an explosive hat-trick in Town's 4-0 win, but by that time Ipswich were too far behind to make the play-offs and eventually finished eighth. In the FA Cup third round home tie against Manchester United, a Sunday game televised live by the BBC, Town put up a tremendous fight before going down 2-1, while their interest in the Littlewoods Cup was ended by eventual winners Luton and in the Simod Cup by Coventry, both at the fourth round stage. One player on his way was goalkeeper Jon Hallworth, who cost Oldham £125,000. The death occurred on 16 October 1987 of the club's president, Lady Blanche Cobbold, who was 89, and former groundsman Freddie Blake also died that season at the age of 83.

Searching for the Right Formula

Ipswich gave debuts to three players in the opening game of the 1988-89 season – goalkeeper Craig Forrest, who had travelled all the way from Canada to serve his apprenticeship, central defender David Linighan, who cost a club record £300,000 fee from Shrewsbury, and utility man David Hill, an £80,000 buy from Scunthorpe. Town started with a seven-game unbeaten league run that included Linighan's return to Gay Meadow, where Simon Milton's hat-trick helped to earn a 5-1 win. But they then hit a barren spell, winning just once in seven games and not even scoring in five of them. Mark Brennan, who the previous season had become the club's youngest-ever captain despite making no attempt to disguise his distaste for the tactics dictated by John Duncan, had departed, Middlesbrough pipping Norwich for his signature when his Portman Road contract expired.

By far the most significant change, however, saw Charlie Woods assume a new role as assistant to the manager, with coach Peter Trevivian in effect stepping into his shoes as Duncan's right-hand man with direct input as to how the first team prepared and the tactics they would adopt. Town broke new ground when they signed Soviet Union international sweeper Sergei Baltacha, only to realize that he could not be accommodated in his usual role as Duncan was against changing his preferred system of operating with a flat back four. The first Soviet star to turn out in the Football League, he was handed an unorthodox role on the right of midfield and marked his debut with the opening goal in Town's 5-1 home win over Mick Mills' Stoke.

Scottish midfielder Ian Redford was signed from Dundee United at a cost of £200,000, while Town introduced youth players Chris Kiwomya, David Gregory and Gavin Johnson, along with Michael Cheetham, who had been spotted playing for the Army. Ian Juryeff, on loan from Leyton Orient, made substitute appearances, while Ron Fearon had a 21-game run in goal, and Town used a total of 25 players, the same as the previous season, as manager Duncan searched in vain for a promotion formula.

They finished with a seven-game unbeaten run, including five straight wins and four without conceding a goal, but despite collecting seven points more than the previous season they were again eighth. Duncan was experiencing disciplinary problems and Dalian Atkinson, who had on at least one occasion broken a Friday night curfew prior to an away game, was fined £500 for his outspoken comments when a newspaper quoted him as saying: 'Play me or sell me.' He was given his answer when Ipswich accepted a £450,000 bid from Sheffield Wednesday, apparently being in such a rush to conclude the deal that they did not insist on a sell-on clause, something that surprised Owls boss Ron Atkinson, who later sold the player to Real Sociedad for £1.7 million, which represented a handsome profit.

The 1989-90 season was one of frustration for Ipswich's supporters, their spirits only being lifted, briefly, by a 13-game unbeaten run that saw Town climb to fifth in the Second Division. But their progress came to an abrupt end with a 5-0 thrashing at Port Vale on New Year's Day. Prior to the good run getting under way, there had been demonstrations against manager John Duncan because the team's start to the season saw them lying 17th in October, and the unrest quickly returned, lasting through to the end of the season as some supporters allowed their anger to boil over with heated, on-the-pitch protests, including the burning of a managerial effigy, something never previously seen at Portman Road.

Duncan continued to ring the changes, signing full-back Neil Thompson, a former nappy salesman, from Scarborough, then spending a record £350,000 to sign Brian Gayle from Manchester City. But one deal that did not go ahead would have seen David Lowe join Nottingham Forest in return for Lee Chapman and £400,000, the Ipswich player picking up an injury that jettisoned the proposed transaction. Despite an unexpected FA Cup win at Leeds, the general mood at Portman Road was one of depression and it was on results in the league that the manager was being judged. Despite three wins from the last four games, which enabled Town to finish ninth with just four points fewer than the previous year, it was not enough to keep Duncan in a job and he was sacked within three days of the season ending, although it soon became clear that the change had been anticipated some time earlier in the Portman Road boardroom.

The Right Man for the Job?

It was in the serene surroundings of Glemham Hall, the majestic home of Ipswich chairman Patrick Cobbold, that the Town directors convened to interview John Lyall for the managerial vacancy, although it may have been more a case of the experienced former West Ham boss, who had landed a lucrative job as a consultant to Terry Venables at Tottenham Hotspur, quizzing the board about their ambitions. Apparently, he was late after driving from his home in the Essex countryside and, after listing his conditions and terms, it is said he went for a stroll in the Glemham Hall gardens before returning to hear whether or not they were acceptable.

The Town directors were convinced that Lyall, bitterly upset at the circumstances of his departure from Upton Park following the Hammers' relegation in 1989, was the man to lead them forward and he in turn relished his return to the sharp end, anxious to prove

John Lyall arrived at Portman Road with a point to prove.

a point to those behind his dismissal at West Ham. His appointment did not cause major upheaval, more a minor reshuffle of the backroom team as Peter Trevivian reverted to running the youth team, while Lyall introduced another ex-Upton Park stalwart, Mick McGiven, as first team coach.

Lyall and McGiven chose to make the daily journey from the London area, rather than move to East Anglia. This made it difficult for them to integrate locally and one area of Town's day-to-day activities that seemed to suffer was their relationship with the local media, neither of the two newcomers having been used to speaking to newspaper, radio and television representatives on such a regular basis.

Transfer activity saw John Wark depart for a second time from Portman Road, this time to join Middlesbrough in a £50,000 deal after he felt he was worth more than John Lyall was prepared to pay, while the largely unused Sergei Baltacha moved to Scotland to join St Johnstone and Mich D'Avray also quit in favour of a switch to Dutch football. Lyall's first signing was veteran goalkeeper Phil Parkes and he must have created a new record when he appeared in the last three games of that season, by which time he was approaching his 41st birthday, and conceded a penalty in each of them. In pre-season games David Linighan, who had fallen out of favour at the end of John Duncan's spell in charge, was handed the captaincy, but once the action got under way for real there was no reason for optimism as Town lost their first two games and failed to score in either of them.

Lyall turned the corner with two straight wins but it was clear he felt the need to strengthen his squad. Having failed to land Martin Foyle from Oxford United in September – his £500,000 offer was rejected – it was not until January 1991 that he was successful in landing a former West Ham player, Steve Whitton, for £150,000 from Sheffield Wednesday. Soon afterwards he brought in another ex-Hammer, Paul Goddard, who had cost Millwall £800,000, but who had been given a tough time by supporters at the Den who were unwilling to forgive his past. He was released and immediately snapped up by Lyall and they were to prove two very useful signings, although the 1990-91 season petered out to a disappointing end, with Town finishing below mid-table in 14th place – their worst for 25 years – while West Ham finished second and won promotion back to the First Division.

Lyall successfully introduced Chris Kiwomya as a first team regular and he finished as top scorer with 12 league goals, while the hard-working Steve Palmer, a Cambridge University graduate, also began to establish himself in midfield. Homesick youngster Chris Swailes, who later returned as a

George Burley signing, left in March 1991 to join Peterborough United for £10,000. The following month there was a major announcement, when chairman Patrick Cobbold announced he was standing down to be replaced by John Kerr.

Defying the Odds

The bookmakers rated Ipswich as no better than 25-1 outsiders for the Second Division title in the 1991-92 season and it seemed the Town fans were of a similar opinion regarding their team's chances. The first home game was on a Tuesday night, Port Vale were the visitors and the paying customers were less than impressed. Only 8,937 turned out, the lowest attendance for any opening home game in the club's history and more than 1,000 down on the previous low, for a Southern League fixture with Folkestone in 1937.

On the first day of the season, incidentally, Marcus Stewart had marked his Bristol Rovers debut with a goal in the 3-3 draw with Ipswich at Twerton Park, Bath. Slowly but surely, however, John Lyall began to exert his influence and his coaching prowess was never in doubt as he masterminded a remarkable turnaround that saw Town clinch the Second Division title for the fifth time in their history and book a place in the inaugural Premier League. It was a fantastic achievement on modest resources and rapped out a message, loud and clear, that he was far from being the spent force West Ham had suggested he was when they dismissed him three years earlier.

From an individual point of view, the undoubted success story of the season centred on John Wark, who enjoyed a new lease of life in returning to Ipswich for a third time. Told by Middlesbrough boss Lennie Lawrence to move to the area, rather than commute from his home in Suffolk and live part of the week in a flat on Teesside, he refused and parted company with the club. Thinking he would quickly be fixed up elsewhere, he was amazed to find that clubs like Falkirk, in Scotland, wanted to have a look at him before committing themselves. Feeling he had nothing to prove he declined, but south of the border only Orient and Colchester, then in the Conference, showed any interest. Wark was convinced he could do better, but in the absence of any concrete offers he came close to signing on the dole.

'When I got to the front door of the office I became very nervous,' he recalled. 'I knew I couldn't go ahead with it. I turned back and, as things worked out, it was the best move I could have made.'

Solo training sessions were not the answer as he strived for peak fitness, so he asked Ipswich if he could train at Portman Road and, when they agreed, he quietly went about his business. It was when they asked him to turn out for the reserves that it dawned on the Town management team that he still had plenty to offer. He remained in the background, but Ipswich's decision to sell Brian Gayle to Sheffield United for £800,000, a price too good to refuse, was instrumental in giving Wark's career the kiss of life.

The management had earmarked Tony Humes to fill the void left by Gayle's departure, but he fractured his arm in the eighth game of the season at Newcastle and, in fact, never played for Town again as a loan move to Wrexham became permanent. Old campaigner Wark was summoned and found himself on the bench for a Rumbelows Cup tie at Derby. He wasn't needed that night, but three days later he appeared for the entire second half of a 2-1 league win at Grimsby, after which he was in the side right through to the end of the season, which he capped in style with the fans' Player of the Year award and a new contract. An injury to new signing Eddie Youds, who cost £250,000 from Everton but was crocked on his debut at Derby, also helped Wark to establish himself as a key member of the title-winning

50 Greatest Players

JOHN WARK   Midfielder

Joined Ipswich Town: July 1973 (as an apprentice)

Debut: v Leeds United, 27 March 1975, FA Cup

Appearances: 679   **Goals:** 179

Left Ipswich Town: 19 March 1984   **For:** Liverpool

John launched his career as a defender, but it was as a goalscoring midfielder that he became best known before reverting to defence once again at the end of an illustrious career. Twice he left Portman Road, for Liverpool and Middlesbrough, but he returned each time. He was a box-to-box player who never shirked his defensive responsibilities, but his uncanny knack for being in the right place at the right time earned him well over 100 goals, while his accuracy from the penalty spot also served the club well. An FA Cup winner in 1978, three years later his goals helped to win the UEFA Cup and that season also saw him crowned PFA Player of the Year, the only Ipswich player to have gained the prestigious award. He won Scottish youth honours, eight Under-23 caps and 29 senior caps, three of them in his time with Liverpool. After his retirement he worked as a community coach and a scout at Portman Road before joining Portsmouth, then Coventry, as chief scout, only for the Sky Blues' relegation in 2001 to cost him his job.

side, and his defensive partnership with David Linighan was instrumental in the club's unexpected, but not undeserved, success.

A run of five straight wins in late March and early April put Town ten points clear at the top of the table. Last-gasp goals played a part, with Neil Thompson netting in the 89th minute to clinch victory at Southend and then Steve Whitton converting a stoppage-time penalty at home to Wolves to earn another three points. The Southend game saw the league debut of tall defender Phil Whelan, who marked the occasion with a goal, and he was on target again in his next game, against Wolves. Ipswich suffered from the promotion jitters during the run-in, their ten-point lead eventually being whittled down to four, and a goalless stalemate at home to Grimsby, when victory would have ensured promotion, was particularly frustrating since a bumper crowd of 22,393 – the team's success had seen the fans flock back – turned out in celebratory mood. But a 1-1 draw in the penultimate game at Oxford, when Jim Magilton opened the scoring for the home side and Gavin Johnson levelled within two minutes, was enough to launch the championship party and it continued a week later at Portman Road when the trophy was presented to the team and an excited crowd before a 3-1 win over Brighton. The inevitable open-top bus parade and civic reception followed 24 hours later and there was much to anticipate for Ipswich supporters with a new-look football structure taking shape.

Their performances against Liverpool in the FA Cup inspired confidence that they would be able to cope with the demands of Premier League football. Town took two games to dispose of Hartlepool in the third round, then defeated Bournemouth 3-0 to set up a visit from Liverpool in the fifth round. A 0-0 home draw with Graeme Souness' team earned them an Anfield replay in which they forced extra-time before going down, rather unluckily, 3-2 to the eventual winners.

The 1991-92 season had seen Patrick Cobbold become president in succession to his late mother, but he remained on the board, and Murray Sangster, who retired after 28 years' service as a director, became a vice-president.

Landmarks during the season included Paul Goddard's goal in the 2-1 win over Middlesbrough, which was Town's 3,000th in the Football League, and when Scottish veteran John Wark converted a penalty in the 4-0 home win over Tranmere, on St Andrew's Day, it was his 50th spot-kick success from 58 attempts. John Carruthers, the Carlisle-based scout responsible for launching many a career at Portman Road, retired and continued to work

50 Greatest Players

ROMEO ZONDERVAN   Midfielder

Joined Ipswich Town: 21 March 1984   **From:** West Bromwich Albion

Debut: v Watford, 24 March 1984, League

Appearances: 325   **Goals:** 20

Left Ipswich Town: May 1992   **For:** NAC Breda

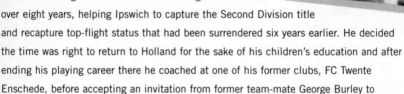

There was genuine concern for Town's top-flight status when Romeo was signed in a £70,000, deadline-day move in 1984 and he helped to bring about a change in fortune, scoring twice in eight appearances as relegation fears were banished by an impressive climax to the season. Capped six times by Holland before he arrived at Portman Road, he was a hard-working player, a tremendous athlete who operated from box-to-box in his time as a midfielder and loved to race forward when used at right-back. He remained a regular choice for over eight years, helping Ipswich to capture the Second Division title and recapture top-flight status that had been surrendered six years earlier. He decided the time was right to return to Holland for the sake of his children's education and after ending his playing career there he coached at one of his former clubs, FC Twente Enschede, before accepting an invitation from former team-mate George Burley to become Ipswich's first full-time European scout.

part-time on behalf of the club. Sponsors Fisons renewed their sponsorship agreement, which was worth £225,000 over three years to the club, and skipper David Linighan forced his way into the PFA Second Division select team.

There was one big-name departure, though, when Romeo Zondervan returned to Holland with NAC Breda, putting his children's education ahead of the undeniable lure of Premier League football with Ipswich. Another change saw Portman Road become an all-seater stadium as both the Churchmans and North Stands were converted during the close season.

Chapter Twelve: 1992-95
Back in the Big Time

John Lyall only reinforced his squad with one major signing – Welsh midfielder Geraint Williams – as Ipswich joined the football revolution triggered by the formation of the new FA Premier League and its controversial partnership with the satellite broadcaster BSkyB, whose demands on behalf of a growing army of subscribers meant that football would never be the same again.

Town's home clash with Aston Villa was only one of nine top-flight games that day, as two fixtures had been moved to accommodate live coverage on the Sunday afternoon and Monday evening, a now-familiar pattern. Another change saw the introduction of what was commonly called the back-pass rule, which meant that a goalkeeper could no longer handle the ball when it was deliberately played to him by a colleague, unless it was headed or chested by the outfield player.

New signing Williams, who cost £650,000 from Derby County, proved to be something of a lucky mascot as Ipswich made an impressive start to the season by avoiding defeat in each of their opening eight league games. In the ninth, when he was absent through injury, Town crashed 4-2 at Oldham, but by Boxing Day they had lost just twice in a 22-game run that featured eight wins and 12 draws. They then suffered successive defeats, but won their next two, at Tottenham and at home to Manchester United, in the space of three days. Amazingly, Frank Yallop scored on each occasion – his first goals in four-and-a-half years.

Clive Baker, the former Norwich City goalkeeper who had been signed on a free transfer from Coventry City, had taken over in goal after Craig Forrest was sent off in the 0-0 home draw with Sheffield United and he held his place for the remainder of the season with some impressive displays. Bobby Robson, in charge of Sporting Lisbon at the time, did his former club a favour when he recommended two players who were surplus to requirements in Portugal. Bulgarian international Bontcho Guentchev became a regular and popular choice, but Macedonian-born Australian cap Vlado Bozinoski made minimal impact and was on his way before the season ended.

Sadly, Town could not maintain the form that had seen them collect a very creditable 42 points from 26 games and they were unable to win any of their next 13. Only a home victory over Norwich, surprise title contenders who eventually finished third, in a game televised live by the BSkyB cameras, guaranteed their Premier League status for another year. The Canaries were doubled that season by Town, who also took four points off champions Manchester United. There were emotional scenes on the last day of the season as the fixture list determined that the great Brian Clough's final game in charge of Nottingham Forest, who had already been relegated, would be at Portman Road. Clough, ever the showman, milked the generous applause as he brought the curtain down on a colourful and controversial, but most of all successful, career.

It seemed incredible that Ipswich finished just three points better off than relegated Crystal Palace, having lost just two games more than third-placed Norwich, but it could be attributed to the fact that only Palace were able to match their tally of 16 draws. Palace, Forest and Arsenal were the only sides who scored fewer goals than John Lyall's team, while 13 others conceded either the same number of goals, or more. Whatever way one examined the statistics, however, for Ipswich to have survived was a great achievement at the end of a season in which they had proved stubborn opposition.

They were grateful to the 17-goal partnership of Chris Kiwomya and Jason Dozzell, who developed a fine understanding. Kiwomya, who benefited greatly from Lyall's coaching and had ended speculation about his future the previous season when he signed a new contract, was one of the quickest players around and Town played to his strength when they frequently knocked the ball in behind opposing defences at the earliest opportunity.

Ipswich had also advanced to the quarter-final stage of both cup competitions. In the FA Cup they eliminated Plymouth, Tranmere and Grimsby, against whom Guentchev claimed a hat-trick, before eventual winners Arsenal handed out something of a lesson as they triumphed 4-2 at Portman Road. The Gunners also won the Coca-Cola Cup and it was the runners-up, Sheffield Wednesday, who ended Town's interest in a Hillsborough replay after Wigan, Portsmouth and Aston Villa had been accounted for, mainly by six-goal Kiwomya who boosted his overall tally to 17, way ahead of any of his team-mates. But John Lyall, who had spent exactly £1 million to recruit Whitton, Youds and Williams, was not fooled by Ipswich's showing after an absence from the big-time of six years. He had pinpointed areas of the squad that he felt required strengthening,

50 Greatest Players

JASON DOZZELL   **Forward**

Joined Ipswich Town: 12 December 1984   **From:** Juniors

Debut: v Coventry City, 4 February 1984, League

Appearances: 416   **Goals:** 73

Left Ipswich Town: 1 August 1993   **For:** Tottenham Hotspur

Jason was still attending Chantry High School when Ipswich boss Bobby Ferguson named him as a substitute for a first-team game at home to Coventry when the club's First Division status was in the balance. That was a story in itself, but what followed was the stuff of fairytales as the youngster, just 16 years and 57 days old, climbed off the bench with less than half an hour gone to rewrite the record books. One minute from the end he scored Town's third goal in a 3-1 win to become not only the club's youngest-ever first-team player, but also the youngest to score a First Division goal. On the Monday morning, while his picture was splashed all over the local and national papers, he was back at his desk and it was a further ten months before he signed professional forms. Tall and languid, but extremely skilful and quick-thinking, Jason won England Under-21 honours before joining Tottenham for a then record fee. He returned to Portman Road, briefly, in the 1997-98 season and then had a spell at Northampton before joining Colchester to take his league appearances beyond the 500 mark. He was forced to retire in September 2001 because of a long-term toe injury.

while he was also forced to replace Jason Dozzell who had opted for a move to Tottenham that earned Town £1.75 million.

Calling for the Reinforcements

Lyall spent £400,000 on Paul Mason from Aberdeen and a further £750,000 on Ian Marshall from Oldham in readiness for the 1993-94 season and both players contributed to the team's outstanding start, when they won their first three games without conceding a goal. Marshall found the net in each of them after he and Mason both netted on their debut and the powerfully-built striker could hardly have hoped for a better introduction to life as an Ipswich player. Frustrated at Oldham boss Joe Royle's persistence in fielding him in a defensive role, it was the opportunity to play up front that appealed to him most about joining Town and he must have felt he had proved a point when he found the net at his old stamping ground on the season's opening day.

Intriguingly, John Lyall had decided to take a step back, allowing Mick McGiven to take charge of team affairs. Lyall still had input – his spying missions to watch future opponents led to him dictating tactics – but McGiven took charge of the daily coaching. Their three successive victories took Town to the top of the renamed Premiership, but they then hit a lean period of eight games without a win that sent them crashing down the table.

With a transfer surplus at his disposal, Lyall turned to an old favourite in Stuart Slater in an effort to boost the squad. Sudbury-born Slater, a Town fan as a youngster, had been lured to West Ham to start his career and several impressive displays had persuaded Celtic to take him north of the border in a big-money move. The Glasgow giants decided to cut their losses in unloading Slater on Town, but his contribution of just one goal in 35 appearances that season was disappointing. It was not difficult to sympathize with Slater's plight because he was a likeable character who genuinely had affection for the club and desperately wanted to succeed, although playing in a struggling side whose confidence was being sapped almost by the week was doing him no favours.

Fighting for Survival

A 2-0 win at Wimbledon, while certainly welcome, offered only brief respite from what was clearly an uphill struggle and it emerged that dressing room unrest was playing a part in Town's troubles. David Linighan's non-appearance for the second half of a 4-1 home defeat by Sheffield Wednesday was virtually brushed aside by Mick McGiven in the post-match press conference. McGiven perfected the art of saying as little as possible on such occasions and when he explained that Linighan had an injury there seemed no reason to disbelieve him. Even when quizzed by reporters who had learned the real truth – Linighan was so upset at stinging criticism delivered in his direction during the half-time briefing that he refused to budge for the second half – McGiven continued to insist the player was injured and it was an embarrassing episode for the club that, with proper handling, could have been avoided.

Linighan was absent from the next game, a 2-2 draw at struggling Swindon when John Wark, celebrating his 600th appearance, scored both goals, but he returned to the fold as Town managed to put together a seven-game unbeaten run to the end of the year. Particularly pleasing to supporters was the pre-Christmas home win over Norwich, made possible by Canary star Gary Megson's last-gasp own goal.

But Ipswich were earning themselves an unwanted reputation for their negative tactics, especially away from home, although no one at Portman Road was inclined to apologize when sheer hard work and organisation earned results like a 0-0 draw at Manchester United to bring home a precious point.

As in the previous year, however, Town were really up against it during the second half of the campaign and after losing 2-1 at home to Liverpool on New Year's Day they only managed two wins right through to the end of the season.

Ipswich went into their final game at Blackburn with their Premiership status hanging by a thread and later, with emotions running high up and down the country, it seemed they were actually down. Only Swindon were definitely relegated at the start of play that day and it would be two from a group of five – Ipswich, Southampton, Sheffield United, Everton and Oldham – who would accompany them. Late in the day, with only a few minutes remaining in all the key games, Town's fate seemed to have been sealed as they played out a 0-0 draw at Ewood Park and Sheffield United, by then their closest rivals, were hanging on for a point at Chelsea. There was despair among the travelling supporters as John Lyall urged his team forward in search of the goal that would clinch survival – until news filtered through of a dramatic development at Stamford Bridge. Mark Stein had scored a late, late winner for Chelsea and so Sheffield United were down and the point Ipswich earned was enough to enable them to scrape clear in real Houdini fashion.

There were emotional scenes on the pitch, as Lyall hugged his players, and the relief at their escape from the jaws of disaster was palpable. It was time to reflect and fans were quick to recall the most exciting game of the season had been the 3-2 home win over Sheffield United. No one realized it at the time, of course, but Stuart Slater's only goal that season turned out to be worth its weight in gold.

Ipswich may have been well drilled defensively – they kept clean sheets in exactly one third of their league games and conceded fewer goals than ninth-placed QPR – but they suffered from an acute shortage of goals scored. They were the Premiership's lowest scorers and after top marksman Ian Marshall on ten came Chris Kiwomya with half as many. Marshall, incidentally, only made 28 league starts as injuries took their toll, but he was also the club's leading marksman in terms of cup goals. In the FA Cup he was on target in both third round games against Swindon and the fourth round victory over Tottenham, but after drawing at Molineux it was Wolves who won through in the Portman Road replay.

Town's interest in the Coca-Cola Cup ended in the third round at Liverpool when their scorers in a 3-2 defeat were Paul Mason and Ian Marshall, both born on Merseyside. It said a lot about the 1993-94 season that John Wark was again the fans' choice as Player of the Year, for the fourth time in six seasons, and he was to figure prominently in a major backroom reshuffle that summer.

Backroom Changes

John Lyall did not enjoy a close relationship with the Ipswich supporters. He kept his distance, chose not to appear at many social events and rarely opened up in the press. He was a bit of a stranger to the fans, even after four years at the helm, and was dependent, therefore, on results to win them over. Having escaped relegation so narrowly the previous season, with Mick McGiven in charge of team affairs, it was widely expected that Lyall would seize control again and lead from the front.

He decided, instead, to introduce a brand new partnership. Neither Paul Goddard nor John Wark lacked experience in the game, but it seemed a brave gamble to give them responsibility for coaching the first team as Mick McGiven took up a new role as football development officer, which meant he was responsible for everything outside the first team.

Goddard retired as a player, but Wark vowed to carry on as the pair worked in tandem, with Lyall remaining in overall charge. Realizing the need to strengthen the squad, Town smashed their transfer record with the £1 million purchase of Steve Sedgley from Tottenham, a player who could perform in midfield or as a central defender, and they also captured Danish import Claus Thomsen who, coincidentally, also proved adept in the same two areas of the field. Great curiosity was aroused when Lyall and chief scout Charlie Woods headed for South America on a scouting trip, with one report, which appeared in a national newspaper and was then picked up locally, even suggesting their target was Argentinian international striker Gabriel Batistuta, at that time playing for Italian side Fiorentina. But the two players they did bring back with them were unknowns by comparison.

Uruguayan striker Adrian Paz and Argentinian full-back Mauricio Taricco looked rather bemused by all the attention they were receiving at the Portman Road media conference, but the smile of satisfaction on the face of manager John Lyall suggested he had pulled off something of a transfer coup. He described Paz as being a typical English centre-forward and even invited local journalists to view the video tape that featured the long-haired player in action and which, presumably, had first brought him to Lyall's attention. He was an international player, it was stressed, who had played for Penarol, the former world club champions, while it was hinted that Taricco, capped at Under-21 level by Argentina but the holder of an Italian passport, was more of a long-term signing.

Taricco, though, was given an almost immediate debut, in the home leg of a Coca-Cola Cup tie against Bolton, and it proved such a nightmare that nothing more was seen of him at first team level that season. Paz, on the other hand, started in style as Ipswich, having won just one of their opening six league games, *Mauricio Taricco (above) and Adrian Paz were* defeated Manchester United 3-2 at *the surprise outcome of a scouting trip to* Portman Road, a performance *South America.* that gave no hint of the despair to follow in what gradually unfolded as the worst season in the club's history.

Entering Freefall

Having crashed out of the Coca-Cola Cup as Bolton added to their 3-0 success at Portman Road with a 1-0 win in the return game, Town saw precious points slip away and gained just one win, at home to Leeds, in a nine-game sequence that reaped just four points out of a possible 27. The alarm bells were ringing and the strain clearly showed as Lyall and Kevin Keegan had an angry verbal exchange at St James' Park after a 1-1 draw, the Newcastle manager being critical of Town's negative approach.

The rumour mill was working overtime, too, with suggestions that the Portman Road hierarchy were none too impressed with on-the-field events and changes were imminent. Ipswich's next game was at home to Manchester City and from the poor turnout, just 13,504, it was obvious

Great Managers – 1990-94

JOHN LYALL

John Lyall arrived at Ipswich in 1990 with a point to prove – to football as a whole, but in particular to his previous employers at West Ham – and there can be no question that he succeeded. Hurt at the way he was abruptly discarded by the Hammers after 34 years' service to the club, following relegation to the old Second Division in 1989, he rose to the challenge on offer at Portman Road. Lyall moved up the coaching ladder at Upton Park after an injury-plagued spell as a player saw him make a mere 34 appearances in three years and he succeeded Ron Greenwood in 1974 to embark on a 15-year stint as manager that had more highs than lows.

His task at Ipswich was clearly defined. He was expected to lead the club back to the big-time and he did so in only his second season, not only clinching promotion, but winning the Second Division title in style with a team that started the campaign as 25-1 outsiders. He was not a big spender, preferring to recruit tried-and-tested players he already knew well and to nurture the club's young talent. It is all too easily forgotten, for example, that future stars like Richard Wright and Kieron Dyer were all initially groomed for stardom by Lyall.

It was Lyall who led Ipswich into the inaugural Premier League and, initially at least, all was well as his well-drilled team defied the odds to survive. But he removed himself into the background in his fourth year in charge, promoting Mick McGiven to run the first team and they only hung on by the skin of their teeth.

His decision to put Paul Goddard and John Wark in dual charge of the side the following season backfired as Town lost valuable ground early in the campaign, to the extent that they were looking relegation certainties by the time he resigned on 5 December 1994.

His choice was to turn his back on the game, but he could retire in the knowledge that Ipswich, despite their precarious position in the Premier League, were in far better health than before his appointment.

that the fans' patience, too, was close to breaking point. As his team slumped to a 2-1 defeat, which meant that Town had won just three of their opening 17 league games, Lyall was the main target for supporters' abuse and, having taken the weekend to think carefully about his next move, he duly resigned on the Monday morning. Even the Town players returning from the training ground to Portman Road just after noon on 5 December 1994 had no idea Lyall had gone. Chairman John Kerr immediately called a press conference, at which he announced that Paul Goddard would be in caretaker charge until the appointment of a new manager which would take place as soon as possible.

Already stressful times became even more traumatic when director and president, Patrick Cobbold, collapsed and died suddenly at his Glemham Hall home, another huge blow at a time when only the most optimistic of fans would have given the club a remote chance of escaping the drop. As the search for Lyall's successor got under way, Town plunged to a 4-1 defeat at Nottingham Forest and then gained successive draws at home to Wimbledon and at West Ham.

There was no shortage of contenders for the job, ex-skipper Mick Mills being quick to seek permission from his employers, Sheffield Wednesday, where he was chief scout, to be interviewed. Graham Turner, David Pleat, Mike Walker and Goddard, considered by many to be worth the gamble, were all mentioned. Two other former players, Russell Osman and Alan Brazil, also declared their intention to apply. Howard Kendall, a championship winner with Everton, was granted an interview and brought along his boots, so keen was he to commence work straight away.

Turning to an Old Face

But, eventually, it was to George Burley that the directors turned to fill the gap, having been won over by his enthusiasm at the interview stage. Burley had cut his teeth in management at Ayr United and in the summer of 1994 returned south to join Colchester, where he briefly sought the advice of his former boss, Bobby Ferguson. Over Christmas it transpired that Burley had resigned after just a few months at Layer Road and he watched the Boxing Day draw at Upton Park before taking charge for the home defeat by Arsenal two days later. His appointment caused ill feeling between Town and Colchester, even though the

Despite only limited managerial experience, with Ayr United and Colchester, George Burley's enthusiasm won over the Town board.

Essex club had originally granted permission for an approach to Burley, and the saga dragged on before Ipswich were ordered to compensate their neighbours.

Burley appointed his friend and former youth team colleague, Dale Roberts, who had also been with him at Ayr, as his assistant and Mick McGiven negotiated a pay-off before eventually becoming reserve coach at Chelsea. Lyall, meanwhile, melted into the background and turned his back on the game.

A new manager, perhaps, but it was still obvious that Town needed a miracle to save their season. As if their plight at the wrong end of the Premiership was not bad enough, they also suffered a humiliating FA Cup third round defeat at Wrexham.

Burley's first win saw Adam Tanner mark his debut with a goal in the 4-1 thrashing of fellow strugglers Leicester City and Town could not have chosen a better way of getting over the disastrous trip to Wales than by rewriting the record books.

Ipswich had made countless trips to Anfield over the years without recording a single win, so it was generally felt that the game on 14 January 1995 offered next to no chance of success. Tanner, however, completed a remarkable few days when his long-distance shot took a slight deflection and flew into the roof of the net. Could Burley pull off the impossible and haul Ipswich clear?

In their next game they were leading until near the end, when his nephew, Craig Burley, netted Chelsea's equalizer in a 2-2 draw which marked the debut, as a substitute, of the new manager's first signing, experienced striker Lee Chapman, who cost £70,000 from West Ham. Chapman's first, and only, goal for the club earned a 2-1 home win over Southampton, with Town's opener being scored by Scottish striker Alex Mathie, who was Burley's second buy at £500,000 from Newcastle. The money to recruit Mathie was raised by the sale of Chris Kiwomya to Arsenal for £1.5 million and Eddie Youds to Bradford City for £175,000, which also left enough in reserve to bring Chris Swailes back to Portman Road from Doncaster and he became the manager's third purchase at a cost of £225,000.

Ipswich had managed three wins and a draw in eight league games at the start of 1995 – hardly championship form, but a huge improvement on what had gone before – when they headed for Manchester United and what turned out to be their lowest point in years.

It was no contest and with United leading 3-0 at the break the only interest centred on how many goals they would eventually score.

They stopped at nine, although shell-shocked Town keeper Craig Forrest admitted afterwards that it probably should have been an even heavier defeat. John Wark may have been struggling with flu symptoms, but it was an embarrassing display by a Town side run off their feet by an in-form home outfit. Harsh words were apparently exchanged at the end, with Steve Sedgley later admitting that his own personal feud with the manager resulted in him throwing in the captain's armband.

United boss Alex Ferguson, however, felt for his opposite number, still finding his feet in top-flight management, and later admitted: 'I didn't want them to score ten. You could have set our performance to music, but it's unthinkable for a manager to lose 10-0. George was emotional at the end. It was hard for him. I said "I'm sorry about that, but you just have to do it". He just walked away and never came in for a drink. I didn't blame him. I felt genuinely sorry for him. But I spoke to him after that about his team and he might have paid attention to what I said. I told him to stand by his principles and he would get there in the long run. You need patience in life and to get real quality you need to persevere. The worst thing you can be is blind to what's wrong.'

Ipswich were not in a position to reject any realistic offers and Phil Whelan was next to depart, joining Middlesbrough on deadline day for £300,000, although an administrative error meant the deal was not completed in time for him to appear for Boro that season and his career was put on hold until the start of the following campaign.

The Old Trafford result knocked the stuffing out of Ipswich and they never recovered, losing their next six games. That meant a run of eight defeats on the trot, seven of them without even scoring. In their final 14 games of the season they triumphed just once, when 17-year-old Richard Wright made his debut in goal and celebrated with the first of many clean sheets as Coventry were beaten 2-0 at Portman Road.

The end could not come quickly enough and they duly finished bottom, having lost 29 of their 42 games, collecting a mere 27 points in the process. They used 34 players, more than in any other season, and gave debuts to 15, beating the 1946-47 record. Claus Thomsen was the leading league marksman with only five goals, yet another record, and no one had to be reminded that it was the worst season in the club's history. Most of the damage had been done, of course, during the early part of the campaign, but it was now George Burley's job to be ruthless in determining which changes he wanted to make in order to halt the slump and revive the club.

Chapter Thirteen: 1995-98
Picking up the Pieces

Many dismissed David Sheepshanks' ideas and vision for the club as fanciful – he would prove those doubters wrong.

Four days before the start of the 1995-96 season, chairman John Kerr stepped down to be replaced by David Sheepshanks. So Ipswich were under new management in more ways than one and the new supremo wasted no time in making his mark, delivering a stirring speech at a press conference when he unveiled a five-year plan that envisaged a return to Europe at the turn of the century.

Sheepshanks became the club's first genuine hands-on chairman, devoting long hours to devising a solid business plan and making it clear he was in overall charge, while in no way undermining Burley's authority when it came to team matters. The new man inherited a difficult task, admitting the club was 'haemorrhaging to death' financially, but pledging to do his bit to supply a transfusion of new ideas. He provided much-needed boardroom energy and leadership, combined with solid support for the manager, and pledged to create greater PR awareness, improved access for the media, a more prolific youth system, more involvement with the community and increased investment in commercial opportunities – all of which was designed to restore the club's Premiership status at the earliest opportunity and to put the club on a solid financial footing once again. Some people mocked his ambition, others just shook their heads and dismissed his ideas as fanciful, but all were forced to eat their words as he kept his promise and duly delivered.

Sheepshanks, an Old Etonian, never kidded himself it would be easy, but even his critics were full of admiration for the enthusiastic way in which he tackled his task and there is no doubt that his dynamic leadership rubbed off on those around him, while the Portman Road stadium is the living proof of a vision still not totally fulfilled.

The brewers, Greene King, were unveiled as Town's new sponsors, but supporters were slow to snap up season tickets for the club's return to the First Division, which made it even more difficult to continue paying a number of players Premiership-style wages. Mick Stockwell, rewarded with a testimonial when Bobby Robson brought his Porto team to Portman Road in an attractive curtain-raiser, was appointed captain and George Burley was encouraged by the pre-season tour to Finland that had, he felt, improved dressing room morale.

But preparations could have gone more smoothly – David Linighan broke a toe while on holiday in Portugal, both Steve Sedgley and Paul Mason were placed on the transfer list, Craig Forrest was unwilling to play in friendly

50 Greatest Players

DAVID LINIGHAN   Defender

Joined Ipswich Town: 23 June 1988

From: Shrewsbury Town

Debut: v Stoke City, 27 August 1988, League

Appearances: 327   **Goals:** 13

Left Ipswich Town: 26 January 1996   **For:** Blackpool

It was John Duncan who signed David, who served an apprenticeship as a joiner before switching to full-time football, and he became a permanent fixture in the side for the best part of seven years. His own personal highlight was to captain the side that won the Second Division title under John Lyall in 1992, thereby booking a place in the inaugural Premier League and he was a defensive hero before Town bowed to the inevitable and were relegated three years later. A tough, hard-tackling defender who was dominant in the air, he served the club with distinction and his brother, Andy, also had a successful career with Norwich, Arsenal and Crystal Palace. After three years with Blackpool, he had a spell north of the border with Dunfermline, where former Ipswich colleague Gavin Johnson was a team-mate, and then returned south to play for Mansfield before dropping into the Nationwide Conference with Southport.

games in case it jeopardised his chances of a move and Adrian Paz had departed. It had been rumoured that Mauricio Taricco would also be unloaded and he seemed to be in the depths of despair as he opened his heart, begging for a first team chance that few felt would ever come his way. It was just as well Town decided to persevere with their first-ever Argentinian, while Forrest's future was also resolved as he signed a two-year contract and started the season as first choice keeper.

Bontcho Guentchev was released to join Luton, while one of a large group of Dutch trialists was kept on. Gus Uhlenbeek, a right-sided player of devastating pace who had started out with Ajax, cost £100,000 from Top Ost. He went straight into the side on the opening day of the season for a disappointing 3-1 away defeat by Barry Fry's Birmingham City, after which Town took ten points from their next four games with Alex Mathie helping himself to six goals as he took the early honours in his own personal duel with strike partner Ian Marshall, the pair having staked a friendly £50 wager as to who would score most often.

After Mathie's hat-trick destroyed Sunderland at home, Ipswich were third, but they slipped down the table to below the half-way point as a result of winning just two of their next 13 league games. As he struggled for results, manager Burley was at the same time trying to change the personnel. Steve Palmer went to Watford for £135,000 in September 1995 and it represented something of a coup when the Town boss eventually persuaded Tony Mowbray to leave Celtic for £300,000 the following month.

Burley had earmarked Mowbray for the captaincy and the following month allowed an ex-skipper, David Linighan, to depart for Blackpool in an £80,000 deal. It was clear, as the first anniversary of his appointment loomed, that he was reshaping his squad. Mowbray's arrival coincided with the dismal run, but he was ultimately responsible for a change of fortune as Town climbed back into the First Division's top six courtesy of a ten-game unbeaten sequence.

Sadly for the inspirational Mowbray, and Ipswich, he was injured as he stretched to make a tackle during a narrow 1-0 defeat at Sunderland and his season was over. It was a huge blow to Town's promotion hopes, but the team recovered to win four and draw one of their next six games and despite a later sequence of just one win in five, they gained two consecutive victories and knew that a third in their last game of the season, at home to Millwall, could still reserve a play-off place.

Town were odds-on favourites against a team battling desperately to avoid the drop, but they could not score and a goalless draw did neither side any good. While Ipswich finished seventh, allowing Leicester to leapfrog over them en route to a Premiership return, Millwall dropped into the Second Division.

Looking back on that season, the highlights included a remarkable recovery at Oakwell when Ipswich stormed back from 3-0 down with three goals in the closing stages to earn an unexpected point, while a controversial decision by referee Kevin Lynch denied Town a similar outcome in the East Anglian derby at Carrow Road. The official blew his whistle and pointed to the spot, only to change his mind after consulting a linesman and instead awarded the Canaries a free-kick for offside. Town, for whom John Wark had already netted from the spot and was relishing the chance to stage an action replay, went down 2-1 and an angry George Burley was prompted to ask: 'Who was offside, the invisible man?'

In the return game, however, Ipswich won by the same scoreline after a late own goal by Robert Ullathorne, whose backpass struck a divot, deceiving goalkeeper Bryan Gunn as he swung and missed his clearance, and the ball trundled over the line, much to the delight of the home crowd.

There may have been eventual disappointment in the league campaign, but Ipswich made national headlines when they knocked out big-spending Blackburn in the FA Cup, holding them to a goalless draw at Portman Road and then going through when Paul Mason hit a glorious long-range winner in extra-time at Ewood Park. Goalkeeper Richard Wright, just 18 and replacing Craig Forrest from the line-up in the first game, marked his first FA Cup appearance with a world-class save from England striker Alan Shearer, who took time to congratulate him afterwards. On an emotion-charged night for the Town fans who had travelled north, they were joined in the celebrations afterwards by chairman David Sheepshanks as he deserted his privileged place in the directors' box and rushed to congratulate the players.

Mason revelled in the FA Cup that season, also scoring the only goal to see off Walsall in the fourth round, and he was on target again as Aston Villa won 3-1 at Portman Road in the fifth. Alun Armstrong, little realising what the future had in store for him, scored Stockport's first goal in their 2-1 second leg win at Ipswich in the Coca-Cola Cup, after the sides had drawn 1-1 at Edgeley Park, and Town's first, and last, venture into the Anglo-Italian Cup saw them beat Serie B opponents Reggiana, Foggia and Salernitana, draw with Brescia and then slump to defeat at the semi-final stage, to Port Vale.

Starting to Take Shape

Young players like Richard Wright, James Scowcroft and Tony Vaughan all blossomed during George Burley's first season in charge, with the manager, who signed a new three-year contract soon after the campaign ended, claiming: 'We got our credibility back, both as a team and as a club.'

Mauricio Taricco, who had been so close to being released, confirmed his undoubted class and Town's achievement in scoring more goals than any other side in the three divisions of the Football League, or the Premiership, owed much to their strike force of Ian Marshall and Alex Mathie, who between them contributed 37 of the team's 79 league goals.

The outcry among supporters, therefore, when Ipswich accepted an £800,000 Leicester bid for Marshall shortly after the 1996-97 season got under way, was to be expected. Those who voiced the opinion that the club would regret the decision were chorusing 'told you so' as Town made an indifferent start, while a crowd of just 9,767 for the first home game against Reading suggested the supporters would have to be won over. Ipswich found Marshall difficult to replace as they won just one of their first six league games and then, after four without losing, they slumped again, winning just one in nine and at one stage were down in 17th place.

Manager Burley strengthened his squad in the summer of 1996 with the arrival of Dutch winger Bobby Petta from Feyenoord, after he impressed during a trial period, and former Burnley midfielder Danny Sonner, who had also shown up well after parting company with German lower league side Preussen Cologne. Both arrived on free transfers as cash was in short supply at Portman Road, a factor that influenced the directors' decision to cash in on Marshall, and the team's inconsistency during the first half of the 1996-97 campaign led to some poor home attendances and a feeling that the play-offs would again prove to be out of Town's range.

That feeling was compounded when they went to Tranmere and lost 3-0, meaning that they had won six, drawn seven and lost eight of their first 21 league games. But December triggered an amazing transformation, with Town picking up the Performance of the Month award for their 2-1 win at runaway leaders, Bolton, which was to be the champions' only home defeat that season. It spurred Town on, and of their 25 fixtures through to the end of the season they won 14, drew seven and lost just four, earning them fourth place in the table just six points adrift of second-placed Barnsley, who were promoted automatically.

So Ipswich were not only in the play-offs, but firm favourites to see off fifth-placed Sheffield United, who had twice been beaten 3-1 in the regular

Kieron Dyer made his first appearance mid-way through the 1996-97 campaign, three days before his 18th birthday, a Boxing Day triumph over Crystal Palace.

league programme, the Portman Road game being memorable for a Neil Gregory hat-trick.

Mauricio Taricco turned on the style to such an extent that he polled most votes in the fans' Player of the Year poll, while defender Chris Swailes, making the most of a second chance at the club, was another success story. His failure to command a regular place led to him being placed on the transfer list at his own request, but the £900,000 sale of Claus Thomsen to Everton, after he had starred for Denmark in the Euro 96 tournament staged in England, then the absence of Jason Cundy, led to him being recalled. Not only that, he came off the list and was happy to sign a new contract.

Cundy had seized the chance of a £200,000 permanent move to Portman Road that season, having been frozen out at Tottenham and given a new lease of life during a successful loan spell with Ipswich. His arrival was a major turning point for Town. Youth product Richard Naylor made the breakthrough, too, and scored five senior goals, only for his season to end in March because of tendinitis in both knees, a problem that was to plague him for years to come.

James Scowcroft continued his impressive progress, helping to compensate for the long-term loss of Alex Mathie, who was out of action as early as October and then, having undergone surgery on both shoulders, sat out the remainder of the campaign. Town also had a close look at St Lucian striker Earl John, keen to try his luck in England after a spell in Portugal, but he was restricted to a few minutes as a substitute before moving on to Rotherham and Plymouth. Young goalkeeper Richard Wright also enhanced his reputation, keeping five successive clean sheets, a new club record, towards the end of the season.

Mid-way through the campaign George Burley decided he could not keep Kieron Dyer under wraps any longer. Three days before his 18th birthday he made a brief appearance as substitute in the Boxing Day triumph over

Crystal Palace, a sweet success for Town and their fans as derisory comments by visiting boss Dave Bassett, made after the teams' goalless stalemate at Selhurst Park three months earlier, were again rammed down his throat, Ipswich having also inflicted a 4-1 Coca-Cola Cup defeat over the Eagles.

Dyer was introduced again for the defeat at Huddersfield, then he was given his full debut in the FA Cup third round defeat at Nottingham Forest. Slightly built, it was feared he would be brushed aside too easily, but any doubts as to whether he could cope were quickly dispelled by his early performances and it was clear that he was the most exciting new player to be introduced from within the club in many years. Another home-grown product, Adam Tanner, who had been given his chance soon after George Burley's arrival at the club, heaped disgrace on himself and Town when he tested positive for cocaine during a routine drugs test. The club stood by him and in January 1997 he appeared before a Football Association disciplinary commission, when it was felt he escaped lightly with a three-month ban.

On the eve of the play-off game at Bramall Lane there was another bombshell, when Jason Cundy delivered the news that he was suffering from testicular cancer. Cundy had undergone surgery to remove a testicle, the real reason for his absence from the side being put down to more run-of-the-mill problems, and he fought a brave battle to overcome the disease, not only keeping his promise to return to action, but supporting a Suffolk-based awareness campaign.

Whirlwind Town may have breezed through the second half of the season, but midfielder Geraint Williams urged caution – 'we all start level now and there are no favourites' – against a side renowned for their battling qualities. Wise words, as it turned out, because after a 1-1 draw at Bramall Lane, when Mick Stockwell cancelled out Jan-Aage Fjortoft's opener, Town could not capitalise on home advantage in the return game. United went ahead twice, Town hit back twice and then the visitors levelled the aggregate score at 3-3 on 90 minutes. A tense period of extra time followed.

But there was no further scoring and Ipswich bowed out on the away goals rule, left to reflect on a late Steve Sedgley effort that came back off a post and how they failed to overcome a United side handicapped by an injury to goalkeeper Alan Kelly and the sending-off of Nick Henry, both of which appeared inexplicably to have tipped the scales in the home side's favour.

Pushing for the Top Flight

It was a busy summer of transfer activity at Portman Road as George Burley set about reshaping his side for another promotion challenge. Experienced defender Mark Venus arrived from Wolves, with Steve Sedgley moving in the opposite direction and Town also pocketing in the region of £350,000, while cash-strapped Bournemouth could not refuse an £800,000 offer for their energetic midfielder and captain, Matt Holland, a player Burley quickly tipped to become skipper of Ipswich in the not too distant future.

Goalkeeper Craig Forrest, having accepted his chances of overtaking Richard Wright were remote, joined West Ham for £500,000, and Town plugged the gap by signing Lee Bracey from Bury for a modest £40,000. Young defender Tony Vaughan, having reached the end of his contract, signed for Manchester City, with a tribunal determining the fee at £1.35 million.

Town were left to rue the one who got away, however, after Kevin Phillips had agreed terms in George Burley's office only for the Town board to show reluctance to sanction his purchase from Watford. Had the Hornets been prepared to settle for £250,000, the deal would have gone ahead, but Ipswich, at the time uncertain of the outcome of Vaughan's tribunal, refused to stump up any more and the player instead moved to Sunderland, who were only too willing to meet Watford's asking price.

While Phillips quickly discovered his scoring touch in the North East, eventually netting 29 times in the league, Town were finding goals hard to come by during the early stages of the 1997-98 season. In an effort to boost the output they introduced Mark Stein on loan from Chelsea; in fact, they were to use the loan system several times that season with mixed results. David Kerslake, Andy Legg and David Whyte all checked in for a time and Town even opened the door for a return to the club by Jason Dozzell, who had been

Bournemouth could not refuse an £800,000 offer for their livewire midfielder Matt Holland, which would prove to be money well spent by George Burley.

Great Matches

FOOTBALL LEAGUE FIRST DIVISION   **Portman Road, 21 February 1998**
Ipswich Town 5   Norwich City 0   **Attendance: 21,858**
Mathie 3
Petta 2

There is nothing like a win over arch-rivals Norwich City and when it is achieved by a record-equalling scoreline it has a special glow to it.

The writing was on the wall for the Canaries after just 64 seconds when Alex Mathie netted with a venomous right-foot shot that flew past a startled Andy Marshall. There was no way back for Norwich after 27 minutes when Mathie to beat the offside flag and drill his shot low inside Marshall's left-hand post. Mathie completed his hat-trick just before the break, turning in Stockwell's cross to ensure a place in the record books.

The Scottish striker failed to appear after the interval and it was winger Bobby Petta's turn to catch the eye with a further two goals as Town piled on the agony for the men in yellow. Petta's first was an absolute gem to leave the Canaries in total disarray after 56 minutes and nine minutes from the end skipper Matt Holland held off the challenge of substitute Danny Mills to enable the Dutchman to complete the rout.

Ipswich Town: Wright, Stockwell (Sonner), Clapham, Dyer, Mowbray, Cundy, Uhlenbeek, Holland, Johnson, Mathie (Scowcroft), Petta.

Norwich City: Marshall, Sutch, Segura (Kenton), Grant, Fleming, Jackson, Forbes (Llewellyn), Fleck (Mills), Coote, Carey, Eadie.

Referee: C. Wilkes (Gloucester).

released by Tottenham. He played eight league games before they announced they would not be pursuing their interest, a decision shrouded in mystery.

When Ipswich reached November having won just three of their opening 15 league games and occupying a bottom four slot, they decided to enter the transfer market and signed striker David Johnson from Bury for a fee reported as £1.1 million, made up of £800,000 plus £300,000-rated defender Chris Swailes, which made it a new club record. Around the same time, ex-player Bryan Hamilton returned as first team coach after losing his job as manager of the Northern Ireland national team, and the two new arrivals had an immediate effect.

Johnson, a former England schoolboy international who had started his career at Manchester United, was an instant success when he netted on his debut, a 1-1 draw at Wolves, and that sent Town on an incredible run that was even more impressive than the second-half surge of the previous campaign.

50 Greatest Players

MATT HOLLAND   **Midfielder**

Joined Ipswich Town: August 1997   **From:** Bournemouth

Debut: v QPR, 9 August 1997, League

Appearances: 214*   **Goals:** 36*

*up to summer 2001

In terms of value for money, Matt is one of the finest acquisitions in the club's history, his debut season in the Premiership completing four years without missing a single game since his £800,000 move from Bournemouth. A Manchester United fan and Old Trafford regular as a schoolboy, he launched his career with West Ham, but was loaned to non-league Farnborough and then Bournemouth before completing a move to the south coast in 1995. He was appointed captain at Dean Court and Ipswich boss George Burley confirmed he was destined for a similar role at Portman Road when he brought him to the club. An energetic midfielder who catches the eye for his wholehearted approach, he has an amazing disciplinary record of just two bookings in his career to date – one with his previous club and another in four years with Ipswich. He is eligible for the Republic of Ireland through his grandmother and has established himself in their squad, scoring his first goal in the World Cup qualifier in Portugal in October 2000, and netting again to keep the Republic on course for the 2002 spectacular in the Far East.

They lost two of their next seven league games, then the season really took off. They suffered just one defeat in a magnificent 23-game run that reaped 56 points and saw them yet again clinch a play-off place. Johnson contributed 20 league goals as he struck up a powerful partnership with the fit-again Alex Mathie, who in turn weighed in with 13, including a hat-trick against Norwich. Bobby Petta, who had made little impact during his first season at the club, netted twice against the Canaries during a lengthy purple patch; Holland claimed ten league goals; and left-back Jamie Clapham, originally signed on loan from Tottenham, looked a bargain at £300,000.

Richard Wright, who kept 21 clean sheets in all competitions, and Matt Holland, who won the supporters' Player of the Year award to cap an outstanding first season at Ipswich, were both ever-present, while Mick Stockwell had a 100 per cent appearance record in the league. But injuries took their toll elsewhere. Town had to cope without Mark Venus for a large part of the season, while Tony Mowbray only started half the league games and the previous season's top scorer, Paul Mason, was not seen after the first game. Richard Naylor only managed five substitute outings in the league and another stand-by striker, Neil Gregory, moved to Colchester in a £50,000 deal in January 1998.

But both Kieron Dyer and, to a lesser extent, James Scowcroft, established themselves as key members of George Burley's squad, as did Jason Cundy, only absent from five league games as he confirmed his recovery from cancer. Geraint Williams was dropped for the visit to West Bromwich Albion, when Cundy's late header secured all three points, and although he returned two games later, that was the last that was seen of him that term.

Town went goal crazy in the month of February, rattling in five goals in three successive home games against Huddersfield, Norwich and Oxford, and when they also went nap against Port Vale, as part of a five-game winning run that ended the regular league season, it seemed they were in tremendous shape going into the play-offs, where their opponents would be Charlton.

Falling at the Final Hurdle

One of Ipswich's worst displays of the season had seen them crushed 3-0 at The Valley, but they had won the return game 3-1 and were not overawed

50 Greatest Players

RICHARD WRIGHT   Goalkeeper

Joined Ipswich Town: July 1994   From: School

Debut: v Coventry City, 6 May 1995, League

Appearances: 291

Left Ipswich Town: July 2001   For: Arsenal

Richard became the first Ipswich goalkeeper to play for England when he was capped against Malta in the summer of 2000, prior to being a member of the squad at the European Championships in Holland and Belgium when he was not called upon. He has completed a full set of international honours – schoolboy, youth, Under-21 and senior – and is tipped to become the No.1 choice in the near future. Richard was in the first team at the age of 17, just before the club was relegated from the Premiership, but he played a significant part in helping Ipswich regain top-flight status, keeping a record number of clean sheets along the way. Just as he did on his England debut, he saved a penalty in the 2000 play-off final at Wembley against Barnsley, and there was relief all round when he pledged his future to the club shortly afterwards. Assured performances during the 2000-01 campaign led to his inclusion in Sven-Goran Eriksson's first squads, but it came as a massive blow when he announced his departure for Arsenal, in a bid to lay claim to the England No.1 shirt.

at the prospect of taking on Alan Curbishley's team. The first game was a disaster for Jamie Clapham, if only for the fact that he turned a 12th-minute cross past his own keeper.

There was no further scoring and the anticipated football classic instead deteriorated into a niggly, disjointed affair that saw nine players cautioned and the visitors' former Norwich defender, Danny Mills, dismissed. Tempers continued to flare even after the final whistle and Mauricio Taricco had blood pouring from a nose wound after an alleged clash in the players' lounge area with opposition winger, Neil Heaney.

Charlton had gone 12 hours without conceding a goal and for the must-win second leg George Burley opted for Gus Uhlenbeek's pace, axing Clapham from the starting line-up. An outstanding Shaun Newton goal after 36 minutes was enough to put Charlton firmly in control and as the game wore on it became increasingly obvious that there was going to be no way back for Town. They were destined for First Division football for at least another season.

Ironically, Ipswich had beaten Charlton over two games to launch their Coca-Cola Cup campaign, before seeing off Torquay to set up a third round visit from Manchester United, who fielded a weakened side and whose manager, Alex Ferguson, did not seem over-concerned when they were beaten 2-0, Town's second goal on the stroke of half-time being a wonder strike by Mauricio Taricco. It needed an extra-time winner from Tony Mowbray to overcome Oxford at the Manor Ground and Ipswich's next opponents, with some people starting to talk about a possible Wembley appearance, were Chelsea.

Town performed gallantly to hold the Premiership side to a 2-2 draw and would have probably edged through to the last four had substitute Bobby Petta scored from a 112th-minute chance when he had only visiting keeper Ed de Goey to beat rather than struck an upright. Ipswich, who had played the better football, seemed to lose their nerve in the penalty shoot-out while the big-money visitors confidently converted their spot-kicks.

Town needed a replay to eliminate Bristol Rovers at the third round stage of the FA Cup, then Sheffield United held them at Portman Road in the fourth when Dean Saunders netted on the rebound eight minutes from the end after his penalty was pushed out by Richard Wright. David Johnson had put Ipswich ahead, but in the Bramall Lane replay he cracked a 42nd-minute penalty against a post, an expensive error since Don Hutchison had converted from the spot after 13 minutes and that was enough to see the Blades advance into the last 16.

Chapter Fourteen: 1998-2001
Push for the Premiership

The most significant event of the 1998 close season saw Bryan Hamilton depart from Portman Road. Having been offered a two-year contract to continue as first team coach, he decided instead to accept a three-year deal with arch-rivals Norwich, where his role was to assist new boss Bruce Rioch and to oversee the club's academy set-up. What might have been a major upheaval was avoided, however, as George Burley turned to fellow countryman Stewart Houston, a former Manchester United and Scotland player, to take over. Best known for his part in Arsenal's success when he was Highbury boss George Graham's right-hand man, he also had a spell as the Gunners' stand-in manager and a brief stint in charge of QPR under his belt.

A trio of free transfer signings – untried youngsters Sean Friars and Terry Bowes from Liverpool and Arsenal, together with Dutch left-back Marco Holster from Heracles – confirmed Town were in no position to spend big money on new recruits. They released Geraint Williams, but were rocked by the departure of Gus Uhlenbeek after a remarkable turnaround. Having rejoined his colleagues for pre-season training at Orwell Park School, the out-of-contract Dutchman confirmed he had agreed a new deal with manager George Burley and was all set to commit himself to Town.

But the *Evening Star* quickly had to change its first edition story when a fax arrived from Portman Road stating that Uhlenbeek was, in fact, going to join Fulham. The player later explained that a call from Craven Cottage boss Kevin Keegan on his mobile telephone, during a break in training, led to his dramatic change of mind and saw him head for London and the Second Division champions-to-be, where he confirmed the salary on offer was greater than he would have earned by staying at Ipswich.

When Ipswich did decide it was necessary to enter the transfer market, it was a few weeks into the season when they spent a modest £50,000 on defender Manuel Thetis, a Frenchman who had been playing in Spain with Seville. Goals were in short supply at the start of the campaign as Town completed a hat-trick of successive goalless draws and then lost 2-0 at home to Sunderland, leaving them in 18th position. Richard Wright saved a penalty in the opening game at Grimsby, which was to prove new boy

Holster's only senior start of the entire campaign, but the goalkeeper was perhaps fortunate to remain on the field after his challenge on Lee Nogan.

Ex-Town defender Chris Swailes relished his return with Bury and helped them to earn a point and, in the third 0-0 stalemate, the woodwork denied both Mick Stockwell and Mark Venus at Portsmouth. Three headers saw Town win comfortably at Port Vale and they scored three times in four games on the trot, also beating Bradford and Bristol City and drawing at Oxford when Thetis made his first appearance in a 3-3 draw.

An unfortunate 1-0 defeat at Vicarage Road, when Ipswich outplayed Watford but lost to a fifth-minute penalty conceded by Richard Wright, was followed by three straight wins in which Town did not concede a goal and climbed to third in the table. The sequence was ended when Norwich triumphed by the only goal at Portman Road in a game Kieron Dyer missed through injury. His midfield place went to on-loan Arsenal player Paolo Vernazza, who was in turn replaced by another loanee, Jonathan Hunt from Derby. Ipswich had sold Danny Sonner to Sheffield Wednesday for £75,000, the figure stipulated in his contract, and pulled in a further £400,000 when striker Alex Mathie, no longer guaranteed a regular place, returned north of the border to join Dundee United.

It was felt the two departures would be enough to balance the books, but after three successive wins over Stockport, West Brom and Wolves, which saw Town move into second place behind leaders Sunderland, came the bombshell news that the board had negotiated a £1.775 million deal to take Mauricio Taricco to Tottenham, a move in which Charlie Woods, having quit Portman Road to become Spurs' new chief scout a few months earlier, had undoubtedly played a part. There was uproar among supporters with whom Taricco was a firm favourite, and chairman David Sheepshanks struggled to placate them, insisting the club had no choice but to sell as their bankers demanded a rising overdraft had to be substantially reduced.

The fans may have felt there was a glimmer of hope when Taricco suffered an ankle injury in the closing stages of his 170th and final game, at home to Wolves, that saw his transfer temporarily shelved. Supporters were waving 'Don't go Mauricio' banners as David Johnson's 89th-minute goal earned a point in a 2-2 draw at Huddersfield, a game that saw Mick Stockwell limp off and require an ankle operation. The fans' protests were in vain, however, and the deal was eventually concluded. The Wolves game was also memorable for goalkeeper Richard Wright, who attended the birth of his first child, Harry, that afternoon and then made it a double celebration with a clean sheet, one of 26 he kept for Town that season.

50 Greatest Players

MAURICIO TARICCO   Defender

Joined Ipswich Town: 1995   **From:** Argentinos Juniors

Debut: v Bolton Wanderers, 9 September 1994, League

Appearances: 170   **Goals:** 7

Left Ipswich Town: 9 November 1998   **For:** Tottenham Hotspur

Mauricio, the first Argentinian player to represent the club, proved to be one of the bargain buys of all time when he was spotted during a scouting trip to South America by then manager John Lyall and recruited at a cost of just £175,000. He took time to settle in England, often pleading for a first-team chance after George Burley arrived as manager, but he had to be patient before eventually breaking into the side and only then after it seemed he was destined to return home. Equally at home in either full-back position, he quickly won over the supporters with his wholehearted approach and he showed no lack of enterprise or skill going forward. The measure of his popularity with the fans was demonstrated when he won their annual Player of the Year poll in 1998. The same people whose votes earned him the accolade were up in arms when he was sold to Spurs for what seemed a cut-price £1.775 million, the club explaining that they were forced into the deal for financial reasons. Mauricio did well at White Hart Lane until a pelvic injury curtailed his progress early in the 2000-01 season.

Taricco's departure and Stockwell's injury paved the way for John Kennedy's introduction to the first team, while the lack of cash at manager George Burley's disposal was further emphasised by the loan signings of West Ham pair Lee Hodges and Samassi Abou. The latter plugged the gap while David Johnson underwent a cartilage operation, but Town's attacking options suffered another blow when James Scowcroft was carried off with a broken collar bone in a home defeat by Barnsley.

It was in the next game, when Richard Naylor's late goal sealed a 2-1 win at Sheffield United, that youngster Titus Bramble demonstrated his immense potential as he appeared on the scene for the first time and Town remained second until successive defeats, at home by Grimsby and at Sunderland, saw them drop to fifth place. Dutch full-back Fabian Wilnis, who cost £200,000 from De Graafschap, made his debut against the Mariners, while yet another loanee, Jim Magilton from Sheffield Wednesday, made his bow at the Stadium of Light. Town used the loan system to bring in another new face, Marlon Harewood from Nottingham Forest, to fill in for the absent Scowcroft, but another double blow was just around the corner.

Changes Behind the Scenes

Stewart Houston could not reject the opportunity to once again team up with George Graham at Tottenham, creating a vacancy that John Gorman, out of work since leaving his post as assistant manager of England in the wake of Glenn Hoddle's departure, agreed to fill. But in Gorman's first game, a 3-2 home win over Watford, an injury to the scorer of the first goal Kieron Dyer proved costly. It later transpired that he had a cracked left fibula, suffered in an earlier challenge with Micah Hyde, and Dyer claimed a new Football League record as the first player to score with a broken leg.

Manuel Thetis, whose first goal for the club had beaten Tranmere a fortnight earlier, also scored the only goal away at West Bromwich Albion, but had to suffer the indignity of being the first Ipswich player to be sent off that season after he got involved in a dust-up with Sean Flynn. Town finalised a £682,500 deal for Jim Magilton and their casualties were all back in time for the run-in, only for vital points to be dropped as they managed just two wins in their last six games and surrendered the second automatic promotion spot to Bradford.

It meant that Town were in the play-offs for the third year in a row and this time their opponents were sixth-placed Bolton, who scored six minutes from the end of the first leg at the Reebok Stadium. It was to prove to be a precious lead as Kieron Dyer's last-gasp header at Portman Road made it 2-1 and took the second leg into extra-time. Bob Taylor's second goal restored the visitors' advantage and Matt Holland's strike four minutes from the end was not enough to prevent Ipswich's heartache as they lost on the away goals rule.

Town's interest in both cup competitions was brief. In the Worthington Cup they drew 1-1 at Exeter in the first round, first leg, and completed the job with a convincing 5-1 victory in the return game. Substitute Paul Mason cracked in Town's fifth, which seemed significant since he was out of contract and had been promised a new deal if he could prove his fitness, but it was not enough to convince George Burley and Mason, who had made a habit of scoring special goals, was soon being told his services were no longer required.

Second Division Luton were Ipswich's next opponents, a 2-1 first leg lead proving insufficient as they were sent packing after extra-time at Kenilworth Road on a night when Richard Wright looked a pale shadow of the England goalkeeper he was to become. In the FA Cup, an own goal by John McGreal gifted Town victory in a third round tie at Tranmere and they returned to Merseyside in the fourth round, losing 1-0 at Everton.

Kieron Dyer's immediate reaction, within hours of the play-off knock out by Bolton, was to insist he was staying at Portman Road, but another 24 hours on and it emerged that he was on his way. The club insisted he asked for a transfer and issued a press release to that effect, but the player and his representatives argued that they had only requested to be kept informed of interest from the Premiership, of which there was plenty. When it came to matching Ipswich's £6 million valuation, however, it was Ruud Gullit and Newcastle United who took the plunge while others hesitated and what may have seemed an expensive gamble quickly proved to be a sound investment as Dyer established himself both in the top flight and with England, which guaranteed Town a further £500,000 payment.

George Burley invested some of the Dyer windfall immediately, spending £750,000 on John McGreal from Tranmere and £500,000 on Crewe Alexandra midfielder Jermaine Wright, who put Town ahead of an alternative move to Nottingham Forest. Burley, who had released Jason Cundy, also brought in experienced goalkeeper Mike Salmon from Charlton after out-of-contract Lee Bracey accepted an offer from Hull City. Swedish striker Jonas Axeldahl, who had been playing in Italy, was also recruited on

50 Greatest Players

KIERON DYER   **Midfielder**

Joined Ipswich Town: July 1995   **From:** School

Debut: v Crystal Palace, 26 December 1996, League

Appearances: 113   **Goals:** 12

Left Ipswich Town: July 1999   **For:** Newcastle United

Youth product Kieron was an instant hit with Town supporters who loved his effervescent style, revelling in situations where he could run at opponents and use his pace and trickery. He quickly became a fixture in the first team, although his versatility meant he played as a wing-back on either flank before settling down in a central midfield role. It was not long before he was at the centre of transfer speculation, his consistency earning him England squad recognition during Glenn Hoddle's time in charge, and he departed for Newcastle in a deal worth £6 million in July 1999. Ipswich pocketed a further £500,000 as a result of him gaining senior international honours under Kevin Keegan, to go with those at youth, Under-21 and B levels, and he was again selected by a third England boss, Sven-Goran Eriksson, although injury forced him to withdraw. Such has been his impact at Newcastle that there have been links with other clubs, including Leeds United and Manchester United, and his transfer value has soared to the £20 million mark.

a free transfer, while Bobby Petta confirmed what many had suspected for some months, that he would be on the move when his contract expired, when he agreed a lucrative deal with Glasgow giants Celtic.

Another major change saw first team coach John Gorman reject an offer to stay on at Portman Road and this time the club did not have to look far for a replacement, as experienced defender Tony Mowbray, who had made no secret of his desire to become a coach, jumped at the chance to launch a new chapter of his career. Club legend John Wark, who had been obviously disappointed to be overlooked the previous year when Colin Suggett replaced Charlie Woods as chief scout, which left him with only a part-time scouting role, also decided to move on and was appointed chief scout of First Division Portsmouth.

50 Greatest Players

TONY MOWBRAY   **Defender**

Joined Ipswich Town: 6 October, 1995   **From:** Celtic

Debut: v Wolves, 7 October 1995, League

Appearances: 152   **Goals:** 8

Left Ipswich Town: 30 June 2000 (became first team coach)

George Burley's determination to sign Tony in a £300,000 deal paid handsome dividends, even if his early progress at Portman Road was blighted by injury problems. Quickly installed as club captain, the inspirational defender proved a massive influence on those around him as he regained full fitness and became a defensive rock.

Tony was a player to whom others looked up, as much for his strong personality as his leadership qualities or what he had already achieved in a career that started with local club Middlesbrough, with whom he gained England B honours, and performances that earned him cult status at Celtic.

He was the manager's first choice to become the new first team coach at Portman Road in the summer of 1999 and was recalled early in the season that followed, his presence giving the side a defensive stability. He could hardly have made more of an impact, rallying his team-mates for a determined promotion push, and he rounded off the campaign in style when he headed a vital goal in the play-off final defeat of Barnsley at Wembley. That proved to be a fitting farewell to Tony the player as he concentrated on his coaching responsibilities in Town's first season back in the Premiership, warranting a large slice of the credit for the way Ipswich performed upon their return to the top flight.

The Road to Glory

Town's new-look side were the early-season leaders of the First Division, with a six-game unbeaten run that saw them rattle in 17 goals for the loss of only six, but the sequence was ended when Manuel Thetis was punished for a tackle on Stan Lazaridis just ten minutes into the home clash with Birmingham City and Paul Furlong scored the only goal from the spot. Ipswich paid £800,000 to Blackburn for former England Under-21 defender Gary Croft and he was an instant hero with the winning goal on his debut against Manchester City.

Within days, however, he was making headlines for all the wrong reasons, when it was revealed he had been arrested for a string of motoring offences and attempting to pervert the course of justice. Croft was jailed for three months on 10 December and, after his release the following month, made history as the first professional to wear an electronic tag in games. He was not the only player in trouble with the authorities and when Adam Tanner heaped further shame on the club by being convicted of drink-driving, Town responded by telling him he was finished at Portman Road. Tanner, banned by the FA three years earlier after a drugs test found traces of cocaine, revealed he had been receiving treatment at the same clinic where England star Paul Merson battled against drink, drug and gambling problems in 1994.

A 2-1 defeat at Grimsby was followed by another, 4-1 at home to QPR, in which Jim Magilton was sent off, and manager George Burley made the decision to give player-coach Tony Mowbray his first start of the season in the home clash with Charlton, which resulted in a 4-2 victory. David Johnson was on target in that game and the following day flew to Scotland to meet Craig Brown, who had been alerted to the Town player's availability. Despite having played for his native Jamaica and the England B team, because his appearances were all in friendly games his international future had not been resolved. He had been called up by Wales, but failed to appear because of injury and it was an embarrassing episode for all concerned when, having pledged his future to the Scots, it became apparent that he was not eligible after all.

Nothing, however, was to divert Town's promotion bid off course and they put together an 18-game unbeaten league run, at the tail end of which supporters had a brand new hero. Fans had been speculating for some time about the identity of George Burley's latest transfer target, especially when the Ipswich boss revealed he was poised to spend a new record fee on the mystery man, and eventually it transpired that Huddersfield's Marcus

Martijn Reuser, a former Ajax player and capped once by Holland, made an immediate impact, scoring on his debut in the match against Fulham.

Stewart was the player he wanted. The Yorkshire club's initial reluctance to accept Town's £2.5 million bid – with a further £250,000 to follow if Stewart helped bring Premiership football to Portman Road – was understandable, since they were also involved in the promotion race, and it was a major surprise when they eventually agreed to sell to one of their closest rivals.

The deal, financed by the cash surplus remaining from Kieron Dyer's departure seven months earlier, showed that Ipswich meant business and Stewart could hardly have asked for a better start with his new employers. A goal on his debut in a 2-0 win at Barnsley was followed by the winner against former club Huddersfield, just seven days later as he made a memorable first appearance at Portman Road.

50 Greatest Players

MARCUS STEWART   Forward

Joined Ipswich Town: 1 February 2000   **From:** Huddersfield Town

Debut: v Barnsley, 5 February 2000, League

Appearances: 54*   **Goals:** 26*

*up to summer 2001

Marcus was an instant favourite with Ipswich fans when he scored on his debut at Barnsley and then netted the winner in a 2-1 defeat at home to his former club Huddersfield. An England schoolboy cap who started his career with local club Bristol Rovers, he scored twice in the first leg of the play-off semi-final at Bolton and was also on target in the final at Wembley as Ipswich booked their return to the Premiership. That meant a further £250,000 was on its way to Huddersfield, as part of the transfer agreement, but it was obvious that Town had landed themselves a real bargain when he was in sizzling form for much of the 2000-01 campaign. As one of the country's leading marksmen – he was even the Premiership's top scorer for a while – he was linked with an England call-up. But for a late injury he would probably have improved upon his excellent 21-goal tally.

At first, it seemed that David Johnson and Marcus Stewart would hit it off together, but after his initial burst, the club's record signing never managed to find the net again as he struggled with both injuries and a loss of form. Bogey team Crewe Alexandra were beaten at Portman Road before Town managed just two points from five games, the last in that horror sequence being a 2-0 home defeat by Norwich, who had caretaker boss Bryan Hamilton in charge for the first time.

Ipswich arrested the slide by winning at Tranmere and then it was time for a fresh injection of talent in the shape of Dutch loanee Martijn Reuser, a former Ajax player who had been capped once by Holland and who had been back on loan at the Amsterdam giants from Vitesse Arnhem when Town's Euro scout, Romeo Zondervan, decided he had something to offer. Reuser's debut as a substitute saw him score the only goal against Fulham in the 90th minute and he was to prove something of a lucky mascot, even if Ipswich missed out yet again on automatic promotion, pipped by Manchester City, despite taking 15 points from their last six games.

And so to the play-offs for the fourth year in a row, with Town again being pitted against Bolton, the team who had shattered their promotion dream 12 months earlier. When Ipswich were 2-0 down at the Reebok Stadium inside the first 26 minutes, and both Tony Mowbray and David Johnson had been forced to withdraw through injury, they seemed to be on their way out again. But Marcus Stewart's long-range strike brought them back into it before the break and the same player struck again after 65 minutes to level the score. Town finished well on top, although they also had to be grateful to goalkeeper Richard Wright for an excellent save to thwart Claus Jensen when the Dane was clean through.

The headline of the Ipswich Evening Star *of Thursday 18 May 2000 says it all as Town's fans celebrate victory over Barnsley in the First Division Play-off semi-final.*

Great Matches

FIRST DIVISION PLAY-OFF FINAL

Wembley Stadium, London, 29 May 2000

Ipswich Town 4   **Barnsley 2**   **Attendance: 73,427**

Mowbray
Naylor
Stewart
Reuser

Hignett 2 (1 pen)

Tears of joy ran down the cheeks of Ipswich players and supporters alike as they celebrated the realization of a Premiership dream. Having failed at the semi-final stage of the play-offs in the three previous seasons, there was no denying the all-round relief that a return ticket to the big-time was finally theirs. The atmosphere was electric – better, even, than the FA Cup final of 1978 according to some observers lucky enough to have been present each time.

It was to be a nerve-racking afternoon for both sides although the Yorkshire club made the more promising start, taking a seventh-minute lead. Barnsley's No.1 danger man, Craig Hignett, let fly with a long-distance drive that beat Richard Wright, came down off the underside of the bar and rebounded off the hapless keeper into the net. David Johnson was replaced by Naylor midway through the first half and within six minutes Town were level, player-coach Tony Mowbray rising at the far post to head home from a Jim Magilton corner.

On the stroke of half-time, goalkeeper Wright was penalised for a challenge on Hignett, but he regained his composure to keep out Darren Barnard's spot-kick.

Seven minutes after the restart Naylor put Ipswich in front and they were well in command when Marcus Stewart headed a Jamie Clapham cross past Barnsley keeper Kevin Miller in the 58th minute to make the score 3-1. The Tykes reduced the leeway after 77 minutes when Mowbray fouled Geoff Thomas in the area and Hignett succeeded where Barnard failed, from the spot. They were denied an equaliser seven minutes later, thanks to Wright's fabulous save from a close-in header by Georgi Hristov.

In the closing stages, Martijn Reuser broke clear to smash the ball high past Miller and any fears that Barnsley could force the game into extra-time quickly evaporated. The scenes that followed will live long in the memory of those present as Town finally put years of heartbreak behind them and launched themselves into a promotion party.

Ipswich Town: R. Wright, McGreal, Mowbray, Venus, Croft, J. Wright (Wilnis), Magilton, Holland, Clapham, Johnson (Naylor), Stewart (Reuser).

Barnsley: Miller, Curtis (Eaden), Chettle, Morgan, Barnard, Brown, Hignett, Tinkler (Thomas), Appleby, Shipperley, Dyer (Hristov).

Referee: T. Heilbron (Co. Durham).

The return game was one of the most remarkable ever played at Portman Road and on a night of almost unbearable tension Town triumphed 5-3 thanks to extra-time goals by Jamie Clapham and Martijn Reuser after Jim Magilton had claimed his first senior hat-trick and Bolton were reduced to nine men. Ipswich had finally negotiated the play-off semis at the fourth time of asking and were Wembley-bound to meet Barnsley in the last club game at the famous old stadium before the bulldozers were due to move in.

Town sold over 37,000 tickets for what developed into another nail-biter. Town fell behind after only six minutes and David Johnson was an early casualty, but once Tony Mowbray levelled and Richard Wright saved a penalty he conceded just before the break, they gradually overpowered Dave Bassett's team to win 4-2 and clinch their long-awaited Premiership return.

If the scenes at Wembley brought a tear to the eye, the open-top bus parade to a packed Cornhill was every bit as emotional and revived memories of how supporters had celebrated the FA Cup and UEFA Cup victories. For chairman David Sheepshanks, five years at the helm and now leading the club back to the big-time, the moment had finally arrived when he could stand on the Town Hall balcony and scream: 'We are Premier League!'

50 Greatest Players

HERMANN HREIDARSSON   Defender

Joined Ipswich Town: 17 August 2000   **From:** Wimbledon

Debut: v Tottenham Hotspur, 19 August 2000, League

Appearances: 45*   **Goals:** 1*

*up to summer 2001

Hermann proved another astute, value-for-money signing by Ipswich boss George Burley, who handed over a club record fee of £4 million to Wimbledon in order to bolster his squad prior to the return to the Premiership. The powerful Icelandic international had been relegated with both the Dons and Crystal Palace – he also had a spell with Brentford in the Second Division – but he looked a class act from day one. A superb athlete with a powerful left foot, Hermann showed he had plenty to offer, whether in his more accustomed position in the centre of defence or at left-back, where his surging runs were often the launching pad for many a Town goal. Strong in the air and also quick off the mark, his value soared on the back of his performances during an excellent first season at Portman Road and there were no objections when it came to handing over the £500,000 bonus promised to Wimbledon if Hermann helped the club to retain its top-flight status.

Back with the Big Boys

Ipswich wasted no time in preparing for their Premiership return and negotiated a £1 million fee to clinch the permanent transfer of Dutch star Martijn Reuser. They also returned to Holland and recruited teenage prospects Nabil Abidallah and Guillermo Graaven from Ajax, much to the annoyance of the Amsterdam club, which represented something of a coup as neither player had committed himself and Town were perfectly within their rights in snapping up the duo.

Experienced former England defender John Scales was also snapped up on a free transfer from Tottenham, but Ipswich lost out to Charlton for Bolton star Claus Jensen, after both clubs had agreed a £4 million fee, and also failed to persuade Moroccan international Hassan Kachloul to move from Southampton. They did, however, shatter their transfer record to spend £4 million on Icelandic international defender Hermann Hreidarsson from Wimbledon on the eve of the new campaign.

Long-serving utility player Mick Stockwell was released, and Marco Holster and Manuel Thetis departed before the end of the season. Town boss George Burley and all his players made no apologies for emphasising that to finish fourth bottom, and thereby avoiding what most

50 Greatest Players

MICK STOCKWELL   Midfielder

Joined Ipswich Town: July 1981   **From:** School

Debut: v Coventry City, 26 December 1985, League

Appearances: 611   **Goals:** 44

Left Ipswich Town: June 2000   **For:** Colchester United

Little could Mick have realised, when he arrived at Portman Road straight from school soon after Ipswich had won the UEFA Cup in 1981, that he would eventually complete 19 seasons with the club. His versatility was one of his greatest assets and he played full-back, wing-back, midfield and even, during an injury crisis, as a striker. Mick joined a long list of heroes when he was voted the supporters' Player of the Year in 1993. Hard-working and athletic, he qualified for a testimonial and the man who originally signed him, Bobby Robson, brought Porto to Ipswich for the game. Sadly for Mick, he was released as Town regained their Premiership status and he followed the well-worn route to Colchester United, quickly establishing himself as a favourite with Layer Road fans who warmed to his wholehearted approach. Mick finished his first season with the Essex club as their top scorer with 11 goals.

experts regarded as inevitable relegation, would be an excellent achievement, and there were a number of encouraging signs as a new era dawned, not least in pre-season home games against AZ Alkmaar and Fiorentina.

Far from having to woo support, the club found themselves turning away potential customers and for 9,000 season ticket applicants there was only disappointment. But Ipswich responded to the problem of limited accommodation by pressing ahead with plans to erect a new South Stand, part of which was in use prior to the end of the 2000-01 season, and then to replace the North Stand, work on which started immediately after the season was over, as part of a multi-million pound redevelopment scheme aimed at giving Portman Road a brand-new look and boosting capacity to beyond the 30,000 mark.

On the opening day of the season the Town coach was stuck in traffic and it took a call from John Scales to the secretary at White Hart Lane, who in turn arranged a police escort, to prevent what could have been an embarrassing return to the Premiership. Mark Venus scored the first top-flight goal of the new campaign to give Ipswich a flying start, but Tottenham took advantage of defensive slackness by the visitors to emerge 3-1 victors. Town's first home game was against Manchester United, the reigning champions, and Fabian Wilnis scored a magnificent opener, later cancelled out by David Beckham's cunning free-kick.

There was plenty of praise, however, for Ipswich's performance, not least from United boss Sir Alex Ferguson, who declared: 'If they continue to play like that they will not go down.' A home win over Sunderland followed three days later, courtesy of a wonderful solo goal by defensive giant Titus Bramble, and those who felt successive defeats at Leicester and at home to Aston Villa signalled the end of Town's encouraging start to life back in the Premiership were quickly eating their words. Slovenian international defender Amir Karic, spotted by George Burley during a scouting trip to Euro 2000, was on board by this time following a £700,000 move from Maribor.

A shock 2-1 success at Leeds was the first of nine away wins – only Leeds and Manchester United could boast as many – as Ipswich confounded their critics in spectacular style, winning friends up and down the country for their enterprising play. Starting with that win at Elland Road, they went on a six-game unbeaten run and then lost only three times in their next ten Premiership fixtures, reaching the turn of the year with some impressive results, including a 1-0 win at Liverpool.

It was at Anfield that Alun Armstrong made his debut after a £500,000 move from Middlesbrough and he was to prove to be an outstanding bargain as he contributed seven Premiership goals by the end of the season. But the scoring honours went to Marcus Stewart, at one time the top-flight's leading marksman and touted for England honours as he found the net in seven games on the trot, and ended with a total of 21 in all competitions. That tally may have been greater but for injury and suspension, as he was forced to serve a three-game ban following his dismissal in the home defeat by Leeds. To compensate for his absence, Town signed Celtic striker Mark Burchill on loan to the end of the season, at which point they decided against making the move permanent.

Defying the Critics

Town survived a spell of five successive defeats, three of them in the league to Chelsea, Leeds and Arsenal, before finding their feet again and re-entering the transfer market, selling David Johnson to Nottingham Forest for £3 million and recruiting full-back Chris Makin from Sunderland in a £1.25 million deal. Bobby Robson was given a magnificent welcome back to Portman Road, but there was no happy return as his Newcastle side were beaten 1-0, a result that kept Ipswich, unbelievably, on course for a Champions League place as they entered the last lap of what had long since been described as a fairytale season.

Unfortunately, a 2-1 defeat at Charlton saw them lose valuable ground, but they still went into their final game, at Derby, along with Liverpool and Leeds as contenders to join Manchester United and Arsenal in the biggest club tournament of them all. Town recorded their only away draw of the season at Pride Park, but even a victory would not have been enough, although it said much about their season that some supporters were still disappointed at having to make do with a UEFA Cup slot.

A remarkable campaign in which Ipswich finished fifth and returned to Europe for the first time in 19 years was reflected by George Burley being crowned Manager of the Year, which earned him a new five-year contract. Burley said: 'We have exceeded all expectations – including our own. It is no secret that we began the season thinking that finishing 17th would be a fantastic achievement, so to qualify for Europe has been nothing short of phenomenal.'

It was a season when so many players grasped the opportunity to show they could perform at the highest level, when manager George Burley's shrewd transfer market dealings paid handsome dividends and when the club's collective spirit shone through on a regular basis. Far from being an

Great Managers – 1994-present

GEORGE BURLEY

Such was Town's impact during the 2000-01 season that many observers feel George Burley is destined to become the most successful manager in the club's history. A tall order, when you consider the achievements of Alf Ramsey and Bobby Robson, but Burley, the first ex-Ipswich player to take charge of the club, appears to have all the right credentials.

He inherited a hopeless task in 1994 and relegation six months later took no one by surprise. But it is the way he has hauled the club back from the brink, with solid backing from upstairs, that has been impressive.

There is more than a hint of Robson in Burley – hardly surprising, given their time together at Portman Road – and he appears to have inherited his mentor's eye for a bargain in the transfer market, always a useful managerial trait. Burley literally talked himself into the job. There were other, far more experienced applicants, but the directors liked his determination to succeed and were sold on his vision for the club when they interviewed him.

Maybe his achievements north of the border with Ayr United and in just six months at nearby Colchester United could best be described as modest, but Ipswich presented Burley with a true test of his skills as a manager and he has passed with flying colours. A model of consistency as a player, he is devoted to Ipswich, but may well find himself in the same situation as Robson did more than once, in being a target for more glamorous clubs. Still only 45, his best years in management may yet be ahead of him and Town wisely invested in his talents by awarding him a deal that ties him to the club until 2006. Do not be surprised, however, if he stays on a lot longer than that.

overnight success, Ipswich reaped the rewards for their long-term planning and chairman David Sheepshanks insisted: 'Continuous improvement is the order of the day. We will not get carried away, but I believe it is realistic to be planning to establish Ipswich Town in the top half of the Premiership with genuine ambitions of European football year on year.'

It was their 'all for one' attitude, more than anything else, that carried them through, players visibly growing in confidence as one good result generally followed another, and although their interest in the FA Cup was short-lived, a win over Morecambe being followed by defeat at Sunderland, they were close to making the final of the Worthington Cup. Having disposed of Millwall, Arsenal, Coventry and Manchester City, they faced Birmingham over two legs at the semi-final stage. They took a narrow 1-0 lead to St Andrews, but their hopes of making the final at the Millennium Stadium in Cardiff were sunk in the mud as Birmingham stormed to a 4-1 success, after extra-time, to clinch a 4-2 aggregate victory.

That disappointment was soon forgotten, however, and Town's status in the Premiership enabled them to secure a new shirt sponsorship deal with Ipswich-based energy company TXU Europe, worth a basic £4 million over three years, but with performance incentives that could take the total to £7 million.

As manager George Burley continued to plan for the future, he signed Spanish star Pablo Counago on a free transfer from Celta Vigo after seeing him score twice for the Spanish Under-21 side against England. He also looked to have succeeded, at last, in persuading Hassan Kachloul to join Town after his contract at Southampton expired, but having given his word the Moroccan changed his mind and instead moved to Aston Villa.

There was further disappointment for supporters when they learned that goalkeeper Richard Wright was joining Arsenal for £5 million. It was explained that Wright had only agreed to sign a new contract if it included a clause agreeing he could talk to any of three nominated clubs, one of which was Arsenal, should they match the stipulated valuation. Anxious to pursue his international career, and convinced he would have more chance of doing so at Highbury than at Portman Road, Wright seized the opportunity. The blow of losing Wright, who had been compared to the legendary Gordon Banks by Burley, was cushioned, however, as Town snapped up Andy Marshall from neighbours Norwich, where he had been crowned Player of the Year, but decided against renewing his contract.

Marshall's arrival was followed by the club's investment in promising young defender Chris Hogg, the England Under-15 schoolboy captain for whom they handed over an initial £150,000 to York City. Then Burley continued his summer spending when he paid £800,000 for highly-rated Hartlepool midfielder Tommy Miller, a former schoolboy signing at Ipswich who had been released several years earlier. His next move, as the start of the new season loomed, was to spend in excess of £8 million, silencing those supporters who had voiced their concern at the club's lack of big-money transfer activity.

Protracted negotiations were finally concluded for 30-year-old Nigerian winger Finidi George, a European Cup winner with Ajax in 1995 who cost in excess of £3 million from Spanish club Real Mallorca. Then Burley took everyone by surprise when he decided to bring in a new goalkeeper. His first target was Derby's Estonian international, Mart Poom, but the Rams rejected Town's £4.5 million bid and Burley instead switched his attention to Matteo Sereni of Italian Serie B club Sampdoria, for whom he paid a new club record fee of £5 million. Still he wasn't finished and Argentinian midfielder Sixto Peralta arrived on a season-long loan from Inter Milan, while Danish Under-21 player Thomas Gaardsoe, also a midfielder, took Burley's pre-season spending to £10 million when he was signed from Aalborg. Ipswich went a long way towards balancing the books when they took their summer transfer income to £8 million by selling James Scowcroft to Leicester City, long-term admirers of the home-grown former England Under-21 star, in a £3 million deal. And so ended a hectic round of transfers that had seen eight players of six different nationalities introduced into an increasingly cosmopolitan squad. As the new North Stand began to take shape and the 2001-2002 campaign got under way, chairman David Sheepshanks stressed: 'If I say I'd be happy to finish in the top half, it sounds unambitious. But I'd be very satisfied if that's what we did. It would mean that we had really managed to establish ourselves. The UEFA Cup is very exciting, and we will go for it, don't you worry, but the Premiership is the be-all and end-all. People would rightly say that I'm nuts if I said we could actually win it in the next year or two, but in a few years' time, why not?' On 30 August 2001 Sheepshanks hosted a UEFA Cup reunion to mark the 20th anniversary of one of the club's most memorable successes, reassembling manager Bobby Robson and the other heroes of 1981.

Recalling the early stages of his eventful reign as chairman, he said: 'The old joke about Ipswich was that the only boardroom crisis was if the white wine ran out, but that wore very thin. We had to wear our ambition on our sleeve. People kept grumbling that nothing was as good as in Robson's day, but we had to turn the past into a springboard, not a millstone.' His five-year plan duly fulfilled, Sheepshanks and manager Burley were in no mood for self-congratulation. Instead they simply set themselves and the club new targets, which may once have been regarded as out of range but now appear very much within Ipswich's grasp.

Finidi George became an instant hero, scoring twice on his debut against Derby County.

The Ipswich Town Directory

Club Information

- Formed in 1878 as the Ipswich Association FC to distinguish it from the Ipswich Football Club who played rugby. The two clubs amalgamated in 1888 and rugby was dropped in 1893
- Joined Norfolk & Suffolk League in 1899
- Turned professional on 1st May 1936
- Elected to Football League in 1938
- Ground: Portman Road, Ipswich, Suffolk IP1 2DA
- Tel: 01473 400500 Fax: 01473 400040
- Website: www.itfc.co.uk

Honours

- League Division 1 champions: 1961-62
- Runners-up: 1980-81, 1981-82
- Division 1 Play-off winners: 1999-2000
- Division 2 champions: 1960-61, 1967-68, 1991-92
- Division 3 (South) champions: 1953-54, 1956-57
- FA Cup winners: 1978
- Football League Cup semi-finalists: 1981-82, 1984-85
- Texaco Cup winners: 1972-1973
- European Cup: 1962-63 (1st Rd)
- European Cup-Winners' Cup: 1978-79 (3rd Rd)
- UEFA Cup winners: 1980-81
- UEFA Cup: 1973-74 (quarter-finals); 1974-75 (1st Rd); 1975-76 (2nd Rd); 1977-78 (3rd Rd); 1979-80 (2nd Rd); 1980-81 (winners); 1981-82 (1st Rd); 1982-83 (1st Rd)

Records

- Record victory: 10-0 v Floriana (H) European Cup Preliminary Rd 2nd leg, 25 September 1962
- Record league win: 7-0 v Portsmouth (H) Division 2, 7 November 1964; 7-0 v Southampton (H) Division 1, 2 February 1974; 7-0 v W.B.A. (H) Division 1, 6 November 1976
- Record FA Cup win: 11-0 v Cromer (H) 3rd Qualifying Rd, 31 October 1936
- Record defeat: 1-10 v Fulham (A) Division 1, 26 December 1963
- Most points gained in a season (2pts): 64, Division 3 (South), 1953-54, 1956-57
- Most points gained in a season (3pts): 87, Division 1, 1999-00
- Most league goals in season: 106, Division 3 (South), 1955-56
- Highest league scorer in season: Ted Phillips, 41, Division 3 (South), 1956-57
- Most senior appearances: Mick Mills, 737 (1966-1982)
- Most league goals: Ray Crawford 204 (1958-63 and 1966-69)
- Most league goals in a game: 5, Alan Brazil v Southampton, Division 1, 16 February 1982
- Most capped player (with club): Allan Hunter, 47 for Northern Ireland
- Youngest league player: Jason Dozzell, aged 16 years 56 days v Coventry City (H), Division 1, 4 February 1984
- Oldest league player: Mick Burns, aged 43 years 219 days v Gateshead (H), FA Cup 3rd Rd, 12 January 1952
- Record signing: £5 million for Matteo Sereni from Sampdoria, August 2001
- Record sale: £6 million for Keiron Dyer to Newcastle United, July 1999
- Record attendance: 38,010 v Leeds United, FA Cup 6th Rd, 8 March 1975
- Record attendance (all-seater stadium): 25,004 v Manchester City, FA Carling Premiership, 7 May 2001
- Most first-class matches played in season: 66 (42 League, 5 FA Cup, 7 League Cup, 12 UEFA Cup) in 1980-81
- Undefeated in league matches: 23 (1979-80)
- Matches without a league win: 21 (1963-64)
- Successive league wins: 8 (1953-54)
- Successive league defeats: 10 (1954-55)

50 Greatest Players

Nothing is more likely to provoke debate among football fans than to compile a list of their club's 50 greatest players of all time. So it is with Ipswich Town, with no two supporters likely to concur. The following list is based on the authors' own personal opinions, taking into account the players' own personal qualities, achievements and length of service, and also considering the results of various fans' polls spread over a period of several years. Far from settling the argument once and for all, it is designed to spark further discussion on the subject.

No.1 Kevin Beattie (Defender) – 307 games, 32 goals. Town's best-ever player who only fell short in terms of achievement because his career was tragically cut short by injury (see page 170).

No.2 Mick Mills (Defender) – 741 games, 30 goals. Inspirational captain for club and country who played more games for Town than anyone else. Awarded the MBE for services to the game (see page 176).

No.3 John Wark (Midfielder) – 679 games, 179 goals. Versatile performer, the club's most capped Scotsman with an amazing eye for goal and an incredible record from the penalty spot (see page 202).

No.4 Bill Baxter (Defender) – 459 games, 22 goals. Outstanding athlete, player and captain, and a huge favourite with supporters after he remained loyal to Town and spanned two different eras (see page 115).

No.5 Ray Crawford (Forward) – 353 games, 227 goals. The statistics say it all about a player whose scoring record on behalf of Town will never be beaten. Also the club's first-ever England international (see page 98).

No.6 Frans Thijssen (Midfielder) – 170 games, 16 goals. Dutch international, one of the most gifted individuals ever to play for Town. His skills made him virtually impossible to dispossess (see page 178).

No.7 Arnold Muhren (Midfielder) – 214 games, 29 goals. A player of outstanding pedigree whose arrival at Portman Road signalled the dawn of an exciting and successful era (see page 175).

No.8 Allan Hunter (Defender) – 355 games, 10 goals. He enjoyed cult status with supporters who loved his often-unconventional style. Captained Northern Ireland and was revered by his team-mates (see page 171).

No.9 Terry Butcher (Defender) – 351 games, 21 goals. Captained Ipswich and England, and thought nothing of spilling blood on behalf of both (see page 192).

No.10 Paul Mariner (Forward) – 339 games, 135 goals. The complete centre-forward, his early promise with Ipswich led to international recognition and he became an England regular (see page 182).

No.11 Ted Phillips (Forward) – 293 games, 179 goals. Powerful, robust forward who formed a lethal partnership with Ray Crawford and was considered unlucky never to win England honours (see page 97).

No.12 John Elsworthy (Wing-half) – 433 games, 52 goals. Loyal one-club servant and the only player to win two Third Division (South), one Second Division and one First Division winner's medals (see page 102).

No.13 Tommy Parker (Wing-half/inside-forward) – 465 appearances, 100 goals. Captained Ipswich to their first major title and set an appearance record that stood for years (see page 73).

No.14 Jimmy Leadbetter (Winger) – 373 appearances, 49 goals. Highly influential player, the secret weapon behind the club's League Championship success in 1962 (see page 105).

No.15 George Burley (Defender) – 500 appearances, 11 goals. Classy full-back who made his debut at 17 and is the only ex-player to go on and manage the club (see page 189).

No.16 Alan Brazil (Forward) – 210 appearances, 80 goals. Outstanding finisher who excelled in staying ice-cool in one-on-one situations with the opposition goalkeeper (see page 179).

No.17 Kieron Dyer (Midfielder) – 113 appearances, 12 goals. From his early appearances it was obvious Town had unearthed a diamond with the ability to win many England caps (see page 232).

No.18 Colin Viljoen (Midfielder) – 372 appearances, 54 goals. A player of amazing vision, he was the man who made Ipswich tick for a great many years and deserved his England honours (see page 151).

No.19 Trevor Whymark (Forward) – 335 appearances, 104 goals. Renowned for his unselfish play, goal-scoring prowess and aerial ability (see page 153).

No.20 Clive Woods (Winger) – 338 appearances, 31 goals. A box of tricks who terrorised opponents at his peak and was a clear winner of the Man of the Match award at the FA Cup Final in 1978 (see page 156).

No.21 Russell Osman (Defender) – 385 appearances, 21 goals. Uncompromising defender for club and country, the only ever-present in Town's memorable UEFA Cup-winning campaign (see page 188).

No.22 Eric Gates (Forward) – 384 appearances, 96 goals. Diminutive player big on talent whose role behind the front two foxed opponents. Deserved his England recognition (see page 187).

No.23 David Johnson (Forward) – 178 appearances, 46 goals. Pacy striker who gained England honours and formed a tremendous club partnership alongside Trevor Whymark (see page 136).

No.24 Paul Cooper (Goalkeeper) – 575 appearances. One of Bobby Robson's best signings at just £23,000, he gave outstanding service and established a reputation for saving penalty kicks (see page 195).

No.25 Andy Nelson (Defender) – 214 appearances, 0 goals. Strong, commanding centre-half who captained the club to the Second Division and First Division titles in successive seasons (see page 104).

No.26 Brian Talbot (Midfielder) – 227 appearances, 31 goals. Energetic player who gained England honours at Portman Road (see page 152).

No.27 Tom Garneys (Forward) – 273 appearances, 143 goals. Top scorer in his first seasons at Portman Road, he helped the club to capture the Third Division (South) title on two occasions (see page 76).

No.28 Roy Bailey (Goalkeeper) – 346 appearances. Agile goalkeeper who played an important part in helping Ipswich secure the League Championship in 1962 (see page 99).

No.29 Mick Stockwell (Midfielder) – 611 appearances, 44 goals. Outstanding servant who played in most outfield positions and never gave less than 100 per cent in every game he played (see page 239).

No.30 Matt Holland (Midfielder) – 214 appearances, 36 goals. Inspired signing, he completed his first four seasons without missing a game and captained Ipswich to their Premiership return (see page 225).

No.31 Ken Malcolm (Defender) – 291 appearances, 2 goals. Tough full-back whose commitment was total and who only missed a League Championship medal because of injury (see page 101).

No.32 Danny Hegan (Midfielder) – 230 appearances, 38 goals. Cultured inside-forward with a hint of mischief as he unlocked opposition defences and created chances for others (see page 112).

No.33 Larry Carberry (Defender) – 283 appearances, 0 goals. Tremendous full-back whose stay at Portman Road coincided with some of the club's most memorable years (see page 103).

No.34 Jason Dozzell (Forward) – 416 appearances, 73 goals. Immensely talented, he scored on his debut and went on to give excellent service (see page 207).

No.35 Roy Stephenson (Winger) – 163 appearances, 26 goals. Player specially targeted by Alf Ramsey and whose first two seasons saw him gain Second Division and First Division winner's medals (see page 89).

No.36 Richard Wright (Goalkeeper) – 291 appearances. A star in the making even before his first team debut at the age of 17 and the only Town keeper to play for England (see page 226).

No.37 Jimmy McLuckie (Inside-forward) – 57 appearances, 3 goals. The club's first professional captain who was one of the country's top players when he joined Town in the Southern League (see page 55).

No.38 Roger Osborne (Midfielder) – 149 appearances, 10 goals. Hard-working and enthusiastic, he has a special place in the club's history for his FA Cup-winning goal at Wembley in 1978 (see page 159).

No.39 Steve McCall (Defender/Midfielder) – 331 appearances, 12 goals. Solid, dependable and versatile, he slotted into the UEFA Cup-winning side and enjoyed a long career in football (see page 186).

No.40 Mick Lambert (Winger) – 263 appearances, 45 goals. Fast, direct player with an eye for goal, as well as the ability to lay on scoring chances for others (see page 155).

No.41 Dai Rees (Defender) – 385 appearances, 1 goal. Strong centre-half whose total commitment was his trademark throughout a distinguished stay at Portman Road (see page 77).

No.42 Jimmy Robertson (Winger) – 98 appearances, 12 goals. The Scot's contribution towards keeping Ipswich in the First Division in the early 70s should never be under-estimated (see page 121).

No.43 Billy Reed (Winger) – 169 appearances, 46 goals. The Welshman was the first Ipswich player to win senior international honours and also gained two Third Division (South) winner's medals (see page 75).

No.44 Bryan Hamilton (Midfielder) – 199 appearances, 56 goals. Northern Ireland international with an uncanny knack of being in the right place at the right time, as reflected in his scoring record (see page 133).

No.45 Mauricio Taricco (Defender) – 170 appearances, 7 goals. Argentinian full-back whose enthusiasm and skill endeared him to Town fans who were up in arms when he was sold (see page 230).

No.46 Tony Mowbray (Defender) – 152 appearances, 8 goals. Commanding figure whose presence lifted others and who led by example as he helped Town regain Premiership status (see page 233).

No.47 Marcus Stewart (Forward) – 54 appearances, 26 goals. Striker whose scoring record says it all. Once the club's record signing, he set the Premiership alight in his first season there (see page 235).

No.48 David Linighan (Defender) – 327 appearances, 13 goals. Led the club to the old Second Division title in 1992 and gave his all to help them survive two seasons in the Premiership (see page 217).

No.49 Hermann Hreidarsson (Defender) – 45 appearances, 1 goal. One-time record signing whose first season saw him become one of the main stars in Ipswich's return to the Premiership (see page 238).

No.50 Romeo Zondervan (Midfielder) – 325 appearances, 20 goals. A former Dutch international, he was an industrious, talented player who helped secure Premiership status in 1992 (see page 204).

Results and Tables 1890-2001

The following pages include details of every official match played by Ipswich Town. League matches appear first, followed by individual cup competitions. The opponents played at home are written in capital letters, and appear in upper and lower case for away games. The date of the match, the score, Ipswich Town's goalscorers and the match attendances are also included. Full league and cup appearances and the goalscorers are featured separately. The final league table is included at the bottom of each page as well as a Fact File which notes particularly interesting facts and figures for the season. In both the league and cup appearances and goalscorers tables the category 'other' includes matches in the Divisional Play-offs, the Anglo-Italian Cup, the Full Members Cup, the Texaco Cup, and the FA Charity Shield. Details of the war years are not included as the club did not play between 1939 and 1945.

Ipswich's first league experience began in 1899 when they took part in the Norfolk & Suffolk League. Prior to this they had been competing regularly in the Amateur Cup and the Suffolk Senior Cup. Their inaugural season in the N & S League saw them finish fourth out of eight. They continued to compete in this league until 1907 when they joined the Southern Amateur League. They were champions four times during their spell in this league – in 1921-22, 1929-30, 1932-33 and 1933-34. They joined the Eastern Counties League for one season (1935-36) before they turned professional and entered the Southern League.

Key:
1Q – first qualifying round etc; RQ – Regional Qualifying Round
RQF – Regional quarter-final; PRd – Preliminary Round
XPRd – Extra Preliminary Round
Rd1 – first round; Rd2 – second round etc
1L – 1st leg; 2L – 2nd leg
R – replay; 2R – second replay
SQF – Southern quarter-final, SSF – Southern semi-final
QF – quarter-final; SF – semi-final
SF/1L – semi-final first leg etc
F – final
aet – after extra time

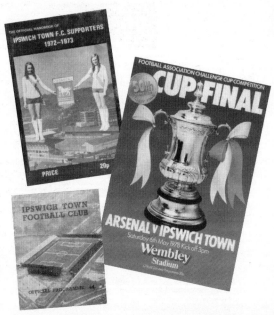

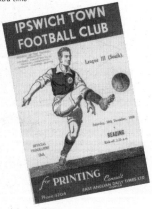

Pre-League FA Cup Results 1890-1936

Season 1890-91

FA Cup

DATE	OPPONENTS		SCORE	GOALSCORERS
Oct 4	READING	(RQ1) W	2-0	Sheringham, Turner S
Oct 25	Norwich Thorpe	(RQ2) W	4-0	Turner P, Kent, Peacock
Nov 15	HUNTINGTON COUNTY	(RQ3) W	5-2	Sheringham, Turner P 2, Kent
Dec 6	93RD HIGHLANDERS	(RQF) L	1-4	Kent

Season 1891-92

FA Cup

DATE	OPPONENTS		SCORE	GOALSCORERS
Oct 3	Old Westminsters	(RQ1) L	0-5	

Season 1892-93

FA Cup

DATE	OPPONENTS		SCORE	GOALSCORERS
Oct 15	OLD WYKEHAMISTS	(RQ1) W	4-0	Kent, Haward, Turner S 2
Oct 29	Old Westminsters	(RQ2) L	1-4	Josselyn

Season 1930-31

FA Cup

DATE	OPPONENTS		SCORE	GOALSCORERS
Sep 6	HARWICH & PARKESTON	(XPRd) W	5-0	Birtchenall 2, Green 2, Smith L
Sep 20	LEISTON WORKS	(PRd) W	5-2	Taylor, Groom, Birtchenall, Green 2
Oct 4	SEVERALLS ATHLETIC	(1QRd) W	6-1	Green 5, Groom
Oct 18	CRITTALLS ATHLETIC	(2QRd) L	2-3	Birtchenall, Watson

Season 1931-32

FA Cup

DATE	OPPONENTS		SCORE	GOALSCORERS
Sep 19	Leiston Works	(PRd) L	2-3	Gibbs, Russell

Season 1932-33

FA Cup

Sep 3	KIRKLEY	(XPRd) D	0-0	
Sep 8	Kirkley	(R) W	3-2	Jones, Rodwell, Groom
Sep 17	Cambridge Town	(PRd) D	2-2	Stopher, Rodwell
Sep 21	CAMBRIDGE TOWN	(R) L	1-2	Tubby

Season 1933-34

FA Cup

Sep 2	Gorleston	(XPRd) L	2-3	Wells, Cowley

Season 1934-35

FA Cup

Sep 15	NORWICH ST BARNABAS	(PRd) W	3-2	Tubby, Groom, o.g.
Sep 29	NORWICH YMCA	(1QRd) D	1-1	Green
Oct 3	NORWICH YMCA	(R) W	4-2	Sowerby 2, Clements, Nedd
Oct 13	FROST ATHLETIC	(2QRd) W	2-0	Green, Stopher
Oct 27	Gorleston	(3QRd) L	0-2	

Season 1935-36

FA Cup

Oct 5	YARMOUTH TOWN	(1QRd) D	0-0	
Oct 10	Yarmouth Town	(R) L	1-4	Hetherington

Season 1936-37

Southern League

DATE	OPPONENTS	SCORE	GOALSCORERS	ATTENDANCE
Aug 29	TUNBRIDGE WELLS RANGERS	W 4-1	Dobson, Williams, Bruce, Blackwell	14,211
Sep 12	Margate	W 1-0	Williams	4,305
Sep 26	Guildford City	W 3-2	Bruce, Dobson 2	3,094
Oct 10	Tunbridge Wells Rangers	W 2-0	Carter, Blackwell	3,925
Oct 24	Dartford	D 0-0		3,500
Nov 7	Folkestone	W 3-1	Perrett, Williams, Carter	3,000
Nov 18	TORQUAY UNITED RESERVES	D 0-0		4,800
Nov 21	Exeter City Reserves	D 2-2	Carter, Dobson	1,000
Dec 2	DARTFORD	W 3-1	Williams, Little, Sowerby	5,000
Dec 5	NEWPORT COUNTY RESERVES	D 1-1	Mulraney	8,100
Dec 19	PLYMOUTH ARGYLE RESERVES	W 4-3	McLuckie, Bruce, Carter 2	8,100
Dec 25	Norwich City Reserves	W 2-0	McLuckie, Carter	9,800
Dec 26	NORWICH CITY RESERVES	L 1-3	Mulraney	15,242
Dec 30	BATH CITY	D 1-1	Blackwell	5,256
Jan 9	BARRY TOWN	W 4-1	Bruce, Carter, o.g. 2	8,245
Jan 16	Yeovil & Petters United	D 4-4	Carter 3, Williams	4,200
Jan 27	Aldershot Reserves	W 2-1	Blackwell, Perrett	975
Feb 6	ALDERSHOT RESERVES	W 1-0	Cowie	8,500
Feb 13	Cheltenham Town	W 3-1	Bruce 2, Carter	1,900
Feb 20	GUILDFORD CITY	W 4-1	Blackwell 2, Bruce 2	8,200
Feb 27	Bath City	W 3-2	Carter, Bruce, McLuckie	1,880
Mar 3	EXETER CITY RESERVES	W 6-0	Perrett, Bruce, Carter, Blackwell 2, Dobson	4,700
Mar 6	MARGATE	W 3-2	Bruce, Dobson 2	10,150
Mar 13	Plymouth Argyle Reserves	D 1-1	McLuckie	5,000
Mar 20	FOLKESTONE	L 0-1		10,149
Apr 3	Torquay United Reserves	D 2-2	Carter 2	1,500
Apr 10	Newport County Reserves	W 2-1	Sowerby, Carter	4,850
Apr 17	YEOVIL & PETTERS UNITED	W 3-0	Cowie, Carter, Edwards	10,238
Apr 24	CHELTENHAM TOWN	W 3-0	Perrett, McLuckie, Carter	7,200
May 1	Barry Town	L 0-3		4,562

FA Cup

Sep 19	EASTERN COUNTIES UTD	(PRd) W 7-0	Blackwell 3, Dobson 2, Carter, Bruce	6,700
Oct 3	STOWMARKET	(1QRd) W 8-0	Carter 3, Bruce 3, Little, Perrett	7,500
Oct 17	Lowestoft Town	(2QRd) D 1-1	Blackwell	3,675
Oct 21	LOWESTOFT TOWN	(R) W 7-1	Perrett 3 (3 pen), Williams 2, Carter, Dobson	5,500
Oct 31	CROMER	(3QRd) W 11-0	Dobson 2, Williams 2, Bruce 2, McLuckie 2, Blackwell 2, Carter	4,200
Nov 14	CAMBRIDGE TOWN	(4QRd) W 2-1	Clements, Blackwell	8,500
Nov 28	WATFORD	(Rd1) W 2-1	Bruce, Carter	18,229
Dec 12	SPENNYMOOR UNITED	(Rd2) L 1-2	Carter	12,491

League & Cup Appearances

PLAYER	LEAGUE	CUP COMPETITION FA CUP	TOTAL
Blackwell	20	7	27
Bruce	25	6	31
Carter	29	8	37
Clements		1	1
Cowie	27	7	34
Cross	1		1
Dobson	23	4	27
Edwards	7		7
Hays	3		3
Houldsworth	29	8	37
Jobson	1	3	4
Little	2	4	6
Mauldsey	1		1
McLuckie	27	8	35
Mulraney	10		10
Parry	28	7	35
Perrett	25	7	32
Shufflebottom	9	1	10
Smith	1		1
Sowerbutts	1		1
Sowerby	12	2	14
Thomson	27	8	35
Williams	22	7	29

Goalscorers

PLAYER	LEAGUE	CUP COMPETITION FA CUP	TOTAL
Carter	18	8	26
Bruce	11	7	18
Blackwell	8	7	15
Dobson	7	5	12
Williams	5	4	9
Perrett	4	4	8
McLuckie	5	2	7
Cowie	2		2
Mulraney	2		2
Sowerby	2		2
Little	1	1	2
Clements		1	1
Edwards	1		1
Opp's o.gs.	2		2

Fact File

After starting with a win against Tunbridge Wells Rangers, Ipswich played 12 games before suffering their first defeat as a professional club.

MANAGER: Mick O'Brien

CAPTAIN: Jimmy McLuckie

TOP SCORER: Jack Carter

BIGGEST WIN: 11-0 v Cromer (H), 31 October 1936, FA Cup 3rd Qualifying Round

HIGHEST ATTENDANCE: 18,229 v Watford, 28 November 1936, FA Cup 1st Round

Final Southern League Table

		P	W	D	L	F	A	PTS
1	IPSWICH TOWN	30	19	8	3	68	35	46
2	NORWICH CITY RES	30	18	5	7	70	35	41
3	FOLKESTONE	30	17	4	9	71	61	38
4	BATH CITY	30	15	5	10	66	52	35
5	MARGATE	30	15	4	11	61	49	34
6	GUILFORD CITY	30	15	4	11	54	60	34
7	YEOVIL & PETTERS	30	15	3	12	77	69	33
8	NEWPORT CO RES	30	11	8	11	72	68	30
9	PLYMOUTH ARG RES	30	11	8	11	64	58	30
10	BARRY TOWN	30	12	4	14	58	72	28
11	CHELTENHAM TOWN	30	10	4	16	61	70	24
12	EXETER CITY RES	30	8	7	15	57	78	23
13	DARTFORD	30	9	5	16	41	55	23
14	TORQUAY UTD RES	30	8	5	17	45	76	21
15	TUNBRIDGE WELLS R	30	7	6	17	62	64	20
16	ALDERSHOT RES	30	7	6	17	47	72	20

Season 1937-38

Southern League

DATE	OPPONENTS	SCORE	GOALSCORERS	ATTENDANCE
Aug 28	FOLKESTONE	W 2-1	Alsop, Astill	9,943
Sep 4	Colchester United	D 3-3	Williams, Alsop, Perrett (pen)	11,000
Sep 11	BARRY TOWN	W 4-1	Alsop, Astill, Bruce, Perrett	7,558
Sep 15	Dartford	W 1-0	Edwards	1,400
Sep 18	YEOVIL & PETTERS UNITED	W 3-2	Bruce 3 (1 pen)	9,941
Oct 2	TORQUAY UNITED RESERVES	W 4-1	Edwards 2, Alsop, Bruce	6,750
Oct 16	NEWPORT COUNTY RESERVES	W 8-2	Little, Mulraney, Alsop 3, Astill 3	7,866
Oct 23	Barry Town	L 0-5		2,000
Oct 30	SWINDON TOWN RESERVES	L 2-3	Mulraney, Little	7,451
Nov 6	TUNBRIDGE WELLS RANGERS	W 3-1	Little 3	7,210
Dec 4	EXETER CITY RESERVES	W 5-0	Edwards, Perrett (pen), Astill 2, Mulraney	6,734
Dec 11	Bath City	W 4-3	Little, Astill, Edwards 2	1,500
Dec 18	Swindon Town Reserves	D 2-2	Astill, McLuckie	3,392
Dec 25	Norwich City Reserves	L 2-3	Edwards, Astill	7,100
Dec 27	NORWICH CITY RESERVES	L 1-2	Alsop	13,643
Jan 15	Exeter City Reserves	W 2-1	Alsop, McLuckie	1,500
Jan 22	GUILDFORD CITY	W 3-0	Alsop 2, Perrett (pen)	9,100
Jan 29	Folkestone	L 0-2		2,350
Feb 5	COLCHESTER UNITED	W 3-2	Astill, Perrett, Little	23,890
Feb 12	Bristol Rovers Reserves	D 2-2	Little, Astill	1,570
Feb 19	BATH CITY	W 2-0	Jones, Mulraney	8,140
Feb 26	Tunbridge Wells Rangers	D 0-0		2,560
Mar 12	Yeovil & Petters United	D 1-1	Taylor	3,656
Mar 19	CHELTENHAM TOWN	W 3-1	Mulraney 2, Taylor	8,540
Mar 26	Guildford City	L 2-3	Alsop, Perrett	5,366
Apr 2	Cheltenham Town	W 2-1	Alsop 2	3,428
Apr 9	DARTFORD	W 5-1	Alsop 2, Little 2, Mulraney	7,043
Apr 15	Plymouth Argyle Reserves	L 1-2	Mulraney	7,000
Apr 18	PLYMOUTH ARGYLE RESERVES	L 2-3	Jones, McLuckie	12,647
Apr 20	Aldershot Reserves	W 5-2	Alsop 2, Perrett, McLuckie, Britton o.g.	1,550
Apr 23	Newport County Reserves	L 1-2	Alsop	1,250
Apr 27	Torquay United Reserves	D 2-2	Jones, Taylor	1,100
Apr 30	ALDERSHOT RESERVES	W 7-0	Alsop 4, Taylor 2, Jones	5,327
May 4	BRISTOL ROVERS RESERVES	W 2-0	Alsop, Little	5,484

FA Cup

Nov 13	Hoffman Athletic	(4Q) W 3-0	Alsop, Mulraney 2	3,400
Nov 27	Yeovil & Petters United	(Rd1) L 1-2	Astill	6,446

League & Cup Appearances

PLAYER	LEAGUE	CUP COMPETITION FA CUP	TOTAL
Alsop	24	2	26
Astill	27	2	29
Bruce	17	2	19
Burns H	1		1
Carter	2		2
Cowie	7	1	8
Edwards	10		10
Houldsworth	27	2	29
Jones	12		12
Little	28	2	30
McLuckie	32	1	33
Mulraney	22	2	24
Parry	34	2	36
Perrett	32	2	34
Rodger	33	2	35
Shufflebottom	32	2	34
Sowerbutts	7		7
Taylor	13		13
Thomson	1		1
Williams	13		13

Goalscorers

PLAYER	LEAGUE	CUP COMPETITION FA CUP	TOTAL
Alsop	24	1	25
Astill	12	1	13
Little	11		11
Mulraney	8	2	10
Perrett	7		7
Edwards	7		7
Bruce	5		5
Taylor	5		5
McLuckie	4		4
Jones	4		4
Williams	1		1
Opp's o.gs.	1		1

Fact File

Even though they did not win the Southern League, Ipswich were elected to the Football League at the expense of Gillingham.

MANAGER: Scott Duncan

CAPTAIN: Jimmy McLuckie

TOP SCORER: Gilbert Alsop

BIGGEST WIN: 7-0 v Aldershot Reserves, 30 April 1938, Southern League

HIGHEST ATTENDANCE: 23,890 v Colchester United, 5 February 1938, Southern League

Final Southern League Table

		P	W	D	L	F	A	Pts
1	GUILDFORD CITY	34	22	5	7	94	60	49
2	PLYMOUTH ARG RES	34	18	9	7	98	58	43
3	IPSWICH TOWN	34	19	6	9	89	54	44
4	YEOVIL & PETTERS	34	14	14	6	72	45	42
5	NORWICH CITY RES	34	15	11	8	77	55	41
6	COLCHESTER UNITED	34	15	8	11	90	58	38
7	BRISTOL ROVERS RES	34	14	8	12	63	62	36
8	SWINDON TOWN RES	34	14	7	13	70	76	35
9	TUNBRIDGE WELLS R	34	14	6	14	68	74	34
10	ALDERSHOT RES	34	10	12	12	42	55	32
11	CHELTENHAM TOWN	34	13	5	16	72	68	31
12	EXETER CITY RES	34	13	5	16	71	75	31
13	DARTFORD	34	9	11	14	51	70	29
14	BATH CITY	34	9	9	16	45	65	27
15	FOLKESTONE	34	10	6	18	58	82	26
16	NEWPORT CO RES	34	10	6	18	56	86	26
17	BARRY TOWN	34	8	7	19	50	88	23
18	TORQUAY UTD RES	34	8	7	19	46	81	23

Season 1938-39

Football League Division Three South

DATE	OPPONENTS	SCORE	GOALSCORERS	ATTENDANCE
Aug 27	SOUTHEND UNITED	W 4-2	Jones 2, Alsop, Davies	19,242
Aug 29	Walsall	W 1-0	Mulraney	13,700
Sep 3	Exeter City	L 0-3		9,800
Sep 7	BOURNEMOUTH	L 0-2		12,547
Sep 10	CARDIFF CITY	L 1-2	Alsop	16,180
Sep 17	Northampton Town	L 0-2		13,422
Sep 24	Reading	L 1-2	Chadwick	10,500
Oct 1	BRISTOL ROVERS	D 0-0		12,753
Oct 8	Brighton & Hove Albion	L 0-2		10,000
Oct 15	NEWPORT COUNTY	L 1-4	Mulraney	13,810
Oct 22	Notts County	L 1-2	Chadwick	12,000
Oct 29	TORQUAY UNITED	W 1-0	Davies	12,722
Nov 5	Swindon Town	D 1-1	Chadwick	10,437
Nov 12	PORT VALE	W 2-0	Chadwick, Curran	13,628
Nov 19	Watford	D 0-0		8,442
Dec 3	Bristol City	L 2-3	Davies, Chadwick	7,822
Dec 17	Clapton Orient	D 1-1	Fletcher	6,500
Dec 26	MANSFIELD TOWN	W 5-1	Fletcher (pen), Mulraney, Jones, Chadwick 2	3,562
Dec 27	Mansfield Town	W 1-0	Chadwick	6,500
Dec 31	EXETER CITY	D 2-2	Fletcher (pen), Bell	12,114
Jan 14	Cardiff City	L 1-2	Fletcher	14,000
Jan 18	CRYSTAL PALACE	W 2-1	Chadwick, Jones	5,219
Jan 21	NORTHAMPTON TOWN	W 2-0	Jones, Chadwick	11,135
Feb 4	Bristol Rovers	D 3-3	Jones, Fletcher 2 (1 pen)	7,209
Feb 11	BRIGHTON & HOVE ALBION	D 0-0		13,340
Feb 18	Newport County	L 2-3	Jones, Chadwick	11,700
Feb 25	NOTTS COUNTY	L 0-2		10,141
Mar 4	Torquay United	D 1-1	Little	6,000
Mar 11	SWINDON TOWN	W 3-1	Chadwick 2, Jones	11,724
Mar 18	Port Vale	D 0-0		6,000
Mar 25	WATFORD	W 5-1	Mulraney, Davies 2, Little, Chadwick	11,447
Apr 1	Crystal Palace	L 0-3		13,764
Apr 7	Queens Park Rangers	D 0-0		15,161
Apr 8	BRISTOL CITY	W 4-0	Mulraney 3, Fillingham	12,834
Apr 10	QUEENS PARK RANGERS	W 1-0	Chadwick	18,963
Apr 15	Aldershot	L 1-3	Fletcher	6,000
Apr 19	Southend United	D 0-0		3,700
Apr 22	CLAPTON ORIENT	W 3-0	Little, McLuckie, Fletcher	10,394
Apr 26	ALDERSHOT	W 7-2	Little 2, Mulraney, Fletcher, Davies, Chadwick 2	8,061
Apr 29	WALSALL	W 1-0	Davies	11,427
May 3	READING	W 2-1	Little, Bell	9,527
May 6	Bournemouth	D 0-0		3,500

FA Cup

DATE	OPPONENTS		SCORE	GOALSCORERS	ATTENDANCE
Nov 26	STREET	(Rd1)	W 7-0	Chadwick 4, Davies 2, Fletcher (pen)	15,208
Dec 10	TORQUAY UNITED	(Rd2)	W 4-1	Little 2, Chadwick, Jones	16,356
Jan 7	Aston Villa	(Rd3)	D 1-1	Hutcheson	34,910
Jan 11	ASTON VILLA	(R)	L 1-2	Jones	28,194

League & Cup Appearances

PLAYER	LEAGUE	CUP COMPETITION FA CUP	TOTAL
Alsop	9		9
Bell	25	4	29
Burns	42	4	46
Chadwick	34	4	38
Cope	4		4
Cowie	6		6
Curran	7	1	8
Dale	40	4	44
Davies	32	3	35
Fillingham	29	2	31
Fletcher	29	4	33
Hutcheson		2	2
Jones	21	2	23
Little	32	3	35
McGourty	1		1
McLuckie	41	4	45
Morris	1		1
Mulraney	28	3	31
Parry	42	4	46
Perrett	16		16
Rimmer	3		3
Rodger	9		9
Shufflebottom	2		2
Williams	9		9

Goalscorers

PLAYER	LEAGUE	CUP COMPETITION FA CUP	TOTAL
Chadwick	17	5	22
Fletcher	9	1	10
Jones	8	2	10
Davies	7	2	9
Mulraney	8		8
Little	6	2	8
Alsop	2		2
Bell	2		2
Curran	1		1
Fillingham	1		1
Hutcheson		1	1
McLuckie	1		1

Final Division Three South Table

		P	W	D	L	F	A	Pts
1	NEWPORT CO	42	22	11	9	58	45	55
2	CRYSTAL PALACE	42	20	12	10	71	52	52
3	BRIGHTON & HA	42	19	11	12	68	49	49
4	WATFORD	42	17	12	13	62	51	46
5	READING	42	16	14	12	69	59	46
6	QPR	42	15	14	13	68	49	44
7	IPSWICH TOWN	42	16	12	14	62	52	44
8	BRISTOL C	42	16	12	14	61	63	44
9	SWINDON T	42	18	8	16	72	77	44
10	ALDERSHOT	42	16	12	14	53	66	44
11	NOTTS CO	42	17	9	16	59	54	43
12	SOUTHEND U	42	16	9	17	61	64	41
13	CARDIFF C	42	15	11	16	61	65	41
14	EXETER C	42	13	14	15	65	82	40
15	BOURNEMOUTH	42	13	13	16	52	58	39
16	MANSFIELD T	42	12	15	15	44	62	39
17	NORTHAMPTON T	42	15	8	19	51	58	38
18	PORT VALE	42	14	9	19	52	58	37
19	TORQUAY U	42	14	9	19	54	70	37
20	CLAPTON ORIENT	42	11	13	18	53	55	35
21	WALSALL	42	11	11	20	68	69	33
22	BRISTOL R	42	10	13	19	55	61	33

Fact File

Ipswich's final position of seventh was the highest position any club had achieved in their debut season.

MANAGER: Scott Duncan

CAPTAIN: Jimmy McLuckie

TOP SCORER: Fred Chadwick

BIGGEST WIN: 7-0 v Street, 26 November 1938, FA Cup 1st Round

HIGHEST ATTENDANCE: 28,194 v Aston Villa, 11 January 1939, FA Cup 3rd Round replay

Season 1939-40

Football League Division Three South

DATE	OPPONENTS	SCORE	GOALSCORERS	ATTENDANCE
Aug 26	Clapton Orient	D 2-2	Mulraney, Little	11,018
Aug 30	BRISTOL ROVERS	W 2-0	Mitcheson, Chadwick	8,884
Sep 2	NORWICH CITY	D 1-1	Chadwick	10,792

League & Cup Appearances

PLAYER	LEAGUE	CUP COMPETITION FA CUP	TOTAL
Bell	3		3
Burns	3		3
Chadwick	3		3
Dale	3		3
Fletcher	3		3
Hick	3		3
Little	3		3
McLuckie	3		3
Mitcheson	3		3
Mulraney	3		3
O'Mahoney	3		3

Goalscorers

PLAYER	LEAGUE	CUP COMPETITION FA CUP	TOTAL
Chadwick	2		2
Little	1		1
Mitcheson	1		1
Mulraney	1		1

Fact File

On 29 September 1939, the Ipswich Town board of directors finally declared that operations at Portman Road would be closed down due to the war – they were the first League club to do so.

MANAGER: Scott Duncan
CAPTAIN: Jimmy McLuckie
TOP SCORER: Fred Chadwick
BIGGEST WIN: 2-0 v Bristol Rovers (H), 30 August 1939, Division Three South
HIGHEST ATTENDANCE: 10,792 v Norwich City, 2 September 1939, Division Three South

Final Division Three South Table

		P	W	D	L	F	A	Pts
1	READING	3	2	1	0	8	2	5
2	EXETER C	3	2	1	0	5	3	5
3	CARDIFF C	3	2	0	1	5	5	4
4	CRYSTAL PALACE	3	2	0	1	8	9	4
5	BRIGHTON & HA	3	1	2	0	5	4	4
6	IPSWICH TOWN	3	1	2	0	5	3	4
7	NOTTS CO	2	2	0	0	6	3	4
8	SOUTHEND U	3	1	1	1	3	3	3
9	BRISTOL C	3	1	1	1	5	5	3
10	CLAPTON ORIENT	3	0	3	0	3	3	3
11	MANSFIELD T	3	1	1	1	8	8	3
12	NORWICH C	3	1	1	1	4	4	3
13	TORQUAY U	3	0	3	0	4	4	3
14	BOURNEMOUTH	3	1	1	1	13	4	3
15	WALSALL	3	1	1	1	3	3	3
16	NORTHAMPTON T	3	1	0	2	2	12	2
17	QPR	3	0	2	1	4	5	2
18	WATFORD	3	0	2	1	4	5	2
19	BRISTOL R	3	0	1	2	2	7	1
20	PORT VALE	2	0	1	1	0	1	1
21	ALDERSHOT	3	0	1	2	3	4	1
22	SWINDON T	3	0	1	2	2	4	1

Season 1945-46

Football League Division Three (South - North)

DATE	OPPONENTS	SCORE	GOALSCORERS	ATTENDANCE
Aug 25	Port Vale	L 2-3	Little, Smythe	6,080
Sep 1	PORT VALE	L 0-1		11,512
Sep 8	NOTTS COUNTY	W 1-0	Parlane	10,786
Sep 12	Walsall	L 0-3		10,605
Sep 15	Notts County	D 1-1	O'Mahoney	9,142
Sep 22	NORTHAMPTON TOWN	W 2-1	Hornby, Day	11,259
Sep 29	Northampton Town	D 3-3	Day 3	
Oct 6	Queens Park Rangers	L 0-2		15,000
Oct 13	QUEENS PARK RANGERS	W 2-1	Edwards, Gillespie	15,171
Oct 20	CLAPTON ORIENT	W 3-1	Gillespie, Edwards, Biggs	11,298
Oct 27	Clapton Orient	L 1-2	Edwards, Gillespie	4,500
Nov 3	Watford	L 3-4	Parker T 2, Day	5,000
Oct 10	WATFORD	W 4-2	Parker T, Little (pen), Day 2	9,437
Dec 1	Norwich City	L 0-4		16,000
Dec 19	NORWICH CITY	D 0-0		5,040
Dec 22	Mansfield Town	W 2-1	Day, Trenter	2,608
Dec 25	Southend United	L 0-2		
Dec 26	SOUTHEND UNITED	W 3-1	Trenter 2, Gillespie	11,778
Dec 29	WALSALL	W 5-3	Day 3, Trenter, Stow	9,471

Division Three (South) Cup

DATE	OPPONENTS	SCORE	GOALSCORERS	ATTENDANCE
Jan 12	Queens Park Rangers	L 1-4	Day	12,500
Jan 19	QUEENS PARK RANGERS	W 1-0	Trenter	9,524
Jan 26	Southend United	L 1-2	Little	5,336
Feb 2	SOUTHEND UNITED	W 2-1	Day, Little	9,570
Feb 9	Norwich City	L 0-1		10,731
Feb 16	NORWICH CITY	W 4-0	Trenter, Gillespie, Day, Roy	14,980
Feb 23	PORT VALE	W 1-0	McCormack	8,106
Mar 2	Port Vale	L 1-4	Little	3,235
Mar 9	MANSFIELD TOWN	W 2-1	O'Mahoney 2 (2 pen)	9,865
Mar 16	Mansfield Town	L 0-3		4,452
Mar 23	Notts County	L 0-1		9,966
Mar 30	NOTTS COUNTY	L 1-2	Little	9,156
Apr 6	Watford	W 1-0	o.g.	4,517
Apr 13	WATFORD	D 2-2	Little, Day	10,196
Apr 20	Reading	L 0-2		10,385
Apr 22	READING	W 2-1	Parker T, o.g.	12,636

FA Cup

Nov 17	Wisbech	(Rd1/1L) W 3-0	Fletcher, Little 2	4,356
Nov 24	Wisbech	(Rd1/2L) W 5-0	Parker T 3, Price 2	10,598
Dec 8	Queens Park Rangers	(Rd2/1L) L 0-4		12,000
Dec 15	QUEENS PARK RANGERS	(Rd2/2L) L 0-2		10,571

Final Division Three (South - North) Table

		P	W	D	L	F	A	Pts
1	QPR	16	11	3	2	38	11	25
2	Walsall	16	10	4	2	34	18	24
3	Mansfield T	16	8	4	4	24	15	20
4	Southend U	16	7	5	4	22	21	19
5	Norwich C	16	7	2	7	27	25	16
6	Ipswich Town	16	7	1	8	19	24	15
7	Clapton Orient	16	6	3	7	22	31	15
8	Port Vale	16	5	4	7	21	25	14
9	Northampton T	16	5	2	9	27	29	12
10	Watford	16	5	1	10	23	35	11
11	Notts Co	16	5	0	11	17	31	10

MANAGER: Scott Duncan

CAPTAIN: Jimmy McLuckie

TOP SCORER: Albert Day

BIGGEST WIN: 5-0 v Wisbech (H), 24 November 1945, FA Cup 1st Round 2nd Leg

HIGHEST ATTENDANCE: 15,171 v QPR, 13 October 1945, Division Three (South - North)

League & Cup Appearances

PLAYER	LEAGUE	CUP COMPETITION FA CUP	TOTAL
Antonio	3	3	6
Baird	1	1	2
Bell	36	4	40
Biggs	5		5
Burns	4		4
Coleman	1		1
Combe	1		1
Connor	1		1
Day	21		21
Edwards	11	3	14
Fitzsimmons	1		1
Fletcher	3	3	6
Forder	1		1
Fox	15	2	17
Gillespie	26		26
Harris	12		12
Hick	1		1
Hobbis	1		1
Hornby	1		1
Jones	1		1
Little	25	4	29
Maskell	1		1
McCormack	2		2
McLuckie	17	3	20
McNally	1		1
Mitcheson	2		2
Mulraney	1		1
Newman	1	1	2
Noonan	2		2
O'Mahoney	36	3	39
Parker T	12	4	16
Parlane	3		3
Parry	31	4	35
Perrett	14		14
Price	10	4	14
Robinson	1		1
Ross	1		1
Roy	12		12
Saphin	27	3	30
Sayers	2		2
Smyth	7	2	9
Somerfield	1	1	2
Southam	11		11
Stow	8		8
Tadman	1		1
Toothill	4		4
Trenter	15		15
Wardlaw	2	3	5
Williams		1	1

Goalscorers

PLAYER	LEAGUE	CUP COMPETITION FA CUP	TOTAL
Day	15		15
Little	7	2	9
Parker T	4	3	7
Trenter	6		6
Gillespie	4		4
Edwards	3		3
O'Mahoney	3		3
Price		2	2
Roy	2		2
Biggs	1		1
Fletcher		1	1
Hornby	1		1
McCormack	1		1
Parlane	1		1
Smythe	1		1
Stow	1		1
Opp's o.gs.	2		2

Fact File

To ease travel problems, the decision was made to regionalize the Third Division. Ipswich appeared in the South section with ten other clubs.

Season 1946-47

Football League Division Three South

DATE	OPPONENTS	SCORE	GOALSCORERS	ATTENDANCE
Aug 31	Leyton Orient	D 2-2	Connor 2	12,000
Sep 4	BRISTOL ROVERS	L 0-2		12,012
Sep 7	NORWICH CITY	W 5-0	Day 3, Parker T 2	20,120
Sep 12	Southend United	D 1-1	Connor	8,500
Sep 14	WATFORD	W 2-0	Connor, Roy	14,142
Sep 21	Walsall	L 2-4	Parker T, Day	9,000
Sep 28	READING	W 2-0	Day, Fox	16,009
Oct 5	Crystal Palace	D 1-1	O'Mahoney (pen)	20,820
Oct 12	TORQUAY UNITED	D 1-1	Baird	14,605
Oct 19	Notts County	W 2-1	Parker T 2	18,000
Oct 26	NORTHAMPTON TOWN	L 1-2	Baird	12,696
Nov 2	Aldershot	L 1-4	Day	6,000
Nov 9	BRIGHTON & HOVE ALBION	L 1-2	Parker T	11,774
Nov 16	Exeter City	D 0-0		10,000
Nov 23	PORT VALE	W 2-1	Little, Parker S	13,001
Dec 7	SWINDON TOWN	W 3-1	Roy, Parker T, Parker S	9,871
Dec 21	CARDIFF CITY	L 0-1		12,288
Dec 25	Queens Park Rangers	W 3-1	Parker T, Gillespie, Parker S	15,000
Dec 26	QUEENS PARK RANGERS	D 1-1	Day	20,267
Dec 28	LEYTON ORIENT	D 0-0		13,126
Jan 1	Bournemouth	D 1-1	Day	8,000
Jan 4	Norwich City	W 1-0	Parker S	23,167
Jan 11	Bristol City	W 2-1	Little, Day	16,543
Jan 18	Watford	L 0-2		9,000
Jan 25	WALSALL	W 2-1	Day 2	9,846
Feb 1	Reading	W 3-1	Day 2, Chadwick	6,955
Feb 8	CRYSTAL PALACE	D 1-1	Parker S	9,168
Feb 15	Torquay United	D 0-0		6,500
Mar 15	Brighton & Hove Albion	D 0-0		6,000
Mar 22	EXETER CITY	W 2-1	Day, O'Mahoney	11,066
Mar 29	Port Vale	L 0-1		10,378
Apr 4	Mansfield Town	L 3-4	Pole, O'Mahoney (pen), Parker T	5,000
Apr 5	BRISTOL CITY	W 3-2	Pole, Parker S, Lang	16,022
Apr 7	Mansfield Town	W 2-1	Parker S, Pole	15,126
Apr 12	Swindon Town	L 1-2	Pole	13,209
Apr 19	BOURNEMOUTH	W 2-1	Pole, Little	11,153
Apr 26	Cardiff City	L 2-3	O'Mahoney (pen), Parker S	40,000
May 3	SOUTHEND UNITED	W 1-0	Little	12,426
May 10	Bristol Rovers	D 1-1	Parker S	10,459
May 17	NOTTS COUNTY	L 1-2	Parker T	10,229
May 26	ALDERSHOT	D 1-1	Parker T	9,883
May 31	Northampton Town	D 2-2	Clarke G, Parker S	3,200

FA Cup

Nov 30	TORQUAY UNITED	(Rd1) W 2-0	Parker S, Parker T	13,828
Dec 14	Walsall	(Rd2) D 0-0		11,000
Dec 18	WALSALL	(R) L 0-1		11,500

League & Cup Appearances

PLAYER	LEAGUE	CUP COMPETITION FA CUP	TOTAL
Baird	40	3	43
Bell	40	3	43
Brown	1		1
Brownlow	1		1
Burns	41	3	44
Chadwick	6		6
Clarke, G	1		1
Clarke, W	3		3
Connor	12		12
Day	25		25
Fox	11		11
Gillespie	6		6
Green	4		4
Lang	5		5
Little	33	3	36
Mackay	5	2	7
O'Mahoney	40	3	43
Parker, S	27	3	30
Parker, T	40	3	43
Parry	15		15
Perrett	32	3	35
Pole	14		14
Roy	15	2	17
Rumbold	42	3	45
Smith	2	2	4
Smythe	1		1

Goalscorers

PLAYER	LEAGUE	CUP COMPETITION FA CUP	TOTAL
Day	14		14
Parker, T	11	1	12
Parker, S	10	1	11
Pole	5		5
Connor	4		4
O'Mahoney	4		4
Little	4		4
Baird	2		2
Roy	2		2
Fox	1		1
Chadwick	1		1
Clarke, G	1		1
Gillespie	1		1
Lang	1		1

Fact File

The first league derbies between Norwich and Town start with a splendid double for Ipswich.

MANAGER: Scott Duncan
CAPTAIN: Matthew O'Mahoney
TOP SCORER: Albert Day
BIGGEST WIN: 5-0 v Norwich City (H), 7 September 1946, Division Three South
HIGHEST ATTENDANCE: 20,267 v QPR, 26 December 1946, Division Three South

Final Division Three South Table

		P	W	D	L	F	A	Pts
1	Cardiff C	42	30	6	6	93	30	66
2	QPR	42	23	11	8	74	40	57
3	Bristol C	42	20	11	11	94	56	51
4	Swindon T	42	19	11	12	84	73	49
5	Walsall	42	17	12	13	74	59	46
6	Ipswich Town	42	16	14	12	61	53	46
7	Bournemouth	42	18	8	16	72	54	44
8	Southend U	42	17	10	15	71	60	44
9	Reading	42	16	11	15	83	74	43
10	Port Vale	42	17	9	16	68	63	43
11	Torquay U	42	15	12	15	52	61	42
12	Notts Co	42	15	10	17	63	63	40
13	Northampton T	42	15	10	17	72	75	40
14	Bristol R	42	16	8	18	59	69	40
15	Exeter C	42	15	9	18	60	69	39
16	Watford	42	17	5	20	61	76	39
17	Brighton & HA	42	13	12	17	54	72	38
18	Crystal Palace	42	13	11	18	49	62	37
19	Leyton Orient	42	12	8	22	54	75	32
20	Aldershot	42	10	12	20	48	78	32
21	Norwich C	42	10	8	24	64	100	28
22	Mansfield T	42	9	10	23	48	96	28

Season 1947-48

Football League Division Three South

DATE	OPPONENTS	SCORE	GOALSCORERS	ATTENDANCE
Aug 23	NOTTS COUNTY	W 2-0	Parker S 2	14,073
Aug 27	Southend United	L 2-3	Day, Rumbold	13,000
Aug 30	Swansea Town	D 1-1	Parker T	26,000
Sep 3	SOUTHEND UNITED	W 4-0	Day, Parker T 2, Maffey	11,410
Sep 6	BOURNEMOUTH	D 1-1	Pole	15,835
Sep 10	Exeter City	L 0-1		9,000
Sep 13	Norwich City	W 5-1	Parker T, Jennings, Parker S 2, Day	23,356
Sep 17	EXETER CITY	W 2-0	Parker T, Jennings	12,627
Sep 20	Bristol City	L 0-4		23,009
Sep 27	READING	W 1-0	Parker T	15,195
Oct 4	Walsall	W 2-1	Day, Baird	18,394
Oct 11	BRIGHTON & HOVE ALBION	W 4-0	Jennings 2, Parker S, Rumbold (pen)	14,573
Oct 18	Watford	W 3-2	Parker S 2, Jennings	9,000
Oct 25	QUEENS PARK RANGERS	W 1-0	Jennings	24,361
Nov 1	Port Vale	L 1-4	Rumbold (pen)	18,000
Nov 8	SWINDON TOWN	L 0-1		14,787
Nov 15	Torquay United	L 0-3		8,000
Nov 22	CRYSTAL PALACE	W 3-0	Parker T 2, Little	12,387
Dec 25	Newport County	L 1-3	Pole	13,000
Dec 27	NEWPORT COUNTY	W 3-0	Perrett, Day 2	11,880
Jan 3	SWANSEA TOWN	W 3-2	Little, Pole, Rumbold (pen)	13,352
Jan 10	Aldershot	W 1-0	Jennings	6,500
Jan 17	Bournemouth	L 0-4		15,000
Jan 24	Brighton & Hove Albion	L 1-4	Little	10,000
Jan 31	NORWICH CITY	L 1-2	Little	19,689
Feb 7	BRISTOL CITY	W 1-0	Parker T	10,862
Feb 14	Reading	W 2-1	Jennings, Perrett	15,347
Feb 21	WALSALL	W 3-1	Little, Jennings, Day	7,897
Mar 6	WATFORD	L 1-3	Jennings	11,644
Mar 13	Queens Park Rangers	L 0-2		21,500
Mar 20	PORT VALE	W 2-1	Parker S, Jennings	11,100
Mar 26	Leyton Orient	D 1-1	Parker S	25,000
Mar 27	Swindon Town	W 1-0	Day	14,440
Mar 29	LEYTON ORIENT	W 1-0	Bell	16,239
Apr 3	TORQUAY UNITED	W 2-1	Baird, Jennings	11,008
Apr 10	Crystal Palace	L 1-2	Day	18,000
Apr 15	Notts County	W 1-0	Rumbold (pen)	33,515
Apr 17	ALDERSHOT	W 2-0	Perrett, Little	12,065
Apr 21	NORTHAMPTON TOWN	W 5-2	Jennings 2, Pole, Day, Smalley o.g.	9,285
Apr 24	Northampton Town	L 2-4	Parker T, Day	5,000
Apr 28	Bristol Rovers	L 0-2		8,722
May 1	BRISTOL ROVERS	L 0-4		10,604

FA Cup

Nov 9	Swindon Town	(Rd1) L 2-4	Parker S, Parker T	20,382

League & Cup Appearances

PLAYER	LEAGUE	CUP COMPETITION FA CUP	TOTAL
Baird	42	1	43
Bell	35	1	36
Brown	23		23
Burns	19	1	20
Clarke	1		1
Day	35		35
Green	33	1	34
Jennings	36	1	37
Little	35	1	36
Maffey	5		5
Mitchell	1		1
O'Mahoney	5		5
Parker S	32	1	33
Parker T	42	1	43
Parry	17		17
Perrett	38	1	39
Pole	17	1	18
Rumbold	42	1	43
Smythe	1		1
Stevenson	3		3

Goalscorers

PLAYER	LEAGUE	CUP COMPETITION FA CUP	TOTAL
Jennings	14		14
Day	11		11
Parker T	10	1	11
Parker S	9	1	10
Little	6		6
Rumbold	5		5
Pole	4		4
Perrett	3		3
Baird	2		2
Bell	1		1
Maffey	1		1
Opp's o.gs.	1		1

Final Division Three South Table

		P	W	D	L	F	A	Pts
1	QPR	42	26	9	7	74	37	61
2	BOURNEMOUTH	42	24	9	9	76	35	57
3	WALSALL	42	21	9	12	70	40	51
4	IPSWICH TOWN	42	23	3	16	67	61	49
5	SWANSEA T	42	18	12	12	70	52	48
6	NOTTS CO	42	19	8	15	68	59	46
7	BRISTOL C	42	18	7	17	77	65	43
8	PORT VALE	42	16	11	15	63	54	43
9	SOUTHEND U	42	15	13	14	51	58	43
10	READING	42	15	11	16	56	58	41
11	EXETER C	42	15	11	16	55	63	41
12	NEWPORT CO	42	14	13	15	61	73	41
13	CRYSTAL PALACE	42	13	13	16	49	49	39
14	NORTHAMPTON T	42	14	11	17	58	72	39
15	WATFORD	42	14	10	18	57	79	38
16	SWINDON T	42	10	16	16	41	46	36
17	LEYTON ORIENT	42	13	10	19	51	73	36
18	TORQUAY U	42	11	13	18	63	62	35
19	ALDERSHOT	42	10	15	17	45	67	35
20	BRISTOL R	42	13	8	21	71	75	34
21	NORWICH C	42	13	8	21	61	76	34
22	BRIGHTON & HA	42	11	12	19	43	73	34

Fact File

By a quirk of fate Ipswich played Bristol Rovers in three consecutive league games in 1948 – the last two games of this season and the first one of next season.

MANAGER: Scott Duncan
CAPTAIN: Dave Bell
TOP SCORER: Bill Jennings
BIGGEST WIN: 5-1 v Norwich City, 13 September 1947, Division Three South
HIGHEST ATTENDANCE: 24,361 v QPR, 25 October 1947, Division Three South

Season 1948-49

Football League Division Three South

DATE	OPPONENTS	SCORE	GOALSCORERS	ATTENDANCE
Aug 21	Bristol Rovers	W 6-1	Jennings 2, Parker T, Dempsey 2, Rumbold	16,314
Aug 25	TORQUAY UNITED	W 5-1	Jennings 2, Little, Parker T 2,	15,472
Aug 28	NEWPORT COUNTY	W 5-1	Brown J, Parker T, Little, Jennings, Rumbold (pen)	17,900
Sep 1	Torquay United	D 1-1	Jennings	11,400
Sep 4	Swansea Town	L 0-2		30,000
Sep 9	Notts County	L 2-9	Jennings, Dempsey	32,820
Sep 11	READING	W 3-2	Jennings, Parker T, Little	14,294
Sep 15	NOTTS COUNTY	W 3-2	Jennings, Parker T 2	21,262
Sep 18	Crystal Palace	D 1-1	McGinn	18,000
Sep 25	WATFORD	L 1-2	Harris o.g.	15,060
Oct 2	Bournemouth	L 2-4	Stirling o.g., Jennings	19,564
Oct 9	Northampton Town	D 1-1	Parker T	9,550
Oct 16	NORWICH CITY	L 1-2	Dempsey	24,569
Oct 23	Port Vale	W 2-1	Parker T, Brown J	14,000
Oct 30	MILLWALL	W 1-0	Parker S	14,009
Nov 6	Swindon Town	L 0-4		14,000
Nov 13	LEYTON ORIENT	D 2-2	Dempsey, Rumbold (pen)	12,434
Nov 20	Exeter City	W 3-1	Jennings 2, Parker T	9,167
Dec 18	BRISTOL ROVERS	L 0-1		8,751
Dec 25	Walsall	L 1-2	Parker T	12,956
Dec 27	WALSALL	W 3-2	McGinn, Parker S 2	10,432
Jan 1	Newport County	L 0-3		10,000
Jan 15	SWANSEA TOWN	W 2-0	Rumbold, Brown J	12,200
Jan 22	Reading	L 1-2	Jennings	14,571
Jan 29	BRISTOL CITY	W 2-0	Parker S, Jennings	11,190
Feb 5	CRYSTAL PALACE	W 3-2	Parker S 2, Jennings	10,226
Feb 12	BRIGHTON & HOVE ALBION	D 2-2	Brown J, Parker S	10,695
Feb 19	Watford	W 2-1	Parker S, Rumbold (pen)	12,000
Feb 26	BOURNEMOUTH	W 1-0	Brown J	13,289
Mar 5	NORTHAMPTON TOWN	W 4-2	Jennings 2, Parker S, Parker T	10,443
Mar 12	Norwich City	L 0-2		35,126
Mar 19	PORT VALE	W 4-1	Jennings, Brown J 3	10,722
Mar 26	Millwall	D 0-0		23,175
Apr 2	SWINDON TOWN	W 4-2	Jennings, Parker S, Baird, Rumbold (pen)	12,908
Apr 6	Aldershot	L 0-2		6,000
Apr 9	Leyton Orient	D 1-1	Little	9,000
Apr 15	Southend United	D 1-1	Jennings	17,000
Apr 16	EXETER CITY	D 2-2	Jennings 2	13,552
Apr 18	SOUTHEND UNITED	L 1-3	Jennings	13,336
Apr 23	Bristol City	L 0-2		9,692
Apr 30	ALDERSHOT	W 4-1	Perrett, Parker T, Parker S, Brown J	7,841
May 7	Brighton & Hove Albion	L 1-6	Brown J	11,066

FA Cup

Dec 4	ALDERSHOT	(Rd1) L 0-3	13,220

League & Cup Appearances

PLAYER	LEAGUE	CUP COMPETITION FA CUP	TOTAL
Baird	37	1	38
Bell	41	1	42
Brown (J)	41	1	42
Brown (T)	42	1	43
Clarke	1		1
Day	3		3
Dempsey	22	1	23
Gibson	1		1
Graham		1	1
Hayes	3		3
Jennings	37	1	38
Little	35	1	36
McGinn	8		8
Mitchell	1		1
Nielson	1		1
O'Mahoney	13		13
Parker S	22		22
Parker T	41	1	42
Parry	30	1	31
Perrett	42	1	43
Rees	6		6
Rumbold	35		35

Goalscorers

PLAYER	LEAGUE	CUP COMPETITION FA CUP	TOTAL
Jennings	23		23
Parker T	13		13
Parker S	11		11
Brown J	10		10
Rumbold	6		6
Dempsey	5		5
Little	4		4
McGinn	2		2
Baird	1		1
Perrett	1		1
Opp's o.gs.	2		2

Fact File

Ipswich started and finished the season with away games which had a 6-1 scoreline, one in their favour, one against.

MANAGER: Scott Duncan
CAPTAIN: Dave Bell
TOP SCORER: Bill Jennings
BIGGEST WIN: 6-1 v Bristol Rovers (A), 21 August 1948, Division Three South
HIGHEST ATTENDANCE: 24,569 v Norwich City, 16 October 1948, Division Three South

Final Division Three South Table

		P	W	D	L	F	A	Pts
1	SWANSEA T	42	27	8	7	87	34	62
2	READING	42	25	5	12	77	50	55
3	BOURNEMOUTH	42	22	8	12	69	48	52
4	SWINDON T	42	18	15	9	64	56	51
5	BRISTOL R	42	19	10	13	61	51	48
6	BRIGHTON & HA	42	15	18	9	55	55	48
7	IPSWICH TOWN	42	18	9	15	78	77	45
8	MILLWALL	42	17	11	14	63	64	45
9	TORQUAY U	42	17	11	14	65	70	45
10	NORWICH C	42	16	12	14	67	49	44
11	NOTTS CO	42	19	5	18	102	68	43
12	EXETER C	42	15	10	17	63	76	40
13	PORT VALE	42	14	11	17	51	54	39
14	WALSALL	42	15	8	19	56	64	38
15	NEWPORT CO	42	14	9	19	68	92	37
16	BRISTOL C	42	11	14	17	44	62	36
17	WATFORD	42	10	15	17	41	54	35
18	SOUTHEND U	42	9	16	17	41	46	34
19	LEYTON ORIENT	42	11	12	19	58	80	34
20	NORTHAMPTON T	42	12	9	21	51	62	33
21	ALDERSHOT	42	11	11	20	48	59	33
22	CRYSTAL PALACE	42	8	11	23	38	76	27

Season 1949-50

Football League Division Three South

DATE	OPPONENTS	SCORE	GOALSCORERS	ATTENDANCE
Aug 20	BOURNEMOUTH	L 1-2	O'Brien	15,148
Aug 22	Bristol Rovers	L 0-2		17,508
Aug 27	Crystal Palace	L 0-2		19,100
Aug 31	BRISTOL ROVERS	W 3-1	Brown J, Jennings, O'Brien	12,708
Sep 3	WATFORD	D 1-1	Brown J	14,410
Sep 5	Port Vale	D 2-2	Parker T, O'Brien	12,000
Sep 10	Reading	L 1-3	Parker T	17,491
Sep 17	LEYTON ORIENT	D 4-4	O'Brien, Gibbons 2, Parker S	13,074
Sep 24	Exeter City	D 1-1	Parker S	9,000
Oct 1	NOTTINGHAM FOREST	L 1-2	O'Brien	16,486
Oct 8	Northampton Town	W 2-1	Parker S, O'Brien	13,373
Oct 15	NORWICH CITY	W 3-0	Brown J 3	26,161
Oct 22	Newport County	L 0-1		11,419
Oct 2⁹	BRISTOL CITY	D 0-0		12,717
Nov 5	Brighton & Hove Albion	L 1-2	Parker S	5,451
Nov 12	WALSALL	L 1-5	Parker T	10,749
Nov 19	Millwall	L 1-3	Baird (pen)	17,165
Dec 3	Torquay United	D 2-2	Parker S, O'Brien	7,500
Dec 17	Bournemouth	L 0-4		10,130
Dec 24	CRYSTAL PALACE	D 4-4	O'Brien, Myles 2, Jennings	9,520
Dec 26	Notts County	L 0-2		40,192
Dec 27	NOTTS COUNTY	L 0-4		22,983
Dec 31	Watford	L 0-6		10,424
Jan 14	READING	W 2-0	Parker S, Brown J	10,585
Jan 21	Leyton Orient	L 0-4		10,000
Jan 28	SWINDON TOWN	W 3-1	Driver, Mitchell (pen), Brown J	9,160
Feb 4	EXETER CITY	W 1-0	Gibbons	11,431
Feb 11	ALDERSHOT	W 1-0	Brown J	9,989
Feb 18	Nottingham Forest	L 0-2		20,542
Feb 25	NORTHAMPTON TOWN	D 2-2	Parker S, Mitchell (pen)	11,174
Mar 4	Norwich City	D 1-1	Parker S	32,438
Mar 11	NEWPORT COUNTY	W 1-0	Driver	12,688
Mar 18	Bristol City	L 2-4	O'Brien 2	12,389
Mar 25	BRIGHTON & HOVE ALBION	D 2-2	Parker S, Pole	12,702
Apr 1	Walsall	W 3-1	Pole 2, McCrory	8,765
Apr 7	Southend United	D 2-2	Driver, Pole	20,000
Apr 8	MILLWALL	L 0-3		13,045
Apr 10	SOUTHEND UNITED	L 1-3	O'Brien	11,686
Apr 15	Swindon Town	W 3-0	Driver, Parker S 2	10,000
Apr 22	TORQUAY UNITED	W 3-1	Parker S 2, Brown J	12,632
Apr 29	Aldershot	L 0-5		6,000
May 6	PORT VALE	W 2-1	McCrory, Driver	12,451

FA Cup

Nov 26	BRIGHTON & HOVE ALBION	(Rd1)	W 2-1	Brown J, Baird (pen)	12,265
Dec 10	Chelmsford City	(Rd2)	D 1-1	Brown J	11,327
Dec 14	Chelmsford City	(R)	W 1-0*	Parker S	10,968
Jan 7	West Ham United	(Rd3)	L 1-5	Parker S	25,000

* after extra time

League & Cup Appearances

PLAYER	LEAGUE	CUP COMPETITION FA CUP	TOTAL
Baird	39	4	43
Bell	30	3	33
Brown J	35	4	39
Brown T	42	4	46
Clarke	10	3	13
Dobson	3		3
Driver	18		18
Elsworthy	1		1
Feeney	12		12
Fletcher	5		5
Gibbons	11	2	13
Green	9		9
Hayes	6		6
Jennings	20	2	22
Jones	8		8
Little	11	4	15
McCrory	12		12
Mitchell	40	4	44
Myles	3		3
O'Brien	41	4	45
Parker S	34	4	38
Parker T	36	4	40
Perrett	3		3
Pole	6		6
Rees	11		11
Roberts	1		1
Rumbold	2	1	3
Smith	8	1	9
Snell	5		5

Goalscorers

PLAYER	LEAGUE	CUP COMPETITION FA CUP	TOTAL
Parker S	13	2	15
O'Brien	11		11
Brown J	9	2	11
Driver	5		5
Pole	4		4
Gibbons	3		3
Parker T	3		3
Baird	1	1	2
Jennings	2		2
McCrory	2		2
Mitchell	2		2
Myles	2		2

Fact File

Sammy McCrory became the first Town player to be sent off since they joined the Football League when he was dismissed at Aldershot in the last away game of the season.

MANAGER: Scott Duncan

CAPTAIN: Dave Bell

TOP SCORER: Stanley Parker

BIGGEST WIN: 3-0 v Norwich City (H), 15 October 1949, Division Three South; 3-0 v Swindon Town (A), 15 April 1950, Division Three South

HIGHEST ATTENDANCE: 26,161 v Norwich City, 15 October 1949, Division Three South

Final Division Three South Table

		P	W	D	L	F	A	Pts
1	NOTTS CO	42	25	8	9	95	50	58
2	NORTHAMPTON T	42	20	11	11	72	50	51
3	SOUTHEND U	42	19	13	10	66	48	51
4	NOTTINGHAM F	42	20	9	13	67	39	49
5	TORQUAY U	42	19	10	13	66	63	48
6	WATFORD	42	16	13	13	45	35	45
7	CRYSTAL PALACE	42	15	14	13	55	54	44
8	BRIGHTON & HA	42	16	12	14	57	69	44
9	BRISTOL R	42	19	5	18	51	51	43
10	READING	42	17	8	17	70	64	42
11	NORWICH C	42	16	10	16	65	63	42
12	BOURNEMOUTH	42	16	10	16	57	56	42
13	PORT VALE	42	15	11	16	47	42	41
14	SWINDON T	42	15	11	16	59	62	41
15	BRISTOL C	42	15	10	17	60	61	40
16	EXETER C	42	14	11	17	63	75	39
17	IPSWICH TOWN	42	12	11	19	57	86	35
18	LEYTON ORIENT	42	12	11	19	53	85	35
19	WALSALL	42	9	16	17	61	62	34
20	ALDERSHOT	42	13	8	21	48	60	34
21	NEWPORT CO	42	13	8	21	67	98	34
22	MILLWALL	42	14	4	24	55	63	32

Season 1950-51

Football League Division Three South

DATE	OPPONENTS	SCORE	GOALSCORERS	ATTENDANCE
Aug 19	NORTHAMPTON TOWN	D 1-1	Brown J	15,807
Aug 23	LEYTON ORIENT	D 2-2	Driver, Brown J	12,455
Aug 26	PLYMOUTH ARGYLE	W 2-0	McCrory, O'Brien	15,552
Aug 31	Leyton Orient	L 0-2		16,000
Sep 2	Reading	L 0-2		17,527
Sep 4	Port Vale	L 0-1		16,000
Sep 9	SOUTHEND UNITED	W 1-0	McCrory	12,955
Sep 13	PORT VALE	D 2-2	McCrory 2	10,696
Sep 16	Exeter City	L 0-2		10,000
Sep 23	BOURNEMOUTH	W 1-0	Elsworthy	12,331
Sep 30	Gillingham	W 1-0	Roberts	12,853
Oct 7	Nottingham Forest	D 0-0		26,588
Oct 14	TORQUAY UNITED	W 3-1	Driver, Roberts, Jennings	14,271
Oct 21	Aldershot	W 1-0	Roberts	9,000
Oct 28	SWINDON TOWN	W 4-1	Jennings, Roberts, McCrory 2	12,944
Nov 4	Colchester United	W 3-2	McCrory, Wookey, Driver	14,037
Nov 11	BRISTOL ROVERS	L 2-3	McCrory (pen), Myles	15,315
Nov 18	Crystal Palace	W 3-1	McCrory 3	12,065
Dec 2	Newport County	W 2-1	McCrory 2	11,492
Dec 16	Northampton Town	L 1-2	o.g.	7,078
Dec 23	Plymouth Argyle	L 1-2	Warne	13,860
Dec 25	MILLWALL	W 2-1	McCrory, Roberts	12,981
Dec 26	Millwall	L 0-4		17,922
Dec 30	READING	L 0-2		10,295
Jan 6	WALSALL	W 3-1	Myles, Driver, Warne	9,500
Jan 13	Southend United	L 0-1		8,000
Jan 20	EXETER CITY	W 1-0	Warne	10,446
Jan 27	Walsall	L 0-2		9,334
Feb 3	Bournemouth	L 1-2	Warne	9,617
Feb 10	BRIGHTON & HOVE ALBION	W 3-0	Driver, Warne, Roberts	10,979
Feb 17	GILLINGHAM	W 5-1	Warne 2, Driver, Parker T, McCrory (pen)	9,081
Feb 24	NOTTINGHAM FOREST	L 1-3	Roberts	17,595
Mar 3	Torquay United	W 1-0	Brown J	6,500
Mar 10	ALDERSHOT	W 5-2	Warne, Driver, McCrory (pen), Brown J, o.g.	9,803
Mar 17	Swindon Town	L 0-2		7,003
Mar 23	Watford	W 2-0	Warne 2	7,272
Mar 24	COLCHESTER UNITED	W 3-0	Driver 2, McCrory	19,033
Mar 26	WATFORD	W 2-1	McCrory 2 (1 pen)	13,490
Mar 31	Bristol Rovers	D 1-1	Roberts	16,885
Apr 7	CRYSTAL PALACE	D 1-1	Driver	10,956
Apr 11	NORWICH CITY	L 0-1		24,239
Apr 14	Brighton & Hove Albion	L 0-4		10,763
Apr 18	Bristol City	L 1-2	Roberts	10,314
Apr 21	NEWPORT COUNTY	W 2-1	Warne, Brown J	10,330
Apr 28	Norwich City	W 3-1	McCrory 2 (1 pen), Dobson	30,137
May 5	BRISTOL CITY	W 2-0	Driver, Brown J	10,728

FA Cup

Nov 25	Leyton Orient	(Rd1) W 2-1	Jennings, Parker T	10,560
Dec 9	Brighton & Hove Albion	(Rd2) L 0-2		14,411

Fact File

Between 28 October and 2 December McCrory scored in five consecutive league games.

MANAGER: Scott Duncan

CAPTAIN: Tommy Parker/Len Tyler

TOP SCORER: Sammy McCrory

BIGGEST WIN: 5-1 v Gillingham (H), 17 February 1951, Division Three South

HIGHEST ATTENDANCE: 24,239 v Norwich City, 11 April 1951, Division Three South

League & Cup Appearances

PLAYER	LEAGUE	CUP COMPETITION FA CUP	TOTAL
Baird	44	2	46
Brown J	22		22
Brown T	3		3
Burns	43	2	45
Clarke	1		1
Deacon	2		2
Dobson	2		2
Driver	44	2	46
Elsworthy	2		2
Feeney	44	2	46
Green	1		1
Jennings	9	2	11
Jones	6		6
McCrory	45	2	47
Murchison	4		4
Myles	4		4
O'Brien	9		9
Parker S	11		11
Parker T	45	2	47
Pole	2		2
Rees	46	2	48
Roberts	35	2	37
Tyler	45	2	47
Warne	22		22
Wookey	15	2	17

Goalscorers

PLAYER	LEAGUE	CUP COMPETITION FA CUP	TOTAL
McCrory	21		21
Driver	11		11
Warne	11		11
Roberts	9		9
Brown J	6		6
Jennings	2	1	3
Myles	2		2
Parker T	1	1	2
Dobson	1		1
Elsworthy	1		1
O'Brien	1		1
Wookey	1		1
Opp's o.gs.	2		2

Final Division Three South Table

		P	W	D	L	F	A	Pts
1	NOTTINGHAM F	46	30	10	6	110	40	70
2	NORWICH C	46	25	14	7	82	45	64
3	READING	46	21	15	10	88	53	57
4	PLYMOUTH ARG	46	24	9	13	85	55	57
5	MILLWALL	46	23	10	13	80	57	56
6	BRISTOL R	46	20	15	11	64	42	55
7	SOUTHEND U	46	21	10	15	92	69	52
8	IPSWICH TOWN	46	23	6	17	69	58	52
9	BOURNEMOUTH	46	22	7	17	65	57	51
10	BRISTOL C	46	20	11	15	64	59	51
11	NEWPORT CO	46	19	9	18	77	70	47
12	PORT VALE	46	16	13	17	60	65	45
13	BRIGHTON & HA	46	13	17	16	71	79	43
14	EXETER C	46	18	6	22	62	85	42
15	WALSALL	46	15	10	21	52	62	40
16	COLCHESTER U	46	14	12	20	63	76	40
17	SWINDON T	46	18	4	24	55	67	40
18	ALDERSHOT	46	15	10	21	56	88	40
19	LEYTON ORIENT	46	15	8	23	53	75	38
20	TORQUAY U	46	14	9	23	64	81	37
21	NORTHAMPTON T	46	10	16	20	55	67	36
22	GILLINGHAM	46	13	9	24	69	101	35
23	WATFORD	46	9	11	26	54	88	29
24	CRYSTAL PALACE	46	8	11	27	33	84	27

Season 1951-52

Football League Division Three South

DATE	OPPONENTS	SCORE	GOALSCORERS	ATTENDANCE
Aug 18	SOUTHEND UNITED	W 4-1	Roberts 2, Driver, Garneys	15,828
Aug 22	Millwall	L 0-4		18,000
Aug 25	Newport County	L 1-2	Myles	12,062
Aug 29	MILLWALL	W 3-0	Driver 2, Garneys	11,165
Sep 1	READING	W 4-2	McCrory, Garneys, Driver 2	12,328
Sep 5	BRIGHTON & HOVE ALBION	W 5-0	Garneys, McCrory 2, Parker T, o.g.	13,263
Sep 8	Northampton Town	L 0-1		13,802
Sep 12	Brighton & Hove Albion	L 1-5	McCrory	11,730
Sep 15	PORT VALE	W 2-0	Driver, Myles	9,284
Sep 22	Bristol City	W 2-0	Garneys 2	20,555
Sep 29	PLYMOUTH ARGYLE	D 2-2	Roberts, Myles	15,633
Oct 6	Exeter City	L 1-2	Garneys	7,000
Oct 13	COLCHESTER UNITED	L 0-2		19,275
Oct 20	Crystal Palace	L 1-3	McCrory	20,965
Oct 27	SWINDON TOWN	L 1-5	McCrory (pen)	11,570
Nov 3	Leyton Orient	L 0-2		10,232
Nov 10	WALSALL	L 0-1		10,076
Nov 17	Shrewsbury Town	W 2-0	Driver, McCrory	8,048
Dec 1	Watford	D 1-1	McCrory	10,645
Dec 8	BRISTOL ROVERS	L 1-2	Driver	9,545
Dec 22	NEWPORT COUNTY	W 3-1	Driver, McCrory, Dobson	9,619
Dec 25	NORWICH CITY	L 0-2		15,821
Dec 26	Norwich City	L 0-2		32,011
Dec 29	Reading	L 0-4		15,101
Jan 5	NORTHAMPTON TOWN	W 3-2	Roberts 2, Parker T	10,071
Jan 19	Port Vale	D 0-0		10,500
Jan 26	BRISTOL CITY	D 1-1	Garneys	9,136
Jan 30	TORQUAY UNITED	W 2-0	Garneys 2	4,015
Feb 2	BOURNEMOUTH	W 3-1	Elsworthy, McCrory, Garneys	11,685
Feb 9	Plymouth Argyle	L 0-2		19,039
Feb 16	EXETER CITY	L 2-4	Elsworthy, o.g.	9,839
Feb 23	Bournemouth	D 2-2	Garneys, Havenga	9,968
Mar 1	Colchester United	L 0-1		15,175
Mar 8	CRYSTAL PALACE	D 1-1	McCrory	10,352
Mar 15	Swindon Town	W 2-1	McCrory 2	7,733
Mar 22	LEYTON ORIENT	W 1-0	McCrory	11,096
Mar 29	Walsall	W 3-1	Garneys, Havenga, Gaynor	3,173
Apr 5	SHREWSBURY TOWN	W 1-0	Garneys	10,227
Apr 11	Gillingham	D 1-1	McCrory	14,100
Apr 12	Aldershot	D 1-1	Garneys (pen)	7,500
Apr 14	GILLINGHAM	D 1-1	Murchison	12,550
Apr 19	WATFORD	W 3-0	Elsworthy 2, o.g.	8,901
Apr 23	ALDERSHOT	L 2-3	Roberts, McCrory (pen)	7,726
Apr 26	Bristol Rovers	L 0-1		12,134
Apr 30	Southend United	L 0-5		6,500
May 3	Torquay United	L 0-2		5,563

FA Cup

Nov 29	Merthyr Tydfil	(Rd1) D 2-2	McCrory, Garneys	10,300
Dec 5	MERTHYR TYDFIL	(R) W 1-0	Roberts	10,132
Dec 15	EXETER CITY	(Rd2) W 4-0	Garneys 2, Dobson, Driver	11,819
Jan 12	GATESHEAD	(Rd3) D 2-2	Garneys, Myles (pen)	11,819
Jan 16	Gateshead	(R) D 3-3	Dobson 2, Roberts	13,723
Jan 21	Gateshead*	(2R) L 1-2	Garneys	7,470

* played at Bramall Lane, Sheffield, result after extra time

League & Cup Appearances

PLAYER	LEAGUE	CUP COMPETITION FA CUP	TOTAL
Acres	2		2
Baird	14		14
Ball	4		4
Burns	12	1	13
Clarke	11		11
Deacon	20	3	23
Dobson	13	3	16
Driver	24	5	29
Elsworthy	17	1	18
Feeney	40	6	46
Fletcher	3		3
Garneys	45	6	51
Gaynor	12		12
Green	5	1	6
Havenga	12		12
Jones	3	2	5
McCrory	40	3	43
Murchison	29	6	35
Myles	10	3	13
Parker T	45	6	51
Parry	34	5	39
Rees	34	6	40
Roberts	37	6	43
Snell	2		2
Trenter	2		2
Tyler	28	3	31
Warne	8		8

Goalscorers

PLAYER	LEAGUE	CUP COMPETITION FA CUP	TOTAL
Garneys	15	5	20
McCrory	16	1	17
Driver	9	1	10
Roberts	6	2	8
Dobson	1	3	4
Elsworthy	4		4
Myles	3	1	4
Havenga	2		2
Parker T	2		2
Gaynor	1		1
Murchison	1		1
Opp's o.gs.	3		3

Fact File

During the season Ipswich employed 27 players and nine of them wore the outside right shirt at various stages of the campaign.

MANAGER: Scott Duncan

CAPTAIN: Tommy Parker

TOP SCORER: Tom Garneys

BIGGEST WIN: 5-0 v Brighton & Hove Albion (H), 5 September 1951, Division Three South

HIGHEST ATTENDANCE: 19,275 v Colchester United, 13 October 1951, Division Three South

Final Division Three South Table

		P	W	D	L	F	A	Pts
1	PLYMOUTH ARG	46	29	8	9	107	53	66
2	READING	46	29	3	14	112	60	61
3	NORWICH C	46	26	9	11	89	50	61
4	MILLWALL	46	23	12	11	74	53	58
5	BRIGHTON & HA	46	24	10	12	87	63	58
6	NEWPORT CO	46	21	12	13	77	76	54
7	BRISTOL R	46	20	12	14	89	53	52
8	NORTHAMPTON T	46	22	5	19	93	74	49
9	SOUTHEND U	46	19	10	17	75	66	48
10	COLCHESTER U	46	17	12	17	56	77	46
11	TORQUAY U	46	17	10	19	86	98	44
12	ALDERSHOT	46	18	8	20	78	89	44
13	PORT VALE	46	14	15	17	50	66	43
14	BOURNEMOUTH	46	16	10	20	69	75	42
15	BRISTOL C	46	15	12	19	58	69	42
16	SWINDON T	46	14	14	18	51	68	42
17	IPSWICH TOWN	46	16	9	21	63	74	41
18	LEYTON ORIENT	46	16	9	21	55	68	41
19	CRYSTAL PALACE	46	15	9	22	61	80	39
20	SHREWSBURY T	46	13	10	23	62	86	36
21	WATFORD	46	13	10	23	57	81	36
22	GILLINGHAM	46	11	13	22	71	81	35
23	EXETER C	46	13	9	24	65	86	35
24	WALSALL	46	13	5	28	55	94	31

Season 1952-53

Football League Division Three South

DATE	OPPONENTS	SCORE	GOALSCORERS	ATTENDANCE
Aug 23	Colchester United	D 0-0		14,674
Aug 27	NORWICH CITY	W 2-1	Garneys 2	21,033
Aug 30	READING	L 1-2	Garneys	12,891
Sep 3	Norwich City	L 0-1		28,713
Sep 6	Bournemouth	L 1-2	Brown	10,736
Sep 9	Bristol City	L 2-4	Garneys, o.g.	6,635
Sep 13	SOUTHEND UNITED	D 0-0		11,211
Sep 17	BRISTOL CITY	W 1-0	Elsworthy	7,118
Sep 20	Watford	L 0-1		17,126
Sep 24	SHREWSBURY TOWN	W 2-1	Garneys, Elsworthy	7,006
Sep 27	BRIGHTON & HOVE ALBION	W 1-0	Elsworthy	10,993
Oct 1	CRYSTAL PALACE	W 2-0	Elsworthy, Callaghan	5,783
Oct 4	Newport County	W 3-1	Havenga, Garneys 2	9,645
Oct 11	COVENTRY CITY	W 3-0	Garneys, Elsworthy	13,375
			Callaghan	
Oct 18	Exeter City	D 1-1	Garneys	13,000
Oct 25	BRISTOL ROVERS	L 1-5	Garneys	14,829
Nov 1	Millwall	L 2-3	Gaynor, Garneys	22,484
Nov 8	GILLINGHAM	D 1-1	Callaghan	9,440
Nov 15	Walsall	W 3-1	Garneys, Brown, Ball	5,724
Nov 29	Queens Park Rangers	D 2-2	Gaynor, Parker	8,857
Dec 13	Aldershot	D 1-1	Garneys	4,676
Dec 20	COLCHESTER UNITED	D 2-2	Elsworthy, Jones	12,572
Dec 26	Leyton Orient	L 1-3	Brown	6,597
Jan 3	READING	D 1-1	Elsworthy	10,531
Jan 14	TORQUAY UNITED	D 2-2	Elsworthy, o.g.	4,108
Jan 17	BOURNEMOUTH	W 2-1	Brown, Garneys	9,630
Jan 24	Southend United	L 0-2		6,500
Jan 31	Torquay United	L 1-4	Garneys	5,432
Feb 7	WATFORD	D 1-1	Elsworthy	8,177
Feb 14	Brighton & Hove Albion	W 4-1	Garneys 2, Brown	8,149
			Elsworthy	
Feb 21	NEWPORT COUNTY	W 3-0	Elsworthy, Brown,	10,019
			Garneys	
Feb 28	Coventry City	L 0-2		14,000
Mar 7	EXETER CITY	L 0-1		8,867
Mar 14	Bristol Rovers	L 0-3		21,224
Mar 21	MILLWALL	L 1-6	Parker	9,373
Mar 25	LEYTON ORIENT	L 0-1		3,116
Mar 28	Gillingham	D 1-1	Murchison	8,868
Apr 4	WALSALL	W 5-0	Elsworthy, Parker 2	6,801
			Ball, o.g.	
Apr 6	NORTHAMPTON TOWN	D 1-1	Elsworthy	12,049
Apr 7	Northampton Town	L 0-2		12,307
Apr 11	Shrewsbury Town	D 2-2	Rees, Parker	8,294
Apr 15	SWINDON TOWN	D 1-1	Brown	5,478
Apr 18	QUEENS PARK RANGERS	L 0-1		8,372
Apr 22	Crystal Palace	D 1-1	Dobson	10,007
Apr 25	Swindon Town	L 0-2		8,518
May 1	ALDERSHOT	W 2-1	Brown, Dobson	4,595

FA Cup

Nov 22	BOURNEMOUTH	(Rd1) D 2-2	Garneys, Elsworthy	10,337
Nov 26	Bournemouth	(R) D 2-2*	Elsworthy, Garneys	7,294
Dec 1	Bournemouth †	(R2) W 3-2	Garneys 2, Gaynor	4,756
Dec 6	Bradford City	(Rd2) D 1-1	Elsworthy	13,348
Dec 10	BRADFORD CITY	(R) W 5-1	Garneys, Brown 2,	9,350
			Elsworthy 2	
Jan 10	Everton	(Rd3) L 2-3	Garneys, Brown	42,252

* after extra time
† played at Highbury

Fact File

This was the first season since becoming a professional club that Ipswich failed to score in their opening game.

MANAGER: Scott Duncan

CAPTAIN: Tommy Parker

TOP SCORER: Tom Garneys

BIGGEST WIN: 5-0 v Walsall (H), 4 April 1953, Division Three South

HIGHEST ATTENDANCE: 14,829 v Bristol Rovers, 25 October 1952, Division Three South

League & Cup Appearances

PLAYER	LEAGUE	CUP COMPETITION	TOTAL
		FA CUP	
Acres	27	5	32
Ball	28	6	34
Brown	35	6	41
Callaghan	13		13
Clarke	9		9
Deacon	31	6	37
Dobson	10		10
Elsworthy	39	6	45
Feeney	30		30
Garneys	34	6	40
Gaynor	35	5	40
Havenga	7		7
Higgins	2		2
Jones	13		13
Murchison	7		7
Myles	46	6	52
Newman	18	5	23
Parker	45	6	51
Parry	28		28
Rees	39	6	45
Snell	6		6
Tennant	4		4

Goalscorers

PLAYER	LEAGUE	CUP COMPETITION	TOTAL
		FA CUP	
Garneys	18	6	24
Elsworthy	13	5	18
Brown	9	3	12
Parker	5		5
Callaghan	3		3
Gaynor	2	1	3
Ball	2		2
Dobson	1		1
Havenga	1		1
Jones	1		1
Murchison	1		1
Rees	1		1
Opp's o.gs.	3		3

Final Division Three South Table

		P	W	D	L	F	A	PTS
1	BRISTOL R	46	26	12	8	92	46	64
2	MILLWALL	46	24	14	8	82	44	62
3	NORTHAMPTON T	46	26	10	10	109	70	62
4	NORWICH C	46	25	10	11	99	55	60
5	BRISTOL C	46	22	15	9	95	61	59
6	COVENTRY C	46	19	12	15	77	62	50
7	BRIGHTON & HA	46	19	12	15	81	75	50
8	SOUTHEND U	46	18	13	15	69	74	49
9	BOURNEMOUTH	46	19	9	18	74	69	47
10	WATFORD	46	15	17	14	62	63	47
11	READING	46	19	8	19	69	64	46
12	TORQUAY U	46	18	9	19	87	88	45
13	CRYSTAL PALACE	46	15	13	18	66	82	43
14	LEYTON ORIENT	46	16	10	20	68	73	42
15	NEWPORT CO	46	16	10	20	70	82	42
16	IPSWICH TOWN	46	13	15	18	60	69	41
17	EXETER C	46	13	14	19	61	71	40
18	SWINDON T	46	14	12	20	64	79	40
19	ALDERSHOT	46	12	15	19	61	77	39
20	QPR	46	12	15	19	61	82	39
21	GILLINGHAM	46	12	15	19	55	74	39
22	COLCHESTER U	46	12	14	20	59	76	38
23	SHREWSBURY T	46	12	12	22	68	91	36
24	WALSALL	46	7	10	29	56	118	24

Season 1953-54

Football League Division Three South

DATE	OPPONENTS	SCORE	GOALSCORERS	ATTENDANCE
Aug 19	Walsall	W 2-0	Myles, McLuckie	13,075
Aug 22	COLCHESTER UNITED	W 3-0	McLuckie 2, Reed	18,130
Aug 26	TORQUAY UNITED	W 2-1	Garneys 2	11,476
Aug 29	Millwall	W 2-1	Dobson, Parker	18,121
Sep 2	Torquay United	D 1-1	McLuckie	7,692
Sep 5	LEYTON ORIENT	W 3-1	Brown, Garneys, Elsworthy	13,851
Sep 9	GILLINGHAM	W 6-1	Myles (pen), Reed, McLuckie, Parker 2, Brown	12,458
Sep 12	Reading	L 1-3	Reed	17,330
Sep 16	Gillingham	D 1-1	Brown	7,000
Sep 17	ALDERSHOT	W 4-0	Reed, Crowe, McLuckie, Garneys	15,379
Sep 24	Swindon Town	W 2-1	Crowe, Garneys	13,417
Sep 31	WALSALL	W 3-0	Reed, Garneys, Elsworthy	15,026
Nov 7	Shrewsbury Town	D 1-1	Parker	10,227
Nov 14	EXETER CITY	D 1-1	McLuckie	15,125
Nov 28	NORWICH CITY	D 1-1	Reed	25,961
Dec 5	Queens Park Rangers	L 1-3	Reed	13,760
Dec 19	Colchester United	W 2-1	Reed, Elsworthy	10,316
Dec 25	Coventry City	W 3-1	Reed, Parker, Brown	16,820
Dec 26	COVENTRY CITY	W 4-1	Elsworthy 3 (1 pen), McLuckie	18,922
Jan 2	MILLWALL	D 1-1		15,178
Jan 16	Leyton Orient	W 2-1	Parker (pen), Elsworthy	17,306
Jan 23	READING	L 0-1		18,016
Feb 6	Southend United	L 1-3	Garneys	7,000
Feb 13	BRIGHTON & HOVE ALBION	L 2-3	McLuckie, Reed	16,479
Feb 27	BRISTOL CITY	W 2-1	Garneys 2	14,182
Mar 3	Watford	L 0-1		6,760
Mar 6	Aldershot	L 0-3		6,624
Mar 13	NEWPORT COUNTY	L 1-2	Reed	12,531
Mar 20	Norwich City	W 2-1	Garneys, Crowe	27,079
Mar 25	Northampton Town	L 0-1		7,000
Mar 27	SHREWSBURY TOWN	D 0-0		13,439
Apr 3	Exeter City	W 2-1	Garneys, Callaghan	9,500
Apr 7	SOUTHAMPTON	W 2-1	Reed, Garneys	15,021
Apr 10	QUEENS PARK RANGERS	W 2-1	Garneys, Parker	15,309
Apr 16	CRYSTAL PALACE	W 2-0	Garneys, Phillips	18,290
Apr 17	Southampton	D 1-1	Garneys	17,562
Apr 19	Crystal Palace	D 1-1	Crowe	15,568
Apr 24	SWINDON TOWN	W 2-0	Callaghan, Crowe	17,802
Apr 26	Newport County	W 2-1	Callaghan, Garneys	11,258
May 1	NORTHAMPTON TOWN	W 2-1	Phillips, o.g.	22,136

FA Cup

Nov 21	READING	(Rd1) W 4-1	Elsworthy, Crowe, Garneys 2	16,586
Dec 12	WALTHAMSTOW AVENUE	(Rd2) D 2-2	Myles (pen), Brown	18,403
Jan 16	Walthamstow Avenue	(R) W 1-0	Crowe	11,000
Jan 9	OLDHAM ATHLETIC	(Rd3) D 3-3	Garneys, Myles, Reed	16,711
Jan 12	Oldham Athletic	(R) W 1-0	Garneys	16,241
Jan 30	BIRMINGHAM CITY	(Rd4) W 1-0	Reed	25,000
Feb 20	Preston North End	(Rd5) L 1-6	Garneys	34,500

League & Cup Appearances

PLAYER	LEAGUE	CUP COMPETITION FA CUP	TOTAL
Acres	46	7	53
Brown	20	5	25
Callaghan	6		6
Crowe	32	4	36
Dobson	2		2
Elsworthy	33	5	38
Feeney	44	7	51
Fletcher	4		4
Garneys	44	7	51
Jones	2		2
McLuckie	46	7	53
Myles	46	7	53
Parker	46	7	53
Parry	46	7	53
Phillips	4		4
Reed	41	7	48
Rees	41	7	48

Goalscorers

PLAYER	LEAGUE	CUP COMPETITION FA CUP	TOTAL
Garneys	19	5	24
Reed	13	2	15
McLuckie	12		12
Elsworthy	9	1	10
Parker	8		8
Crowe	6	2	8
Brown	4	1	5
Myles	3	2	5
Callaghan	3		3
Phillips	2		2
Acres	1		1
Dobson	1		1
Opp's o.gs.	1		1

Final Division Three South Table

		P	W	D	L	F	A	Pts
1	IPSWICH TOWN	46	27	10	9	82	51	64
2	BRIGHTON & HA	46	26	9	11	86	61	61
3	BRISTOL C	46	25	6	15	88	66	56
4	WATFORD	46	21	10	15	85	69	52
5	NORTHAMPTON T	46	20	11	15	82	55	51
6	SOUTHAMPTON	46	22	7	17	76	63	51
7	NORWICH C	46	20	11	15	73	66	51
8	READING	46	20	9	17	86	73	49
9	EXETER C	46	20	8	18	68	58	48
10	GILLINGHAM	46	19	10	17	61	66	48
11	LEYTON ORIENT	46	18	11	17	79	73	47
12	MILLWALL	46	19	9	18	74	77	47
13	TORQUAY U	46	17	12	17	81	88	46
14	COVENTRY C	46	18	9	19	61	56	45
15	NEWPORT CO	46	19	6	21	61	81	44
16	SOUTHEND U	46	18	7	21	69	71	43
17	ALDERSHOT	46	17	9	20	74	86	43
18	QPR	46	16	10	20	60	68	42
19	BOURNEMOUTH	46	16	8	22	67	70	40
19	SWINDON T	46	15	10	21	67	70	40
21	SHREWSBURY T	46	14	12	20	65	76	40
22	CRYSTAL PALACE	46	14	12	20	60	86	40
23	COLCHESTER U	46	10	10	26	50	78	30
24	WALSALL	46	9	8	29	40	87	26

Fact File

Ipswich recorded eight successive league wins between 23 September and 31 October.

MANAGER: Scott Duncan

CAPTAIN: Tommy Parker

TOP SCORER: Tom Garneys

BIGGEST WIN: 6-1 v Gillingham (H), 9 September 1953, Division Three South

HIGHEST ATTENDANCE: 25,961 v Norwich City, 28 November 1953, Division Three South

Season 1954-55

Football League Division Two

DATE	OPPONENTS	SCORE	GOALSCORERS	ATTENDANCE
Aug 21	Rotherham United	L 2-3	Elsworthy, Garneys	14,594
Aug 25	Middlesbrough	W 1-0	Garneys	23,357
Aug 28	LUTON TOWN	W 3-1	Garneys 2, Reed	20,625
Sep 1	MIDDLESBROUGH	W 6-1	Garneys 2, Crowe 2, Reed, McLuckie	19,782
Sep 4	Hull City	L 2-4	Phillips 2	28,091
Sep 8	Birmingham City	L 0-4		21,238
Sep 11	LINCOLN CITY	L 1-2	Reed	17,831
Sep 15	BIRMINGHAM CITY	L 1-2	Crowe	16,783
Sep 18	Bury	L 1-2	Garneys	15,187
Sep 22	STOKE CITY	L 0-1		15,536
Sep 25	LEEDS UNITED	L 1-2	Garneys	16,716
Oct 2	Nottingham Forest	L 0-2		15,990
Oct 9	Blackburn Rovers	L 1-4	Myles	27,083
Oct 16	FULHAM	L 2-4	Acres, McLuckie	20,059
Oct 23	Port Vale	D 3-3	McLuckie, Malcolm, Grant	14,532
Oct 30	DONCASTER ROVERS	W 5-1	Malcolm, Garneys 4	17,866
Nov 6	Derby County	L 0-2		11,332
Nov 13	WEST HAM UNITED	L 0-3		18,650
Nov 20	Bristol Rovers	L 0-4		19,619
Nov 27	PLYMOUTH ARGYLE	W 2-1	Garneys, Reed	12,826
Dec 4	Swansea Town	L 1-6	Callaghan W	18,150
Dec 11	NOTTS COUNTY	L 0-1		12,442
Dec 18	ROTHERHAM UNITED	D 2-2	Garneys 2 (1 pen)	11,360
Dec 25	Liverpool	L 2-6	Garneys, Parker	24,704
Dec 27	LIVERPOOL	W 2-0	Grant, Reed	19,481
Jan 1	Luton Town	L 2-3	Phillips, Parker (pen)	16,581
Feb 5	BURY	L 2-3	o.g. Garneys	11,394
Feb 12	Leeds United	L 1-4	McLuckie	12,038
Feb 26	BLACKBURN ROVERS	D 1-1	Grant	13,389
Mar 5	Fulham	L 1-4	Garneys	17,179
Mar 9	NOTTINGHAM FOREST	W 2-1	Brown, Garneys	4,937
Mar 12	PORT VALE	W 1-0	Garneys	12,970
Mar 19	Doncaster Rovers	D 1-1	Reed	8,137
Mar 26	DERBY COUNTY	W 2-1	Phillips, Parker (pen)	13,869
Apr 2	West Ham United	L 0-4		24,023
Apr 9	BRISTOL ROVERS	W 1-0	Brown	16,186
Apr 11	Stoke City	L 0-3		20,554
Apr 16	Plymouth Argyle	L 0-2		20,183
Apr 18	HULL CITY	W 2-0	McLuckie, Grant	11,942
Apr 23	SWANSEA TOWN	D 1-1	Brown	18,515
Apr 27	Lincoln City	D 1-1	Elsworthy	8,201
Apr 30	Notts County	L 1-2	McLuckie	10,812

FA Cup

Jan 8	BISHOP AUCKLAND	(Rd3) D 2-2	Garneys, Reed	15,934
Jan 12	Bishop Auckland	(R) L 0-3		9,000

League & Cup Appearances

PLAYER	LEAGUE	CUP COMPETITION FA CUP	TOTAL
Acres	38		38
Brown	21		21
Callaghan H	1		1
Callaghan W	2	1	3
Crowe	18	1	19
Elsworthy	14		14
Feeney	39	2	41
Fletcher	5	1	6
Garneys	24	1	25
Grant	28	2	30
Jones	1		1
Malcolm	19	2	21
McLuckie	40	2	42
McMillan	12		12
Murchison	2		2
Myles	33	1	34
Parker	41	2	43
Parry	30	2	32
Phillips	12	1	13
Reed	40	2	42
Rees	41	2	43
Walls	1		1

Goalscorers

PLAYER	LEAGUE	CUP COMPETITION FA CUP	TOTAL
Garneys	20	1	21
Reed	6	1	7
McLuckie	6		6
Grant	4		4
Phillips	4		4
Brown	3		3
Crowe	3		3
Parker	3		3
Elsworthy	2		2
Malcolm	2		2
Acres	1		1
Callaghan W	1		1
Myles	1		1
Opp's o.gs.	1		1

Fact File

Billy Reed became the first player to earn an international cap while on Ipswich's books when he played for Wales against both Yugoslavia and Scotland.

MANAGER: Scott Duncan
CAPTAIN: Tommy Parker
TOP SCORER: Tom Garneys
BIGGEST WIN: 6-1 v Middlesbrough (H), 1 September 1954, Division Two
HIGHEST ATTENDANCE: 20,625 v Luton Town, 28 August 1954, Division Two

Final Division Two Table

		P	W	D	L	F	A	Pts
1	BIRMINGHAM C	42	22	10	10	92	47	54
2	LUTON T	42	23	8	11	88	53	54
3	ROTHERHAM U	42	25	4	13	94	64	54
4	LEEDS U	42	23	7	12	70	53	53
5	STOKE C	42	21	10	11	69	46	52
6	BLACKBURN R	42	22	6	14	114	79	50
7	NOTTS CO	42	21	6	15	74	71	48
8	WEST HAM U	42	18	10	14	74	70	46
9	BRISTOL R	42	19	7	16	75	70	45
10	SWANSEA T	42	17	9	16	86	83	43
11	LIVERPOOL	42	16	10	16	92	96	42
12	MIDDLESBROUGH	42	18	6	18	73	82	42
13	BURY	42	15	11	16	77	72	41
14	FULHAM	42	14	11	17	76	79	39
15	NOTTINGHAM F	42	16	7	19	58	62	39
16	LINCOLN C	42	13	10	19	68	79	36
17	PORT VALE	42	12	11	19	48	71	35
18	DONCASTER R	42	14	7	21	58	95	35
19	HULL C	42	12	10	20	44	69	34
20	PLYMOUTH ARG	42	12	7	23	57	82	31
21	IPSWICH TOWN	42	11	6	25	57	92	28
22	DERBY CO	42	7	9	26	53	82	23

Season 1955-56

Football League Division Three South

DATE	OPPONENTS	SCORE	GOALSCORERS	ATTENDANCE
Aug 20	TORQUAY UNITED	L 0-2		15,796
Aug 24	SOUTHAMPTON	W 4-2	Garneys, McLuckie, Parker 2	12,545
Aug 27	Newport County	L 1-2	Garneys	8,595
Aug 31	Southampton	D 2-2	Parker 2 (1 pen)	9,988
Sep 3	SWINDON TOWN	W 6-2	Parker 3, Garneys, Grant, Reed	13,238
Sep 7	WALSALL	W 5-2	Elsworthy, Garneys, Reed 3	13,527
Sep 10	Queens Park Rangers	D 1-1	Parker	11,763
Sep 15	Walsall	W 3-1	Parker, Garneys, McLuckie	12,496
Sep 17	NORTHAMPTON TOWN	W 1-0	Yeoman o.g.	17,629
Sep 21	SHREWSBURY TOWN	W 2-1	Garneys, Grant	12,627
Sep 24	Aldershot	W 3-0	Grant, Brown, Garneys	7,502
Sep 28	Brighton & Hove Albion	L 0-3		13,642
Oct 1	CRYSTAL PALACE	D 3-3	Parker 2, Reed	15,332
Oct 8	BOURNEMOUTH	W 1-0	Garneys	17,084
Oct 15	Gillingham	D 0-0		12,193
Oct 22	MILLWALL	W 6-2	Parker 2 (1 pen), Reed, Grant 3	13,707
Oct 29	Reading	W 5-1	Blackman, Grant 3, Reed	10,070
Nov 5	WATFORD	D 0-0		16,194
Nov 12	Brentford	L 2-3	McLuckie, Acres	14,795
Nov 26	Southend United	W 3-2	Grant, Parker, Blackman	13,340
Dec 3	EXETER CITY	D 2-2	Blackman, Grant	14,638
Dec 17	Torquay United	D 2-2	Myles, Reed	7,173
Dec 24	NEWPORT COUNTY	W 3-2	Brown, Parker, Reed	12,438
Dec 26	Colchester United	D 3-3	Parker 2 (1 pen), Grant	13,176
Dec 27	COLCHESTER UNITED	W 3-1	McLuckie, Blackman, Reed	22,644
Dec 31	Swindon Town	W 1-0	Parker	10,909
Jan 7	COVENTRY CITY	W 1-0	Garneys	14,991
Jan 14	QUEENS PARK RANGERS	W 4-1	Parker 2, Garneys 2	12,168
Jan 21	Northampton Town	W 5-0	Garneys 3, Parker, Reed	13,103
Feb 4	ALDERSHOT	W 2-1	Parker, Reed	12,974
Feb 11	Crystal Palace	L 0-1		5,738
Feb 18	Bournemouth	D 1-1	Parker	8,514
Feb 25	GILLINGHAM	D 1-1	Parker	12,957
Mar 3	Millwall	W 5-0	Grant 3, Elsworthy, Garneys	7,404
Mar 10	READING	D 3-3	Leadbetter, Parker 2	15,053
Mar 17	Watford	W 2-0	Garneys, Parker	9,450
Mar 24	BRENTFORD	D 1-1	Lowden o.g.	13,672
Mar 30	NORWICH CITY	W 4-1	Garneys, Elsworthy, Parker, Grant	22,984
Mar 31	Coventry City	L 1-3	Garneys	15,369
Apr 2	Norwich City	L 2-3	Acres, Garneys	31,054
Apr 7	SOUTHEND UNITED	W 3-0	Leadbetter, Parker, McLuckie	13,484
Apr 14	Exeter City	D 2-2	Blackman, Parker	6,607
Apr 21	LEYTON ORIENT	W 2-0	McLuckie, Blackman	22,344
Apr 25	BRIGHTON & HOVE ALBION	W 2-1	Blackman, Snell	18,223
Apr 28	Shrewsbury Town	D 1-1	Leadbetter	7,308
May 3	Leyton Orient	W 2-1	Leadbetter, Blackman	15,379

FA Cup

Nov 19	Peterborough United	(Rd1) L 1-3	Parker	20,843

League & Cup Appearances

PLAYER	LEAGUE	CUP COMPETITION FA CUP	TOTAL
Acres	43	1	44
Ashcroft	7		7
Bailey	2		2
Baker	20		20
Blackman	13	1	14
Brown	8		8
Deacon	1		1
Elsworthy	43	1	44
Feeney	5		5
Garneys	36		36
Grant	35	1	36
Leadbetter	22		22
Macrow	1		1
Malcolm	43	1	44
McLuckie	38	1	39
McMillan	37	1	38
Millward	3		3
Myles	26	1	27
Parker	44	1	45
Reed	30	1	31
Rees	46	1	47
Snell	3		3

Goalscorers

PLAYER	LEAGUE	CUP COMPETITION FA CUP	TOTAL
Parker	30	1	31
Garneys	19		19
Grant	16		16
Reed	12		12
Blackman	8		8
McLuckie	6		6
Leadbetter	4		4
Elsworthy	3		3
Acres	2		2
Brown	2		2
Myles	1		1
Snell	1		1
Opp's o.gs.	2		2

Fact File

A tele-recording of part of the Peterborough v Ipswich FA Cup tie was shown in *Sports Special* by the BBC on 19 November 1955. This was the first time that Ipswich Town had appeared on television.

MANAGER: Alf Ramsey

CAPTAIN: Tommy Parker

TOP SCORER: Tommy Parker

BIGGEST WIN: 5-0 v Northampton Town (A), 21 January 1956, Division Three South; 5-0 v Millwall (A), 3 March 1956, Division Three South

HIGHEST ATTENDANCE: 22,984 v Norwich City, 30 March 1956, Division Three South

Final Division Three South Table

		P	W	D	L	F	A	Pts
1	LEYTON ORIENT	46	29	8	9	106	49	66
2	BRIGHTON & HA	46	29	7	10	112	50	65
3	IPSWICH TOWN	46	25	14	7	106	60	64
4	SOUTHEND U	46	21	11	14	88	80	53
5	TORQUAY U	46	20	12	14	86	63	52
6	BRENTFORD	46	19	14	13	69	66	52
7	NORWICH C	46	19	13	14	86	82	51
8	COVENTRY C	46	20	9	17	73	60	49
9	BOURNEMOUTH	46	19	10	17	63	51	48
10	GILLINGHAM	46	19	10	17	69	71	48
11	NORTHAMPTON T	46	20	7	19	67	71	47
12	COLCHESTER U	46	18	11	17	76	81	47
13	SHREWSBURY T	46	17	12	17	69	66	46
14	SOUTHAMPTON	46	18	8	20	91	81	44
15	ALDERSHOT	46	12	16	18	70	90	40
16	EXETER C	46	15	10	21	58	77	40
17	READING	46	15	9	22	70	79	39
18	QPR	46	14	11	21	64	86	39
19	NEWPORT CO	46	15	9	22	58	79	39
20	WALSALL	46	15	8	23	68	84	38
21	WATFORD	46	13	11	22	52	85	37
22	MILLWALL	46	15	6	25	83	100	36
23	CRYSTAL PALACE	46	12	10	24	54	83	34
24	SWINDON T	46	8	14	24	34	78	30

Season 1956-57

Football League Division Three South

DATE	OPPONENTS	SCORE	GOALSCORERS	ATTENDANCE
Aug 18	Torquay United	L 1-4	Leadbetter	9,842
Aug 22	Bournemouth	L 0-1		12,365
Aug 25	MILLWALL	L 0-2		13,678
Aug 29	BOURNEMOUTH	W 1-0	Leadbetter	11,651
Sep 1	Brighton & Hove Albion	L 2-3	Leadbetter (pen), Phillips	15,177
Sep 6	Walsall	L 0-2		9,399
Sep 8	GILLINGHAM	D 1-1	Phillips	11,659
Sep 12	WALSALL	D 2-2	Phillips 2	10,389
Sep 15	Swindon Town	L 1-3	Phillips	8,409
Sep 19	COVENTRY CITY	W 4-0	Phillips 2, Garneys 2	9,272
Sep 22	BRENTFORD	W 4-0	Garneys, Grant 2, Millward	12,888
Sep 24	Coventry City	D 1-1	Millward	19,253
Sep 29	Aldershot	L 1-3	Millward	5,223
Oct 6	COLCHESTER UNITED	W 3-1	Phillips 3	20,321
Oct 13	Newport County	L 0-1		12,687
Oct 20	READING	W 4-2	Phillips 2, Garneys 2	11,671
Oct 27	Plymouth Argyle	W 2-1	Millward, Garneys	12,679
Nov 3	QUEENS PARK RANGERS	W 4-0	Phillips 3, Garneys	12,778
Nov 10	Northampton Town	L 1-2	Myles	9,655
Nov 24	Crystal Palace	W 3-1	Phillips, Garneys, Reed	10,431
Dec 1	EXETER CITY	W 3-0	Elsworthy, Phillips, Millward	11,933
Dec 15	TORQUAY UNITED	W 6-0	Elsworthy, Phillips 2, Garneys, Snell, Leadbetter (pen)	12,783
Dec 22	Millwall	D 2-2	Phillips, Reed	8,319
Dec 25	Watford	L 1-2	Garneys	4,544
Dec 26	WATFORD	W 4-1	Phillips 3, Reed	11,348
Dec 29	BRIGHTON & HOVE ALBION	W 4-0	Phillips 2, Garneys 2	15,631
Jan 12	Gillingham	D 1-1	Nekrews o.g.	6,191
Jan 19	SWINDON TOWN	W 4-1	Reed 2, Leadbetter 2	13,375
Jan 26	SHREWSBURY TOWN	W 5-1	Phillips 3, Reed, Leadbetter	15,101
Feb 2	Brentford	D 1-1	Phillips	10,538
Feb 9	ALDERSHOT	W 4-1	Leadbetter, Reed, Phillips, Millward	15,407
Feb 16	Colchester United	D 0-0		18,593
Feb 23	NEWPORT COUNTY	W 5-0	Millward 2, Phillips 2, Myles	13,548
Mar 2	Reading	W 3-1	Phillips 3	10,481
Mar 9	SOUTHAMPTON	W 2-0	Reed 2	18,831
Mar 16	Queens Park Rangers	W 2-0	Andrews o.g., Phillips	12,339
Mar 23	NORTHAMPTON TOWN	L 0-1		17,144
Mar 28	Shrewsbury Town	D 1-1	Leadbetter (pen)	3,789
Mar 30	Southend United	L 0-2		8,754
Apr 6	CRYSTAL PALACE	W 4-2	Reed, Elsworthy, Blackman,Phillips	12,559
Apr 13	Exeter City	W 2-1	Leadbetter, Phillips	5,753
Apr19	Norwich City	W 2-1	Millward, Phillips	28,783
Apr 20	PLYMOUTH ARGYLE	W 2-1	Leadbetter, Blackman	16,752
Apr 22	NORWICH CITY	W 3-1	Phillips 2, Leadbetter	21,755
Apr 27	SOUTHEND UNITED	D 3-3	Blackman 2, Elsworthy	20,085
May 1	Southampton	W 2-0	Leadbetter, Acres	10,946

FA Cup

Nov 7	HASTINGS UNITED	(Rd1) W 4-0	Leadbetter (pen), Garneys, Phillips 2	13,481
Dec 8	Watford	(Rd2) W 3-1	Garneys, Phillips 2	13,913
Jan 5	FULHAM	(Rd3) L 2-3	Phillips, Garneys	22,199

Fact File

With 41 goals from 41 games, Ted Phillips was the highest scorer in the entire Football League.

MANAGER: Alf Ramsey

CAPTAIN: Doug Rees/Basil Acres

TOP SCORER: Ted Phillips

BIGGEST WIN: 6-0 v Torquay United (H), 15 December 1956, Division Three South

HIGHEST ATTENDANCE: 21,755 v Norwich City, 22 April 1957, Division Three South

League & Cup Appearances

PLAYER	LEAGUE	CUP COMPETITION FA CUP	TOTAL
Acres	22		22
Bailey	46	3	49
Blackman	12		12
Carberry	25	3	28
Deacon	4		4
Elsworthy	39	3	42
Garneys	28	3	31
Grant	12		12
Leadbetter	45	3	48
Macrow	1		1
Malcolm	43	3	46
McLuckie	14		14
Millward	35	3	38
Myles	41	3	44
Parker	3		3
Phillips	41	3	44
Reed	37	3	40
Rees	45	3	48
Snell	11		11
Thrower	2		2

Goalscorers

PLAYER	LEAGUE	CUP COMPETITION FA CUP	TOTAL
Phillips	41	5	46
Garneys	12	3	15
Leadbetter	13	1	14
Reed	10		10
Millward	9		9
Blackman	4		4
Elsworthy	4		4
Grant	2		2
Myles	2		2
Acres	1		1
Snell	1		1
Opp's o.gs.	2		2

Final Division Three South Table

		P	W	D	L	F	A	Pts
1	IPSWICH TOWN	46	25	9	12	101	54	59
2	TORQUAY U	46	24	11	11	89	64	59
3	COLCHESTER U	46	22	14	10	84	56	58
4	SOUTHAMPTON	46	22	10	14	76	52	54
5	BOURNEMOUTH	46	19	14	13	88	62	52
6	BRIGHTON & HA	46	19	14	13	86	65	52
7	SOUTHEND U	46	18	12	16	73	65	48
8	BRENTFORD	46	16	16	14	78	76	48
9	SHREWSBURY T	46	15	18	13	72	79	48
10	QPR	46	18	11	17	61	60	47
11	WATFORD	46	18	10	18	72	75	46
12	NEWPORT CO	46	16	13	17	65	62	45
13	READING	46	18	9	19	80	81	45
14	NORTHAMPTON T	46	18	9	19	66	73	45
15	WALSALL	46	16	12	18	80	74	44
16	COVENTRY C	46	16	12	18	74	84	44
17	MILLWALL	46	16	12	18	64	84	44
18	PLYMOUTH ARG	46	16	11	19	68	73	43
19	ALDERSHOT	46	15	12	19	79	92	42
20	CRYSTAL PALACE	46	11	18	17	62	75	40
21	EXETER C	46	12	13	21	61	79	37
22	GILLINGHAM	46	12	13	21	54	85	37
23	SWINDON T	46	15	6	25	66	96	36
24	NORWICH C	46	8	15	23	61	94	31

Season 1957-58

Football League Division Two

DATE	OPPONENTS	SCORE	GOALSCORERS	ATTENDANCE
Aug 24	Blackburn Rovers	D 0-0		24,406
Aug 28	BARNSLEY	W 3-0	Garneys, Pickett, Rees Derek	20,468
Aug 31	ROTHERHAM UNITED	L 1-2	Leadbetter	21,436
Sep 4	Barnsley	L 1-5	Siddall	12,272
Sep 7	NOTTS COUNTY	W 2-1	Millward, Siddall	17,018
Sep 11	FULHAM	D 1-1	Acres	19,645
Sep 14	Lincoln City	L 1-2	Millward	12,579
Sep 18	Fulham	D 0-0		16,221
Sep 21	BRISTOL ROVERS	W 3-2	Phillips, Millward, Rees Derek	20,441
Sep 28	Derby County	D 2-2	Phillips 2	18,510
Oct 5	SWANSEA TOWN	L 0-1		19,861
Oct 12	Huddersfield Town	L 0-3		15,276
Oct 19	GRIMSBY TOWN	W 3-2	Elsworthy, Millward, Garneys	18,734
Oct 26	Stoke City	L 1-5	Millward	17,482
Nov 2	BRISTOL CITY	W 4-2	Phillips 3 (1 pen), Garneys	17,681
Nov 9	Cardiff City	D 1-1	Garneys	16,490
Nov 16	LIVERPOOL	W 3-1	Phillips 2, Garneys	20,591
Nov 23	Middlesbrough	L 2-5	Garneys, Phillips (pen)	20,522
Nov 30	LEYTON ORIENT	W 5-3	Phillips 2, Garneys, Millward 2	17,412
Dec 7	Charlton Athletic	L 1-4	Garneys	9,813
Dec 14	DONCASTER ROVERS	W 2-0	Garneys, Johnstone (pen)	13,576
Dec 21	BLACKBURN ROVERS	W 2-1	Millward, Garneys	16,023
Dec 25	West Ham United	D 1-1	Rees Derek	25,515
Dec 26	WEST HAM UNITED	W 2-1	Siddall 2	21,899
Dec 28	Rotherham United	W 4-1	Rees Derek 2, Garneys 2	11,612
Jan 11	Notts County	W 3-0	Garneys, Rees Derek, Reed	13,612
Jan 18	LINCOLN CITY	D 1-1	Leadbetter	16,384
Feb 1	Bristol Rovers	L 1-3	Reed	21,524
Feb 8	DERBY COUNTY	D 2-2	Millward, Rees Derek	15,951
Feb 15	Swansea Town	D 0-0		10,136
Feb 22	MIDDLESBROUGH	D 1-1	Garneys (pen)	17,768
Mar 1	Grimsby Town	W 2-0	Millward, Garneys	13,263
Mar 8	STOKE CITY	L 1-3	Rees Derek	17,169
Mar 15	Bristol City	L 0-1		20,101
Mar 22	CARDIFF CITY	W 3-1	Rees Derek 2, Garneys	13,469
Mar 29	Liverpool	L 1-3	Rees Derek	24,026
Apr 5	HUDDERSFIELD TOWN	W 4-0	Rees Derek, Pickett, Garneys (pen), Millward	15,712
Apr 7	SHEFFIELD UNITED	W 1-0	Siddall	20,126
Apr 8	Sheffield United	D 1-1	Garneys	20,991
Apr 12	Leyton Orient	L 0-2		10,105
Apr 19	CHARLTON ATHLETIC	L 1-4	Garneys	22,615
Apr 26	Doncaster Rovers	D 1-1	Rees Derek	7,045

FA Cup

Jan 4	Crystal Palace	(Rd3) W 1-0	McLuckie	21,939
Jan 25	Manchester United	(Rd4) L 0-2		53,550

League & Cup Appearances

PLAYER	LEAGUE	CUP COMPETITION FA CUP	TOTAL
Acres	18	2	20
Bailey	38	2	40
Blackman	2		2
Carberry	28		28
Deacon	4		4
Elsworthy	38	2	40
Garneys	33	2	35
Johnstone	6		6
Leadbetter	42	2	44
Lundstrum	5		5
Malcolm	38	2	40
McLuckie	3	1	4
McMillan	4		4
Millward	41	2	43
Myles	6	1	7
Phillips	11		11
Pickett	37	1	38
Reed	7	1	8
Rees Derek	31	2	33
Rees Doug	41	2	43
Siddall	28		28
Snell	1		1

Goalscorers

PLAYER	LEAGUE	CUP COMPETITION FA CUP	TOTAL
Garneys	19		19
Rees D	13		13
Millward	11		11
Phillips	11		11
Siddall	5		5
Leadbetter	2		2
Pickett	2		2
Reed	2		2
Acres	1		1
Elsworthy	1		1
Johnstone	1		1
McLuckie		1	1

Fact File

Even though he played only 11 times this season, Ted Phillips still averaged a goal a game.

MANAGER: Alf Ramsey
CAPTAIN: Douglas Rees/Reg Pickett
TOP SCORER: Tom Garneys
BIGGEST WIN: 4-0 v Huddersfield Town (H), 5 April 1958, Division Two
HIGHEST ATTENDANCE: 22,615 v Charlton Athletic, 19 April 1958, Division Two

Final Division Two Table

		P	W	D	L	F	A	Pts
1	WEST HAM U	42	23	11	8	101	54	57
2	BLACKBURN R	42	22	12	8	93	57	56
3	CHARLTON ATH	42	24	7	11	107	69	55
4	LIVERPOOL	42	22	10	10	79	54	54
5	FULHAM	42	20	12	10	97	59	52
6	SHEFFIELD U	42	21	10	11	75	50	52
7	MIDDLESBROUGH	42	19	7	16	83	74	45
8	IPSWICH TOWN	42	16	12	14	68	69	44
9	HUDDERSFIELD T	42	14	16	12	63	66	44
10	BRISTOL R	42	17	8	17	85	80	42
11	STOKE C	42	18	6	18	75	73	42
12	LEYTON ORIENT	42	18	5	19	77	79	41
13	GRIMSBY T	42	17	6	19	86	83	40
14	BARNSLEY	42	14	12	16	70	74	40
15	CARDIFF C	42	14	9	19	63	77	37
16	DERBY CO	42	14	8	20	60	81	36
17	BRISTOL C	42	13	9	20	63	88	35
18	ROTHERHAM U	42	14	5	23	65	101	33
19	SWANSEA T	42	11	9	22	72	99	31
20	LINCOLN C	42	11	9	22	55	82	31
21	NOTTS CO	42	12	6	24	44	80	30
22	DONCASTER R	42	8	11	23	56	88	27

Season 1958-59

Football League Division Two

DATE	OPPONENTS	SCORE	GOALSCORERS	ATTENDANCE
Aug 23	Scunthorpe United	D 1-1	Garneys	13,317
Aug 27	LEYTON ORIENT	W 2-1	Rees Derek, Millward	16,796
Aug 30	SHEFFIELD WEDNESDAY	L 0-2		19,837
Sep 4	Leyton Orient	L 0-2		11,766
Sep 6	Fulham	L 2-3	Rees Derek, Curtis	33,714
Sep 10	DERBY COUNTY	D 1-1	Curtis	15,292
Sep 13	LINCOLN CITY	W 4-1	Rees Derek, Curtis 2, Middleton o.g.	14,498
Sep 17	Derby County	L 2-3	Rees Derek, Pickett	19,020
Sep 20	Sunderland	W 2-0	Rees Derek 2	26,970
Sep 27	STOKE CITY	L 0-2		17,616
Oct 4	Swansea Town	L 2-4	Crawford 2	12,594
Oct 11	Cardiff City	W 2-1	Millward, Crawford	20,357
Oct 18	HUDDERSFIELD TOWN	D 0-0		14,578
Oct 25	Barnsley	L 0-3		11,736
Nov 1	CHARLTON ATHLETIC	W 3-1	Berry 2, Crawford	15,941
Nov 8	Sheffield United	L 0-2		17,628
Nov 15	BRIGHTON & HOVE ALBION	W 5-3	Crawford 3, Johnstone 2	13,006
Nov 22	Grimsby Town	W 3-2	Leadbetter, Crawford 2	9,724
Nov 29	LIVERPOOL	W 2-0	Crawford, Rees Derek	15,634
Dec 6	Middlesbrough	W 3-2	Crawford 2, Berry	25,946
Dec 13	ROTHERHAM UNITED	W 1-0	Crawford	12,126
Dec 20	SCUNTHORPE UNITED	W 3-1	Crawford, Phillips, Rees Derek	13,204
Dec 26	BRISTOL ROVERS	L 0-2		15,808
Dec 27	Bristol Rovers	D 1-1	Myles	20,587
Jan 3	Sheffield Wednesday	L 1-3	Crawford	25,085
Jan 17	FULHAM	L 1-2	Leadbetter	15,960
Jan 31	Lincoln City	L 1-3	Rees Derek	9,784
Feb 7	SUNDERLAND	L 0-2		16,745
Feb 16	Stoke City	L 0-1		11,213
Feb 21	SWANSEA TOWN	W 3-2	Crawford 3	11,023
Mar 7	Huddersfield Town	L 0-3		9,604
Mar 14	BARNSLEY	W 3-1	Crawford 2, Phillips	11,122
Mar 21	Charlton Athletic	L 1-5	Johnstone	15,301
Mar 27	Bristol City	L 0-3		20,117
Mar 28	CARDIFF CITY	D 3-3	Phillips 2, Crawford	12,159
Mar 30	BRISTOL CITY	D 1-1	Phillips	13,549
Apr 4	Brighton & Hove Albion	L 1-4	Phillips	20,739
Apr 11	GRIMSBY TOWN	W 2-1	Crawford 2	12,208
Apr 18	Liverpool	L 1-3	Millward	16,415
Apr 23	Rotherham United	W 2-1	Crawford, Millward	13,069
Apr 25	MIDDLESBROUGH	W 2-1	Phillips 2 (1 pen)	11,927
Apr 30	SHEFFIELD UNITED	W 1-0	Crawford	10,455

FA Cup

Jan 10	HUDDERSFIELD TOWN	(Rd3) W 1-0	Crawford (pen)	14,521
Jan 24	Stoke City	(Rd4) W 1-0	Rees Derek	27,062
Feb 14	LUTON TOWN	(Rd5) L 2-5	Rees Derek 2	26,700

League & Cup Appearances

PLAYER	LEAGUE	CUP COMPETITION FA CUP	TOTAL
Acres	7		7
Bailey	42	3	45
Belcher	3	3	6
Berry	33	3	36
Carberry	39	3	42
Crawford	30	3	33
Curtis	8		8
Deacon	1		1
Elsworthy	11		11
Garneys	4		4
Garrett	1		1
Johnstone	29	3	32
Leadbetter	39	3	42
Malcolm	36	3	39
Millward	21	3	24
Myles	4		4
Owne	3		3
Phillips	22		22
Pickett	37	1	38
Rees Derek	33	3	36
Rees Doug	6		6
Siddall	17		17
Snell	36	3	39

Goalscorers

PLAYER	LEAGUE	CUP COMPETITION FA CUP	TOTAL
Crawford	25	1	26
Rees Derek	9	3	12
Phillips	8		8
Curtis	4		4
Millward	4		4
Berry	3		3
Johnstone	3		3
Leadbetter	2		2
Garneys	1		1
Myles	1		1
Pickett	1		1
Opp's o.gs.	1		1

Final Division Two Table

		P	W	D	L	F	A	Pts
1	SHEFFIELD W	42	28	6	8	106	48	62
2	FULHAM	42	27	6	9	96	61	60
3	SHEFFIELD U	42	23	7	12	82	48	53
4	LIVERPOOL	42	24	5	13	87	62	53
5	STOKE C	42	21	7	14	72	58	49
6	BRISTOL R	42	18	12	12	80	64	48
7	DERBY CO	42	20	8	14	74	71	48
8	CHARLTON ATH	42	18	7	17	92	90	43
9	CARDIFF C	42	18	7	17	65	65	43
10	BRISTOL C	42	17	7	18	74	70	41
11	SWANSEA T	42	16	9	17	79	81	41
12	BRIGHTON & HA	42	15	11	16	74	90	41
13	MIDDLESBROUGH	42	15	10	17	87	71	40
14	HUDDERSFIELD T	42	16	8	18	62	55	40
15	SUNDERLAND	42	16	8	18	64	75	40
16	IPSWICH TOWN	42	17	6	19	62	77	40
17	LEYTON ORIENT	42	14	8	20	71	78	36
18	SCUNTHORPE U	42	12	9	21	55	84	33
19	LINCOLN C	42	11	7	24	63	93	29
20	ROTHERHAM U	42	10	9	23	42	82	29
21	GRIMSBY T	42	9	10	23	62	90	28
22	BARNSLEY	42	10	7	25	55	91	27

Fact File

Ray Crawford set a new club record by scoring in six successive games from 15 November to 20 December.

MANAGER: Alf Ramsey

CAPTAIN: Reg Pickett

TOP SCORER: Ray Crawford

BIGGEST WIN: 4-1 v Lincoln City (H), 13 September 1958, Division Two

HIGHEST ATTENDANCE: 19,837 v Sheffield Wednesday, 30 August 1958, Division Two

The Essential History of Ipswich Town

Football League Division Two

DATE	OPPONENTS	SCORE	GOALSCORERS	ATTENDANCE
Aug 22	HUDDERSFIELD TOWN	L 1-4	Rees	14,441
Aug 26	SWANSEA TOWN	W 4-1	Berry, Phillips 3	11,146
Aug 29	Leyton Orient	L 1-4	Phillips	14,162
Sep 3	Swansea Town	L 1-2	Crawford	16,118
Sep 5	LINCOLN CITY	W 3-0	Berry 2, Crawford	13,042
Sep 7	Bristol Rovers	L 1-2	Phillips	24,093
Sep 12	Aston Villa	L 1-3	Crawford	33,747
Sep 16	BRISTOL ROVERS	W 3-0	Curtis, Leadbetter, Phillips	10,865
Sep 19	SUNDERLAND	W 6-1	Curtis 3, Phillips 3 (1 pen)	14,941
Sep 26	Portsmouth	W 2-0	Leadbetter, Curtis	16,646
Oct 3	STOKE CITY	W 4-0	Curtis 4	16,102
Oct 10	Scunthorpe United	D 2-2	Crawford, Phillips (pen)	11,408
Oct 17	ROTHERHAM UNITED	L 2-3	Crawford, Siddall	15,783
Oct 24	Cardiff City	L 2-3	Lundstrum, Leadbetter	20,223
Oct 31	HULL CITY	W 2-0	Crawford 2	12,738
Nov 7	Sheffield United	L 0-1		14,692
Nov 14	MIDDLESBROUGH	W 1-0	Crawford	12,975
Nov 21	Derby County	L 0-3		14,890
Nov 28	PLYMOUTH ARGYLE	D 3-3	Phillips 2 (1 pen), Leadbetter	11,368
Dec 5	Liverpool	L 1-3	Crawford	24,843
Dec 12	CHARLTON ATHLETIC	D 1-1	Phillips (pen)	10,881
Dec 19	Huddersfield Town	L 1-3	Phillips	10,648
Dec 26	BRIGHTON & HOVE ALBION	W 3-0	Phillips 2, Crawford	13,947
Dec 28	Brighton & Hove Albion	W 4-1	Phillips 2, Crawford 2	16,171
Jan 2	LEYTON ORIENT	W 6-3	Millward 3, Leadbetter, Crawford, Phillips	11,740
Jan 16	Lincoln City	W 1-0	Leadbetter	8,542
Jan 23	ASTON VILLA	W 2-1	Dugdale o.g., Crawford	19,283
Feb 6	Sunderland	W 1-0	Crawford	18,636
Feb 13	PORTSMOUTH	D 1-1	Phillips (pen)	12,502
Feb 27	SCUNTHORPE UNITED	W 1-0	Phillips	12,829
Mar 5	Rotherham United	W 4-1	Crawford, Millward, Owen, Phillips	11,454
Mar 12	CARDIFF CITY	D 1-1	Elsworthy	18,776
Mar 19	Plymouth Argyle	L 1-3	Owen	14,898
Mar 26	SHEFFIELD UNITED	W 2-0	Phillips, Crawford	19,048
Mar 30	Stoke City	W 2-1	Millward, Crawford	4,070
Apr 2	Middlesbrough	L 1-4	Leadbetter	13,336
Apr 9	DERBY COUNTY	D 1-1	Leadbetter	11,618
Apr 15	BRISTOL CITY	L 1-3	Rees	13,055
Apr 16	Charlton Athletic	W 3-1	Phillips, Hewie o.g. Rees	15,495
Apr 18	Bristol City	L 1-5	Curtis	11,140
Apr 23	LIVERPOOL	L 0-1		12,049
Apr 30	Hull City	L 0-2		5,719

FA Cup

Jan 9	PETERBOROUGH UNITED (Rd3)	L 2-3	Millward, Phillips	26,000

League & Cup Appearances

PLAYER	LEAGUE	CUP COMPETITION FA CUP	TOTAL
Acres	14		14
Bailey	42	1	43
Belcher	24		24
Berry	5		5
Carberry	34	1	35
Crawford	36	1	37
Curtis	18		18
Deacon	3		3
Elsworthy	20	1	21
Leadbetter	42	1	43
Lundstrum	8		8
Malcolm	33	1	34
Millward	21	1	22
Myles	4		4
Nelson	42	1	43
Owen	18	1	19
Phillips	42	1	43
Pickett	36	1	37
Rees	10		10
Siddall	10		10

Goalscorers

PLAYER	LEAGUE	CUP COMPETITION FA CUP	TOTAL
Phillips	24	1	25
Crawford	18		18
Curtis	10		10
Leadbetter	8		8
Millward	5	1	6
Berry	3		3
Rees	3		3
Owen	2		2
Elsworthy	1		1
Lundstrum	1		1
Siddall	1		1
Opp's o.gs.	2		2

Final Division Two Table

		P	W	D	L	F	A	Pts
1	Aston Villa	42	25	9	8	89	43	59
2	Cardiff C	42	23	12	7	90	62	58
3	Liverpool	42	20	10	12	90	66	50
4	Sheffield U	42	19	12	11	68	51	50
5	Middlesbrough	42	19	10	13	90	64	48
6	Huddersfield T	42	19	9	14	73	52	47
7	Charlton Ath	42	17	13	12	90	87	47
8	Rotherham U	42	17	13	12	61	60	47
9	Bristol R	42	18	11	13	72	78	47
10	Leyton Orient	42	15	14	13	76	61	44
11	Ipswich Town	42	19	6	17	78	68	44
12	Swansea T	42	15	10	17	82	84	40
13	Lincoln C	42	16	7	19	75	78	39
14	Brighton & HA	42	13	12	17	67	76	38
15	Scunthorpe U	42	13	10	19	57	71	36
16	Sunderland	42	12	12	18	52	65	36
17	Stoke C	42	14	7	21	66	83	35
18	Derby Co	42	14	7	21	61	77	35
19	Plymouth Arg	42	13	9	20	61	89	35
20	Portsmouth	42	10	12	20	59	77	32
21	Hull C	42	10	10	22	48	76	30
22	Bristol C	42	11	5	26	60	97	27

Fact File

The 6-1 victory over Sunderland was the first time that two Ipswich players had scored hat-tricks in the same match.

MANAGER: Alf Ramsey
CAPTAIN: Reg Pickett
TOP SCORER: Ted Phillips
BIGGEST WIN: 6-1 v Sunderland (H), 19 September 1959, Division Two
HIGHEST ATTENDANCE: 19,283 v Aston Villa, 28 January 1960, Division Two

Season 1960-61

Football League Division Two

DATE	OPPONENTS	SCORE	GOALSCORERS	ATTENDANCE
Aug 20	Leyton Orient	W 3-1	Rees 2, Crawford	14,798
Aug 25	Scunthorpe United	L 0-4		11,130
Aug 27	DERBY COUNTY	W 4-1	Owen, Crawford, Rees, Elsworthy	12,309
Aug 30	SCUNTHORPE UNITED	W 2-0	Crawford 2	12,426
Sep 3	Bristol Rovers	D 1-1	Phillips (pen)	15,467
Sep 7	Brighton & Hove Albion	W 4-2	Crawford 3, Phillips	12,595
Sep 10	LIVERPOOL	W 1-0	Phillips	13,521
Sep 13	BRIGHTON & HOVE ALBION	W 4-0	Phillips 2, Crawford 2	14,672
Sep 17	Rotherham United	D 1-1	Phillips	8,873
Sep 24	SOUTHAMPTON	D 3-3	Stephenson, Phillips 2	15,318
Oct 1	Leeds United	W 5-2	Crawford 3, Stephenson, Phillips	13,582
Oct 8	Charlton Athletic	W 2-0	Phillips, Millward	12,671
Oct 15	SHEFFIELD UNITED	L 0-1		19,529
Oct 22	Stoke City	W 4-2	Crawford 2, Phillips, Millward	8,052
Oct 29	SWANSEA TOWN	L 0-3		11,178
Nov 5	Luton Town	L 2-3	Crawford 2	11,221
Nov 12	LINCOLN CITY	W 3-1	Phillips, Millward, Crawford	10,197
Nov 19	Portsmouth	L 0-1		11,482
Nov 26	HUDDERSFIELD TOWN	W 4-2	Phillips (pen), Millward, Crawford, Stephenson	11,056
Dec 3	Sunderland	L 0-2		21,251
Dec 10	PLYMOUTH ARGYLE	W 3-1	Crawford 2, Phillips	11,798
Dec 17	LEYTON ORIENT	W 6-2	Crawford 3, Owen o.g., Leadbetter, Phillips (pen)	9,803
Dec 26	Norwich City	W 3-0	Crawford 2, Phillips	30,884
Dec 27	NORWICH CITY	W 4-1	Phillips (pen), Crawford 2, Millward	23,321
Jan 14	BRISTOL ROVERS	W 3-2	Millward, Stephenson 2	11,946
Jan 21	Liverpool	D 1-1	Phillips	33,401
Feb 4	ROTHERHAM UNITED	D 1-1	Crawford	12,225
Feb 11	Southampton	D 1-1	Stephenson	19,946
Feb 18	LEEDS UNITED	W 4-0	Crawford, Phillips 2, Rees	13,125
Feb 25	CHARLTON ATHLETIC	W 2-1	Crawford 2	14,365
Mar 7	Sheffield United	W 3-1	Phillips, Crawford 2	35,057
Mar 11	STOKE CITY	W 2-1	Phillips, Elsworthy	16,578
Mar 18	Plymouth Argyle*	W 2-1	Phillips, Crawford	9,879
Mar 25	LUTON TOWN	L 0-1		21,744
Mar 31	MIDDLESBROUGH	W 3-1	Leadbetter, Crawford 2	22,239
Apr 1	Huddersfield Town	W 3-1	Phillips 2, Crawford	16,459
Apr 3	Middlesbrough	L 1-3	Phillips	12,996
Apr 8	PORTSMOUTH	D 2-2	Phillips (pen), Curtis	18,538
Apr 15	Lincoln City	W 4-1	Crawford, Leadbetter, Phillips, Stephenson	7,820
Apr 22	SUNDERLAND	W 4-0	Elsworthy, Crawford, Curtis, Phillips (pen)	21,115
Apr 24	Derby County	W 4-1	Stephenson 2, Crawford, Curtis	13,121
Apr 29	Swansea Town	L 1-2	Phillips	18,239

* played at Torquay

FA Cup

Jan 7	Southampton	(Rd3) L 1-7	Page o.g.	20,422

League Cup

Oct 11	BARNSLEY	(Rd1) L 0-2		11,189

Fact File

Ray Crawford and Ted Phillips scored 70% of Ipswich's goals between them – no other player reached double figures.

MANAGER: Alf Ramsey

CAPTAIN: Andy Nelson

TOP SCORER: Ray Crawford

BIGGEST WIN: 6-2 v Leyton Orient (H), 17 December 1960, Division Two

HIGHEST ATTENDANCE: 23,231 v Norwich City, 27 December 1960, Division Two

MAJOR TRANSFERS IN: Bill Baxter from Broxburn; John Compton from Chelsea; Roy Stephenson from Leicester

League & Cup Appearances

PLAYER	LEAGUE	CUP COMPETITION		TOTAL
		FA CUP	LC	
Bailey	38	1	1	40
Baxter	19			19
Carberry	42	1	1	44
Crawford	42	1	1	44
Compton	3			3
Curtis	5			5
Elsworthy	39	1	1	41
Hall	4			4
Laurel	3		1	4
Leadbetter	42	1	1	44
Malcolm	41	1	1	43
Millward	19	1	1	21
Nelson	39	1		40
Owen	8			8
Phillips	42	1	1	44
Pickett	24	1	1	26
Rees	16			16
Siddall	3		1	4
Stephenson	33	1		34

Goalscorers

PLAYER	LEAGUE	CUP COMPETITION		TOTAL
		FA CUP	LC	
Crawford	40			40
Phillips	30			30
Stephenson	9			9
Millward	6			6
Rees	4			4
Curtis	3			3
Elsworthy	3			3
Leadbetter	3			3
Owen	1			1
Opp's o.gs.	1	1		2

Final Division Two Table

		P	W	D	L	F	A	Pts
1	Ipswich Town	42	26	7	9	100	55	59
2	Sheffield U	42	26	6	10	81	51	58
3	Liverpool	42	21	10	11	87	58	52
4	Norwich C	42	20	9	13	70	53	49
5	Middlesbrough	42	18	12	12	83	74	48
6	Sunderland	42	17	13	12	75	60	47
7	Swansea T	42	18	11	13	77	73	47
8	Southampton	42	18	8	16	84	81	44
9	Scunthorpe U	42	14	15	13	69	64	43
10	Charlton Ath	42	16	11	15	97	91	43
11	Plymouth Arg	42	17	8	17	81	82	42
12	Derby Co	42	15	10	17	80	80	40
13	Luton T	42	15	9	18	71	79	39
14	Leeds U	42	14	10	18	75	83	38
15	Rotherham U	42	12	13	17	65	64	37
16	Brighton & HA	42	14	9	19	61	75	37
17	Bristol R	42	15	7	20	73	92	37
18	Stoke C	42	12	12	18	51	59	36
19	Leyton Orient	42	14	8	20	55	78	36
20	Huddersfield T	42	13	9	20	62	71	35
21	Portsmouth	42	11	11	20	64	91	33
22	Lincoln C	42	8	8	26	48	95	24

Season 1961-62

Football League Division One

DATE	OPPONENTS	SCORE	GOALSCORERS	ATTENDANCE
Aug 19	Bolton Wanderers	D 0-0		16,708
Aug 22	Burnley	L 3-4	Phillips 2, Crawford	24,577
Aug 26	MANCHESTER CITY	L 2-4	Betts o.g., Leadbetter	21,473
Aug 29	BURNLEY	W 6-2	Crawford 2, Stephenson, Moran, Phillips, Leadbetter	23,835
Sep 2	West Bromwich Albion	W 3-1	Moran 2, Crawford	19,016
Sep 5	BLACKBURN ROVERS	W 2-1	Stephenson, Phillips	24,928
Sep 9	BIRMINGHAM CITY	W 4-1	Crawford, Phillips 2, Moran	20,017
Sep 16	Everton	L 2-5	Phillips, Moran	35,259
Sep 18	Blackburn Rovers	D 2-2	Phillips 2 (1 pen)	19,904
Sep 23	FULHAM	L 2-4	Crawford 2	23,050
Sep 30	Sheffield Wednesday	W 4-1	Phillips 2, Crawford, Leadbetter	26,565
Oct 7	WEST HAM UNITED	W 4-2	Crawford 2, Phillips 2	28,059
Oct 14	Sheffield United	L 1-2	Leadbetter	22,194
Oct 21	TOTTENHAM HOTSPUR	W 3-2	Phillips, Crawford 2	28,778
Oct 28	Blackpool	D 1-1	Phillips	19,773
Nov 4	NOTTINGHAM FOREST	W 1-0	Phillips	19,068
Nov 11	Wolverhampton Wanderers	L 0-2		21,711
Nov 18	MANCHESTER UNITED	W 4-1	Phillips 2, Crawford, Elsworthy	25,755
Nov 25	Cardiff City	W 3-0	Phillips 2, Moran	22,823
Dec 2	CHELSEA	W 5-2	Crawford 3, Moran, Stephenson	22,726
Dec 9	Aston Villa	L 0-3		31,924
Dec 16	BOLTON WANDERERS	W 2-1	Crawford 2	16,587
Dec 23	Manchester City	L 0-3		18,376
Dec 26	LEICESTER CITY	W 1-0	Crawford	18,146
Jan 13	WEST BROMWICH ALBION	W 3-0	Stephenson, Moran, Leadbetter	18,378
Jan 20	Birmingham City	L 1-3	Crawford	26,968
Feb 3	EVERTON	W 4-0	Phillips, Moran, Elsworthy, Crawford	22,572
Feb 10	Fulham	W 2-1	Stephenson, Crawford	25,209
Feb 24	West Ham United	D 2-2	Leadbetter, Phillips (pen)	27,763
Mar 3	SHEFFIELD UNITED	W 4-0	Moran, Leadbetter, Crawford 2	20,158
Mar 9	SHEFFIELD WEDNESDAY	W 2-1	Crawford, Stephenson	23,713
Mar 14	Tottenham Hotspur	W 3-1	Crawford, Phillips 2	51,098
Mar 17	BLACKPOOL	D 1-1	Moran	22,450
Mar 24	Nottingham Forest	D 1-1	Moran	26,053
Mar 28	Leicester City	W 2-0	Crawford, Stephenson	19,068
Mar 31	WOLVERHAMPTON WANDERERS	W 3-2	Phillips (pen), Crawford, Moran	23,153
Apr 7	Manchester United	L 0-5		24,976
Apr 14	CARDIFF CITY	W 1-0	Moran	17,693
Apr 20	ARSENAL	D 2-2	Phillips (pen), Leadbetter	30,649
Apr 21	Chelsea	D 2-2	Crawford, Phillips	28,462
Apr 23	Arsenal	W 3-0	Phillips, Crawford 2	44,694
Apr 28	ASTON VILLA	W 2-0	Crawford 2	28,932

FA Cup

Jan 6	LUTON TOWN	(Rd3) D 1-1	Phillips	18,450
Jan 10	Luton Town	(R) D 1-1*	Elsworthy	23,818
Jan 15	Luton Town†	(2R) W 5-1	Moran, Phillips 2 (1 pen), Stephenson 2	29,438
Jan 27	Norwich City	(Rd4) D 1-1	Leadbetter	39,890
Jan 30	NORWICH CITY	(R) L 1-2	Crawford	29,796

*after extra time
† played at Highbury

League Cup

Sep 11	MANCHESTER CITY	(Rd1) W 4-2	Moran 2, Crawford 2	14,919
Oct 3	Swansea Town	(Rd2) D 3-3	Phillips, Stephenson, Crawford	13,541
Oct 24	SWANSEA TOWN	(R) W 3-2	Phillips (pen), Moran, Stephenson	11,010
Nov 21	Aston Villa	(Rd3) W 3-2	Leadbetter, Phillips 2 (1 pen)	22,000
Dec 11	Blackburn Rovers	(Rd4) L 1-4	Phillips (pen)	11,071

MANAGER: Alf Ramsey

CAPTAIN: Andy Nelson

TOP SCORER: Ray Crawford

BIGGEST WIN: 6-2 v Burnley (H), 29 August 1961, Division One

HIGHEST ATTENDANCE: 30,649 v Arsenal, 20 April 1962, Division One

MAJOR TRANSFERS IN: Doug Moran from Falkirk

League & Cup Appearances

PLAYER	LEAGUE	CUP COMPETITION		TOTAL
		FA CUP	LC	
Bailey	37	4	3	44
Baxter	40	5	5	50
Carberry	42	5	4	51
Crawford	41	5	4	50
Compton	39	5	5	49
Curtis	4		1	5
Elsworthy	41	5	5	51
Hall	5	1	2	8
Leadbetter	41	3	5	49
Malcolm	3			3
Millward			1	1
Moran	42	5	5	52
Nelson	42	5	5	52
Owen	1	2	1	4
Phillips	40	5	5	50
Pickett	3			3
Stephenson	41	5	4	50

Goalscorers

PLAYER	LEAGUE	CUP COMPETITION		TOTAL
		FA CUP	LC	
Crawford	33	1	3	37
Phillips	28	3	5	36
Moran	14	1	3	18
Stephenson	7	2	2	11
Leadbetter	8	1	1	10
Elsworthy	2	1		3
Opp's o.gs.	1			1

Fact File

Despite scoring 93 goals, only six different players scored during the season.

Final Division One Table

		P	W	D	L	F	A	Pts
1	IPSWICH TOWN	42	24	8	10	93	67	56
2	BURNLEY	42	21	11	10	101	67	53
3	TOTTENHAM H	42	21	10	11	88	69	52
4	EVERTON	42	20	11	11	88	54	51
5	SHEFFIELD U	42	19	9	14	61	69	47
6	SHEFFIELD W	42	20	6	16	72	58	46
7	ASTON VILLA	42	18	8	16	65	56	44
8	WEST HAM U	42	17	10	15	76	82	44
9	WBA	42	15	13	14	83	67	43
10	ARSENAL	42	16	11	15	71	72	43
11	BOLTON W	42	16	10	16	62	66	42
12	MANCHESTER C	42	17	7	18	78	81	41
13	BLACKPOOL	42	15	11	16	70	75	41
14	LEICESTER C	42	17	6	19	72	71	40
15	MANCHESTER U	42	15	9	18	72	75	39
16	BLACKBURN R	42	14	11	17	50	58	39
17	BIRMINGHAM C	42	14	10	18	65	81	38
18	WOLVERHAMPTON W	42	13	10	19	73	86	36
19	NOTTINGHAM F	42	13	10	19	63	79	36
20	FULHAM	42	13	7	22	66	74	33
21	CARDIFF C	42	9	14	19	50	81	32
22	CHELSEA	42	9	10	23	63	94	28

Season 1962-63

Football League Division One

DATE	OPPONENTS	SCORE	GOALSCORERS	ATTENDANCE
Aug 18	BLACKBURN ROVERS	D 3-3	Moran, Crawford 2	19,062
Aug 20	Blackpool	L 0-1		23,305
Aug 25	Sheffield United	L 1-2	Crawford	23,703
Aug 28	BLACKPOOL	W 5-2	Phillips, Moran, Crawford 2, James o.g.	21,294
Sep 1	NOTTINGHAM FOREST	D 1-1	Leadbetter	19,645
Sep 5	Manchester City	L 1-2	Crawford	25,252
Sep 8	Bolton Wanderers	W 3-1	Crawford, Thrower, Moran	17,790
Sep 11	MANCHESTER CITY	D 0-0		18,849
Sep 15	Liverpool	D 1-1	Crawford	40,121
Sep 22	WOLVERHAMPTON WANDERERS	L 2-3	Moran, Crawford	25,468
Sep 29	Aston Villa	L 2-4	Crawford 2	31,860
Oct 6	LEICESTER CITY	L 0-1		19,000
Oct 13	Fulham	D 1-1	Baxter	22,966
Oct 20	WEST BROMWICH ALBION	D 1-1	Crawford	19,141
Oct 27	Everton	L 1-3	Moran	39,692
Nov 3	MANCHESTER UNITED	L 3-5	Crawford, Blackwood 2	18,475
Nov 10	Leyton Orient	W 2-1	Blackwood, Baxter	13,929
Nov 17	BIRMINGHAM CITY	L 1-5	Phillips	16,775
Nov 24	Arsenal	L 1-3	Blackwood	25,038
Dec 1	SHEFFIELD WEDNESDAY	W 2-0	Crawford 2	17,166
Dec 8	Burnley	L 1-3	Phillips	19,498
Dec 15	Blackburn Rovers	W 1-0	Crawford	8,564
Dec 21	SHEFFIELD UNITED	W 1-0	Phillips	17,055
Dec 26	Tottenham Hotspur	L 0-5		36,297
Feb 23	Leicester City	L 0-3		31,258
Mar 2	FULHAM	L 0-1		18,226
Mar 5	LIVERPOOL	D 2-2	Phillips, Stephenson	14,063
Mar 9	West Bromwich Albion	L 1-6	Crawford	10,746
Mar 16	TOTTENHAM HOTSPUR	L 2-4	Baxter, Crawford	23,679
Mar 19	EVERTON	L 0-3		19,712
Mar 23	Manchester United	W 1-0	Leadbetter	32,798
Mar 30	ARSENAL	D 1-1	Phillips (pen)	16,686
Apr 6	Birmingham City	W 1-0	Stephenson	17,013
Apr 12	West Ham United	W 3-1	Moran, Phillips, Crawford	23,170
Apr 13	LEYTON ORIENT	D 1-1	Moran	18,677
Apr 15	WEST HAM UNITED	L 2-3	Crawford, Stephenson	21,988
Apr 20	Sheffield Wednesday	W 3-0	Crawford 3	17,268
Apr 27	BURNLEY	W 2-1	Crawford, Phillips	18,645
May 4	Wolverhampton Wanderers	D 0-0		15,832
May 10	Nottingham Forest	L 1-2	Stephenson	13,055
May 17	BOLTON WANDERERS	W 4-1	Stephenson, Moran, Crawford, Phillips	19,088
May 21	ASTON VILLA	D 1-1	Moran	17,230

FA Cup

Jan 9	Mansfield Town	(Rd3) W 3-2	Leadbetter 3	17,032
Jan 30	Leicester City	(Rd4) L 1-3	Blackwood	26,054

European Cup

Sep 18	Floriana	(PRd/1L) W 4-1	Crawford 2, Phillips 2	15,784
Sep 25	FLORIANA	(PRd/2L) W10-0	Moran 2, Phillips 2 (1 pen), Crawford 5, Elsworthy	25,287
Nov 14	AC Milan	(Rd1/1L) L 0-3		7,607
Nov 28	AC MILAN	(Rd1/2L) W 2-1	Crawford, Blackwood	25,001

Charity Shield

Aug 11	TOTTENHAM HOTSPUR		L 1-5	Stephenson	20,067

MANAGER: Alf Ramsey/Jackie Milburn

CAPTAIN: Andy Nelson

TOP SCORER: Ray Crawford

BIGGEST WIN: 10-0 v Floriana (H), 25 September 1962, European Cup

HIGHEST ATTENDANCE: 25,468 v Wolverhampton Wanderers, 22 September 1962, Division One

MAJOR TRANSFERS IN: Bobby Blackwood from Heart of Midlothian

MAJOR TRANSFERS OUT: Dermot Curtis to Exeter City; Reg Pickett to Shrewsbury Town

League & Cup Appearances

PLAYER	LEAGUE	CUP COMPETITION		OTHER	TOTAL
		FA CUP	EC		
Bailey	35	2	4	1	42
Baxter	42	2	4	1	49
Blackwood	19	2	4		25
Carberry	29	2	2	1	34
Crawford	42	2	4	1	49
Compton	34	2	3	1	40
Curtis	6				6
Dougan	1				1
Elsworthy	33	2	3	1	39
Hall	7				7
Laurel	1		1		2
Leadbetter	35	2	1	1	39
Malcolm	18		3		21
Millward	3				3
Moran	32		4	1	37
Nelson	39	2	3	1	45
Phillips	35	2	3	1	41
Pickett	3		1		4
Stephenson	41	2	4	1	48
Thrower	7				7

Goalscorers

PLAYER	LEAGUE	CUP COMPETITION		OTHER	TOTAL
		FA CUP	EC		
Crawford	25		8		33
Phillips	9		4		13
Moran	9		2		11
Stephenson	5			1	6
Blackwood	4	1	1		6
Leadbetter	2	3			5
Baxter	3				3
Elsworthy	1				1
Thrower	1				1
Opp's o.gs.	1				1

Fact File

The 10-0 victory over Floriana is still Ipswich's record victory as a professional club.

Final Division One Table

		P	W	D	L	F	A	Pts
1	EVERTON	42	25	11	6	84	42	61
2	TOTTENHAM H	42	23	9	10	111	62	55
3	BURNLEY	42	22	10	10	78	57	54
4	LEICESTER C	42	20	12	10	79	53	52
5	WOLVERHAMPTON W	42	20	10	12	93	65	50
6	SHEFFIELD W	42	19	10	13	77	63	48
7	ARSENAL	42	18	10	14	86	77	46
8	LIVERPOOL	42	17	10	15	71	59	44
9	NOTTINGHAM F	42	17	10	15	67	69	44
10	SHEFFIELD U	42	16	12	14	58	60	44
11	BLACKBURN R	42	15	12	15	79	71	42
12	WEST HAM U	42	14	12	16	73	69	40
13	BLACKPOOL	42	13	14	15	58	64	40
14	WBA	42	16	7	19	71	79	39
15	ASTON VILLA	42	15	8	19	62	68	38
16	FULHAM	42	14	10	18	50	71	38
17	IPSWICH TOWN	42	12	11	19	59	78	35
18	BOLTON W	42	15	5	22	55	75	35
19	MANCHESTER U	42	12	10	20	67	81	34
20	BIRMINGHAM C	42	10	13	19	63	90	33
21	MANCHESTER C	42	10	11	21	58	102	31
22	LEYTON ORIENT	42	6	9	27	37	81	21

Season 1963-64

Football League Division One

DATE	OPPONENTS	SCORE	GOALSCORERS	ATTENDANCE
Aug 24	BURNLEY	W 3-1	Crawford 2, Moran	23,000
Aug 28	Manchester United	L 0-2		39,921
Aug 30	West Ham United	D 2-2	Baxter, Phillips	27,599
Sep 3	MANCHESTER UNITED	L 2-7	Moran 2	28,113
Sep 7	Sheffield Wednesday	L 1-3	Phillips	18,198
Sep 14	EVERTON	D 0-0		20,099
Sep 18	Bolton Wanderers	L 0-6		12,917
Sep 21	Birmingham City	L 0-1		19,095
Sep 28	WEST BROMWICH ALBION	L 1-2	Moran	13,859
Oct 1	BOLTON WANDERERS	L 1-3	Colrain	11,363
Oct 5	Arsenal	L 0-6		31,803
Oct 9	Sheffield United	L 1-3	Moran	18,946
Oct 12	CHELSEA	L 1-3	Moran	15,703
Oct 19	Blackpool	D 2-2	Baxter, Hegan	14,666
Oct 26	LIVERPOOL	L 1-2	Hegan	16,322
Nov 2	Nottingham Forest	L 1-3	Hegan	21,109
Nov 9	STOKE CITY	L 0-2		15,013
Nov 16	Wolverhampton Wanderers	L 1-2	Phillips	17,891
Nov 23	TOTTENHAM HOTSPUR	L 2-3	Phillips, Elsworthy	25,014
Nov 30	Aston Villa	D 0-0		16,353
Dec 7	BLACKBURN ROVERS	D 0-0		15,500
Dec 14	Burnley	L 1-3	Baker	10,558
Dec 20	WEST HAM UNITED	W 3-2	Blackwood, Moran, Baker	11,730
Dec 26	Fulham	L 1-10	Baker	19,374
Dec 28	FULHAM	W 4-2	Baxter, Hegan, Broadfoot, Baker	15,808
Jan 11	SHEFFIELD WEDNESDAY	L 1-4	Baker	15,199
Jan 18	Everton	D 1-1	Blackwood	38,242
Feb 1	BIRMINGHAM CITY	W 3-2	Hegan, Blackwood 2	13,349
Feb 8	West Bromwich Albion	L 1-2	Blackwood	13,476
Feb 18	ARSENAL	L 1-2	Baker	17,483
Feb 22	Chelsea	L 0-4		20,703
Feb 29	SHEFFIELD UNITED	W 1-0	Baxter	11,465
Mar 7	Liverpool	L 0-6		35,575
Mar 21	Stoke City	L 1-9	Broadfoot	16,135
Mar 28	NOTTINGHAM FOREST	W 4-3	Leadbetter, Blackwood 2, Colrain	12,017
Mar 30	LEICESTER CITY	D 1-1	Colrain	16,265
Mar 31	Leicester City	L 1-2	Baker	15,925
Apr 4	Tottenham Hotspur	L 3-6	Baker 3	25,115
Apr 11	ASTON VILLA	W 4-3	Broadfoot 2, Baker, Baxter	11,658
Apr 14	WOLVERHAMPTON WANDERERS	W 1-0	Baker	15,928
Apr 18	Blackburn Rovers	L 1-3	Moran	10,341
Apr 25	BLACKPOOL	W 4-3	Baker 3, Gratrix o.g.	11,187

FA Cup

Jan 4	OLDHAM ATHLETIC	(Rd3) W 6-3	Broadfoot, Hegan 2, Baker 3	15,304
Jan 25	STOKE CITY	(Rd4) D 1-1	Baxter	21,949
Jan 29	Stoke City	(R) L 0-1		34,162

League Cup

Sep 25	WALSALL	(Rd2) D 0-0		8,568
Oct 03	Walsall	(R) L 0-1		6,632

League & Cup Appearances

PLAYER	LEAGUE	CUP COMPETITION		TOTAL
		FA CUP	LC	
Bailey	27	3	2	32
Baker	20	2		22
Baxter	42	3	2	47
Bevis	5			5
Blackwood	28	3	1	32
Bolton	32	3	1	36
Broadfoot	29	3		32
Carberry	10		2	12
Colrain	15		2	17
Compton	35	3	1	39
Crawford	6			6
Davin	26	3		29
Dougan	16	1	2	19
Elsworthy	23			23
Hegan	21	3	1	25
Leadbetter	17	2	1	20
Moran	30	2	2	34
Nelson	26	2	1	29
Phillips	20		1	21
Stephenson	22		2	24
Thorburn	10			10
Thrower	1		1	2
Treacy	1			1

Goalscorers

PLAYER	LEAGUE	CUP COMPETITION		TOTAL
		FA CUP	LC	
Baker	15	3		18
Moran	8			8
Blackwood	7			7
Hegan	5	2		7
Baxter	5	1		6
Broadfoot	4	1		5
Phillips	4			4
Colrain	3			3
Crawford	2			2
Elsworthy	1			1
Leadbetter	1			1
Opp's o.gs.	1			1

Fact File

Ipswich conceded 121 goals in league games – a club record.

MANAGER: Jackie Milburn

CAPTAIN: Andy Nelson/Bill Baxter

TOP SCORER: Gerry Baker

BIGGEST WIN: 6-3 v Oldham Athletic (H), 4 January 1964, FA Cup 3rd Round

HIGHEST ATTENDANCE: 28,113 v Manchester United, 3 September 1963, Division One

MAJOR TRANSFERS IN: Gerry Baker from Hibernian; Jack Bolton from Raith; Joe Broadfoot from Millwall; John Colrain from Clyde; Danny Hegan from Sunderland

MAJOR TRANSFERS OUT: John Compton to Bournemouth; Doug Moran to Dundee U; Ray Crawford to Wolverhampton Wanderers

Final Division One Table

		P	W	D	L	F	A	Pts
1	LIVERPOOL	42	26	5	11	92	45	57
2	MANCHESTER U	42	23	7	12	90	62	53
3	EVERTON	42	21	10	11	84	64	52
4	TOTTENHAM H	42	22	7	13	97	81	51
5	CHELSEA	42	20	10	12	72	56	50
6	SHEFFIELD W	42	19	11	12	84	67	49
7	BLACKBURN R	42	18	10	14	89	65	46
8	ARSENAL	42	17	11	14	90	82	45
9	BURNLEY	42	17	10	15	71	64	44
10	WBA	42	16	11	15	70	61	43
11	LEICESTER C	42	16	11	15	61	58	43
12	SHEFFIELD U	42	16	11	15	61	64	43
13	NOTTINGHAM F	42	16	9	17	64	68	41
14	WEST HAM U	42	14	12	16	69	74	40
15	FULHAM	42	13	13	16	58	65	39
16	WOLVERHAMPTON W	42	12	15	15	70	80	39
17	STOKE C	42	14	10	18	77	78	38
18	BLACKPOOL	42	13	9	20	52	73	35
19	ASTON VILLA	42	11	12	19	62	71	34
20	BIRMINGHAM C	42	11	7	24	54	92	29
21	BOLTON W	42	10	8	24	48	80	28
22	IPSWICH TOWN	42	9	7	26	56	121	25

Season 1964-65

Football League Division Two

DATE	OPPONENTS	SCORE	GOALSCORERS	ATTENDANCE
Aug 22	Cardiff City	D 0-0		16,911
Aug 25	COVENTRY CITY	L 1-3	Blackwood	17,252
Aug 29	PRESTON NORTH END	L 1-5	Broadfoot	12,823
Sep 1	Coventry City	L 3-5	Baker, Hegan, Brogan	37,782
Sep 5	Norwich City	L 1-2	Baker	25,087
Sep 12	Plymouth Argyle	D 1-1	Brogan	20,775
Sep 15	NORTHAMPTON TOWN	D 0-0		13,520
Sep 19	BOLTON WANDERERS	L 1-4	Thrower	12,558
Sep 26	Middlesbrough	W 4-2	Brogan 2, Broadfoot, Colrain	15,593
Sep 29	Northampton Town	L 2-3	Colrain, Broadfoot	14,886
Oct 3	NEWCASTLE UNITED	W 3-1	Brogan, Hegan 2 (1 pen)	14,444
Oct 7	Crystal Palace	D 1-1	Colrain	22,690
Oct 10	ROTHERHAM UNITED	D 4-4	Hegan, Colrain 2, Broadfoot	13,756
Oct 17	Swansea Town	D 1-1	Colrain	10,508
Oct 24	DERBY COUNTY	W 2-1	Baker, Hegan	12,781
Oct 31	Swindon Town	L 1-3	Colrain	14,301
Nov 7	PORTSMOUTH	W 7-0	Broadfoot, Hegan 2, Brogan 3, Baker	12,356
Nov 14	Manchester City	L 0-4		16,835
Nov 21	CHARLTON ATHLETIC	D 1-1	Baxter (pen)	13,807
Nov 28	Leyton Orient	D 0-0		7,009
Dec 5	BURY	W 1-0	Baker	9,118
Dec 12	CARDIFF CITY	D 1-1	Baker	10,010
Dec 19	Preston North End	L 1-4	Broadfoot	11,835
Dec 26	HUDDERSFIELD TOWN	W 3-2	McNeil, Nicholson o.g., Coddington o.g.	11,608
Dec 28	Huddersfield Town	D 0-0		10,596
Jan 2	NORWICH CITY	W 3-0	Baker 2, Broadfoot	25,863
Jan 16	PLYMOUTH ARGYLE	D 2-2	Reeves o.g., Brogan	12,106
Jan 23	Bolton Wanderers	D 0-0		13,557
Feb 6	MIDDLESBROUGH	W 5-2	Treacy 2, Baker, Brogan, Coddington o.g.	11,071
Feb 13	Newcastle United	D 2-2	Baker, Treacy	29,459
Feb 20	Rotherham United	D 2-2	Colrain, Hardy o.g.	7,333
Feb 27	SWANSEA TOWN	W 3-0	Broadfoot, Baker, Brogan	12,141
Mar 5	Bury	W 1-0	Treacy	6,300
Mar 13	SWINDON TOWN	D 0-0		12,454
Mar 20	Portsmouth	W 2-0	Treacy, Broadfoot	7,920
Mar 27	MANCHESTER CITY	W 4-1	Brogan, Baker 2, Baxter	12,709
Apr 3	Charlton Athletic	L 0-4		11,471
Apr 10	LEYTON ORIENT	D 1-1	Baker	11,730
Apr 17	Derby County	W 3-2	Brogan, Colrain, Broadfoot	11,800
Apr 19	SOUTHAMPTON	W 2-0	Colrain, Baker	15,241
Apr 21	Southampton	D 1-1	Harper	11,377
Apr 24	CRYSTAL PALACE	W 3-2	Baker, Broadfoot, Baxter	14,631

FA Cup

Jan 9	Swindon Town	(Rd3) W 2-1	Brogan 2	14,802
Jan 30	Tottenham Hotspur	(Rd4) L 0-5		43,992

League Cup

Sep 23	Coventry City	(Rd2) L 1-4	Colrain	14,778

League & Cup Appearances

PLAYER	LEAGUE	CUP COMPETITION		TOTAL
		FA CUP	LC	
Bailey	8	1		9
Baker	36	1		37
Baxter	37	2		39
Bevis		2		2
Blackwood	15	1		1
Bolton	18		1	19
Broadfoot	36	2	1	39
Brogan	40	2	1	43
Carberry	8		1	9
Colrain	23		1	24
Davin	26	2		28
Elsworthy	3			3
Hancock	20			20
Harper	7			7
Hegan	31	2	1	34
Leadbetter	19	2	1	22
Lea	24	2		26
McNeil	37	2	1	40
Nelson	5			5
Smith	12			12
Stephenson	7			7
Thompson	7			7
Thorburn	14			14
Thrower	17	2	1	20
Treacy	12	1		13

Goalscorers

PLAYER	LEAGUE	CUP COMPETITION		TOTAL
		FA CUP	LC	
Baker	16			16
Brogan	13	2		15
Broadfoot	12			12
Colrain	10		1	11
Hegan	7			7
Treacy	5			5
Baxter	3			3
Blackwood	1			1
Harper	1			1
McNeil	1			1
Thrower	1			1
Opp's o.gs.	4			4

Fact File

Ipswich did not record their first win of the season until their ninth game – their longest start without a win since turning professional.

MANAGER: Jackie Milburn/Bill McGarry

CAPTAIN: Billy Baxter/Mick McNeil

TOP SCORER: Gerry Baker

BIGGEST WIN: 7-0 v Portsmouth (H), 7 November 1964, Division Two

HIGHEST ATTENDANCE: 25,863 v Norwich City, 2 January 1965, Division Two

MAJOR TRANSFERS IN: Frank Brogan from Celtic; Mick McNeil from Middlesbrough; Cyril Lea from Leyton Orient; Ken Hancock from Port Vale

MAJOR TRANSFERS OUT: Bobby Blackwood to Colchester United; Larry Carberry to Barrow

Final Division Two Table

		P	W	D	L	F	A	Pts
1	NEWCASTLE U	42	24	9	9	81	45	57
2	NORTHAMPTON T	42	20	16	6	66	50	56
3	BOLTON W	42	20	10	12	80	58	50
4	SOUTHAMPTON	42	17	14	11	83	63	48
5	IPSWICH TOWN	42	15	17	10	74	67	47
6	NORWICH C	42	20	7	15	61	57	47
7	CRYSTAL PALACE	42	16	13	13	55	51	45
8	HUDDERSFIELD T	42	17	10	15	53	51	44
9	DERBY CO	42	16	11	15	84	79	43
10	COVENTRY C	42	17	9	16	72	70	43
11	MANCHESTER C	42	16	9	17	63	62	41
12	PRESTON NE	42	14	13	15	76	81	41
13	CARDIFF C	42	13	14	15	64	57	40
14	ROTHERHAM U	42	14	12	16	70	69	40
15	PLYMOUTH ARG	42	16	8	18	63	79	40
16	BURY	42	14	10	18	60	66	38
17	MIDDLESBROUGH	42	13	9	20	70	76	35
18	CHARLTON ATH	42	13	9	20	64	75	35
19	LEYTON ORIENT	42	12	11	19	50	72	35
20	PORTSMOUTH	42	12	10	20	56	77	34
21	SWINDON T	42	14	5	23	63	81	33
22	SWANSEA T	42	11	10	21	62	84	32

Season 1965-66

Football League Division Two

DATE	OPPONENTS	SCORE	GOALSCORERS	ATTENDANCE
Aug 21	PRESTON NORTH END	W 1-0	Baker	14,548
Aug 24	Huddersfield Town	L 0-1		11,448
Aug 28	Charlton Athletic	L 0-2		10,887
Aug 31	HUDDERSFIELD TOWN	D 2-2	Colrain, Broadfoot	14,283
Sep 4	PLYMOUTH ARGYLE	W 4-1	Hegan, Newman o.g., Lea, Colrain	12,739
Sep 7	MIDDLESBROUGH	W 2-1	Baxter, Lea	15,478
Sep 11	Portsmouth	L 0-1		13,959
Sep 14	Middlesbrough	L 2-3	Baker, Colrain	15,221
Sep 18	BOLTON WANDERERS	W 2-0	Baker, Brogan	12,775
Sep 25	Norwich City	L 0-1		26,407
Oct 9	BURY	L 3-4	McNeil, Brogan, Baker	12,025
Oct 16	Southampton	W 2-1	Brogan, Hegan	19,050
Oct 23	DERBY COUNTY	D 2-2	Baker, Colrain (pen)	12,336
Oct 30	Cardiff City	L 0-1		8,325
Nov 6	CARLISLE UNITED	H 1-0	Bolton (J)	10,784
Nov 13	Coventry City	L 1-3	Brogan	23,195
Nov 20	BRISTOL CITY	D 0-0		8,939
Nov 27	Manchester City	L 1-2	Spearritt	19,416
Dec 4	ROTHERHAM UNITED	D 0-0		10,279
Dec 11	Wolverhampton Wanderers	L 1-4	Hegan	19,072
Dec 18	SOUTHAMPTON	W 3-0	Kellard, Baxter, Brogan	9,773
Dec 27	Crystal Palace	L 1-3	Baker	16,064
Jan 1	Bury	D 1-1	Bolton (J)	5,258
Jan 8	COVENTRY CITY	W 1-0	Hegan	13,054
Jan 15	Derby County	D 2-2	Baker, Spearritt	14,717
Jan 29	Preston North End	W 1-0	Kellard	11,879
Feb 5	CHARLTON ATHLETIC	L 1-4	Hegan	10,690
Feb 11	CRYSTAL PALACE	D 2-2	Brogan, Kellard	9,132
Feb 19	Plymouth Argyle	L 0-3		11,361
Feb 26	PORTSMOUTH	W 1-0	Baker	9,109
Mar 2	Bolton Wanderers	L 1-3	Crawford	9,180
Mar 19	NORWICH CITY	W 2-0	Crawford, Baxter (pen)	22,690
Mar 26	BIRMINGHAM CITY	L 0-1		9,351
Apr 2	Carlisle United	L 1-3	Spearritt	7,555
Apr 8	Leyton Orient	W 4-1	Brogan, Spearritt, Hegan 2	7,406
Apr 9	CARDIFF CITY	W 2-1	Baker, Baxter (pen)	10,392
Apr 11	LEYTON ORIENT	W 3-2	Crawford 2, Baker	13,352
Apr 23	MANCHESTER CITY	D 1-1	Crawford	15,995
Apr 30	Rotherham United	D 0-0		9,431
May 3	Birmingham City	L 1-4	Brogan	9,331
May 7	WOLVERHAMPTON WANDERERS	W 5-2	Crawford 2, Baker, Hawkins o.g., Hegan	14,201
May 10	Bristol City	L 1-4	Crawford	13,893

FA Cup

Jan 22	Southport	(Rd3) D 0-0		7,689
Jan 25	SOUTHPORT	(R) L 2-3	Baker, Brogan	15,459

League Cup

Sep 21	Brighton & Hove Albion	(Rd2) W 2-1	Baker, Brogan	13,498
Oct 13	Workington	(Rd3) D 1-1	Colrain (pen)	8,649
Oct 20	Workington	(R) W 3-1	Colrain (pen), Brogan, Broadfoot	9,965
Nov 3	DARLINGTON	(Rd4) W 2-0	Baker 2	8,470
Nov 17	Cardiff City	(Rd5) L 1-2	Brogan	7,858

League & Cup Appearances

PLAYER	LEAGUE	CUP COMPETITION		TOTAL
		FA CUP	LC	
Baker	38	2	3	43
Baxter	42	2	5	49
Bevis	1			1
Bolton J	19	1	2	22
Bolton R	9			9
Broadfoot	16		4	20
Brogan	40	2	5	47
Colrain	17 (1)		3	20 (1)
Crawford	12			12
Davin	25	2	4	31
Hancock	41	2	5	48
Harper C	6			6
Harper D	26 (2)	2	1	29 (2)
Hegan	39	1	5	45
Kellard	13	2		15
Lea	38 (1)	2	5	45 (1)
McNeil	37		5	44
Mills	2			2
Smith	10 (1)		4	14 (1)
Spearritt	17 (1)		1	18 (1)
Thompson	4 (1)	1	1	6 (1)
Treacy	4 (1)		1	5 (1)
Walsh	6 (1)	1	1	8 (1)

Goalscorers

PLAYER	LEAGUE	CUP COMPETITION		TOTAL
		FA CUP	LC	
Baker	11	1	3	15
Brogan	8	1	3	12
Crawford	8			8
Hegan	8			8
Colrain	4		2	6
Baxter	4			4
Spearritt	4			4
Kellard	3			3
Bolton	2			2
Broadfoot	1		1	2
Lea	2			2
McNeil	1			1
Opp's o.gs.	2			2

Fact File

Dave Harper was the first ever Ipswich substitute when he took over from Frank Brogan at Charlton on 28 August 1965.

MANAGER: Bill McGarry

CAPTAIN: Cyril Lea

TOP SCORER: Gerry Baker

BIGGEST WIN: 5-2 v Wolverhampton Wanderers (H), 7 May 1966, Division Two

HIGHEST ATTENDANCE: 22,690 v Norwich City, 19 March 1966, Division Two

MAJOR TRANSFERS IN: Ray Crawford from WBA; Bobby Kellard from Crystal Palace

MAJOR TRANSFERS OUT: Joe Broadfoot to Northampton; Bobby Kellard to Portsmouth

Final Division Two Table

		P	W	D	L	F	A	Pts
1	MANCHESTER C	42	22	15	5	76	44	59
2	SOUTHAMPTON	42	22	10	10	85	56	54
3	COVENTRY C	42	20	13	9	73	53	53
4	HUDDERSFIELD T	42	19	13	10	62	36	51
5	BRISTOL C	42	17	17	8	63	48	51
6	WOLVERHAMPTON W	42	20	10	12	87	61	50
7	ROTHERHAM U	42	16	14	12	75	74	46
8	DERBY CO	42	16	11	15	71	68	43
9	BOLTON W	42	16	9	17	62	59	41
10	BIRMINGHAM C	42	16	9	17	70	75	41
11	CRYSTAL PALACE	42	14	13	15	47	52	41
12	PORTSMOUTH	42	16	8	18	74	78	40
13	NORWICH C	42	12	15	15	52	52	39
14	CARLISLE U	42	17	5	20	60	63	39
15	IPSWICH TOWN	42	15	9	18	58	66	39
16	CHARLTON ATH	42	12	14	16	61	70	38
17	PRESTON NE	42	11	15	16	62	70	37
18	PLYMOUTH ARG	42	12	13	17	54	63	37
19	BURY	42	14	7	21	62	76	35
20	CARDIFF C	42	12	10	20	71	91	34
21	MIDDLESBROUGH	42	10	13	19	58	86	33
22	LEYTON ORIENT	42	5	13	24	38	80	23

Season 1966-67

Football League Division Two

DATE	OPPONENTS	SCORE	GOALSCORERS	ATTENDANCE
Aug 20	Cardiff City	W 2-0	Crawford, Brogan	7,628
Aug 23	HUDDERSFIELD TOWN	W 3-0	Baker, Brogan (pen), Spearritt	13,570
Aug 27	WOLVERHAMPTON WANDERERS	W 3-1	Hegan 2, Brogan	17,219
Aug 30	Huddersfield Town	L 0-1		12,434
Sep 3	Norwich City	W 2-1	Crawford, Baker	19,129
Sep 6	DERBY COUNTY	W 4-3	Baxter, Baker, Crawford 2	15,686
Sep 10	Bristol City	D 1-1	Baker	12,971
Sep 17	CARLISLE UNITED	L 1-2	Crawford	14,314
Sep 24	Blackburn Rovers	W 2-1	Baker 2	16,523
Sep 28	Derby County	D 2-2	Baker, Spearritt	18,442
Oct 1	BOLTON WANDERERS	D 2-2	Brogan, Crawford	16,019
Oct 8	BIRMINGHAM CITY	W 3-2	Crawford 2, o.g.	15,122
Oct 15	Portsmouth	L 2-4	Baker 2	12,042
Oct 22	HULL CITY	W 5-4	Brogan 2 (1 pen), Crawford 3	20,024
Oct 29	Plymouth Argyle	D 1-1	Crawford	19,048
Nov 5	NORTHAMPTON TOWN	W 6-1	Woods, Brogan 3 (2 pen), Crawford, Baker	12,820
Nov 12	Millwall	L 0-1		20,900
Nov 19	ROTHERHAM UNITED	W 3-0	Houghton, Baker, Crawford	13,499
Nov 26	Preston North End	L 0-2		14,122
Dec 3	BURY	W 2-0	Baker, Crawford	12,353
Dec 9	Coventry City	L 0-5		25,724
Dec 17	CARDIFF CITY	D 0-0		11,166
Dec 20	Charlton Athletic	L 1-2	Baker	9,650
Dec 26	CHARLTON ATHLETIC	D 0-0		16,096
Dec 31	Wolverhampton Wanderers	D 0-0		28,425
Jan 4	BRISTOL CITY	D 0-0		13,876
Jan 21	Carlisle United	L 1-2	Crawford	11,812
Feb 4	BLACKBURN ROVERS	D 1-1	Crawford	16,292
Feb 11	Bolton Wanderers	D 1-1	Crawford	12,565
Feb 25	Birmingham City	D 2-2	Brogan, Crawford	18,491
Mar 4	PLYMOUTH ARGYLE	D 1-1	Brogan (pen)	13,734
Mar 18	Hull City	D 1-1	Brogan	22,775
Mar 25	PORTSMOUTH	W 4-2	Viljoen 3, Crawford	13,699
Mar 27	Crystal Palace	W 2-0	Broadfoot, Brogan	16,029
Mar 28	CRYSTAL PALACE	W 2-0	Harper D, Viljoen	17,167
Apr 1	Northampton Town	D 1-1	McNeil	13,129
Apr 8	MILLWALL	W 4-1	Hegan, Viljoen, Broadfoot, Brogan	20,130
Apr 15	Rotherham United	W 2-0	Hegan 2	8,928
Apr 18	NORWICH CITY	L 0-2		28,047
Apr 22	PRESTON NORTH END	D 0-0		12,758
Apr 28	Bury	W 2-1	Crawford, Brogan	5,760
May 6	COVENTRY CITY	D 1-1	Viljoen	18,945

FA Cup

Jan 28	SHREWSBURY TOWN	(Rd3) W 4-1	Brogan, Crawford, Harper D, Hegan	14,906
Feb 18	CARLISLE UNITED	(Rd4) W 2-0	Crawford, Brogan	22,836
Mar 11	Manchester City	(Rd5) D 1-1	Crawford	47,075
Mar 14	MANCHESTER CITY	(R) L 0-3		30,155

League Cup

Sep 13	Brentford	(Rd2) W 4-2	Hegan, Baker, Woods, Spearritt	5,860
Oct 4	Birmingham City	(Rd3) L 1-2	Crawford	15,116

Fact File

Colin Viljoen scored a hat-trick on his league debut against Portsmouth in a 4-2 victory at Portman Road.

MANAGER: Bill McGarry

CAPTAIN: Cyril Lea

TOP SCORER: Ray Crawford

BIGGEST WIN: 6-1 v Northampton Town (H), 5 November 1966, Division Two

HIGHEST ATTENDANCE: 30,155 v Manchester City, 14 March 1967, FA Cup 5th Round replay

MAJOR TRANSFERS IN: Joe Broadfoot from Millwall; Billy Houghton from Watford; Charlie Woods from Crystal Palace

MAJOR TRANSFERS OUT: Dave Harper to Swindon Town

League & Cup Appearances

PLAYER	LEAGUE	CUP COMPETITION		TOTAL
		FA CUP	LC	
Baker	30	4	2	36
Barnard	8	1		9
Baxter	42	3	2	47
Bolton	7 (1)	0 (1)		7 (2)
Broadfoot	15	3		18
Brogan	35	4	1	40
Carroll	11			11
Crawford	42	4	2	48
Hancock	42	4	2	48
Harper C	2 (2)			2 (2)
Harper D	37	4	2	43
Hegan	37	4	2	43
Houghton	38	3	2	43
Jefferson		1		1
Lea	37 (2)	4	2	43 (2)
McNeil	16 (1)	4		20 (1)
Mills	21 (1)	1	2	24 (1)
Mitchell	0 (2)			0 (2)
Spearritt	22 (3)		2	24 (3)
Viljoen	10			10
Woods	10 (2)		1	11 (2)

Goalscorers

PLAYER	LEAGUE	CUP COMPETITION		TOTAL
		FA CUP	LC	
Crawford	21	3	1	25
Brogan	15	2		17
Baker	13		1	14
Hegan	5	1	1	7
Viljoen	6			6
Spearritt	2		1	3
Broadfoot	2			2
Harper D	1	1		2
Woods	1		1	2
Baxter	1			1
Houghton	1			1
McNeil	1			1
Opp's o.gs.	1			1

Final Division Two Table

		P	W	D	L	F	A	Pts
1	COVENTRY C	42	23	13	6	74	43	59
2	WOLVERHAMPTON W	42	25	8	9	88	48	58
3	CARLISLE U	42	23	6	13	71	54	52
4	BLACKBURN R	42	19	13	10	56	46	51
5	IPSWICH TOWN	42	17	16	9	70	54	50
6	HUDDERSFIELD T	42	20	9	13	58	46	49
7	CRYSTAL PALACE	42	19	10	13	61	55	48
8	MILLWALL	42	18	9	15	49	58	45
9	BOLTON W	42	14	14	14	64	58	42
10	BIRMINGHAM C	42	16	8	18	70	66	40
11	NORWICH C	42	13	14	15	49	55	40
12	HULL C	42	16	7	19	77	72	39
13	PRESTON NE	42	16	7	19	65	67	39
14	PORTSMOUTH	42	13	13	16	59	70	39
15	BRISTOL C	42	12	14	16	56	62	38
16	PLYMOUTH ARG	42	14	9	19	59	58	37
17	DERBY CO	42	12	12	18	68	72	36
18	ROTHERHAM U	42	13	10	19	61	70	36
19	CHARLTON ATH	42	13	9	20	49	53	35
20	CARDIFF C	42	12	9	21	61	87	33
21	NORTHAMPTON T	42	12	6	24	47	84	30
22	BURY	42	11	6	25	49	83	28

Season 1967-68

Football League Division Two

DATE	OPPONENTS	SCORE	GOALSCORERS	ATTENDANCE
Aug 9	Middlesbrough	W 2-0	Crawford, Baker	25,916
Aug 21	Blackpool	D 0-0		19,634
Aug 26	BRISTOL CITY	W 5-0	Brogan 3, Hegan, Viljoen	13,702
Aug 29	BLACKPOOL	D 1-1	Crawford	18,434
Sep 2	Birmingham City	D 0-0		25,463
Sep 6	Blackburn Rovers	L 1-2	Spearritt	13,610
Sep 9	BOLTON WANDERERS	D 1-1	Brogan	14,903
Sep 16	Huddersfield Town	W 4-1	Viljoen, Baker, Hegan, Carroll	11,554
Sep 23	NORWICH CITY	D 0-0		24,873
Sep 30	CARLISLE UNITED	W 3-1	Wigg 2, Spearritt	14,183
Oct 7	Cardiff City	D 1-1	Houghton	11,282
Oct 14	DERBY COUNTY	W 4-0	Spearritt 2, Crawford, Brogan	15,785
Oct 21	Preston North End	D 1-1	Crawford	13,740
Oct 28	CHARLTON ATHLETIC	W 3-2	Crawford, Baker, Spearritt	16,286
Nov 11	ASTON VILLA	W 2-1	Spearritt, Brogan	17,748
Nov 18	Rotherham United	W 3-1	Hegan, Woods, Brogan (pen)	6,068
Nov 25	PLYMOUTH ARGYLE	D 1-1	Spearritt	14,928
Dec 2	Queens Park Rangers	L 0-1		16,266
Dec 9	PORTSMOUTH	L 1-2	Hegan	14,928
Dec 16	MIDDLESBROUGH	L 1-2	Crawford	12,724
Dec 22	Bristol City	D 1-1	Baxter	17,628
Dec 26	MILLWALL	W 2-1	Brogan 2 (2 pen)	18,085
Dec 30	Millwall	D 1-1	Hunt	13,137
Jan 6	BIRMINGHAM CITY	W 2-1	Wigg 2	16,701
Jan 20	HUDDERSFIELD TOWN	W 2-0	Viljoen, Crawford	14,945
Feb 3	Norwich City	W 4-3	Viljoen 3, Houghton	30,022
Feb 10	Carlisle United	L 1-4	Viljoen	17,111
Feb 24	CARDIFF CITY	W 4-2	Brogan, O'Rourke 2, Crawford	15,580
Mar 2	Derby County	W 3-2	Brogan 2, O'Rourke	20,723
Mar 9	Bolton Wanderers	W 2-1	O'Rourke 2	8,511
Mar 16	PRESTON NORTH END	W 4-0	Brogan (pen), Hegan, O'Rourke, Crawford	19,558
Mar 23	Charlton Athletic	W 1-0	Brogan	13,453
Mar 30	CRYSTAL PALACE	D 2-2	Crawford, Baker	24,981
Apr 6	Aston Villa	D 2-2	Crawford, Brogan (pen)	19,851
Apr 13	ROTHERHAM UNITED	W 2-0	Crawford 2	22,146
Apr 15	Hull City	D 1-1	O'Rourke	19,558
Apr 16	HULL CITY	W 2-0	Brogan (pen), Hegan	24,615
Apr 20	Plymouth Argyle	W 1-0	O'Rourke	9,956
Apr 27	QUEENS PARK RANGERS	D 2-2	O'Rourke, Crawford	28,000
May 1	Crystal Palace	W 3-1	Brogan, Crawford, O'Rourke	19,994
May 4	Portsmouth	W 2-1	O'Rourke 2	25,891
May 11	BLACKBURN ROVERS	D 1-1	Crawford	27,952

FA Cup

Jan 27	Chelsea	(Rd3) L 0-3		42,986

League Cup

Sep 12	SOUTHAMPTON	(Rd2) W 5-2	Brogan (pen), Crawford 4	17,202
Oct 11	Stoke City	(Rd3) L 1-2	Crawford	14,815

League & Cup Appearances

PLAYER	LEAGUE	CUP COMPETITION		TOTAL
		FA CUP	LC	
Baker	11		2	13
Barnard	2 (1)			2 (1)
Baxter	41	1	2	44
Bolton	5			5
Broadfoot	4 (1)		0 (1)	4 (2)
Brogan	36	1	1	38
Carroll	38	1	2	41
Crawford	39	1	2	42
Hancock	42	1	2	45
Harper	1 (1)			1 (1)
Hegan	41		2	43
Houghton	41	1	2	44
Hunt	8 (1)	1		9 (1)
Jefferson	28 (2)	1		29 (2)
Lea	4		1	5
McNeil	10 (3)		1	11 (3)
Mills	9 (1)	1	1 (1)	11 (2)
Morris	14			14
O'Rourke	15			15
Spearritt	19 (1)	1	2	22 (1)
Viljoen	39	1	2	42
Wigg	5			5
Woods	9 (2)	0 (1)		9 (3)
Wosahlo	1			1

Goalscorers

PLAYER	LEAGUE	CUP COMPETITION		TOTAL
		FA CUP	LC	
Crawford	16		5	21
Brogan	17		1	18
O'Rourke	12			12
Spearritt	7			7
Viljoen	7			7
Hegan	6			6
Wigg	4			4
Baker	3			3
Baxter	2			2
Houghton	2			2
Carroll	1			1
Hunt	1			1
Woods	1			1

Fact File

John O'Rourke joined the club in February 1968 and played in their last 15 games, scoring 12 goals and helping to earn promotion to the top flight.

MANAGER: Bill McGarry

CAPTAIN: Billy Baxter

TOP SCORER: Ray Crawford

BIGGEST WIN: 5-0 v Bristol City (H), 26 August 1967, Division Two

HIGHEST ATTENDANCE: 28,000 v QPR, 27 April 1968, Division Two

MAJOR TRANSFERS IN: Bobby Hunt from Millwall; Peter Morris from Mansfield Town; John O'Rourke from Middlesbrough

MAJOR TRANSFERS OUT: Gerry Baker to Coventry City; Ron Bolton to Bournemouth

Final Division Two Table

		P	W	D	L	F	A	Pts
1	IPSWICH TOWN	42	22	15	5	79	44	59
2	QPR	42	25	8	9	67	36	58
3	BLACKPOOL	42	24	10	8	71	43	58
4	BIRMINGHAM C	42	19	14	9	83	51	52
5	PORTSMOUTH	42	18	13	11	68	55	49
6	MIDDLESBROUGH	42	17	12	13	60	54	46
7	MILLWALL	42	14	17	11	62	50	45
8	BLACKBURN R	42	16	11	15	56	49	43
9	NORWICH C	42	16	11	15	60	65	43
10	CARLISLE U	42	14	13	15	58	52	41
11	CRYSTAL PALACE	42	14	11	17	56	56	39
12	BOLTON W	42	13	13	16	60	63	39
13	CARDIFF C	42	13	12	17	60	66	38
14	HUDDERSFIELD T	42	13	12	17	46	61	38
15	CHARLTON ATH	42	12	13	17	63	68	37
16	ASTON VILLA	42	15	7	20	54	64	37
17	HULL C	42	12	13	17	58	73	37
18	DERBY CO	42	13	10	19	71	78	36
19	BRISTOL C	42	13	10	19	48	62	36
20	PRESTON NE	42	12	11	19	43	65	35
21	ROTHERHAM U	42	10	11	21	42	76	31
22	PLYMOUTH ARG	42	9	9	24	38	72	27

Season 1968-69

Football League Division One

DATE	OPPONENTS	SCORE	GOALSCORERS	ATTENDANCE
Aug 10	WOLVERHAMPTON WANDERERS	W 1-0	O'Rourke	25,840
Aug 14	Sunderland	L 0-3		30,037
Aug 17	Leicester City	W 3-1	Crawford, O'Rourke, Hegan	26,014
Aug 20	LEEDS UNITED	L 2-3	O'Rourke, Crawford	30,388
Aug 24	ARSENAL	L 1-2	Crawford	25,825
Aug 27	QUEENS PARK RANGERS	W 3-0	Morris, Hegan, Crawford	24,049
Aug 31	Manchester City	D 1-1	Crawford	31,303
Sep 7	Sheffield Wednesday	L 1-1	Crawford	26,770
Sep 14	LIVERPOOL	L 0-2		24,514
Sep 21	Southampton	D 2-2	O'Rourke, Crawford	19,599
Sep 28	STOKE CITY	W 3-1	Crawford 2, Brogan (pen)	20,943
Oct 5	Chelsea	L 1-3	Crawford	31,625
Oct 8	Queens Park Rangers	L 1-2	O'Rourke	17,992
Oct 12	NEWCASTLE UNITED	L 1-4	O'Rourke	20,763
Oct 19	Nottingham Forest*	W 2-1	Crawford, O'Rourke	21,148
Oct 26	TOTTENHAM HOTSPUR	L 0-1		30,251
Nov 2	Burnley	L 0-1		14,741
Nov 9	EVERTON	D 2-2	Crawford, Morris	23,049
Nov 16	Manchester United	D 0-0		45,796
Nov 23	WEST HAM UNITED	D 2-2	Morris, Viljoen	28,996
Nov 30	Coventry City	W 2-0	O'Rourke, Hunt	26,770
Dec 7	WEST BROMWICH ALBION	W 4-1	Viljoen, O'Rourke 2, Brogan	19,725
Dec 14	Newcastle United	L 1-2	O'Rourke	26,440
Dec 21	NOTTINGHAM FOREST	L 2-3	Hegan, Morris	18,739
Dec 26	CHELSEA	L 1-3	Hunt	24,083
Jan 11	BURNLEY	W 2-0	Crawford, Mills	18,858
Jan 18	Everton	D 2-2	Crawford 2	41,725
Feb 1	MANCHESTER UNITED	W 1-0	Dunne o.g.	30,837
Feb 12	Leeds United	L 0-2		24,494
Feb 18	Arsenal	W 2-0	Crawford, O'Rourke	23,891
Mar 1	Wolverhampton Wanderers	D 1-1	O'Rourke	25,600
Mar 11	MANCHESTER CITY	W 2-1	Wigg, O'Rourke	24,313
Mar 18	Tottenham Hotspur	D 2-2	Wigg, Jefferson	21,608
Mar 21	West Ham United	W 3-1	Woods, Wigg, O'Rourke	32,574
Mar 25	COVENTRY CITY	D 0-0		20,519
Apr 4	SUNDERLAND	W 1-0	Wigg	24,021
Apr 5	Stoke City	L 1-2	O'Rourke	15,187
Apr 12	SOUTHAMPTON	D 0-0		19,933
Apr 19	Liverpool	L 0-4		40,449
Apr 23	West Bromwich Albion	D 2-2	Mills, Wigg	21,426
Apr 25	SHEFFIELD WEDNESDAY	W 2-0	Viljoen, Wigg	17,780
May 3	LEICESTER CITY	W 2-1	Viljoen, Lambert	22,017

*played at Meadow Lane

FA Cup

Jan 4	Everton	(Rd3) L 1-2	O'Rourke	49,047

League Cup

Sep 3	NORWICH CITY	(Rd2) L 2-4	McNeil, Crawford	23,087

League & Cup Appearances

PLAYER	LEAGUE	CUP COMPETITION		TOTAL
		FA CUP	LC	
Barnard	7 (1)		1	8 (1)
Baxter	39	1	1	41
Bell	1			1
Best	21	1		22
Brogan	31 (1)		1	32 (1)
Bugg	3			3
Carroll	15 (2)		1	16 (2)
Crawford	30	1	1	32
Hancock	18		1	19
Harper	4			4
Hegan	38	1	1	40
Houghton	28	1	1	30
Hunt	4 (7)			4 (7)
Jefferson	40	1		41
Lambert	2			2
Lea	0 (1)			0 (1)
McNeil	3		1	4
Miller	1			1
Mills	35 (1)		1	36 (1)
Morris	33 (1)	1	1	35 (1)
O'Rourke	39	1		40
Spearritt	4 (5)		1	5 (5)
Stacey	3			3
Viljoen	37 (1)	1	1	39 (1)
Wigg	10			10
Woods	16 (4)	0 (1)		16 (5)

Goalscorers

PLAYER	LEAGUE	CUP COMPETITION		TOTAL
		FA CUP	LC	
Crawford	16		1	17
O'Rourke	16	1		17
Wigg	6			6
Morris	4			4
Viljoen	4			4
Hegan	3			3
Brogan	2			2
Hunt	2			2
Mills	2			2
Jefferson	1			1
Lambert	1			1
McNeil			1	1
Woods	1			1
Opp's o.gs.	1			1

Fact File

Cyril Lea took over as caretaker manager after the departure of Bill McGarry for two months until Bobby Robson was appointed.

MANAGER: Bill McGarry/Bobby Robson

CAPTAIN: Billy Baxter

TOP SCORER: Ray Crawford

BIGGEST WIN: 4-1 v WBA (H), 7 December 1968, Division One

HIGHEST ATTENDANCE: 30,837 v Manchester United, 1 February 1969, Division One

MAJOR TRANSFERS IN: David Best from Oldham Athletic; Steve Stacey from Wrexham

MAJOR TRANSFERS OUT: Ray Crawford to Charlton Athletic; Ken Hancock to Tottenham Hotspur; Danny Hegan to WBA; Billy Houghton to Leicester City; Eddie Spearritt to Brighton; Steve Stacey to Chester City

Final Division One Table

		P	W	D	L	F	A	Pts
1	LEEDS U	42	27	13	2	66	26	67
2	LIVERPOOL	42	25	11	6	63	24	61
3	EVERTON	42	21	15	6	77	36	57
4	ARSENAL	42	22	12	8	56	27	56
5	CHELSEA	42	20	10	12	73	53	50
6	TOTTENHAM H	42	14	17	11	61	51	45
7	SOUTHAMPTON	42	16	13	13	57	48	45
8	WEST HAM U	42	13	18	11	66	50	44
9	NEWCASTLE U	42	15	14	13	61	55	44
10	WBA	42	16	11	15	64	67	43
11	MANCHESTER U	42	15	12	15	57	53	42
12	IPSWICH TOWN	42	15	11	16	59	60	41
13	MANCHESTER C	42	15	10	17	64	55	40
14	BURNLEY	42	15	9	18	55	82	39
15	SHEFFIELD W	42	10	16	16	41	54	36
16	WOLVERHAMPTON W	42	10	15	17	41	58	35
17	SUNDERLAND	42	11	12	19	43	67	34
18	NOTTINGHAM F	42	10	13	19	45	57	33
19	STOKE C	42	9	15	18	40	63	33
20	COVENTRY C	42	10	11	21	46	64	31
21	LEICESTER C	42	9	12	21	39	68	30
22	QPR	42	4	10	28	39	95	18

Season 1969-70

Football League Division One

DATE	OPPONENTS	SCORE	GOALSCORERS	ATTENDANCE
Aug 9	NOTTINGHAM FOREST	D 0-0		19,310
Aug 12	DERBY COUNTY	L 0-1		20,551
Aug 16	Chelsea	L 0-1		29,613
Aug 20	Derby County	L 1-3	Brogan	31,467
Aug 23	COVENTRY CITY	L 0-1		18,280
Aug 27	Southampton	L 2-4	Collard, Brogan	20,598
Aug 30	Tottenham Hotspur	L 2-3	Wigg, Viljoen	33,333
Sep 6	NEWCASTLE UNITED	W 2-0	Wigg, O'Rourke	18,328
Sep 13	West Bromwich Albion	D 2-2	O'Rourke, Collard	21,173
Sep 16	WOLVERHAMPTON WANDERERS	D 1-1	Viljoen (pen)	22,462
Sep 20	EVERTON	L 0-3		23,258
Sep 27	Burnley	W 1-0	Hunt	12,366
Oct 4	SHEFFIELD WEDNESDAY	W 1-0	Lambert	17,067
Oct 11	Manchester United	L 1-2	Mills	52,281
Oct 18	LIVERPOOL	D 2-2	Wigg, Brogan	23,266
Oct 25	Arsenal	D 0-0		22,458
Nov 1	MANCHESTER CITY	D 1-1	McNeil	24,128
Nov 8	Leeds United	L 0-4		26,497
Nov 15	CRYSTAL PALACE	W 2-0	Hill 2	18,046
Nov 18	CHELSEA	L 1-4	Viljoen	20,941
Nov 22	Stoke City	D 3-3	Lambert, Collard, Viljoen (pen)	19,287
Nov 29	WEST HAM UNITED	W 1-0	Hill	17,454
Dec 6	Sunderland	L 1-2	Viljoen	12,739
Dec 13	WEST BROMWICH ALBION	L 0-1		18,379
Dec 20	Newcastle United	L 0-4		19,411
Dec 26	Coventry City	L 1-3	Wigg	32,649
Dec 27	TOTTENHAM HOTSPUR	W 2-0	Woods Charlie, Hill	24,658
Jan 10	Everton	L 0-3		42,510
Jan 17	BURNLEY	L 0-1		17,801
Jan 24	Wolverhampton Wanderers	L 0-2		24,636
Jan 31	Sheffield Wednesday	D 2-2	Hill, Mills	17,630
Feb 10	MANCHESTER UNITED	L 0-1		29,755
Feb 28	Manchester City	L 0-1		29,376
Mar 7	STOKE CITY	D 1-1	Viljoen (pen)	16,146
Mar 14	West Ham United	D 0-0		20,934
Mar 21	SUNDERLAND	W 2-0	Pitt o.g., Whymark	20,781
Mar 24	Liverpool	L 0-2		29,548
Mar 28	Crystal Palace	D 1-1	Woods Charlie	27,499
Mar 31	ARSENAL	W 2-1	Baxter, Clarke	25,716
Apr 4	SOUTHAMPTON	W 2-0	Robertson, Carroll (pen)	21,757
Apr 10	Nottingham Forest	L 0-1		10,589
Apr 21	LEEDS UNITED	W 3-2	Robertson 2, Clarke	16,936

FA Cup

Jan 3	MANCHESTER UNITED	(Rd3) L 0-1		29,503

League Cup

Sep 3	COLCHESTER UNITED	(Rd2) W 4-0	Carroll, Mills, Brogan 2 (2 pen)	19,019
Sep 24	WEST BROMWICH ALBION	(Rd3) D 1-1	Woods Charlie	19,250
Oct 1	West Bromwich Albion	(R) L 0-2		24,697

League & Cup Appearances

PLAYER	LEAGUE	CUP COMPETITION		TOTAL
		FA CUP	LC	
Barnard	1			1
Baxter	41	1	3	45
Bell	1			1
Best	40	1	3	44
Brogan	19 (1)	0 (1)	1	20 (2)
Bugg	1			1
Carroll	42	1	3	46
Clarke	7			7
Collard	30		2	32
Harper	17 (1)	1	0 (1)	18 (2)
Hill	17 (1)	1		18 (1)
Hunt	4 (1)		1 (1)	5 (2)
Jefferson	24		2	26
Lambert	17 (1)		2	19 (1)
McNeil	18 (1)	1	1	20 (1)
Miller	0 (1)			0 (1)
Mills	40	1	3	44
Morris	29 (2)	1	1	31 (2)
O'Rourke	15		2	17
Robertson	7			7
Sivell	1			1
Viljoen	34	1	3	38
Whymark	6 (2)			6 (2)
Wigg	20 (2)	1	3	24 (2)
Woods Charlie	30 (9)	1	3	34 (9)
Woods Clive	1 (2)			1 (2)
Wosahlo	0 (1)			0 (1)

Goalscorers

PLAYER	LEAGUE	CUP COMPETITION		TOTAL
		FA CUP	LC	
Viljoen	6			6
Brogan	3		2	5
Hill	4			4
Wigg	4			4
Mills	3		1	4
Collard	3			3
Robertson	3			3
Woods Charlie	2		1	3
Clarke	2			2
Lambert	2			2
O'Rourke	2			2
Carroll	1		1	2
Baxter	1			1
Hunt	1			1
McNeil	1			1
Whymark	1			1
Opp's o.g.s.	1			1

Fact File

Colin Viljoen was Ipswich's top scorer with just six goals – the first season that the club's leading scorer has failed to reach double figures.

MANAGER: Bobby Robson

CAPTAIN: Billy Baxter

TOP SCORER: Colin Viljoen

BIGGEST WIN: 4-0 v Colchester United (H), 3 September 1969, League Cup 2nd Round

HIGHEST ATTENDANCE: 29,755 v Manchester United, 10 February 1970, Division One

MAJOR TRANSFERS IN: Frank Clarke from QPR; Ian Collard from WBA; Mick Hill from Sheffield United; Jimmy Robertson from Arsenal

MAJOR TRANSFERS OUT: Frank Brogan to Halifax Town; John O'Rourke to Coventry City; Ron Wigg and Charlie Woods to Watford

Final Division One Table

		P	W	D	L	F	A	Pts
1	EVERTON	42	29	8	5	72	34	66
2	LEEDS U	42	21	15	6	84	49	57
3	CHELSEA	42	21	13	8	70	50	55
4	DERBY CO	42	22	9	11	64	37	53
5	LIVERPOOL	42	20	11	11	65	42	51
6	COVENTRY C	42	19	11	12	58	48	49
7	NEWCASTLE U	42	17	13	12	57	35	47
8	MANCHESTER U	42	14	17	11	66	61	45
9	STOKE C	42	15	15	12	56	52	45
10	MANCHESTER C	42	16	11	15	55	48	43
11	TOTTENHAM H	42	17	9	16	54	55	43
12	ARSENAL	42	12	18	12	51	49	42
13	WOLVERHAMPTON W	42	12	16	14	55	57	40
14	BURNLEY	42	12	15	15	56	61	39
15	NOTTINGHAM F	42	10	18	14	50	71	38
16	WBA	42	14	9	19	58	66	37
17	WEST HAM U	42	12	12	18	51	60	36
18	IPSWICH TOWN	42	10	11	21	40	63	31
19	SOUTHAMPTON	42	6	17	19	46	67	29
20	CRYSTAL PALACE	42	6	15	21	34	68	27
21	SUNDERLAND	42	6	14	22	30	68	26
22	SHEFFIELD W	42	8	9	25	40	71	25

Season 1970-71

Football League Division One

DATE	OPPONENTS	SCORE	GOALSCORERS	ATTENDANCE
Aug 15	Stoke City	D 0-0		17,039
Aug 18	COVENTRY CITY	L 0-2		21,199
Aug 22	NOTTINGHAM FOREST	D 0-0		19,150
Aug 26	Derby County	L 0-2		30,869
Aug 29	Southampton	L 0-1		18,724
Sep 1	WOLVERHAMPTON WANDERERS	L 2-3	Viljoen 2 (1 pen)	18,705
Sep 5	BURNLEY	W 3-0	Baxter, Clarke, Viljoen (pen)	15,993
Sep 12	Everton	L 0-2		41,596
Sep 19	MANCHESTER UNITED	W 4-0	Viljoen 2 (1 pen), Whymark, Clarke	27,777
Sep 26	Chelsea	L 1-2	Clarke	38,541
Oct 3	WEST BROMWICH ALBION	D 2-2	Viljoen, Clarke	17,578
Oct 10	Huddersfield Town	L 0-1		17,944
Oct 17	STOKE CITY	W 2-0	Clarke (pen), Hill	18,170
Oct 24	LIVERPOOL	W 1-0	Hill	22,576
Oct 31	Manchester City	L 0-2		27,317
Nov 7	WEST HAM UNITED	W 2-1	Hill, Mills	22,993
Nov 14	Newcastle United	D 0-0		25,657
Nov 21	ARSENAL	L 0-1		22,867
Nov 28	Blackpool	W 2-0	Hill, Viljoen	13,048
Dec 5	CRYSTAL PALACE	L 1-2	Viljoen	19,457
Dec 12	Leeds United	D 0-0		29,675
Dec 19	NOTTINGHAM FOREST	W 1-0	Baxter	14,085
Jan 9	Coventry City	L 0-1		19,938
Jan 16	DERBY COUNTY	L 0-1		20,332
Jan 30	BLACKPOOL	W 2-1	Hammond, Lambert	17,512
Feb 6	Crystal Palace	L 0-1		23,482
Feb 20	Arsenal	L 2-3	Robertson 2	39,872
Feb 23	LEEDS UNITED	L 2-4	Hill, Viljoen	27,281
Feb 26	MANCHESTER CITY	W 2-0	Viljoen, Clarke	20,686
Mar 13	NEWCASTLE UNITED	W 1-0	Robertson	17,065
Mar 20	West Ham United	D 2-2	Bell, Robertson	25,957
Mar 23	TOTTENHAM HOTSPUR	L 1-2	Hill	21,718
Mar 27	Burnley	D 2-2	Lambert, Morris	13,479
Mar 29	Liverpool	L 1-2	Lambert	41,817
Apr 3	SOUTHAMPTON	L 1-3	Woods	16,389
Apr 6	EVERTON	D 0-0		20,288
Apr 10	Tottenham Hotspur	L 0-2		28,708
Apr 12	West Bromwich Albion	W 1-0	Robertson	12,684
Apr 17	HUDDERSFIELD TOWN	W 2-0	Hill, Clarke	16,626
Apr 24	Manchester United	L 2-3	Morris, Clarke	31,662
Apr 28	Wolverhampton Wanderers	D 0-0		18,827
May 1	CHELSEA	D 0-0		24,708

FA Cup

Jan 11	Newcastle United	(Rd3) D 1-1	Mills	32,100
Jan 13	NEWCASTLE UNITED	(R) W 2-1	Viljoen, Hill	21,429
Jan 23	West Bromwich Albion	(Rd4) D 1-1	Clarke	27,178
Jan 26	WEST BROMWICH ALBION	(R) W 3-0	Clarke, Robertson, Clarke	25,998
Feb 13	Stoke City	(Rd5) D 0-0		36,809
Feb 16	STOKE CITY	(R) L 0-1		30,229

League Cup

Sep 8	ARSENAL	(Rd2) D 0-0		21,552
Sep 28	Arsenal	(R) L 0-4		26,542

Fact File

Ipswich's visit to Chelsea on 26 September caused controversy when referee Roy Capey awarded Chelsea a goal when Alan Hudson's shot clearly went through the side netting.

MANAGER: Bobby Robson

CAPTAIN: Bill Baxter/Mick Mills

TOP SCORER: Colin Viljoen

BIGGEST WIN: 4-0 v Manchester United (H), 19 September 1970, Division One

HIGHEST ATTENDANCE: 30,229 v Stoke City, 16 February 1971, FA Cup 5th Round replay

MAJOR TRANSFERS OUT: Bill Baxter to Hull; Bobby Hunt to Charlton

League and Cup Appearances

PLAYER	LEAGUE	CUP COMPETITION		TOTAL
		FA CUP	LC	
Barnard	0 (1)			0 (1)
Baxter	24	3	2	29
Bell	23	4		27
Best	18		2	20
Carroll	8		1	9
Clarke	36	6	2	44
Collard	15 (2)	4 (1)	0 (1)	19 (4)
Hammond	29	6	1	36
Harper	13			13
Hill	26	6		32
Hunt	0 (1)			0 (1)
Jefferson	20 (1)	1		21 (1)
Lambert	11 (6)	0 (2)	0 (1)	11 (9)
McNeil	19	6	2	27
Miller	3 (3)			3 (3)
Mills	42	6	2	50
Morris	41	6	2	49
Robertson	40	6	2	48
Shanahan	3 (1)			3 (1)
Sivell	24	6		30
Viljoen	31 (1)	6	2	39 (1)
Whymark	8 (2)		2	10 (2)
Woods	28 (5)	0 (1)	2	30 (6)

Goalscorers

PLAYER	LEAGUE	CUP COMPETITION		TOTAL
		FA CUP	LC	
Viljoen	10	2		12
Clarke	8	2		10
Hill	7	1		8
Robertson	5	1		6
Lambert	3			3
Baxter	2			2
Morris	2			2
Mills	1		1	2
Bell	1			1
Hammond	1			1
Whymark	1			1
Woods	1			1

Final Division One Table

		P	W	D	L	F	A	Pts
1	ARSENAL	42	29	7	6	71	29	65
2	LEEDS U	42	27	10	5	72	30	64
3	TOTTENHAM H	42	19	14	9	54	33	52
4	WOLVERHAMPTON W	42	22	8	12	64	54	52
5	LIVERPOOL	42	17	17	8	42	24	51
6	CHELSEA	42	18	15	9	52	42	51
7	SOUTHAMPTON	42	17	12	13	56	44	46
8	MANCHESTER U	42	16	11	15	65	66	43
9	DERBY CO	42	16	10	16	56	54	42
10	COVENTRY C	42	16	10	16	37	38	42
11	MANCHESTER C	42	12	17	13	47	42	41
12	NEWCASTLE U	42	14	13	15	44	46	41
13	STOKE C	42	12	13	17	44	48	37
14	EVERTON	42	12	13	17	54	60	37
15	HUDDERSFIELD T	42	11	14	17	40	49	36
16	NOTTINGHAM F	42	14	8	20	42	61	36
17	WBA	42	10	15	17	58	75	35
18	CRYSTAL PALACE	42	12	11	19	39	57	35
19	IPSWICH TOWN	42	12	10	20	42	48	34
20	WEST HAM U	42	10	14	18	47	60	34
21	BURNLEY	42	7	13	22	29	63	27
22	BLACKPOOL	42	4	15	23	34	66	23

Season 1971-72

Football League Division One

DATE	OPPONENTS	SCORE	GOALSCORERS	ATTENDANCE
Aug 14	EVERTON	D 0-0		23,757
Aug 17	COVENTRY CITY	W 3-1	Clarke 2 (1 pen), Hamilton	19,269
Aug 21	Southampton	D 0-0		17,931
Aug 23	West Ham United	D 0-0		25,714
Aug 28	LEEDS UNITED	L 0-2		26,658
Aug 31	DERBY COUNTY	D 0-0		18,687
Sep 4	Manchester United	L 0-1		44,852
Sep 11	LEICESTER CITY	L 1-2	Clarke (pen)	18,483
Sep 18	West Bromwich Albion	W 2-1	Robertson, Clarke	18,885
Sep 25	NEWCASTLE UNITED	D 0-0		18,720
Oct 2	Tottenham Hotspur	L 1-2	Collard	33,562
Oct 9	NOTTINGHAM FOREST	D 1-1	Harper	16,285
Oct 16	Everton	D 1-1	Hill	31,590
Oct 23	STOKE CITY	W 2-1	Hill 2	17,677
Oct 30	Arsenal	L 1-2	Hill	39,065
Nov 6	WOLVERHAMPTON WANDERERS	W 2-1	Hill, Belfitt	21,938
Nov 13	Crystal Palace	D 1-1	Belfitt	18,462
Nov 20	HUDDERSFIELD TOWN	W 1-0	Hill	16,168
Nov 27	Sheffield United	L 0-7		26,233
Dec 4	LIVERPOOL	D 0-0		21,362
Dec 11	Manchester City	L 0-4		26,900
Dec 18	MANCHESTER UNITED	D 0-0		29,213
Dec 27	Chelsea	L 0-2		43,896
Jan 1	WEST BROMWICH ALBION	L 2-3	Hill, Belfitt	16,883
Jan 8	Leeds United	D 2-2	Hunter, Clarke	32,194
Jan 22	Coventry City	D 1-1	Hunter	18,183
Jan 29	WEST HAM UNITED	W 1-0	Morris	22,757
Feb 12	Stoke City	D 3-3	Lambert 2, Miller	20,244
Feb 19	ARSENAL	L 0-1		28,657
Feb 26	Wolverhampton Wanderers	D 2-2	Belfitt 2	19,349
Mar 4	CRYSTAL PALACE	L 0-2		17,221
Mar 11	NOTTINGHAM FOREST	W 2-0	Viljoen, Whymark	9,872
Mar 18	SOUTHAMPTON	D 1-1	Whymark	15,528
Mar 22	Derby County	L 0-1		26,738
Mar 25	Leicester City	L 0-1		19,769
Apr 1	CHELSEA	L 1-2	Viljoen (pen)	24,319
Apr 3	TOTTENHAM HOTSPUR	W 2-1	Want o.g., Belfitt	24,302
Apr 5	Newcastle United	W 1-0	Whymark	22,979
Apr 8	Huddersfield Town	W 3-1	Belfitt, Morris, Robertson	12,139
Apr 15	SHEFFIELD UNITED	D 0-0		17,052
Apr 18	MANCHESTER CITY	W 2-1	Whymark, Harper	24,464
Apr 22	Liverpool	L 0-2		54,316

FA Cup

Jan 15	Peterborough United	(Rd3) W 2-0	Viljoen, Hill	16,973
Feb 5	Birmingham City	(Rd4) L 0-1		40,708

League Cup

Sep 7	MANCHESTER UNITED	(Rd2) L 1-3	Robertson	28,143

League & Cup Appearances

PLAYER	LEAGUE	CUP COMPETITION		TOTAL
		FA CUP	LC	
Belfitt	26	2		28
Bell	7		1	8
Best	27	2	1	30
Carroll	1			1
Clarke	18 (3)		1	19 (3)
Collard	13 (1)			13 (1)
Hamilton	8 (8)		0 (1)	8 (9)
Hammond	15		1	16
Harper	42	2	1	45
Hill	20 (1)	2	1	23 (1)
Hunter	35	2		37
Jefferson	42	2	1	45
Lambert	14 (2)			14 (2)
McNeil	1	1		2
Miller	29 (1)	1 (1)	1	31 (2)
Mills	35	2	1	38
Morris	29 (2)	2	1	32 (2)
Robertson	40	2	1	43
Sivell	15			15
Viljoen	32	2		34
Whymark	12 (2)			12 (2)
Woods	1 (4)			1 (4)

Goalscorers

PLAYER	LEAGUE	CUP COMPETITION		TOTAL
		FA CUP	LC	
Hill	7	1		8
Belfitt	7			7
Clarke	5			5
Whymark	4			4
Robertson	2		1	3
Viljoen	2	1		3
Harper	2			2
Hunter	2			2
Lambert	2			2
Morris	2			2
Collard	1			1
Hamilton	1			1
Miller	1			1
Opp's o.gs.	1			1

Fact File

Allan Hunter was signed during the season and he went on to become the club's most capped player.

MANAGER: Bobby Robson

CAPTAIN: Mick Mills

TOP SCORER: Mick Hill

BIGGEST WIN: 3-1 v Coventry City (H), 17 August 1971, Division One; 3-1 v Huddersfield Town (A), 8 April 1972, Division One

HIGHEST ATTENDANCE: 29,231 v Manchester United, 18 December 1971, Division One

MAJOR TRANSFERS IN: Rod Belfitt from Leeds; Bryan Hamilton from Linfield; Allan Hunter from Blackburn

MAJOR TRANSFERS OUT: Jimmy Robertson to Stoke City

Final Division One Table

		P	W	D	L	F	A	Pts
1	Derby Co	42	24	10	8	69	33	58
2	Leeds U	42	24	9	9	73	31	57
3	Liverpool	42	24	9	9	64	30	57
4	Manchester C	42	23	11	8	77	45	57
5	Arsenal	42	22	8	12	58	40	52
6	Tottenham H	42	19	13	10	63	42	51
7	Chelsea	42	18	12	12	58	49	48
8	Manchester U	42	19	10	13	69	61	48
9	Wolverhampton W	42	18	11	13	65	57	47
10	Sheffield U	42	17	12	13	61	60	46
11	Newcastle U	42	15	11	16	49	52	41
12	Leicester C	42	13	13	16	41	46	39
13	Ipswich Town	42	11	16	15	39	53	38
14	West Ham U	42	12	12	18	47	51	36
15	Everton	42	9	18	15	37	48	36
16	WBA	42	12	11	19	42	54	35
17	Stoke C	42	10	15	17	39	56	35
18	Coventry C	42	9	15	18	44	67	33
19	Southampton	42	12	7	23	52	80	31
20	Crystal Palace	42	8	13	21	39	65	29
21	Nottingham F	42	8	9	25	47	81	25
22	Huddersfield T	42	6	13	23	27	59	25

Season 1972-73

Football League Division One

DATE	OPPONENTS	SCORE	GOALSCORERS	ATTENDANCE
Aug 12	Manchester United	W 2-1	Whymark, Hamilton	51,549
Aug 15	NORWICH CITY	L 1-2	Hamilton	29,544
Aug 19	BIRMINGHAM CITY	W 2-0	Miller, Whymark	17,775
Aug 23	Leeds United	D 3-3	Hamilton, Beattie, Belfitt	32,461
Aug 26	Newcastle United	W 2-1	Lambert, Viljoen	24,601
Aug 29	Sheffield United	D 0-0		23,522
Sep 2	TOTTENHAM HOTSPUR	D 1-1	Viljoen	23,140
Sep 9	Southampton	W 2-1	Hamilton, Belfitt	13,919
Sep 16	STOKE CITY	W 2-0	Belfitt 2	17,754
Sep 23	Chelsea	L 0-2		29,647
Sep 30	LEICESTER CITY	L 0-2		17,811
Oct 7	WEST HAM UNITED	D 1-1	Hamilton	22,218
Oct 14	Arsenal	L 0-1		34,196
Oct 21	DERBY COUNTY	W 3-1	Belfitt, Beattie, Whymark	16,948
Oct 28	Everton	D 2-2	Lambert, Belfitt	30,185
Nov 4	LEEDS UNITED	D 2-2	Madeley o.g., Whymark	27,547
Nov 11	Norwich City	D 0-0		34,640
Nov 18	Wolverhampton Wanderers	W 1-0	Whymark	14,888
Dec 2	Manchester City	D 1-1	Johnson	27,839
Dec 5	COVENTRY CITY	W 2-0	Johnson, Whymark	17,786
Dec 9	CRYSTAL PALACE	W 2-1	Johnson 2	18,079
Dec 16	LIVERPOOL	D 1-1	Lambert	25,990
Dec 23	West Bromwich Albion	L 0-2		12,147
Dec 26	CHELSEA	W 3-0	Beattie, Whymark, Hollins o.g.	26,229
Dec 30	Birmingham City	W 2-1	Johnson, Hamilton	32,705
Jan 6	NEWCASTLE UNITED	W 1-0	Whymark	19,609
Jan 20	Tottenham Hotspur	W 1-0	Hamilton	33,014
Jan 27	SOUTHAMPTON	D 2-2	Viljoen (pen), Hamilton	19,629
Feb 17	MANCHESTER UNITED	W 4-1	Hamilton 2, Harper, Viljoen (pen)	31,857
Feb 24	Liverpool	L 1-2	Johnson	43,875
Mar 2	West Ham United	W 1-0	Johnson	37,004
Mar 10	ARSENAL	L 1-2	Whymark	34,636
Mar 17	WEST BROMWICH ALBION	W 2-0	Beattie, Viljoen (pen)	17,614
Mar 24	EVERTON	L 0-1		20,580
Mar 31	Coventry City	L 1-2	Beattie	16,933
Apr 4	Stoke City	L 0-1		18,319
Apr 7	MANCHESTER CITY	D 1-1	Lambert	19,107
Apr 14	Crystal Palace	D 1-1	Hamilton	29,218
Apr 21	WOLVERHAMPTON WANDERERS	W 2-1	Morris, Whymark	23,932
Apr 24	Leicester City	D 1-1	Lambert	20,373
Apr 28	SHEFFIELD UNITED	D 1-1	Whymark	19,271
Apr 30	Derby County	L 0-3		20,382

FA Cup

Jan 13	Chelmsford City	(Rd3) W 3-1	Harper, Johnson, Hamilton	15,557
Feb 3	Chelsea	(Rd4) L 0-2		36,491

League Cup

Sep 5	Newport County	(Rd2) W 3-0	Lambert, Collard, Miller	9,516
Oct 3	STOKE CITY	(Rd3) L 1-2	Viljoen	14,387

Texaco Cup

Sep 12	ST JOHNSTONE	(Rd1/1L) W 4-2	Belfitt 2, Whymark 2	11,777
Sep 27	St Johnstone	(Rd1/2L) W 2-0	Whymark, Woods	5,500
Oct 24	WOLVERHAMPTON W	(Rd2/1L) W 2-1	Belfitt, Lambert	14,264
Nov 7	Wolverhampton W	(Rd2/2L) W 1-0	Hamilton	12,029
Nov 14	Newcastle United	(SF/1L) D 1-1	Whymark, Woods	22,531
Apr 10	NEWCASTLE UNITED	(SF/2L) W 1-0	Hamilton	18,904
May 4	NORWICH CITY	(F/1L) W 2-1	Morris 2	29,700
May 7	Norwich City	(F/2L) W 2-1	Whymark, Woods	35,798

MANAGER: Bobby Robson

CAPTAIN: Mick Mills

TOP SCORER: Trevor Whymark

BIGGEST WIN: 4-1 v Manchester United (H), 17 February 1973, Division One

HIGHEST ATTENDANCE: 31,857 v Manchester United, 17 February 1973, Division One

MAJOR TRANSFERS IN: David Johnson from Everton

MAJOR TRANSFERS OUT: Rod Belfitt to Everton; Frank Clarke to Carlisle United; Derek Jefferson to Wolverhampton; Mick Hill to Crystal Palace

League & Cup Appearances

PLAYER	LEAGUE	CUP COMPETITION		OTHER	TOTAL
		FA CUP	LC		
Beattie	37 (1)	1	2	8	48 (1)
Belfitt	14	1	3		18
Best	40	2	2	7	51
Collard	12 (3)		2	3	17 (3)
Clarke	1 (1)		0 (1)		1 (2)
Hamilton	42	2	2	8	54
Hammond	1 (1)				1 (1)
Harper	35	2	2	8	47
Hill	0 (1)	1			1 (1)
Hunter	41	2	2	8	53
Jefferson	9				9
Johnson	27		2	4	33
Keeley	1				1
Lambert	40	2	2	8	52
Miller	3 (5)		0 (1)	1 (1)	4 (7)
Mills	42	2	2	8	54
Morris	31 (2)	2		7	40 (2)
Peddelty	2	1			3
Sivell	2	1			3
Viljoen	40	2	2	5	49
Whymark	41	2	2	8	53
Woods	1 (4)		1 (3)		2 (7)

Goalscorers

PLAYER	LEAGUE	CUP COMPETITION		OTHER	TOTAL
		FA CUP	LC		
Whymark	11		5		16
Hamilton	11	1		2	14
Belfitt	6		3		9
Johnson	7	1			8
Lambert	5		1	1	7
Viljoen	5		1		6
Beattie	5				5
Morris	1		2		3
Harper	1	1			2
Miller	1		1		2
Woods			2		2
Collard			1		1
Opp's o.gs.	2				2

Fact File

Ipswich fielded the same side for 11 consecutive matches from 7 November 1972 to 6 January 1973.

Final Division One Table

		P	W	D	L	F	A	Pts
1	LIVERPOOL	42	25	10	7	72	42	60
2	ARSENAL	42	23	11	8	57	43	57
3	LEEDS U	42	21	11	10	71	45	53
4	IPSWICH TOWN	42	17	14	11	55	45	48
5	WOLVERHAMPTON W	42	18	11	13	66	54	47
6	WEST HAM U	42	17	12	13	67	53	46
7	DERBY CO	42	19	8	15	56	54	46
8	TOTTENHAM H	42	16	13	13	58	48	45
9	NEWCASTLE U	42	16	13	13	60	51	45
10	BIRMINGHAM C	42	15	12	15	53	54	42
11	MANCHESTER C	42	15	11	16	57	60	41
12	CHELSEA	42	13	14	15	49	51	40
13	SOUTHAMPTON	42	11	18	13	47	52	40
14	SHEFFIELD U	42	15	10	17	51	59	40
15	STOKE C	42	14	10	18	61	56	38
16	LEICESTER C	42	10	17	15	40	46	37
17	EVERTON	42	13	11	18	41	49	37
18	MANCHESTER U	42	12	13	17	44	60	37
19	COVENTRY C	42	13	9	20	40	55	35
20	NORWICH C	42	11	10	21	36	63	32
21	CRYSTAL PALACE	42	9	12	21	41	58	30
22	WBA	42	9	10	23	38	62	28

Season 1973-74

Football League Division One

DATE	OPPONENTS	SCORE	GOALSCORERS	ATTENDANCE
Aug 25	LEICESTER CITY	D 1-1	Munro o.g.	20,116
Aug 27	West Ham United	D 3-3	Whymark, Johnson 2	23,335
Sep 1	Everton	L 0-3		32,469
Sep 4	NEWCASTLE UNITED	L 1-3	Whymark	21,766
Sep 8	MANCHESTER UNITED	W 2-1	Johnson, Lambert	22,005
Sep 12	Newcastle United	L 1-3	Johnson	30,231
Sep 15	Stoke City	D 1-1	Woods	17,096
Sep 22	BURNLEY	W 3-2	Hamilton 2, Harper	19,136
Sep 29	Birmingham City	W 3-0	Lambert, Hamilton, Harper	26,919
Oct 6	TOTTENHAM HOTSPUR	D 0-0		23,903
Oct 13	Chelsea	W 3-2	Hamilton, Johnson 2	25,111
Oct 20	Arsenal	D 1-1	Lambert	28,344
Oct 27	WOLVERHAMPTON WANDERERS	W 2-0	Morris, Hamilton	20,882
Nov 3	Coventry City	W 1-0	Whymark	18,699
Nov 10	DERBY COUNTY	W 3-0	Lambert 2, Beattie	23,551
Nov 17	Liverpool	L 2-4	Johnson, Hamilton	37,420
Nov 24	MANCHESTER CITY	W 2-1	Whymark 2	19,210
Dec 8	LEEDS UNITED	L 0-3		27,313
Dec 15	Southampton	L 0-2		14,663
Dec 22	BIRMINGHAM CITY	W 3-0	Lambert 2, Hammond	15,457
Dec 26	Norwich City	W 2-1	Johnson (pen), Lambert	30,072
Dec 29	Manchester United	L 0-2		36,365
Jan 1	EVERTON	W 3-0		23,444
Jan 12	STOKE CITY	D 1-1	Johnson	18,583
Jan 19	Leicester City	L 0-5		24,208
Feb 2	SOUTHAMPTON	W 7-0	Lambert, Whymark 2, Beattie, Mills, Hamilton 2	20,046
Feb 5	WEST HAM UNITED	L 1-3	Hamilton	25,734
Feb 9	Burnley	W 1-0	Morris	15,470
Feb 23	Tottenham Hotspur	D 1-1	Whymark	26,289
Feb 26	CHELSEA	D 1-1	Mills	22,414
Mar 2	NORWICH CITY	D 1-1	Hamilton	24,998
Mar 9	Wolverhampton Wanderers	L 1-3	Woods	23,984
Mar 12	Sheffield United	W 3-0	Johnson, Morris, Hamilton	10,832
Mar 16	ARSENAL	D 2-2	Whymark, Hamilton	22,275
Mar 23	Derby County	L 0-2		23,860
Mar 30	COVENTRY CITY	W 3-0	Johnson, Talbot 2	17,404
Apr 6	Manchester City	W 3-1	Johnson, Hamilton, Morris	22,269
Apr 12	Queens Park Rangers	W 1-0	Whymark	27,567
Apr 13	LIVERPOOL	D 1-1	Whymark	33,292
Apr 15	QUEENS PARK RANGERS	W 1-0	Johnson	26,093
Apr 20	Leeds United	L 2-3	Talbot, Hamilton	46,015
Apr 27	SHEFFIELD UNITED	L 0-1		22,391

FA Cup

Jan 5	SHEFFIELD UNITED	(Rd3)	W 3-2	Hamilton, Beattie 2	17,929
Jan 26	Manchester United	(Rd4)	W 1-0	Beattie	37,177
Feb 16	Liverpool	(Rd5)	L 0-2		45,340

League Cup

Oct 8	LEEDS UNITED	(Rd2)	W 2-0	Johnson, Hamilton	26,279
Oct 31	Fulham	(Rd3)	D 2-2	Whymark, Woods	8,964
Nov 14	FULHAM	(R)	W 2-1	Viljoen, Mills	21,355
Nov 21	BIRMINGHAM CITY	(Rd4)	L 1-3	Miller	12,228

UEFA Cup

Sep 19	REAL MADRID	(Rd1/1L)	W 1-0	Rubinan o.g.	25,280
Oct 3	Real Madrid	(Rd1/2L)	D 0-0		80,000
Oct 24	Lazio	(Rd2/1L)	W 4-0	Whymark 4	26,433
Nov 7	Lazio	(Rd2/2L)	L 2-4	Viljoen (pen), Johnson	20,000
Nov 28	FC TWENTE	(Rd3/1L)	W 1-0	Whymark	18,918
Dec 2	FC Twente	(Rd3/2L)	W 2-1	Morris, Hamilton	18,000
Mar 6	LOKOMOTIV LEIPZIG	(QF/1L)	W 1-0	Beattie	26,466
Mar 20	Lokomotiv Leipzig	(QF/2L)	L 0-1*		57,000

* after extra time, lost 3-4 on penalties

League & Cup Appearances

PLAYER	LEAGUE	CUP COMPETITION			TOTAL
		FA CUP	LC	UEFA	
Beattie	42	3	4	8	57
Best	22	1	4	5	32
Burley	20	3		2	25
Collard	8 (1)		1	2 (1)	11 (2)
Cooper	1				1
Gates	0 (6)			0 (1)	0 (7)
Hamilton	41 (1)	3	4	8	56 (1)
Hammond	7 (1)		2	2 (2)	11 (3)
Harper	14		2	4	20
Hunter	34	3	4	7	48
Johnson	40	3	3	7 (1)	53 (1)
Keeley	3		1		4
Lambert	26	3	3	3	35
Miller	2 (3)		1	1 (1)	4 (4)
Mills	42	3	4	8	57
Morris	36	3	3 (1)	6 (1)	48 (2)
Osborne	3 (6)			0 (1)	3 (7)
Peddelty	5				5
Sivell	19	2		3	24
Talbot	15	1		2	18
Twamley	1				1
Viljoen	24	2 (1)	4	6	36 (1)
Whymark	39	3	3	8	53
Woods	18 (9)		0 (2)	5 (1)	24 (12)

Goalscorers

PLAYER	LEAGUE	CUP COMPETITION			TOTAL
		FA CUP	LC	UEFA	
Hamilton	16	1	1	1	19
Whymark	11		1	5	17
Johnson	13		1	1	15
Lambert	9				9
Beattie	2	3		1	6
Morris	4			1	5
Woods	3		1		4
Mills	2		1		3
Talbot	3				3
Harper	2				2
Viljoen				2	2
Hammond	1				1
Miller			1		1
Opp's o.gs.	1			1	2

Fact File

Ipswich took part in their first ever penalty shoot out in the quarter-final of the UEFA Cup, losing out to Lokomotiv Leipzig 3-4.

Final Division One Table

		P	W	D	L	F	A	Pts
1	LEEDS U	42	24	14	4	66	31	62
2	LIVERPOOL	42	22	13	7	52	31	57
3	DERBY Co	42	17	14	11	52	42	48
4	IPSWICH TOWN	42	18	11	13	67	58	47
5	STOKE C	42	15	16	11	54	42	46
6	BURNLEY	42	16	14	12	56	53	46
7	EVERTON	42	16	12	14	50	48	44
8	QPR	42	13	17	12	56	52	43
9	LEICESTER C	42	13	16	13	51	41	42
10	ARSENAL	42	14	14	14	49	51	42
11	TOTTENHAM H	42	14	14	14	45	50	42
12	WOLVERHAMPTON W	42	13	15	14	49	49	41
13	SHEFFIELD U	42	14	12	16	44	49	40
14	MANCHESTER C	42	14	12	16	39	46	40
15	NEWCASTLE U	42	13	12	17	49	48	38
16	COVENTRY C	42	14	10	18	43	54	38
17	CHELSEA	42	12	13	17	56	60	37
18	WEST HAM U	42	11	15	16	55	60	37
19	BIRMINGHAM C	42	12	13	17	52	64	37
20	SOUTHAMPTON	42	11	14	17	47	68	36
21	MANCHESTER U	42	10	12	20	38	48	32
22	NORWICH C	42	7	15	20	37	62	29

MANAGER: Bobby Robson

CAPTAIN: Mick Mills

TOP SCORER: Bryan Hamilton

BIGGEST WIN: 7-0 v Southampton (H), 2 February 1974, Division One

HIGHEST ATTENDANCE: 32,285 v Liverpool, 13 April 1974, Division One

MAJOR TRANSFERS IN: Paul Cooper from Birmingham

MAJOR TRANSFERS OUT: David Best to Portsmouth; Geoff Hammond to Manchester City; Peter Morris to Norwich City

1974-75

Football League Division One

DATE	OPPONENTS	SCORE	GOALSCORERS	ATTENDANCE
Aug 17	Tottenham Hotspur	W 1-0	Johnson	26,344
Aug 20	Arsenal	W 1-0	Lambert	31,027
Aug 24	BURNLEY	W 2-0	Talbot (pen), Whymark	22,361
Aug 27	ARSENAL	W 3-0	Lambert 2, Beattie	27,510
Aug 31	Sheffield United	L 1-3	Lambert	17,963
Sep 7	EVERTON	W 1-0	Woods	23,393
Sep 14	Luton Town	W 4-1	Talbot 2 (1 pen), Hamilton, Whymark	17,577
Sep 21	CHELSEA	W 2-0	Talbot, Johnson	23,111
Sep 24	STOKE CITY	W 3-1	Viljoen, Hamilton, Whymark	24,469
Sep 28	Newcastle United	L 0-1		43,520
Oct 5	Queens Park Rangers	L 0-1		19,494
Oct 12	LEEDS UNITED	D 0-0		29,817
Oct 15	Burnley	L 0-1		17,711
Oct 19	West Ham United	L 0-1		23,543
Oct 26	MANCHESTER CITY	D 1-1	Hamilton	25,177
Nov 2	LIVERPOOL	W 1-0	Talbot	30,575
Nov 9	Wolverhampton Wanderers	L 1-2	Woods	20,123
Nov 16	COVENTRY CITY	W 4-0	Johnson 3, Talbot	21,176
Nov 23	Derby County	L 0-2		24,341
Nov 30	CARLISLE UNITED	W 3-1	Hamilton, Johnson, Lambert	20,193
Dec 7	Middlesbrough	L 0-3		23,735
Dec 14	TOTTENHAM HOTSPUR	W 4-0	Viljoen, Beattie, Lambert, Osborne	20,812
Dec 20	Leicester City	W 1-0	Whymark	18,636
Dec 26	LUTON TOWN	L 0-1		23,406
Dec 28	Birmingham City	W 1-0	Osborne	30,266
Jan 11	MIDDLESBROUGH	W 2-0	Osborne, Johnson	24,720
Jan 18	Carlisle United	L 1-2	Whymark	13,054
Feb 1	WOLVERHAMPTON WANDERERS	W 2-0	Beattie, Viljoen	22,184
Feb 8	Liverpool	L 2-5	Beattie, Whymark	47,421
Feb 22	Coventry City	L 1-3	Hunter	16,980
Feb 25	DERBY COUNTY	W 3-0	Johnson, Hamilton, Beattie	23,132
Mar 1	SHEFFIELD UNITED	L 0-1		21,813
Mar 15	NEWCASTLE UNITED	W 5-4	Hamilton 3, Hunter, Johnson	23,070
Mar 18	Stoke City	W 2-1	Whymark, Mills	28,109
Mar 22	Everton	D 1-1	Whymark	46,269
Mar 29	LEICESTER CITY	W 2-1	Woods, Viljoen	28,745
Mar 31	Chelsea	D 0-0		35,005
Apr 1	BIRMINGHAM CITY	W 3-2	Collard, Woods, Lambert	27,417
Apr 12	QUEENS PARK RANGERS	W 2-1	Hamilton, Whymark	28,684
Apr 19	Leeds United	L 1-2	Talbot	30,174
Apr 23	Manchester City	D 1-1	Hamilton	29,391
Apr 26	WEST HAM UNITED	W 4-1	Talbot, Whymark, Beattie, Hunter	31,642

FA Cup

Jan 4	Wolverhampton Wanderers	(Rd3) W 2-1	Viljoen, Johnson	28,542
Jan 25	LIVERPOOL	(Rd4) W 1-0	Mills	34,709
Feb 15	ASTON VILLA	(Rd5) W 3-2	Johnson, Hamilton 2	31,297
Mar 8	LEEDS UNITED	(Rd6) D 0-0		38,010
Mar 11	Leeds United	(R)(aet) D 1-1	Johnson	50,074
Mar 25	Leeds United	(2R)(aet) D 0-0		35,195
Mar 27	Leeds United*	(R3) W 3-2	Whymark, Hamilton, Woods	19,510
Apr 5	West Ham United**	(SF) D 0-0		58,000
Apr 9	West Ham United†	(R) L 1-2	Jennings o.g.	45,344

* played at Filbert Street, Leicester
** played at Villa Park, Birmingham
† played at Stamford Bridge, London

League Cup

Sep 10	Coventry City	(Rd2) W 2-1	Whymark, Hamilton	13,066
Oct 8	HEREFORD UNITED	(Rd3) W 4-1	Johnson, Talbot, Hunter, Whymark	16,337
Nov 12	STOKE CITY	(Rd4) W 2-1	Hamilton, Johnson	20,661
Dec 4	Norwich City	(Rd5) D 1-1	Whymark	34,802
Dec 10	NORWICH CITY	(R) L 1-2	Johnson	29,228

UEFA Cup

Sep 18	FC TWENTE	(Rd1/1L) D 2-2	Hamilton, Talbot	28,047
Oct 2	FC Twente*	(Rd1/2L) D 1-1	Hamilton	18,000

* lost on away goals rule

Fact File

The attendance at the FA Cup 6th round tie with Leeds of 38,010 was a new ground record for Portman Road.

League & Cup Appearances

PLAYER	LEAGUE	CUP COMPETITION			TOTAL
		FA CUP	LC	UEFA	
Austin	2				2
Beattie	37	8	5	2	52
Burley	31	9	2	2	44
Collard	5 (2)	1	0 (1)		6 (3)
Cooper	2				2
Gates	0 (6)		0 (2)		0 (8)
Hamilton	33 (2)	6	4	2	45 (2)
Harper	10	3	2		15
Hunter	36	7	4	2	49
Johnson	35	7	4	2	48
Lambert	31 (5)	7	2 (2)		40 (7)
Mills	42	9	5		56
Osborne	10 (2)	1 (3)	0 (1)		11 (6)
Peddelty	6	1	1		8
Roberts	1				1
Sivell	40	9	5	2	56
Talbot	40	9	5	2	56
Twamley	1				1
Viljoen	37	9	5	2	53
Wark	3	2			5
Whymark	40	8	5	2	55
Woods	20 (16)	6 (2)	5	2	33 (18)

Goalscorers

PLAYER	LEAGUE	CUP COMPETITION			TOTAL
		FA CUP	LC	UEFA	
Hamilton	10	3	2	2	17
Johnson	9	3	3		15
Whymark	10	1	3		14
Talbot	8		1	1	10
Lambert	7				7
Beattie	6				6
Viljoen	4	1			5
Woods	4	1			5
Hunter	3		1		4
Osborne	3				3
Mills	1	1			2
Collard	1				1
Opp's o.g.s.	1				1

MANAGER: Bobby Robson

CAPTAIN: Mick Mills

TOP SCORER: Bryan Hamilton

BIGGEST WIN: 4-0 v Coventry (H), 16 November 1974, Division One; 4-0 v Tottenham (H), 14 December 1974, Division One

HIGHEST ATTENDANCE: 38,010 v Leeds United, 8 March 1975, FA Cup 6th Round

MAJOR TRANSFERS OUT: Ian Collard to Portsmouth

Final Division One Table

		P	W	D	L	F	A	PTS
1	DERBY CO	42	21	11	10	67	49	53
2	LIVERPOOL	42	20	11	11	60	39	51
3	IPSWICH TOWN	42	23	5	14	66	44	51
4	EVERTON	42	16	18	8	56	42	50
5	STOKE C	42	17	15	10	64	48	49
6	SHEFFIELD U	42	18	13	11	58	51	49
7	MIDDLESBROUGH	42	18	12	12	54	40	48
8	MANCHESTER C	42	18	10	14	54	54	46
9	LEEDS U	42	16	13	13	57	49	45
10	BURNLEY	42	17	11	14	68	67	45
11	QPR	42	16	10	16	54	54	42
12	WOLVERHAMPTON W	42	14	11	17	57	54	39
13	WEST HAM U	42	13	13	16	58	59	39
14	COVENTRY C	42	12	15	15	51	62	39
15	NEWCASTLE U	42	15	9	18	59	72	39
16	ARSENAL	42	13	11	18	47	49	37
17	BIRMINGHAM C	42	14	9	19	53	61	37
18	LEICESTER C	42	12	12	18	46	60	36
19	TOTTENHAM H	42	13	8	21	52	63	34
20	LUTON T	42	11	11	20	47	65	33
21	CHELSEA	42	9	15	18	42	72	33
22	CARLISLE U	42	12	5	25	43	59	29

Season 1975-76

Football League Division One

DATE	OPPONENTS	SCORE	GOALSCORERS	ATTENDANCE
Aug 16	NEWCASTLE UNITED	L 0-3		27,680
Aug 20	Tottenham Hotspur	D 1-1	Viljoen	28,311
Aug 23	Leeds United	L 0-1		30,912
Aug 26	BURNLEY	D 0-0		23,579
Aug 30	BIRMINGHAM CITY	W 4-2	Johnson, Hamilton, Whymark 2 (1 pen)	22,659
Sep 6	Coventry City	D 0-0		17,622
Sep 13	LIVERPOOL	W 2-0	Johnson, Austin	28,151
Sep 20	Manchester United	L 0-1		50,513
Sep 23	NORWICH CITY	W 2-0	Beattie, Hamilton	35,077
Sep 27	MIDDLESBROUGH	L 0-3		22,321
Oct 4	Derby County	L 0-1		26,056
Oct 11	Stoke City	W 1-0	Hamilton	21,975
Oct 18	LEICESTER CITY	D 1-1	Whymark	23,418
Oct 25	Manchester City	D 1-1	Hamilton	30,644
Nov 1	ASTON VILLA	W 3-0	Peddelty, Whymark, Hamilton	24,687
Nov 8	Wolverhampton Wanderers	L 0-1		16,191
Nov 15	QUEENS PARK RANGERS	D 1-1	Peddelty	25,543
Nov 22	Leicester City	D 0-0		20,115
Nov 29	SHEFFIELD UNITED	D 1-1	Whymark	20,802
Dec 6	Everton	D 3-3	Lambert, Johnson, Woods	24,601
Dec 13	LEEDS UNITED	W 2-1	Lambert, Peddelty	26,855
Dec 20	Newcastle United	D 1-1	Talbot	25,098
Dec 26	ARSENAL	W 2-0	Woods, Hunter	28,476
Dec 27	West Ham United	W 2-1	Lambert, Peddelty	32,741
Jan 10	Liverpool	D 3-3	Whymark 2, Gates	40,547
Jan 17	COVENTRY CITY	D 1-1	Osborne	23,543
Jan 31	TOTTENHAM HOTSPUR	L 1-2	Johnson	24,049
Feb 7	Burnley	W 1-0	Beattie (pen)	17,307
Feb 17	WOLVERHAMPTON WANDERERS	W 3-0	Beattie 2, Whymark	19,301
Feb 21	Queens Park Rangers	L 1-3	Lambert	22,593
Mar 6	Aston Villa	D 0-0		32,477
Mar 13	STOKE CITY	D 1-1	Osborne	22,812
Mar 20	Sheffield United	W 2-1	Johnson, Mills	15,220
Mar 27	EVERTON	W 1-0	Whymark (pen)	22,370
Mar 31	Norwich City	L 0-1		31,021
Apr 3	Middlesbrough	L 0-2		15,000
Apr 7	MANCHESTER CITY	W 2-1	Lambert, Whymark	21,290
Apr 10	MANCHESTER UNITED	W 3-0	Lambert, Whymark, Johnson	33,438
Apr 13	Birmingham City	L 0-3		20,497
Apr 17	Arsenal	W 2-1	Bertschin, Sharkey	26,937
Apr 19	WEST HAM UNITED	W 4-0	Bertschin, Talbot, Whymark, Peddelty	28,217
Apr 24	DERBY COUNTY	L 2-6	Lambert, Whymark	26,971

FA Cup

Jan 3	Halifax Town	(Rd3) W 3-1	Lambert 3	23,426
Jan 24	WOLVERHAMPTON W	(Rd4) D 0-0		30,110
Jan 27	Wolverhampton Wanderers	(R) L 0-1		31,333

League Cup

Sep 9	Leeds United	(Rd2) L 2-3	Johnson, Hunter	15,318

UEFA Cup

Sep 17	Feyenoord	(Rd1/1L) W 2-1	Whymark, Johnson	30,000
Oct 1	FEYENOORD	(Rd1/2L) W 2-0	Woods, Whymark	30,411
Oct 22	FC Bruges	(Rd2/1L) W 3-0	Gates, Peddelty, Austin	28,719
Nov 5	FC Bruges	(Rd2/2L) L 0-4		30,000

League & Cup Appearances

PLAYER	LEAGUE	CUP COMPETITION			TOTAL
		FA CUP	LC	UEFA	
Austin	8 (9)	1 (1)		0 (2)	9 (12)
Beattie	29	3	1	3	36
Bertschin	2 (1)				2 (1)
Burley	42	3	1	3	49
Cooper	40	3	1	4	48
Gates	7 (6)	0 (1)		1 (2)	8 (9)
Hamilton	18	1	4		23
Hunter	40	2	1	4	47
Johnson	32 (3)	3	1	4	40 (3)
Lambert	30 (1)	3	1	0 (3)	34 (4)
Mills	42	3	1	4	50
Osborne	33 (3)	1	4		38 (3)
Peddelty	27	1	2		30
Roberts	1				1
Sharkey	12 (1)				12 (1)
Sivell	2				2
Talbot	19	3	1		23
Tibbot	2	1			3
Turner	0 (1)				0 (1)
Viljoen	9	1		3	13
Wark	3		1		4
Whymark	40	2	1	4	47
Woods	24 (7)	3	0 (1)	4	31 (8)

Goalscorers

PLAYER	LEAGUE	CUP COMPETITION			TOTAL
		FA CUP	LC	UEFA	
Whymark	13			2	15
Lambert	7	3			10
Johnson	6		1	1	8
Peddelty	5			1	6
Hamilton	5				5
Beattie	4				4
Woods	2			1	3
Bertschin	2				2
Osborne	2				2
Talbot	2				2
Austin	1			1	2
Gates	1			1	2
Hunter	1		1		2
Mills	1				1
Sharkey	1				1
Viljoen	1				1

Fact File

Keith Bertschin scored in each of his first two games for the club, at the end of the season.

Final Division One Table

		P	W	D	L	F	A	Pts
1	LIVERPOOL	42	23	14	5	66	31	60
2	QPR	42	24	11	7	67	33	59
3	MANCHESTER U	42	23	10	10	68	42	56
4	DERBY CO	42	21	11	10	75	58	53
5	LEEDS U	42	21	9	12	65	46	51
6	IPSWICH TOWN	42	16	14	12	54	48	46
7	LEICESTER C	42	13	19	10	48	51	45
8	MANCHESTER C	42	16	12	15	64	46	43
9	TOTTENHAM H	42	14	15	13	63	63	43
10	NORWICH C	42	16	10	16	58	58	42
11	EVERTON	42	15	12	15	60	66	42
12	STOKE C	42	15	11	16	48	50	41
13	MIDDLESBROUGH	42	15	10	17	46	45	40
14	COVENTRY C	42	13	14	15	47	57	40
15	NEWCASTLE U	42	15	9	18	71	62	39
16	ASTON VILLA	42	11	17	14	51	59	39
17	ARSENAL	42	13	10	19	47	53	36
18	WEST HAM U	42	13	10	19	48	71	36
19	BIRMINGHAM C	42	13	7	22	57	75	33
20	WOLVERHAMPTON W	42	10	10	22	51	68	30
21	BURNLEY	42	9	10	23	43	66	28
22	SHEFFIELD U	42	6	10	26	33	82	22

MANAGER: Bobby Robson

CAPTAIN: Mick Mills

TOP SCORER: Trevor Whymark

BIGGEST WIN: 4-0 v West Ham United (H), 19 April 1976, Division One

HIGHEST ATTENDANCE: 35,077 v Norwich City, 23 September 1975, Division One

MAJOR TRANSFERS IN: None

MAJOR TRANSFERS OUT: Bryan Hamilton to Everton; David Johnson to Liverpool

Season 1976-77

Football League Division One

DATE	OPPONENTS	SCORE	GOALSCORERS	ATTENDANCE
Aug 21	TOTTENHAM HOTSPUR	W 3-1	Lambert 2, Bertschin	28,490
Aug 24	Everton	D 1-1	Beattie	33,070
Aug 28	QUEENS PARK RANGERS	D 2-2	Abbott o.g, Beattie (pen)	24,470
Sep 4	Aston Villa	L 2-5	Wark, Bertschin	36,916
Sep 11	LEICESTER CITY	D 0-0		19,610
Sep 18	Stoke City	L 1-2	Whymark	20,171
Sep 25	ARSENAL	W 3-1	Osborne, Gates, Beattie (pen)	25,469
Oct 2	Bristol City	W 2-1	Whymark, Osborne	21,114
Oct 16	West Ham United	W 2-0	Woods 2	24,534
Oct 23	MANCHESTER CITY	W 1-0	Whymark	25,113
Oct 30	Manchester United	W 1-0	Woods	57,416
Nov 6	WEST BROMWICH ALBION	W 7-0	Whymark 4, Wark, Beattie, Mariner	25,373
Nov 20	LEEDS UNITED	D 1-1	Talbot	30,918
Nov 23	SUNDERLAND	W 3-1	Whymark, Beattie, Burley	24,323
Nov 27	Middlesbrough	W 2-0	Mariner, Talbot	20,070
Dec 4	LIVERPOOL	W 1-0	Mariner	35,109
Dec 7	Birmingham City	W 4-2	Mariner, Wark, Talbot 2	31,161
Dec 18	DERBY COUNTY	D 0-0		23,234
Dec 27	Coventry City	D 1-1	Bertschin	28,269
Jan 3	MANCHESTER UNITED	W 2-1	Greenhoff B o.g, Woods	30,105
Jan 15	EVERTON	W 2-0	Whymark, Wark	25,570
Jan 22	Tottenham Hotspur	L 0-1		35,126
Feb 12	ASTON VILLA	W 1-0	Woods	29,766
Feb 15	NORWICH CITY	W 5-0	Wark (pen), Whymark 3, Mariner	34,726
Feb 19	Leicester City	L 0-1		21,134
Feb 26	STOKE CITY	L 0-1		25,293
Mar 5	Arsenal	W 4-1	Talbot, Wark (pen), Bertschin, Mariner	34,688
Mar 9	Newcastle United	D 1-1	Wark	31,790
Mar 12	BRISTOL CITY	W 1-0	Wark (pen)	24,548
Mar 16	West Bromwich Albion	L 0-4		22,659
Mar 19	Sunderland	L 0-1		35,376
Mar 22	WEST HAM UNITED	W 4-1	Taylor T o.g., Mariner 3	27,287
Apr 2	Manchester City	L 1-2	Whymark	42,780
Apr 5	COVENTRY CITY	W 2-1	Mariner, Burley	23,616
Apr 9	Norwich City	W 1-0	Whymark	31,088
Apr 11	BIRMINGHAM CITY	W 1-0	Bertschin	29,025
Apr 16	Leeds United	L 1-2	Bertschin	28,578
Apr 23	MIDDLESBROUGH	L 0-1		23,348
Apr 30	Liverpool	L 1-2	Wark (pen)	56,044
May 7	NEWCASTLE UNITED	W 2-0	Osborne, Wark	24,760
May 14	Derby County	D 0-0		24,491
May 16	Queens Park Rangers	L 0-1		19,171

FA Cup

Jan 8	BRISTOL CITY	(Rd3) W 4-1	Mariner 2, Whymark Gates	25,157
Jan 29	WOLVERHAMPTON W	(Rd4) D 2-2	Mariner, Burley	32,996
Feb 2	Wolverhampton Wanderers	(R) L 0-1		33,686

League Cup

Aug 31	BRIGHTON & HOVE ALBION	(Rd2) D 0-0		16,027
Sep 7	Brighton & Hove Albion	(R) L 1-2	Lambert	26,748

League & Cup Appearances

PLAYER	LEAGUE	CUP COMPETITION		TOTAL
		FA CUP	LC	
Beattie	30 (1)	1	2	33 (1)
Bertschin	17 (12)		1	18 (12)
Burley	40	3	2	45
Cooper	34	3	1	38
Gates	6 (6)	0 (2)		6 (8)
Geddis	0 (2)			0 (2)
Hunter	36	2	2	40
Lambert	8 (3)		2	10 (3)
Mariner	28	3		31
Mills	37	3	2	42
Osborne	34	3		37
Peddelty	4			4
Roberts	12 (1)	3		15 (1)
Sharkey	5		1	6
Sivell	8		1	9
Talbot	42	3	2	47
Tibbott	11 (2)			11 (2)
Turner	3 (1)		1	4 (1)
Wark	33	3	2	38
Whymark	36	3	2	41
Woods	38 (3)	3	1 (1)	42 (4)

Goalscorers

PLAYER	LEAGUE	CUP COMPETITION		TOTAL
		FA CUP	LC	
Whymark	14	1		15
Mariner	10	3		13
Wark	10			10
Bertschin	6			6
Beattie	5			5
Talbot	5			5
Woods	5			5
Osborne	3			3
Burley	2	1		3
Lambert	2		1	3
Gates	1	1		2
Opps o.gs.	3			3

Fact File

Ipswich went 15 League games without defeat from 25 September 1976 to 15 January 1977, winning 12 of them.

Final Division One Table

		P	W	D	L	F	A	Pts
1	LIVERPOOL	42	23	11	8	62	33	57
2	MANCHESTER C	42	21	14	7	60	34	56
3	IPSWICH TOWN	42	22	8	12	66	39	56
4	ASTON VILLA	42	22	7	13	76	50	51
5	NEWCASTLE U	42	18	13	11	64	49	49
6	MANCHESTER U	42	18	11	13	71	62	47
7	WBA	42	16	13	13	62	56	45
8	ARSENAL	42	16	11	15	64	59	43
9	EVERTON	42	14	14	14	62	64	42
10	LEEDS U	42	15	12	15	48	51	42
11	LEICESTER C	42	12	18	12	47	60	42
12	MIDDLESBROUGH	42	14	13	15	40	45	41
13	BIRMINGHAM C	42	13	12	17	63	61	38
14	QPR	42	13	12	17	47	52	38
15	DERBY CO	42	9	19	14	50	55	37
16	NORWICH C	42	14	9	19	47	64	37
17	WEST HAM U	42	11	14	17	46	65	36
18	BRISTOL C	42	11	13	18	38	48	35
19	COVENTRY C	42	10	15	17	48	59	35
20	SUNDERLAND	42	11	12	19	46	54	34
21	STOKE C	42	10	14	18	28	51	34
22	TOTTENHAM H	42	12	9	21	48	72	33

MANAGER: Bobby Robson

CAPTAIN: Mick Mills

TOP SCORER: Trevor Whymark

BIGGEST WIN: 7-0 v WBA (H), 6 November 1976, Division One

HIGHEST ATTENDANCE: 35,109 v Liverpool, 4 December 1976, Division One

MAJOR TRANSFERS IN: Paul Mariner from Plymouth Argyle

MAJOR TRANSFERS OUT: Keith Bertschin to Birmingham City; John Peddelty to Plymouth Argyle; Pat Sharkey to Millwall

Season 1977-78

Football League Division One

DATE	OPPONENTS	SCORE	GOALSCORERS	ATTENDANCE
Aug 20	ARSENAL	W 1-0	Geddis	30,154
Aug 24	Derby County	D 0-0		19,809
Aug 27	Manchester United	D 0-0		57,904
Sep 3	CHELSEA	W 1-0	Talbot	21,063
Sep 10	Leeds United	L 1-2	Mariner	24,380
Sep 17	LIVERPOOL	D 1-1	Whymark	30,069
Sep 24	Middlesbrough	D 1-1	Mariner	19,843
Oct 1	NEWCASTLE UNITED	W 2-1	Mills, Gates	21,626
Oct 4	Nottingham Forest	L 0-4		26,845
Oct 8	West Bromwich Albion	L 0-1		22,918
Oct 15	BIRMINGHAM CITY	W 5-2	Mariner, Mills, Woods, Whymark 2 (1 pen)	21,313
Oct 22	Coventry City	D 1-1	Mariner	20,014
Oct 29	WEST HAM UNITED	L 0-2		27,330
Nov 5	MANCHESTER CITY	W 1-0	Mariner	24,575
Nov 12	Leicester City	L 1-2	Talbot	13,779
Nov 19	EVERTON	D 3-3	Mariner, Whymark 2 (1 pen)	22,790
Nov 26	Wolverhampton Wanderers	D 0-0		18,468
Dec 3	ASTON VILLA	W 2-0	Whymark, Gates	20,908
Dec 10	Bristol City	L 0-2		24,701
Dec 17	LEICESTER CITY	W 1-0	Whymark	16,905
Dec 26	Norwich City	L 0-1		27,887
Dec 27	QUEENS PARK RANGERS	W 3-2	Geddis 2, Mills	22,440
Dec 31	DERBY COUNTY	L 1-2	Mariner	20,870
Jan 2	Arsenal	L 0-1		43,705
Jan 14	MANCHESTER UNITED	L 1-2	Mariner	23,321
Jan 21	Chelsea	L 3-5	Osborne, Wark, Mariner	26,044
Feb 4	LEEDS UNITED	L 0-1		24,120
Feb 25	Newcastle United	W 1-0	Woods	22,521
Mar 4	WEST BROMWICH ALBION	D 2-2	Mills, Wark	20,130
Mar 18	COVENTRY CITY	D 1-1	Woods	21,110
Mar 21	MIDDLESBROUGH	D 1-1	Wark (pen)	17,789
Mar 24	West Ham United	L 0-3		23,867
Mar 25	Queens Park Rangers	D 3-3	Wark, Burley, Mariner	15,563
Mar 27	NORWICH CITY	W 4-0	Talbot 2, Geddis, Mills	29,989
Apr 1	Manchester City	L 1-2	Mariner	34,975
Apr 11	Birmingham City	D 0-0		19,289
Apr 15	Everton	L 0-1		33,402
Apr 18	Liverpool	D 2-2	Whymark, Lambert	40,044
Apr 22	BRISTOL CITY	W 1-0	Mills	22,523
Apr 25	NOTTINGHAM FOREST	L 0-2		30,062
Apr 29	Aston Villa	L 1-6	Whymark	30,955
May 9	WOLVERHAMPTON WANDERERS	L 1-2	Wark	25,904

FA Cup

Jan 7	Cardiff City	(Rd3) W 2-0	Mariner 2	13,584
Jan 28	HARTLEPOOL UNITED	(Rd4) W 4-1	Viljoen 2 (1 pen), Mariner, Talbot	24,207
Feb 18	Bristol Rovers	(Rd5) D 2-2	Turner 2	23,543
Feb 24	BRISTOL ROVERS	(R) W 3-0	Mills, Mariner, Woods	29,090
Mar 11	Millwall	(Rd6) W 6-1	Burley, Mariner 3, Wark, Talbot	23,082
Apr 4	West Bromwich Albion*	(SF) W 3-1	Talbot, Mills, Wark	50,922
May 6	Arsenal**	(F) W 1-0	Osborne	100,000

*played at Highbury; **played at Wembley

League Cup

Aug 30	NORTHAMPTON TOWN	(Rd2) W 5-0	Whymark 2 (2 pen), Gates, Woods, Mariner	15,276
Oct 25	Burnley	(Rd3) W 2-1	Whymark 2	9,607
Nov 29	MANCHESTER CITY	(Rd4) L 1-2	Whymark (pen)	22,120

UEFA Cup

Sep 14	Landskrona Bois	(Rd1/1L) W 1-0	Whymark	7,156
Sep 28	LANDSKRONA BOIS	(Rd1/2L) W 5-0	Whymark 4 (1 pen), Mariner	18,741
Oct 19	LAS PALMAS	(Rd2/1L) W 1-0	Gates	22,195
Nov 2	Las Palmas	(Rd2/2L) D 3-3	Mariner 2, Tibbott	22,000
Nov 23	BARCELONA	(Rd3/1L) W 3-0	Gates, Whymark, Talbot	33,663
Dec 7	Barcelona	(Rd3/2L) L 0-3*		24,000

*lost on penalties

MANAGER: Bobby Robson

CAPTAIN: Mick Mills

TOP SCORER: Paul Mariner

BIGGEST WIN: 6-1 v Millwall (A), 11 March 1978, FA Cup 6th Round

HIGHEST ATTENDANCE: 33,663 v Barcelona, 23 November 1977, UEFA Cup 3rd Round 1st Leg

MAJOR TRANSFERS OUT: Colin Viljoen to Manchester City

League & Cup Appearances

PLAYER	LEAGUE	CUP COMPETITION			TOTAL
		FA CUP	LC	UEFA	
Beattie	14	3	1	3	21
Brazil	0 (2)	0 (1)			0 (3)
Burley	31	6	2	3	42
Butcher	3				3
Cooper	40	7	3	6	56
Gates	23 (1)	1	3	6	33 (1)
Geddis	20 (6)	2	0 (1)	0 (4)	22 (11)
Hunter	37	7	3	6	53
Lambert	0 (9)	1 (3)	0 (1)	0 (1)	1 (14)
Mariner	37	7	3	6	53
Mills	34	7	2	5	48
Osborne	24 (2)	3 (1)	2	4 (1)	33 (4)
Osman	28	4	2	3 (1)	37 (1)
Overton	1				1
Parkin	0 (1)	0 (1)			0 (2)
Roberts	3		1	0 (1)	4 (1)
Sivell	1				1
Stirk	6		1	1	8
Talbot	40	7	3	6	56
Tibbott	28	1	2	5	36
Turner	9 (5)	5			14 (5)
Viljoen	10	4		0 (2)	14 (2)
Wark	18	6 (1)		0 (1)	24 (2)
Whymark	19 (1)		3	6	28 (1)
Woods	36	6	2	6	50

Goalscorers

PLAYER	LEAGUE	CUP COMPETITION			TOTAL
		FA CUP	LC	UEFA	
Mariner	11	7	1	3	22
Whymark	9		5	6	20
Mills	6	2			8
Talbot	4	3		1	8
Wark	5	2			7
Woods	3	1	1		5
Gates	2		1	2	5
Geddis	4				4
Osborne	1	1			2
Burley	1	1			2
Viljoen	2				2
Turner	2				2
Lambert	1				1
Tibbott			1		1

Fact File

Ipswich went to Millwall on 13 August for a pre-season friendly and won 6-1. Incredibly, they repeated this score when they visited the Den in an FA Cup 6th Round tie seven months later.

Final Division One Table

		P	W	D	L	F	A	Pts
1	NOTTINGHAM F	42	25	14	3	69	24	64
2	LIVERPOOL	42	24	9	9	65	34	57
3	EVERTON	42	22	11	9	76	45	55
4	MANCHESTER C	42	20	12	10	74	51	52
5	ARSENAL	42	21	10	11	60	37	52
6	WBA	42	18	14	10	62	53	50
7	COVENTRY C	42	18	12	12	75	62	48
8	ASTON VILLA	42	18	10	14	57	42	46
9	LEEDS U	42	18	10	14	63	53	46
10	MANCHESTER U	42	16	10	16	67	63	42
11	BIRMINGHAM C	42	16	9	17	55	60	41
12	DERBY CO	42	14	13	15	54	59	41
13	NORWICH C	42	11	18	13	52	66	40
14	MIDDLESBROUGH	42	12	15	15	42	54	39
15	WOLVERHAMPTON W	42	12	12	18	51	64	36
16	CHELSEA	42	11	14	17	46	69	36
17	BRISTOL C	42	11	13	18	49	53	35
18	IPSWICH TOWN	42	11	13	18	47	61	35
19	QPR	42	9	15	18	47	64	33
20	WEST HAM U	42	12	8	22	52	69	32
21	NEWCASTLE U	42	6	10	26	42	78	22
22	LEICESTER C	42	5	12	25	26	70	22

Season 1978-79

Football League Division One

DATE	OPPONENTS	SCORE	GOALSCORERS	ATTENDANCE
Aug 19	West Bromwich Albion	L 1-2	Woods	21,700
Aug 22	LIVERPOOL	L 0-3		28,114
Aug 26	MANCHESTER UNITED	W 3-0	Mariner 2, Talbot	21,802
Sep 2	Middlesbrough	D 0-0		14,427
Sep 9	ASTON VILLA	L 0-2		22,189
Sep 16	Wolverhampton Wanderers	W 3-1	Mariner, Muhren, Whymark	16,409
Sep 23	BRISTOL CITY	L 0-1		20,168
Sep 30	Southampton	W 2-1	Mariner 2	21,264
Oct 7	Coventry City	D 2-2	Osman, Woods	21,859
Oct 14	EVERTON	L 0-1		22,676
Oct 21	Nottingham Forest	L 0-1		28,911
Oct 28	QUEENS PARK RANGERS	W 2-1	Gates, Mariner	20,717
Nov 4	Arsenal	L 1-4	Mariner	35,269
Nov 11	WEST BROMWICH ALBION	L 0-1		20,914
Nov 18	Manchester United	L 0-2		42,109
Nov 21	MIDDLESBROUGH	W 2-1	Burley, Woods	17,570
Nov 25	Manchester City	W 2-1	Gates, Talbot	38,256
Dec 2	LEEDS UNITED	L 2-3	Beattie, Wark (pen)	22,526
Dec 9	Tottenham Hotspur	L 0-1		33,882
Dec 16	BOLTON WANDERERS	W 3-0	Mariner, Gates, Talbot	16,593
Dec 26	NORWICH CITY	D 1-1	Mills	26,336
Dec 30	CHELSEA	W 5-1	Osman, Muhren 2, Wark, Mariner	21,439
Jan 20	WOLVERHAMPTON WANDERERS	W 3-1	Wark 2 (1 pen), Mariner	17,965
Feb 3	Bristol City	L 1-3	Mariner	17,025
Feb 10	SOUTHAMPTON	D 0-0		19,520
Feb 24	Everton	W 1-0	Mariner	29,031
Feb 28	Derby County	W 1-0	Woods	15,935
Mar 3	NOTTINGHAM FOREST	D 1-1	Brazil	27,198
Mar 13	COVENTRY CITY	D 1-1	Muhren	16,095
Mar 17	ARSENAL	W 2-0	Wark, Rix o.g.	26,407
Mar 24	Liverpool	L 0-2		43,243
Mar 31	MANCHESTER CITY	W 2-1	Geddis, Brazil	20,773
Apr 3	Birmingham City	D 1-1	Muhren	12,499
Apr 7	Leeds United	D 1-1	Gates	24,153
Apr 14	Norwich City	W 1-0	Thijssen	25,061
Apr 16	DERBY COUNTY	W 2-1	Mariner, Mills	19,899
Apr 17	BIRMINGHAM CITY	W 3-0	Gates, Butcher, Brazil	17,676
Apr 21	Bolton Wanderers	W 3-2	Brazil 2, Wark	20,073
Apr 28	TOTTENHAM HOTSPUR	W 2-1	Muhren, Brazil	28,179
May 2	Aston Villa	D 2-2	Muhren 2	26,636
May 5	Chelsea	W 3-2	Brazil 2, Woods	15,462
May 11	Queens Park Rangers	W 4-0	Gates 2, Brazil, Butcher	9,819

FA Cup

Jan 10	CARLISLE UNITED	(Rd3) W 3-2	Beattie, Muhren, Wark (pen)	17,660
Jan 27	ORIENT	(Rd4) D 0-0		23,377
Jan 30	Orient	(R) W 2-0	Mariner 2	13,672
Feb 26	BRISTOL ROVERS	(Rd5) W 6-1	Brazil 2, Mills, Muhren, Geddis, Mariner	23,231
Mar 10	LIVERPOOL	(Rd6) L 0-1		31,322

League Cup

Aug 30	Blackpool	(Rd2) L 0-2		10,029

European Cup-Winners' Cup

Sep 13	AZ '67 Alkmaar	(Rd1/1L) D 0-0		18,000
Sep 27	AZ '67 ALKMAAR	(Rd1/2L) W 2-0	Mariner, Wark (pen)	21,330
Oct 18	SW INNSBRUCK	(Rd2/1L) W 1-0	Wark (pen)	19,958
Nov 1	SW Innsbruck	(Rd2/2L) D 1-1	Burley	18,000
Mar 7	BARCELONA	(QF/1L) W 2-1	Gates 2	29,197
Mar 21	Barcelona	(QF/2L) L 0-1*		100,000

* lost on away goals rule

Charity Shield

Aug 12	Nottingham Forest**	L 0-5		68,000

** played at Wembley

MANAGER: Bobby Robson

CAPTAIN: Mick Mills

TOP SCORER: Paul Mariner

BIGGEST WIN: 6-1 v Bristol Rovers (H), 26 February 1979, FA Cup 5th Round

HIGHEST ATTENDANCE: 29,197 v Barcelona, 7 March 1979, European Cup-Winners' Cup quarter-final 2nd Leg

MAJOR TRANSFERS IN: Arnold Muhren and Frans Thijssen from FC Twente

MAJOR TRANSFERS OUT: Dave Geddis to Aston Villa; Mick Lambert to Peterborough; Brian Talbot to Arsenal; Trevor Whymark to Derby

---

League & Cup Appearances

PLAYER	LEAGUE	CUP COMPETITION			OTHER	TOTAL
		FA CUP	LC	ECWC		
Beattie	19 (1)	3		3		26 (1)
Brazil	14 (5)	1 (1)		2		17 (6)
Burley	38	5	1	6	1	51
Butcher	21	1	2			24
Cooper	41	5	1	6	1	54
Gates	20 (2)	1	2 (1)	1		24 (3)
Geddis	6 (9)	0 (1)		2 (3)		8 (13)
Hunter	4			2 (1)		6 (1)
Lambert	1 (3)		0 (1)			1 (4)
Mariner	33	5	1	4	1	44
Mills	42	5	1	6	1	55
Muhren	41	5		2		48
Osman	39	5	1	6	1	52
Parkin	3 (1)		1		1	5 (1)
Roberts	1					1
Sivell	1					1
Talbot	21	1	1	4	1	27
Thijssen	16	1				17
Tibbott	11	4		5		20
Turner					0 (1)	0 (1)
Wark	42	5	1	6	1	55
Whymark	8 (5)	3 (1)	1	3	1	16 (5)
Woods	41	5	1	5	1	53

Goalscorers

PLAYER	LEAGUE	CUP COMPETITION			OTHER	TOTAL
		FA CUP	LC	ECWC		
Mariner	13	3		1		17
Brazil	9	2				11
Muhren	8	2				10
Gates	7			2		9
Wark	6	1		2		9
Woods	5					5
Mills	2	1				3
Talbot	3					3
Beattie	1	1				2
Burley	1		1			2
Butcher	2					2
Geddis	1	1				2
Osman	2					2
Thijssen	1					1
Whymark	1					1
Opp's o.gs.	1					1

Fact File

This season marked the beginning of the Dutch era at Ipswich with the arrival of Muhren and Thijssen. Muhren's debut against Liverpool found him isolated in midfield as the ball constantly by-passed him, but Robson quickly adjusted the tactics to showcase the brilliant skills of these Dutch masters.

Final Division One Table

		P	W	D	L	F	A	Pts
1	LIVERPOOL	42	30	8	4	85	16	68
2	NOTTINGHAM F	42	21	18	3	61	26	60
3	WBA	42	24	11	7	72	35	59
4	EVERTON	42	17	17	8	52	40	51
5	LEEDS U	42	18	14	10	70	52	50
6	IPSWICH TOWN	42	20	9	13	63	49	49
7	ARSENAL	42	17	14	11	61	48	48
8	ASTON VILLA	42	15	16	11	59	49	46
9	MANCHESTER U	42	15	15	12	60	63	45
10	COVENTRY C	42	14	16	12	58	68	44
11	TOTTENHAM H	42	13	15	14	48	61	41
12	MIDDLESBROUGH	42	15	10	17	57	50	40
13	BRISTOL C	42	15	10	17	47	51	40
14	SOUTHAMPTON	42	12	16	14	47	53	40
15	MANCHESTER C	42	13	13	16	58	56	39
16	NORWICH C	42	7	23	12	51	57	37
17	BOLTON W	42	12	11	19	54	75	35
18	WOLVERHAMPTON W	42	13	8	21	44	68	34
19	DERBY CO	42	10	11	21	44	71	31
20	QPR	42	6	13	23	45	73	25
21	BIRMINGHAM C	42	6	10	26	37	64	22
22	CHELSEA	42	5	10	27	44	92	20

The Essential History of Ipswich Town

Season 1979-80

Football League Division One

DATE	OPPONENTS	SCORE	GOALSCORERS	ATTENDANCE
Aug 8	NOTTINGHAM FOREST	L 0-1		27,371
Aug 21	Arsenal	W 2-0	Hunter, Muhren	33,245
Aug 25	Wolverhampton Wanderers	L 0-3		22,025
Sep 1	STOKE CITY	W 3-1	Brazil, Mariner, Wark	17,539
Sep 8	BRISTOL CITY	W 1-0	Woods	16,915
Sep 15	Brighton & Hove Albion	L 0-2		23,608
Sep 22	EVERTON	D 1-1	Wark	19,251
Sep 29	Crystal Palace	L 1-4	Gates	29,885
Oct 6	Leeds United	L 1-2	Mariner	19,342
Oct 9	ARSENAL	L 1-2	Brazil	21,527
Oct 13	LIVERPOOL	L 1-2	Mariner	25,310
Oct 20	Manchester United	L 0-1		50,816
Oct 27	MIDDLESBROUGH	W 1-0	Brazil	17,593
Nov 3	Nottingham Forest	L 0-2		24,593
Nov 10	ASTON VILLA	D 0-0		17,807
Nov 17	Derby County	W 1-0	Mariner	16,699
Nov 24	SOUTHAMPTON	W 3-1	Gates, Wark, Brazil	18,685
Dec 1	Coventry City	L 1-4	Wark (pen)	16,439
Dec 8	MANCHESTER CITY	W 4-0	Mills, Gates 3	18,221
Dec 15	Bolton Wanderers	W 1-0	Brazil	10,929
Dec 21	TOTTENHAM HOTSPUR	W 3-1	Gates, Mariner, Muhren	18,852
Dec 26	Norwich City	D 3-3	Gates, Muhren, Wark	24,335
Dec 29	WOLVERHAMPTON WANDERERS	W 1-0	Butcher	22,333
Jan 1	WEST BROMWICH ALBION	W 4-0	Mariner, Wark (pen), Osman, Thijssen	22,477
Jan 12	Stoke City	W 1-0	Mariner	15,253
Jan 19	Bristol City	W 3-0	Gates, Brazil, Mariner	14,218
Feb 2	BRIGHTON & HOVE ALBION	D 1-1	Wark (pen)	22,494
Feb 9	Everton	W 4-0	Mariner, Brazil 2, Gates	31,218
Feb 19	CRYSTAL PALACE	W 3-0	Gates, Wark, Brazil	23,012
Feb 23	Liverpool	D 1-1	Gates	47,566
Mar 1	MANCHESTER UNITED	W 6-0	Brazil 2, Mariner 3, Thijssen	30,120
Mar 11	Middlesbrough	D 1-1	Mariner	18,712
Mar 14	LEEDS UNITED	W 1-0	Mariner	23,120
Mar 22	Aston Villa	D 1-1	Wark	22,386
Mar 29	DERBY COUNTY	D 1-1	Gates	19,718
Apr 2	Tottenham Hotspur	W 2-0	Mariner, Osman	26,423
Apr 5	NORWICH CITY	W 4-2	Wark 3 (2 pen), Mariner	28,968
Apr 7	West Bromwich Albion	D 0-0		19,844
Apr 12	COVENTRY CITY	W 3-0	Butcher, Mariner, Brazil	20,502
Apr 19	Southampton	W 1-0	Muhren	22,028
Apr 26	BOLTON WANDERERS	W 1-0	Gates	21,447
May 3	Manchester City	L 1-2	Hunter	31,648

FA Cup

Jan 5	Preston North End	(Rd3) W 3-0	Mariner 2, Brazil	16,986
Jan 26	Bristol City	(Rd4) W 2-1	Wark, Mariner	19,608
Feb 16	CHESTER	(Rd5) W 2-1	Burley, Wark	26,353
Mar 8	Everton	(Rd6) L 1-2	Beattie	45,104

League Cup

Aug 29	COVENTRY CITY	(Rd2/1L) L 0-1		13,217
Sep 4	Coventry City	(Rd2/2L) D 0-0		16,705

UEFA Cup

Sep 19	Skeid Oslo	(Rd1/1L) W 3-1	Mills, Turner, Mariner	3,190
Oct 3	SKEID OSLO	(Rd1/2L) W 7-0	Muhren 2, McCall 2, Wark, Mariner, Thijssen,	13,440
Oct 24	Grasshoppers	(Rd2/1L) D 0-0		16,000
Nov 7	GRASSHOPPERS	(Rd2/2L) D 1-1*	Beattie	19,574

* lost on away goals rule

MANAGER: Bobby Robson

CAPTAIN: Mick Mills

TOP SCORER: Paul Mariner

BIGGEST WIN: 7-0 v Skied Oslo (H), 3 October 1979, UEFA Cup 1st Round 2nd Leg

HIGHEST ATTENDANCE: 30,120 v Manchester United (H), 1 March 1980, Division One

MAJOR TRANSFERS IN: Kevin O'Callaghan from Millwall

MAJOR TRANSFERS OUT: Noel Parkinson to Bristol Rovers; Clive Woods to Norwich City

League & Cup Appearances

PLAYER	LEAGUE	CUP COMPETITION			TOTAL
		FA CUP	LC	UEFA	
Beattie	10	0 (2)		2	12 (2)
Brazil	31 (4)	4	2	2 (1)	39 (5)
Burley	38	4	2	4	48
Butcher	36	4	2	4	46
Cooper	40	4	2	4	50
D'Avray	1 (1)				1 (1)
Gates	34 (2)	4	1 (1)	2	41 (3)
Hunter	16			2	18
Mariner	41	3	2	4	50
McCall	3 (7)			2	5 (7)
Mills	37	4	2	3	46
Muhren	37	4	2	3	46
O'Callaghan	1 (3)				1 (3)
Osborne	4 (2)				4 (2)
Osman	42	4	2	4	52
Parkin			1		1
Parkinson		0 (2)			(2)
Sivell	2				2
Thijssen	37	4	2	3	46
Turner	3 (4)			1 (1)	4 (5)
Wark	40 (1)	4	2	3	49 (1)
Woods	9	1	1		11

Goalscorers

PLAYER	LEAGUE	CUP COMPETITION			TOTAL
		FA CUP	LC	UEFA	
Mariner	17	3		2	22
Wark	12	2		1	15
Gates	13				13
Brazil	12	1			13
Muhren	4			2	6
Thijssen	2			1	3
Beattie		1		1	2
Butcher	2				2
Hunter	2				2
Osman	2				2
McCall				2	2
Mills	1			1	2
Burley		1			1
Turner				1	1
Woods	1				1

Fact File

The 6-0 home defeat of Manchester United in March included two missed penalties by Ipswich. With regular penalty king John Wark unavailable, Thijssen and Beattie both had spot kicks saved by Gary Bailey.

Final Division One Table

		P	W	D	L	F	A	Pts
1	LIVERPOOL	42	25	10	7	81	30	60
2	MANCHESTER U	42	24	10	8	65	35	58
3	IPSWICH TOWN	42	22	9	11	68	39	53
4	ARSENAL	42	18	16	8	52	36	52
5	NOTTINGHAM F	42	20	8	14	63	43	48
6	WOLVERHAMPTON W	42	19	9	14	58	47	47
7	ASTON VILLA	42	16	14	12	51	50	46
8	SOUTHAMPTON	42	18	9	15	65	53	45
9	MIDDLESBROUGH	42	16	12	14	50	44	44
10	WBA	42	11	19	12	54	50	41
11	LEEDS U	42	13	14	15	46	50	40
12	NORWICH C	42	13	14	15	58	66	40
13	CRYSTAL PALACE	42	12	16	14	41	50	40
14	TOTTENHAM H	42	15	10	17	52	62	40
15	COVENTRY C	42	16	7	19	56	66	39
16	BRIGHTON & HA	42	11	15	16	47	57	37
17	MANCHESTER C	42	12	13	17	43	66	37
18	STOKE C	42	13	10	19	44	58	36
19	EVERTON	42	9	17	16	43	51	35
20	BRISTOL C	42	9	13	20	37	66	31
21	DERBY CO	42	11	8	23	47	67	30
22	BOLTON W	42	5	15	22	38	73	25

Season 1980-81

Football League Division One

DATE	OPPONENTS	SCORE	GOALSCORERS	ATTENDANCE
Aug 16	Leicester City	W 1-0	Wark	21,640
Aug 19	BRIGHTON & HOVE ALBION	W 2-0	Wark, Gates	21,568
Aug 23	Stoke City	D 2-2	Brazil, Gates	10,722
Aug 30	EVERTON	W 4-0	Brazil, Wark, Butcher, Mariner	20,879
Sep 6	ASTON VILLA	W 1-0	Thijssen	23,192
Sep 13	Crystal Palace	W 2-1	Wark, Gates	24,282
Sep 20	COVENTRY CITY	W 2-0	Wark 2	20,507
Sep 27	Wolverhampton Wanderers	W 2-0	Brazil, Mariner	18,503
Oct 4	LEEDS UNITED	D 1-1	Wark	24,087
Oct 11	Liverpool	D 1-1	Thijssen	48,084
Oct 18	MANCHESTER UNITED	D 1-1	Mariner	28,451
Oct 25	Sunderland	W 2-0	Muhren, Brazil	32,368
Nov 1	WEST BROMWICH ALBION	D 0-0		23,043
Nov 8	Southampton	D 3-3	Gates, Wark, Mariner	21,261
Nov 11	Brighton & Hove Albion	L 0-1		17,055
Nov 15	LEICESTER CITY	W 3-1	Gates, Williams o.g., D'Avray	19,892
Nov 22	Nottingham Forest	W 2-1	Brazil, Wark (pen)	24,423
Dec 6	Manchester City	D 1-1	Muhren	35,215
Dec 13	LIVERPOOL	D 1-1	Brazil	32,274
Dec 17	Tottenham Hotspur	L 3-5	Mariner 2, Gates	22,741
Dec 20	Birmingham City	W 3-1	Mariner, Wark, Brazil	16,161
Dec 26	NORWICH CITY	W 2-0	Brazil, Wark	27,890
Dec 27	Arsenal	D 1-1	Wark (pen)	42,818
Jan 10	NOTTINGHAM FOREST	W 2-0	Mariner, Muhren	25,701
Jan 13	BIRMINGHAM CITY	W 5-1	Wark, Butcher, Mariner, Muhren, Brazil	21,158
Jan 17	Everton	D 0-0		25,516
Jan 31	STOKE CITY	W 4-0	Wark (pen), Brazil 2, Gates	23,843
Feb 7	CRYSTAL PALACE	W 3-2	Mariner, Wark (pen), Gilbert o.g.	25,036
Feb 17	MIDDLESBROUGH	W 1-0	Brazil	24,781
Feb 21	WOLVERHAMPTON WANDERERS	W 3-1	Wark, Gates, Beattie	24,218
Feb 28	Coventry City	W 4-0	Brazil, Gates, McCall, Osman	17,557
Mar 14	TOTTENHAM HOTSPUR	W 3-0	Gates, Wark (pen), Brazil	32,052
Mar 21	Manchester United	L 1-2	Butcher	46,685
Mar 28	SUNDERLAND	W 4-1	Muhren, Mariner 2, Thijssen	25,450
Mar 31	Leeds United	L 0-3		26,462
Apr 4	West Bromwich Albion	L 1-3	Brazil	22,216
Apr 14	Aston Villa	W 2-1	Brazil, Gates	47,495
Apr 18	ARSENAL	L 0-2		30,935
Apr 20	Norwich City	L 0-1		26,083
Apr 25	MANCHESTER CITY	W 1-0	Butcher	22,684
May 2	Middlesbrough	L 1-2	Mariner	15,503
May 13	SOUTHAMPTON	L 2-3	Brazil, Wark	19,504

FA Cup

Jan 3	ASTON VILLA	(Rd3) W 1-0	Mariner	27,721
Jan 24	Shrewsbury Town	(Rd4) D 0-0		18,000
Jan 27	SHREWSBURY TOWN	(R) W 3-0	Gates 2, Wark	27,543
Feb 14	CHARLTON ATHLETIC	(Rd5) W 2-0	Wark, Mariner	30,221
Mar 7	Nottingham Forest	(Rd6) D 3-3	Mariner, Anderson o.g. Thijssen	34,796
Mar 10	NOTTINGHAM FOREST	(R) W 1-0	Muhren	31,060
Apr 11	Manchester City*	(SF)(aet) L 0-1		46,537

*played at Villa Park

League Cup

Aug 26	Middlesbrough	(Rd2/1L) L 1-3	Wark	14,459
Sep 2	MIDDLESBROUGH	(Rd2/2L) W 3-0	Osman, Mariner 2	14,780
Sep 23	NORWICH CITY	(Rd3) D 1-1	Osman	26,462
Oct 8	Norwich City	(R) W 3-1	Mariner 2, Muhren	24,523
Oct 28	Birmingham City	(Rd4) L 1-2	Wark (pen)	18,968

UEFA Cup

Sep 17	ARIS SALONIKA	(Rd1/1L) W 5-1	Wark 4 (3 pen), Mariner	20,872
Oct 1	Aris Salonika	(Rd1/2L) L 1-3	Gates	40,000
Oct 22	BOHEMIANS	(Rd2/1L) W 3-0	Wark 2, Beattie	17,163
Nov 5	Bohemians	(Rd2/2L) L 0-2		16,000
Nov 26	WIDZEW LODZ	(Rd3/1L) W 5-0	Wark 3, Brazil, Mariner	20,445
Dec 10	Widzew Lodz	(Rd3/2L) L 0-1		9,000
Mar 4	St Etienne	(Rd4/1L) W 4-1	Mariner 2, Muhren, Wark	42,000
Mar 18	ST ETIENNE	(Rd4/2L) W 3-1	Butcher, Wark (pen), Mariner	30,141
Apr 8	FC KÖLN	(SF/1L) W 1-0	Wark	24,780
Apr 22	FC Köln	(SF/2L) W 1-0	Butcher	55,000
May 6	AZ '67 ALKMAAR	(F/1L) W 3-0	Wark (pen), Thijssen, Mariner	27,532
May 20	AZ '67 Alkmaar	(F/2L) L 2-4	Thijssen, Wark	28,500

League & Cup Appearances

PLAYER	LEAGUE	CUP COMPETITION			TOTAL
		FA CUP	LC	UEFA	
Beattie	7	2		2 (6)	11 (6)
Brazil	35	7	4	12	58
Burley	23	2	4	5	34
Butcher	40	7	5	12	64
Cooper	38	7	5	11	61
D'Avray	1 (4)		1	0 (1)	2 (5)
Gates	37	7	5	11	60
Hunter	1				1
Mariner	36	7	4	11	58
McCall	30 (1)	4 (1)	2	9 (1)	45 (3)
Mills	33	6	5	10	54
Muhren	41	7	5	12	65
O'Callaghan	11 (13)	0 (4)	1 (1)	0 (5)	12 (23)
Osborne	1				1
Osman	42	7	5	12	66
Parkin	2 (2)				2 (2)
Sivell	4		1		5
Steggles	6		2		8
Thijssen	31	7	4	10	52
Turner	3 (1)			0 (1)	3 (2)
Wark	40	7	5	12	64

Goalscorers

PLAYER	LEAGUE	CUP COMPETITION			TOTAL
		FA CUP	LC	UEFA	
Wark	18	2	2	14	36
Mariner	13	3	4	6	26
Brazil	17			1	18
Gates	11	2		1	14
Muhren	5	1	1	1	8
Butcher	4			2	6
Thijssen	3	1		2	6
Osman	1	2			3
Beattie	1			1	2
D'Avray	1				1
McCall	1				1
Opp's o.gs.	2	1			3

MANAGER: Bobby Robson

CAPTAIN: Mick Mills

TOP SCORER: John Wark

BIGGEST WIN: 5-0 v Widzew Lodz (H), 26 November 1980, UEFA Cup 3rd Round 1st Leg

HIGHEST ATTENDANCE: 32,052 v Tottenham Hotspur, 14 March 1981, Division One

MAJOR TRANSFERS IN: None

MAJOR TRANSFERS OUT: None

Final Division One Table

		P	W	D	L	F	A	Pts
1	ASTON VILLA	42	26	8	8	72	40	60
2	IPSWICH TOWN	42	23	10	9	77	43	56
3	ARSENAL	42	19	15	8	61	45	53
4	WBA	42	20	12	10	60	42	52
5	LIVERPOOL	42	17	17	8	62	46	51
6	SOUTHAMPTON	42	20	10	12	76	56	50
7	NOTTINGHAM F	42	19	12	11	62	44	50
8	MANCHESTER U	42	15	18	9	51	36	48
9	LEEDS U	42	17	10	15	39	47	44
10	TOTTENHAM H	42	14	15	13	70	68	43
11	STOKE C	42	12	18	12	51	60	42
12	MANCHESTER C	42	14	11	17	56	59	39
13	BIRMINGHAM C	42	13	12	17	50	61	38
14	MIDDLESBROUGH	42	16	5	21	53	61	37
15	EVERTON	42	13	10	19	55	58	36
16	COVENTRY C	42	13	10	19	48	68	36
17	SUNDERLAND	42	14	7	21	52	53	35
18	WOLVERHAMPTON W	42	13	9	20	43	55	35
19	BRIGHTON & HA	42	14	7	21	54	67	35
20	NORWICH C	42	13	7	22	49	73	33
21	LEICESTER C	42	13	6	23	40	67	32
22	CRYSTAL PALACE	42	6	7	29	47	83	19

Season 1981-82

Football League Division One

DATE	OPPONENTS	SCORE	GOALSCORERS	ATTENDANCE
Aug 29	SUNDERLAND	D 3-3	Wark, Gates 2	24,060
Sep 1	Birmingham City	D 1-1	Brazil	17,328
Sep 5	Manchester United	W 2-1	Brazil, Wark	45,645
Sep 12	LIVERPOOL	W 2-0	Neal o.g., Wark (pen)	27,603
Sep 19	Notts County	W 4-1	Brazil 2, Wark, Muhren	12,559
Sep 22	WEST BROMWICH ALBION	W 1-0	Deehan o.g.	20,524
Sep 26	LEEDS UNITED	W 2-1	Butcher, Gates	22,319
Oct 3	Southampton	L 3-4	Wark 2 (1 pen), Mariner	22,552
Oct 10	WOLVERHAMPTON WANDERERS	W 1-0	O'Callaghan	20,498
Oct 17	Everton	L 1-2	Gates	25,146
Oct 24	ARSENAL	W 2-1	Mariner, Mills	24,362
Oct 31	Aston Villa	W 1-0	Osman	32,652
Nov 7	SWANSEA CITY	L 2-3	Mariner, Muhren	24,190
Nov 21	Stoke City	L 0-2		13,802
Nov 28	MANCHESTER CITY	W 2-0	Wark (pen), D'Avray	20,476
Dec 5	Middlesbrough	W 1-0	D'Avray	13,577
Jan 3	BIRMINGHAM CITY	W 3-2	Mariner 2, Brazil	19,188
Jan 16	Coventry City	W 4-2	Wark, Muhren, Mariner, Brazil	11,719
Jan 30	NOTTS COUNTY	L 1-3	Thijssen	21,570
Feb 6	Liverpool	L 0-4		41,316
Feb 16	SOUTHAMPTON	W 5-2	Brazil 5	20,264
Feb 20	Leeds United	W 2-0	Brazil, Mills	20,287
Feb 27	Wolverhampton Wanderers	L 1-2	Gates	12,439
Mar 2	West Ham United	L 0-2		24,846
Mar 6	EVERTON	W 3-0	Wark, Brazil, Gates	19,360
Mar 13	Arsenal	L 0-1		25,977
Mar 17	Nottingham Forest	D 1-1	Wark (pen)	16,686
Mar 20	ASTON VILLA	W 3-1	Wark, McCall, Gates	20,407
Mar 27	Swansea City	W 2-1	Brazil, Gates	20,750
Mar 30	BRIGHTON & HOVE ALBION	W 3-1	Brazil 2, Wark	19,361
Apr 3	COVENTRY CITY	W 1-0	Wark	20,411
Apr 7	Sunderland	D 1-1	Steggles	11,845
Apr 10	Tottenham Hotspur	L 0-1		45,215
Apr 13	WEST HAM UNITED	W 3-2	Brazil, Wark (pen), Osman	28,767
Apr 17	STOKE CITY	W 2-0	Mariner, Wark	20,309
Apr 20	MANCHESTER UNITED	W 2-1	Wark 2	25,763
Apr 24	Manchester City	D 1-1	Brazil	30,329
May 1	Middlesbrough	W 3-1	Wark, Muhren, Brazil	17,980
May 5	West Bromwich Albion	W 2-1	Gates, Brazil	12,564
May 8	Brighton & Hove Albion	W 1-0	Mariner	17,786
May 15	NOTTINGHAM FOREST	L 1-3	Brazil	19,937
May 17	TOTTENHAM HOTSPUR	W 2-1	Mills, Brazil	20,764

FA Cup

Jan 2	Birmingham City	(Rd3) W 3-2	Brazil 2, Wark	17,236
Jan 23	Luton Town	(Rd4) W 3-0	Brazil, Gates 2	20,188
Feb 13	Shrewsbury Town	(Rd5) L 1-2	D'Avray	13,965

League Cup

Oct 7	Leeds United	(Rd2/1L) W 1-0	Gates	16,994
Oct 27	LEEDS UNITED	(Rd2/2L) W 3-0	Gates, Mariner, Steggles	16,464
Nov 10	BRADFORD CITY	(Rd3) D 1-1	Wark	13,694
Dec 2	Bradford City	(R)(aet) W 3-2	O'Callaghan, Muhren, Turner	13,518
Dec 15	Everton	(Rd4) W 3-2	Gates, Brazil, Wark	15,759
Jan 18	WATFORD	(Rd5) W 2-1	Wark, Brazil	20,817
Feb 2	LIVERPOOL	(SF/1L) L 0-2		26,690
Feb 9	Liverpool	(SF/2L) D 2-2	Gates, Brazil	34,933

UEFA Cup

Sep 16	ABERDEEN	(Rd1/1L) D 1-1	Thijssen	18,535
Sep 30	Aberdeen	(Rd1/2L) L 1-3	Wark (pen)	25,000

MANAGER: Bobby Robson

CAPTAIN: Mick Mills

TOP SCORER: Alan Brazil

BIGGEST WIN: 5-2 v Southampton (H), 16 February 1982, Division One

HIGHEST ATTENDANCE: 28,767 v West Ham United, 13 April 1982, Division One

MAJOR TRANSFERS IN: None

MAJOR TRANSFERS OUT: Allan Hunter to Colchester United; Arnold Muhren to Manchester United

---

League & Cup Appearances

PLAYER	LEAGUE	CUP COMPETITION			TOTAL
		FA CUP	LC	UEFA	
Brazil	35	3	6 (1)	2	46 (1)
Burley	29	3	6		38
Butcher	27	1	6	2	36
Cooper	32	3	8	2	45
D'Avray	12 (1)	0 (1)	1	0 (1)	13 (2)
Gates	38	3	7	2	50
Gernon	4				4
Hunter		1		1	2
Jackson	1				1
Mariner	25	2	5	1	33
McCall	42	3	7	2	54
Mills	42	3	8	2	55
Muhren	42	3	8	2	55
O'Callaghan	7 (12)	1 (1)	2 (1)	1 (1)	11 (15)
Osman	39	3	7	2	51
Parkin	5 (1)				5 (1)
Sivell	9				9
Steggles	18	1	3		22
Thijssen	12		5 (1)	2	19 (1)
Turner	1 (2)		0 (2)		1 (4)
Wark	42	3	8	2	55

Goalscorers

PLAYER	LEAGUE	CUP COMPETITION			TOTAL
		FA CUP	LC	UEFA	
Brazil	22	3	3		28
Wark	18	1	3	1	23
Gates	9	2	4		15
Mariner	8		1		9
Muhren	4		1		5
D'Avray	2	1			3
Mills	3				3
Osman	2				2
O'Callaghan	1		1		2
Steggles	1		1		2
Thijssen	1			1	2
Butcher	1				1
McCall	1				1
Turner			1		1
Opps' o.gs	2				2

Fact File

When he made his debut for Ipswich against Manchester United at Portman Road in April 1982, goalkeeper John Jackson became the oldest player to play for the club.

Final Division 1 Table

		P	W	D	L	F	A	Pts
1	LIVERPOOL	42	26	9	7	80	32	87
2	IPSWICH TOWN	42	26	5	11	75	53	83
3	MANCHESTER U	42	22	12	8	59	29	78
4	TOTTENHAM H	42	20	11	11	67	48	71
5	ARSENAL	42	20	11	11	48	37	71
6	SWANSEA C	42	21	6	15	58	51	69
7	SOUTHAMPTON	42	19	9	14	72	67	66
8	EVERTON	42	17	13	12	56	50	64
9	WEST HAM U	42	14	16	12	66	57	58
10	MANCHESTER C	42	15	13	14	49	50	58
11	ASTON VILLA	42	15	12	15	55	53	57
12	NOTTINGHAM F	42	15	12	15	42	48	57
13	BRIGHTON & HA	42	13	13	16	43	52	52
14	COVENTRY C	42	13	11	18	56	62	50
15	NOTTS CO	42	13	8	21	61	69	47
16	BIRMINGHAM C	42	10	14	18	53	61	44
17	WBA	42	11	11	20	46	57	44
18	STOKE C	42	12	8	22	44	63	44
19	SUNDERLAND	42	11	11	20	38	58	44
20	LEEDS U	42	10	12	20	39	61	42
21	WOLVERHAMPTON W	42	10	10	22	32	63	40
22	MIDDLESBROUGH	42	8	15	19	34	52	39

Season 1982-83

Football League Division One

DATE	OPPONENTS	SCORE	GOALSCORERS	ATTENDANCE
Aug 28	Brighton & Hove Albion	D 1-1	Gates	13,641
Aug 31	TOTTENHAM HOTSPUR	L 1-2	Brazil	24,968
Sep 4	COVENTRY CITY	D 1-1	Mariner	16,662
Sep 7	West Ham United	D 1-1	Wark	21,963
Sep 11	Manchester United	L 1-3	Mariner	43,140
Sep 18	STOKE CITY	L 2-3	Brazil, Wark	19,119
Sep 25	Notts County	W 6-0	Mariner 2, Brazil, Wark, Thijssen, McCall	8,454
Oct 2	LIVERPOOL	W 1-0	D'Avray	24,342
Oct 9	ARSENAL	L 0-1		20,792
Oct 16	Luton Town	D 1-1	Brazil	13,378
Oct 23	Birmingham City	D 0-0		12,051
Oct 30	WEST BROMWICH ALBION	W 6-1	Gates, Thijssen, Wark 4	20,011
Nov 6	Nottingham Forest	L 1-2	McCall	17,461
Nov 13	MANCHESTER CITY	W 1-0	Wark	19,523
Nov 20	Southampton	D 1-1	Thijssen	18,449
Nov 27	Coventry City	D 1-1	Brazil	9,550
Nov 27	SWANSEA CITY	W 3-1	Osman, Burley, Wark	17,849
Dec 4	Sunderland	W 3-2	Gates, Brazil 2	15,000
Dec 11	EVERTON	L 0-2		17,512
Dec 18	Watford	L 1-2	Mariner	18,048
Dec 27	NORWICH CITY	L 2-3	Osman, Mariner	29,596
Dec 29	Aston Villa	D 1-1	Wark	21,912
Jan 1	SOUTHAMPTON	W 2-1	Mariner, Osman	18,866
Jan 15	BRIGHTON & HOVE ALBION	W 2-0	Wark, Brazil	17,092
Jan 22	Stoke City	L 0-1		14,026
Feb 5	MANCHESTER UNITED	D 1-1	Wark	23,531
Feb 12	Liverpool	L 0-1		34,976
Feb 26	LUTON TOWN	W 3-0	Brazil, Wark, Putney	18,615
Mar 5	BIRMINGHAM CITY	W 3-1	Putney, Osman, Brazil	16,436
Mar 12	West Bromwich Albion	L 1-4	Wark	12,892
Mar 19	NOTTINGHAM FOREST	W 2-0	Mariner 2	17,534
Mar 22	Arsenal	D 2-2	Wark, Putney	17,639
Mar 26	Manchester City	W 1-0	Wark	21,845
Apr 2	ASTON VILLA	L 1-2	McCall	19,912
Apr 4	Norwich City	D 0-0		23,476
Apr 9	NOTTS COUNTY	D 0-0		15,924
Apr 16	Tottenham Hotspur	L 1-3	Mariner	30,557
Apr 23	SUNDERLAND	W 4-1	Wark 2, Mariner, Turner	16,193
Apr 30	Swansea City	D 1-1	Mariner	8,568
May 3	WEST HAM UNITED	L 1-2	D'Avray	18,690
May 7	WATFORD	W 3-1	McCall, Wark 2	19,921
May 14	Everton	D 1-1	Mariner	17,420

FA Cup

Jan 8	Charlton Athletic	(Rd3) W 3-2	Thijssen, Wark 2 (1 pen)	16,699
Jan 29	GRIMSBY TOWN	(Rd4) W 2-0	Osman, McCall	21,455
Feb 19	Norwich City	(Rd5) L 0-1		28,001

League Cup

Oct 4	LIVERPOOL	(Rd2/1L) L 1-2	Wark	19,329
Oct 26	Liverpool	(Rd2/2L) L 0-2		17,698

UEFA Cup

Sep 15	Roma	(Rd1/1L) L 0-3		60,334
Sep 29	ROMA	(Rd1/2L) W 3-1	Gates, Butcher, McCall	17,751

Fact File

Ipswich's 6-0 win at Notts County in September 1982 was their biggest ever away win.

MANAGER: Bobby Ferguson

CAPTAIN: Mick Mills

TOP SCORERS: John Wark/Paul Mariner

BIGGEST WIN: 6-0 v Notts County (A), 25 September 1982, Division One

HIGHEST ATTENDANCE: 29,596 v Norwich City, 27 December 1982, Division One

MAJOR TRANSFERS IN: Tony Kinsella from Millwall; Trevor Putney from Brentwood

MAJOR TRANSFERS OUT: Alan Brazil to Tottenham Hotspur; Mick Mills to Southampton; Frans Thijssen to Vancouver

League & Cup Appearances

PLAYER	LEAGUE	CUP COMPETITION			TOTAL
		FA CUP	LC	UEFA	
Barnes	6				6
Brazil	28	3	2	2	35
Burley	31		2	2	35
Butcher	42	3	2	2	49
Cooper	35	2	1	1	39
D'Avray	13 (4)		1	1	15 (4)
Gates	24	1	1	2	28
Gernon	26	3	1		30
Kinsella	3 (1)				3 (1)
Linford			0 (1)		0 (1)
Mariner	37	3	1	1	42
McCall	42	3	2	2	49
Mills	11		2	2	15
O'Callaghan	20 (8)	2	1 (1)	0 (1)	23 (10)
Osman	38	3	2	2	45
Parkin	4 (2)				4 (2)
Putney	17 (3)	1			18 (3)
Sivell	7	1	1	1	10
Steggles	9	2			11
Thijssen	27 (2)	3	1	2	33 (2)
Turner	0 (5)	0 (1)			0 (6)
Wark	42	3	2	2	49

Goalscorers

PLAYER	LEAGUE	CUP COMPETITION			TOTAL
		FA CUP	LC	UEFA	
Wark	20	2	1		23
Mariner	13				13
Brazil	10				10
McCall	4	1		1	6
Osman	4	1			5
Gates	3		1		4
Thijssen	3	1			4
Putney	3				3
D'Avray	2				2
Burley	1				1
Butcher	1		1		1
Turner	1				1

Final Division One Table

		P	W	D	L	F	A	Pts
1	LIVERPOOL	42	24	10	8	87	37	82
2	WATFORD	42	22	5	15	74	57	71
3	MANCHESTER U	42	19	13	8	56	38	70
4	TOTTENHAM H	42	20	9	13	65	50	69
5	NOTTINGHAM F	42	20	9	13	62	50	69
6	ASTON VILLA	42	21	5	16	62	50	68
7	EVERTON	42	18	10	14	66	48	64
8	WEST HAM U	42	20	4	18	68	62	64
9	IPSWICH TOWN	42	15	13	14	64	50	58
10	ARSENAL	42	16	10	16	58	56	58
11	WBA	42	15	12	15	51	49	57
12	SOUTHAMPTON	42	15	12	15	54	58	57
13	STOKE C	42	16	9	17	53	64	57
14	NORWICH C	42	14	12	16	52	58	54
15	NOTTS CO	42	15	7	20	55	71	52
16	SUNDERLAND	42	12	14	16	48	61	50
17	BIRMINGHAM C	42	12	14	16	40	55	50
18	LUTON T	42	12	13	17	65	84	49
19	COVENTRY C	42	13	9	20	48	59	48
20	MANCHESTER C	42	13	8	21	47	70	47
21	SWANSEA C	42	10	11	21	51	69	41
22	BRIGHTON & HA	42	9	13	20	38	68	40

The Essential History of Ipswich Town

Football League Division One

DATE	OPPONENTS	SCORE	GOALSCORERS	ATTENDANCE
Aug 27	TOTTENHAM HOTSPUR	W 3-1	Gates 2, Mariner	26,185
Aug 30	Watford	D 2-2	Gates, O'Callaghan	15,388
Sep 3	Notts County	W 2-0	Fashanu o.g., Mariner	9,023
Sep 6	EVERTON	W 3-0	Mariner, Wark, Turner	16,543
Sep 10	STOKE CITY	W 5-0	Burley, Gates, Wark 2 (1 pen), Mariner	16,315
Sep 17	Birmingham City	L 0-1		13,159
Sep 24	WEST BROMWICH ALBION	L 3-4	Wark (pen), Gates, Mariner	16,611
Oct 1	Coventry City	W 2-1	Mariner, O'Callaghan	10,492
Oct 15	QUEENS PARK RANGERS	L 0-2		17,959
Oct 22	LEICESTER CITY	D 0-0		14,994
Oct 29	Southampton	L 2-3	Mariner 2	18,515
Nov 5	West Ham United	L 1-2	Osman	20,682
Nov 12	ARSENAL	W 1-0	Gates	21,652
Nov 19	Nottingham Forest	L 1-2	Butcher	14,979
Nov 26	LIVERPOOL	D 1-1	Wark (pen)	23,826
Dec 3	Sunderland	D 1-1	Gates	15,555
Dec 10	MANCHESTER UNITED	L 0-2		19,779
Dec 17	Aston Villa	L 0-4		16,548
Dec 26	WOLVERHAMPTON WANDERERS	W 3-1	Mariner, O'Callaghan, McCall	14,477
Dec 27	Norwich City	D 0-0		25,679
Dec 31	NOTTS COUNTY	W 1-0	Mariner	14,146
Jan 2	West Bromwich Albion	L 1-2	Gates	11,199
Jan 14	Tottenham Hotspur	L 0-2		25,832
Jan 21	BIRMINGHAM CITY	L 1-2	D'Avray	12,900
Feb 4	COVENTRY CITY	W 3-1	Mariner, Brennan, Dozzell	13,406
Feb 11	Stoke City	L 0-1		10,315
Feb 21	SOUTHAMPTON	L 0-3		14,934
Feb 25	Leicester City	L 0-2		11,399
Mar 3	WEST HAM UNITED	L 0-3		17,297
Mar 10	Arsenal	L 1-4	Gates	24,000
Mar 13	Luton Town	L 1-2	Putney	8,776
Mar 17	Everton	L 0-1		18,013
Mar 24	WATFORD	D 0-0		14,956
Mar 31	LUTON TOWN	W 3-0	Gates, Putney, D'Avray	14,570
Apr 7	Queens Park Rangers	L 0-1		12,251
Apr 14	NOTTINGHAM FOREST	D 2-2	Zondervan, D'Avray	15,429
Apr 21	Wolverhampton Wanderers	W 3-0	D'Avray, Osman, Sunderland	6,611
Apr 23	NORWICH CITY	W 2-0	Zondervan, Sunderland	22,135
Apr 28	Liverpool	D 2-2	Gates 2	32,069
May 5	SUNDERLAND	W 1-0	Osman	17,657
May 7	Manchester United	W 2-1	D'Avray, Sunderland	44,257
May 12	ASTON VILLA	W 2-1	Gates, D'Avray	20,043

FA Cup

Jan 7	Cardiff City	(Rd3) W 3-0	Gates 3	10,118
Jan 28	Shrewsbury Town	(Rd4) L 0-2		11,110

League Cup

Oct 5	BLACKBURN ROVERS	(Rd2/1L) W 4-3	Mariner, Wark 3 (1 pen)	11,478
Nov 26	Blackburn Rovers	(Rd2/2L) W 2-1	Hamilton o.g., Wark	8,990
Nov 9	QUEENS PARK RANGERS	(Rd3) W 3-2	Wark 2, Mariner	12,343
Nov 30	NORWICH CITY	(Rd4) L 0-1		25,570

League & Cup Appearances

PLAYER	LEAGUE	CUP COMPETITION		TOTAL
		FA CUP	LC	
Barnes	10 (1)			10 (1)
Brennan	19		1 (1)	20 (1)
Burley	28	2	4	34
Butcher	34	2	4	40
Cooper	36	1	4	41
Cranson	8			8
D'Avray	17 (6)	1 (1)	0 (2)	18 (9)
Dozzell	0 (5)			0 (5)
Gates	37	2	3	42
Gernon	19	1 (1)	3	23 (1)
Kinsella	4 (1)	1	1	6 (1)
Mariner	23	1	4	28
McCall	42	2	4	48
O'Callaghan	23 (2)	2	4	29 (2)
Osman	37	2	3	42
Parkin	18 (3)	2	4	21 (3)
Putney	32 (3)		3	35 (3)
Sivell	6	1		7
Steggles	5		1	6
Sunderland	15			15
Turner	3 (7)			3 (7)
Wark	32	2	4	38
Yallop	6			6
Zondervan	8			8

Goalscorers

PLAYER	LEAGUE	CUP COMPETITION		TOTAL
		FA CUP	LC	
Gates	13	3		16
Mariner	12		2	14
Wark	5		6	11
D'Avray	6			6
Osman	3			3
Sunderland	3			3
O'Callaghan	2			2
Putney	2			2
Zondervan	2			2
Brennan	1			1
Burley	1			1
Butcher	1			1
Dozzell	1			1
McCall	1			1
Turner	1			1
Opp's o.gs.	1		1	2

Fact File

When he came on as a substitute against Coventry City in the league game in February 1984 Jason Dozzell became the youngest player to appear and score for the club.

MANAGER: Bobby Ferguson

CAPTAIN: Paul Mariner/Terry Butcher

TOP SCORER: Eric Gates

BIGGEST WIN: 5-0 v Stoke City (H), 10 September 1983, Division One

HIGHEST ATTENDANCE: 25,570 v Norwich City, 30 November 1983, League Cup

MAJOR TRANSFERS IN: Alan Sunderland from Arsenal; Romeo Zondervan from WBA

MAJOR TRANSFERS OUT: Paul Mariner to Arsenal; John Wark to Liverpool

Final Division One Table

		P	W	D	L	F	A	Pts
1	LIVERPOOL	42	22	14	6	73	32	80
2	SOUTHAMPTON	42	22	11	9	66	38	77
3	NOTTINGHAM F	42	22	8	12	76	45	74
4	MANCHESTER U	42	20	14	8	71	41	74
5	QPR	42	22	7	13	67	37	73
6	ARSENAL	42	19	9	15	74	60	63
7	EVERTON	42	16	14	12	44	42	62
8	TOTTENHAM H	42	17	10	15	64	65	61
9	WEST HAM U	42	17	9	16	60	55	60
10	ASTON VILLA	42	17	9	16	59	61	60
11	WATFORD	42	16	9	17	68	77	57
12	IPSWICH TOWN	42	15	8	19	55	57	53
13	SUNDERLAND	42	13	13	16	42	53	52
14	NORWICH C	42	12	15	15	48	49	51
15	LEICESTER C	42	13	12	17	65	68	51
16	LUTON T	42	14	9	19	53	66	51
17	WBA	42	14	9	19	48	62	51
18	STOKE C	42	13	11	18	44	63	50
19	COVENTRY C	42	13	11	18	57	77	50
20	BIRMINGHAM C	42	12	12	18	39	50	48
21	NOTTS CO	42	10	11	21	50	72	41
22	WOLVERHAMPTON W	42	6	11	25	27	80	29

Season 1984-85

Football League Division One

DATE	OPPONENTS	SCORE	GOALSCORERS	ATTENDANCE
Aug 25	West Ham United	D 0-0		19,032
Aug 28	LUTON TOWN	D 1-1	Gates	15,331
Sep 1	MANCHESTER UNITED	D 1-1	Sunderland	20,434
Sep 4	Everton	D 1-1	Gates	22,314
Sep 8	Leicester City	L 1-2	Gates	10,737
Sep 15	ARSENAL	W 2-1	Osman, Zondervan	24,508
Sep 22	Sheffield Wednesday	D 2-2	Gates 2	25,558
Sep 29	ASTON VILLA	W 3-0	Gates, Osman, Sunderland	15,630
Oct 6	Newcastle United	L 0-3		25,094
Oct 13	QUEENS PARK RANGERS	D 1-1	Gates (pen)	15,733
Oct 20	WEST BROMWICH ALBION	W 2-0	Gates, Sunderland	14,154
Oct 27	Chelsea	L 0-2		19,213
Nov 3	WATFORD	D 3-3	Brennan, Butcher, D'Avray	15,680
Nov 10	Coventry City	L 0-1		8,790
Nov 17	TOTTENHAM HOTSPUR	L 0-3		21,894
Nov 24	Liverpool	L 0-2		34,918
Dec 1	SOUTHAMPTON	L 0-1		14,113
Dec 8	Stoke City	W 2-0	D'Avray, Putney	7,925
Dec 15	SUNDERLAND	L 0-2		12,493
Dec 22	Manchester United	L 0-3		35,168
Dec 26	Nottingham Forest	L 0-2		17,123
Dec 29	EVERTON	L 0-2		16,045
Jan 1	NORWICH CITY	W 2-0	Dozzell, Gates	21,710
Feb 2	Aston Villa	L 1-2	Osman	15,051
Mar 2	CHELSEA	W 2-0	Cranson, Wilson	17,735
Mar 16	Queens Park Rangers	L 0-3		9,518
Mar 19	Arsenal	D 1-1	Dozzell	18,365
Mar 23	NEWCASTLE UNITED	D 1-1	Gates	14,366
Mar 30	Luton Town	L 1-3	Gates	12,640
Apr 3	West Bromwich Albion	W 2-1	D'Avray, Wilson	8,112
Apr 6	NOTTINGHAM FOREST	W 1-0	Sunderland	16,296
Apr 8	Norwich City	W 2-0	Butcher, D'Avray	18,227
Apr 13	SHEFFIELD WEDNESDAY	L 1-2	D'Avray	16,268
Apr 16	Watford	L 1-3	Sunderland	16,074
Apr 20	Tottenham Hotspur	W 3-2	Brennan, Gates (pen), Sunderland	20,348
Apr 23	LEICESTER CITY	W 2-0	D'Avray, Sunderland	13,666
Apr 27	LIVERPOOL	D 0-0		24,484
May 4	Southampton	L 0-3		16,156
May 6	STOKE CITY	W 5-1	Gates, Putney, Wilson 3	14,150
May 11	Sunderland	W 2-0	Wilson 2	9,389
May 14	COVENTRY CITY	D 0-0		14,038
May 17	WEST HAM UNITED	L 0-1		19,326

FA Cup

DATE	OPPONENTS		SCORE	GOALSCORERS	ATTENDANCE
Jan 4	Bristol Rovers	(Rd3)	W 2-1	Dozzell, Brennan	12,257
Jan 26	GILLINGHAM	(Rd4)	W 3-2	Wilson, Sage o.g., Dozzell	16,547
Mar 4	SHEFFIELD WEDNESDAY	(Rd5)	W 3-2	Zondervan, Burley, Sunderland	17,459
Mar 9	Everton	(Rd6)	D 2-2	Wilson, Zondervan	36,468
Mar 13	EVERTON	(R)	L 0-1		27,737

League Cup

DATE	OPPONENTS		SCORE	GOALSCORERS	ATTENDANCE
Sep 25	DERBY COUNTY	(Rd2/1L)	W 4-2	Gates, Osman, Sunderland, Putney	10,809
Oct 10	Derby County	(Rd2/2L)	D 1-1	D'Avray	14,374
Oct 30	NEWCASTLE UNITED	(Rd3)	D 1-1	Gates	15,084
Nov 7	Newcastle United	(R)	W 2-1	D'Avray, Gates	22,982
Nov 20	QUEENS PARK RANGERS	(Rd4)	W 2-1	D'Avray, Zondervan	18,879
Jan 23	QUEENS PARK RANGERS	(Rd5)	D 0-0		16,143
Jan 28	Queens Park Rangers	(R)	W 2-1	D'Avray, Zondervan	14,563
Feb 23	NORWICH CITY	(SF/1L)	W 1-0	D'Avray	27,404
Mar 6	Norwich City	(SF/2L)	L 0-2		23,545

League & Cup Appearances

PLAYER	LEAGUE	CUP COMPETITION		TOTAL
		FA CUP	LC	
Brennan	35 (1)	5	8	48 (1)
Burley	37	3	9	49
Butcher	41	5	9	55
Cole	0 (2)			0 (2)
Cooper	36	4	9	49
Cranson	19 (1)	5	6	30 (1)
D'Avray	30 (3)	2	7 (1)	39 (4)
Dozzell	9 (5)	2	4	15 (5)
Gates	41	4	8	53
Gernon	13			13
Grew	6		1	7
McCall	31	5	9	45
O'Callaghan	10 (5)		2 (1)	12 (6)
Osman	29	2 (2)	6	37 (2)
Parkin	6 (5)		0 (1)	6 (6)
Putney	27	4	9	40
Steggles	6			6
Sunderland	23 (3)	2 (1)	5 (1)	30 (5)
Wilson	15 (2)	4		19 (2)
Yallop	7 (3)	2		9 (3)
Zondervan	41	5	8	54

Goalscorers

PLAYER	LEAGUE	CUP COMPETITION		TOTAL
		FA CUP	LC	
Gates	13		3	16
D'Avray	6		5	11
Sunderland	7	1	1	9
Wilson	7	2		9
Zondervan	1	2	2	5
Osman	3		1	4
Dozzell	2	2		4
Brennan	2	1		3
Putney	2		1	3
Butcher	2			2
Cranson	1			1
Burley	1			1
Opp's o.g.	1			1

Fact File

Victory at Bristol Rovers in the FA Cup in January 1985 meant that Ipswich had survived the 3rd Round of the tournament for 15 consecutive years.

Final Division One Table

		P	W	D	L	F	A	Pts
1	EVERTON	42	28	6	8	88	43	90
2	LIVERPOOL	42	22	11	9	68	35	77
3	TOTTENHAM H	42	23	8	11	78	51	77
4	MANCHESTER U	42	22	10	10	77	47	76
5	SOUTHAMPTON	42	19	11	12	56	47	68
6	CHELSEA	42	18	12	12	63	48	66
7	ARSENAL	42	19	9	14	61	49	66
8	SHEFFIELD W	42	17	14	11	58	45	65
9	NOTTINGHAM F	42	19	7	16	56	48	64
10	ASTON VILLA	42	15	11	16	60	60	56
11	WATFORD	42	14	13	15	81	71	55
12	WBA	42	16	7	19	58	62	55
13	LUTON T	42	15	9	18	57	61	54
14	NEWCASTLE U	42	13	13	16	55	70	52
15	LEICESTER C	42	15	6	21	65	73	51
16	WEST HAM U	42	13	12	17	51	68	51
17	IPSWICH TOWN	42	13	11	18	46	57	50
18	COVENTRY C	42	15	5	22	47	64	50
19	QPR	42	13	11	18	53	72	50
20	NORWICH C	42	13	10	19	46	64	49
21	SUNDERLAND	42	10	10	22	40	62	40
22	STOKE C	42	3	8	31	24	91	17

MANAGER: Bobby Ferguson

CAPTAIN: Terry Butcher

TOP SCORER: Eric Gates

BIGGEST WIN: 5-1 v Stoke City, 6 May 1985, Division One

HIGHEST ATTENDANCE: 27,404 v Norwich City, 23 February 1985, League Cup semi-final

MAJOR TRANSFERS IN: Mark Grew from Oldham; Kevin Wilson from Derby

MAJOR TRANSFERS OUT: Kevin O'Callaghan to Portsmouth; Russell Osman to Leicester City

The Essential History of Ipswich Town

Football League Division One

DATE	OPPONENTS	SCORE	GOALSCORERS	ATTENDANCE
Aug 17	Queens Park Rangers	L 0-1		12,466
Aug 20	MANCHESTER UNITED	L 0-1		18,777
Aug 24	TOTTENHAM HOTSPUR	W 1-0	Zondervan	17,758
Aug 26	Liverpool	L 0-5		29,383
Aug 31	SOUTHAMPTON	D 1-1	Cranson	11,588
Sep 7	West Bromwich Albion	W 2-1	Putney, Sunderland	7,733
Sep 14	BIRMINGHAM CITY	L 0-1		11,616
Sep 21	ASTON VILLA	L 0-3		11,598
Sep 28	Leicester City	L 0-1		7,290
Oct 1	Luton Town	L 0-1		8,533
Oct 5	Nottingham Forest	L 1-3	Atkins	12,120
Oct 12	NEWCASTLE UNITED	D 2-2	Cole, Zondervan	12,536
Oct 19	Arsenal	L 0-1		19,522
Oct 26	WEST HAM UNITED	L 0-1		16,849
Nov 2	CHELSEA	L 0-2		15,324
Nov 9	Manchester City	D 1-1	Gleghorn	20,853
Nov 16	EVERTON	L 3-4	D'Avray, Wilson, Butcher	13,910
Nov 23	Oxford United	L 3-4	Wilson, Brennan (pen), Dozzell	9,387
Nov 30	SHEFFIELD WEDNESDAY	W 2-1	D'Avray 2	12,918
Dec 7	Manchester United	L 0-1		37,981
Dec 14	QUEENS PARK RANGERS	W 1-0	Wilson	12,032
Dec 21	Tottenham Hotspur	L 0-2		18,845
Dec 26	Coventry City	W 1-0	D'Avray	9,356
Dec 28	LUTON TOWN	D 1-1	Gleghorn	16,155
Jan 1	WATFORD	D 0-0		15,922
Jan 11	Birmingham City	W 1-0	Wilson	6,856
Jan 18	Southampton	L 0-1		13,164
Feb 1	LIVERPOOL	W 2-1	D'Avray, Wilson	20,551
Mar 8	NOTTINGHAM FOREST	W 1-0	Butcher	12,658
Mar 11	ARSENAL	L 1-2	Dozzell	13,967
Mar 15	Newcastle United	L 1-3	Wilson	18,851
Mar 22	WEST BROMWICH ALBION	W 1-0	Butcher	12,100
Mar 29	Watford	D 0-0		14,988
Mar 31	COVENTRY CITY	W 1-0	Brennan	13,485
Apr 5	Chelsea	D 1-1	Brennan	13,072
Apr 8	LEICESTER CITY	L 0-2		11,718
Apr 12	MANCHESTER CITY	D 0-0		13,986
Apr 16	Aston Villa	L 0-1		13,611
Apr 19	Everton	L 0-1		39,055
Apr 26	OXFORD UNITED	W 3-2	Dozzell, Butcher, Atkins	17,827
Apr 30	West Ham United	L 1-2	Wilson	31,121
May 3	Sheffield Wednesday	L 0-1		22,369

FA Cup

Jan 4	BRADFORD CITY	(Rd3) D 4-4	Evans o.g., Wilson, Brennan, D'Avray	13,003
Jan 13	Bradford City*	(R) W 1-0	Brennan	10,108
Jan 25	West Ham United	(Rd4) D 0-0		25,035
Feb 4	WEST HAM UNITED	(R)(aet) D 1-1	Dozzell	25,384
Feb 6	WEST HAM UNITED	(2R)(aet) L 0-1		14,515

*played at Elland Road, Leeds

League Cup

Sep 23	DARLINGTON	(Rd2/1L) W 3-1	Wilson 2, Yallop	7,664
Oct 8	Darlington	(Rd2/2L) W 4-1	Wilson 3, Dozzell	3,321
Oct 29	Grimsby Town	(Rd3) W 2-0	Cole, Wilson	6,684
Nov 26	SWINDON TOWN	(Rd4) W 6-1	Brennan, Wilson, Butcher 2, Cole 2	12,083
Jan 21	Liverpool	(Rd5) L 0-3		19,762

MANAGER: Bobby Ferguson

CAPTAIN: Terry Butcher

TOP SCORER: Kevin Wilson

BIGGEST WIN: 6-1 v Swindon Town (H), 26 November 1985, League Cup 4th Round

HIGHEST ATTENDANCE: 25,384 v West Ham United, 4 February 1986, FA Cup 4th Round replay

MAJOR TRANSFERS IN: Ian Atkins from Everton; Nigel Gleghorn from Seaham Red Star; Neill Rimmer from Everton

MAJOR TRANSFERS OUT: George Burley to Sunderland; Terry Butcher to Rangers; Trevor Putney to Norwich City; Kevin Steggles to Southend

League & Cup Appearances

PLAYER	LEAGUE	CUP COMPETITION		TOTAL
		FA CUP	LC	
Atkins	20 (1)		4	24 (1)
Atkinson	0 (1)			0 (1)
Brennan	40	5	5	50
Burley	6			6
Butcher	27	5	2	34
Cole	12 (6)	0 (1)	2 (1)	14 (8)
Cooper	36	5	5	46
Cranson	42	5	5	52
D'Avray	24 (2)	5	2	31 (2)
Dozzell	38 (3)	5	5	48 (3)
Gernon	11		2	13
Gleghorn	17 (4)	2	0 (1)	19 (5)
Hallworth	6			6
McCall	33	5	4	42
Parkin	13 (1)		1	14 (1)
Putney	18 (3)	4	3	25 (3)
Rimmer	1 (1)			1 (1)
Steggles	5 (1)		2	7 (1)
Stockwell	3 (5)	2	0 (1)	5 (6)
Sunderland	13 (4)		1	14 (4)
Wilson	37 (2)	5	4	47 (2)
Yallop	32 (2)	5	5	42 (2)
Zondervan	28	3 (1)	2	33 (1)

Goalscorers

PLAYER	LEAGUE	CUP COMPETITION		TOTAL
		FA CUP	LC	
Wilson	7	1	7	15
D'Avray	5	1		6
Butcher	4		2	6
Brennan	3	2	1	6
Dozzell	3	1	1	5
Cole	1		3	4
Atkins	2			2
Gleghorn	2			2
Zondervan	2			2
Cranson	1			1
Putney	1			1
Sunderland	1			1
Yallop			1	1
Opps. o.gs.		1		1

Fact File

In January 1987 Ipswich progressed beyond the FA Cup 3rd Round for the 16th consecutive season by beating Bradford City.

Final Division One Table

		P	W	D	L	F	A	Pts
1	LIVERPOOL	42	26	10	6	89	37	88
2	EVERTON	42	26	8	8	87	41	86
3	WEST HAM U	42	26	6	10	74	40	84
4	MANCHESTER U	42	22	10	10	70	36	76
5	SHEFFIELD W	42	21	10	11	63	54	73
6	CHELSEA	42	20	11	11	57	56	71
7	ARSENAL	42	20	9	13	49	47	69
8	NOTTINGHAM F	42	19	11	12	69	53	68
9	LUTON T	42	18	12	12	61	44	66
10	TOTTENHAM H	42	19	8	15	74	52	65
11	NEWCASTLE U	42	17	12	13	67	72	63
12	WATFORD	42	16	11	15	69	62	59
13	QPR	42	15	7	20	53	64	52
14	SOUTHAMPTON	42	12	10	20	51	62	46
15	MANCHESTER C	42	11	12	19	43	57	45
16	ASTON VILLA	42	10	14	18	51	67	44
17	COVENTRY C	42	11	10	21	48	71	43
18	OXFORD U	42	10	12	20	62	80	42
19	LEICESTER C	42	10	12	20	54	76	42
20	IPSWICH TOWN	42	11	8	23	32	55	41
21	BIRMINGHAM C	42	8	5	29	30	73	29
22	WBA	42	4	12	26	35	89	24

Season 1986-87

Football League Division Two

DATE	OPPONENTS	SCORE	GOALSCORERS	ATTENDANCE
Aug 23	GRIMSBY TOWN	D 1-1	Wilson	12,455
Aug 30	Portsmouth	D 1-1	Brennan	11,849
Sep 2	OLDHAM ATHLETIC	L 0-1		10,316
Sep 6	SHREWSBURY TOWN	W 1-0	D'Avray	9,399
Sep 13	West Bromwich Albion	W 4-3	Deehan 3, Wilson	9,031
Sep 20	SUNDERLAND	D 1-1	D'Avray	12,824
Sep 27	Birmingham City	D 2-2	Brennan, Wilson	7,227
Oct 4	Hull City	L 1-2	Deehan	6,872
Oct 11	BRIGHTON & HOVE ALBION	W 1-0	D'Avray	11,215
Oct 18	Bradford City*	W 4-3	Gleghorn 3, Dozzell	5,348
Oct 21	Plymouth Argyle	L 0-2		12,569
Oct 25	STOKE CITY	W 2-0	Wilson 2	11,054
Nov 1	HUDDERSFIELD TOWN	W 3-0	Atkins, Deehan 2	10,211
Nov 8	Derby County	L 1-2	Stockwell	14,145
Nov 15	Crystal Palace	D 3-3	Wilson 3	7,138
Nov 22	BARNSLEY	W 1-0	Wilson	10,150
Nov 29	Blackburn Rovers	D 0-0		4,951
Dec 6	SHEFFIELD UNITED	D 2-2	Wilson, Gleghorn	11,022
Dec 13	Reading	W 4-1	Wilson 2, Brennan 2	6,935
Dec 19	PLYMOUTH ARGYLE	W 3-0	Wilson, Brennan 2	11,538
Dec 26	Millwall	L 0-1		4,737
Dec 27	CRYSTAL PALACE	W 3-0	Cole, Deehan, Wilson	15,007
Jan 1	LEEDS UNITED	W 2-0	Zondervan, Gleghorn	14,125
Jan 3	Shrewsbury Town	L 1-2	Dozzell	4,783
Jan 24	Grimsby Town	D 1-1	Deehan	4,981
Feb 7	PORTSMOUTH	L 0-1		18,670
Feb 14	Oldham Athletic	L 1-2	Wilson	5,584
Feb 21	BIRMINGHAM CITY	W 3-0	Deehan, Cole, Cranson	10,005
Feb 28	Sunderland	L 0-1		11,789
Mar 3	WEST BROMWICH ALBION	W 1-0	Brennan	9,843
Mar 14	BRADFORD CITY	W 1-0	Deehan	10,330
Mar 21	Brighton & Hove Albion	W 2-1	Wilson, D'Avray	8,393
Mar 25	Stoke City	D 0-0		11,805
Mar 28	HULL CITY	D 0-0		10,240
Apr 4	DERBY COUNTY	L 0-2		16,533
Apr 11	Huddersfield Town	W 2-1	Gleghorn 2	5,888
Apr 18	Leeds United	L 2-3	Humes 2	24,839
Apr 21	MILLWALL	D 0-0		10,957
Apr 25	Barnsley	L 1-2	Cranson	5,536
May 2	BLACKBURN ROVERS	W 3-1	Wilson 3	10,657
May 4	Sheffield United	D 0-0		8,324
May 9	READING	H 1-1	Wilson	16,036

*played at Odsal Stadium, Bradford

FA Cup

Jan 10	BIRMINGHAM CITY	(Rd3) L 0-1		11,616

League Cup

Sep 23	Scunthorpe United	(Rd2/1L) W 2-1	Dozzell, Deehan	3,919
Oct 7	SCUNTHORPE UNITED	(Rd2/2L) W 2-0	Brennan, Wilson	6,587
Oct 28	Cambridge United	(Rd 3) L 0-1		8,893

Full Members Cup

Sep 16	PLYMOUTH ARGYLE	(Rd1) W 3-2	Dozzell, Gleghorn, Wilson	5,752
Nov 25	Reading	(Rd2) W 2-0	Deehan, Wilson	3,058
Dec 2	ASTON VILLA	(Rd3) W 1-0	Wilson	8,224
Jan 31	Manchester City	(Rd4) W 3-2	Brennan, Wilson, Humes	11,027
Mar 11	Blackburn Rovers	(Rd5) L 0-3		12,060

Play-offs

May 14	CHARLTON ATHLETIC	(SF/1L) D 0-0		18,465
May 17	Charlton Athletic	(SF/2L) L 1-2	McCall	11,234

MANAGER: Bobby Ferguson

CAPTAIN: Ian Atkins

TOP SCORER: Kevin Wilson

BIGGEST WIN: 4-1 v Reading (A), 13 December 1986, Division Two

HIGHEST ATTENDANCE: 18,670 v Portsmouth, 7 February 1987, Division Two

MAJOR TRANSFERS IN: John Deehan from Norwich City

MAJOR TRANSFERS OUT: Paul Cooper to Leicester City; Irvin Gernon to Northampton Town; Steve McCall to Sheffield Wednesday; Tommy Parkin to Grimsby; Kevin Wilson to Chelsea

League & Cup Appearances

PLAYER	LEAGUE	CUP COMPETITION		OTHER	TOTAL
		FA CUP	LC		
Atkins	40	1	3	6	50
Atkinson	3 (5)		1 (1)	0 (1)	4 (7)
Brennan	37	1	3	7	48
Cole	11 (5)	1	1	1 (1)	14 (6)
Cooper	36	1	3	5	45
Cranson	32	0 (1)	1	5	38 (1)
D'Avray	14 (5)		0 (1)	0 (2)	14 (8)
Deehan	29	1	3	5	38
Dozzell	42	1	3	7	53
Gernon	3		1		4
Gleghorn	28 (3)	1	3	3	35 (3)
Hallworth	6			2	8
Humes	21 (1)		1	5	27 (1)
McCall	26	1	1	5	33
O'Donnell	8 (2)	2	3 (2)		13 (4)
Parkin	1 (2)		1 (1)		2 (3)
Rimmer	0 (1)		1		1 (1)
Stockwell	16 (5)	1(1)	2 (1)		19 (7)
Wilson	42	1	3	7	53
Yallop	30 (1)	1	1	5 (1)	37 (2)
Zondervan	39	1	2	6	48

Goalscorers

PLAYER	LEAGUE	CUP COMPETITION		OTHER	TOTAL
		FA CUP	LC		
Wilson	20		1	4	25
Deehan	10		1	1	12
Brennan	7		1	1	9
Gleghorn	7			1	8
D'Avray	4				4
Dozzell	2		1	1	4
Humes	2			1	3
Cole	2				2
Cranson	2				2
Atkins	1				1
Stockwell	1				1
Zondervan	1				1
McCall				1	1

Fact File

Ipswich played the whole league season without conceding a goal at the North Stand end of the Portman Road ground.

Final Division Two Table

		P	W	D	L	F	A	Pts
1	DERBY CO	42	25	9	8	64	38	84
2	PORTSMOUTH	42	23	9	10	53	28	78
3	OLDHAM ATH	42	22	9	11	65	44	75
4	LEEDS U	42	19	11	12	58	44	68
5	IPSWICH TOWN	42	17	13	12	59	43	64
6	CRYSTAL PALACE	42	19	5	18	51	53	62
7	PLYMOUTH ARG	42	16	13	13	62	57	61
8	STOKE C	42	16	10	16	63	53	58
9	SHEFFIELD U	42	15	13	14	50	49	58
10	BRADFORD C	42	15	10	17	62	62	55
11	BARNSLEY	42	14	13	15	49	52	55
12	BLACKBURN R	42	15	10	17	45	55	55
13	READING	42	14	11	17	52	59	53
14	HULL C	42	13	14	15	41	55	53
15	WBA	42	13	12	17	51	49	51
16	MILLWALL	42	14	9	19	39	45	51
17	HUDDERSFIELD T	42	13	12	17	54	61	51
18	SHREWSBURY T	42	15	6	21	41	53	51
19	BIRMINGHAM C	42	11	17	14	47	59	50
20	SUNDERLAND	42	12	12	18	49	59	48
21	GRIMSBY T	42	10	14	18	39	59	44
22	BRIGHTON & HA	42	9	12	21	37	54	39

Season 1987-88

Football League Division Two

DATE	OPPONENTS	SCORE	GOALSCORERS	ATTENDANCE
Aug 15	ASTON VILLA	D 1-1	Gleghorn	14,580
Aug 18	Plymouth Argyle	D 0-0		11,901
Aug 22	Shrewsbury Town	D 0-0		3,611
Aug 29	STOKE CITY	W 2-0	Hemming o.g., Lowe	11,149
Sep 1	Blackburn Rovers	L 0-1		6,074
Sep 5	LEEDS UNITED	W 1-0	Lowe	11,163
Sep 12	Millwall	L 1-2	Brennan	6,356
Sep 19	SWINDON TOWN	W 3-2	Yallop (pen), Brennan, D'Avray	10,460
Sep 26	Crystal Palace	W 2-1	Cranson, Lowe	10,828
Sep 30	Leicester City	D 1-1	Woods	11,533
Oct 3	BARNSLEY	W 1-0	Lowe	10,992
Oct 10	Hull City	L 0-1		6,962
Oct 17	MANCHESTER CITY	W 3-0	Rimmer 2, Harbey	12,711
Oct 20	Middlesbrough	L 1-3	D'Avray	10,491
Oct 24	SHEFFIELD UNITED	W 1-0	Lowe	11,949
Oct 31	Bournemouth	D 1-1	Brennan	8,105
Nov 3	HUDDERSFIELD TOWN	W 3-0	Woods, Lowe, Brennan	9,984
Nov 7	READING	W 2-1	Lowe 2	11,508
Nov 14	West Bromwich Albion	D 2-2	Rimmer, Lowe	8,457
Nov 21	OLDHAM ATHLETIC	W 2-0	Brennan, Lowe	11,007
Nov 28	Birmingham City	L 0-1		6,718
Dec 5	BRADFORD CITY	W 4-0	Stockwell, Gleghorn, Zondervan 2 (2 pen)	13,707
Dec 18	SHREWSBURY TOWN	W 2-0	Zondervan (pen), D'Avray	9,930
Dec 26	CRYSTAL PALACE	L 2-3	Lowe 2	17,200
Dec 28	Swindon Town	L 2-4	Lowe, Brennan	12,429
Jan 1	Stoke City	W 2-1	Lowe, D'Avray	9,976
Jan 2	MILLWALL	D 1-1	D'Avray	13,710
Jan 16	Aston Villa	L 0-1		20,201
Jan 30	BLACKBURN ROVERS	L 0-2		12,803
Feb 6	Leeds United	L 0-1		19,564
Feb 13	PLYMOUTH ARGYLE	L 1-2	Deehan	10,476
Feb 20	LEICESTER CITY	L 0-2		11,084
Feb 27	Barnsley	W 3-2	Atkinson 2, Atkins (pen)	6,482
Mar 5	Manchester City	L 0-2		17,402
Mar 12	HULL CITY	W 2-0	Woods, Lowe	9,728
Mar 19	BOURNEMOUTH	L 1-2	Woods	10,208
Mar 26	Sheffield United	L 1-4	Zondervan (pen)	8,753
Apr 2	Reading	D 1-1	Lowe	9,953
Apr 4	WEST BROMWICH ALBION	D 1-1	Yallop	10,665
Apr 8	Huddersfield Town	W 2-1	Atkinson 2	4,023
Apr 23	MIDDLESBROUGH	W 4-0	Atkinson 3, D'Avray	12,773
Apr 30	Oldham Athletic	L 1-3	D'Avray	5,018
May 2	BIRMINGHAM CITY	W 1-0	Atkinson	11,067
May 7	Bradford City	W 3-2	D'Avray, Dozzell, Milton	16,017

FA Cup

Jan 10	MANCHESTER UNITED	(Rd3) L 1-2	Humes	23,012

League Cup

Sep 22	NORTHAMPTON TOWN	(Rd2/1L) D 1-1	Zondervan	8,645
Oct 7	Northampton Town	(Rd2/2L) W 4-2	Harbey, D'Avray 2, Lowe	8,316
Oct 27	SOUTHEND UNITED	(Rd3) W 1-0	Harbey	13,444
Nov 17	LUTON TOWN	(Rd4) L 0-1		15,643

Full Members Cup

Nov 10	MIDDLESBROUGH	(Rd1) W 1-0	Woods	6,108
Dec 1	WEST BROMWICH ALBION	(Rd2) W 2-1	Zondervan, Gleghorn	5,308
Jan 25	WATFORD	(Rd3) W 5-2	Lowe, D'Avray, Wark 2, Deehan	7,460
Feb 9	Coventry City	(QF) L 0-2		7,607

MANAGER: John Duncan

CAPTAIN: Ian Cranson/Ian Atkins/Romeo Zondervan

TOP SCORER: David Lowe

BIGGEST WIN: 4-0 v Bradford City (H), 5 December 1987, Division Two; 4-0 v Middlesbrough (H), 23 April 1988, Division Two

HIGHEST ATTENDANCE: 23,012 v Manchester United, 10 January 1988, FA Cup 3rd Round

MAJOR TRANSFERS IN: Graham Harbey from Derby County; David Lowe from Wigan; Neil Woods from Rangers

MAJOR TRANSFERS OUT: Ian Atkins to Birmingham; Mark Brennan to Middlesbrough; Ian Cranson to Sheffield Wednesday; Nigel Gleghorn to Manchester City; Jon Hallworth to Oldham Athletic

League & Cup Appearances

PLAYER	LEAGUE	CUP COMPETITION FA CUP	CUP COMPETITION LC	OTHER	TOTAL
Atkins	13 (3)	1	1	3	18 (3)
Atkinson	13 (4)		1		14 (4)
Bernal	4 (5)			0 (2)	4 (7)
Brennan	34 (2)	1	4	4	43 (2)
Carson	1				1
Cole	1 (1)				1 (1)
Cranson	29	1	3	2	35
D'Avray	26 (3)	1	4	1 (1)	3 (4)
Deehan	16 (4)	0 (1)		2 (2)	18 (7)
Dozzell	35 (4)	1	4	2	42 (4)
Fearon	10				10
Gleghorn	11 (5)	0 (1)	0 (1)	2 (2)	1 (9)
Hallworth	33	1	4	4	42
Harbey	34 (1)	1	4	4	43 (1)
Humes	23 (4)	1	2	4	30 (4)
Lowe	41	1	3	3	48
Milton	7 (1)	0 (2)			7 (3)
O'Donnell	1 (1)				1 (1)
Rimmer	18 (1)	3	0 (1)		21 (2)
Stockwell	42 (1)	0 (1)	4	4	50 (2)
Wark	5 (2)		2		7 (2)
Wilson	5 (1)				5 (1)
Woods	12 (7)			2	14 (7)
Yallop	41	1	4	4	50
Zondervan	29	1	3	1	34

Goalscorers

PLAYER	LEAGUE	CUP COMPETITION FA CUP	CUP COMPETITION LC	OTHER	TOTAL
Lowe	17		1	1	19
D'Avray	7		2	1	10
Atkinson	8				8
Brennan	6				6
Zondervan	4	1		1	6
Woods	4			1	5
Gleghorn	2			1	3
Harbey	1		2		3
Rimmer	3				3
Deehan	1			1	2
Wark				2	2
Yallop	2				2
Atkins	1				1
Cranson	1				1
Dozzell	1				1
Humes	1				1
Milton	1				1
Stockwell	1				1
Opp's o.gs.	1				1

Fact File

Dalian Atkinson scored 6 goals in the last 5 games of the season to register 8 in all.

Final Division Two Table

		P	W	D	L	F	A	Pts
1	MILLWALL	44	25	7	12	72	52	82
2	ASTON VILLA	44	22	12	10	68	41	78
3	MIDDLESBROUGH	44	22	12	10	63	36	78
4	BRADFORD C	44	22	11	11	74	54	77
5	BLACKBURN R	44	21	14	9	68	52	77
6	CRYSTAL PALACE	44	22	9	13	86	59	75
7	LEEDS U	44	19	12	13	61	51	69
8	IPSWICH TOWN	44	19	9	16	61	52	66
9	MANCHESTER C	44	19	8	17	80	60	65
10	OLDHAM ATH	44	18	11	15	72	64	65
11	STOKE C	44	17	11	16	50	57	62
12	SWINDON T	44	16	11	17	73	60	59
13	LEICESTER C	44	16	11	17	62	61	59
14	BARNSLEY	44	15	12	17	61	62	57
15	HULL C	44	14	15	15	54	60	57
16	PLYMOUTH ARG	44	16	8	20	65	67	56
17	BOURNEMOUTH	44	13	10	21	56	68	49
18	SHREWSBURY T	44	11	16	17	42	54	49
19	BIRMINGHAM C	44	11	15	18	41	66	48
20	WBA	44	12	11	21	50	69	47
21	SHEFFIELD U	44	13	7	24	45	74	46
22	READING	44	10	12	22	44	70	42
23	HUDDERSFIELD T	44	6	10	28	41	100	28

Season 1988-89

Football League Division Two

DATE	OPPONENTS	SCORE	GOALSCORERS	ATTENDANCE
Aug 27	Stoke City	D 1-1	Humes	8,639
Sep 3	SUNDERLAND	W 2-0	Atkinson, Dozzell	12,835
Sep 10	Leicester City	W 1-0	Atkinson	10,816
Sep 17	WATFORD	W 3-2	Milton, Atkinson, Lowe	14,644
Sep 20	Shrewsbury Town	W 5-1	Milton 3, Dozzell, Yallop	4,154
Sep 24	BRADFORD CITY	D 1-1	Atkinson	13,074
Oct 1	West Bromwich Albion	W 2-1	Lowe, Dozzell	9,357
Oct 4	Crystal Palace	L 0-2		10,325
Oct 8	MANCHESTER CITY	W 1-0	Dozzell	15,521
Oct 15	OXFORD UNITED	L 1-2	Dozzell	13,039
Oct 22	Barnsley	L 0-2		6,325
Oct 25	PORTSMOUTH	L 0-1		14,796
Oct 29	Bournemouth	L 0-1		6,648
Nov 5	LEEDS UNITED	L 0-1		11,755
Nov 8	WALSALL	W 3-1	Wark 2 (2 pen), Stockwell	9,067
Nov 12	Swindon Town	W 3-2	Atkinson, Dozzell, Zondervan	7,246
Nov 19	BRIGHTON & HOVE ALBION	L 2-3	Lowe, Stockwell	12,386
Nov 26	Birmingham City	L 0-1		5,932
Dec 3	PLYMOUTH ARGYLE	D 2-2	Lowe, D'Avray	9,929
Dec 10	Blackburn Rovers	L 0-1		7,258
Dec 16	OLDHAM ATHLETIC	W 2-1	Dozzell, Wark	8,982
Dec 26	Chelsea	L 0-3		17,621
Dec 31	Hull City	D 1-1	Redford	7,800
Jan 2	LEICESTER CITY	W 2-0	Linighan, Milton	14,037
Jan 14	Walsall	W 4-2	Wark (pen), Dozzell, Kiwomya, Redford	4,623
Jan 21	STOKE CITY	W 5-1	Baltacha, Dozzell 2, Kiwomya, Yallop	14,692
Feb 4	CRYSTAL PALACE	L 1-2	Wark	14,569
Feb 11	Manchester City	L 0-4		22,145
Feb 21	BARNSLEY	W 2-0	Dozzell, Milton	9,995
Feb 25	Oxford United	D 1-1	Linighan	6,086
Feb 28	Portsmouth	W 1-0	Milton	7,145
Mar 4	SWINDON TOWN	L 1-2	Milton	11,542
Mar 11	Leeds United	W 4-2	Atkinson, Milton, Wark 2 (1 pen)	19,639
Mar 14	BOURNEMOUTH	W 3-1	Wark, Atkinson 2	10,747
Mar 18	SHREWSBURY TOWN	W 2-0	Atkinson 2	10,913
Mar 25	Sunderland	L 0-4		13,859
Mar 28	CHELSEA	L 0-1		22,950
Apr 1	Watford	L 2-3	Milton, Wark	12,054
Apr 4	Oldham Athletic	L 0-4		5,182
Apr 8	HULL CITY	D 1-1	Swan o.g.	10,191
Apr 15	Bradford City	D 2-2	D'Avray, Zondervan	9,691
Apr 22	West Bromwich Albion	W 2-1	Humes, Wark (pen)	12,047
Apr 29	BIRMINGHAM CITY	W 4-0	Wark, Lowe 2, Zondervan	9,975
May 1	Plymouth Argyle	W 1-0	Humes	6,484
May 6	Brighton & Hove Albion	W 1-0	D'Avray	8,616
May 13	BLACKBURN ROVERS	W 2-0	Wark 2 (2 pen)	10,861

FA Cup

Jan 7	Nottingham Forest	(Rd3) L 0-3		20,743

League Cup

Sep 26	Port Vale	(Rd2/1L) L 0-1		6,545
Oct 10	PORT VALE	(Rd2/2L) W 3-0	Dozzell, Atkinson 2	8,869
Nov 1	LEYTON ORIENT	(Rd3) W 2-0	Stockwell, Dozzell	9,751
Nov 30	Aston Villa	(Rd4) L 2-6	Atkinson, Stockwell	16,284

Full Members Cup

Nov 23	Oxford United	(Rd1) W 3-2	Lowe 2, Zondervan	1,560
Dec 20	NORWICH CITY	(Rd2) W 1-0	Milton	18,024
Jan 10	BLACKBURN ROVERS	(Rd3) W 1-0	Stockwell	8,115
Jan 24	NOTTINGHAM FOREST	(QF) L 1-3	Dozzell	16,495

MANAGER: John Duncan

CAPTAIN: Romeo Zondervan

TOP SCORERS: Dalian Atkinson/Jason Dozzell/John Wark

BIGGEST WIN: 5-1 v Shrewsbury Town (A), 20 September 1988 Division Two; 5-1 v Stoke City (H), 21 January 1989 Division Two

HIGHEST ATTENDANCE: 22,950 v Chelsea, 28 March 1989

MAJOR TRANSFERS IN: Sergei Baltacha from Dinamo Kiev; David Hill from Scunthorpe; David Linighan from Shrewsbury Town; Ian Redford from Dundee United

MAJOR TRANSFERS OUT: Dalian Atkinson to Sheffield Wednesday

League & Cup Appearances

PLAYER	LEAGUE	CUP COMPETITION		OTHER	TOTAL
		FA CUP	LC		
Atkinson	33 (1)		3	2	38 (1)
Baltacha	19 (1)			1	20 (1)
Cheetham	1 (2)	0 (1)		0 (1)	1 (4)
D'Avray	24 (8)		2	1 (2)	27 (10)
Dozzell	29	1	3	4	37
Fearon	18	1		2	21
Forrest	28		4	2	34
Gregory	0 (2)			0 (1)	0 (3)
Harbey	19 (4)	1	3 (1)	4	27 (5)
Hill	35 (1)	1	2 (1)	3	41 (2)
Humes	26		2		28
Johnson	4				4
Juryeff	0 (2)				0 (2)
Kiwomya	16 (10)	1	1	2	20 (10)
Linighan	40 (1)	1	3	3	47 (1)
Lowe	30 (2)		4	2 (1)	36 (3)
Mayes				0 (1)	0 (1)
Milton	25 (10)		3	1 (1)	29 (11)
O'Donnell	1 (1)	0 (1)	1	1	3 (2)
Redford	22 (2)	1	1	3	27 (2)
Stockwell	20 (3)	1	4	3	28 (3)
Wark	41	1	3	4	49
Woods	0 (1)				0 (1)
Yallop	38 (2)	1	3	4	46 (2)
Zondervan	37	1	2	2	42

Goalscorers

PLAYER	LEAGUE	CUP COMPETITION		OTHER	TOTAL
		FA CUP	LC		
Atkinson	10		3		13
Dozzell	11	1		1	13
Wark	13				13
Milton	10			1	11
Lowe	6	1		2	9
Stockwell	2	2		1	5
Zondervan	3		1		4
Dozzell	3				3
Humes	3				3
Kiwomya	2				2
Linighan	2				2
Redford	2				2
Yallop	2				2
Baltacha	1				1
Opp's o.gs.	1				1

Fact File

Sergei Baltacha became the first Russian to play in the Football League when he made a scoring debut against Stoke City in January 1989.

Final Division Two Table

		P	W	D	L	F	A	Pts
1	CHELSEA	46	29	12	5	96	50	99
2	MANCHESTER C	46	23	13	10	77	53	82
3	CRYSTAL PALACE	46	23	12	11	71	49	81
4	WATFORD	46	22	12	12	74	48	78
5	BLACKBURN R	46	22	11	13	74	59	77
6	SWINDON T	46	20	16	10	68	53	76
7	BARNSLEY	46	20	14	12	66	58	74
8	IPSWICH TOWN	46	22	7	17	71	61	73
9	WBA	46	18	18	10	65	41	72
10	LEEDS U	46	17	16	13	59	50	67
11	SUNDERLAND	46	16	15	15	60	60	63
12	BOURNEMOUTH	46	18	8	20	53	62	62
13	STOKE C	46	15	14	17	57	72	59
14	BRADFORD C	46	13	17	16	52	59	56
15	LEICESTER C	46	13	16	17	56	63	55
16	OLDHAM ATH	46	11	21	14	75	72	54
17	OXFORD U	46	14	12	20	62	70	54
18	PLYMOUTH ARG	46	14	12	20	55	66	54
19	BRIGHTON & HA	46	14	9	23	57	66	51
20	PORTSMOUTH	46	13	12	21	53	62	51
21	HULL C	46	11	14	21	52	68	47
22	SHREWSBURY T	46	8	18	20	40	67	42
23	BIRMINGHAM C	46	8	11	27	31	76	35
24	WALSALL	46	5	16	25	41	80	31

Season 1989-90

Football League Division Two

DATE	OPPONENTS	SCORE	GOALSCORERS	ATTENDANCE
Aug 19	BARNSLEY	W 3-1	Woods, Humes, Lowe	12,100
Aug 22	Sunderland	W 4-2	Lowe 2, Milton, Dozzell	15,965
Aug 26	Sheffield United	L 0-2		13,600
Sep 2	BOURNEMOUTH	D 1-1	Dozzell	11,425
Sep 9	Leeds United	D 1-1	Milton	22,972
Sep 16	WOLVERHAMPTON WANDERERS	L 1-3	Westley o.g.	14,324
Sep 23	Oxford United	D 2-2	Redford, Penney o.g.	5,131
Sep 27	Brighton & Hove Albion	L 0-1		9,770
Sep 30	STOKE CITY	D 2-2	D'Avray, Dozzell	10,389
Oct 7	NEWCASTLE UNITED	W 2-1	Wark (pen), Lowe	13,679
Oct 14	Swindon Town	L 0-3		8,039
Oct 18	Bradford City	L 0-1		7,350
Oct 21	PLYMOUTH ARGYLE	W 3-0	Kiwomya 2, Milton	10,362
Oct 28	Portsmouth	W 3-2	Milton 2, Dozzell	7,914
Oct 31	WATFORD	W 1-0	Thompson (pen)	12,587
Nov 4	WEST BROMWICH ALBION	W 3-1	Kiwomya, Lowe, Milton	12,028
Nov 11	Blackburn Rovers	D 2-2	May o.g, Wark (pen)	7,913
Nov 18	Leicester City	W 1-0	Stockwell	11,664
Nov 25	OLDHAM ATHLETIC	D 1-1	Kiwomya	12,304
Dec 2	Barnsley	W 1-0	Humes	6,097
Dec 9	SUNDERLAND	D 1-1	Wark	13,833
Dec 26	WEST HAM UNITED	W 1-0	Stockwell	24,365
Dec 30	MIDDLESBROUGH	W 3-0	Stockwell, Humes, Donowa	14,290
Jan 1	Port Vale	L 0-5		8,617
Jan 13	SHEFFIELD UNITED	D 1-1	Lowe	16,787
Jan 20	Bournemouth	L 1-3	Thompson (pen)	7,464
Feb 10	Wolverhampton Wanderers	L 1-2	Dozzell	18,781
Feb 17	LEEDS UNITED	D 2-2	Kiwomya, Wark	17,102
Feb 24	Oldham Athletic	L 1-4	Wark	10,193
Mar 3	LEICESTER CITY	D 2-2	Wark, Lowe	12,237
Mar 6	Stoke City	D 0-0		10,815
Mar 10	BRIGHTON & HOVE ALBION	W 2-1	Wark, Milton	10,886
Mar 13	OXFORD UNITED	W 1-0	Pennyfather	10,380
Mar 17	Newcastle United	L 1-2	Milton	20,521
Mar 20	SWINDON TOWN	W 1-0	Dozzell	11,856
Mar 24	BRADFORD CITY	W 1-0	Wark	11,074
Mar 31	Plymouth Argyle	L 0-1		6,793
Apr 7	Watford	D 3-3	Stuart 2, Wark	11,158
Apr 10	PORTSMOUTH	L 0-1		11,062
Apr 14	PORT VALE	W 3-2	Wark, Dozzell, Thompson (pen)	10,509
Apr 17	West Ham United	L 0-2		25,178
Apr 21	HULL CITY	L 0-1		9,380
Apr 25	Middlesbrough	W 2-1	Lowe, Milton	15,233
Apr 28	BLACKBURN ROVERS	W 3-1	Milton, Lowe 2	11,007
May 1	Hull City	L 3-4	Lowe 2, Redford	5,306
May 5	West Bromwich Albion	W 3-1	Lowe, Milton, Dozzell	11,567

FA Cup

Jan 6	Leeds United	(Rd3)	W 1-0	Dozzell	26,766
Jan 27	Barnsley	(Rd4)	L 0-2		14,440

League Cup

Sep 19	TRANMERE ROVERS	(Rd2/1L)	L 0-1		7,757
Oct 3	Tranmere Rovers	(Rd2/2L)	L 0-1		10,050

Full Members Cup

Nov 21	WATFORD	(Rd2)	W 4-1	Gregory 3, Redford	5,078
Dec 21	WIMBLEDON	(Rd3)	W 3-1	Milton, Thompson (pen), Johnson	7,918
Jan 23	CHELSEA	(SSF)	L 2-3	Donowa, Gregory	13,365

MANAGER: John Duncan

CAPTAIN: Romeo Zondervan

TOP SCORER: David Lowe

BIGGEST WIN: 4-2 v Sunderland (A), 22 August 1989, Division Two

HIGHEST ATTENDANCE: 24,365 v West Ham United, 28 December 1989, Division Two

MAJOR TRANSFERS IN: Louie Donowa from Willem II; Brian Gayle from Manchester City; Glenn Pennyfather from Crystal Palace; Neil Thompson from Scarborough Town

MAJOR TRANSFERS OUT: Sergei Baltacha to St Johnstone; Louie Donowa to Bristol City; Mich D'Avray to Leicester City; Graham Harbey to WBA; Neil Woods to Bradford City

League & Cup Appearances

PLAYER	LEAGUE	CUP COMPETITION		OTHER	TOTAL
		FA CUP	LC		
Baltacha	3 (5)		1		4 (5)
Cheetham	0 (1)				0 (1)
D'Avray	8 (4)		1		9 (4)
Donowa	17 (6)	2	0 (2)	2 (1)	21 (9)
Dozzell	46	2	2	3	53
Forrest	45	2	2	3	52
Gayle	20	0 (1)			20 (1)
Gregory	1 (3)	1		2	4 (3)
Harbey	0 (1)				0 (1)
Hill	1 (1)		1		2 (1)
Humes	17 (7)	2	2		21 (7)
Johnson	3 (3)		0 (1)	0 (1)	3 (5)
Kiwomya	19 (10)	1	1	1	21 (10)
Linighan	41	1	2	1	47
Lowe	31 (3)	1	2	1	35 (3)
Meade	0 (1)				0 (1)
Milton	41	2	1	3	47
Neville	1				1
Palmer	3 (2)		2		5 (2)
Pennyfather	7 (1)		0 (1)		7 (2)
Redford	14 (4)	1		1	16 (4)
Stockwell	34	2	1	2 (1)	39 (1)
Stuart	5				5
Thompson	44 (1)	2	2	3	51 (1)
Wark	41	2	1	3	47
Woods	3 (4)			2	5 (4)
Yallop	31	1 (1)	0 (1)	3	35 (2)
Zondervan	30		2	1	33

Goalscorers

PLAYER	LEAGUE	CUP COMPETITION		OTHER	TOTAL
		FA CUP	LC		
Lowe	13				13
Milton	11			1	12
Wark	10				10
Dozzell	8	1			9
Kiwomya	5				5
Gregory				4	4
Thompson	3			1	4
Humes	3				3
Redford	2			1	3
Stockwell	3				3
Donowa	1			1	2
Stuart	2				2
D'Aray	1				1
Johnson				1	1
Pennyfather	1				1
Woods	1				1
Opp's o.gs.	3				3

Final Division Two Table

		P	W	D	L	F	A	Pts
1	LEEDS U	46	24	13	9	79	52	85
2	SHEFFIELD U	46	24	13	9	78	58	85
3	NEWCASTLE U	46	22	14	10	80	55	80
4	SWINDON T	46	20	14	12	79	59	74
5	BLACKBURN R	46	19	17	10	74	59	74
6	SUNDERLAND	46	20	14	12	70	64	74
7	WEST HAM U	46	20	12	14	80	57	72
8	OLDHAM ATH	46	19	14	13	70	57	71
9	IPSWICH TOWN	46	19	12	15	67	66	69
10	WOLVERHAMPTON W	46	18	13	15	67	60	67
11	PORT VALE	46	15	16	15	62	57	61
12	PORTSMOUTH	46	15	16	15	62	65	61
13	LEICESTER C	46	15	14	17	67	79	59
14	HULL C	46	14	16	16	58	65	58
15	WATFORD	46	14	15	17	58	60	57
16	PLYMOUTH ARG	46	14	13	19	58	63	55
17	OXFORD U	46	15	9	22	57	66	54
18	BRIGHTON & HA	46	15	9	22	56	72	54
19	BARNSLEY	46	13	15	18	49	71	54
20	WBA	46	12	15	19	67	71	51
21	MIDDLESBROUGH	46	13	11	22	52	63	50
22	BOURNEMOUTH	46	12	12	22	57	76	48
23	BRADFORD C	46	9	14	23	44	68	41
24	STOKE C	46	6	19	21	35	63	37

Season 1990-91

Football League Division Two

DATE	OPPONENTS	SCORE	GOALSCORERS	ATTENDANCE
Aug 25	SHEFFIELD WEDNESDAY	L 0-2		17,284
Aug 28	Swindon Town	L 0-1		10,817
Sep 1	West Bromwich Albion	W 2-1	Humes, Thompson	10,318
Sep 8	BLACKBURN ROVERS	W 2-1	Gregory, Stockwell	10,953
Sep 15	Millwall	D 1-1	Kiwomya	12,604
Sep 19	West Ham United	L 1-3	Milton	18,764
Sep 22	BRISTOL ROVERS	W 2-1	Gayle, Kiwomya	11,084
Sep 29	WATFORD	D 1-1	Gayle	11,351
Oct 2	Barnsley	L 1-5	Thompson (pen)	6,934
Oct 6	Plymouth Argyle	D 0-0		5,935
Oct 13	PORT VALE	W 3-0	Milton 2, Stockwell	10,369
Oct 20	NEWCASTLE UNITED	W 2-1	Gayle, Milton	15,567
Oct 23	Oldham Athletic	L 0-2		13,170
Oct 27	Leicester City	W 2-1	Stockwell 2	11,053
Nov 3	BRIGHTON & HOVE ALBION	L 1-3	Stockwell	11,437
Nov 10	Hull City	D 3-3	Dozzell, Redford, Kiwomya	5,294
Nov 17	NOTTS COUNTY	D 0-0		10,778
Nov 24	BRISTOL CITY	D 1-1	Dozzell	10,037
Dec 1	Wolverhampton Wanderers	D 2-2	Dozzell, Redford	15,803
Dec 8	SWINDON TOWN	D 1-1	Redford (pen)	9,358
Dec 15	Sheffield Wednesday	D 2-2	Milton, Redford	19,333
Dec 21	Portsmouth	D 1-1	Palmer	7,010
Dec 26	MIDDLESBROUGH	L 0-1		12,508
Dec 29	CHARLTON ATHLETIC	D 4-4	Stockwell, Thompson, Dozzell, Milton	11,719
Jan 1	Oxford United	L 1-2	Thompson	5,103
Jan 12	WEST BROMWICH ALBION	W 1-0	Whitton	11,036
Jan 19	Blackburn Rovers	W 1-0	Whitton	8,256
Feb 2	MILLWALL	L 0-3		13,338
Feb 23	HULL CITY	W 2-0	Goddard 2	9,900
Mar 2	WOLVERHAMPTON WANDERERS	D 0-0		13,350
Mar 9	Bristol City	L 2-4	Dozzell, Goddard	11,474
Mar 16	Watford	D 1-1	Linighan	7,732
Mar 18	Port Vale	W 2-1	Glover o.g., Thompson	5,820
Mar 22	PLYMOUTH ARGYLE	W 3-1	Morgan o.g, Goddard 2	9,842
Mar 30	Middlesbrough	D 1-1	Linighan	15,140
Apr 2	PORTSMOUTH	D 2-2	Dozzell, Thompson (pen)	11,314
Apr 6	Charlton Athletic	D 1-1	Linighan	6,443
Apr 10	Bristol Rovers	L 0-1		4,983
Apr 13	OXFORD UNITED	D 1-1	Kiwomya	9,135
Apr 17	WEST HAM UNITED	L 0-1		20,290
Apr 20	Newcastle United	D 2-2	Kiwomya 2	17,638
Apr 25	BARNSLEY	W 2-0	Kiwomya, Goddard	7,379
Apr 27	OLDHAM ATHLETIC	L 1-2	Kiwomya	12,332
May 4	LEICESTER CITY	W 3-2	Houghton, Gayle, Kiwomya	11,347
May 7	Notts County	L 1-3	Humes	6,902
May 11	Brighton & Hove Albion	L 1-2	Kiwomya	12,281

FA Cup

Jan 5	Southampton	(Rd3) L 2-3	Dozzell 2	15,101

League Cup

Sep 25	Shrewsbury Town	(Rd2/1L) D 1-1	Redford	2,764
Oct 9	SHREWSBURY TOWN	(Rd2/2L) W 3-0	Redford, Kiwomya, Milton	7,306
Oct 30	SOUTHAMPTON	(Rd3) L 0-2		15,573

Full Members Cup

Dec 12	Wimbledon	(Rd2) W 2-0	Redford, Kiwomya	1,787
Jan 22	OXFORD UNITED	(Rd3) W 2-1	Milton, Dozzell	7,465
Feb 27	Norwich City	(SSF) L 0-2		16,225

MANAGER: John Lyall

CAPTAIN: David Linighan

TOP SCORER: Chris Kiwomya

BIGGEST WIN: 3-0 v Shrewsbury Town (H), 9 October 1990, League Cup; 3-0 v Port Vale (H), 13 October 1990, Division Two

HIGHEST ATTENDANCE: 20,290 v West Ham United, 17 April 1991, Division Two

MAJOR TRANSFERS IN: Paul Goddard from Millwall; Steve Whitton from Sheffield Wednesday

MAJOR TRANSFERS OUT: David Hill to Scunthorpe

League & Cup Appearances

PLAYER	LEAGUE	CUP COMPETITION		OTHER	TOTAL
		FA CUP	LC		
Dozzell	27 (3)	1	0 (1)	3	31 (4)
Forrest	43	1		3	50
Gayle	33		3		36
Goddard	18 (1)			1	19 (1)
Gregory	14 (7)	3		0 (1)	17 (8)
Hill	18 (5)		3		21 (5)
Houghton	7 (1)				7 (1)
Humes	15 (1)			1	16 (1)
Johnson	5 (2)			2	7 (2)
Kiwomya	34 (3)	1	3	1	39 (3)
Linighan	45	1	3	2	51
Lowe	12 (1)	1		2	15 (1)
Milton	27 (4)	1	3	3	34 (4)
Palmer	18 (5)	1		2 (1)	21 (6)
Parkes	3				3
Pennyfather		0 (1)			0 (1)
Redford	23 (3)	1	3	1	28 (3)
Stockwell	44	1	3	3	51
Thompson	33 (5)	1	0 (1)	2	36 (6)
Whitton	10			2	12
Yallop	44 (1)	1	3	3	51 (1)
Zondervan	33 (1)		3	2	38 (1)

Goalscorers

PLAYER	LEAGUE	CUP COMPETITION		OTHER	TOTAL
		FA CUP	LC		
Kiwomya	10			1	12
Dozzell	6	2		1	9
Milton	6		1	1	8
Redford	4		2	1	7
Goddard	6				6
Stockwell	6				6
Thompson	6				6
Gayle	4				4
Linighan	3				3
Humes	2				2
Whitton	2				2
Gregory	1				1
Houghton	1				1
Palmer	1				1
Opp's o.gs.	2				2

Fact File

Phil Parkes played in the last three games of the season and conceded a penalty in each game.

Final Division Two Table

		P	W	D	L	F	A	Pts
1	OLDHAM ATH	46	25	13	8	83	53	88
2	WEST HAM U	46	24	15	7	60	34	87
3	SHEFFIELD W	46	22	16	7	80	51	82
4	NOTTS CO	46	23	11	12	76	55	80
5	MILLWALL	46	20	13	13	70	51	73
6	BRIGHTON & HA	46	21	7	18	63	69	70
7	MIDDLESBROUGH	46	20	9	17	66	47	69
8	BARNSLEY	46	19	12	15	63	48	69
9	BRISTOL C	46	20	7	19	68	71	67
10	OXFORD U	46	14	19	13	69	66	61
11	NEWCASTLE U	46	14	17	15	49	56	59
12	WOLVERHAMPTON W	46	13	19	14	63	63	58
13	BRISTOL R	46	15	13	18	56	59	58
14	IPSWICH TOWN	46	13	18	15	60	68	57
15	PORT VALE	46	15	12	19	56	64	57
16	CHARLTON ATH	46	13	17	16	57	61	56
17	PORTSMOUTH	46	14	11	21	58	70	53
18	PLYMOUTH ARG	46	12	17	17	54	68	53
19	BLACKBURN R	46	14	10	22	51	66	52
20	WATFORD	46	12	15	19	45	59	51
21	SWINDON T	46	12	14	20	65	73	50
22	LEICESTER C	46	14	8	24	60	83	50
23	WBA	46	10	18	18	52	61	48
24	HULL C	46	10	15	21	57	85	45

Season 1991-92

Football League Division Two

DATE	OPPONENTS	SCORE	GOALSCORERS	ATTENDANCE
Aug 17	Bristol Rovers	D 3-3	Dozzell, Goddard, Stockwell	6,444
Aug 20	PORT VALE	W 2-1	Kiwomya, Thompson (pen)	8,937
Aug 24	MIDDLESBROUGH	W 2-1	Dozzell, Goddard	9,822
Aug 31	Blackburn Rovers	W 2-1	Kiwomya, Goddard	8,898
Sep 3	SWINDON TOWN	L 1-4	Kiwomya	11,002
Sep 7	SOUTHEND UNITED	W 1-0	Thompson (pen)	12,732
Sep 14	Barnsley	L 0-1		6,786
Sep 17	Newcastle United	D 1-1	Kiwomya	16,336
Sep 21	BRISTOL CITY	W 4-2	Thompson, Linighan, Kiwomya, Goddard	9,692
Sep 28	Grimsby Town	W 2-1	Lowe, Johnson	6,621
Oct 5	OXFORD UNITED	W 2-1	Milton, Whitton	9,922
Oct 12	Brighton & Hove Albion	D 2-2	Milton, Dozzell	9,010
Oct 19	MILLWALL	D 0-0		11,175
Oct 26	Portsmouth	D 1-1	Milton	8,007
Oct 30	Charlton Athletic	D 1-1	Whitton	6,939
Nov 2	Leicester City	D 2-2	Wark, Johnson	11,331
Nov 5	SUNDERLAND	L 0-1		9,768
Nov 9	CAMBRIDGE UNITED	L 1-2	Stockwell	20,586
Nov 16	Derby County	L 0-1		12,493
Nov 23	Wolverhampton Wanderers	W 2-1	Linighan, Dozzell	11,915
Nov 30	TRANMERE ROVERS	W 4-0	Milton, Thompson, Linighan, Wark (pen)	11,072
Dec 7	Plymouth Argyle	L 0-1		4,986
Dec 20	Swindon Town	D 0-0		7,404
Dec 26	CHARLTON ATHLETIC	W 2-0	Kiwomya 2	13,826
Dec 28	BLACKBURN ROVERS	W 2-1	Johnson, Dozzell	17,657
Jan 1	Port Vale	W 2-1	Kiwomya 2	8,075
Jan 11	Middlesbrough	L 0-1		15,104
Jan 18	BRISTOL ROVERS	W 1-0	Milton	10,435
Feb 1	Millwall	W 3-2	Dozzell, Thompson, Kiwomya	8,847
Feb 8	PORTSMOUTH	W 5-2	Dozzell 2, Kiwomya 2, Awford o.g.	13,494
Feb 21	Tranmere Rovers	W 1-0	Milton	9,161
Feb 29	PLYMOUTH ARGYLE	W 2-0	Kiwomya, Whitton	12,852
Mar 7	Watford	W 1-0	Whitton	9,199
Mar 14	LEICESTER CITY	D 0-0		16,174
Mar 17	WATFORD	L 1-2	Dozzell	12,484
Mar 21	Cambridge United	D 1-1	Milton	9,766
Mar 28	DERBY COUNTY	W 2-1	Dozzell 2	15,305
Mar 31	BARNSLEY	W 2-0	Kiwomya 2	14,148
Apr 4	Southend United	W 2-1	Whelan, Thompson	10,003
Apr 7	WOLVERHAMPTON WANDERERS	W 2-1	Whelan, Whitton (pen)	17,379
Apr 11	NEWCASTLE UNITED	W 3-2	Whitton (pen), Wark, Kiwomya	20,673
Apr 14	Sunderland	L 0-3		22,131
Apr 18	Bristol City	L 1-2	Whitton (pen)	16,931
Apr 21	GRIMSBY TOWN	D 0-0		22,393
Apr 25	Oxford United	D 1-1	Johnson	10,525
May 2	BRIGHTON & HOVE ALBION	W 3-1	Whitton 2 (1 pen), Johnson	26,803

FA Cup

Jan 4	HARTLEPOOL UNITED	(Rd3) D 1-1	Dozzell	12,507
Jan 15	Hartlepool United	(R) W 2-0	Dozzell, Milton	8,500
Feb 5	BOURNEMOUTH	(Rd4) W 3-0	Dozzell, Whitton, Kiwomya	17,193
Feb 16	LIVERPOOL	(Rd5) D 0-0		26,104
Feb 26	Liverpool	(R) L 2-3	Johnson, Dozzell	27,355

League Cup

Sep 25	Derby County	(Rd2/1L) D 0-0		10,215
Oct 8	DERBY COUNTY	(Rd2/2L) L 0-2		8,982

Full Members Cup

Oct 2	Bristol Rovers	(Rd1) W 3-1	Dozzell, Lowe 2	1,490
Oct 22	LUTON TOWN*	(Rd2)(aet) D 1-1	Lowe	5,750
Nov 26	Chelsea**	(SQF)(aet) D 2-2	Kiwomya 2	6,325

* won 2-1 on penalties; ** lost 3-4 on penalties

MANAGER: John Lyall

CAPTAIN: David Linighan

TOP SCORER: Chris Kiwomya

BIGGEST WIN: 4-0 v Tranmere Rovers (H), 30 November 1991, Division Two

HIGHEST ATTENDANCE: 26,803 v Brighton, 2 May 1992, Division Two

MAJOR TRANSFERS IN: Eddie Youds from Everton

MAJOR TRANSFERS OUT: Brian Gayle to Sheffield United; Tony Humes to Wrexham

League and Cup Appearances

PLAYER	LEAGUE	CUP COMPETITION		OTHER	TOTAL
		FA CUP	LC		
Dozzell	45	5	1	3	54
Edmonds	0 (2)			0 (1)	0 (3)
Forrest	46	5	2	3	56
Gayle	5				5
Goddard	19 (5)	0 (1)	1	1	21 (6)
Gregory	0 (1)		0 (1)	1	1 (2)
Humes	5				5
Johnson	33 (9)	5	1	1	40 (9)
Kiwomya	43	5	2	1	51
Linighan	36	5	2	2	45
Lowe	7 (7)		1	2 (1)	10 (8)
Milton	31 (3)	5	1	3	40 (3)
Moncur	5 (1)				5 (1)
Palmer	16 (7)	5		1 (1)	22 (8)
Pennyfather	2 (1)		0 (1)		2 (2)
Stockwell	46	5	2	2	55
Thompson	45	5	2	3	55
Wark	36 (1)	5	1	3	45 (1)
Whelan	8			1	9
Whitton	43	5	2	2	52
Yallop	9 (8)	0 (1)	2	2 (1)	13 (10)
Youds	1				1
Zondervan	25 (3)	0 (1)	2	2	29 (4)

Goalscorers

PLAYER	LEAGUE	CUP COMPETITION		OTHER	TOTAL
		FA CUP	LC		
Kiwomya	16	1		2	19
Dozzell	11	4		1	16
Whitton	9	1			10
Milton	7	1			8
Johnson	5	1			6
Thompson	6				6
Goddard	4				4
Lowe	1			3	4
Linighan	3				3
Wark	3				3
Stockwell	2				2
Whelan	2				2
Opp's o.gs.	1				1

Fact File

Paul Goddard's goal in Town's 2-1 win over Middlesbrough in August 1991 was Ipswich's 3,000th goal in the Football League.

Final Division Two Table

		P	W	D	L	F	A	Pts
1	Ipswich Town	46	24	12	10	70	50	84
2	Middlesbrough	46	23	11	12	58	41	80
3	Derby Co	46	23	9	14	69	51	78
4	Leicester C	46	23	8	15	62	55	77
5	Cambridge U	46	19	17	10	65	47	74
6	Blackburn R	46	21	11	14	70	53	74
7	Charlton Ath	46	20	11	15	54	48	71
8	Swindon T	46	18	15	13	69	55	69
9	Portsmouth	46	19	12	15	65	51	69
10	Watford	46	18	11	17	51	48	65
11	Wolverhampton W	46	18	10	18	61	54	64
12	Southend U	46	17	11	18	63	63	62
13	Bristol R	46	16	14	16	60	63	62
14	Tranmere R	46	14	19	13	56	56	61
15	Millwall	46	17	10	19	64	71	61
16	Barnsley	46	16	11	19	46	57	59
17	Bristol C	46	13	15	18	55	71	54
18	Sunderland	46	14	11	21	61	65	53
19	Grimsby T	46	14	11	21	47	62	53
20	Newcastle U	46	13	13	20	66	84	52
21	Oxford U	46	13	11	22	66	73	50
22	Plymouth Arg	46	13	9	24	42	64	48
23	Brighton & HA	46	12	11	23	56	77	47
24	Port Vale	46	10	15	21	42	59	45

Season 1992-93

FA Premier League

DATE	OPPONENTS	SCORE	GOALSCORERS	ATTENDANCE
Aug 15	ASTON VILLA	D 1-1	Johnson	16,818
Aug 18	Wimbledon	W 1-0	Johnson	4,954
Aug 22	Manchester United	D 1-1	Kiwomya	31,704
Aug 25	LIVERPOOL	D 2-2	Dozzell, Kiwomya	20,109
Aug 30	TOTTENHAM HOTSPUR	D 1-1	Wark	20,100
Sep 1	Middlesbrough	D 2-2	Wark, Goddard	14,255
Sep 5	Queens Park Rangers	D 0-0		12,806
Sep 12	WIMBLEDON	W 2-1	Stockwell 2	13,333
Sep 19	Oldham Athletic	L 2-4	Wark, Thompson	11,150
Sep 26	SHEFFIELD UNITED	D 0-0		16,353
Oct 3	LEEDS UNITED	W 4-2	Kiwomya, Wark 2 (1 pen), Dozzell	21,200
Oct 17	Chelsea	L 1-2	Whitton	16,072
Oct 24	CRYSTAL PALACE	D 2-2	Dozzell 2	17,861
Oct 31	Nottingham Forest	W 1-0	Dozzell	21,411
Nov 7	SOUTHAMPTON	D 0-0		15,722
Nov 21	Sheffield Wednesday	D 1-1	Kiwomya	24,270
Nov 28	EVERTON	W 1-0	Johnson	18,032
Dec 5	Coventry City	D 2-2	Kiwomya, Whitton (pen)	11,294
Dec 12	MANCHESTER CITY	W 3-1	Stockwell, Johnson, Goddard	16,833
Dec 21	Norwich City	W 2-0	Kiwomya, Thompson	20,032
Dec 26	Arsenal	D 0-0		26,198
Dec 28	BLACKBURN ROVERS	W 2-1	Guentchev, Kiwomya	21,431
Jan 9	OLDHAM ATHLETIC	L 1-2	Kiwomya	15,025
Jan 16	Sheffield United	L 0-3		16,758
Jan 27	Tottenham Hotspur	W 2-0	Yallop, Guentchev	23,738
Jan 30	MANCHESTER UNITED	W 2-1	Kiwomya, Yallop	22,068
Feb 6	Aston Villa	L 0-2		25,395
Feb 9	QUEENS PARK RANGERS	D 1-1	Thompson	17,354
Feb 20	Liverpool	D 0-0		36,680
Feb 27	Leeds United	L 0-1		28,848
Mar 2	MIDDLESBROUGH	L 0-1		15,430
Mar 10	SHEFFIELD WEDNESDAY	L 0-1		16,538
Mar 13	Southampton	L 3-4	Linighan, Goddard, Kiwomya	15,428
Mar 20	COVENTRY CITY	D 0-0		16,698
Mar 24	Everton	L 0-3		15,638
Apr 3	Manchester City	L 1-3	Johnson	20,680
Apr 6	CHELSEA	D 1-1	Guentchev	17,444
Apr 10	ARSENAL	L 1-2	Wark (pen)	20,358
Apr 12	Blackburn Rovers	L 1-2	Milton	14,071
Apr 19	NORWICH CITY	W 3-1	Dozzell 2, Stockwell	21,087
May 1	Crystal Palace	L 1-3	Gregory	18,881
May 8	NOTTINGHAM FOREST	W 2-1	Milton, Whitton (pen)	22,093

FA Cup

Jan 12	PLYMOUTH ARGYLE	(Rd3) W 3-1	Thompson, Dozzell, Whitton	12,803
Jan 23	Tranmere Rovers	(Rd4) W 2-1	Dozzell, Guentchev	13,683
Feb 13	GRIMSBY TOWN	(Rd5) W 4-0	Guentchev 3, Wark	17,894
Mar 6	ARSENAL	(Rd6) L 2-4	Kiwomya, Guentchev	22,054

League Cup

Sep 22	Wigan Athletic	(Rd2/1L) D 2-2	Johnson, Robertson o.g.	2,684
Oct 6	WIGAN ATHLETIC	(Rd 2/2L) W 4-0	Johnson, Kiwomya 3	7,305
Oct 27	Portsmouth	(Rd3) W 1-0	Thompson	10,773
Dec 2	Aston Villa	(Rd4) D 2-2	Kiwomya 2	21,545
Dec 15	ASTON VILLA	(R) W 1-0	Kiwomya	19,196
Jan 19	SHEFFIELD WEDNESDAY	(Rd5) D 1-1	Whitton (pen)	19,374
Feb 3	Sheffield Wednesday	(R) L 0-1		26,328

MANAGER: John Lyall

CAPTAIN: David Linighan

TOP SCORER: Chris Kiwomya

BIGGEST WIN: 4-0 v Wigan Athletic (H), 6 October 1992, League Cup 2nd Round; 4-0 v Grimsby Town (H), 13 February 1993, FA Cup 5th Round

HIGHEST ATTENDANCE: 22,093 v Nottingham Forest, 8 May 1993, FA Premier League

MAJOR TRANSFERS IN: Clive Baker from Coventry; Bontcho Guentchev from Sporting Lisbon; Geraint Williams from Derby County

MAJOR TRANSFERS OUT: Jason Dozzell to Tottenham Hotspur

League and Cup Appearances

PLAYER	LEAGUE	CUP COMPETITION		TOTAL
		FA CUP	LC	
Baker	30 (1)	4	5	39 (1)
Bozinoski	3 (6)	0 (1)	1 (1)	4 (8)
Dozzell	41	4	7	52
Forrest	11		2	13
Goddard	19 (6)	1 (1)	4	24 (7)
Gregory	1 (2)		0 (1)	1 (3)
Guentchev	19 (2)	4	2	25 (2)
Johnson	39 (1)	4	7	50 (1)
Kiwomya	38	3	7	48
Linighan	42	3	7	52
Milton	7 (5)			7 (5)
Palmer	4 (3)			4 (3)
Pennyfather	2 (2)		1	3 (2)
Petterson	1			1
Stockwell	38 (1)	3	5 (1)	46 (2)
Thompson	31	4	7	42
Wark	36 (1)	4	6 (1)	46 (2)
Whelan	28 (4)	2 (1)	5 (1)	35 (6)
Whitton	20 (4)	3	4	27 (4)
Williams	37	4	4 (1)	45 (1)
Yallop	5 (1)	1 (1)	2	8 (2)
Youds	10 (6)	0 (1)	1 (2)	11 (9)

Goalscorers

PLAYER	LEAGUE	CUP COMPETITION		TOTAL
		FA CUP	LC	
Kiwomya	10	1	6	17
Dozzell	7	2		9
Guentchev	3	5		8
Johnson	5		2	7
Wark	6	1		7
Thompson	3	1	1	5
Whitton	3	1	1	5
Stockwell	4			4
Goddard	3			3
Milton	2			2
Yallop	2			2
Gregory	1			1
Linighan	1			1
Opp's o.gs.		1		1

Fact File

Clive Baker became the club's first goalkeeper substitute when he replaced Whelan after Craig Forrest had been sent off early in the home game with Sheffield United in September 1992.

Final Premier League Table

		P	W	D	L	F	A	Pts
1	MANCHESTER U	42	24	12	6	67	31	84
2	ASTON VILLA	42	21	11	10	57	40	74
3	NORWICH CITY	42	21	9	12	61	65	72
4	BLACKBURN R	42	20	11	11	68	46	71
5	QPR	42	17	12	13	63	56	63
6	LIVERPOOL	42	16	11	15	62	55	59
7	SHEFFIELD W	42	15	14	13	55	51	59
8	TOTTENHAM H	42	16	11	15	60	66	59
9	MANCHESTER C	42	15	12	15	56	51	57
10	ARSENAL	42	15	11	16	40	38	56
11	CHELSEA	42	14	14	14	51	54	56
12	WIMBLEDON	42	14	12	16	57	47	54
13	EVERTON	42	15	8	19	53	55	53
14	SHEFFIELD U	42	14	10	18	54	53	52
15	COVENTRY C	42	13	13	16	52	57	52
16	IPSWICH TOWN	42	12	16	14	50	55	52
17	LEEDS UNITED	42	12	15	15	57	62	51
18	SOUTHAMPTON	42	13	11	18	54	61	50
19	OLDHAM A	42	13	10	19	63	74	49
20	CRYSTAL P	42	11	16	15	48	61	49
21	MIDDLESBROUGH	42	11	11	20	54	75	44
22	NOTTINGHAM F	42	10	10	22	41	62	40

Season 1993-94

FA Premier League

DATE	OPPONENTS	SCORE	GOALSCORERS	ATTENDANCE
Aug 14	Oldham Athletic	W 3-0	Marshall, Palmer, Mason	12,182
Aug 17	SOUTHAMPTON	W 1-0	Marshall	14,569
Aug 21	CHELSEA	W 1-0	Marshall	17,582
Aug 25	Norwich City	L 0-1		19,189
Aug 28	Sheffield United	D 1-1	Whitton	17,932
Aug 31	NEWCASTLE UNITED	D 1-1	Kiwomya	19,126
Sep 11	Arsenal	L 0-4		28,563
Sep 18	ASTON VILLA	L 1-2	Marshall	16,617
Sep 26	TOTTENHAM HOTSPUR	D 2-2	Milton, Marshall	19,411
Oct 2	Queens Park Rangers	L 0-3		12,292
Oct 17	LEEDS UNITED	D 0-0		17,548
Oct 25	Wimbledon	W 2-0	Mason, Stockwell	7,756
Oct 30	EVERTON	L 0-2		15,078
Nov 8	SHEFFIELD WEDNESDAY	L 1-4	Marshall	15,070
Nov 20	Swindon Town	D 2-2	Wark 2 (1 pen)	13,343
Nov 24	Manchester United	D 0-0		43,300
Nov 27	BLACKBURN ROVERS	W 1-0	Youds	14,582
Dec 4	OLDHAM ATHLETIC	D 0-0		12,004
Dec 8	Southampton	W 1-0	Kiwomya	9,028
Dec 11	Chelsea	D 1-1	Kiwomya	12,508
Dec 18	NORWICH CITY	W 2-1	Wark (pen), Megson o.g.	19,498
Dec 27	WEST HAM UNITED	D 1-1	Linighan	21,024
Jan 1	LIVERPOOL	L 1-2	Marshall	22,355
Jan 15	Leeds United	D 0-0		31,317
Jan 22	WIMBLEDON	D 0-0		12,372
Feb 2	Coventry City	L 0-1		11,265
Feb 5	Manchester City	L 1-2	Marshall	28,188
Feb 12	Everton	D 0-0		19,588
Feb 22	SHEFFIELD UNITED	W 3-2	Linighan, Marshall, Slater	10,747
Mar 5	ARSENAL	L 1-5	Dixon o.g.	18,656
Mar 12	Aston Villa	W 1-0	Johnson	23,732
Mar 19	Tottenham Hotspur	D 1-1	Kiwomya	26,653
Mar 23	Newcastle United	L 0-2		32,216
Mar 26	QUEENS PARK RANGERS	L 1-3	Guentchev	15,182
Mar 29	MANCHESTER CITY	D 2-2	Linighan, Guentchev (pen)	13,099
Apr 2	West Ham United	L 1-2	Mason	18,307
Apr 4	COVENTRY CITY	L 0-2		12,633
Apr 9	Liverpool	L 0-1		30,485
Apr 16	SWINDON TOWN	D 1-1	Marshall	14,934
Apr 23	Sheffield Wednesday	L 0-5		23,475
May 1	MANCHESTER UNITED	L 1-2	Kiwomya	22,559
May 7	Blackburn Rovers	D 0-0		20,633

FA Cup

Jan 8	Swindon Town	(Rd3) D 1-1	Marshall	12,105
Jan 18	SWINDON TOWN	(R)(aet) W 2-1	Stockwell, Marshall	12,796
Jan 29	TOTTENHAM HOTSPUR	(Rd4) W 3-0	Marshall, Johnson, Thompson	22,539
Feb 19	Wolverhampton Wanderers	(Rd5) D 1-1	Wark	28,234
Mar 2	WOLVERHAMPTON W	(R) L 1-2	Palmer	19,385

League Cup

Sep 21	CAMBRIDGE UNITED	(Rd2/1L) W 2-1	Milton, Whitton	8,645
Oct 5	Cambridge United	(Rd2/2L) W 2-0	Marshall, Kiwomya	6,979
Oct 27	Liverpool	(Rd3) L 2-3	Marshall, Mason (pen)	19,058

League and Cup Appearances

PLAYER	LEAGUE	CUP COMPETITION		TOTAL
		FA CUP	LC	
Baker	15			15
Durrant	3 (4)			3 (4)
Forrest	27	5	3	35
Goddard	3 (1)		0 (1)	3 (2)
Guentchev	9 (15)	2 (2)	2	13 (17)
Johnson	16	3		19
Kiwomya	34 (3)	2	1	37 (3)
Linighan	38	5	3	46
Marshall	28 (1)	5	3	36 (1)
Mason	18 (4)	1 (2)	3	22 (6)
Milton	11 (4)		2 (1)	13 (5)
Palmer	31 (5)	2 (3)		33 (8)
Slater	28	5	2	35
Stockwell	42	5	3	50
Thompson	32	5	3	40
Wark	38	5	3	46
Whelan	28 (1)		1	29 (1)
Whitton	7 (4)	0 (1)	1 (1)	8 (6)
Williams	34	5	3	42
Yallop	2 (5)		0 (1)	2 (6)
Youds	18 (5)	5		23 (5)

Goalscorers

PLAYER	LEAGUE	CUP COMPETITION		TOTAL
		FA CUP	LC	
Marshall	10	3	2	15
Kiwomya	5		1	6
Mason	3		1	4
Wark	3	1		4
Linighan	3			3
Guentchev	2			2
Johnson	1	1		2
Milton	1		1	2
Palmer	1	1		2
Stockwell	1	1		2
Whitton	1		1	2
Slater	1			1
Thompson		1		1
Youds	1			1
Opp's o.gs.	2			2

Fact File

Ian Marshall joined Ipswich after John Lyall said he would play him as a striker rather than a defender, where his previous club, Oldham, deployed him. He promptly scored in his first five league games, including the season opener at Oldham.

MANAGER: John Lyall

CAPTAIN: David Linighan

TOP SCORER: Ian Marshall

BIGGEST WIN: 3-0 v Tottenham Hotspur (H), 29 January 1994, FA Cup 4th Round

HIGHEST ATTENDANCE: 22,559 v Manchester United, 1 May 1994, FA Premier League

MAJOR TRANSFERS IN: Ian Marshall from Oldham Athletic; Paul Mason from Aberdeen; Stuart Slater from Celtic

MAJOR TRANSFERS OUT: Steve Whitton to Colchester United

Final Premier League Table

		P	W	D	L	F	A	Pts
1	MANCHESTER U	42	27	11	4	80	38	92
2	BLACKBURN R	42	25	9	8	63	36	84
3	NEWCASTLE U	42	23	8	11	82	41	77
4	ARSENAL	42	18	17	7	53	28	71
5	LEEDS U	42	18	16	8	65	39	70
6	WIMBLEDON	42	18	11	13	56	53	65
7	SHEFFIELD W	42	16	16	10	76	54	64
8	LIVERPOOL	42	17	9	16	59	55	60
9	QPR	42	16	12	14	62	61	60
10	ASTON VILLA	42	15	12	15	46	50	57
11	COVENTRY C	42	14	14	14	43	45	56
12	NORWICH C	42	12	17	13	65	61	53
13	WEST HAM U	42	13	13	16	47	58	52
14	CHELSEA	42	13	12	17	49	53	51
15	TOTTENHAM H	42	11	12	19	54	59	45
16	MANCHESTER C	42	9	18	15	38	49	45
17	EVERTON	42	12	8	22	42	63	44
18	SOUTHAMPTON	42	12	7	23	49	66	43
19	IPSWICH TOWN	42	9	16	17	35	58	43
20	SHEFFIELD U	42	8	18	16	42	60	42
21	OLDHAM ATH	42	9	13	20	42	68	40
22	SWINDON T	42	5	15	22	47	100	30

Season 1994-95

FA Premier League

DATE	OPPONENTS	SCORE	GOALSCORERS	ATTENDANCE
Aug 20	NOTTINGHAM FOREST	L 0-1		18,882
Aug 23	Wimbledon	D 1-1	Milton	5,853
Aug 27	Queens Park Rangers	W 2-1	Yates o.g., Guentchev	12,456
Aug 30	TOTTENHAM HOTSPUR	L 1-3	Kiwomya	22,559
Sep 10	Aston Villa	L 0-2		22,241
Sep 19	NORWICH CITY	L 1-2	Wark (pen)	17,447
Sep 24	MANCHESTER UNITED	W 3-2	Mason 2, Sedgley	22,559
Oct 1	Southampton	L 1-3	Marshall	13,246
Oct 10	Coventry City	L 0-2		9,526
Oct 16	SHEFFIELD WEDNESDAY	L 1-2	Wark	13,075
Oct 23	Chelsea	L 0-2		15,068
Oct 29	LIVERPOOL	L 1-3	Paz	22,513
Nov 1	LEEDS UNITED	W 2-0	Sedgley, Williams	15,956
Nov 5	Crystal Palace	L 0-3		13,349
Nov 19	BLACKBURN ROVERS	L 1-3	Thomsen	17,329
Nov 26	Newcastle United	D 1-1	Thomsen	34,459
Dec 3	MANCHESTER CITY	L 1-2	Mason	13,504
Dec 10	Nottingham Forest	L 1-4	Thomsen	21,340
Dec 16	WIMBLEDON	D 2-2	Milton, Sedgley	11,367
Dec 26	West Ham United	D 1-1	Thomsen	20,562
Dec 28	ARSENAL	L 0-2		22,054
Dec 31	Everton	L 1-4	Sedgley	25,659
Jan 2	LEICESTER CITY	W 4-1	Kiwomya 2, Tanner, Yallop	15,803
Jan 14	Liverpool	W 1-0	Tanner	32,733
Jan 21	CHELSEA	D 2-2	Slater, Wark (pen)	17,296
Jan 28	Blackburn Rovers	L 1-4	Wark (pen)	21,325
Feb 4	CRYSTAL PALACE	L 0-2		15,570
Feb 22	Manchester City	L 0-2		21,430
Feb 25	SOUTHAMPTON	W 2-1	Mathie, Chapman	16,076
Feb 28	NEWCASTLE UNITED	L 0-2		18,639
Mar 4	Manchester United	L 0-9		43,804
Mar 8	Tottenham Hotspur	L 0-3		24,930
Mar 20	Norwich City	L 0-3		17,510
Apr 1	ASTON VILLA	L 0-1		15,710
Apr 5	Leeds United	L 0-4		28,600
Apr 11	QUEENS PARK RANGERS	L 0-1		11,767
Apr 15	Arsenal	L 1-4	Marshall	36,818
Apr 17	WEST HAM UNITED	D 1-1	Thomsen	19,099
Apr 29	Leicester City	L 0-2		15,248
May 6	COVENTRY CITY	W 2-0	Marshall, Pressley o.g.	12,893
May 9	EVERTON	L 0-1		14,951
May 14	Sheffield Wednesday	L 1-4	Mathie	30,213

FA Cup

Jan 7	Wrexham	(Rd3) L 1-2	Linighan	8,324

League Cup

Sep 21	BOLTON WANDERERS	(Rd2/1L) L 0-3		7,787
Oct 5	Bolton Wanderers	(Rd2/2L) L 0-1		8,212

League and Cup Appearances

PLAYER	LEAGUE	CUP COMPETITION		TOTAL
		FA CUP	LC	
Baker	2	1		3
Chapman	9 (7)			9 (7)
Cotterell	0 (2)		0 (1)	0 (3)
Ellis	1			1
Forrest	36		2	38
Gregory, D	0 (1)			0 (1)
Gregory, N	1 (2)			1 (2)
Guentchev	11 (5)		2	13 (5)
Johnson	14 (3)	0 (1)	2	16 (4)
Kiwomya	13 (2)	1	0 (1)	14 (3)
Linighan	31 (1)	1	1 (1)	33 (2)
Marshall	14 (4)			14 (4)
Mason	19 (2)	1		20 (2)
Mathie	13			13
Milton	19 (6)		1	20 (6)
Morgan	1			1
Norfolk	1 (2)			1 (2)
Palmer	10 (2)		1	11 (2)
Paz	13 (4)	0 (1)		13 (5)
Sedgley	26	1	2	29
Slater	22 (5)	1	2	25 (5)
Stockwell	14 (1)			14 (1)
Swailes	4			4
Tanner	9 (1)	1		10 (1)
Taricco			1	1
Thompson	9 (1)			9 (1)
Thomsen	31 (2)	1	2	34 (2)
Vaughan	10	1		11
Wark	26	2		28
Whelan	12 (1)	1		13 (1)
Williams	38		2	40
Wright	3			3
Yallop	41	1	2	44
Youds	9 (1)			9 (1)

Goalscorers

PLAYER	LEAGUE	CUP COMPETITION		TOTAL
		FA CUP	LC	
Thomsen	5			5
Sedgley	4			4
Wark	4			4
Kiwomya	3			3
Marshall	3			3
Mason	3			3
Mathie	2			2
Milton	2			2
Tanner	2			2
Chapman	1			1
Guentchev	1			1
Linighan		1		1
Paz	1			1
Slater	1			1
Williams	1			1
Yallop	1			1
Opp's o.gs.	2			2

Fact File

Adam Tanner's goal at Liverpool gave Ipswich their first ever Ànfield win.

MANAGER: John Lyall/George Burley

CAPTAIN: David Linighan

TOP SCORER: Claus Thomsen

BIGGEST WIN: 4-1 v Leicester City (H), 2 January 1995, FA Premier League

HIGHEST ATTENDANCE: 22,559 v Tottenham, 30 August 1994, FA Premier League; 22,559 v Manchester United, 24 September 1994, FA Premier League

MAJOR TRANSFERS IN: Lee Chapman from West Ham; Alex Mathie from Newcastle; Adrian Paz from Penarol; Steve Sedgley from Tottenham; Chris Swailes from Doncaster; Mauricio Taricco from Argentinos Juniors; Claus Thomsen from Aarhus

MAJOR TRANSFERS OUT: David Gregory to Peterborough; Bontcho Guentchev to Luton; Gavin Johnson to Luton; Chris Kiwomya to Arsenal; Eddie Youds to Bradford City

Final Premier League Table

		P	W	D	L	F	A	PTS
1	BLACKBURN R	42	27	8	7	80	39	89
2	MANCHESTER U	42	26	10	6	77	28	88
3	NOTTINGHAM F	42	22	11	9	72	43	77
4	LIVERPOOL	42	21	11	10	65	37	74
5	LEEDS U	42	20	13	9	59	38	73
6	NEWCASTLE U	42	20	12	10	67	47	72
7	TOTTENHAM H	42	16	14	12	66	58	62
8	QPR	42	17	9	16	61	59	60
9	WIMBLEDON	42	15	11	16	48	65	56
10	SOUTHAMPTON	42	12	18	12	61	63	54
11	CHELSEA	42	13	15	14	50	55	54
12	ARSENAL	42	13	12	17	52	49	51
13	SHEFFIELD W	42	13	12	17	49	57	51
14	WEST HAM U	42	13	11	18	44	48	50
15	EVERTON	42	11	17	14	44	51	50
16	COVENTRY C	42	12	14	16	44	62	50
17	MANCHESTER C	42	12	13	17	53	64	49
18	ASTON VILLA	42	11	15	16	51	56	48
19	CRYSTAL PALACE	42	11	12	19	34	49	45
20	NORWICH C	42	10	13	19	37	54	43
21	LEICESTER C	42	6	11	25	45	80	29
22	IPSWICH TOWN	42	7	6	29	36	93	27

Season 1995-96

Football League Division One

DATE	OPPONENTS	SCORE	GOALSCORERS	ATTENDANCE
Aug 12	Birmingham City	L 1-3	Marshall	18,910
Aug 19	CRYSTAL PALACE	W 1-0	Mathie	12,681
Aug 26	West Bromwich Albion	D 0-0		14,470
Aug 30	STOKE CITY	W 4-1	Slater 2, Mathie 2	10,848
Sep 2	SUNDERLAND	W 3-0	Mathie 3	12,390
Sep 9	Huddersfield Town	L 1-2	Sedgley (pen)	12,057
Sep 12	Oldham Athletic	D 1-1	Marshall	5,622
Sep 16	WATFORD	W 4-2	Gregory N 2, Thomsen, Uhlenbeek	11,441
Sep 23	CHARLTON ATHLETIC	L 1-5	Thomsen	12,815
Sep 30	Sheffield United	D 2-2	Marshall 2	12,567
Oct 7	WOLVERHAMPTON WANDERERS	L 1-2	Sedgley (pen)	15,335
Oct 14	Derby County	D 1-1	Sedgley	13,034
Oct 22	LUTON TOWN	L 0-1		9,123
Oct 28	Reading	W 4-1	Uhlenbeek, Mathie, Mason, Williams	10,281
Nov 4	GRIMSBY TOWN	D 2-2	Mason 2	10,250
Nov 11	Millwall	L 1-2	Mason	11,360
Nov 19	Norwich City	L 1-2	Wark (pen)	17,862
Nov 22	SOUTHEND UNITED	D 1-1	Uhlenbeek	9,757
Nov 25	PORTSMOUTH	W 3-2	Milton, Marshall, Thompson	10,286
Dec 3	Wolverhampton Wanderers	D 2-2	Marshall, Mowbray	20,867
Dec 9	Charlton Athletic	W 2-0	Stockwell, Marshall	10,316
Dec 16	SHEFFIELD UNITED	D 1-1	Tuttle o.g.	9,630
Dec 22	BARNSLEY	D 2-2	Marshall, Mathie	11,791
Jan 1	PORT VALE	W 5-1	Milton, Sedgley, Marshall, Mathie 2	9,926
Jan 13	Crystal Palace	D 1-1	Mathie	14,097
Jan 20	BIRMINGHAM CITY	W 2-0	Milton 2	12,540
Feb 3	WEST BROMWICH ALBION	W 2-1	Marshall, Mowbray	10,798
Feb 10	Stoke City	L 1-3	Scowcroft	12,239
Feb 20	Sunderland	L 0-1		14,052
Feb 24	Watford	W 3-2	Uhlenbeek, Mathie 2	11,872
Mar 3	LEICESTER CITY	W 4-2	Wark, Milton, Marshall 2	9,817
Mar 9	Barnsley	D 3-3	Marshall 2, Milton	7,705
Mar 13	Leicester City	W 2-0	Marshall, Mathie	17,783
Mar 16	TRANMERE ROVERS	L 1-2	Marshall	11,759
Mar 19	OLDHAM ATHLETIC	W 2-1	Mason 2	9,674
Mar 23	Port Vale	L 1-2	Marshall	7,277
Mar 30	Luton Town	W 2-1	Milton 2	9,151
Apr 2	DERBY COUNTY	W 1-0	Vaughan	16,210
Apr 6	READING	L 1-2	Mathie	17,328
Apr 8	Grimsby Town	L 1-2	Scowcroft	5,904
Apr 14	NORWICH CITY	W 2-1	Marshall, Ullathorne o.g.	20,355
Apr 17	Tranmere Rovers	L 2-5	Mason, Marshall	6,008
Apr 20	Southend United	L 1-2	Milton	8,363
Apr 27	Portsmouth	W 1-0	Mathie	12,954
May 1	HUDDERSFIELD TOWN	W 2-1	Mathie 2	17,473
May 5	MILLWALL	D 0-0		17,290

FA Cup

Jan 6	BLACKBURN ROVERS	(Rd3) D 0-0		21,236
Jan 16	Blackburn Rovers	(R)(aet) W 1-0	Mason	19,606
Feb 13	WALSALL	(Rd4) W 1-0	Mason	18,489
Feb 17	ASTON VILLA	(Rd5) L 1-3	Mason	20,748

League Cup

Sep 19	Stockport County	(Rd2/1L) D 1-1	Sedgley	4,865
Oct 3	STOCKPORT COUNTY	(Rd2/2L) L 1-2	Thomsen	8,250

Anglo-Italian Cup

Sep 5	REGGIANA	W 2-1	Mathie, Tanner	9,525
Oct 11	Brescia	D 2-2	Sedgley, Mason	1,300
Nov 8	Foggia	W 1-0	Mason	2,000
Dec 13	SALERNITANA	W 2-0	Mowbray, Gregory	6,429
Jan 23	PORT VALE	(English SF) L 2-4	Mason, Gregory	5,831

MANAGER: George Burley

CAPTAINS: Geraint Williams/Tony Mowbray

TOP SCORERS: Ian Marshall/Alex Mathie

BIGGEST WIN: 5-1 v Port Vale (H), 1 January 1996, Division One

HIGHEST ATTENDANCE: 20,748 v Aston Villa, 17 February 1996, FA Cup 5th Round

MAJOR TRANSFERS IN: Tony Mowbray from Celtic; Gus Uhlenbeek from Tops SV

MAJOR TRANSFERS OUT: Lee Chapman to Swansea; David Linighan to Blackpool; Steve Palmer to Watford; Stuart Slater to Watford; Neil Thompson to Barnsley

League and Cup Appearances

PLAYER	LEAGUE	CUP COMPETITION FA CUP	LC	OTHER	TOTAL
Appleby	0 (3)			1	1 (3)
Barber	1				1
Chapman	2 (4)	1		2	5 (4)
Durrant				0 (1)	0 (1)
Forrest	21	1	1	3	26
Gregory, N	5 (12)	0 (1)	2	3 (2)	10 (15)
Linighan	2		1	1	4
Marshall	35	4			39
Mason	24 (2)	2 (1)		3	29 (3)
Mathie	39	2	1	4	46
Milton	34 (3)	4	0 (2)	4 (1)	42 (6)
Mowbray	19	4		3	26
Norfolk				1	1
Palmer	5			1	6
Petterson	1				1
Scowcroft	13 (10)	2	0 (1)	1 (2)	16 (13)
Sedgley	40	4	2	3	49
Slater	11 (6)		2	2 (2)	15 (8)
Stockwell	33 (4)	3	1	2	39 (4)
Swailes	4 (1)				4 (1)
Tanner	3 (7)			3 (1)	6 (8)
Taricco	36 (3)	3	2	3	44 (3)
Thompson	5				5
Thomsen	36 (1)	3		2 (1)	43 (2)
Uhlenbeek	37 (3)	1 (3)	2	4	44 (6)
Vaughan	19 (6)		1	2	22 (6)
Wark	13 (1)	2	1	2	18 (1)
Williams	42	4	2	2	50
Wright	23	3	1	2	29
Yallop	3 (4)	1	1	1 (2)	6 (6)

Goalscorers

PLAYER	LEAGUE	CUP COMPETITION FA CUP	LC	OTHER	TOTAL
Marshall	19				19
Mathie	18			1	19
Mason	7	3		3	13
Milton	9				9
Sedgley	4	1		1	6
Gregory, N	2			2	4
Uhlenbeek	4				4
Mowbray	2		1		3
Thomsen	2		1		3
Scowcroft	2				2
Slater	2				2
Wark	2				2
Stockwell	1				1
Tanner				1	1
Thompson	1				1
Vaughan	1				1
Williams	1				1
Opp's o.gs.	2				2

Final Division One Table

		P	W	D	L	F	A	Pts
1	SUNDERLAND	46	22	17	7	59	33	83
2	DERBY CO	46	21	16	9	71	51	79
3	CRYSTAL PALACE	46	20	15	11	67	48	75
4	STOKE C	46	20	13	13	60	49	73
5	LEICESTER C	46	19	14	13	66	60	71
6	CHARLTON ATH	46	17	20	9	57	45	71
7	Ipswich Town	46	19	12	15	79	69	69
8	HUDDERSFIELD T	46	17	12	17	61	58	63
9	SHEFFIELD U	46	16	14	16	57	54	62
10	BARNSLEY	46	14	18	14	60	66	60
11	WBA	46	16	12	18	60	68	60
12	PORT VALE	46	15	15	16	59	66	60
13	TRANMERE R	46	14	17	15	64	60	59
14	SOUTHEND U	46	15	14	17	52	61	59
15	BIRMINGHAM C	46	15	13	18	61	64	58
16	NORWICH C	46	14	15	17	59	55	57
17	GRIMSBY T	46	14	14	18	55	69	56
18	OLDHAM ATH	46	14	14	18	54	50	56
19	READING	46	13	17	16	54	63	56
20	WOLVERHAMPTON W	46	13	16	17	56	62	55
21	PORTSMOUTH	46	13	13	20	61	69	52
22	MILLWALL	46	13	13	20	43	63	52
23	WATFORD	46	10	18	18	62	70	48
24	LUTON T	46	11	12	23	40	64	45

Season 1996-97

Football League Division One

DATE	OPPONENTS	SCORE	GOALSCORERS	ATTENDANCE
Aug 16	Manchester City	L 0-1		29,126
Aug 24	READING	W 5-2	Vaughan 2, Sedgley (pen), Taricco, Scowcroft	9,767
Aug 27	GRIMSBY TOWN	D 1-1	Mason	9,762
Aug 31	Oldham Athletic	D 3-3	Mathie 2, Stockwell	5,339
Sep 7	HUDDERSFIELD TOWN	L 1-3	Mason	10,661
Sep 10	Crystal Palace	D 0-0		12,520
Sep 14	Sheffield United	W 3-1	Sedgley, Scowcroft 2	14,261
Sep 20	CHARLTON ATHLETIC	W 2-1	Sedgley, Mathie	10,558
Sep 28	West Bromwich Albion	D 0-0		15,606
Oct 1	BARNSLEY	D 1-1	Mathie	9,041
Oct 11	Norwich City	L 1-3	Sonner	20,256
Oct 15	Birmingham City	L 0-1		15,664
Oct 19	PORTSMOUTH	D 1-1	Mason	10,514
Oct 26	TRANMERE ROVERS	L 0-2		11,003
Oct 30	Queens Park Rangers	W 1-0	Mason	10,562
Nov 2	Oxford United	L 1-3	Tanner	7,903
Nov 9	SOUTHEND UNITED	D 1-1	Stockwell	10,146
Nov 16	Bradford City	L 1-2	Cundy	10,504
Nov 19	SWINDON TOWN	W 3-2	Scowcroft, Creaney, Sedgley (pen)	7,086
Nov 23	PORT VALE	W 2-1	Tanner, Mason	9,491
Nov 30	Tranmere Rovers	L 0-3		10,127
Dec 7	WOLVERHAMPTON WANDERERS	D 0-0		12,048
Dec 14	Bolton Wanderers	W 2-1	Scowcroft 2	13,314
Dec 21	STOKE CITY	D 1-1	Mason	10,159
Dec 26	CRYSTAL PALACE	W 3-1	Tanner (pen), Mason, Naylor	16,020
Dec 28	Huddersfield Town	L 0-2		11,467
Jan 1	Charlton Athletic	D 1-1	Tanner (pen)	10,186
Jan 18	Barnsley	W 2-1	Mason, Cundy	9,872
Jan 25	WEST BROMWICH ALBION	W 5-0	Holmes o.g., Scowcroft, Stockwell, Naylor, Mason	9,381
Feb 1	Southend United	D 0-0		7,232
Feb 8	QUEENS PARK RANGERS	W 2-0	Naylor, Gregory	12,983
Feb 15	Port Vale	D 2-2	Mason, Stockwell	6,115
Feb 22	OXFORD UNITED	W 2-1	Naylor, Stockwell	11,483
Mar 1	Wolverhampton Wanderers	D 0-0		26,700
Mar 4	BRADFORD CITY	W 3-2	Sedgley (pen), Sonner, Gregory	9,367
Mar 8	Stoke City	W 1-0	Taricco	11,933
Mar 15	BOLTON WANDERERS	L 0-1		16,187
Mar 18	SHEFFIELD UNITED	W 3-1	Gregory 3	10,374
Mar 22	Reading	L 0-1		10,058
Mar 31	Grimsby Town	L 1-2	Mason	6,268
Apr 5	OLDHAM ATHLETIC	W 4-0	Scowcroft, Williams, Stockwell, Gregory	11,730
Apr 12	Swindon Town	W 4-0	Swailes, Stockwell, Sedgley (pen), Gudmundsson	8,591
Apr 18	NORWICH CITY	W 2-0	Taricco, Mason	22,397
Apr 22	MANCHESTER CITY	W 1-0	Sedgley (pen)	15,824
Apr 25	Portsmouth	W 1-0	Scowcroft	12,101
May 4	BIRMINGHAM CITY	D 1-1	Gudmundsson	20,570

FA Cup

Jan 4	Nottingham Forest	L 0-3		14,681

League Cup

Aug 20	BOURNEMOUTH	(Rd1/1L) W 2-1	Marshall, Mason	6,163
Sep 3	Bournemouth	(Rd1/2L) W 3-0	Scowcroft, Mathie, Stockwell	4,119
Sep 17	Fulham	(Rd2/1L) D 1-1	Milton	6,947
Sep 24	FULHAM	(Rd2/2L) W 4-2	Sonner, Sedgley (pen), Mathie 2	6,825
Oct 22	CRYSTAL PALACE	(Rd3) W 4-1	Mason 2, Mathie 2	8,390
Nov 26	GILLINGHAM	(Rd4) W 1-0	Naylor	15,070
Jan 21	LEICESTER City	(Rd5) L 0-1		20,793

Play-offs

May 10	Sheffield United	(SF/1L) D 1-1	Stockwell	22,312
May 14	SHEFFIELD UNITED	(SF/2L) D 2-2*	Scowcroft, Gudmundsson	21,467

after extra time, lost on away goals rule

MANAGER: George Burley

CAPTAIN: Tony Mowbray

TOP SCORER: Paul Mason

BIGGEST WIN: 5-0 v WBA (H), 25 January 1997, Division One

HIGHEST ATTENDANCE: 22,397 v Norwich, 18 April 1997, Division One

MAJOR TRANSFERS IN: Jason Cundy from Tottenham; Bobby Petta from Feyenoord; Danny Sonner from Preussen Köln

MAJOR TRANSFERS OUT: Claus Thomsen to Everton; Ian Marshall to Leicester

League and Cup Appearances

PLAYER	LEAGUE	CUP COMPETITION		OTHER	TOTAL
		FA CUP	LC		
Creaney	6				6
Cundy	13	1	2		16
Dyer	2 (11)	1		1 (1)	4 (12)
Forrest	6		2		8
Gregory	10 (7)		0 (1)	1 (1)	11 (9)
Gudmundsson	2 (6)			1 (1)	3 (7)
Howe	2 (1)	1			3 (1)
Jean	0 (1)				0 (1)
Marshall	2		1		3
Mason	41 (2)	1	6	1	48 (2)
Milton	8 (15)		3 (2)		11 (17)
Mathie	11 (1)		5		16 (1)
Mowbray	8		1		9
Naylor	19 (8)		0 (1)	1 (3)	20 (12)
Niven	2				2
Petta	1 (5)		1		2 (5)
Scowcroft	40 (1)	1	6	2	49 (1)
Sedgley	39		6	2	47
Sonner	22 (7)	1	5 (1)		28 (8)
Stockwell	42 (1)	1	6 (1)	2	51 (2)
Swailes	23	2	2		27
Tanner	10 (6)	1	1		12 (6)
Taricco	41	1	5	2	49
Thomsen	10 (1)	1	4		15 (1)
Uhlenbeek	34 (4)	1	3 (3)	2	40 (7)
Vaughan	27 (5)		4 (2)	2	33 (7)
Wark	2		1		3
Williams	43	1	6	2	52
Wright	40	1	5	2	48

Goalscorers

PLAYER	LEAGUE	CUP COMPETITION		OTHER	TOTAL
		FA CUP	LC		
Mason	12		3		15
Scowcroft	9		1	1	11
Mathie	4		5		9
Stockwell	7		1	1	9
Sedgley	7		1		8
Gregory	6				6
Naylor	4		1		5
Tanner	4				4
Gudmundsson	2			1	3
Sonner	2		1		3
Taricco	3				3
Cundy	2				2
Vaughan	2				2
Creaney	1				1
Marshall			1		1
Milton			1		1
Swailes	1				1
Williams	1				1
Opp's o.gs.	1				1

Final Division One Table

		P	W	D	L	F	A	Pts
1	BOLTON W	46	28	14	4	100	53	98
2	BARNSLEY	46	22	14	10	76	55	80
3	WOLVERHAMPTON W	46	22	10	14	68	51	76
4	IPSWICH TOWN	46	20	14	12	68	50	74
5	SHEFFIELD U	46	20	13	13	75	52	73
6	CRYSTAL PALACE	46	19	14	13	78	48	71
7	PORTSMOUTH	46	20	8	18	59	53	68
8	PORT VALE	46	17	16	13	58	55	67
9	QPR	46	18	12	16	64	60	66
10	BIRMINGHAM C	46	17	15	14	52	48	66
11	TRANMERE R	46	17	14	15	63	56	65
12	STOKE C	46	18	10	18	51	57	64
13	NORWICH C	46	17	12	17	63	68	63
14	MANCHESTER C	46	17	10	19	59	60	61
15	CHARLTON ATH	46	16	11	19	52	66	59
16	WBA	46	14	15	17	68	72	57
17	OXFORD U	46	16	9	21	64	68	57
18	READING	46	15	12	19	58	67	57
19	SWINDON T	46	15	9	22	52	71	54
20	HUDDERSFIELD T	46	13	15	18	48	61	54
21	BRADFORD C	46	12	12	22	47	72	48
22	GRIMSBY T	46	11	13	22	60	81	46
23	OLDHAM ATH	46	10	13	23	51	66	43
24	SOUTHEND U	46	8	15	23	42	86	39

Season 1997-98

Football League Division One

DATE	OPPONENTS	SCORE	GOALSCORERS	ATTENDANCE
Aug 9	Queens Park Rangers	D 0-0		17,614
Aug 23	Bradford City	L 1-2	Dyer	13,913
Aug 30	WEST BROMWICH ALBION	D 1-1	Stein	13,508
Sep 2	SWINDON TOWN	W 2-1	Venus, Sonner	11,246
Sep 13	Huddersfield Town	D 2-2	Edmondson o.g., Dyer	9,313
Sep 20	STOKE CITY	L 2-3	Scowcroft, Holland	10,665
Sep 26	Norwich City	L 1-2	Stein	18,911
Oct 4	MANCHESTER CITY	W 1-0	Mathie	14,322
Oct 18	Oxford United	L 0-1		7,594
Oct 21	Crewe Alexandra	D 0-0		4,730
Oct 25	BURY	W 2-0	Tanner (pen), Dozzell	10,478
Oct 28	Birmingham City	D 1-1	Holland	16,778
Nov 1	Charlton Athletic	L 0-3		12,672
Nov 4	STOCKPORT COUNTY	L 0-2		8,938
Nov 9	SHEFFIELD UNITED	D 2-2	Legg, Gregory	9,695
Nov 15	Wolverhampton Wanderers	D 1-1	Johnson	21,937
Nov 22	Reading	W 4-0	Holland, Johnson, Scowcroft, Naylor	9,400
Nov 29	NOTTINGHAM FOREST	L 0-1		17,580
Dec 2	MIDDLESBROUGH	D 1-1	Johnson	13,619
Dec 6	Tranmere Rovers	D 1-1	Johnson	5,720
Dec 13	PORTSMOUTH	W 2-0	Cundy, Johnson	11,641
Dec 20	Port Vale	W 3-1	Mathie 2, Johnson	5,784
Dec 26	BIRMINGHAM CITY	L 0-1		17,459
Dec 28	Swindon Town	W 2-0	Johnson (pen), Petta	10,609
Jan 10	QUEENS PARK RANGERS	D 0-0		12,672
Jan 17	Middlesbrough	D 1-1	Johnson	30,081
Jan 27	West Bromwich Albion	W 3-2	Holland, Scowcroft, Cundy	12,403
Jan 31	BRADFORD CITY	W 2-1	Mathie 2	11,864
Feb 7	Stoke City	D 1-1	Holland	11,416
Feb 14	HUDDERSFIELD TOWN	W 5-1	Holland, Johnson 2, Mathie, Naylor	10,509
Feb 18	Manchester City	W 2-1	Petta, Dyer	27,156
Feb 21	NORWICH CITY	W 5-0	Mathie 3, Petta 2	21,858
Feb 24	OXFORD UNITED	W 5-2	Mathie, Johnson 3 (1 pen), Holland	11,824
Feb 28	Sunderland	D 2-2	Petta, Dyer	35,114
Mar 3	Sheffield United	W 1-0	Holland	14,120
Mar 7	CHARLTON ATHLETIC	W 3-1	Stockwell, Cundy, Johnson	19,831
Mar 14	Stockport County	W 1-0	Johnson	8,939
Mar 21	WOLVERHAMPTON WANDERERS	W 3-0	Johnson, Holland, Scowcroft	21,510
Mar 28	READING	W 1-0	Scowcroft	19,075
Apr 5	Nottingham Forest	L 1-2	Scowcroft	22,292
Apr 11	TRANMERE ROVERS	D 0-0		18,039
Apr 13	Portsmouth	W 1-0	Johnson	15,040
Apr 18	PORT VALE	W 5-1	Johnson 2, Petta 2, Mathie	16,205
Apr 25	Bury	W 1-0	Stockwell	7,830
Apr 28	SUNDERLAND	W 2-0	Holland, Mathie	20,902
May 3	CREWE ALEXANDRA	W 3-2	Johnson, Stockwell, Mathie	19,105

FA Cup

Jan 3	Bristol Rovers	(Rd3)	D 1-1	Stockwell	8,610
Jan 13	BRISTOL ROVERS	(R)	W 1-0	Johnson	11,362
Jan 24	SHEFFIELD UNITED	(Rd4)	D 1-1	Johnson	14,654
Feb 3	Sheffield United	(R)	L 0-1		14,144

League Cup

Aug 13	Charlton Athletic	(Rd1/1L)	W 1-0	Venus	6,598
Aug 26	CHARLTON ATHLETIC	(Rd1/2L)	W 3-1	Stein, Brown o.g., Scowcroft	10,989
Sep 16	TORQUAY UNITED	(Rd2/1L)	D 1-1	Stockwell	8,031
Sep 23	Torquay United	(Rd2/2L)	W 3-0	Holland 2, Dyer	3,598
Oct 14	MANCHESTER UNITED	(Rd3)	W 2-0	Mathie, Taricco	22,173
Nov 18	Oxford United	(Rd4)	W 2-1	Dozzell, Mowbray	5,723
Jan 7	CHELSEA	(Rd5)(aet)	D 2-2*	Taricco, Mathie	22,088

* lost 1-4 on penalties

Play-offs

May 10	CHARLTON ATHLETIC	(SF/1L)	L 0-1		21,681
May 13	Charlton Athletic	(SF/2L)	L 0-1		15,585

MANAGER: George Burley

CAPTAIN: Tony Mowbray

TOP SCORER: David Johnson

BIGGEST WIN: 5-0 v Norwich (H), 21 February 1998, Division One

HIGHEST ATTENDANCE: 22,173 v Manchester United, 14 October 1997, League Cup 3rd Round

MAJOR TRANSFERS IN: Matt Holland from Bournemouth

MAJOR TRANSFERS OUT: Steve Sedgley to Wolverhampton Wanderers

---

League and Cup Appearances

PLAYER	LEAGUE	CUP COMPETITION		OTHER	TOTAL
		FA CUP	LC		
Brown	1				1
Clapham	22			1	23
Cundy	40 (1)	3	6	2	51 (1)
Dozzell	8		2		10
Dyer	41	2	7	2	52
Gregory	2 (6)		0 (2)		2 (8)
Holland	46	4	7	2	59
Johnson	30 (1)		4	2	36 (1)
Keeble	0 (1)				0 (1)
Kennedy	0 (1)				0 (1)
Kerslake	2 (5)			1 (1)	3 (6)
Legg	6		1		7
Mason	1		1		2
Mathie	25 (12)	0 (2)	3 (2)	2	30 (16)
Milton	7 (13)		1 (1)		8 (14)
Mowbray	23 (2)	2	4		29 (2)
Naylor	0 (5)				0 (5)
Petta	28 (4)	3 (1)	3 (2)	2	36 (7)
Scowcroft	19 (12)	4	5	0 (2)	28 (14)
Sonner	6 (17)	0 (1)	1 (1)	0 (1)	7 (20)
Stein	6 (1)		3 (1)		9 (2)
Stockwell	46	4	6	2	58
Swailes	3 (2)	1			4 (2)
Tanner	14 (4)	3 (1)	0 (1)		17 (6)
Taricco	41	4	6	2	53
Uhlenbeek	6 (5)		2	1 (1)	9 (6)
Venus	12 (2)	1	5	2	20 (2)
Whyte	2				2
Williams	23	4	7		34
Wright	46	4	7	2	59

Goalscorers

PLAYER	LEAGUE	CUP COMPETITION		OTHER	TOTAL
		FA CUP	LC		
Johnson	20	2			22
Mathie	13		2		15
Holland	10		2		12
Petta	7				7
Scowcroft	6		1		7
Dyer	4		1		5
Stockwell	3	1	1		5
Cundy	3				3
Stein	2		1		3
Dozzell	1		1		2
Naylor	2				2
Taricco			2		2
Venus	1		1		2
Gregory	1				1
Legg	1				1
Mowbray			1		1
Sonner	1				1
Tanner	1				1
Opp's o.gs.	1		1		2

Final Division One Table

		P	W	D	L	F	A	Pts
1	NOTTINGHAM F	46	28	10	8	82	42	94
2	MIDDLESBROUGH	46	27	10	9	77	41	91
3	SUNDERLAND	46	26	12	8	86	50	90
4	CHARLTON ATH	46	26	10	10	80	49	88
5	IPSWICH TOWN	46	23	14	9	77	43	83
6	SHEFFIELD U	46	19	17	10	69	54	74
7	BIRMINGHAM C	46	19	17	10	60	35	74
8	STOCKPORT CO	46	19	8	19	71	69	65
9	WOLVERHAMPTON W	46	18	11	17	57	53	65
10	WBA	46	16	12	17	50	56	61
11	CREWE ALEX	46	18	5	23	58	65	59
12	OXFORD U	46	16	10	20	60	64	58
13	BRADFORD C	46	14	15	17	46	59	57
14	TRANMERE R	46	14	14	18	54	57	56
15	NORWICH C	46	14	13	19	52	69	55
16	HUDDERSFIELD T	46	14	11	21	50	72	53
17	BURY	46	11	19	16	42	58	52
18	SWINDON T	46	14	10	22	42	73	52
19	PORT VALE	46	13	10	23	56	66	49
20	PORTSMOUTH	46	13	10	23	51	63	49
21	QPR	46	10	19	17	51	63	49
22	MANCHESTER C	46	12	12	22	56	57	48
23	STOKE C	46	11	13	22	44	74	46
24	READING	46	11	9	26	39	78	42

Season 1998-99

Football League Division One

DATE	OPPONENTS	SCORE	GOALSCORERS	ATTENDANCE
Aug 9	Grimsby Town	D 0-0		7,211
Aug 15	BURY	D 0-0		13,267
Aug 22	Portsmouth	D 0-0		12,002
Aug 29	SUNDERLAND	L 0-2		15,813
Aug 31	Port Vale	W 3-0	Scowcroft, Johnson, Holland	5,485
Sep 8	BRADFORD CITY	W 3-0	Scowcroft 2, Venus	11,596
Sep 12	Oxford United	D 3-3	Scowcroft, Johnson, Dyer	6,632
Sep 19	BRISTOL CITY	W 3-1	Johnson 2, Scowcroft	13,657
Sep 26	Watford	L 0-1		13,109
Sep 29	Tranmere Rovers	W 2-0	Johnson, Scowcroft	5,072
Oct 3	CRYSTAL PALACE	W 3-0	Venus (pen), Taricco, Mathie	16,837
Oct 17	SWINDON TOWN	W 1-0	Johnson	13,212
Oct 20	NORWICH CITY	L 0-1		22,079
Oct 24	Stockport County	W 1-0	Dyer	7,432
Oct 31	WEST BROMWICH ALBION	W 2-0	Johnson	15,568
Nov 3	WOLVERHAMPTON WANDERERS	W 2-0	Scowcroft, Stockwell	14,680
Nov 7	Huddersfield Town	D 2-2	Venus, Johnson	14,240
Nov 14	Barnsley	W 1-0	Johnson	15,996
Nov 21	BOLTON WANDERERS	L 0-1		17,225
Nov 28	Crewe Alexandra	W 3-0	Scowcroft 3 (1 pen)	5,165
Dec 2	Queens Park Rangers	D 1-1	Holland	12,449
Dec 5	BIRMINGHAM CITY	W 1-0	Petta	15,901
Dec 12	BARNSLEY	L 0-2		16,021
Dec 20	Sheffield United	W 2-1	Abou, Naylor	12,944
Dec 26	PORTSMOUTH	W 3-0	Naylor 2, Dyer	21,805
Dec 28	Wolverhampton Wanderers	L 0-1		24,636
Jan 9	GRIMSBY TOWN	L 0-1		15,575
Jan 17	Sunderland	L 1-2	Holland	39,835
Jan 30	PORT VALE	W 1-0	Clapham	16,328
Feb 6	Bury	W 3-0	Venus (pen), Mowbray, Harewood	4,750
Feb 13	Bradford City	D 0-0		15,024
Feb 20	OXFORD UNITED	W 2-1	Holland, Venus (pen)	16,920
Feb 27	Bristol City	W 1-0	Naylor	14,065
Mar 2	WATFORD	W 3-2	Dyer, Venus, Johnson	18,818
Mar 6	TRANMERE ROVERS	W 1-0	Thetis	15,929
Mar 9	Crystal Palace	L 2-3	Johnson, Clapham	16,360
Mar 13	HUDDERSFIELD TOWN	W 3-0	Magilton, Johnson, Petta	17,170
Mar 20	West Bromwich Albion	W 1-0	Thetis	15,552
Apr 3	Swindon Town	W 6-0	Venus 2 (2 pen), Scowcroft, Mowbray, Clapham, Wilnis	10,337
Apr 5	QUEENS PARK RANGERS	W 3-1	Johnson, Scowcroft, Holland	22,162
Apr 11	Norwich City	D 0-0		19,511
Apr 17	Bolton Wanderers	L 0-2		19,894
Apr 20	STOCKPORT COUNTY	W 1-0	Magilton	17,056
Apr 24	CREWE ALEXANDRA	L 1-2	Venus (pen)	20,845
May 2	Birmingham City	L 0-1		27,685
May 9	SHEFFIELD UNITED	W 4-1	Magilton, Scowcroft, Dyer, Naylor	21,689

FA Cup

Jan 2	Tranmere Rovers	(Rd3) W 1-0	McGreal o.g.	7,223
Jan 23	Everton	(Rd4) L 0-1		28,854

League Cup

Aug 11	Exeter City	(Rd1/1L) D 1-1	Holland	3,233
Aug 18	EXETER CITY	(Rd1/2L) W 5-1	Taricco, Holland, Stockwell, Mathie, Mason	7,952
Sep 15	LUTON TOWN	(Rd2/1L) W 2-1	Scowcroft, Thetis	9,032
Sep 22	Luton Town	(Rd2/2L)(aet) L 2-4	Johnson, Davis S o.g.	5,655

Play-offs

May 16	Bolton Wanderers	(SF/1L) L 0-1		18,295
May 19	BOLTON WANDERERS*	(SF/2L) W 4-3	Holland 2, Dyer 2	21,755

* after extra-time, lost on away goals rule

MANAGER: George Burley

CAPTAIN: Tony Mowbray

TOP SCORERS: David Johnson/James Scowcroft

BIGGEST WIN: 6-0 v Swindon Town (A), 3 April 1999, Division One

HIGHEST ATTENDANCE: 22,162 v QPR, 5 April 1999, Division One

MAJOR TRANSFERS IN: Jim Magilton from Sheffield Wednesday; Manuel Thetis from Sevila; Fabian Wilnis from De Graafschap

MAJOR TRANSFERS OUT: Kieron Dyer to Newcastle United; Alex Mathie to Dundee United; Danny Sonner to Sheffield Wednesday; Mauricio Taricco to Tottenham Hotspur

---

League and Cup Appearances

PLAYER	LEAGUE	CUP COMPETITION		OTHER	TOTAL
		FA CUP	LC		
Abou	5				5
Bramble	2 (2)	0 (1)			2 (3)
Brown	0 (1)				0 (1)
Clapham	45 (1)	2	3 (1)	2	52 (2)
Cundy	1 (3)				1 (3)
Dyer	36 (1)	2	4	2	44 (1)
Harewood	5 (1)				5 (1)
Hodges	0 (4)				0 (4)
Holland	46	2	4	2	54
Holster	1 (9)	0 (1)	0 (1)		1 (11)
Hunt	2 (4)				2 (4)
Johnson	41 (1)	2	4	2	49 (1)
Kennedy	6 (1)	1			7 (1)
Logan	0 (2)				0 (2)
Magilton	19			2	21
Mason			0 (1)		0 (1)
Mathie	2 (6)		1 (1)		3 (7)
Mowbray	40	2	2	2	46
Naylor	10 (20)	1 (1)	1 (1)	0 (2)	12 (24)
Petta	26 (6)	2	4	1	33 (6)
Scowcroft	29 (3)		2	2	33 (3)
Sonner	0 (4)		0 (2)		0 (6)
Stockwell	23 (7)	1	4	0 (2)	28 (9)
Tanner	13 (6)	0 (1)	1 (1)		14 (8)
Taricco	16		4		20
Thetis	29 (2)	2	2	1 (1)	34 (3)
Venus	44	2	4	2	52
Vernazza	2				2
Wilnis	17 (1)	1		2	20 (1)
Wright	46	2	4	2	54

Goalscorers

PLAYER	LEAGUE	CUP COMPETITION		OTHER	TOTAL
		FA CUP	LC		
Johnson	13		1		14
Scowcroft	13		1		14
Holland	5		2	2	9
Venus	9				9
Dyer	5			2	7
Naylor	5				5
Clapham	3				3
Magilton	3				3
Stockwell	2		1		3
Thetis	2		1		3
Mathie	1		1		2
Mowbray	2				2
Petta	2				2
Taricco	1		1		2
Abou	1				1
Harewood	1				1
Mason			1		1
Wilnis	1				1
Opp's o.gs.	1		1		2

Final Division One Table

		P	W	D	L	F	A	Pts
1	SUNDERLAND	46	31	12	3	91	28	105
2	BRADFORD C	46	26	9	11	82	47	87
3	IPSWICH TOWN	46	26	8	12	69	32	86
4	BIRMINGHAM C	46	23	14	11	66	37	81
5	WATFORD	46	21	14	11	65	56	77
6	BOLTON W	46	20	16	10	78	59	76
7	WOLVERHAMPTON W	46	19	16	11	64	43	73
8	SHEFFIELD U	46	18	11	17	71	66	67
9	NORWICH C	46	15	17	14	62	61	62
10	HUDDERSFIELD T	46	15	16	15	62	71	61
11	GRIMSBY T	46	17	10	19	40	52	61
12	WBA	46	16	11	19	69	76	59
13	BARNSLEY	46	14	17	15	59	56	59
14	CRYSTAL PALACE	46	14	16	16	58	71	58
15	TRANMERE R	46	12	20	14	63	61	56
16	STOCKPORT CO	46	12	17	17	49	60	53
17	SWINDON T	46	13	11	22	59	81	50
18	CREWE ALEX	46	12	12	22	54	78	48
19	PORTSMOUTH	46	11	14	21	57	73	47
20	QPR	46	12	11	23	52	61	47
21	PORT VALE	46	13	8	25	45	75	47
22	BURY	46	10	17	19	35	60	47
23	OXFORD U	46	10	14	22	48	71	44
24	BRISTOL C	46	9	15	22	57	80	42

Season 1999-2000

Football League Division One

DATE	OPPONENTS	SCORE	GOALSCORERS	ATTENDANCE
Aug 7	NOTTINGHAM FOREST	W 3-1	Naylor, Johnson, Scowcroft	20,830
Aug 15	Swindon Town	W 4-1	Johnson 2, Naylor 2	6,195
Aug 21	BOLTON WANDERERS	W 1-0	Johnson	17,696
Aug 28	Sheffield United	D 2-2	Scowcroft, Johnson	12,455
Aug 30	BARNSLEY	W 6-1	Johnson 2, Venus, Naylor, Scowcroft, Magilton	18,037
Sep 11	Portsmouth	D 1-1	Scowcroft	16,034
Sep 18	BIRMINGHAM CITY	L 0-1		19,758
Sep 26	MANCHESTER CITY	W 2-1	Johnson, Croft	19,406
Oct 2	Grimsby Town	L 1-2	Magilton	6,531
Oct 16	QUEENS PARK RANGERS	L 1-4	Holland	17,544
Oct 19	CHARLTON ATHLETIC	W 4-2	Scowcroft, Venus, Johnson, Stockwell	17,940
Oct 23	Walsall	W 1-0	Naylor	6,526
Oct 27	Manchester City	L 0-1		32,799
Oct 30	GRIMSBY TOWN	W 2-0	Clapham, Naylor	16,617
Nov 2	Huddersfield Town	L 1-3	Holland	12,093
Nov 6	Blackburn Rovers	D 2-2	Holland, Mowbray	18,512
Nov 12	TRANMERE ROVERS	D 0-0		14,514
Nov 21	Norwich City	D 0-0		19,948
Nov 24	WOLVERHAMPTON WANDERERS	W 1-0	Scowcroft	15,731
Nov 27	CREWE ALEXANDRA	W 2-1	Johnson 2	15,211
Dec 5	Nottingham Forest	W 1-0	Holland	15,724
Dec 7	Crystal Palace	D 2-2	Holland, Johnson	13,176
Dec 18	WEST BROMWICH ALBION	W 3-1	Johnson, Scowcroft, Midgley	14,712
Dec 26	Fulham	D 0-0		17,255
Dec 28	STOCKPORT COUNTY	W 1-0	Scowcroft	20,671
Jan 3	Port Vale	W 2-1	Holland, Scowcroft	6,808
Jan 15	SWINDON TOWN	W 3-0	Stockwell, Naylor 2	17,326
Jan 22	Bolton Wanderers	D 1-1	Holland	11,924
Jan 29	SHEFFIELD UNITED	D 1-1	Johnson (pen)	17,350
Feb 5	Barnsley	W 2-0	Scowcroft, Stewart	17,601
Feb 12	HUDDERSFIELD TOWN	W 2-1	Scowcroft, Stewart	21,233
Feb 19	Crewe Alexandra	W 2-1	Clapham, Wright J	6,393
Feb 27	Birmingham City	D 1-1	Johnson	20,493
Mar 4	PORTSMOUTH	L 0-1		20,305
Mar 7	BLACKBURN ROVERS	D 0-0		18,871
Mar 11	Wolverhampton Wanderers	L 1-2	Scowcroft	22,652
Mar 19	NORWICH CITY	L 0-2		21,760
Mar 22	Tranmere Rovers	W 2-0	Holland, Johnson	6,933
Mar 25	FULHAM	W 1-0	Reuser	20,168
Apr 4	West Bromwich Albion	D 1-1	Holland	12,536
Apr 8	PORT VALE	W 3-0	Scowcroft, Johnson, Holland	19,663
Apr 15	Stockport County	W 1-0	Johnson	8,501
Apr 22	Queens Park Rangers	L 1-3	Magilton (pen)	14,920
Apr 25	CRYSTAL PALACE	W 1-0	Johnson	18,798
Apr 29	Charlton Athletic	W 3-1	Magilton, Johnson, Reuser	20,043
May 7	WALSALL	W 2-0	Johnson 2	21,908

FA Cup

Dec 13	SOUTHAMPTON	(Rd3)	L 0-1		14,383

League Cup

Apr 11	Brentford	(Rd1/1L)	W 2-0	Johnson, Clapham	4,825
Apr 24	BRENTFORD	(Rd1/2L)	W 2-0	Scowcroft, Clapham	9,748
Sep 14	Crewe Alexandra	(Rd2/1L)	L 1-2	Venus	4,759
Sep 21	CREWE ALEXANDRA	(Rd2/2L)	D 1-1	Scowcroft	9,689

Play-offs

May 14	Bolton Wanderers	(SF/1L)	D 2-2	Stewart 2	18,814
May 17	BOLTON WANDERERS	(SF/2L)	W 5-3	Magilton 3 (1 pen), Clapham (pen), Reuser	21,543
May 29	Barnsley*	(F)	W 4-2	Mowbray, Naylor, Stewart, Reuser	73,427

* played at Wembley

MANAGER: George Burley

CAPTAIN: Matt Holland

TOP SCORER: David Johnson

BIGGEST WIN: 6-1 v Barnsley (H), 30 August 1999, Division One

HIGHEST ATTENDANCE: 21,908 v Walsall, 7 May 2000, Division One

MAJOR TRANSFERS IN: Gary Croft from Blackburn Rovers; John McGreal from Tranmere Rovers; Martijn Reuser from Ajax; Marcus Stewart from Huddersfield Town; Jermaine Wright from Crewe Alexandra

League and Cup Appearances

PLAYER	LEAGUE	CUP COMPETITION		OTHER	TOTAL
		FA CUP	LC		
Axeldal	1 (15)	0 (1)	0 (3)		1 (19)
Brown	20 (5)	1	2	1 (1)	24 (6)
Clapham	44 (2)	1	4	3	52 (2)
Clegg	3				3
Croft	14 (7)			2 (1)	16 (8)
Friars	0 (1)				0 (1)
Holland	46	1	4	3	54
Johnson	44	1	4	3	52
Logan	0 (1)				0 (1)
Magilton	33 (5)	1	3	3	40 (5)
McGreal	34	1	4	1	40
Midgley	1 (3)				1 (3)
Mowbray	35 (1)	1		3	39 (1)
Naylor	19 (17)	0 (1)	3 (1)	0 (2)	22 (21)
Reuser	2 (6)			0 (3)	2 (9)
Scowcroft	40 (1)	1	3 (1)	2	46 (2)
Stewart	9 (1)			3	12 (1)
Stockwell	21 (14)	1	3 (1)		25 (15)
Thetis	15 (1)		3	1	19 (1)
Venus	28		3	3	34
Wilnis	30 (5)	1	1 (1)	1 (1)	33 (7)
Wright, J	21 (13)	0 (1)	3 (1)	1	25 (14)
Wright, R	46	1	4	3	54

Goalscorers

PLAYER	LEAGUE	CUP COMPETITION		OTHER	TOTAL
		FA CUP	LC		
Johnson	22		1		23
Scowcroft	13		2		15
Holland	10				10
Naylor	8			1	9
Magilton	4			3	7
Clapham	2		2	1	5
Stewart	2			3	5
Reuser	2			2	4
Venus	2		1		3
Mowbray	1			1	2
Stockwell	1		1		2
Croft	1				1
Midgley	1				1
Wright, J	1				1

Fact File

Jim Magilton's hat-trick in the play-off semi-final over Bolton in May 2000 was the first hat-trick of his professional career.

Final Division One Table

		P	W	D	L	F	A	Pts
1	CHARLTON A	46	27	10	9	79	45	91
2	MANCHESTER C	46	26	11	9	78	40	89
3	IPSWICH TOWN	46	25	12	9	71	42	87
4	BARNSLEY	46	24	10	12	88	67	82
5	BIRMINGHAM C	46	22	11	13	65	44	77
6	BOLTON W	46	21	13	12	69	50	76
7	WOLVERHAMPTON W	46	21	11	14	64	48	74
8	HUDDERSFIELD T	46	21	11	14	62	49	74
9	FULHAM	46	17	16	13	49	41	67
10	QPR	46	16	18	12	62	53	66
11	BLACKBURN R	46	15	17	14	55	51	62
12	NORWICH C	46	14	15	17	45	50	57
13	TRANMERE R	46	15	12	19	57	68	57
14	NOTTINGHAM F	46	14	14	18	53	55	56
15	CRYSTAL PALACE	46	13	15	18	57	67	54
16	SHEFFIELD U	46	13	15	18	59	71	54
17	STOCKPORT CO	46	13	15	18	55	67	54
18	PORTSMOUTH	46	13	12	21	55	66	51
19	CREWE ALEX	46	14	9	23	46	67	51
20	GRIMSBY T	46	13	12	21	41	67	51
21	WBA	46	10	19	17	43	60	49
22	WALSALL	46	11	13	22	52	77	46
23	PORT VALE	46	7	15	24	48	69	36
24	SWINDON T	46	8	12	26	38	77	36

Season 2000-01

FA Premier League

DATE	OPPONENTS	SCORE	GOALSCORERS	ATTENDANCE
Aug 19	Tottenham Hotspur	L 1-3	Venus	36,148
Aug 22	MANCHESTER UNITED	D 1-1	Wilnis	22,007
Aug 26	SUNDERLAND	W 1-0	Bramble	21,830
Sep 6	Leicester City	L 1-2	Magilton (pen)	19,598
Sep 9	ASTON VILLA	L 1-2	Stewart	22,065
Sep 16	Leeds United	W 2-1	Scowcroft, Wright J	35,552
Sep 23	ARSENAL	D 1-1	Stewart	22,030
Sep 30	Everton	W 3-0	McGreal, Stewart 2	32,597
Oct 14	WEST HAM UNITED	D 1-1	Stewart	22,243
Oct 21	Bradford City	W 2-0	Petrescu o.g., Clapham	17,045
Oct 28	MIDDLESBROUGH	W 2-1	Naylor, Venus	21,771
Nov 4	Newcastle United	L 1-2	Stewart	50,922
Nov 11	CHARLTON ATHLETIC	W 2-0	Holland, Stewart	22,263
Nov 20	Coventry City	W 1-0	Wilnis	19,322
Nov 25	Manchester City	W 3-2	Stewart 2, Hreidarsson	33,741
Dec 2	DERBY COUNTY	L 0-1		22,003
Dec 10	Liverpool	W 1-0	Stewart	43,509
Dec 16	SOUTHAMPTON	W 3-1	Scowcroft, Bridge o.g., Armstrong	22,228
Dec 23	Manchester United	L 0-2		67,597
Dec 26	CHELSEA	D 2-2	Scowcroft, Stewart	22,237
Dec 30	TOTTENHAM HOTSPUR	W 3-0	Stewart, Armstrong, Clapham	22,234
Jan 1	Sunderland	L 1-4	Stewart	46,053
Jan 14	LEICESTER CITY	W 2-0	Stewart, Scowcroft	22,002
Jan 20	Chelsea	L 1-4	Stewart	34,948
Feb 3	LEEDS UNITED	L 1-2	Venus	22,015
Feb 10	Arsenal	L 0-1		38,011
Feb 24	EVERTON	W 2-0	Holland, Armstrong	22,220
Mar 4	BRADFORD CITY	W 3-1	Reuser 2, Burchill	21,820
Mar 10	Aston Villa	L 1-2	Armstrong	28,216
Mar 17	West Ham United	W 1-0	Reuser	26,046
Apr 2	Southampton	W 3-0	Stewart 3 (1 pen)	15,244
Apr 10	LIVERPOOL	D 1-1	Armstrong	23,504
Apr 14	NEWCASTLE UNITED	W 1-0	Stewart (pen)	24,028
Apr 16	Middlesbrough	W 2-1	Armstrong 2	34,294
Apr 21	COVENTRY CITY	W 2-0	Reuser, Wright J	24,612
Apr 30	Charlton Athletic	L 1-2	Reuser	20,043
May 7	MANCHESTER CITY	W 2-1	Holland, Reuser	25,004
May 19	Derby County	D 1-1	Carbonari o.g.	33,239

FA Cup

Jan 6	Morecambe	(Rd3) W 3-0	Stewart, Armstrong, Wright J	5,923
Jan 27	Sunderland	(Rd4) L 0-1		33,626

League Cup

Sep 19	Millwall	(Rd2/1L) L 0-2		8,068
Sep 26	MILLWALL	(Rd2/2L)(aet) W 5-0	Johnson 2, Bramble, Holland, Magilton	13,008
Nov 1	Arsenal	(Rd3) W 2-1	Clapham, Scowcroft	26,105
Nov 28	COVENTRY CITY	(Rd4) W 2-1	Bramble, Johnson	19,563
Dec 19	Manchester City	(Rd5)(aet) W 2-1	Holland, Venus	31,252
Jan 9	BIRMINGHAM CITY	(SF/1L) W 1-0	Stewart (pen)	21,684
Jan 31	Birmingham City	(SF/2L)(aet) L 1-4	Scowcroft	28,624

Fact File

Ipswich failed to score in just three of their Premier League games during the 2000-01 season.

MANAGER: George Burley

CAPTAIN: Matt Holland

TOP SCORER: Marcus Stewart

BIGGEST WIN: 5-0 v Millwall (H), 26 September 2000, League Cup

HIGHEST ATTENDANCE: 25,004 v Manchester City, 7 May 2001, FA Premier League

MAJOR TRANSFERS IN: Alun Armstrong from Middlesbrough; Hermann Hreidarsson from Wimbledon; Chris Makin from Sunderland

MAJOR TRANSFERS OUT: David Johnson to Nottingham Forest; Mick Stockwell to Colchester

League and Cup Appearances

PLAYER	LEAGUE	CUP COMPETITION		TOTAL
		FA CUP	LC	
Abidallah	0 (2)			0 (2)
Armstrong	15 (6)	2		17 (2)
Bramble	23 (3)	2	4 (1)	29 (4)
Branagan	2		1	3
Brown	0 (4)			0 (4)
Burchill	2 (5)			2 (5)
Clapham	28 (7)	0 (2)	7	35 (9)
Croft	6 (2)	1	3 (1)	10 (3)
Holland	38	2	6 (1)	46 (1)
Hreidarsson	35 (1)	2	7	44 (1)
Johnson	6 (8)		5	11 (8)
Karic			0 (3)	0 (3)
Logan		0 (1)		0 (1)
Magilton	32 (1)	1 (1)	6	39 (2)
Makin	10			10
McGreal	25 (3)	1	5	31 (3)
Naylor	5 (8)	0 (1)	1 (1)	6 (10)
Reuser	13 (13)	1	3 (4)	17 (17)
Scales	2		2	4
Scowcroft	22 (12)	1 (1)	5 (2)	28 (15)
Stewart	33 (1)	2	3 (2)	38 (3)
Venus	23 (2)	1	3	27 (2)
Wilnis	27 (2)	2	5 (1)	34 (3)
Wright, J	35 (2)	2	5 (2)	42 (4)
Wright R	36	2	6	44

Goalscorers

PLAYER	LEAGUE	CUP COMPETITION		TOTAL
		FA CUP	LC	
Stewart	19	1	1	21
Armstrong	7	1		8
Reuser	6			6
Scowcroft	4		2	6
Holland	3		2	5
Venus	3		1	4
Bramble	1		2	3
Clapham	2		1	3
Johnson			3	3
Wright, J	2	1		3
Magilton	1		1	2
Wilnis	2			2
Burchill	1			1
Hreidarsson	1			1
McGreal	1			1
Naylor	1			1
Opp's o.gs.	3			3

Final Premier League Table

		P	W	D	L	F	A	Pts
1	MANCHESTER UNITED	38	24	8	6	79	31	80
2	ARSENAL	38	20	10	8	63	38	70
3	LIVERPOOL	38	20	9	9	71	39	69
4	LEEDS UNITED	38	20	8	10	64	43	68
5	IPSWICH TOWN	38	20	6	12	57	42	66
6	CHELSEA	38	17	10	11	68	45	61
7	SUNDERLAND	38	15	12	11	46	41	57
8	ASTON VILLA	38	13	15	10	46	43	54
9	CHARLTON ATHLETIC	38	14	10	14	50	57	52
10	SOUTHAMPTON	38	14	10	14	40	48	52
11	NEWCASTLE UNITED	38	14	9	15	44	50	51
12	TOTTENHAM HOTSPUR	38	13	10	15	47	54	49
13	LEICESTER CITY	38	14	6	18	39	51	48
14	MIDDLESBROUGH	38	9	15	14	44	44	42
15	WEST HAM UNITED	38	10	12	16	45	50	42
16	EVERTON	38	11	9	18	45	59	42
17	DERBY COUNTY	38	10	12	16	37	59	42
18	MANCHESTER CITY	38	8	10	20	41	65	34
19	COVENTRY CITY	38	8	10	20	36	63	34
20	BRADFORD CITY	38	5	11	22	30	70	26

Complete Players' Career Records

(records up to and including season 2000-01)
Others = Divisional Play-offs, the Anglo-Italian Cup, the Full Members Cup, the Texaco Cup and the FA Charity Shield

Player		Birthplace	From	Year Joined	Year Left	To	League App	Sub	Goals
Abidallah	Nabil	Amsterdam	Ajax	2000		Still at club	0	2	0
Abou	Samassi	Gagnoa	West Ham	1998	1999	Loan	5	0	1
Acres	Basil	Brantham	Brantham	1950	1960	Retired	217		6
Alsop	Gilbert	Coalpit Heath	WBA	1937	1939	Walsall	9		2
Appleby	Richard	Middlesbrough	Newcastle	1995	1996	Swansea	0	3	0
Armstrong	Alun	Gateshead	Middlesbrough	2000		Still at club	15	6	7
Ashcroft	Charles	Croston	Liverpool	1955	1957	Coventry	7		0
Astil	Leonard	Wolverhampton	Blackburn	1937	1938	Colchester	0		0
Atkins	Ian	Birmingham	Everton	1985	1988	Birmingham	73	4	4
Atkinson	Dalian	Shrewsbury	Apprentice	1985	1989	Sheffield W	49	11	18
Austin	Terence	Isleworth	Crystal Palace	1973	1976	Plymouth	10	9	1
Axeldahl	Jonas	Holm	Foggia	1999	2000	Cambridge United	1	15	0
Bailey	Roy	Epsom	Crystal Palace	1956	1965	South Africa	315		0
Baird	Henry	Belfast	Huddersfield	1946	1951	Coaching staff	216		6
Baker	Clive	North Walsham	Coventry City	1992	1995	Retired	47	1	0
Baker	Gerard	New York	Hibernian	1963	1967	Coventry	135		58
Baker	William	Penrhiwceiber	Cardiff City	1955	1957	Retired	20		0
Ball	Joseph	Walsall	Banbury Spencer	1951	1954	Aldershot	32		2
Baltacha	Sergei	Ukraine	Dinamo Kiev	1989	1990	St Johnstone	22	6	1
Barnard	Christopher	Cardiff	Southend United	1966	1970	Torquay United	18	3	0
Barnes	David	Paddington	Coventry City	1982	1984	Wolverhampton	16	1	0
Baxter	William	Edinburgh	Broxburn Athletic	1960	1971	Hull City	409		21
Beattie	Kevin	Carlisle	Apprentice	1971	1982	Colchester	225	3	24
Belcher	James	Stepney	Crystal Palace	1958	1961	Brentford	27		0
Belfitt	Roderick	Doncaster	Leeds United	1971	1972	Everton	40		13
Bell	Dave	Goverbridge	Derby County	1938	1950	Retired	171		3
Bell	Robert	Cambridge	Tottenham	1967	1971	Blackburn	32		1
Bernal	Andrew	Canberra, Aus	Sporting Gijon	1987	1987	Australia	4	5	0
Berry	Peter	Aldershot	Crystal Palace	1958	1961	Retired	38		6
Bertschin	Keith	Enfield	Barnet	1973	1977	Birmingham	19	13	8
Best	David	Wareham	Oldham	1968	1974	Portsmouth	168		0
Bevis	David	Southampton	Juniors	1959	1966	Cambridge City	6		0
Blackman	Ronald	Portsmouth	Nottingham Forest	1955	1958	Tonbridge	27		12
Blackwell	Jack	Sheffield	Boston	1936	1937	Unknown	0		0
Blackwood	Robert	Edinburgh	Hearts	1962	1965	Colchester	62		12
Bolton	John	Lesmahagow	Raith Rovers	1963	1966	Morton	69		2
Bolton	Ronald	Golborne	Bournemouth	1965	1967	Bournemouth	21	1	0
Bozinoski	Vlado	Macedonia	Sporting Lisbon	1992	1992	Sporting Lisbon	3	6	0
Bramble	Titus	Ipswich	Trainee	1998		Still at club	25	5	1
Brazil	Alan	Glasgow	Apprentice	1977	1983	Tottenham	143	11	70
Branagan	Keith	Fulham	Bolton	2000		Still at club	2		0
Brennan	Mark	Rossendale	Apprentice	1983	1988	Middlesbrough	165	3	19
Broadfoot	Joseph	Lewisham	Millwall	1963	1965	Northampton			
			Millwall	1967	1969	Retired	100	1	19
Brogan	Francis	Glasgow	Glasgow Celtic	1964	1971	Halifax	201	2	58
Brown	John	Belfast	Barry Town	1948	1951	Retired	98		25
Brown	Thomas	Troon	Glenathon Jnrs	1938	1951	Bury Town	111		0
Brown	Thomas	Galashiels	Annbanks Jnrs	1952	1956	Walsall	84		17
Brown	Wayne	Barking	Trainee	1996		Still at club	21	10	0
Bruce	Robert	Paisley	Sheffield W	1936	1938	Mossley	0		0
Bugg	Alec	Needham Market	Juniors	1967	1970	Bournemouth	4		0
Burchill	Mark	Broxburn	Glasgow Celtic	2001	2001	Loan	2	5	1
Burley	George	Cumnock	Apprentice	1973	1985	Sunderland	394		6
Burns	Mick	Lee Holme	Preston	1938	1952	Retired	157		0
Butcher	Terence	Singapore	Juniors	1976	1986	Glasgow Rangers	271		16
Callaghan	William	Glasgow	Great Perth Jnrs	1952	1955	Sudbury Town	21		7
Carberry	Lawrence	Liverpool	Bootle	1956	1965	Barrow	257		0
Carroll	Thomas	Dublin	Cambridge City	1966	1971	Birmingham	115	2	2
Carter	John	Aylesbury	Reading	1936	1938	Yeovil	0		0
Chadwick	Frederick	Manchester	Newport	1938	1947	Bristol Rovers	40		18
Chapman	Lee	Lincoln	West Ham	1995	1996	Swansea	11	11	1
Cheetham	Michael	Amsterdam	Basingstoke	1988	1989	Cambridge	1	3	0
Clapham	James	Lincoln	Tottenham	1998		Still at club	139	10	7
Clarke	Frank	Willenhall	QPR	1970	1973	Carlisle United	62	4	15
Clarke	George	Ipswich	Bramford Rd OB	1946	1954	Retired	34		1

FAC Apps	Sub	Goals	FLC Apps	Sub	Goals	European Apps	Sub	Goals	Others Apps	Sub	Goals	Totals Apps	Sub	Goals
0	0	0	0	0	0	0	0	0	0	0	0	0	2	0
0	0	0	0	0	0	0	0	0	0	0	0	5	0	1
15		0	0		0	0		0	0		0	232		6
0		0	0		0	0		0	0		0	9		2
0	0	0	0	0	0	0	0	0	1	0	0	1	3	0
2	0	1	0	0	0	0	0	0	0	0	0	17	6	8
0		0	0		0	0		0	0		0	7		0
2		1	0		0	0		0	0		0	2		1
2		0	8		0	0		0	9		0	92	4	4
0	0	0	5	1	3	0	0	0	2	1	0	56	13	21
1	1	0	0	0	0	0	2	1	0	0	0	11	12	2
0	1	0	0	3	0	0	0	0	0	0	0	1	19	0
19		7	0		0	4		0	1		0	346		0
11	1	0	0		0	0		0	0		0	227		7
5	0	0	5	0	0	0	0	0	0	0	0	57	1	0
9	4	7	4		0	0		0	0		0	151		66
0	0	0	0		0	0		0	0		0	20		0
6	0	0	0		0	0		0	0		0	38		2
0	0	0	1		0	0	0	0	1	0	0	24	6	1
1	0	0	1		0	0		0	0	0	0	20	3	0
0	0	0	0		0	0	0	0	0	0	0	16	1	0
23	1	22	0		0	4		0	1		0	459		22
24	2	5	16		0	23	6	3	8	0	0	296	11	32
2	0	0	0		0	0		0	0		0	29		0
2		1	0		0	0		0	3		3	46		16
16	0	0	0		0	0		0	0		0	187		3
4	0	1	0		0	0		0	0		0	37		1
0	0	0	0		0	0	0	0	0	2	0	4	7	0
3		0	0		0	0		0	0		0	41		6
0	0	0	1		0	0	0	0	0	0	0	20	13	8
7		0	12		0	5		0	7		0	199		0
2	0	0	0		0	0		0	0		0	8		0
1		0	0		0	0	0	0	0	0	0	28	0	12
7	7	0	0		0	0		0	0		0	7		7
5	1	2	0		0	4		1	0		0	73		14
4	0	4	0		0	0		0	0		0	77		2
0	1	0	0		0	0	0	0	0	0	0	21	2	0
0	1	0	1	1	0	0	0	0	0	0	0	4	8	0
2	1	0	4	1	2	0	0	0	0	0	0	31	7	3
18	2	6	14	1	3	20	1	1	0	0	0	195	15	80
0		0	1		0	0		0	0		0	3		0
12	0	3	21	1	2	0	0	0	11	0	1	209	4	25
8	0	1	5	1	1	0	0	0	0	0	0	113	2	21
10	1	5	9		6	0	0	0	0	0	0	220	3	69
5	2	0	0		0	0		0	0		0	103		27
5	0	0	0		0	0		0	0		0	116		0
11	4	0	0		0	0		0	0		0	95		21
1	0	0	2	0	0	0	0	0	1	1	0	25	11	0
8	7	0	0		0	0		0	0		0	8		7
0		0	0		0	0		0	0		0	4		0
0	0	0	0	0	0	0	0	0	0	0	0	2	5	1
43	4	35	0		0	27		1	1		0	500		11
11	0	0	0		0	0		0	0		0	168		0
28	0	30	2		0	22		3	0		0	351		21
1	0	0	0		0	0		0	0		0	22		7
15	0	8	0		0	2		0	1		0	283		0
2	0	0	7	0	1	0	0	0	0	0	0	124	2	3
8	8	0	0		0	0		0	0		0	8		8
4	5	0	0		0	0		0	0		0	44		23
0	0	0	1	0	0	0	0	0	2	0	0	14	11	1
0	1	0	0	0	0	0	0	0	1	0	0	1	5	0
3	0	0	14	1	3	0	0	0	6	0	1	162	11	11
6	0	2	3	0	0	0	0	0	0	1	0	71	5	17
3	0	0	0		0	0		0	0		0	37		1

The Essential History of Ipswich Town

Player		Birthplace	From	Year Joined	Year Left	To	League App	Sub	Goals
Clarke	Willie	Newport	Amateur	1947	1950	Unknown	3		0
Clegg	Michael	Ashton under Lyne	Manchester Utd	2000	2000	Loan	3		0
Cole	Michael	Hillingdon	Apprentice	1983	1988	Fulham	24	14	3
Collard	Ian	Hetton-le-Hole	WBA	1969	1975	Portsmouth	83	9	5
Colrain	John	Glasgow	Clyde	1963	1966	Glentoran	55	1	17
Compton	John	Poplar	Chelsea	1960	1964	Bournemouth	111		0
Connor	John	Todmorden	Albion Rovers	1944	1946	Carlisle United	12		4
Cooper	Paul	Brierley Hill	Birmingham	1974	1987	Leicester	447		0
Cope	Jack	Ellesmere Port	Bury	1938	1939	Unknown	4		0
Cotterell	Leo	Cambridge	Trainee	1993	1996	Bournemouth	0	2	0
Cowie	Charles	Falkirk	Barrow	1936	1939	Training staff	6		0
Cranson	Ian	Easington	Apprentice	1982	1988	Sheffield W	130	1	5
Crawford	Raymond	Portsmouth	Portsmouth	1958	1963	Wolverhampton }			
			WBA	1966	1969	Charlton }	320		204
Creaney	Gerard	Coatbridge	Manchester City	1996	1996	Loan	6		1
Croft	Gary	Burton on Trent	Blackburn	1999		Still at club	20	9	1
Crowe	Alexander	Motherwell	St Mirren	1953	1953	Unknown	50		9
Cundy	Jason	Wimbledon	Tottenham	1996	199	Portsmouth	54	4	5
Curran	Pat	Sunderland	Sunderland	1938	1939	Watford	7		1
Curtis	Dermot	Dublin	Bristol City	1958	1963	Exeter City	41		17
Dale	William	Manchester	Manchester City	1938	1939	Unknown	40		
Davies	Albert	Cardiff	Cardiff City	1938	1939	Army	32		7
Davin	Joseph	Dumbarton	Hibernian	1963	1966	Morton	77		0
D'Avray	Mich	Johannesburg	Apprentice	1979	1990	South Africa	170	43	38
Day	Albert	Camberwell	Brighton	1946	1949	Watford	63		25
Deacon	David	Broome	Bungay	1950	1960	Cambridge United	66		0
Deehan	John	Solihull	Norwich City	1986	1988	Manchester City	45	4	11
Dempsey	John	Cumbernauld	Queen of South	1948	1949	Retired	22		5
Dobson	George	Sheffield	Rotherham	1936	1937	Unknown	0		0
Dobson	Robert	Frimley	Wisbech Town	1949	1954	Cambridge	30		5
Donowa	Brian	Ipswich	Willem II Tiburg	1989	1990	Bristol City	17	6	1
Dougan	George	Glasgow	Yiewsley	1963	1965	South Africa	17		0
Dozzell	Jason	Ipswich	Apprentice	1984	1993	Tottenham }			
			Tottenham	1997	1997	Northampton }	320	20	53
Driver	Allenby	Blackwell	Norwich City	1950	1952	Walsall	86		25
Durrant	Lee	Great Yarmouth	Trainee	1992	1996	Unknown	3	4	0
Dyer	Keiron	Ipswich	Trainee	1997	1999	Newcastle	79	12	9
Edmonds	Darren	Watford	Leeds United	1991	1992	Scarborough	0	2	0
Edwards	David	Bargoed	Gloucester City	1939	1946	Swindon	0		0
Elsworthy	John	Newport	Newport County	1949	1965	Retired	396		44
Fearon	Ronald	Romford	Sutton United	1987	1993	Sutton United	28		0
Feeney	James	Belfast	Swansea	1950	1956	Retired	214		0
Fillingham	Thomas	Bulwell	Birmingham	1938	1939	Retired	29		1
Fletcher	Charles	London	Plymouth	1938	1945	Clapton Orient	29		9
Fletcher	Leonard	Hammersmith	RAF Didcot	1949	1955	Falkirk	20		0
Forrest	Craig	Vancouver	Apprentice	1985	1997	West Ham	263		0
Fox	Geoffrey	Bristol	MCW	1945	1947	Bristol Rovers	11		1
Garneys	Thomas	West Ham	Brentford	1951	1959	Retired	248		123
Gates	Eric	Ferryhill	Apprentice	1972	1985	Sunderland	267	29	73
Gayle	Brian	Kingston	Manchester City	1990	1991	Sheffield Utd	58	0	4
Gaynor	James	Dublin	Shamrock Rovers	1952	1953	Aldershot	47		3
Geddis	David	Carlisle	Apprentice	1975	1979	Aston Villa	26	17	5
Gernon	Frederick	Birmingham	Apprentice	1980	1987	Gillingham	76	0	0
Gibbons	John	Charlton	QPR	1949	1950	Tottenham	11		3
Gillespie	Ian	Plymouth	Crystal Palace	1946	1947	Colchester	6		1
Gleghorn	Nigel	Seaham	Seaham Red Star	1985	1988	Manchester City	56	12	11
Goddard	Paul	Harlington	Millwall	1991	1993	Youth coach	59	13	13
Grant	Wilfred	Ashington	Cardiff City	1954	1957	Llanelli	75		22
Green	Donald	Needham Market	Bramford	1947	1952	Stowmarket	52		0
Gregory	David	Hadleigh	Trainee	1987	1995	Peterborough	16	16	2
Gregory	Neil	Ndola	Trainee	1992	1998	Colchester	18	27	9
Grew	Mark	Bilston	Leicester City	1984	1986	Port Vale	6		0
Gudmundsson	Niklas	Sweden	Blackburn	1997	1997	Loan	2	6	2
Guentchev	Bontcho	Tchoshevo	Sporting Lisbon	1992	1995	Luton Town	39	22	6
Hall	Wilfred	St Helens	Stoke City	1960	1963	Macclesfield	16		0
Hallworth	Jonathan	Hazel Grove	Apprentice	1983	1989	Oldham	45		0
Hamilton	Bryan	Belfast	Linfield	1971	1975	Everton	142	11	43
Hammond	Geoffrey	Sudbury	Juniors	1968	1974	Manchester City	52	3	2
Hancock	Kenneth	Hanley	Port Vale	1964	1969	Tottenham	163		0
Harbey	Graham	Chesterfield	Derby County	1987	1989	WBA	53	6	1
Harewood	Marlon	Hampstead	Nottingham Forest	1999	1999	Loan	5	1	1
Harper	Colin	Ipswich	Juniors	1964	1977	Port Vale	144	4	5

FAC Apps	Sub	Goals	FLC Apps	Sub	Goals	European Apps	Sub	Goals	Others Apps	Sub	Goals	Totals Apps	Sub	Goals
0		0	0		0	0		0	0		0	3		0
0		0	0		0	0		0	0		0	3		0
0	2	0	3	1	3	0	0	0	1	1	0	28	18	6
5	1	0	5	1	1	2	2	0	3	0	0	98	13	6
0	0	0	6	0	3	0	0	0	0	0	0	61	1	20
10		0	6		0	3		0	1		0	131		0
0		0	0		0	0		0	0		0	12		4
45		0	43		0	34		0	6		0	575		0
0		0	0		0	0		0	0		0	4		0
0	0	0	0	1	0	0	0	0	0	0	0	0	3	0
0		0	0		0	0		0	0		0	6	0	0
11	1	0	15	0	0	0	0	0	7	0	0	163	2	5
18		5	10		10	4		8	1	0	0	353	0	227
0		0	0		0	0		0	0		0	6		1
1	0	0	3	1	0	0	0	0	2	1	0	26	11	1
5		2	0		0	0		0	0		0	55		11
4	0	0	8	0	0	0	0	0	2	0	0	68	4	5
1		0	0		0	0		0	0		0	8		1
0		0	1		0	0		0	0		0	42		17
4		0	0		0	0		0	0		0	44		0
3	2	0	0		0	0		0	0		0	35		9
7		0	4		0	0		0	0		0	88		0
9	2	2	19	4	7	1	2	0	2	3	1	201	54	48
0		0	0		0	0		0	0		0	63		25
9		0	0		0	0		0	0		0	75		0
1	0	0	3	1	1	0	0	0	7	2	2	56	7	14
1		0	0		0	0		0	0		0	23		5
4	5	0	0		0	0		0	0		0	4		5
3	3	0	0		0	0		0	0		0	33		8
2	0	0	0	2	0	0	0	0	2	1	1	21	9	2
1		0	2		0	0		0	0		0	20		0
22	0	12	31	1	3	0	0	0	22	0	4	395	21	73
7	1	0	0		0	0		0	0		0	93		26
0	0	0	0	0	0	0	0	0	0	1	0	3	5	0
5	0	0	11	0	1	0	0	0	5	1	2	100	13	12
0	0	0	0	0	0	0	0	0	0	1	0	0	3	0
3		0	0		0	0		0	0		0	3		0
27	7	0	6		0	3		1	1		0	433		52
1		0	0		0	0		0	2		0	31		0
18	0	0	0	0	0	0	0	0	0	0	0	232	0	0
2		0	0		0	0		0	0		0	31		1
7	2	0	0		0	0		0	0		0	36		11
1		0	0		0	0		0	0		0	21		0
14	0	19	0		0	0		0	14	0	0	310		0
2		0	0		0	0		0	0		0	13		1
25	20	0	0		0	0		0	0		0	273		143
23	3	8	28	1	8	26	6	7	1	0	0	345	39	96
0	1	0	3	0	0	0	0	0	0	0	0	61	1	4
5		1	0		0	0		0	0		0	52		4
2	1	1	0	1	0	2	7	0	0	0	0	30	26	6
4	1	0	7	0	0	0	0	0	0	0	0	87	1	0
2		0	0		0	0		0	0		0	13		3
0		0	0		0	0		0	0		0	6		1
3	1	0	3	2	0	0	0	0	5	2	2	67	17	13
1	2	0	5	1	0	0	0	0	2	0	0	67	16	13
3		0	0		0	0		0	0		0	78		22
2		0	0		0	0		0	0		0	54		0
1	0	0	3	2	0	0	0	0	3	2	4	23	20	6
0	1	0	2	3	0	0	0	0	4	3	2	24	34	11
1		0	0		0	0		0	0		0	7		0
0	0	0	0	0	0	0	0	0	1	1	1	3	7	3
6	2	5	6	0	0	0	0	0	0	0	0	51	24	11
1		0	2		0	0		0	0		0	19		0
1		0	4		0	0		0	6		0	56		0
11	1	5	11	1	3	14	0	3	8	0	2	186	13	56
6	0	0	4	0	0	2	2	0	0	0	0	64	5	2
7		0	10		0	0		0	0		0	180		0
2	0	0	7	1	2	0	0	0	8	0	0	70	7	3
0	0	0	0		0	0		0	0		0	5	1	1
5	0	1	8	1	0	6	0	0	8	0	0	171	5	6

Player		Birthplace	From	Year Joined	Year Left	To	League App	Sub	Goals
Harper	David	Peckham	Millwall	1965	1967	Swindon	70	2	2
Havenga	William	South Africa	Luton Town	1952	1953	Kettering	19		3
Hayes	Hugh	Bangor	Bangor	1946	1950	Bangor	9		0
Hegan	Daniel	Coatbridge	Sunderland	1963	1969	WBA	207		34
Higgins	Augustine	Dublin	Aston Villa	1952	1953	Unknown	2		0
Hill	David	Nottingham	Scunthorpe	1989	1991	Scunthorpe	54	7	0
Hill	Michael	Hereford	Sheffield Utd	1969	1973	Crystal Palace	63	3	18
Hodges	Lee	Plaistow	West Ham	1998	1998	Loan	0	4	0
Holland	Matthew	Bury	Bournemouth	1997		Still at club	176	0	28
Holster	Marco	Weesp	SC Heracles	1998	2000	Holland	1	9	0
Houghton	Scott	Hitchin	Tottenham	1991	1991	Loan	7	1	1
Houghton	William	Hemsworth	Watford	1966	1969	Leicester	107		3
Howe	Stephen	Cramlington	Nottingham Forest	1997	1997	Loan	2	1	0
Hreidarsson	Hermann	Iceland	Wimbledon	2000		Still at club	35	1	1
Humes	Anthony	Blyth	Apprentice	1983	1992	Wrexham	107	13	10
Hunt	Jonathan	Camden	Derby County	1998	1998	Loan	2	4	0
Hunt	Robert	Colchester	Millwall	1967	1970	Charlton	16	10	4
Hunter	Allan	Sion Mills	Blackburn	1971	1982	Colchester	280		8
Hutcheson	John	Falkirk	Chelsea	1938	1939	Crittalls	0		0
Jefferson	Derek	Morpeth	Apprentice	1966	1972	Wolverhampton	163	3	1
Jennings	Henry	Norwich	Northampton	1947	1951	Rochdale	102		41
Johnson	David	Kingston	Bury	1997	2001	Nottingham F	121	10	55
Johnson	David Edward	Liverpool	Everton	1972	1976	Liverpool	134	3	35
Johnson	Gavin	Stowmarket	Trainee	1989	1995	Luton Town	114	18	11
Johnstone	Robert	Edinburgh	West Ham	1957	1959	Canada	35		4
Jones	Frederick	Pontypool	Folkestone	1938	1939	Unknown	21		8
Jones	William	Aberbargoed	Bargoed	1949	1955	Sudbury Town	33		1
Juryeff	Ian	Gosport	Leyton Orient	1989	1989	Loan	0	2	0
Karic	Amir	Oramovica Ponja	NK Maribor	2000		Still at club	0	0	0
Keeley	Glenn	Basildon	Apprentice	1972	1974	Newcastle	4		0
Kellard	Bobby	Edmonton	Crystal Palace	1965	1966	Portsmouth	13		3
Kennedy	John	Newmarket	Trainee	1997	2000	Unknown	6	2	0
Kerslake	David	Stepney	Charlton	1997	1998	Swindon	2	5	0
Kinsella	Antony	Orsett	Tampa Bay	1982	1984	Millwall	7	2	0
Kiwomya	Christopher	Huddersfield	Trainee	1987	1995	Arsenal	197	28	51
Lambert	Michael	Balsham	Newmarket	1967	1979	Peterborough	180	30	39
Lang	Tommy	Larkhall	Queen of South	1946	1947	Retired	5		1
Laurel	John	Bexleyheath	Tottenham	1959	1963	Kings Lynn	4		0
Lea	Cyril	Wrexham	Leyton Orient	1964	1979	Stoke City	103	4	2
Leadbetter	James	Edinburgh	Brighton	1955	1965	Sudbury Town	344		43
Legg	Andrew	Neath	Birmingham	1997	1997	Loan	6		1
Linighan	David	Hartlepool	Shrewsbury	1988	1995	Blackpool	275	2	12
Little	Jackie	Blaydon	Needham Market	1937	1950	Stowmarket	146		20
Logan	Richard	Bury St Edmunds	Trainee	1999		Still at club	0	3	0
Lowe	David	Liverpool	Wigan Athletic	1987	1992	Leicester	121	13	37
Lundstrum	Colin	Colchester	West Ham	1956	1961	Colchester	13		1
McCall	Stephen	Carlisle	Apprentice	1978	1987	Sheffield W	249	8	7
McCrory	Samuel	Belfast	Swansea	1950	1952	Plymouth	97		39
McGinn	Francis	Cambuslang	Wrexham	1948	1949	Unknown	8		2
McGreal	John	Liverpool	Tranmere	1999		Still at club	59	3	1
McLuckie	George	Falkirk	Blackburn	1953	1958	Reading	141		24
McLuckie	Jimmy	Stonehouse	Aston Villa	1936	1947	Clacton	41		1
McMillan	George	Stonehouse	Newarthill Jnrs	1953	1959	Stirling Albion	53		0
McNeil	Michael	Middlesbrough	Middlesbrough	1964	1972	Cambridge City	141	5	4
Mackay	Angus	Glasgow	Hamilton	1946	1947	Exeter City	5		0
Macrow	Geoffrey	East Harling	Thetford Town	1955	1957	Stowmarket	2		0
Maffey	Denis	Sunderland	Walton United	1947	1948	Colchester	5		1
Magilton	Jim	Belfast	Sheffield W	1999		Still at club	84	6	8
Makin	Christopher	Manchester	Sunderland	2001		Still at club	10		0
Malcolm	Kenneth	Aberdeen	Arbroath	1954	1964	Retired	274		2
Mariner	Paul	Bolton	Plymouth	1976	1984	Arsenal	260		96
Marshall	Ian	Liverpool	Oldham	1993	1996	Leicester	79	5	32
Mason	Paul	Liverpool	Aberdeen	1993	1998	Retired	103	10	25
Mathie	Alexander	Bathgate	Newcastle	1995	1998	Dundee United	90	19	38
Midgley	Neil	Cambridge	Trainee	1997	2001	Barnet	1	3	1
Miller	John	Ipswich	Juniors	1968	1974	Norwich City	38	13	2
Mills	Michael	Godalming	Portsmouth	1966	1982	Southampton	588	3	22
Millward	Horace	Sheffield	Southampton	1955	1963	Poole Town	143		35
Milton	Simon	Fulham	Bury Town	1987	1999	Staff	217	64	48
Mitchell	Alexander	Greenock	Bute Athletic	1946	1950	Bury Town	42		2
Mitchell	David	Stoke	Port Vale	1966	1968	Unknown	0	2	0
Moncur	John	Stepney	Tottenham	1991	1991	Loan	5	1	0

Complete Players' Career Records: Harper D – Moncur

FAC Apps	Sub	Goals	FLC Apps	Sub	Goals	European Apps	Sub	Goals	Others Apps	Sub	Goals	Totals Apps	Sub	Goals
6	0	1	3	0	0	0	0	0	0	0	0	79	2	3
0		0	0		0	0		0	0		0	19		3
0		0	0		0	0		0	0		0	9		0
11		3	12		1	0		0	0		0	230		38
0		0	0		0	0		0	0		0	2		0
1	0	0	6	1	0	0	0	0	3	0	0	64	8	0
9	0	2	2	0	0	0	0	0	0	0	0	74	3	20
0	0	0	0	0	0	0	0	0	0	0	0	0	4	0
9	0	0	21	1	6	0	0	0	7	0	2	213	1	36
0	1	0	0	1	0	0	0	0	0	0	0	1	11	0
0		0	0	0	0	0	0	0	0	0	0	7	1	1
5		0	5		0	0		0	0		0	117		3
0	0	0	1	0	0	0	0	0	0	0	0	3	1	0
2	0	0	7	0	0	0	0	0	0	0	0	44	1	1
4	0	1	6	0	0	0	0	0	10	0	1	127	13	12
0	0	0	0	0	0	0	0	0	0	0	0	2	4	0
1	0	0	1	1	0	0		0	0		0	18	11	4
26		0	17		2	21	1	0	10	0	0	354	1	10
2		1	0		0	0		0	0		0	2		1
6	0	0	3	0	0	0		0	0		0	172	3	1
6		1	0		0	0		0	0		0	108		42
7	0	2	13	0	5	0	0	0	7	0	0	148	10	62
15	0	4	8	0	5	13	1	2	4	0	0	174	4	46
12	1	2	10	1	2	0	0	0	3	1	1	139	21	16
3		0	0		0	0		0	0		0	38		4
2		2	0		0	0		0	0		0	23		10
3		0	0		0	0		0	0		0	36		1
0	0	0	0	0	0	0	0	0	0	0	0	0	2	0
0	0	0	0	3	0	0	0	0	0	0	0	0	3	0
0		0	0		0	1		0	0		0	5		0
2		0	0		0	0		0	0		0	15		3
1	0	0	0	0	0	0	0	0	0	0	0	7	2	0
0	0	0	1	1	0	0	0	0	0	0	0	3	6	0
1	0	0	1	0	0	0	0	0	0	0	0	9	2	0
14	0	2	14	1	8	0	0	0	5	1	3	230	30	64
16	5	3	12	5	2	3	4	0	8	0	1	219	44	45
0		0	0		0	0		0	0		0	5		1
0	0	0	1	0	1	0	0	0	0	0	0	6		0
8	0	0	8	0	0	0	0	0	0	0	0	119	4	2
19	5	0	8	1	1	0	0	0	1	0	0	373		49
0		0	1		0	0		0	0		0	7		1
18	0	1	21	0	0	0	0	0	11	0	0	325	2	13
22		5	0		0	0		0	0		0	168		25
0	1	0	0	0	0	0	0	0	0	0	0	0	4	0
3	0	0	10	0	2	0	0	0	10	2	6	144	15	45
0		0	0		0	0		0	0		0	13		1
23	1	1	29	0	0	15	1	3	3	0	1	319	10	12
5		1	0		0	0		0	0		0	102		40
0		0	0		0	0		0	0		0	8		2
2	0	0	9	0	0	0	0	0	1	0	0	71	3	1
11		1	0		0	0		0	0		0	152		25
16		2	0		0	0		0	0		0	57		3
1		0	0		0	0		0	0		0	54		0
16	0	0	11	0	1	0	0	0	0	0	0	168	5	5
2		0	0		0	0		0	0		0	7		0
0		0	0		0	0		0	0		0	2		0
0		0	0		0	0		0	0		0	5		1
2	1	0	9	0	1	0	0	0	5	0	3	100	7	12
0		0	0		0	0		0	0		0	10		0
13	0	1	0		0	3		0	0		0	291		2
31		19	20		8	27		12	1		0	339		135
9	0	3	4	0	3	0	0	0	0	0	0	92	5	38
4	3	3	10	1	5	0	0	0	4	0	3	121	14	36
2	2	0	10	3	8	0	0	0	6	0	1	108	24	47
0	0	0	0	0	0	0	0	0	0	0	0	1	3	1
1	1	0	2	1	2	1	1	0	1	1	0	43	17	4
57	0	5	43	1	2	40	0	1	9	0	0	737	4	30
10		1	2		0	0		0	0		0	155		36
12	0	0	15	8	3	0	0	0	14	2	3	258	74	54
4		0	0		0	0		0	0		0	46		2
0	0	0	0	0	0	0	0	0	0	0	0	0	2	0
0	0	0	0	0	0	0	0	0	0	0	0	5	1	0

The Essential History of Ipswich Town

Player		Birthplace	From	Year Joined	Year Left	To	League App	Sub	Goals
Moran	Douglas	Musselburgh	Falkirk	1961	1964	Dundee United	104		31
Morris	Peter	Shirebrook	Mansfield	1968	1974	Norwich City	213	7	13
Mowbray	Anthony	Saltburn	Glasgow Celtic	1995	2000	1st team coach	125	3	5
Muhren	Arnold	Netherlands	Twente Enschede	1978	1982	Manchester Utd	161		21
Mulraney	Ambrose	Wishaw	Dartford	1936	1945	Birmingham	28		8
Murchison	Ronald	Hurlford	Auchterader	1950	1955	Newmarket	42		2
Myles	Neil	Falkirk	Third Lanark	1949	1960	Clacton Town	223		15
Naylor	Richard	Leeds	Trainee	1995		Still at club	53	58	20
Nelson	Andy	Silvertown	West Ham	1959	1964	Leyton Orient	193		0
Newman	Eric	Romford	Whitton	1950	1953	Chelmsford	18		0
Niven	Stuart	Glasgow	Trainee	1996	2000	Barnet	2		0
Norfolk	Lee	New Zealand	Trainee	1994	1997	Unknown	1	2	0
O'Brien	Joseph	Dublin	Luton Town	1949	1951	Unknown	50		12
O'Callaghan	Kevin	Dagenham	Millwall	1980	1985	Portsmouth	72	43	4
O'Donnell	Christopher	Newcastle	Apprentice	1985	1989	Leeds United	12	4	0
O'Mahoney	Matthew	Kilkenny	Bristol Rovers	1939	1948	Yarmouth Town	58		4
O'Rourke	John	Northampton	Middlesbrough	1968	1969	Coventry	69		30
Osborne	Roger	Ottley	Grundisburgh	1971	1981	Colchester	109	15	9
Osman	Russell	Ilkeston	Apprentice	1976	1985	Leicester	294	0	17
Owen	Aled	Anglesey	Tottenham	1958	1963	Wrexham	30		3
Palmer	Stephen	Brighton	Cambridge Univ	1989	1995	Watford	87	24	2
Parker	Stanley	Worksop	Worksop LBOB	1946	1951	Norwich City	126		43
Parker	Thomas	Hartlepool	HMS *Ganges*	1946	1957	Retired	428		86
Parkes	Phillip	Sedgley	West Ham	1990	1990	Retired	3		0
Parkin	Thomas	Gateshead	Apprentice	1973	1986	Unknown	52	18	0
Parkinson	Noel	Hull	Apprentice	1976	1980	Mansfield	0	0	0
Parry	Brinley	Pontardawe	Swansea	1951	1955	Chelmsford	138		0
Parry	Oswald	Pant	Crystal Palace	1936	1950	Retired	104		0
Paz	Charquero	Montevideo	Penarol	1994	1994	USA	13	4	1
Peddelty	John	Bishop Auckland	Apprentice	1973	1976	Plymouth	44		5
Pennyfather	Glenn	Billericay	Crystal Palace	1989	1993	Bristol City	11	4	1
Perrett	George	Kennington	Fulham	1936	1950	Retired	131		4
Petta	Robert	Rotterdam	Feyenoord	1996	1999	Glasgow Celtic	55	15	9
Petterson	Andrew	Freemantle	Luton Town	1993	1993	Loan ⎤			
			Charlton	1995	1995	Loan ⎦	2		0
Phillips	Edward	Snape	Leiston	1953	1964	Leyton Orient	269		161
Pickett	Reginald	India	Portsmouth	1957	1963	Stevenage Town	140		3
Pole	Harold	Belton	Gorleston	1946	1951	Leyton Orient	39		13
Price	George	Unknown	Amateur	1945	1946	Unknown	0		0
Putney	Trevor	Harold Hill	Brentwood & Warley	1980	1986	Norwich City	94	9	8
Redford	Ian	Perth	Dundee United	1988	1991	Scotland	59	9	8
Reed	William	Rhondda	Brighton	1953	1958	Swansea	155		43
Rees	William	Swansea	Portsmouth	1957	1963	Welling Town	90		29
Rees	Douglas	Neath	Troedyrhiw	1949	1959	Unknown	356		1
Reuser	Martijn	Amsterdam	Vitesse Arnhem	2000		Still at club	15	19	8
Rimmer	Ellis	Birkenhead	Sheffield W	1938	1939	Retired	3		0
Rimmer	Neill	Liverpool	Everton	1985	1988	Wigan	19	3	3
Roberts	James Dale	Newcastle	Apprentice	1974	1980	Hull City	17	1	0
Roberts	James	Larbert	Dundee	1949	1952	Barrow	73		15
Robertson	James	Glasgow	Arsenal	1970	1972	Stoke City	87		10
Rodger	Bob	Dumbarton	Rhyl	1937	1939	Hull City	9		0
Roy	John	Southampton	Aberaman	1946	1947	Yeovil	15		2
Rumbold	George	Alton	Leyton Orient	1946	1950	Retired	121		11
Saphin	Reginald	Kilburn	Amateur	1945	1946	QPR	0		0
Scales	John	Harrogate	Tottenham	2000	2001	Retired	2		0
Scowcroft	James	Bury St Edmunds	Trainee	1994	2001	Leicester	163	39	47
Sedgley	Stephen	Enfield	Tottenham	1994	1997	Wolverhampton	105		15
Shanahan	Terence	Paddington	Tottenham	1969	1971	Blackburn	3	1	0
Sharkey	Patrick	Omagh	Portadown	1973	1977	Mansfield	17	1	1
Shufflebottom	Frank	Chesterfield	Sheffield Utd	1936	1942	Nottingham F	2		0
Siddall	Alfred	Northwich	Bournemouth	1957	1961	Haverhill	58		6
Sivell	Laurence	Lowestoft	Apprentice	1969	1984	Retired	141		0
Slater	Stuart	Sudbury	Glasgow Celtic	1993	1996	Leicester	61	11	4
Smith	George	Bromley	QPR	1949	1950	Unknown	8		0
Smith	John	Liverpool	Army	1945	1946	Unknown	2		0
Smith	Trevor	Lowestoft	Apprentice	1964	1966	Crewe	22	1	0
Smyth	Herbert	Manchester	HMS *Ganges*	1945	1950	Halifax	2		0
Snell	Victor	Ipswich	Juniors	1949	1963	South Africa	64		2
Sonner	Daniel	Wigan	Preussen Koln	1996	1998	Sheffield W	28	28	3
Spearritt	Edward	Lowestoft	Apprentice	1965	1969	Brighton	62	10	13
Stacey	Stephen	Bristol	Wrexham	1968	1970	Bristol City	3		0
Steggles	Kevin	Ditchingham	Apprentice	1978	1987	WBA	49	1	1

Complete Players' Career Records: Moran – Steggles

FAC Apps	Sub	Goals	FLC Apps	Sub	Goals	European Apps	Sub	Goals	Others Apps	Sub	Goals	Totals Apps	Sub	Goals
7		1	7		3	4		2	1		0	123		37
15	0	0	8	1	0	6	1	1	7	0	2	249	9	16
9	0	0	7	0	1	0	0	0	8	0	2	149	3	8
19		3	15		2	19		3	0		0	214		29
5		2	0		0	0		0	0		0	33		10
6		0	0		0	0		0	0		0	48		2
22		3	0		0	0		0	0		0	245		18
1	4	0	6	6	1	0	0	0	0	4	1	60	72	22
11		0	6		0	3		0	1		0	214		0
6		0	0		0	0		0	0		0	24		0
0		0	0		0	0		0	0		0	2		0
0	0	0	0	0	0	0	0	0	1	0	0	2	2	0
4		0	0		0	0		0	0		0	54		12
5	5	0	10	4	1	1	7	0	0	0	0	88	59	5
0	1	0	3	0	0	0	0	0	2	2	0	17	7	0
6		0	0		0	0		0	0		0	64		4
1		1	2		0	0		0	0		0	72		31
8	4	1	2	1	0	8	2	0	0	0	0	127	22	10
30	2	1	28	0	3	29	1	0	1	0	0	382	3	21
3		0	1		0	0		0	0		0	34		3
8	3	1	3	0	0	0	0	0	4	2	0	102	29	3
8		4	0		0	0		0	0		0	134		47
37		7	0		0	0		0	0		0	465		93
0		0	0		0	0		0	0		0	3		0
2	1	0	4	1	0	1	0	0	1	0	0	60	20	0
0	0	0	0	0	0	0	2	0	0	0	0	0	2	0
14		0	0		0	0		0	0		0	152		0
18		0	0		0	0		0	0		0	122		0
0	1	0	0	0	0	0	0	0	0	0	0	13	5	1
3		0	1		0	2		1	0		0	50		6
0	2	0	1	0	0	0	0	0	0	1	0	12	7	1
14		4	0		0	0		0	0		0	145		8
5	1	0	8	2	0	0	0	0	3	0	0	71	18	9
0		0	0		0	0		0	0		0	2		0
13		9	7		5	3		4	1		0	293		179
4		0	1		0	1		0	0		0	146		3
1		0	0		0	0		0	0		0	40		13
4		2	0		0	0		0	0		0	4		2
9	0	0	15	0	1	0	0	0	0	0	0	118	9	9
2	0	0	5	0	2	0	0	0	5	0	2	71	9	12
14		3	0		0	0		0	0		0	169		46
5		3	0		0	0		0	0		0	95		32
29		0	0		0	0		0	0		0	385		1
1	0	0	3	4	0	0	0	0	0	3	2	19	26	10
0		0	0		0	0		0	0		0	3		0
0	0	0	3	0	0	0	0	0	1	1	0	23	4	3
4	0	0	1	0	0	0	1	0	0	0	0	22	2	0
8		2	0		0	0		0	0		0	81		17
8		1	3		1	0		0	0		0	98		12
2		0	0		0	0		0	0		0	11		0
2		0	0		0	0		0	0		0	17		2
5		0	0		0	0		0	0		0	126		11
3		0	0		0	0		0	0		0	3		0
0		0	2		0	0		0	0		0	4		0
9	1	1	21	4	7	0	0	0	7	4	1	200	48	56
5		0	10		2	0		0	5		1	125		18
0	0	0	0	0	0	0	0	0	0	0	0	3	1	0
0	0	0	1	0	0	0	0	0	0	0	0	18	1	1
0		0	0		0	0		0	0		0	2		0
0		0	1		0	0		0	0		0	59		6
19		0	7		0	7		0	1		0	175		0
6	0	0	6	0	0	0	0	0	2	2	0	75	13	4
1		0	0		0	0		0	0		0	9		0
2		0	0		0	0		0	0		0	4		0
0	0	0	4	0	0	0	0	0	0	0	0	26	1	0
2		0	0		0	0		0	0		0	4		0
3		0	0		0	0		0	0		0	67		2
1	1	0	6	4	1	0	0	0	0	1	0	35	34	4
1	0	0	6	0	1	0	0	0	0	0	0	69	10	14
0		0	0		0	0		0	0		0	3		0
3	0	0	6	0	1	2	0	0	0	0	0	60	1	2

The Essential History of Ipswich Town

Player		Birthplace	From	Year Joined	Year Left	To	League App	Sub	Goals
Stein	Earl	Capetown, SA	Chelsea	1997	1997	Loan	6	1	2
Stephenson	Roy	Crook	Leicester City	1960	1965	Lowestoft Town	144		21
Stevenson	W Harry	Derby	Nottingham Forest	1948	1948	Unknown	3		0
Stewart	Marcus	Bristol	Huddersfield	2000		Still at club	42	2	21
Stirk	John	Consett	Apprentice	1973	1978	Watford	6		0
Stockwell	Michael	Chelmsford	Apprentice	1982	2000	Colchester	464	42	35
Stuart	Mark	Chiswick	Plymouth	1990	1990	Loan	5		2
Sowerby	John	NE England	Army	1932	1937	Glasgow Rangers	0		0
Sunderland	Alan	Mexborough	Arsenal	1984		Unknown	51	7	11
Swailes	Christopher	Gateshead	Trainee	1989	1991	Peterborough ⎫			
			Doncaster	1995	1997	Bury ⎭	34	3	1
Talbot	Brian	Ipswich	Apprentice	1970	1979	Arsenal	177		25
Tanner	Adam	Maldon	Trainee	1992	2000	Peterborough	49	24	7
Taricco	Mauricio	Buenos Aires	Argentinos Jnrs	1994	1998	Tottenham	134	3	4
Tennant	David	Ayr	Annbank U	1952	1952	Albion Rovers	4		0
Thetis	Jean-Manuel	France	Seville	1998	2001	Sheffield United	44	3	2
Thijssen	Franz	Netherlands	Twente Enschede	1979	1983	Vancouver W'caps	123	2	10
Thompson	Kenneth	Ipswich	Apprentice	1962	1966	Exeter City	11	1	0
Thompson	Neil	Beverley	Scarborough	1989	1996	Barnsley	199	7	19
Thomsen	Claus	Aarhus	Aarhus	1994	1997	Everton	77	4	7
Thomson	Robert	Scotland	Racing Club de Paris	1936	1950	1st Team Trainer	0		0
Thorburn	James	Lanark	Raith Rovers	1963	1965	St Mirren	24		0
Thrower	Dennis	Ipswich	Juniors	1956	1965	Bury Town	27		2
Tibbott	Leslie	Oswestry	Apprentice	1973	1979	Sheffield Utd	52	2	0
Treacy	Francis	Glasgow	Johnstone Burgh	1961	1966	St Mirren	17	1	5
Trenter	Ronald	Ipswich	Whitton	1946	1951	Clacton Town	2		0
Turner	Robin	Carlisle	Apprentice	1973	1985	Swansea	22	26	2
Twamley	Bruce	Canada	Juniors	1969	1975	Canada	2		0
Tyler	Leonard	Rotherhithe	Millwall	1950	1952	Sittingbourne	73		0
Uhlenbeek	Gustav	Surinam	Tops SV	1995	1998	Fulham	77	12	4
Vaughan	Anthony	Manchester	Trainee	1994	1997	Manchester City	56	11	3
Venus	Mark	Hartlepool	Wolverhampton	1997		Still at club	107	4	15
Vernazza	Paulo	Islington	Arsenal	1998	1998	Loan	2		0
Viljoen	Colin	South Africa	South Africa	1967	1978	Manchester City	303	2	45
Walsh	Roy	Dedham	Apprentice	1965	1967	Southend	6	1	0
Wardlaw	John	Scotland	Morton	1939	1947	Hibernian	0	0	0
Wark	John	Glasgow	Apprentice	1974	1984	Liverpool ⎫			
			Liverpool	1988	1990	Middlesbrough ⎬			
			Middlesbrough	1991	1997	Club scout ⎭	533	6	135
Warne	Raymond	Ipswich	Leiston	1950	1952	Sudbury Town	30		11
Whelan	Philip	Stockport	Juniors	1990	1995	Middlesbrough	76	6	2
Whitton	Stephen	East Ham	Sheffield W	1991	1994	Colchester	80	8	15
Whymark	Trevor	Diss	Diss Town	1969	1979	Vancouver W'caps	249	12	75
Whyte	David	Greenwich	Reading	1997	1998	Bristol Rovers	2		0
Wigg	Ronald	Dunmow	Leyton Orient	1967	1970	Watford	35	2	14
Williams	David	Treorchy	Derby County	1992	1998	Colchester	217		3
Williams	Jackie	Aberdare	Aston Villa	1936	1939	Wrexham	9		0
Wilnis	Fabian	Surinam	De Graafschap	1999		Still at club	74	8	3
Wilson	Kevin	Banbury	Derby County	1985	1987	Chelsea	94	4	34
Wilson	Ulrich	Netherlands	Twente Enschede	1987	1987	Loan	5	1	0
Woods	Charles	Whitehaven	Crystal Palace	1966	1970	Watford	65	17	5
Woods	Clive	Norwich	Norwich Gothic	1969	1980	Norwich City	217	50	24
Woods	Neil	York	Glasgow Rangers	1987	1990	Bradford City	15	12	5
Wookey	Kenneth	Newport	Hereford	1950	1951	Unknown	15		1
Wosahlo	Roger	Cambridge	Chelsea	1967	1968	Peterborough	1	1	0
Wright	Jermaine	Greenwich	Crewe	1999		Still at club	56	15	3
Wright	Richard	Ipswich	Trainee	1995	2001	Arsenal	240		0
Yallop	Frank	Watford	Apprentice	1982	1996	Tampa Bay	289	27	7
Youds	Edward	Liverpool	Everton	1991	1995	Bradford City	38	12	1
Zondervan	Romeo	Surinam	WBA	1984	1992	Holland	270	4	13

The following players have made a single appearance for Ipswich Town – dates with club in brackets.

Barber, Frederick (1995) on loan from Luton Town
Brownlow, John (1946-48)
Callaghan, Henry (1954-56)
Carson, Thomas (1988) on loan from Dundee
Clements, Herbert (1936-38) scored in only appearance
Ellis, Kevin (1995-96)
Garrett, Leonard (1958-61)
Gibson, Joseph (1947-49)
Graham, Thomas (1948-49)

Jackson, John (1981-82)
McGourty, James (1938-39)
Morgan, Philip (1993-95)
Morris, Trevor (1938-39)
Neilson, Thomas (1948-49)
Neville, Christopher (1989)
Overton, Paul (1978-79)
Walls, James (1954-55)

FAC Apps	Sub	Goals	FLC Apps	Sub	Goals	European Apps	Sub	Goals	Others Apps	Sub	Goals	Totals Apps	Sub	Goals
0	0	0	3	1	1	0	0	0	0	0	0	9	2	3
8	2	6	2			4		0	1		1	163		26
0		0	0			0		0	0		0	3		0
2	0	1	3	2	1	0	0	0	3	0	3	50	4	26
0		0	1			1		0	0		0	8		0
28	3	2	43	5	5	0	0	0	22	4	2	557	54	44
0		0	0			0		0	0		0	5		2
2	0	0	0			0		0	0		0	2		0
2	1	1	6	1	1	0	0	0	0	0	0	59	9	13
0		0	3			0		0	2		0	39	3	1
23	3		12		1	14		2	1		0	227		31
5	2	0	2	2	0	0	0	0	3	1	1	59	29	8
8	0	0	18	0	3	0	0	0	7		0	167	3	7
0		0	0			0		0	0		0	4		0
2	0	0	5	0	1	0	0	0	2	1	0	53	4	3
15	0	2	12	1	0	17	0	4	0	0	0	167	3	16
1	0	0	1	0	0	0	0	0	0	0	0	13	1	0
17	0	2	14	1	1	0	0	0	8	0	2	238	8	24
5	0	0	8	0	1	0	0	0	2	1	0	92	5	8
8		0	0			0		0	0		0	8		0
0		0	0			0		0	0		0	24		0
2		0	2			0		0	0		0	31		2
6	0	0	2	0	0	10	0	1	0	0	0	70	2	1
1	0	0	1	0	0	0	0	0	0	0	0	19	1	5
0		0	0			0		0	0		0	2		0
5	1	2	1	2	1	1	3	1	0	1	0	29	33	6
0		0	0			0		0	0		0	2		0
5		0	0			0		0	0		0	78		0
4	3	0	5	3	0	0	0	0	7	1	0	93	19	4
2	0	0	4	2	0	0	0	0	4	0	0	66	13	3
4	0	0	15	0	3	0	0	0	7	0	0	133	4	18
0		0	0			0		0	0		0	2		0
28	1	6	20	0	2	11	2	1	5	0	0	367	5	54
1	0	0	1	0	0	0	0	0	0	0	0	8	1	0
3	0	0	0	0	0	0	0	0	0	0	0	3		0
55	1	12	42	1	12	25	1	18	15	0	2	670	9	179
0	0	0	0	0	0	0	0	0	0	0	0	30		11
3	1	0	6	1	0	0	0	0	1	0	0	86	8	2
8	1	2	7	1	2	0	0	0	4	0	0	99	10	19
21	0	2	20	0	9	23	1	13	9	0	5	322	13	104
0	0	0	0	0	0	0	0	0	0	0	0	2		0
1	0	0	3	0	0	0	0	0	0	0	0	39	2	14
18	0	0	24	1	0	0	0	0	4	0	0	263	1	3
7		4	0			0		0	0		0	16		4
4	0	0	6	2	0	0	0	0	3	1	0	87	11	3
10	0	3	8	0	8	0	0	0	7	0	4	119	4	49
0	0	0	0	0	0	0	0	0	0	0	0	5	1	0
1	1	0	4	1	2	0	0	0	0	0	0	70	19	7
24	3	2	13	4	2	22	1	1	2	2	2	278	60	31
0		0	0			0		0	4		1	19	12	6
2	0	0	0			0		0	0		0	17		1
0		0	0	0	0	0	0	0	0	0	0	1	1	0
2	1	1	8	2	0	0	0	0	1	0	0	67	18	4
13		0	27		0	0	0	0	11		0	291		0
15	3	0	23	2	1	0	0	0	22	4	0	349	36	8
5	1	0	1	2	0	0	0	0	0	0	0	44	15	1
11	2	2	24	0	3	0	0	0	14	0	2	319	6	20

The following players have made a single appearance for Ipswich Town as a substitute – dates with club in brackets.

Friars, Sean (1998-2001)
Jean, Earl (1996)
Keeble, Christopher (1997-2000)
Linford, John (1981-94)
Mayes, Robert (1988-89)
Meade, Raphael (1990)

Club Statistics

Ipswich Town Managers

Mick O'Brien	1936-37	Bobby Robson	1969-82
Scott Duncan	1937-55	Bobby Ferguson	1982-87
Alf Ramsey	1955-63	John Duncan	1987-90
Jackie Milburn	1963-64	John Lyall	1990-94
Bill McGarry	1964-68	George Burley	1994-present

Top appearance-makers

1	Mick Mills	741
2	John Wark	679
3	Mick Stockwell	611
4	Paul Cooper	575
5	George Burley	500
6	Tommy Parker	465
7	Bill Baxter	459
8	John Elsworthy	433
9	Jason Dozzell	415
10 =	Russell Osman	385
	Dai Rees	
	Frank Yallop	
13	Eric Gates	384
14	Jimmy Leadbetter	373
15	Colin Viljoen	372

Top scorers

1	Ray Crawford	227
2	Ted Phillips	181
3	John Wark	179
4	Tom Garneys	143
5	Paul Mariner	135
6	Trevor Whymark	104
7	Eric Gates	96
8	Tommy Parker	93
9	Alan Brazil	80
10	Jason Dozzell	72
11	Francis Brogan	69
12	Gerard Baker	66
13	Chris Kiwomya	64
14	David Johnson	62
15 =	Bryan Hamilton	56
	James Scowcroft	

Players scoring on their debut

Jackie Little	3/10/36	v Stowmarket (H)	FA Cup
Darkie Clements	14/11/36	v Cambridge Town (H)	FA Cup
Bryn Davies	27/8/38	v Southend United (H)	Division 3 (South)
Fred Chadwick	24/9/38	v Reading (A)	Division 3 (South)
Jock Hutcheson	7/1/39	v Aston Villa (A)	FA Cup
Jack Connor	31/8/46	v Clapton Orient (A)	Division 3 (South)
Albert Day	7/9/46	v Norwich City (H)	Division 3 (South)
Stan Parker	23/11/46	v Port Vale (A)	Division 3 (South)
George Clarke	31/5/47	v Northampton Town (A)	Division 3 (South)
John Dempsey	21/8/48	v Bristol Rovers (A)	Division 3 (South)
Francis McGinn	18/9/48	v Crystal Palace (A)	Division 3 (South)
Joe O'Brien	20/8/49	v Bournemouth (H)	Division 3 (South)
Neil Myles	24/12/49	v Crystal Palace (H)	Division 3 (South)
Roy Warne	23/12/50	v Plymouth Argyle (A)	Division 3 (South)
Tom Garneys	18/8/51	v Southend United (H)	Division 3 (South)
George McLuckie	19/8/53	v Walsall (A)	Division 3 (South)
Ron Blackman	29/10/55	v Reading (A)	Division 3 (South)
Brian Siddall	4/9/57	v Barnsley (A)	Division 2
Dermot Curtis	6/9/58	v Fulham (A)	Division 2
Ray Crawford	4/10/58	v Swansea (A)	Division 2
Charlie Woods	13/9/66	v Brentford (A)	League Cup
Colin Viljoen	25/3/67	v Portsmouth (H)	Division 2
Ron Wigg	30/9/67	v Carlisle United (H)	Division 2
John O'Rourke	24/2/68	v Cardiff City (H)	Division 2
Rod Belfitt	6/11/71	v Wolves (H)	Division 1
Keith Bertschin	17/4/76	v Arsenal (A)	Division 1
Jason Dozzell	4/2/84	v Coventry City (H)	Division 1
Kevin Wilson	26/1/85	v Gillingham (H)	FA Cup
Mark Stuart	7/4/90	v Watford (A)	Division 2
Steve Whitton	5/1/61	v WBA (H)	Division 2
Sergei Baltacha	21/1/89	v Stoke City (H)	Division 2
Paul Mason	14/8/93	v Oldham Athletic (A)	Premier League
Ian Marshall	14/8/93	v Oldham Athletic (A)	Premier League
Adam Tanner	2/1/95	v Leicester City (H)	Premier League
Alex Mathie	25/2/95	v Southampton (H)	Premier League
David Johnson	15/11/97	v Wolves (A)	Division 1
Gary Croft	26/9/99	v Manchester City (H)	Division 1
Neil Midgley	18/12/99	v WBA (H)	Division 1
Marcus Stewart	5/2/00	v Barnsley (A)	Division 1
Martijn Reuser	25/3/00	v Fulham (H)	Division 1